AFRICANA STUDIES

A SURVEY OF AFRICA
AND THE AFRICAN DIASPORA

AFRICANA STUDIES

A SURVEY OF AFRICA
AND THE AFRICAN DIASPORA

THIRD EDITION

EDITED BY
MARIO AZEVEDO

CAROLINA ACADEMIC PRESS
DURHAM, NORTH CAROLINA

Library of Congress Cataloging-in-Publication Data

Africana studies : a survey of Africa and the African diaspora / edited by
  Mario Azevedo.— 3rd ed.
    p. cm.
  Includes bibliographical references and index.
  ISBN 0-89089-485-X (alk. paper)
  1. African diaspora. 2. Africa—History. 3. Blacks—History. I. Azevedo,
Mario Joaquim.

  DT16.5.A35 2005
  960—dc22
                                    2005016828

Carolina Academic Press
700 Kent Street
Durham, NC 27701
Telephone (919) 489-7486
Fax (919) 493-5668
E-mail: cap@cap-press.com
www.cap-press.com

Printed in the United States of America

Contents

Contents

Acknowledgments

I am extremely pleased that after years of careful thought, methodical planning, and close consultation with colleagues and friends, *Africana Studies* has finally come to fruition. First and foremost, I wish to thank and congratulate all of the contributors to this unique work who dedicated their time, energies, and talents, to the completion of the project and to its timely submission to the publisher. I appreciate the encouragement I received from Dr. Gwendolyn S. Prater at the conception of the project and the support from Dr. Hunt Davis, Jr., Dr. Marsha Jean Darling, and Dr. Luis Serapiao for suggestions on how to proceed with this work. My colleagues at the University of North Carolina, Charlotte, Dr. Gregory Davis and Dr. Tanure Ojaide, who, like me, teach "Introduction to Afro-American and African Studies," were sources of inspiration. Their contributions add significantly to this volume.

I would also like to acknowledge the role my own students played in the "Introduction to Afro-American and African Studies" course. I used them to classroom test the suitability of the textbook by providing them bound copies of the manuscript as reading materials. Dr. Gregory Davis adopted the same strategy during the Fall 1992 semester. The responses of both classes convinced me that this is a sound and significant undertaking—one that was perhaps long overdue.

My gratitude also goes to Carolina Academic Press, particularly to its untiring editor, Philip Menzies. His vision, patience, and encouragement made the enterprise less onerous for me and the contributors. Last but not least, words of thanks go to my family for patience and understanding, as well as to our departmental secretary, Mrs. Roberta Duff, who spent many hours at the computer preparing the manuscript, and to Mrs. Charlotte Simpson in UNCC Computer Academic Services, who assisted Mrs. Duff and me efficiently and expeditiously whenever we needed a professional and competent hand.

Mario Azevedo

Introduction

Mario Azevedo

This textbook was designed to respond to the present student generation's needs and questions regarding the nature of the disciplines that constitute the African, African American, Afro-Caribbean Studies, and Afro-Latin-American programs, once generically designated as Black Studies. The editor's objective is, first, to make readily available the basic content of these broad fields and discuss their methodologies and themes in an introductory textbook that is comprehensive in its analysis of the experiences, contributions, and aspirations of the peoples of Africa and the scattered African diaspora. The editor's goal has been to provide this material on a reading level that is appropriate to American college freshmen and sophomores. Second, unlike the few textbooks available on the subject at the moment, the present work takes into account, in a single volume, the practical needs of those programs, departments, institutes, or centers that either combine into one unit or split into the fields of African, African American, or Pan-African Studies. In short, this introductory volume attempts to address and represent fairly and adequately the experience and contributions of blacks in Africa, the Americas, and other parts of the world, from the earliest times to the present, and provide a balanced view of the function of the disciplines and the perspectives of those scholars who have labored arduously to make them what they are today and who, by and large, determine their future course.

With these premises in mind, each chapter begins with an introductory statement and a list of the crucial concepts or terms pertinent to the topic, followed by a discussion of the content, as well as the theoretical framework or the controversial interpretations (if any) that have dominated the theme(s) covered, a succinct summary of the chapter, and some study questions to help the student grasp the thrust of the material and to generate class discussion. A short reference list, which may be consulted to get a fuller understanding of the topic and fulfill research interests, concludes each chapter.

The contributors are experienced and respected scholars in the fields of African, African American, and Diaspora Studies, and provide, therefore, a perspective and content that are both relevant and accurate, consonant with the "state of the art" in their own disciplines. Others have been teachers of an introductory course for one or all three fields. The accrued advantage is that, as "toilers in the trenches and frontlines," these contributors are not academics teaching in a platonic world but are classroom educators who, well aware of the needs and the levels of understanding of their students, have made the chapters readable and the content concise and realistic in relation to the common coverage time frame (usually one or two semesters or quarters), rejecting academic dogmatism, single points of view, and tendencies of exclusiveness that have often marred similar academic undertakings.

For years, the editor and many of his colleagues in African American, African, and Pan-African Studies have relied on one or two texts, for lack of better ones. Many of us, to be sure, have tolerated numerous shortcomings in most of the present introductory level textbooks. In general, these texts, without indexes, tend to be ideological, a pitfall the present textbook attempts to avoid or at least minimize. Since we are dealing with young minds, easily impressionable, we prefer a textbook that exposes the students not to a pontificating, dogmatic point of view, but to a variety of perspectives. Moreover, as the textbooks we have used so far focus primarily on the African American experience and leave the African and the Caribbean diaspora Africans in the "tracks of the slave trade," instructors find themselves constantly photocopying or adding supplementary reading materials in order to cover more comprehensively the aggregate experience of all peoples of African descent. Similar shortcomings apply to most textbooks on Africa which we have attempted to use in the past: they focus on Africa and fall short on the diaspora.

Although this work provides a discussion of the basic content, methodologies, and issues in Africana Studies, we realize that some chapters are more relevant than others to specific programs; that a few chapters are more complex in focus and style than most; and that, for some programs, adequate coverage may require two semesters or two quarters rather than one semester or one quarter. Whatever the circumstances, however, the role played by the instructor will be extremely crucial toward the successful use of the textbook. In fact, on certain occasions, only the instructor's specific guidance will allow students to discern what is important, as they attempt to fulfill the course requirements and satisfy any further interests they might develop during the course of the academic year.

Finally, we believe that, unless a superficial coverage of topics is tolerated (which goes against our training and academic standards), a multi-authored volume, in principle, has a better chance of doing justice to the totality of the black experience by combining the knowledge of many. Let it also be said that, to conform with new trends in the fields of African and African Diaspora Studies, the textbook explicitly avoids terms and expressions which elicit negative connotations, such as tribe (for ethnic group, society, or people), paganism, animism, and heathenism (for African traditional religion), brideprice (for bridewealth), huts (for homes or houses), negro (for African American), pygmy (for BaMbuti, Twa), bushman (for Khoi, San), and natives, a term particularly preferred by the British colonial administrators (for Africans). The textbook is not only concerned with providing accurate information to students but also to sensitize (and not indoctrinate) them about the feelings of the people whose culture they are learning.

Insofar as the organization is concerned, the volume is divided into five parts, each with several chapters. Part I focuses on the disciplines that have given us our knowledge of the cultures and experiences of peoples of African descent. Part II traces the evolution and history of the black race and Part III deals with the state of black people and their relationships with each other and the rest of the world, at present, while outlining the challenges the black community is expected to face in the future. Part IV, on the one hand, looks at the specific contributions of black people in a wide array of areas. Part V, on the other, delves into some of the most significant aspects of the social life and values of the black communities scattered across the continents. Part VI, the appendix, provides a chronology of important events in the history of black people and a list of selected periodicals and references that should become part of the student's repertoire of knowledge.

In conclusion, *Africana Studies: A Survey of Africa and The African Diaspora, 3rd Edition* literally introduces students of all racial and ethnic backgrounds to a multidisciplinary as well as an interdisciplinary study of the fields of African and African Diaspora Studies. It focuses on the interaction of cultures, particularly of black people, in the shaping of past and contemporary societies and on the methodologies and key interdisciplinary issues, themes, and problems, all of which provide legitimacy to the two academic fields. Ours is not, as it were, just a textbook on slavery, on colonialism, on racism and discrimination, or on the suffering and hardships of peoples of African origin and descent, or simply on their contributionist record. *Africana Studies* goes beyond that, as it probes into the two related fields and focuses on both the individual and aggregate experiences of black people, not in a vacuum or in isolation, but within the context of the cultural crisscrossing between peoples of African descent and the rest of humankind, across time and space. *Africana Studies* is, therefore, a saga of both the pains and joys (and aspirations) of black people the world over and an exposé of the key to their future, not as a separate and monolithic group but as a dynamic, ever changing part of the world community, yet, with a uniqueness and a heritage worth preserving.

AFRICANA STUDIES

PART I

INTELLECTUAL FOUNDATIONS OF THE BLACK EXPERIENCE

1

African Studies and the State of the Art

Mario Azevedo

Introduction

The study of Africa experienced tremendous expansion both in scope and depth during the past four decades. In England, the University of London's School of Oriental and African Studies has been in existence since 1916, and in France, the 1940s pioneering work on Africa has been superseded by more advanced studies in the field we now call African Studies. Since the 1950s, US scholars have successfully continued their effort to study and understand Africa in a systematic way, using, to the extent possible, scientific methods. Likewise, the former Soviet Union and the Scandinavian countries (Denmark, Norway, and Sweden) established several programs on Africa (such as the well-known African Studies Institute at Uppsala, Sweden) and are devoting more resources to the study of the continent. Even the Japanese have added similar programs to some of their institutions of higher learning, as is the case of Kyoto University, which established the Center for African Studies in 1979, and Tokyo University with its Institute for the Study of Languages and Cultures of Asia and Africa, created as far back as 1964. In fact, the 1950s and 1960s, which the well-known anthropologist Aidan Southall has called "the golden age of Africa," were decades of excitement, novelty, and experimentation.

At that time, scholars, particularly American with strong input from Diaspora African Americans and continental Africans, were determined to correct the traditional disciplines' biases toward Africa and Africans and expend the focus of the existing human sciences. In the social sciences (e.g., history, political science, sociology, economics, geography, psychology, and anthropology), humanities (literature, religion, and philosophy), and fine arts (art, music, dance, and theatre) scholars burnt the midnight oil collecting data on Africa, restoring its history, dispelling myths, and providing an accurate picture of the continent and its people. Even the so-called "hard sciences" (physics, chemistry, biology, mathematics, and statistics) felt the pressure to re-examine the role played by Africans and peoples of African descent in the discovery of new knowledge and the laws of the universe. Today, there at least 52 recognized African Studies departments and programs worldwide and 12 Title VI African Studies Centers in the United States, namely, Boston University, University of California at Los Angeles, University of California at Berkeley, University of Florida, University of Illinois, Indiana University, Michigan State University, Ohio University, Ohio State University, University of Pennsylvania, Stanford University, University of Wisconsin, and Yale University, which provide excellent library resources, grant fellowships to scholars, administer K-12 school outreach programs, promote and teach African languages, and offer strong undergraduate and graduate programs to majors.

✱   This chapter defines the field of African Studies, traces its evolution, examines the nature of its various disciplines, and weighs the impact it has had on our understanding of Africa. However, even though the field of African Studies has been recognized as a legitimate academic pursuit, it still faces many obstacles, including: lack of adequate resources; uneasiness on the part of African authorities to allow research of areas deemed sensitive; lack of coordination and collaboration between American and African institutions; epistemological disagreements; the relevance of scholars' current pursuits to Africa's current conditions; the impact of negative reporting by the electronic and print media; the persistent control of the field and the African Studies Association (ASA) by Western scholars; the role that continental African scholars should play; and its inter-disciplinary nature. The following discussion should provide the undergraduate student with a foundation for the understanding of the "state of the art" or the most updated current state of African Studies and the role played by the social sciences, the humanities, and the arts toward the acceptance of the field within the "academy" [community of scholars] and our knowledge of the African continent itself.

Major terms and concepts: African Studies, "academy," scholar, theoretical framework, ethnocentrism, canon, Eurocentric vs. Afrocentric perspective, causality, applied research, modernization, traditional, class, dependence, Marxism, objectivity, colonial and Pan-African models, equilibrium and conflict theory, structural-functionalism, behavioralism, bourgeois, cultural pluralism, charisma, the military.

Definition and Historical Evolution of African Studies

African Studies is a broad field or area of studies which combines several disciplines in the arts, the humanities, and the social-behavioral sciences for the sole purpose of studying and understanding Africa and its people from all facets — their origins, history, culture, experiences, achievements, contributions, aspirations, and even human and physical environment. A discipline is an organized body of knowledge accumulated over a period of time that has its own canons [rules, methodologies, and specific focus or parameters, e.g., history can only focus on human past and anthropology only on culture and not on culture and government, the latter being the focus of political science], and experts — teachers, writers, and researchers — who set the standards and pass on their knowledge to a generation of students, apprentices, followers, or disciples, hence the use of the word "discipline." Except in the physical sciences where accumulated knowledge usually does not change but is constantly added, in the social sciences, the humanities, and fine arts, old as well as added knowledge can be altered, revised, or discarded altogether as new evidence is uncovered. The major subjects comprising the interdisciplinary field called African Studies are history, political science, anthropology, sociology, religion, literature, music, art, philosophy, geography, linguistics, archaeology, and economics. Africanists [specialists who are trained and experienced and conduct research and publish on Africa] attempt, to the best of their ability, to study the continent using scientific methodology or the rules of scientific inquiry by collecting data systematically, analyzing it [separating the relevant from the non-relevant data], interpreting it [giving it a meaning], and applying or using it in a variety of ways, a phase sometimes known as applied research.

The major questions these disciplines attempt to answer are: why, how, who, when, where, and what lessons. However, the field of African studies deals with human beings whose actions are often unpredictable and cannot be replicated, as, for example, a chemist replicates a compound mixture through repeated experiments in his laboratory. Because people can be actors with hidden motives and idiosyncrasies that are capable of escaping all scientific scrutiny, their motives or "causality" of behavior may be difficult to ascertain. Therefore, conclusions arrived at in the field of African studies cannot be as re-assuring and definitive as those of the natural or "hard" sciences such as physics, mathematics, chemistry, biology, and zoology. Scientists can replicate their experiments over and over again and come up with laws and generalizations that can stand the test of time. In the social-behavioral sciences [those that deal with humans and their behavior], as well as in the humanities [which focus on the interpretation of ideas and emotions] and fine arts [which study and apply aesthetics or the concept of beauty], scholars deal mainly with reasonable theories and opinions, feelings and emotions, probabilities and hypotheses.

Since African Studies deal with Africa, the development of the continent of Africa and its place in world history determine by and large the content and focus of the disciplines involved. These disciplines in turn have the ability to influence and shape the continent's events and processes, particularly those related to the more relevant and appropriate school curriculum. Prior to the 1950s, Africa was not the object of a systematic focus of any traditional discipline, although some historians and anthropologists had already taken the initial steps in that direction. The emergence of the nation-states in Africa during the 1960s, or the decade of Africa's independence, and the subsequent role the continent played in the world community indirectly revolutionized the field of African Studies.

For a long time, Africa was said to have no history and to have contributed nothing to mankind. For example, while Arnold Toynbee, one of the most influential British historians, held the view that Africans had "not contributed positively to any civilization," Oxford University Professor Hugh Trevor-Roper, another British historian, called the African past "nothing but the unrewarding gyrations of barbarous tribes." This belief was prevalent in Europe prior to the twentieth century and was reinforced by misguided nineteenth century social Darwinists who, applying the evolutionary theory of the "survival of the fittest," saw Africans as belonging to an inferior race, one that was destined to extinction. While, on one hand, as Festus Ohaegbulam notes in his *Towards an Understanding of the African Experience from Contemporary and Historical Perspectives*

(1990), German philosopher George Hegel declared that Africa did not constitute part of the history of the world, on the other, such American "scientists" as John Burgess, William Sumner, and Josiah Strong carried out studies designed to prove the inferiority of the black race.

Even though, at times, Western denial of a worthy African past was done unconsciously, it was often a deliberate act to justify and maintain European subjugation of the continent and its people. Europeans claimed that Africans should be enslaved and colonized in order to be saved from extinction and rescued from their own barbaric ways of life. Civilizing Africa was, as the English poet Rudyard Kipling put it, the "white man's burden." As Ohaegbulam further reminds us, British geographer James McQueen expressed more clearly the issue of white superiority when he once wrote that "if we [the British] really wish to do good in Africa, we must teach her savage sons that white men are their superiors." As inferior people, therefore, Africans had nothing to show but so much to learn. Similar writings and pronouncements by prominent Western scholars were commonplace prior to the 1960s.

Festus Ohaegbulam identifies several reasons why Africa was excluded from the academic community. Some of these reasons are summarized below. One was the narrow European definition of history which recognized only written records as sources of knowledge of man's past. Since Africa, except for Egypt, Ethiopia, Nubia, and some early states, such as Mali, had mostly non-literate [with no writing system] languages, its people were excluded from historical consideration. In fact, while Egyptian civilization, prior to the works of scholars such as Anta Cheik Diop of Senegal, was considered to be non-African, the Ethiopian and the Nubian civilizations were attributed to Arabs and fair-skinned outsiders. Two other factors that kept the continent outside the "academy" were the impact of the early missionaries who looked down upon African culture—its music, languages, arts, religion(s), and customs—and the overall inability of the Africans to shape their own destiny as a result of the Atlantic slave trade that began during the fifteenth century and the subsequent European colonial occupation of the continent from the 1880s to the 1960s–1970s.

However, African independence, the changing pattern of world relationships, the student movement of the 1960s in the United States, which, among other things, demanded the establishment of African American and African Studies programs and the creation of autonomous African universities staffed by African scholars had the effect of restoring credit to Africa's pristine contributions to world civilizations, particularly in the fields of art and music. No longer, therefore, did one have to prove that Africa had a history. The acceptance of oral tradition as a valid source of historical knowledge, accomplished through the efforts of scholars such as Jan Vansina (a Belgian historian who worked in Zaire, now the Democratic Republic of Congo), the availability of new written documents, the effort of such archaeologists as Louis Leakey, who worked in Kenya during the 1950s and 1960s, and that of linguists, particularly German, and the involvement of continental African scholars facilitated the development of the field of African Studies.

For the first time, historians read with interest Greco-Roman references to Africa and marvelled at the descriptions of African kingdoms by a number of Arab and non-Arab travelers and scholars, as summarized by Joseph Ki-Zerbo's *Histoire de l'Afrique noire* (1972). Among others, Ki-Zerbo cites the following chroniclers: Al Masoudi (of Baghdad, dead ca. 956), who traveled to Iran, India, and Indonesia, and included in his memoirs two chapters on Africa; Ibn Hawkal (also of Baghdad), author and traveler, who wrote about Africa in 976; Al Bakri, from Cordova (1040–1094), who wrote on ancient Ghana; Al Idris (1099–1164), of Ceuta, Morocco, geographer-traveller, and student at Cordova, who described Africa and Spain in his writings; Aboulfeda (1273–1331), scholar, born in Damascus, who devoted some of his work to the Sudanic states; Al Omari (known as Ibn Fadl Allah), also from Damascus, advisor to sultans in Cairo and Damascus, and author of an encyclopaedia, who described Africa, and made special references to the kingdom of Mali; Ibn Battuta (1303–1377), from Tangier, who travelled to China, the Middle East, East Africa (down to Zanzibar), and West Africa where he was a guest of the emperor of Mali, and left insightful references to the ancient kingdoms of West and East Africa; and Ibn Khaldoun (1332–1406), of Tunis, secretary, minister, ambassador, courtier, traveller, mercenary, and once prisoner, who visited North Africa and Spain and, in 1382, wrote a universal history that describes the Berbers of North Africa.

Ki-Zerbo also enlightens the students of African history about the works of Hassan (*alias* John Leo the African) (1463–1554), born in Granada (Spain) and student at Fez, who left interesting comments about the continent. In fact, Hassan crossed the Sudan around 1507, visited Cairo and Mecca, was captured by pirates and eventually taken to Pope Leo X, who baptized him under the name of Johannes Leo de Medicis. Subsequently, he became a professor at the University of Bologna, Italy, and later returned to Tunisia only to reconvert to Islam. While in Rome, in 1526, he wrote about the continent of Africa and its wonders. In 1520, Mohamad Kate, historian from Timbuktu (ancient Mali), advisor to King Askia Mohamad, wrote of Songhay and the Moroccan invasion in his *Tarikh el-Fettac (Chronicle of the Searcher)*. Finally, "Moor" Es Sadi (or Abderhamane) wrote of the continent in his *Tarikh es-Sudan (Chronicle of Black Lands)* around 1655. Ki-Zerbo further points out that the uncovering of several sources (both from the Middle Ages and the modern era) at the Vatican, from private European collections, monasteries, and other institutions have allowed interested scholars to piece together the missing links of the African past.

The Disciplines and the "State of the Art" in African Studies

History, the "queen" of the social sciences (or the humanities, according to some) has been more responsible for the restoration of the African past than any other discipline. With its rigorous methodology of data collection using every available primary and secondary source (government documents, diaries, memoirs, books, newspapers, oral traditions, witnesses or contemporary actors, fossils, pictorial data, artifacts, etc.) from archives, libraries, excavations, and corroborative materials from other disciplines, the Africanist [Africa-trained] historian, insisting on objectivity, has pioneered the systematic understanding of Africa and provided a foundation for other social sciences and the humanities to utilize their methodologies and thus reach a more comprehensive understanding of the continent and its people.

The historiography of the colonial period treated Africa primarily as an extension of Europe, using European concepts and a Eurocentric point of view. The new Africanist historians brought Africans center-stage, treating them as the primary focus of their work. African scholars, such as Kenneth Onwuka Dike and J.F. Ade Ajayi at Ibadan University, Nigeria, Abu Boahen at Legon, Ghana, Bethwell Ogot at Makerere University, Uganda, Joseph Ki-Zerbo at Ouagadougou (Burkina Faso), and Engelbert Mveng at Yaounde University, Cameroon, were among the trailblazers of this development. In the words of Abiola Irele, once Professor of French at the University of Ibadan, Nigeria (now at Harvard), "It was inevitable that the most significant development should have taken place within the discipline of history. This was the most convenient terrain for taking on the colonizer, so to speak: for repudiating the colonial thesis that Africa had no history before the coming of the white man, that nowhere had the black race displayed an initiative for creating a framework of life and expression with any real human value or significance."

In the United States and England, the critical methodologies of historians such as Jan Vansina, Philip Curtin, the late Basil Davidson, the late Walter Rodney, Rene Pelissier, and many others contributed to the credibility of Africanist history as a legitimate social science with Africa as its focus. Eventually, as a result, Africanist historians came to dominate the field of African Studies and the African Studies Association (ASA). The accomplishment of historians is evidenced by the monumental eight volumes of the *Cambridge History of Africa* edited by J.D. Fage and the completed eight volumes of the *General History of Africa* commissioned by UNESCO, a project that involved some of the best known scholars, including Ajayi, Boahen, Ogot, Ki-Zerbo, and Davidson.

However, pioneering Africanist historians have been criticized by a younger generation of Africans and "radical" scholars who insist that the discipline is too conservative and irrelevant to solving Africa's current problems, partly because it still utilizes a Eurocentric rather than an Afri- or Afro-centric approach to the study of the continent. They point out, for example, that most of the focus has been the history of Europe in Africa, narratives about African kings and chiefs, of wars and empires, of great men and their deeds, of nationalists and trade union leaders, and perhaps of some oppressed segment of society simply to vindicate the past, rather than the account of the masses or the internal dynamics and workings of African societies. Historians are further accused of undertaking "micro-histories" rather than "macro-studies" of the African past, thus rarely presenting a larger picture of the continent as European historians have successfully done regarding their continent. Marxist Africanist historians insist, for example, that a class analysis of Africa must be an intrinsic part of the study of African history.

On methodology, the neo-historians [the new breed of historians, who wish to revise traditional history] argue that the claim of objectivity leads the Africanist historian to nothing, or, as historians A. Temu and B. Swai of the Dar-es-Salaam School, Tanzania, put it in their *Historians and Africanist History: A Critique* (1981), reduces history to a *cul-de-sac*, never venturing "beyond a timid empiricism" [description of facts without analysis or vision of the world]. They point out that ideology and methodology cannot be separated because the mere choice of a specific focus betrays the historian's predisposition, values, and partisanship, thus shattering the claim of objectivity. Temu and Swai sarcastically conclude that the historian's objectivity has been the "objectivity of a eunuch" [that of a castrated man who brags about his sexual escapades]. The claim of the universal applicability of their theories and conclusions (i.e., that generalizations about European history necessarily apply to African history as well) has likewise come under attack. Western academics have, in fact, unwittingly tended to generalize about all societies and cultures using ethnocentric standards, which have often distorted the reality of the world under study. This was clear, for example, when political scientists, sociologists, and economists misapplied to Africa the universality of the modernization theory (to be discussed later in this chapter) during the 1960s.

In the United States, some scholars have coined the term Africology or Afrocology in an attempt to stress the point that Africa is both the object and the subject of inquiry and to distance themselves from the shortcomings and biases of traditional scholarship. Note: The expressions "traditional disciplines" or "traditional scholarship" refer to the disciplines that have been long established and accepted by the "academy," such as history, political science, anthropology, Western music, and Western literature. Non-traditional disciplines would include African studies, African American studies, Women's studies, Jewish Studies, history of science, and art history. It is also interesting to point out that a couple of decades ago some historians toyed with a new popular but shallow methodology called "quantification." This quantitative analysis or statistical analysis in the social sciences was supposed to add a scientific flavor to their work, one that would strengthen their generalizations and allow prediction of human behavior. The attempt has virtually failed because it raised more questions than it provided answers. History or other social sciences are not precise sciences and cannot, therefore, predict human behavior. Thus, most historians have now distanced themselves from this tempting but problematic methodology, which, interestingly, continues to attract political scientists and economists. Along the same lines, the so-called Ibadan and Dar-es-Salaam schools of Africanist historians, of which the late Walter Rodney was the major exponent, further complain that present historiography is dominated by Western historians who continue to misinterpret Africa. Temu and Swai go on to make the interesting point that, even though Leopold von Ranke, the father of modern historiography, advocated objectivity and a dispassionate approach to the study of the past, he himself glorified his Prussian state, and that Lord Ashley, renowned British historian, extolled the virtues of the British empire in which, as we all know, Africans were exploited and treated as sub-humans. Therefore, many new African scholars demand a combination of objectivity, to the extent that it is possible to be objective, and ideology (the latter meaning a "revolutionary consciousness," to use Lansine Kaba's expression)—to make history and other disciplines more relevant to Africa's needs.

Anthropology or the study of culture, first in the form of ethnography [study of technologically less advanced societies or what ethnographers used to call "primitive societies"], began studying Africa before history did. However, the anthropological methodology has encountered the ire of even the most fair-minded Africanists both on the continent and in the West. The first ethnographers, who worked during the 1920s through the 1940s, did their research in collaboration with the colonial administrators whose aim was to understand the African cultures they encountered and facilitate colonization. Some of the ethnographers themselves were colonial administrators who visited their areas of authority and, in their free time, interviewed a few Africans about their most exotic customs and produced sensational monographs. A good example of the latter was Felix Eboue, black-Antillian and governor-general of former French Equatorial Africa (1941–1944), who left several ethnographic treatises on Oubangui-Chari (present Central African Republic). His observations constitute interesting reading because of the unique practices he describes, but are of little scientific value.

These early anthropologists, mostly British and French (Americans entered the field only after 1945), concentrated their attention on the culture of small African social units—which they called "tribes." In most cases, they presented a picture of timeless, static small societies, characterizing their values, to paraphrase Kaba, "as savage or at best as exotic curiosities." It is true, however, that despite their ethnocentric assumptions, the new "social scientists" tended to sympathize with the ethnic groups they studied, and demanded their preservation rather than their elimination by what they called the "superior" European culture.

Thus, although they contributed to our knowledge of some African societies, the first ethnographers, who claimed to be using a scientific approach, were no more than, to use the words of Southall (a former President of the African Studies Association), the "handmaiden of colonialism." No wonder Kaba notes with scorn that "the collusion between this sort of scholarship [that of anthropologists] and the colonial doctrine culminated in the rise of the 'tribal' image of African societies among Westerners..." While they popularized the scientific method of field work and participant-observation [meaning a method whereby researchers observe and participate in the culture they are studying] and sometimes criticized the colonial status quo, anthropologists were seen, up to the 1950s, as allies of colonialism. Their critics charged that they denigrated African cultures and engaged in micro- rather than macro- studies of African societies, while displaying no concern whatsoever for history. Furthermore, as defenders of minority cultures, they showed no regard for the concept of the nation in a culturally divided continent for the simple purpose of preserving exotic "ethnic distinctiveness." In other words, they were fascinated by small societies they characterized as "primitive" and tended to generalize their findings and apply them to the whole continent of Africa. One result of such ethnocentric scholarly arrogance is the strong criticism directed against the works of such well-known anthropologists as E. Evans-Pritchard, who wrote on the Nuer Sudan in 1935. Thus, the claim of objectivity on the part of the early anthropologists has been questioned and characterized, as one African scholar put it, as "another name for Western ethnocentrism and monopoly of the right to interpret other cultures of the world...," and as a subtle way of infusing their "moral values, unrecognized prejudices, covert racism, vested interests and, indeed, political economy upon theory."

In fact, there continues to be concern among continental African anthropologists and others that the damage done by European and some American anthropologists is beyond repair. According to Maxwell Owusu, three conditions must be fulfilled before Western anthropologists are totally accepted in Africa: 1) they must have a mastery of the language of the society they study; 2) they ought to show readiness and commitment to letting African scholars do the necessary and basic research, which requires in-depth cultural knowledge; and 3) they should be willing to engage in a critical and open intellectual dialogue with their African counterparts and abandon their alleged "arrogance." As expected, of course, the younger generation of anthropologists are aware of the errors of their predecessors and are much more careful in their study of and conclusions about African societies. Many of them have, for example, abandoned the use of the term "tribe" for "ethnic group," society, or people; brideprice for brideweatlh; paganism or heathenism for African traditional religion; and huts for homes (or houses). Overall, however, notwithstanding the errors of the past, the works of anthropologists such as Melville Herskovits, founder of the Center for African Studies at Northwestern University in the early 1950s, as well as those of African American sociologists, including E. Franklin Frazier, have contributed to the reintegration of anthropologists as credible social scientists in the field of African Studies. Their influence can be measured by the fact that, from 1957 to 2005, more than eight presidents of the African Studies Association have been anthropologists. In fact, anthropologist, Melville Herskovits, sometimes known as the "Dean of African Studies" in the United States, was the first president.

Just as with the earlier anthropologists, the first sociologists [those who study "the origin, organization, institutions, and development and evolution of human society"] have been highly criticized by continental African scholars. In fact, the first sociologists were undistinguishable from the ethnographers criticized above. Properly trained and unbiased sociologists did not enter the African field until 1945 and expanded their work in Africa only following independence during the 1960s. Thereafter, their major concern was to disengage themselves from anthropology and abandon the tendency to focus their attention on "scientific exoticism" [looking "scientifically" at unimportant and farfetched cultural issues], as was popular among the ethnographers. As Jean Copans writes, sociology was not just "a new specialization, it constituted a complete break on several counts; empirically, as it was taking into consideration the real history of the African peoples; in scale, as it moved on from village to national social groups (from 'mini' to 'maxi');" and theoretically, as it did not ignore the reality of colonialism on the continent.

However, just like other social scientists immediately following independence, sociologists saw Africa as a fertile ground for the testing of their theories on modernization, social change, and development, and assumed that African societies would follow the same developmental pattern as European societies. They were, in essence, evolutionaries who used the European theoretical framework to explain Africa's "transition from feudalism to capitalism" and from a traditional lifestyle to a modern (European) lifestyle. As a result, African (and African American) scholars have seriously questioned the methodologies and assumptions of modern sociologists, casting doubt upon their claim of scientific objectivism [in this case, non-biased treatment of black people] and rejecting one of their major theoretical frameworks, namely, that which looks at black societies through the prism of the white middle class family.

It is understandable, therefore, that a well- known African scholar, O. Onoge, of Nigeria, would echo loudly what many critics feel—that is, insofar as Africa is concerned, sociologists, including Lucy Mair, whom he calls "the Dean of applied functionalism," have demonstrated "amnesia [purposeful ignorance] of the colonial period," bias, and reactionary tendencies. In fact, like many Africans, Onoge still maintains that the "history of African sociology has few redeeming features. In the main [he adds], it is perverse and counter-revolutionary from an African standpoint." Temu and Swai, already mentioned in this chapter, scorn the discipline when they note sarcastically that sociology "...soars into empty abstraction" [meaning that it is too abstract and irrelevant for Africa].

On another level, two female Kenyan sociologists, Diane Kayongo-Male and Philista Onyango in *The Sociology of the African Family* (1984), cast doubt on many research activities undertaken by sociologists in Africa, particularly in reference to the African family. They point out that over-reliance on the survey method [which uses questionnaires and interviews] has been a major problem and that the interviews are usually not private, are conducted by people who are alien to the culture and the language, and that the final product is usually replete with translation misrepresentations. They urge that scholars "place highest reliability on family studies coming from indigenous researchers" and "read clearly to find out exactly how the study was carried out before we jump to unwarranted conclusions about African family life." The criticism, however, seems to have transformed the discipline for the better, making sociology one of the most vibrant and relevant disciplines in African Studies today.

Political scientists, who study government and the decision-making process, were the last ones to enter the field of African Studies for reasons not too difficult to ascertain and, when they did, they entered in full force. In Africa, the colonial administration (1885–1960) was weary of political scientists because they inevitably would have found too many unacceptable features within the governing system. Furthermore, because political education in the schools was forbidden, African political scientists were almost non-existent on the continent during the colonial era. Just prior to and following independence, however, political scientists, particularly Americans, were welcomed and even invited by the new African leaders as advisors, professors, and human resources. Some of the best known names include James Coleman and Carl Rosberg (Nigeria), Henry Bienen (Tanzania), Martin Kilson (Sierra Leone), Aristide Zolberg (Côte d'Ivoire), and Dennis Austin (Ghana). This first wave of political scientists was ebullient about the future of Africa: they enthusiastically talked and wrote of the process of modernization. They viewed Africa's problems of instability, centralization, ethnic and elite competition for resources, political repression, and competing power politics as temporary stages and as the pains of growth, so to speak, in the process toward democratization (the maintenance of multi-party states and the institutionalization of free elections), rapid industrialization, equitable distribution of national resources, an end to intense ethnic loyalties, social mobility, the weakening of obstructive traditional values, urbanization, expansion of literacy, elimination of diseases, and improved infrastructure (new roads, schools, health centers, and communication networks).

Unfortunately, as Naomi Chazan et al. noted in *Politics and Society in Contemporary Africa* (1988), "the modernization theory focused on internal factors to explain political processes in Africa" and underestimated the agrarian nature of African societies, the entrenchment of the bureaucracy and the impact of external factors, such as neo-colonialism, the external debt, and the unfair international trade system. It also showed clear ethnocentric arrogance in its patterning of African realities after Western values. A number of others, however, looked at the various competing cultures on the continent and foresaw the potential for serious political conflict. Unlike the modernization theorists, this group of political scientists emphasized ethnic differences or "tribalism," to use their preferred terminology at the time, group interests, and aspiring leaders, all vying to acquire for themselves and their "cronies" the state's scarce resources. Overall, the themes political scientists dealt with in general, up to the 1970s, were African nationalist

leaders, parties, elections, constitutions, ideologies, political instal
"charismatic" [articulate nationalist] leaders, ethnicity, and intr
tions. Unfortunately, their initial euphoria was shattered in 1963 w
military coup in Sub-Saharan Africa resulted in the assassination of Presi.
vanus Olympio of Togo. Several other military coups followed, including one ι.
puzzled nationalists and pan-Africanists alike: The overthrow of Kwame
Nkrumah, Ghana's first president, by the army in 1966. Prior to 1966, most political scientists had viewed the army as a modernizing force, disciplined and cohesive, and as a professional corps trained at such best military academies as Sand-
hurst (England) and St. Cyr (France), ready to defend the modern state rather
than topple or overthrow it.

As a result of the shock, many political scientists began to revise their theoretical frameworks. In the tradition of Samuel Huttington, they began looking at the
"stress and structural weaknesses" of African institutions which, in their view,
showed extreme "fragility, systemic flaws, and low levels of political culture—
which act[ed] as a sort of magnet to pull the armed forces into the power and legitimacy vacuum." Huttington had postulated that, in the developing world, "the
most important causes of military intervention in politics...[were] not military
but political and reflect[ed] not the social and organizational characteristics of the
military establishment but the political and institutional structure of society." In
other words, the army's behavior simply reflected how inadequate African societies were, with weak and corrupt governments, functioning primarily on the
basis of ethnic loyalties, selfishness, and abuses of citizens' rights. More recent political scientists, however, Samuel Decalo being a good example, have discredited
both theories, and have instead focused their attention on the internal organization of the army itself, namely, its weaknesses and rivalries which are often based
on ethnicity, age, rank, education, personal ambition, and nepotism. These social
scientists have pointed to the inefficient performance of the military as they replace a civilian government, making a mockery of their announced objectives of
ending ethnic conflict and corruption and improving the economy.

As in other disciplines, political scientists have been criticized for distorting
African realities to fit their own personal theoretical framework, explaining
African realities through complicated and exotic terms and concepts such as
"clientelism, dependence, machine politics, corporativism, modernization, cultural pluralism," and so on. In their midst, there has been a conflict between
"bourgeois and non-bourgeois" political scientists, the terms bourgeois and bourgeoisie being negatively used by African Marxists and neo-Marxists to characterize most American scholars and their colleagues on the African continent.
Barongo once wrote that "bourgeois African political scientists have turned political science into an instrument of class domination and exploitation." He advised
them to focus more on the issues of class exploitation and poverty as causes of dependence, the dominant role of the elite, excessive exercise of power, destabilization, and the colonially-inherited political institutions and practices that have cor-
rupted many African leaders.

The reader might wish to know that there are other divisions within the political science "academy," a topic that is suited only for more advanced students. Yet,
for the sake of completeness and for the benefit of the instructor, we will briefly
note them here. There are the traditionalists who use a descriptive quasi-historical
approach to the study of politics and focus mainly on diplomacy, formal institu-

tions, and legal systems such as constitutions, states, and parties. They dominated the discipline prior to 1945. This breed of political scientitsts tended to doubt the validity of scientific methods as applied to human behavior, and, although they carefully studied and observed political behavior, they did not attempt to predict it, as they had no faith in statistical probabilities. Very few traditionalists exist today.

As a result of the changes in world politics in the aftermath of the Second World War (1939–1945), however, a new breed of political scientists, less Euro-centric, emerged in reaction to the traditionalist model, namely, the behavioral-ists, who focused on the concept of the nation-state, calling for the use of scientific methods and theory-building to explain and even predict political behavior. (Patrick McGowan represents the major revisionist in the discipline.) Accordingly, behavioralists attempted to use data quantification (statistics) and measurements (numbers) to predict political behavior and test their "empirical hypotheses." They too are on their way out as relevant political scientists. The structural-func-tionalists ridicule the claims of (social) "scientific" approaches that produce "scientific" results. Instead, they look at international political systems rather than at individual nation-states and use a comparative approach to politics through a focus on such features as legislatures and leaders' roles and assessing how these function. (Immanuel Wallerstein is a proponent of this theory on Africa, and most Marxists and neo-Marxists fall within this category of thinkers.)

Interestingly enough, however, following in the footsteps of Samir Amin, once Director of the *Institut pour le Development Economique et Progres* in Dakar, Senegal, many political scientists are now fascinated by a variety of frameworks focusing on political economy [the interface between politics and the economy], which is popular at the schools of Dar-es-Salaam and Ibadan. Political economy attempts to use the scientific tools of economics and stresses the point that politics are dictated by economic considerations and vice-versa. In this group, one finds the political science activists, Marxists, and proponents of the dependency and underdevelopment theorists. The dependence model views Africa (the *periphery*, the margin or the exploited end of the relationship) as a victim of international capitalism (the *core*, or the center that decides about and benefits from the dependence relationship), and claim that the African masses are exploited by a small African elite—the bourgeoisie or petty bourgeoisie—that renders Africa dependent and underdeveloped. This theory is certainly pessimistic, as it portrays African societies and states as inexorably trapped by a worldwide capitalist conspiracy which controls information and knowledge, technology, wealth, and the economic market. Immanuel Wallerstein (according to Chazan et al.) holds this theory, which also implies that the progress of one nation necessarily "impedes" the progress of other nations.

Although the dependency theory sheds light on the roots of underdevelopment, on social inequalities and economic structures, it falls short as it focuses primarily on factors external to Africa, makes Africans passive receptors rather than actors, neglects the issues of ethnicity, race, and nationalism and provides a totally materialistic perspective of African societies, disregarding the spiritual and intellectual side of life. The statist school, as classified by Chazan et al., on the other hand, which seems to be popular among African scholars as advanced by well-known Africanists such as Carl Rosberg and Robert Jackson, emerged during the 1970s. The statist (a word derived from the word state) emphasizes the state as "the motor force behind social and economic occurrences in Africa," and focuses, therefore, on the autonomy of the state apparatus, on leadership styles, and patron-client relationships. It concludes that the post-colonial state does have the power to mobilize and transform resources but that it has not done so for the benefit of the masses. It blames African leaders for most failures, accuses them of abusing their power for personal gains, and makes them responsible for the continent's chronic international debt. Again, to borrow from Chazan et al., the statist theory, while drawing attention to African "internal dynamics [i.e., the state itself]," confuses the concept of state and government. States remain but governments come and go easily. In addition, it provides no understanding of the relations between state and society or between state and classes, and exaggerates the degree of power of the leaders.

A theory related to the statist model is one expanded by Robert Bates, known as the political choice theory, which sees the state as autonomous or, as Bates put it, asserts "the independent status and determining power of politics." Bates goes on to say in *Essays on the Political Economy of Rural Africa* (1983) that states have their own objectives:

> They want taxes and revenues and intervene in their economic environments to secure them. Politicians want power. And they use the instruments of the state to secure and retain it by manipulating the economy to political advantage. In Africa, political elites have rendered economic markets instruments of political organization.

Whereas the statist approach has been fundamentally negative on the nature and intentions of African states as it portrays them as inexorably linked to the imperfect nature of the leadership, Bate's theory seems to straddle the middle ground, stressing the enormous but not absolute power and autonomy of the state, which has been used to enhance leaders' political gains to the detriment and misery of the masses. Contrary to the dependency theory, the political choice theory sees economic development not as simply related but as subordinate to internal politics. Bates claims that "the political is not merely reducible to the economic; rather, it stands apart from it and can act upon it, often in a manner that is costly in economic terms."

One of the most recent versions of the political choice perspective has been advanced by Naomi Chazan, Robert Mortimer, John Raveland, and Donald Rothchild. They look at the state in Africa as maintaining some degree of autonomy and at political leaders as being able to mobilize resources, the economy, and society to achieve certain goals but also as constrained by historical legacies, demographic pressures, cultural ecology, ideological divisions, and international factors. Thus, while this perception focuses on past errors, its proponents say, it "uncovers components of ongoing processes and elucidates future opportunities and constraints." Unlike the statist theory, the political choice model further posits that a study of politics in Africa should focus on state-society relationships rather than on state-economic relationships or simply on the state itself.

To recapitulate, here is a brief summary of the preceding theories as applied to Africa. 1) The *traditionalists* used historical narrative to study politics and did not believe in the so-called social "scientific" method nor did they attempt to explain "scientifically" current and predict future political behavior in Africa; 2) The *behavioralists* focused on the functioning of the new nation-states in Africa and, un-

like the traditionalists, had faith in using numbers and statistics to explain and predict political behaviour; 3) The *structural-functionalists* study the structures and
functions of political institutions, disregard the claim of "scientism" and compare
nation-states in order to make more realistic generalizations; 4) The *Marxists* focus
on the role of social classes and the resulting exploitation, as well as on the relationship between politics and the economy, and claim that an equitable economic
system would solve all societal ills; 5) The proponents of the *political economy statist school* focus attention on the strong power of the African state and its political
leaders, who thus determine the direction of the economy, and blame the African
leadership for the problems the continent experiences, especially in the economic
sector; 6) Bates' *political choice theory*, like the preceding theory, capitalizes on the
power and autonomy of the state in Africa, making the economy subservient to
politics and the state, and blames the African leadership for the continent's economic mess, a result of their unwise choices; 7) Chazan's (et al.'s) type of *political
choice theory* differs from Bate's in that, although recognizing the power of the
state, points to the various challenges and constraints the leadership faces, including the various colonial legacies, personal ideologies, cultural traditions, and the
inequalities of the international market system.

The new emphases and approaches in the discipline will perhaps make political
scientists less vulnerable to criticism from continental African scholars and others
in the academy. In fact, Barongo, a major critic, gives some credit to the scholars
in the discipline when he observes that, "Ladd's and Lipset's survey of the profession clearly shows that American political scientists in general stand politically to
the right of sociologists but well to the left of the general population."

Geographers have been the least controversial in the field of African studies.
Even during the colonial period, geographers had established several associations
which sent trained and quasi-trained "scientists" to the continent to survey the
terrain for the benefit of diplomats and the army, and for other scientists interested in Africa. As expected, their activity increased following independence. For
a number of developmental reasons, African governments undertook surveys of
different regions of their countries. In general, geographers tend to be less hindered than political scientists or sociologists in their analysis of African affairs.
One reason, as pointed out by critics, is that, at least in their earlier period, they
concentrated on apolitical physical geography and paid little attention to cultural
and demographic geography. Most geographers, including the greatest pioneer,
the late William Hance, have escaped criticism.

Linguists have been less conspicuous in African Studies circles but have played
a vital role in the analysis of cultural origins, and, along with literature experts,
such as Ruth Finnegan, have shed light on African societies, on the possible influences these exerted upon each other, on migratory movements, and on geographical and demographic distribution patterns. Since the 1850s, German missionaries
and linguists (such as Westermann and Homburger) and lovers of oral literature,
collected African folklore, proverbs, riddles, and stories, some of which were later
accepted as valid historical sources. A similar role has been played by musicologists who have strengthened the history of Africa by showing cultural and material contact (through musical instruments, for example) even prior to the 1884–85
partition of the continent. This is exemplified by as works by musicologist Perci-
val Kirby have done in Southern Africa. In other words, one could establish the
nature of contact between two cultures or peoples by studying their musical in-

struments or songs and discover, through similarities, whether or not the two borrowed from each other. If yes, then their history may be linked. These humanists and artists have helped restore the worth and dignity of African traditions and cultural manifestations, often denigrated and neglected during the colonial era. During the post-colonial period, musicologists and ethnomusicologists have pleaded with the African elite and their leaders to preserve their rich but potentially vanishing traditions.

The study of African art has also been a significant component of African Studies. Since 1905, when a mask from the Fang people of Gabon was taken to Europe and its stylistic freedom eventually inspired such artists as Pablo Picasso and Andre Matisse, African art, particularly sculpture, through the recent works of scholars such as Frank Willett and William Fagg, has been gaining acceptance from the academic community. Therefore, earlier ethnography-art specialists, including P. German (on Cameroon, 1910), Gunter Pressman (on Fang of Gabon, 1913), and J. Van Wing (on the former Belgian Congo, 1921–1938), paved the way for the new artists to establish once and for all the fact that art and music are the two most important contributions of Africa to world civilizations.

According to Daniel Biebuyck, however, African art specialists still have a long way to go. Their achievements in the discipline still "lag in range, scope, depth, and comprehensiveness, and…impact on the other academic fields of study." Biebuyck outlines several approaches and themes that need to be explored, including more focus on the neglected areas such as the former Spanish, French, and Portuguese-speaking colonies in Africa; individual African artists; socioeconomic and legal aspects of art; the acquisition of artifacts through purchase and inheritance; labor and acquisition of the primary materials of art and payment of services; taxonomy of materials; and the system of ownership or temporary control and guardianship of an artist's creative possessions. Biebuyck also complains that there is much confusion and uncertainty among the experts themselves regarding the scope and the definition of basic terminology such as art, craft, artistic, material culture, and aesthetics.

The study of African religion by scholars such as John Mbiti, George Parrinder, and Aylard Shorter (in *African Theology*, 1975) has had two effects. The first has been the restoration of Africa's religion(s) to almost the same level of respectability and acceptance as other religions of the world, as a system that attempts to cope with human existence, understand the cosmos, and explain the relationship between humans and the supernatural. These authors have thus attempted to dispel the stereotypes and myths attributed to African religion by nineteenth- and early twentieth-century missionaries who viewed it as nothing more than a series of superstitious beliefs associated with ancestors' "worship" (rather than veneration), with human sacrifice, the drum, and polytheistic practices. The second effect has been to sharpen the similarities of African religion (e.g., belief in one creator of the universe), and differences (e.g., absence of elaborate physical buildings for worship as in the West, of proselytizers or ambulant preachers who strive to convert others and travel from one locality to another, and weekly predictable days of worship) between African religion(s) and Christianity or Islam. African philosophy, on the other hand, is the latest of the disciplines in African Studies. Catholic priest, Placide Temples (who worked in former Zaire and wrote *Bantu Philosophy*, 1945), and John Mbiti, himself an African philosopher and theologian, are known for their pioneering works in this discipline. Again, their studies have refuted claims that Africans are unable to develop or understand complex philosophical systems and that their thought patterns resemble those of a Western child with whom one must talk in symbols and examples. In fact, proponents of these claims attempted to prove the validity of their position by pointing to the round (rather than rectangular) shapes of African homes and the "crooked" or curvilinear rather than straight nature of their paths and traditional walkways. They were trying to make the point that Africans think in a circular fashion.

Notwithstanding the importance of economic development in Africa, economists have been the late-comers into the field of African Studies. Just as the sociologists, however, Africanist economists, during the 1950s and early 1960s, also assumed that African societies would follow the same developmental stages as Western societies. They, therefore, attempted to apply the theoretical models fitting European societies. Essentially, early economists used the traditional vs. the modern framework or the economic stages theory advanced by W. W. Rostow. Rostow identified at least five stages through which all societies are expected to go, and postulated that, once conditions such as enough capital, entrepreneurship spirit, needed skills, existence of foreign exchange [i.e., American dollars, British pounds, and French francs], and sound management practices were present, African economies would advance the same way those of the West did centuries ago.

This unrealistic framework has been replaced by the international-structuralist model, which views the developing world, especially Africa, as helplessly dependent on the capitalist world due to unfair and unequal economic and power relationships. Proponents of the theory see the world as made up of two societies and two economies: the capitalist and the less-developed world and the "haves" and "have-nots" within the developing countries themselves. As social scientists, these economists have tended to focus on policies designed to eradicate poverty and provide employment for all. As Michael Todaro notes, there are two sub-models or versions of the theory, both attempting to explain the reasons for underdevelopment. The first is the neo-colonial dependence sub-model which focuses on the unequal relationships between the Western economies (the core or center) and the developing nations (the periphery or margin). Todaro claims that "landlords, entrepreneurs, merchants, salaried public officials, trade union leaders, etc." in the developing world simply perpetuate the conditions of dependence, as they serve as *compradors (buyers)* of the former, with no power or initiative of their own. The second submodel, which Todaro calls the "false paradigm" model, claims that underdevelopment has been caused and perpetuated by the ill advice of the Western institutions (the UN, UNESCO, the IMF, the World Bank, and others) and their experts, who distort African realities to serve their own economic purposes and test their assumptions and theories on development. Scholars who advance this submodel also hasten to add that, because the training of most of the Third World experts takes place in the West, the cycle of underdevelopment and dependence will continue as the indigenous experts return home simply to apply their irrelevant and distorted theories and end up defending the status quo of the elites. (Both submodels have been advanced by neo-Marxists.) As expected, many African scholars from the continent tend to look with suspicion at these developmental theories. Wang Metuge, for example, characterizes both political scientists and economists as pseudo-scientists who, to gain "scientific credibility," have lately inundated their journals with statistics, expressed in "econometrics" and "politimetrics."

What, then, seems to somewhat unify the scholars from so many persuasions and disciplines in African Studies? Ohaegbulam, referred to earlier, identifies four interdisciplinary models that are implicit in many of the intellectual constructs advanced by Africanists, which are summarized below: the traditional, the colonial, the Marxist, and the pan-African models. Ohaegbulam notes that the traditional model has been proposed by some as the most appropriate for the understanding of Africa and the black experience. Proponents of the model claim that a return to "the source," such as Egypt, to African traditions, to early civilizations, and to Africa's pristine state is a *conditio sine qua non* for any study of black people. One of the weaknesses of the model is that it ignores the fact that Africa is no longer purely traditional: the old and the new either live side by side or have managed to merge.

The colonial model tends to emphasize the colonial period (1885–1960) and its everlasting impact on all African institutions, without, in any way, justifying colonialism. Its proponents maintain that Africa would not be what it is today without the misfortune of colonial domination. They tend to see Africa and African-America, for that matter, as colonies of the West: Africans under neo-colonialism [a new type of colonial domination following Africa's independence during the 1960s and 1970s] and dependence, and black Americans under domestic colonialism, with both people still experiencing "political domination, economic exploitation, and cultural subjugation." One of the problems of this model is that it tends to overlook the African traditional past and its lasting impact. It also looks at the continent from a negative perspective, portraying Africans as struggling helplessly to free themselves from Western colonial and neo-colonial domination and the evil and sinister intentions of the white man.

The Marxist model, increasingly popular during the 1970s, when it was energized by the establishment of the now-defunct "revolutionary" Marxist governments in Angola, Mozambique, Guinea-Bissau, and Ethiopia, posits that the only way to understand accurately the African experience on the continent and in the Diaspora is to "scientifically" analyze the class phenomenon, which is based on the control, ownership, and management of the means of production (property, business, land, equipment, factories, mineral resources). Marxists, or the followers of Karl Marx's philosophy, hold that the major social problems are caused by class differences, which pit the poor against the rich, hence their use of the expression *class struggle*. For Marxists, while the spiritual world does not exist and religion is the *opium* of the people, our actions are fundamentally and primarily motivated by economic considerations, even though we are often not aware of it. Interestingly, Marxists and neo-Marxists [scholars who wish to revise Marxism in light of the fall of socialism and its economic system, as is the case in the former Soviet Union] hold that racism is based on economic factors and that it can be eliminated if social classes are done away with. Thus, according to them, once the economic issue is resolved, race will simply whither away. Such an assertion is certainly problematic as the concept of class in Marxist terms may not be applicable to Africa. Roxborough notes, for example, that "classes in Africa are more complex, and...usually weaker. They are frequently incomplete in the sense that the dominant class, or one fraction of the dominant class, is absent." Rural "classes," are much more important in developing societies than in Europe or America. Furthermore, to believe that racism will vanish when economic conditions become equitable is tantamount to living a utopia or in an unreal world.

The pan-African model, on the other hand, focuses on the commonalities of experiences of black people—slavery, colonialism, racism, imperialism, neo-colonialism, and desire for unity—and on one naturally unifying factor: skin color. The proponents of the model, invoking the ideals and goals of the early pan-Africanist movement led by W. E. B. DuBois, Kwame Nkrumah, George Padmore, Marcus Garvey, and later, by Malcom X and the late Reverend Leon Sullivan, hold that pan-Africanism not only explains the black experience but also provides solutions to black peoples' problems. However, as Ohaegbulam observes, the pan-Africanist framework tends to gloss over or even write off major differences among black people on the continent and in the Diaspora. For example, language, religious beliefs, and even the experience and perception of slavery and freedom are dissimilar in Africa, in the African American community, in the Caribbean, and Latin American countires, such as Brazil. Notwithstanding the shortcomings, however, the pan-Africanist model is a useful comparative teaching tool.

The African Studies Association

The study of Africa acquired enhanced status from the creation of the African Studies Association (ASA) in 1957. The first meeting that led to the establishment of the association took place at the Roosevelt Hotel in New York City under the auspices of the Carnegie Corporation (which provided $6,500 to underwrite the proceedings). The corporation was represented by its President, Dr. Alan Pifer, and some 35 scholars from several disciplines, particularly anthropology, history, and sociology, that met and decided to form the association whose objective would be to collect data and expand knowledge about Africa and its people. In addition, the ASA would stimulate and promote research "in ways appropriate to a scholarly organization" and facilitate communication among interested scholars.

However, some members, particularly African, Caribbean, and African American scholars, came to believe that the ASA should play the role of an active advocate of African causes as well as that of a promoter of knowledge. Likewise, these same scholars began to resent the fact that the association was dominated by white, Anglo male scholars, whose research agendas seemed to them totally irrelevant to Africa's needs. They accused the association's leadership of continuing to play the condescending role of "liberal mediators" and secular "missionaries" of Africa, while collaborating with government agencies such as the State Department, Defense Department, Central Intelligence Agency, and the African American Institute (headquartered in New York). They wished to see the ASA play a major role on critical issues and problems relevant to Africa, such as the liberation of the whole of Southern Africa, especially South Africa, economic development, the strengthening of democratic institutions, health promotion, literacy expansion, and combating the threat posed by military rule on the continent.

These differences burst out in the open in the 1969 ASA meeting in Montreal when, according to Immanuel Wallerstein, a group of black American scholars "seized the platform and put forward a series of demands" they had voiced two years earlier through their splinter African Heritage Studies Association. As a result, the association became much more sensitivity to the views and feelings of minority scholars. Yet, very few African Americans have remained members of the

Association, which lately has been dominated by historians (in 1988, for example, six out of nine Board members were historians), political scientists, and anthropologists. (Unlike Africanist historians, however, Africa-trained anthropologists, artists, musicians, and literature scholars have also their own discipline-specific associations.)

Continental African scholars, as noted earlier, have also been critical of the association's research agenda, have questioned the theoretical premises of some of its members, and resent their control over the canons of the various traditional disciplines. Furthermore, Africans would like to see a more radical approach to scholarship, whereby the researcher is not just a passive onlooker of events occurring in Africa but remains active, embracing African causes throughout his scholarly life. They have also demanded that more credit be given to the work of continental scholars and that blacks have a fairer representation in the association's decision-making process. Some of their concerns are being addressed by the association's Board of Directors. For example, recently, an effort has been made to bring African scholars from the continent to the annual meetings at no cost to them and to guarantee minority representation on the Board.

What is the situation today? Even though the relations between American Africanists and continental African scholars have improved over the years, much of the earlier tension remains and has surfaced openly from time to time. Although the reasons are complex and varied, the most resented is the fact that the field is still dominated by Western Africanists abroad and not by those who arduously "toil in the trenches" of the continent. No one has expressed this problem more succinctly than Thandika Mkandawire whose remarks are summarized below.

First, according to Mkandawire, part of the uneasiness stems from the fact that Anglo-Saxon, male Africanists have remained the "gatekeepers" of African studies and its disciplines, as referees of journals, manuscript reviewers and evaluators, and researchers who are constantly looking for collaborators on the continent to further their personal goals; who act as a police force that not only inspects one's outfit but, above all, is intent on admitting as few Africans as possible through the gates of "the palace," or what we commonly call the "academy," in order not to turn it into a "ghetto." Indeed, this repugnant attitude came to the fore in 1995 when one of the foremost and renowned Africanists, Philip Curtin (at Johns Hopkins University for the past two decades or so), acrimoniously complained in the *Chronicle of Higher Education* that the hiring of many "unqualified" or untrained minorities such as Africans (and African Americans) in the name of affirmative action, and the concomitant rejection of qualified young white graduates, had contributed to the *ghettoization* of African studies units across the country. Confronted that year by members of both black and white races at the annual meeting of the African Studies Association in Orlando, Florida, who accused him of creating divisiveness and injecting racism into the field of African Studies in the United States and elsewhere, Curtin adamantly refused to apologize or recant what, in the view of most members, were unwarranted, insensitive, self-serving, and inaccurate remarks. The debate did not, of course, die in Florida — it has continued.

The second cause of friction, according to Mkandawire, is the "primacy" of dubious deductive "theoretical frameworks" or guiding theories used by many Africanists when they study Africa and its people. As funds become scarce and the pressure to publish increases at the universities, there is the tendency on the part of many scholars to mold reality to fit theories rather than molding one's theory to fit the African reality. Indeed, certain disciplines will not consider a paper to be scholarly unless it is couched in a theory or theoretical framework both before and after the research is completed. Third is the resentment on the part of African scholars when they see their on-going work on the continent almost totally ignored by their Africanist colleagues who are quick to claim *eurekas* ("I single-handedly discovered this") when they come up with new conclusions about Africa. Arguably, American scholars often counter this charge by alleging that the African scholars themselves are unable or, for reasons of suspicion that Western researchers will "steal" their work, are unwilling to share their research agendas until the work is completed.

The fourth source of tension seems to lie on the fact that study protocols or research designs, the conduct of interviews (a popular way of doing research in Africa), and control of important facets of field work are the purview of the Northern Hemisphere or Western scholars, with African scholars in the Southern Hemisphere remaining as onlookers or sometimes as paid collaborators, or study facilitators. Relegated to the receiving-end of the competition for funds and control of the research agendas, Africans, therefore, are reduced to what Mkandwaire calls "barefoot empiricists," similar to men walking without shoes in the streets looking for data. Fifth is the seeming Western Africanists' tendency to simply dismiss as "irrelevant" or unscholarly the publications of continental Africans by either not listing them in their bibliographical entries or listing them as references but never directly citing them. The sixth factor is the propensity for foreign scholars to think that they know best when it comes to Africa, reflected clearly in their "teleological bent" [tendency to predict future events] of the sixties and seventies—to use the author's words—as they pushed forward their modernizing and developmental theories discussed in the preceding sections. Thus, Western scholars are perceived as constantly giving unsolicited advice to African statesmen and continental African scholars. At present, for example, they claim to have all the answers to Africa's problems, from democratic reforms and economic recovery to conflict resolution.

Finally, says Mkandawire, what irks many Africans is Western scholars' "Afro-pessimism" or the "CNN factor," which looks at Africa only in terms of crisis and contributes to "disdain" and "contempt" for all that is African. Indeed, no longer do these Africanists project the image of solidarity and admiration about which they wrote during the 1960s and early 1970s, as Africa entered the period of independence. To prove his point, Mkandawire lists the most common demeaning terms Africanists, especially political scientists and economists, have used in the context of Africa's economic system and state apparatus: pirate capitalism, crony capitalism, nurture capitalism, the state as a lame Leviathan, swollen state, soft state, predatory state, parasitical state, rent-seeking state, over-extended state, kleptocratic state, perverted capitalist state, unsteady state, fallen state, underground state, one that "squats like a bloated toad, simultaneously developed and underdeveloped." Africa is described as moving toward its "final collapse, oblivion, and self-destruction." (In fact, some "experts" have suggested that Africa should be re-colonized or colonized again.)

To be sure, one could say that the tendency to generalize and write only about problems that affect Africa has hurt Africa's ability to redefine its image abroad. To those who are sensitive to the feelings of African scholars and are aware of the resilient tendencies for the West to denigrate Africa, there is no doubt that a residue of arrogance, superiority complex, and scholastic mercilessness surfaces when the worth of scholarship from Africa is evaluated. One way to illustrate this point is to examine the language with which some manuscripts by African scholars are rejected by reviewers of journal articles or book manuscripts. Although rejection of manuscripts submitted by Africanists in the West is at times expressed in unflattering terms, yet (if one is privy to some of the reviewers' comments), the tone of rejection of a continental African's work is often quite appalling. This writer has seen reviews that have classified a Cameroonian Ph.D.'s article submitted for possible publication as "worse than the work of an undergraduate student." Commenting on a Kenyan scholar's article, one reviewer wrote: "Absolutely useless internationally and domestically," "unworthy of our journal" or "our university press." In the majority of the cases where rejection is the end result, there is no constructive criticism to salvage or improve the work submitted. Such an attitude and humiliating characterization should not have a place in academia, but, perhaps to protect their academic turf, many scholars act this way and with much virulence. Under these circumstances, Africanists should understand why, at times, their continental colleagues do not welcome them with open arms when they set foot on African soil in pursuit of their academic goals. Francis B. Nyamnjoh and Natang B. Jua, after discussing the crisis, including the actual violence African universities are experiencing, underscore the minor role to which continental African scholars have been relegated, and conclude by admonishing that "...Only by creating space for African scholarship based on Africa as a unit of analysis in its own right can we begin to correct prevalent situations whereby much is what African states, societies, and economies are *not* (thanks to dogmatic and normative assumptions of mainstream scholarship) but very little of what they actually are. Accepting the research agendas of African scholars may be not just 'a matter of ecumenism or goodwill,' but also the beginnings of a conversation that could enrich scholarship in the West and elsewhere."

Even though, in the process of highlighting the differences between Africanists and African scholars, one should avoid generalizing, most Africanists, both at home and abroad, would not dispute the general accuracy of Mkandawire's earlier remarks. The question is the degree of the pervasiveness of the attitudes he chronicled within the African Studies academy. Does he believe that the differences cannot be resolved? No! Mkandawire, who undoubtedly speaks for many African scholars, advocates tolerance and better understanding between the two groups. Such understanding can be achieved through collaboration on the basis of equal partnership in research and other academic endeavors, through mutual respect of each other's work and open admission that race is a factor to contend with, one which Western scholars, especially Africanists in North America, must strive to overcome in their encounter with continental black scholars. As Gwendolyn Mikell, Director of the African Studies Program at Georgetwon University noted in 1999, the ASA has to forge mutually beneficial relationships with other associations and Africa. The ASA, she wrote, must "overcome the historical hierarchies based on race and nationality that attended [its] creation and early history." After demonstrating the need to forge closer relations with Africa, Mikell addresses the ASA internal problems and concludes by saying: "We cannot cede African studies to either black or white Africanists, but we must insist that our association, our newly trained professionals, and our ASA leadership mirror the cultural and ethnic diversity that is America." African scholars, on their part, must learn to accept as legitimate the training and the skills of their overseas col-

leagues and realize that a diversity of perspectives can only enrich their knowledge and perhaps assist Africa and its institutions to move forward.

In her 1996 African Studies Association presidential address, Iris Burger joined
Mkandawire in echoing the theme of collaboration among scholars across regions
and disciplines and underscored the need to stop the tide of brain drain or the
flight of "human capital" from African universities. She urged members to share
with their continental colleagues the benefits of modern research techniques and
the opportunities offered by the Internet. Yet, the issues of who should speak for
Africans and who holds the "right" perspective on Africa (i.e., is it the Africanist
in America or Europe or the continental African scholar who has the right to lead
the discourse on Africentricity or Afrocentricity?) will continue to liven the debate
within the African Studies academy. While scholars such as Edward Said, Molefi
Asante, and Oyekan Owomoyela, just to mention a few, will continue to impugn
Western scholars of allegedly spreading "tainted" African scholarship through
their Euro-centric perspectives, others wish to see a field of African Studies that
specifically addresses one or all of the following practical themes in Africa: the
primacy of a development-centered focus or sustained development (Ann Seidman); the pursuit of health and gender studies (the latter an agenda pushed forward partly by feminist literature and partly by the Women's Caucus of the
African Studies Association); vigorous research on sexuality in Africa; and a focus
on democratic reforms (Mahmood Mamdani and Claude Ake).

Finally, we should also note that some scholars are uneasy about the debate that
Burger characterizes as the conflict over "epistemological boundaries." A need
arises to reconcile global, interdisciplinary area studies (pronounced dead by such
scholars as Robert Bates) and discipline autonomy, specifically the dichotomy between a local perspective and a global perspective brought into focus recently by
what we have commonly characterized as "village globalization." On this issue,
many would agree with Burger when she notes that " ... at time when 'global' has
become the buzzword in scholarship and policy, we should continue to insist on the
necessity for the contextualized knowledge of language and culture that has been a
strength of area studies and to see local and global knowledge as complementary."
In other words, the two are not mutually exclusive, as globalization always starts
with villagization in an evolutionary process that necessarily binds the beginning
and the end together, that is, the village and the globe, thus the adage "act locally
but think globally." Most likely, however, the complaints of the continental African
scholars will continue, as they are powerless to change the system. Lack of financial
resources to pursue meaningful research activities, the absence of a long tradition of
scholarship on the continent due to historical factors, and the scarcity of publishing
houses and adequate library materials, all contribute to a sense of frustration and
bitterness. Unfortunately, there is no light in sight at the end of the tunnel.

As we conclude this chapter, we owe our readers a brief discussion of the state
of most African universities as we continue to make strides into the twenty-first
century. The situation of many African universities as centers of learning and vigorous, objective research has been deteriorating since the 1970s, the major obstacle being the absence of academic freedom and adequate funding from the state,
which remains the sole significant source of funds for the overwhelming majority
of the institutions of higher learning on the continent. Aware of their power of
leverage, governments choose to close the institutions whenever there is a strong
voice of dissent from students or the faculty. This has happened in Kenya,

Cameroon, Ghana, Nigeria, Chad, Sierra Leone, and in many other African countries. Again, speaking for many African scholars, Thandika Mkandawire writes that the state in Africa "has not hesitated to use its power to bludgeon our skulls, close universities, ban books or generally do everything to silence real or imagined dissidents in institutions of higher learning."

On Kenya, for example, James Mittelman reminds us that research proposals by faculty and students must be approved formally by the president's office and that students and staff have to obtain clearance from this office to travel abroad for a conference. Once a pride of East African institutions of higher learning, Kenyan universities are becoming obsolete. A combination of "political repression and material shortages [of chalk, paper, supplies, current journals, and books] has put a choke hold on academic freedom." While new construction at African universities is virtually at a standstill, in countries such as Nigeria, adds Mittelman, at times university faculty and students are allowed to use the library only one day a week. Dormitory rooms in such countries as Ghana, Nigeria, and Kenya, designed for three or four students, are now housing as many as seven or more students! State of the art computers are still a novelty in most African institutions, and transactions are still done by pen, pencil, and a typewriter.

The precarious conditions under which most African universities operate have been exacerbated by a reduction in research funds out of economic hardships and the demise of the Cold War, which diverted foreign assistance funds away from Africa, resulting in an unprecedented flight of faculty to institutions overseas, causing what has been called Africa's "brain drain." Furthermore, as a result of sustained repression of freedom of expression, much of the research in the social sciences is irrelevant to the practical needs of the Africans and remains distant from public policy. Mkandawire places some of the blame on the African scholars themselves who, following independence during the 1960s, went along with the nationalist ideology that repressed open discussion and controlled any research effort on sensitive issues that could allegedly impede the process of nation building. Their "collaborationist" attitude vis-à-vis the modernization and developmental ideologies of the 1960s and 1970s, which channelled research agendas towards modernizing the newly independent countries, did not help the cause of the institutions of higher learning either.

In the context, development meant nothing more than concentration on programs and studies that would contribute overnight to the "growth of per capita incomes." In most countries, academics were given cars, "mansions," and allowances of all sorts to silence their voices. This strategy, says Mkandawire, was so openly blatant in former Zaire during Mobutu's regime that people in the street amusingly called a state-donated faculty car PTT ("*professeur tais-toi*" or "professor shut up"). Even though the new generation of students and scholars is becoming more vocal against injustices and repression of academic freedom, it has not yet won the war. The obstacles are numerous, as many African leaders, democratic reforms and international outcry notwithstanding, still do not hesitate to imprison students and faculty alike, reduce financial support to the university to a minimum and, quite often, close them indefinitely altogether. The shortage of textbooks, the lack of university presses, continued reliance on Western textbooks and expatriates, and the decline of external funds to support research, make the future of African universities look so bleak that, short of revolution, some experts say, no substantive change for the better is likely to occur.

Summary

The field of African Studies comprises all the disciplines in the humanities, the arts, and the social sciences that focus specifically on Africa and the African peoples from early times to the present. Because these disciplines are different from each other in focus and methodologies, the resulting research conclusions may differ, and tensions among the respective scholars do arise. Despite their differences, however, all studies aim at looking at Africa scientifically in order to provide an accurate understanding of the continent and its people, suggest solutions to pressing problems, and facilitate the exchange of useful information among interested scholars and the public.

As a result of the fact that, for a long time, Africa was left out of the academic world due to such factors as European ethnocentrism, the slave trade, colonialism, and racism, African Studies is a relatively new field which, in fact, did not fully develop until the 1970s. The establishment of the African Studies Association in 1957, the emergence of independent African states during the 1960s, the uncovering of new written sources, the inclusion of oral tradition as a valid historical tool, and the impact of student activism from the civil rights movement in the United States during the 1960s, all facilitated the acceptance and respectability of African Studies within the "academy."

Historically, anthropology, history, sociology, political science, literature, and economics have played a major role in the field, while music, art, geography, linguistics, archaeology, philosophy, and religion have been vital ancillary disciplines in the development of the field and the understanding of Africa. The field of African Studies, which began in the West (Britain, France, and the United States), is still dominated by Western scholars who also control its association, determine by and large the acceptable canons of the disciplines, set the research agenda, and have the resources and access to publishing houses and university presses. As a result, continental African scholars often feel that they are treated as "second class" academics.

Continental Africanists have also questioned some of the Western assumptions including the claim of "scientific objectivity" and are of the opinion that many of the studies undertaken by Africanist scholars are biased and irrelevant or distort the African reality. The debate heightened more recently as a result of the emergence of the Marxist and neo-Marxist school, which insists on thorough analysis of classes and the modes of production as the only viable and accurate basis for a realistic understanding of the development of Africa. Put simply, as Martin Staniland does, the relevant questions that Africanists have been asked to respond to are: What is the intellectual or cultural mission of African Studies? Do scholars have the obligation to commit themselves to solving the problems of Africa through their disciplines? How and who should interpret Africa? What is the role of the non-African scholar? Although the answers have been numerous, Staniland identifies five general responses to these queries.

The "Washingtonian formula," in Staniland's view (prevalent particularly during the 1950s and 1960s), saw African Studies as a partial response to the Cold War and a tool to help preserve the "free world." This mission was, in fact, the condition the American government set for its support of the field during its initial stages, namely, to promote capitalism, democracy, and justice abroad. Consequently, the seeming attempt by the government to interfere in the affairs of the new academic effort in African Studies was one of the reasons of the conflict that erupted at the 1969 Montreal meeting of the African Studies Association. The currently less popular "brokerage and discipline formula," on the other hand, considered African Studies to be a forum and an endeavor to prevent conflicts among cultures and societies, build international "bridges," and foster intercultural understanding. Proponents of the formula emphasize the triple mission of the scholar as "a researcher, educator, and advisor to Africa" (sometimes known as the role of the "secular missionary" or the "liberal mediator," to use Wallerstein's terminology). However, the proponents have also felt that the scholar's most important loyalty was to the discipline itself and that Africa, in a sense, was "a laboratory" for the theories and the evolving methods of the social sciences.

The "developmental formula," on the contrary, holds that African Studies ought to be actively engaged in the "formulation, implementation, and evaluation of policies concerned with increasing the standards of living and expanding opportunities in Africa." Many continental Africans favor this view. Finally, the "advocacy and solidarity formula," for its part, maintains that the Africanist's mission is to "articulate, defend, and promote the interests of groups suffering some form of injustice, oppression, or deprivation." This radical view also has many adepts on the African continent.

No matter what the nature of the debate may be in the future, African Studies is a scientific field whose objective is to establish the fact that Africa and Africans are here to stay and are worth studying. The field has, in fact, done considerable good among American scholars. It is clear, for example, that most Africanist scholars tend to be more sensitive than their counterparts in their views and treatment of Africa and the African people. To borrow from Staniland once again, the commitment and "Afrophilia" are equally prevalent among leftist, radical, liberal, and religious scholars, and even among "moderate conservative postures in domestic politics," with the exception to be found only among "conservative nationalists [for whom only America counts] and white racist groups." Yet, there is no doubt that the field, its scholars, and its official association must be relevant to Africa. Wisdom J. Tottey and Korbla P. Puplampu (2000) discuss several challenges facing the Africanist, including the "intellectual distancing of the disciplines from society, the retrogressive socio-political atmosphere that characterizes some African universities, and the negative attitudes of individual academics." The two scholars conclude by pointing out that "...without a correction of these internal and external deficiencies, it will be difficult to maintain a respectable and beneficial level of research endeavour, integrity, collaboration, and sustainability."

Evidently, differing views and sharp disagreements will continue among scholars, as was illustrated in 1990 when a well-known historian, L. H. Gann, accused the African Studies Association's leadership of discriminating against conservatives, such as himself, and charged in *Issue* (Vol. XVIII, Summer 1990), that the Association was dominated by leftists and Marxists. The charges prompted a stinging reply by four former presidents of the Association: Ann Seidman, Georges Nzongola-Ntalaja, Aidan Southall, and Simon Ottenberg. One can say, however, that, although the criticisms have been at times vicious, the end results have proven healthy for the academic community and have contributed to a marked improvement in the standards of the research activity on Africa. For example, many disciplines require that Ph.D. candidates in African Studies conduct field work in Africa itself for a certain period of time as participant-observers of the groups they might happen to study. There are also common standards among the various African Studies disciplines regarding research design, sampling, interviewing and coding, data analysis, interpretation, and outcome reporting. All these are positive results that critics should not overlook.

Study Questions and Activities

1. Define African Studies and discuss their evolution.
2. Compare and contrast the methodologies and perspectives of historians, anthropologists, and sociologists. How useful are their assumptions and practices?
3. What have been the major problems among scholars within the African Studies field and the African Studies Association?
4. What were the major themes of Africanist scholars during the 1960s? Has the emphasis shifted at present? Compare and contrast the methodologies of a historian, a political scientist, and an anthropologist, and draw a chart outlining the discipline's focus. How useful has each one of them been in the understanding of Africa as it "really" is or was?

References

Claude Ake. "Academic Freedom and Material Base," in M. Diouf and M. Mamdani (eds.). *Academic Freedom in Africa*. Dakar: CODESRIA, 1993.

Delores P. Aldridge and Carlene Young (eds.). *Out of the Revolution: The Development of Africana Studies*. Lanham, MD: Lexington Books, 2000.

Debora P. Amory. "Homosexuality in Africa: Issues and Debates." *Issue*, Vol. XXV, 1(1997): 5–10.

Talmage Anderson (ed.). *Black Studies: Theory, Method, and Cultural Perspectives*. Pullman, WA: University of Washington Press, 1990.

Yolamu Barongo (ed.). *Politcal Science in Africa*. London: Zed Books, 1983.

Robert Bates. "Area Studies and the Discipline." Letter to the *American Political Science Association, Comparative Politics*, Vol. 1 (Winter 1996): 1–2.

Robert Bates. *Essays on the Political Economy of Rural Africa*. Cambridge: Cambridge University Press, 1983.

Daniel Biebuyck. "African Art Studies Since 1957: Achievements and Dimension." *African Studies Review*, Vol. 26, 3/4(September/December 1983): 99–118.

Iris Burger. Contested Boundaries: African Studies Approaching the Millennium." *African Studies Review*, Vol. 40, 2(1997): 1–14.

Byron Caminero-Santangelo. *African Fiction and Joseph Conrad: Reading Postcolonial Intertextuality*. Albany: State University of New York Press, 2005.

Naomi Chazan et al. *Politics and Society in Contemporary Africa*. Boulder, CO: Lynne Rienner Publishers, 1988.

James Coleman, and C. R. D. Halisi. "American Political Science and Tropical Africa." *African Studies Review*, Vol. 26, 3/4(September/December 1983): 25–62.

Jean Copans. "D'un africanisme a l'autre point de vue d'un anthropologue," in *New Dimensions in African Studies*. Ottawa: University of Ottawa Press, 1978.

Philip Curtin et al. *African History*. Boston: Little, Brown, 1978.

Samuel Decalo. *Coups and Army Rule in Africa*. New Haven, CT: Yale University Press, 1976.

E. Evans-Pritchard. *The Nuer*. London: Clarendon Press, 1941.

Michelle Fine, Rosemarie A. Roberts, Maria Elena Torre and with Janice Bloom (eds.). *Echoes of Brown: Youth Documenting and Performing the Legacy of Brown v. Board of Education*. New York: Teachers College Press, 2004.

Andre G. Frank. *Capitalism and Underdevelopment in Latin America*. New York: Monthly Review Press, 1969.

Joseph Greenberg. *The Languages of Africa*, 3rd. ed. Bloomington, IN: Indiana University Research Center, 1970.

Bud Hall. "African Studies: The Formation of Knowledge and Political Commitment," in *New Dimensions in African Studies*, pp. 57–68. Ottawa: University of Ottawa Press, 1978.

Samuel Huttington. *Political Order in Changing Societies*. New Haven, CT: Yale University Press, 1968.

Abiola Irele. "The African Scholar." *Transition*, Vol. 51, 1991: 56–69. *Issue*, Vol. XVIII, 2(Summer 1990): Letters to the Editor.

Bogumil Jewsiewicki. "African Historical Studies: Academic Knowledge as 'Usable Past.'" *African Studies Review*, Vol. 32, 3(December 1989): 1–76.

Lansine Kaba. "Historical Consciousness and Politics in Africa," in Talmage Anderson. *Black Studies*, pp. 43–50. Pullman, WA: University of Washington Press, 1990.

James Katorobo. "Methodological Tendencies and Needs in African Studies," in *New Dimensions in African Studies*, pp. 45—50. Ottawa: University of Ottawa Press, 1978.

Diane Kayongo-Male and Philista Onyango. *The Sociology of the African Family*. London: Longmans, 1984.

Molefi Asante Keta. "More Thoughts on the Africanists' Agenda." *Issue*, Vol. 23, 1(1995): 11–12.

Joseph Ki-Zerbo. *Histoire de l'Afrique noire*. Paris: Hatier, 1972.

Deborah M. LaFond and Gretchen Walsh (eds.). *Research, Reference Service, and Resources for the Study of Africa*. Binghamton, NY: Haworth Information Press, 2004.

Mahmood Mamdani. "A Glimpse of African Studies, Made in USA." *CODESRIA Bulletin*, 2(1990): 7–11.

John Mbiti et al. *Introduction to African Religion*. New York: Praeger, 1975.

Gwendolyn Mikell. "Forging Mutuality: The ASA and Africa in the Coming Decades." *African Studies Review*, Vol. 42, 1(1999): 1–22.

Thandika Mkandawire. "The Social Sciences in Africa: Breaking Local Barriers and Negotiating International Presence." *African Studies Review*, Vol. 40, 2(1997): 15–36.

James A. Mittelman. "Academic Freedom, Transformation and Reconciliation." *Issue*, Vol. XXV, 1(1997): 45–48.

Kagendo Mutua and Beth Blue Swadener (eds.). *Decolonizing Research in Cross-Cultural Contexts: Critical Personal Narratives*. Albany, NY: State University of New York Press, 2004.

Wang Mutege. "Class Interests in the Teaching of Political Science in African Universities," in Barongo (ed.), *Political Science in Africa*, pp. 48—55. London: Zed Books, 1983.

Francis B. Nyamnjoh and Natang B. Jua. "African Universities in Crisis and the Promotion of a Democratic Culture: the Political Economy of Violence in African Educational Systems." *African Studies Review*, Vol. 45, 2(September 2002): 1–26.

Festus Ohaegbulam. *Towards an Understanding of the African Experience*. Lanham, MD: UPA, 1990.

Richard Olanyan. *African History and Culture*. London: Longmans, 1982.

Omu Omoruyi. "Teaching Political Science as a Vocation in Africa," in Barongo (ed.). *Political Science in Africa*, pp. 6—16. London: Zed Books, 1983.

O. Onoge. "Revolutionary Imperatives in African Socialism," in Peter Gutkind and Peter Waterman (eds.). *African Social Studies*, pp. 32—43. New York: Monthly Review Press, 1977.

Owomoyela Oyekan. "With Friends like These...A Critique of Pervasive Anti-Africanisms in Current African Studies Epistemology and Methodology." *African Studies Review*, Vol. 37, 3(December 1994): 77–101.

Margaret Peil. *Social Science Research Methods*. London: Hodder and Stoughton, 1982.

John Edward Phillips (ed.). *Writing African History*. United States: University of Rochester Press, Boydell & Brewer Ltd., US, 2005.

Carl Rosberg and Robert Jackson. *Personal Rule in Black Africa*. Berkeley, CA: University of California Press, 1982.

W. W. Rostrow. *The Struggles of Economic Growth*. London: Cambridge University Press, 1960.

Ian Roxborough. *Theories of Underdeveloment*. New York: Macmillan, 1979.

Edward Said. *Orientalism*. New York: Vintage Books, 1979.

Aylward Shorter. *African Christian Theology*. New York: Orbis Books, 1975.

Aidan Southall. "The Contribution of Anthropology to African Studies." *African Studies Review*, Vol. 26, 3/4(September/December 1983): 63–76.

Martin Staniland. "Who Needs African Studies?" *African Studies Review*, Vol. 26, 3/4 (September/December 1983): 77–98.

Placide Temples. *Bantu Philosophy*. Paris: Presence Africaine, 1959.

A. Temu and B. Swai. *Historians and Africanist History: A Critique*. London: Zed Books, 1981.

Wisdom Tettey and Korbla P. Puplampu. "Social Science Research and the Africanist: The Need for Intellectual and Attitudinal Reconfiguration." *African Studies Review*, Vol. 43, 3(December 2000): 81–102.

Michael Todaro. *Economic Development in the Third World*. New York: Longmans, 1981.

Arnold Toynbee. *War and Civilization*. New York: Oxford University Press, 1950.

Hugh Trevor-Roper. *The Rise of Christian Europe*. New York: Harcourt, Brace, and World, 1965.

Immanuel Wallerstein. "The Evolving Role of the African Scholar in African Studies." *African Studies Review*, Vol. 26, 3/4(September/December 1983): 155–162.

2

African American Studies and the State of the Art

Russell L. Adams

Introduction

The field of African American Studies is a relatively new institutional feature of higher education in America. The focus of this field is on 1) the experiences, 2) the problems, and 3) the prospects of individuals and groups whose heritage, wherever they may be, is African. The field examines the historical records of black people in Africa and the Western hemisphere. The sociological conditions confronting African Americans and Africans (seen from both in-group and out-group perspectives)are stressed. The problems aspect of this new field deals with theoretical questions of several kinds: a) conceptual theory for thinking about how best to *approach* the black experience, b) pedagogical theory or sets of ideas and concepts on how to *study* the black experience, and c) *strategical* or social advocacy theories. As in any field, of course, the experiences, problems, and prospects components in African American Studies frequently overlap. Although the study of the black experience is old, institutional support for it at the level of course concentrations is relatively new. The youthfulness of the field is indicated by the fact that it is known by a variety of names: "Afro-American Studies," "African American Studies," "Africana Studies," "Afro-American and African Studies," "Black Studies," and "Pan-African Studies." At least one department uses the term "Africology." As a generic label, the term "African American Studies" will be used in the following discussion.

Until recently, African American Studies *per se* was a black, community-based endeavor, sparked by the work of the Association for the Study of African American Life and History, itself the legacy of Carter G. Woodson, the "Father of Black History." Although for years a few schools, such as Howard and Fisk universities, had black experience course concentrations within traditional fields and disciplines, African American Studies won institutional visibility only in the late 1960s because of student demand in the wake of the assassination of Dr. Martin Luther King, Jr. Today more than sixty departments of African American Studies exist throughout the nation, primarily in predominantly white colleges and universities. While more than 400 African American Studies programs were funded with "soft" money, some 300 of them still exist. Ten universities offer Master's degrees and Temple University, University of California at Berkeley, Emory University, Harvard University, University of Massachusetts at Amherst, Michigan State University, and Yale University offer a disciplinary or an interdisciplinary Ph.D. degree in African American Studies."

Major terms and concepts: Afrocentricity, Afrocentrism, analytical perspectives, core/boundary, curriculum, Eurocentrism, epistemology, legitimacy, multi-disciplinary, inter-disciplinary, traditional disciplines, field.

Foundation and Structure

As an institutional approach to the black experience, African American Studies takes a variety of forms. In terms of sheer numbers, the most common form is that of the program rather than department. The program enables students to complete either required or elective courses while doing most of their studies in a traditional field. This arrangement permits them to do work in *single* discipline departments and also in the *multi*-disciplinary African American Studies program. Faculty for a program may all be anchored in different traditional departments but teach a course or courses in the program. (Persons teaching full-time in programs, however, usually are not on a "tenure track.") It is generally understood that programs have a shorter life-span than departments, being mainly dependent on elective enrollments for their institutional survival. On the other hand, the program format allows for greater ease in team teaching and interdisciplinary collaboration, a feature used by some institutions to justify this particular configuration of instruction. What has been said about programs applies also to institutes of African American Studies.

The significance of the departmental format, as alluded to above, is largely a measure of the durability of African American Studies departments over time. Of the sixty-odd full-fledged departments organized since 1969, fewer than a half dozen have been abolished or merged. Although the exact number is not known, programs and institutes have declined in far greater proportion, natural consequence of their virtually ad hoc funding and staffing arrangements. From the perspective of impact, however, the department appears to be the most significant. Thus, the most durable African American Studies unit is the department. Incidentally, it may be noted that the often-reported decline in African American Studies as a field has to do more with the decline in the number of programs and institutes rather than departments.

The departmental format also means that a college or university, at least in theory, has accepted African American Studies as an *institutionally* significant area of academic instruction, realizing the aspirations of the pioneers in the African American Studies movement. A regular departmental structure implies that a) funding is from the basic university budgets, b) the college or university tenure rules cover departmental faculty, c) the unit can offer a minor or a major leading to the bachelor of arts degree and or above, and d) it can have a full-time support staff, with standard benefits. It must be pointed out, however, that many institutions also have supported the African American Studies presence on their campuses for non-academic reasons. Some have supported African American Studies departments as "political settlements" with black students; some have funded

Black Studies programs as "insurance" against further demands. Still others have established such units as a handy way of increasing faculty *ethnic diversity*, without having this diversity appear in traditional departments. In any case, a Department of African American Studies is seen as the strongest possible vehicle for assuring the continued presence of this subject on a campus.

The impact of African American student demands for institutional support for the coverage of the black experience went beyond the setting up of institutes, programs, and departments. Many traditional social science and humanities departments have revised their syllabi and/or offered courses to make them more inclusive of the black experience, although proponents of the traditional disciplines say little about these changes—a reticence intended to avoid the impression of responding to black *student* demands. Often revision suggestions are met with overt resistance, as shown most recently by rise of such "canon" preservation groups as the National Association of Scholars and the controversies swirling around multiculturalism.

The simple fact of the major-minor formula for undergraduate instruction, which calls for successful completion of work in both African American Studies as a major and a traditional field as a minor, is often forgotten. Majors in African American Studies typically are required to take an average of thirty or more hours of instruction on various topics and aspects of the black experience and perhaps eighteen to twenty hours in a traditional discipline. Beyond the department, African American Studies majors and minors must also fulfill a given institution's general education and course distribution requirements for graduation. Critics of African American Studies curricula often overlook these *prevailing* institutional prerequisites for a diploma.

While models of African American Studies departments vary significantly in curriculum content, the passage of the years has witnessed a remarkable stability of structure in so far as the delivery of instruction is concerned. The African American pedagogical objectives set forth a quarter century ago, for example, by the Yale University historian John Blassingame in *New Perspectives on Black Studies* (1971) in a "model" department, are still current:

- "to give students a clear conception of the complexity of American life,"
- "to acquaint students with the problems, successes, and failures of America's largest minority group,
- "to enable students to understand the nature of the contemporary racial and social turmoil and to guide them to constructive models of thought about current issues," and
- "to enable students to see the black experience in a world setting."

The same is true of Harvard University's 1969 committee report on African and African American Studies: black students want opportunities to study the black experience for the purposes of black community improvement. This report accurately matched the desires and interest of black students in many other institutions during this period. During the late 1960s, many people felt that major mainstream educational institutions had a direct responsibility to assist in improving society by supporting education and research on the racial front. Knowledge was to be socially relevant and, in the words of a much-quoted slogan of the time, African American Studies departments were to be the embodiments "academic excellence and social responsibility." The Howard University Afro-American Studies departmental catalog of 1975, for example, announced that its departmental goals were to provide "a fundamental understanding of those varied forces which have shaped the Afro-American experience in the Western Hemisphere" and to provide students with a "basic understanding of the special problems of Afro-Americans in contemporary life." The authoritative voice of African American Studies, the National Council for Black Studies, Inc., in a 1996 convention call declared that it "works to

1. establish standards of excellence and provide Afro-American Studies programs in institutions of higher education;
2. facilitate, through consultations and other services, the recruitment of Black Scholars for all levels of teaching and research;
3. assist in the creation and implementation of multicultural education programs and materials for K-12 schools and higher education institutions;
4. promote scholarly Afrocentric research on all aspects of the African World experience;
5. Increase and improve informational resources on Pan African life and culture to be made available to the general public; (and)
6. to provide professional advice to policy makers in education, government and community development."

While the earlier stages of the movement were student-centered, the citation of services show that it covers faculty and administrators within the field and supporters in many different areas beyond campus-bound African American Studies. The African American Studies movement also has been as interested in developing new social science and humanities curricula as in critiquing existing ones. This developmental interest coincides with that of the Ford Foundation, which is now supporting curriculum upgrade initiatives in a number of major institutions. Over the years the National Council for Black Studies has been encouraging member institutions to maximize their curriculum potential around some model of the African American experience. As with the question of objectives, random examination of African American Studies course catalog listings reveals that they do indeed contain significant portions of the original Council model, with its subdivisions of 1) Social Behavioral Studies, 2) Historical Studies and 3) Cultural Studies Areas, each with four levels of treatment corresponding to the standard four levels of study generally required for the undergraduate degree. Allowing for the vagaries of staffing, most undergraduate African American Studies tend to parallel this model. The major variations in curricula are found at the M.A. level. Here students take a limited number of courses in a specific concentration. Doctoral proposals and programs structurally resemble the undergraduate course offerings in their comprehensiveness.

The concepts and polemics of Africentrism have attracted considerable notice *pro* and *con*, but insufficient attention has been given to the variety of actual instruction emphases. Some departments divide their offerings between Africa as a continent and the Black urban experience in North America. The Black Studies Department of Ohio State University perhaps has been in the forefront of this sort of configuration. For nearly two decades under the leadership of Professor James Turner, the Cornell University Africana Studies Department has split its course content between Africa and the Americas, as did the Department of Afro-American Studies at State University of New York at Albany and the University of

North Carolina at Charlotte. The Department of Africology at the University of Wisconsin-Milwaukee has a curriculum which is Afrocentric and diasporan in its geographical and topical coverage of the black presence in the world. Occasionally, a program or department will use an areas/themes approach to orient its curriculum, the example being the Caribbean Studies Program during the Clark-Atlanta University tenure of Professor Richard Long. The Emory University Afro-American Studies faculty in Atlanta and University of California at Santa Barbara both are exploring the possibilities of upgrading their operations to offer the Ph.D.

With the mid-1990s presence of the cultural polymaths Henry Louis Gates and Cornel West, plus infusion of several millions of dollars, the Afro-American Studies operation at Harvard University has attracted the likes of William J. Wilson and bids to dominate academic discourse on the race *relations* aspect of the Black Studies field. With its selection of the academically prolific Manning Marable to head its newly created "Institute for Research in African American Studies," Columbia University has demonstrated a renewed commitment to this new field. Howard University is contemplating a synergistic reconfiguration of its Afro-American Studies Department, African Studies and Research Center and Moorland-Spingarn Research Center to amplify their educational impact on and off the camps. With the addition to its faculty of Ronald Walters, formerly chairman of political science at Howard and Walter Broadnax, late of Harvard, the University of Maryland increased its visibility in the study of race relations. At the time of writing, institutions offering the rare Ph.D. in Afro American Studies included Temple University in Philadelphia and, the University of Massachusetts at Amherst. The Temple University Afro-American graduate program is composed of two major "tracks:" the "Cultural/Aesthetic" and the "Social/Behavioral." The W. E. B. DuBois Department of Afro-American Studies at the University of Massachusetts, Amherst proudly announces that its main objective "is to produce scholars and teachers in the tradition of the Department's namesake, W. E. B. DuBois." Its curriculum consists of a three-track or concentration format: a "History/Politics Track," a "Literature/Culture Track" and a "Public Policy/Community Development Track," serving undergraduate and graduate students. The Afro-American Studies Department at Berkeley divides students' specific fields of emphasis into two general areas: "Issues of Development in the Diaspora" and "Cultural Studies." The former area includes "History of the African Diaspora," "Social and Cultural Institutions," Urban Sociology," "Politics of Culture" and "Political Economy of the Diaspora," courses also common to the above cited departments. The latter area, "Cultural Studies," includes "Comparative Literatures and Cultures," "Critical Theory, Popular Culture, Performance and Film" and "Women's Studies."

Whatever the make-up of announced curricula, the largest proportion of students enrolled in Black Studies programs and departments take African American *social science* courses. Since the major 1976 study of African American Studies operations across the country, repeated surveys have indicated that the typical curriculum is based on the social sciences and humanities fields, with variations as exemplified below. For example, the department of Afro-American Studies at the University of California, Santa Barbara stresses cultural expression, and the University of California, Los Angeles focuses on diasporan history and community development. The disciplines of departmental organizers still influence the focus and character of the curriculum. The Afro-American Studies Department at Howard University, for example, has a pronounced political science orientation and literature orientation, having been established under the leadership of a dean holding a political science doctorate. This tendency is underscored by the experience of the African American Studies program at the University of Maryland, which began with a constitutional historian as chair, evolved in the direction of contemporary public policy analysis under the leadership of a quantitatively-minded economist and is again under the leadership of a highly respected historian. The University of Wisconsin-Milwaukee's Africology Department presents students with two "options:" "Option A: Political Economy" and "Option B: Culture and Society."

In this new field, the construction of curricula is still influenced by faculty availability. Faculty availability, in turn, is a function of institutional location: the more geographically distant from large black population centers, the less attractive to African American prospects. As for location, it is probably no accident that some but obviously not all of the strongest departments are found near populous black off-campus communities. The list of strong departments include Temple University in Philadelphia, Harvard University near Boston with its Roxborough community, University of California-Berkeley, near San Francisco and Oakland, and Ohio State in Columbus. A few notable programs, however, are found in areas with small black populations, the Africana Program at Cornell and the Afro-American Studies departments at University of Washington-Pullman, being examples. A prospective faculty recruit might find him/herself accepting or declining a position as a result of not only location as such but also institutional expectations and competition from other institutions and disciplines.

The generic interdisciplinary African American curriculum models are often greatly altered in practice by the basic educational level of their undergraduate learners. Interdisciplinarity was the theme of the opening symposium of Columbia University's 1996 conference on "The Future of Afro-American Studies." The typical department of African American Studies is inescapably interdisciplinary because it is a species of *intergroup relations*. And no single discipline can adequately explain the interaction of two or more groups in what have been called "segmented" or ethnically plural societies. Interdisciplinarity poses a real pedagogical challenge to African American Studies instructors. Most undergraduates, irrespective of personal or ethnic background, are hard put to understand even one traditional discipline at the undergraduate level. True interdisciplinary learning and teaching require a fairly good grasp of at least two disciplines. This situation, in part, accounts for the somewhat interdisciplinary survey character of the syllabi of many departments. As Professor Gates stated in 1989, "scholarship in black studies tends to bring together insights from several disciplines [precisely] because black studies started as a multidisciplinary field." The slow emergence of doctoral programs, of course, will provide greater opportunities for in-depth interdisciplinary study and research.

Most fields require many years to evolve from areas of awareness to disciplines of practice. After two decades, African American Studies has yet to settle as a discipline. Initially, in the corrective drive against academic exclusion, many Afrocentrist pioneers thought that they could easily construct a reverse mirror image of the curricula they encountered. Few anticipated the difficulty of trying to a) create a new discipline, b) perform corrective functions, c) become race relations generalists; d) do Afro-*loco-parentis* duty; e) work as minority ombudsmen, and f) receive "precisely the same" treatment at tenure time as their opposite race colleagues with far fewer responsibilities. In many instances, black faculty often find themselves functioning as academic social workers and ethnic politicians, with comparatively less time for "pure academics" than their white counterparts. Much of the research done in African American Studies is reinterpretative secondary work, being less time-consuming and expensive than survey and original field investigation. Often secondary analysis is promoted to the position of primary activity, a situation quite common in controversial expositions of ancient African/Egyptian history. Few African Americanists have access to funds for archaeological fieldwork on the African continent or even for extensive domestic survey research. With the passage of time and the expanded presence in higher education of African Americans as a group, however, their share of opportunities for expensive primary research should correspondingly increase.

As stated above the mere existence of the African American Studies movement has had a positive effect on the curricula of many traditional departments. For example, one can now study black political life in the twentieth century in a department of political science, or African American family organization in a department of sociology. Excellent instruction in African economics is available in some economics departments, and an English department with qualified instructors can do a good job on the Harlem Renaissance. A department of philosophy with outstanding individuals such as Lucius Outlaw of Haverford College and Cornel West of Harvard can cross-pollinate African American Studies philosophy offerings. These intellectual cross-currents, however, occur against the ineluctable pull of traditional academic premises and assumptions of Eurocentric universalism. African Americanists thus are constantly involved with thinking through the premises, assumptions and histories undergirding educational communities, including their own. Intellectual independence, a key objective of African American Studies, is a hallmark of their endeavors.

The history of ideological racism in many leading mainstream educational institutions is seen as reason enough for African American Studies departments to be independent. At the turn of the century, when no "mainstream" institution thought the black experience worthy of study and research, white scholars such as William A. Dunning and John W. Burgess, both Columbia University history professors, turned out squads of smugly pro-Southern and anti-black historians of Reconstruction politics to justify the exclusion of blacks from participation in public life for over half a century. Some took to heart Burgess's dictum that "a black skin means membership in a race of men which has never itself succeeded in subjecting passion to reason." In part due to the rise of Nazism and Fascism during the 1930s, American historians began a slow shift toward environmentalist and regionalist perspectives for understanding the South, including its black population. As late as the 1950s, however, as eminent a scholar as Henry Steele Commager could casually refer to African Americans as "Sambos" happy in bondage. Kenneth E. Stampp, a racially more sophisticated scholar, over-corrected in claiming that "innately Negroes *are*, after all, only white men with black skins, nothing more, nothing less," the implication being that since they actually were white, they should be treated fairly.

Like their fellow academics at the end of the last century, the mainstream sociologists tended to posit a genetic model in explaining black failure to achieve white middle-class life-styles and living standards. As a result, the black presence in America was seen as a "problem" to be solved via racial white "uplift" operations. These historical and sociological explanatory perspectives began to change with the 1930s publication of W. E. B. DuBois' *Black Reconstruction in America*. The publication, in 1944, of Gunnar Myrdal's *An American Dilemma*, represented the legitimation of the environmentalist/regionalist explanatory paradigm of the causes of the plight of African Americans. Myrdal, the Swedish-born synthesizer of the empirical research findings of boldly liberal black and white scholars, concluded that the "race problem" was the result of a white supremacist use of social power and ethical hypocrisy in contradictions of the announced principles of the constitution. This book had a pronounced influence on white policy makers and facilitated the spread of environmentalist explanation of social behaviors. In the 1940s, the work of black scholars had to be filtered through the "neutral" hands of a Myrdal in order to have any sort of impact on white America.

In the 1950s, a judicial revolution from above and a social revolution from below brought about the Civil Rights Movement of the 1960s, and greatly eased the way for organized African American Studies. The new cadres of black students admitted to previously "white" institutions in the wake of the assassination of Dr. Martin Luther King, Jr., immediately viewed the existing social science curricula as being implicitly bio-genetic in causal theory, incomplete and morally intolerable. Contemporary white professors were considered intellectually unequipped to take part in determining curricula. Some white professors concurred and demonstrated this by having black students devise their own curricula. Institutional responses to this new situation ranged from that of Dennison University, for example, which was to fund *student* travel to collect information about a Black Studies curriculum. With no institutional standards, this embryonic field had academic charlatans of all colors, with one such individual telling the writer that birth in the black community was a sufficient credential for seeking a teaching job in the field. Despite the high standards of individual African American scholars such as DuBois, Carter G. Woodson, Charles S. Johnson, Ralph Bunche, Ira DeReid, Oliver Cromwell Cox, Charles H. Wesley, E. Franklin Frazier, or John Hope Franklin, initially the newer generation of academic activists celebrated political correctness and activism more than the technical requirements of the field. The "qualifications" issue has yet to be settled, the entire topic now being complicated by the polemics of contemporary political Afrocentrism.

The field of African American studies thus has not yet evolved sufficiently to be classed as a discipline. Its adherents are still struggling among themselves for authoritative and widespread canonical definitions, a common vocabulary and rules of procedure. A combination of youthful minority advocates, political momentum and status quo defensive reactions have greatly complicated core and boundary definitions and developments in African American Studies. Bristling under hostile critiques by conservative scholars, African Americanists have continually pointed out that the so-called "established" disciplines are still defining and re-defining themselves, with virtually no one questioning their basic value. Even more complicated is the matter of the interdisciplinary nature of the field. African American Studies departments recognize that the interwoven nature of the black experience calls for holistic coverage, though they also recognize the impossibility of setting up reverse image, black micro-universities within the confines of the larger ones. Hence, departments now settle for limited "tracks," "options," and "concentrations." Future studies of curriculum construction will doubtless focus on disciplinary questions. In one way or another, however, these departments do attempt to address fundamental issues and problems of knowledge, an inevitable and natural result of their concern with retrieving, correcting and promoting some version of the black presence on the globe. Thus African Americanists pursue their work within a three-ply helix of epistemology, Afrocentricity and ideology.

Epistemology, Afrocentricity, and Ideology

Epistemology is defined by *Webster's Unabridged Dictionary* as "the theory or science of the *methods and grounds* of knowledge, esp. with reference to its limits and validity" (emphasis added). Epistemology involves the examination of the rationales of orientation and the axiologies of choice in interpretations of the social world. African American Studies specialists claim that since the traditional disciplines evolved without an accurate awareness of the nature of the subjective, internal communities of persons of African descent, their vaunted "objectivity" is compromised by their practitioners' a) social distance from blacks, b) basically tourist/anthropologist methods of research on blacks, c) lack of intimate familiarity with the negative effects of the actions of the larger societies on black social formations and psyches, and d) deliberate distortion of the African American and African social record, past and present. The emerging black academic research communities reject the intrinsic elitism and cultural ethnocentrism of establishment academics as flawed at best and degradingly unfair at worst. In their zeal to right ancient errors of perception, some black academics indeed have become somewhat guilty of substituting one exclusivistic vision for that of another. But on balance, Afrocentrists have been seeking to develop their own epistemological versions of social truths.

This rejection of establishment academic perceptions has deep roots in the black intellectual experience. Little-known now, but quite visible during its day, the American Negro Academy, established in 1897 under the leadership of Alexander Crummell, endeavored to provide an educated historical voice for the black experience. Carter G. Woodson, the best-known exponent of this view (and in 1926 the founder of Black History Week, now Month), saw his work as a corrective endeavor. Since the establishment in 1915 of Woodson's Association for the Study of Afro-American Life and History, critical black thought has moved from accepting the "myths of the Negro past" through a rejection of blacks as deviations from the stock of humankind and from the standards of "host" societies to a prideful assertiveness which recently has sprung forth as Afrocentrism. For the first time the concern of professional African Americanists have spilled over into popular media and public discussion. The Afro-Eurocentric battle is larger than any campus; it is a battle over the contents of what every epistemology promotes: a given version of reality which its adherents regard as self-evident, and thus the point of departure for giving it social meaning and significance. Extracted from the polemics of the epistemological contest are the following versions of Africentrism, some of them overlapping, but all of them rejecting epistemologies of marginality and stressing the absolute significance of the experience of black people in human affairs.

The purest form of Afrocentrism posits ancient Africa via Egypt as the source of civilizations, especially Western cultures and their most fundamental ideas and inventions. Art, agriculture, literature, music, philosophy, logic and mathematics all appeared first in a black Egypt, facts contemporary Europeans wish to keep ethnically "clean" by denying their hidden Afro-Asiatic roots. For this group of scholars, this brand of Afrocentrism allows room for personality "centering" in the present to be guided by "Kemetic" centering from full knowledge of the black African/Egyptian past. Adherents to this school of thought assert the primacy of Egyptian Africa as the creative locus of the major ideas and practices which undergird the foundation of humanity. They declare that not only did humankind split off from the simian or ape world in East Africa, but assert that this African segment of humankind generated a still-living stock of ideas during its long history alongside the Nile River Valley. Consequently black people in particular and the remainder of the world in general, should acknowledge their debt to black Egypt (Kemet) and revive those ideas from which sprang earlier black achievements. This school avers that recovery of ancient Egyptian knowledge would fill the contemporary spiritual void and raise the deflated self-esteem of modern descendants of Africans everywhere. The most prominent exponent of this version of Afro-centrism is Dr. Molefe Asante, former chairman of Temple University's African and Afro-American Studies Department. Through his many writings and with the assistance of black professors at other historically white institutions, Asante has made "Afrocentrism" the lightning rod for the ethnic tensions in the on-going cultural wars. This epistemic vision has been called "*Nile Valley*" *Afrocentrism.*

Continental Afrocentrists hold that the entire African continent is the true source of the culture of black trans-Atlantic communities. Adherents of this school celebrate their version of authentic black cultural values and practices in the diaspora and declare that they are prerequisites for the revitalization of African American communities. They hold that a common Afrocentric world view can be synthesized out of the complex of traditional African life and history through careful study of existing artifacts and print materials. *It is a conviction of this group that African social values are more humanistic than those derived from Europe.* For them, the entire continent of Africa and the sum of African history and culture constitute the authentic interpretative foundation for understanding the black experience. Afrocentrists tend to celebrate ancient Ethiopia, Axum, Meroe, Napata on the eastern edge of the continent and medieval Ghana, Mali and Songhai on its western side. They suggest that the ethical foundations of the peace and tranquillity enjoyed by these civilizations at their apex should be rediscovered and put to modern use. Knowledge of the great African kingdoms should be as much part of the modern learners repertoire as that of colonial Portugal, Spain, France and England, not to mention ancient Greece and Rome. The traditional African values and practices, this group declares, could very well be the revivalistic catalyst for the spiritual and secular salvation of a sundered race.

Afrocentric infusionists urge the positive value of infusing or blending Africa-based ideas, concepts, values and historical data into the curricula. This school claims that all Americans can profitably share positive African values, viewpoints, experiences and practices. While such blending would have the effect of reducing stereotypes and enhancing conceptions of others about blacks, sharing would enable people to discern the common humanity of European and African societies. *This group seeks close collaboration with public school curriculum specialists.*

Afrocentric infusionists see black Americans as persons with a rich and valuable ✓
African heritage which has been devalued, underused and ignored to the detriment of this society. Several school systems, mainly in northern urban areas, have attempted to adopt the Afro-infusionist social studies curriculum models, with critics being quite concerned about issues of accuracy and content balance. Perhaps the best known package is the Portland, Oregon *Baseline Essays*, designed to assist public school teachers in revising their instructional units to accommodate Africentric materials. Professor Asa Hilliard of Georgia State University is perhaps the leading advocate of infusionism, even though he also is partial to the Nile Valley School.

Social Afrocentrists, on the other hand, place great stress on the *use of knowledge and resources in protecting and promoting the best interests of black people as members of the localities in which they live.* They do not use African background data as much as the other Afrocentrists. They agree that the heritage of America's black population is insufficiently appreciated, but hold that it is not possible nor desirable to try to reproduce ancient Africa in a world beginning the twenty-first century. Adherents of this school take an interest group approach to the topic of Afrocentrisms and hold that intellectual fads wax and wane but that group interests are permanent. Thus, *social Afrocentrists do not see the black experience as so specialized that only blacks may be involved in exploring it.* This version of Afrocentrism is less "hard line" about who can participate in the work of using education to promote the concerns of African Americans. It recognizes the complexity of human experience and the difficulties in identifying the culturally "African" from the non-African elements which societies absorb over time. Africa per se is more of a target of interest than of inspiration. *In a sense, this conception of Afrocentrism is but a continuation of the integrationist position taken by the first wave of individual black scholars such as W. E. B. DuBois and E. Franklin Frazier in the era of segregation.*

The types of Afrocentrism cited above represent the *thinking* about how to avoid the negative aspects and consequences of traditional curricula and attitudes toward people of African origin, independent of its nuances. The very concept of Afrocentrism has stimulated a great deal of debate about the roles of different epistemic perspectives in guiding instruction and research in the field of African American Studies. At the level of practice, African American studies departments are 1) endeavoring to create an accurate, authentic, and autonomous intellectual vision of the social world, free of the misleading claims of Eurocentric "universality" and "objectivity," 2) still trying to develop and present once-omitted factual material to their students, 3) hoping to evolve from multi-disciplinary to inter-disciplinary instruction, 4) responding more effectively to issues of curriculum balance in the area of cognitive skills, and 5) still constructing their institutional foundations. Despite its developmental problems, the field of African American studies has already made major contributions in the area of ethnic and cultural diversity, by raising anew questions about the nature, content, and direction of American education. In this context, epistemology supplies the grounds for a given explanatory paradigm. Epistemology, then, provides the *given*, the axiomatic premise for thinking about and evaluating social process.

The following is a a brief summary of the most common used *explanatory* ideologies of which students of Africa and African America ought to be aware. One of the most concise discussions of the dual character of epistemic orientations and behavioral analyses is found in an article by Tilden Lemelle entitled "The Status of Black Studies in the Next Decade: The Ideological Imperative," in James Turner (ed.), *The Next Decade: Theoretical and Research Issues in African Studies* (1984). LeMelle classifies black orientations/behaviors into two broad categories: the assimilationist and the self-determinationist. The first category comprises the accommodationist, the reconcilationist, and the liberal idealist. The second category includes the structural, cultural, political and enclave separatists. Booker T. Washington, of course, is known as the great accommodator, supporting industrial individualism and political avoidance on the part of the black community. Dr. Martin Luther King, Jr. and DuBois were quintessential assimilationists and liberal idealists, each believing in open participation in an economically restructured American society. The range of views inherent in the assimiliationist perspective, presumed a continued African American presence *intertwined* in the larger social system. In the self-determinationist camp were the Garveyites who advocated a separate society in the shadow of the existing one here and in Africa, under a single leader, such as Marcus Garvey himself. The various Afro-Islamic groups in America, of course, currently support a structural and cultural separation, their brand of separatism arising out of frustration with American mainstream politics and the shortcomings of the Civil Rights movement of the 1960s. The psychological black nationalist label may be applied to many of the students who demanded the establishment of African American Studies programs (and in some cases, separate cultural facilities), with distinctly social uplift agendas. The point here is that the various perspectives suggested both categories of understanding and ideologies of behavior. The debate on ideological behavior, of late, has brought about much of the controversy over "political correctness."

Socio-Scientific Trends

While Africentricity and other ideologies have emerged as debates over the proper philosophy and perspectives African American activists *should* take toward their work and the best action-oriented strategies they should propose to the African American community, it is helpful to understand what has been the nature of the themes and theories guiding previous *academic* efforts, especially in the context of their usages of the concept of "Community." The term "African American (or Black) Community" has been used to mean a) the collectivity of Americans of African ancestry, and b) blacks as a cohesive socio-political group. The idea of an African American or black community has been used most explicitly in the fields of history, sociology and psychology. These disciplines, respectively, deal with 1) the historical dimensions of the black experiences, 2) the sociological dilemmas of racial stratification and subordination in a democracy and 3) the impact of the community's historical legacy and its contemporary effects on the mentality of black people.

Like most other scholars, African American intellectuals appear to have developed their analytical philosophies in reaction to their own socialization experiences, their individual attitudes toward the canons of their professional disciplines, the major intellectual currents of their eras, and the particular topics, problems and/or questions addressed by them. If these scholars are unified by a single orienting ideology, it would be the ideology of freedom. The individuals and books cited below are to be understood as examples of the themes and theories explaining the character of the black community.

Black scholarly production in the United States originated in the field of history. It began as an effort to have people of African descent seen as complete human beings and not as animated commodities in the economic systems of other peoples. Consequently, the central themes and objectives of black historiography have attacked obliterative racism. In the words of historian Earl E. Thorpe, "the central theme of Black History is the quest of Black Americans for freedom equality and manhood" (sic). John Hope Franklin, the dean of African American historians, has noted several distinct thematic phases in the evolution of black history. From the publication of George Washington Williams' *History of the Negro Race in America* (1883), to about 1915, writes Franklin, "the common objective of the writers of this period was to define and describe the role of Afro-Americans in the life of the nation." The few black historians of the era tried to counteract this by writing amateur histories and biographies as correctives to the widespread belief that no matter where located, Africans were incapable of contributing to history as originators of ideas and artifacts.

The next phase began in 1915 with the founding, by Carter G. Woodson, of the Association for the Study of Negro Life and History. Woodson declared that the objective of his new organization was to "save and publish the records of the Negro, that the race may not become a minor factor in the thought of the world" — hence, the establishment of *Journal of Negro History* in 1916 and the *Negro History Bulletin* a decade later. The practical intent of historical contributionism was the bolstering of community pride and confidence in an era of official racism.

The third phase covers the years between 1935 and 1960, a period which saw the appearance of Nazism overseas, the urbanization of the black community in North America and the beginning of its Civil Rights revolution. In 1933, Woodson wrote *The Mis-Education of the Negro*, a work of epistemology or the study of the ideological foundations of knowledge itself. In this work, he urged blacks, lettered and unlettered alike, not to depend on the majority group for the definition of themselves and of social reality. Two years later, the multi-disciplinary DuBois made a declaration of black intellectual independence with a fresh and provocative interpretation of history. Black history also became overtly critical of how the larger social order was structured and how it functioned. This historical sociology made it easier for historians to use sociology in their pleas for a more equitable society. An excellent example of this is *The Negro in the United States* (1949), a work of sociological history of the American-American community by E. Franklin Frazier, the eminent sociologist.

The fourth and current phase is one in which no level of historical analysis is omitted. Black historiography now includes works from Thomas Holt's *Black Over White: Negro Political Leadership in South Carolina During Reconstruction* (1877) to the global sweep of St. Clair Drake's *Black Folk Here and There* (1990). Moreover, very large numbers of scholars of both races are employing a variety of methods to study and reconstruct the history of the black community from a host of analytical perspectives. Just as African American historians moved from narrative to analysis, so did the black scholars in the field of sociology. Even before emancipation, free blacks were producing narrative reports on the conditions within their communities. In 1897, with his *The Philadelphia Negro*, DuBois did for African American sociology what Carter G. Woodson did for history: he explained, in scientific terms, the black community to itself and the larger society. He and other sociologists such as Charles S. Johnson and E. Franklin Frazier used an evolutionary approach to the study of the black community. Many of these early works measured the development of the black community in terms of rates of growth in income, health, education and occupational diversity.

By the 1940s, as black historians strove to promote racial and community pride via the contributionist approach, African American sociologists sought to understand the contemporary status of the race through a number of theoretical perspectives: acculturation, deprivation, segregation, discrimination. By conceptualizing the social conditions within the white community as the norm, in the black communities' inequalities were seen as negative. The implication of intrinsic human equality espoused by black historians and the sociological observations of group inequalities sparked the search for theories to explain the latter.

Thus began the *pathological* theory of the black community. This hypothesis assumed that the African American community was "ill," and that the white community was not. Sociologists then sought internal and external causes for the "illness" of the community. Some sociologists pointed to the legacy of slavery and hypothesized a culture of black dependency. Others saw the difference in "inappropriate" African cultural "survivals" which had the effect of slowing down the evolution of the race toward technologically oriented culture. Still others wrote of a "culture of poverty." Sociologists who assumed the existence of external sources of the black community's problems called for a return to an interactionist approach as the best way to understand the black community. This meant, again, stressing the conflictive relations and power disparities between the two communities of color. Thus *deprivation* theories were used to guide sociological research on the African American community. The revisionist argument held that persistent racism and discrimination by white America had deprived black communities of opportunities to evolve at the same rate as white immigrant communities. In the 1960s, some scholars defined the black community as an internal *colony*, existing to be exploited by a callous "mother country." Some scholars saw the black community as a "nation within a nation" and several brands of "black nationalism" gained prominence among the more radical black intellectuals.

Internal and external causation theories were blended in the "systems theory" approach, which mainstream sociologists applied to the total social order, an approach that, at bottom, justifies the status quo on a law-and-order basis. In reaction to the inherent conservatism of this conception of the social order, a group of radical sociologists contributed to *The Death of White Sociology*, edited by Joyce Ladner. They called for a new sociology to supersede black community pathology theories and escape the ideological trap of systems theory. They sought a black sociology powerful enough to do this. Major volumes aimed in this direction is *The Truly Disadvantaged* (1987) and *When Work Disappears* (1996) both by William J. Wilson, the most prominent black sociologist of the 1990s. These works place the black community in a vortex of social forces but recognized the role of conscious decision making government as a major factor influencing the quality of life in black America.

The theories of the African American community advocated by black psychologists embody the concatenated effects of its historical past and sociological present. Some psychologists (and social psychologists) have argued that polarities of racial status and dualities of black-white interactions have created a cultural split resulting in a schizoid mentality for African Americans. At the beginning of this century, W. E. B. DuBois, West's model, wrote of this split in *The Souls of Black Folk* (1903) when he asserted in the case of the black Americans that "one ever feels his two-ness, — an American, a Negro; two souls, two thoughts, two unreconciled striving; two warring ideals in one dark body, whose dogged strength alone keeps it from being torn asunder." Although not normally cited as a social psychologist, the philosopher Cornel West in his *Race Matters* (1994) writes as one when explaining the reason for black leadership disarray "is the gross deterioration of personal, familiar, and communal relations among African Americans," relations which "constitute a crucial basis for the development of a collection and critical consciousness and a moral commitment to and courageous engagement with causes beyond that of one's self and family."

In both DuBois and West we find an ethical yearning for psychological wholeness or "one-ness" which would contribute to the strength of community. The functional stress of the "two-ness" or double-consciousness to which they both allude, has created pathological problems for the black community, among them an enervating sense of collective inadequacy and individual impotence. For at least two generations, this has been a common theme of black and white psychologists using "reference group theory," a theory which posits that the basic template of personal identity is the group of which the individual in a socialized member, whatever the status of the group. The unquestioned low status of the African American community in the society thus forces self-concept and self-esteem among blacks to be correspondingly low. The famous 1930s doll-choice experiments of the psychologists Kenneth and Mamie Clark illustrated the pernicious effects of enforced inferior status on the self-concept of black children who showed self-rejection and low-esteem behaviors by their unwillingness to choose dolls in their own self-image. The accepted models of preference were those of Caucasian imagery, especially as related to skin color, hair texture and facial features. Neither nature nor nurture permitted these youngsters to be what they apparently wished to be. In the 1950–1960 period, themes of socially enforced differences and deprivation undergirded arguments aimed at influencing public policy. The results of the doll-choice experiment were key elements in the plaintiffs arguments before the U.S. Supreme Court in the school desegregation case of *Brown v. Board of Education of Topeka* (1954). This essentially environmentalist explanation of diversity was not seriously affected by the spurious black cognitive deficiency arguments of works such as Richard J. Herrnstein and Charles Murray's *The Bell Curve: Intelligence and Class Structure in American Life* (1994).

During the 1960s heyday of the Civil Rights movement, however, the thematic emphases of black psychologists began to shift. Black was "beautiful," including skin, hair and physiognomy. Following the prideful contributionism of the historians of the 1930s and rejecting the pathos of pathogenic sociological themes of the 1940s–1950s, black academics began promoting what Maulana Karenga called the "adaptive vitality" model of black community sociology and psychology. In his *Introduction to Black Studies* (1982) Karenga declared that "the adaptive vitality school contends that adaptation by Blacks to socio-economic pressures and limitations must not be seen as a pathology but a strength." This was the psychological theme of Andrew Billingsley's highly influential *Black Families in White America* (1968), continued in his *Climbing Jacob's Ladder* (1994). Adelbert Jenkins, in the

Psychology of Afro-Americans: A Humanistic Approach (1992), suggested a re-vised model of normality employing a humanistic perspective and based on proven psychological findings. In 1991, William E. Cross in *Shades of Black: Diversity in African American Identity* produced a masterly critique of previous psychological studies and proposed a provocative African American model of the structures and dynamics determining the nature of black identity in contemporary life.

The work of black psychologists suggests that the following tasks are of major interest and importance:

- defining and developing a concept of "normality which is scientifically sound and socially positive;
- creating "treatment" protocols for the African American community strong enough to cover the in-group status diversity of its members; and
- generating implementation strategies powerful enough to neutralize the neg-ative effects of community subordination and socialization in this society.

Whatever the ideological future of Afrocentrism as currently debated, this overview of the themes and theories permeating the work of African American historians, sociologists and psychologists indicates that perspectives arise from the nature of the work done as they do from the work anticipated. Regardless of their individual ideological "isms," black academics are deeply interested in hav-ing their labors make a positive impact in the battle to liberate the African Amer-ican community. By ties of affection and circumstance, black intellectuals are bound to the primary community through which they, as human beings, entered this world. Its struggle is inescapably their own.

Summary

Originating out of the concerns of black students newly present on the campuses of predominantly white institutions of higher education in the later 1960s, African American Studies is a new field of instruction and research. In the context of that socially expansive and innovative time, proponents of African American or Black Studies were keenly disappointed to discover that the black experience was of minor concern to the educational establishment's adherence to "traditional" academic dis-ciplines. More than 60 colleges and universities responded to the African American Studies Movement by establishing full-fledged departments and by setting up more than 400 programs and institutes. Of the various institutional arrangements, the de-partment became the most durable type of unit and constitutes the basis for the fur-ther evolution toward master's and Ph.D. level instruction in the field.

Reluctantly accepted by the academic establishment, professional African Americanists confronted problems of a) faculty recruitment, b) field and discipli-nary definition, d) curriculum construction and d) legitimating a counter-perspec-tive on the nature of the black experience in the world. Since traditional acade-mics had failed formally to explore this experience, the small pool of qualified black academics was the primary source for faculty. Defining the field and creat-ing curricula within it have been especially difficult, for many African American Studies departments have tried to squeeze into small units a reverse-mirror image of the entire range of received historical and social reality.

Thus far, curricula redefinition in this field has evolved around the social sciences and humanities. Most African American Studies departments offer the bachelor of arts degree, although a half-dozen offer the master of arts and two or three now offer the doctorate. When professional African Americanists attempted to share their curricula perspectives with inner city public schools, the theoretical and practical problem of legitimizing African American Studies beyond the college campus attracted much attention among hitherto indifferent segments of both black and white communities. The popular media saw Afrocentrism as "news," one of the rare times an intellectual concept from the black academic community has gone national.

African American scholars have been concerned about the epistemological, political and pedagogical consequences of their endeavors. A review of influential works by African American scholars in history, sociology, and psychology suggests that social and situational circumstances stimulate the evolution of a variety of approaches to the academic treatment of the experience of communities containing persons of African descent. This evolution spans at least a century, and is characterized by the contributions of a small number of especially influential individuals, such as W. E. B. DuBois, Carter G. Woodson, E. Franklin Fraizer, Kenneth and Mamie Clark, to name a few. These scholars were lonely warriors during days of official racial segregation and uncontested white control of public school curricula throughout the nation. In the last two or three decades, a second and larger group of African American intellectual leaders emerged, examples being John Blassingame and Thomas Holt in history, Andrew Billingsley in Sociology and William Cross in psychology. The black intellectual community has not only grown larger in numbers and stronger in resources, but also has produced several public intellectuals, among them Molefe Asante, Derrick Bell, Stephen Carter, Michael Dyson, Gerald Early, Henry Louis Gates, bell hooks, June Jordan, Maulana Karenga, Randall Kennedy, David Lewis, Glenn Loury, Manning Marable, Toni Morrison, Nell Painter, Orlando Patterson, and Cornel West, among others. Whether or not each of these thinkers can be classified as Afrocentrist, at the least they represent the presence of African Americans in the intellectual life of our time.

Afrocentrism, then, is an evolving movement, carrying with it the momentum of previous African American scholarship and concern with epistemological perspectives through which people perceive and evaluate experience. Afrocentrism as ideology arrived on the American educational scene at the precise moment the traditional mono-cultural perspective is being challenged by a nascent multi-culturalism. Afrocentrism appears to be far more disturbing than the multiculturalism because it challenges the very foundations of the old perceptual orders and canons. In contrast, multi-culturalism is at the contributionist/appreciation stage of historical and cultural analysis. When it inevitably advances to the analytical/critical stage, multiculturalism too will come under intense scrutiny.

Afrocentrism has also been nurtured by the persistent and perhaps atavistic racism within the larger society and by color-coded communities in daily life. In reaction to this historically enforced racial separatism, Afrocentrists represent a continuation of the academic and social struggle of African Americans to locate an authentic perspective which reflects the deeper truths about themselves and the society they are seeking to liberate from racial paranoia and color irrationality. Thus, from its inception to the present, as institution, as instruction and as ideology, the African American Studies movement has stimulated discussion and debate about the nature and direction of American education.

The debate among African American scholars has not been limited to episte-mological and science methodology. It has also extended itself to action-oriented approaches or ideological strategies to guarantee the survival of the Black com-munity in a predominantly white repressive society. The image held of the black presence in this society has ranged from the pathological, to the deficiency and de-fective model, on to the adaptive vitality image. African American Studies profes-sionals represent the first large cadre of scholars from within the community. While the African Americans' presence in this society antedates that of the *Mayflower*, only in this century has there emerged from within a body of scholars committed to understanding it and sharing that understanding. Larger than any single individual, this development has generated a healthy debate over the nature of the knowledge process and over what its contents should be.

Study Questions and Activities

1. What factors and attitudes led to omission and distortion of the black experi-ence in the American education system prior to the 1950s?
2. What accounts for the rarity of African American or Black Studies Depart-ments on the campuses of historically black colleges and/or universities?
3. What were the developmental stages of African American Studies prior to the 1960s? Since the 1960s?
4. Identify the strengths and weaknesses of the concept of Afrocentricity as an approach to defining basic knowledge.
5. What is the role of epistemology in the development of a discipline?
6. Compare the ideological assumptions of multiculturalism with the ideological presumptions of Afrocentrism.

References

Russell L. Adams. "Intellectual Questions and Imperatives in the Development of Afro-American Studies." *Journal of Negro Education*, vol. 53, 3 (Summer, 1984): 201–225.

"Africa Dreams." *Newsweek*, September 23, 1991, pp. 42–50.

Abdul Alkalamat et al. *Introduction to Afro-American Studies. A People's Col-lege Primer.* Chicago, IL: Peoples College Press, 1986.

Molefe Asante. *Kemet, Afrocentricity and Knowledge.* Trenton, NJ: Africa World Press, 1990.

John Blassingame. *New Perspectives on Black Studies.* Urbana, IL: University of Illinois Press, 1971.

John Bracey, August Meier and Elliott Rudwick (eds.). *The Black Sociologists: The First Half Century.* Belmont, CA: The Wadsworth Publishing Co., 1971.

John Bracey, August Meier and Elliott Rudwick (eds.) *The Rise of the Ghetto.* Belmont, CA: The Wadsworth Publishing Co., 1971.

James L. Conyers, Jr. (ed.). *Afrocentricity and the Academy: Essays on Theory and Practice.* Jefferson, NC: McFarland, 2003.

William E. Cross, Jr. *Shades of Black: Diversity in African-American Identity.* Philadelphia, PA: Temple University Press, 1991.

Alexander Crummell. "Civilization: The Primal Need of the Race," in Herbert Aptheker. *A Documentary History of the Negro People in the United States.* New York: The Citadel Press, 1951.

Philip T.K Daniel et al. *The National Case for Black Studies: Northern Illinois Black Studies, Four-Year College and University Survey.* DeKalb, IL: Afro-American Studies Program, 1983.

St. Clair Drake and Horace R. Cayton. *Black Metropolis.* New York: Harcourt, Brace, 1945.

W. E. B. DuBois. *Black Reconstruction in America, 1860–1880.* New York: The World Publishing Co., 1964.

———. *The Philadelphia Negro.* Philadelphia: The University Pennsylvania Press, 1899.

Gerald Early. "Understanding Afrocentrism." *Civilization* (July/August 1995): 31–39.

John Ernest. *Liberation Historiography: African American Writers and the Challenge of History, 1794–1861.* Chapel Hill: University of North Carolina Press, 2004.

Walter Fisher. *Ideas for Black Studies: The Morgan State College Program.* Baltimore, MD: The Morgan State College Press, 1971.

John Hope Franklin. "On the Evolution of Scholarship in Afro-American History," in Darlene Clark Hine (ed.). *The State of Afro-American History.* Baton Rouge, LA: Louisiana State University Press, 1986.

E. Franklin Frazier. *The Negro in the United States.* New York: The Macmillan Co., 1947.

Paul Gagnon. "What Should Children Learn." *Atlantic Monthly,* vol. 276, 6 (December, 1995): 65–78.

Henry Louis Gates, Jr. "Academe Must Give Black-Studies Programs Their Due." *The Chronicle of Higher Education* September 20, 1989.

Joyce A. Joyce. *Black Studies as Human Studies: Critical Essays and Interviews.* Albany: State University of New York Press, 2005.

Maulana Karenga. *Introduction to Black Studies.* Los Angeles, CA: Kawaida Publications.

Joyce A. Ladner (ed.). *The Death of White Sociology.* New York: Vintage Books, 1973.

Mary F. Lefkowitz. *Not Out of Africa.* New York: Basic Books, 1996.

———. *"Black Athena" Revisited.* Chapel Hill: The University of North Carolina Press, 1996.

Tilden Lemelle. "The Status of Black Studies in the Second Decade: The Ideological Imperative," in James E. Turner (ed.). *The Next Decade: Theoretical and Research Issues in Africana Studies.* Ithaca, NY: Cornell University Africana Center, 1984.

Wilson Jeremiah Moses. *Creative Conflict in African American Thought: Frederick Douglass, Alexander Crummell, Booker T. Washington, W.E.B. DuBois, and Marcus Garvey.* New York: Cambridge University Press, 2004.

Gunnar Myrdal. *An American Dilemma:The Negro Problem and Modern Democracy.* 2 vols. New York: Harper and Row, 1944.

National Council for Black Studies, Inc. *Black Studies Core Curriculum.* Bloomington, IN, 1971.

Phil Petrie. "Afro-Centrism in a Multicultural Democracy," *American Visions: The Magazine of Afro-American Culture,* vol. 6, 4 (August, 1991): 20–26.

Elaine B. Richardson and Ronald L. Jackson, II (eds.). *African American Rhetoric(s): Interdisciplinary Perspectives.* Carbondale: Southern Illinois University Press, 2004.

William R. Scott (ed.). *Upon These Shores: Themes in the African-American Experience, 1600 to the Present.* New York: Routledge, 2000.

David W. Southern, *Gunnar Myrdal and Black-White Relations: The Use and Abuse of An American Dilemma, 1944–1969.* Baton Rouge, LA: Louisiana State University Press, 1986.

Daniel C. Thompson. *Sociology of the Black Experience.* Westport, CT: Greenwood Press, 1974.

Earl E. Thorpe. *The Central Theme of Black History.* Westport, CT: Greenwood Press, 1960.

Cornel West. *Race Matters.* New York: Vintage Books, 1994.

PART II

PEOPLES OF AFRICAN DESCENT
AND THEIR PLACE IN HISTORY

3

Africa and the Genesis of Humankind

R. Hunt Davis, Jr.

Introduction

Africa has long been considered the cradle of humankind, for it is the only continent where scientists have located evidence for the early evolution of humankind. As with the later development of human societies on the African continent, so it was with early human evolution that the physical environment played a crucial role. But the physical environment is more than just a given—it undergoes gradual change, such as the desiccation of the Sahara Desert that began some 7,000 years ago. Humans also change the environment through their interaction with it, as in the case of the expansion of the African grasslands as agriculturalists cut down the forests to expand their areas of cultivation. The discussion of the African physical environment that follows is thus based on two basic operating assumptions:

1. The physical environment conditions and constrains human activity and, thus, the development of human society, which means that the physical environment plays a central role in historical development; and
2. Humans through their technology have progressively lessened or altered the constraints of the physical environment to the point that today the relationship between human society and the physical environment is vastly different, and vastly more complex, than it was a century ago, let alone several thousand years ago.

Major terms and concepts: Paleolithic age, Neolithic age, a continent of diversity, hominid, *Homo sapiens*, tropics, equator, transhumance, pastoralist, Intertropical Convergence Zone, humus, agricultural revolution, subsistence, Bantu expansion, the iron revolution, feudalism, plateau.

Physical Environment and Human Development

With the above operating assumption in mind, let us turn to the geography of Africa, first considering the size, shape, and geological composition of the continent. The first point to note is that Africa is a vast continent, not a single country. In fact, it is nearly three and a half times the size of the continental United States (the forty-eight contiguous states). It is also a relatively high continent—90 percent of its area is more than 500 feet above sea level, compared with less than 50 percent of Europe. On the other hand, there is only a limited amount of truly high terrain, such as in East Africa, where Mt. Kilimanjaro stands 19,340 feet above sea level and several other mountains range between 14,000 and 17,000 feet. In contrast to the Western Hemisphere, Africa lacks a continental divide. Instead, there is a reverse feature—the great continental fault known as the Rift Valley that runs from the Red Sea through the Ethiopian highlands, down the line of East African lakes and out to sea in Mozambique.

Africa, then, is a vast interior plateau astride the equator. Its most common feature is a series of major internal basins—the Djouf Basin of the middle and upper Niger River; the Chad Basin centering on Lake Chad; the Sudan Basin of the upper Nile; the Congo Basin of the two Congo republics; and the Kalahari Basin of southern Africa. Another feature of the plateau is that the river systems generally have major falls near their mouths as they descend from the inland plateau to the sea. Except for the Gambia, Nile, Niger, and the Senegal Rivers, African river systems are not navigable very far inland from the sea. On the other hand, once inland past the falls, they are as in the case of the Congo River often navigable for long distances.

As would be expected of a continent of nearly 12 million square miles, Africa has five major climatic regions and contains a wide variety of climates and vegetation, even though three-fourths of its surface is in the tropics (between 23.5_N and 23.5_S). To the far north and far south are zones of a Mediterranean style climate, with winter rainfall. Moving into the interior are vast stretches of the Sahara Desert in the north and the Kalahari and Namib Deserts of the south. Bordering the desert areas are broad belts of grassland savanna mixed with light forest, the most widespread ecological type for the continent. Between the grassland zones lies the tropical rain forest. Basically, the climatic zones, which shade gradually into each other, constitute a mirror image except for the fifth zone, that of the East African highlands.

While factors such as latitude, altitude, and temperature affect the continent's vegetation patterns, no factor is more important than rainfall. Basically, the rainfall amounts are heaviest in the equatorial zones and lessen the farther one moves north or south of the equator. There is also a distinct seasonal pattern to the rains, with the heaviest rainfall in the summer months (except for the winter rains at the northern and southern extremes of the continent). Thus, tropical forest regions of West and West Central Africa have rain throughout the year, with total annual amounts often in excess of 80 inches. By way of contrast, the Sahelian border zone south of the Sahara Desert receives up to 20 inches of rain a year, but almost all of it is in the summer months. The result is that farming, except with irrigation, is not possible and the grazing areas for the pastoralists' herds dry up in the winter, forcing a seasonal pattern of migration (transhumance) in search for good pastures. The atmospheric force behind the seasonal rainfall pattern is the Intertropical Convergence Zone (ITCZ), which is a zone of airmass convergence that moves north or south of the equator according to the season. A final feature of the rains is that they are generally very heavy, which can lead to rapid runoff. In East Africa, the Indian Ocean monsoon winds, flowing southward from November through April and reversing course to flow northward from May through October, rather than the ITCZ, constitute the main determinant of the weather.

When it comes to discussing the significance of the physical environment for human activity, soils are another highly important factor. Tropical soils have several general characteristics that are very important for human development. First, they are devoid of humus (decaying matter) since, except at high altitudes, there is no cold season to slow down the decay of vegetation. As a result, they are generally of low fertility and soon become exhausted when farmed. They also leach out readily—especially with the heavy rains that are so typical of most of Africa—and thus lose their limited nutrients. Furthermore, because most African soils have a high iron content, they tend to harden and compact when stripped of their vegetation and exposed to the elements. There are exceptions, such as the volcanic soils of Cameroon, Rwanda, Burundi, and Ethiopia; the fertile silts of the Nile valley and the upper Niger delta; and limited other special situations. Overall, however, African soils are of relatively poor quality and frequently possess a moisture-stressed condition.

The condition of Africa's soils gave rise to agricultural practices which were suitable to the land that was being farmed. A particularly prevalent farming practice was that of "shifting" or "slash and burn" cultivation, where the field would be cleared of vegetation, the vegetation burned (which helped provide nutrients for the soil), and the land farmed for several years until crop yields declined. The field would then be allowed to lie fallow for up to twenty years to enable the soil to regenerate, as a succession of other fields were brought into production and then also allowed to lie fallow. Thus, except for the relatively limited areas of high productivity, the practice in African agriculture was of extensive rather than intensive land use. As shall be seen later in the chapter, it was those areas of the continent with highly productive agricultural lands that were the focal points of the complex societies that gave rise to the early cities and states of the continent.

The mineral resources of the continent have also played a significant role in the development of agriculture and the processes of urbanization and state formation. Africa is, in many ways, a mineral storehouse. In comparison with Europe, for instance, it has extensive mineral holdings. Perhaps the most important of these is iron, which was so critical for the manufacture of tools, weapons, and various other commodities. Some have described Africa in a geological sense as "almost a solid chunk of iron ore," although much of it is of low grade. Gold, which has been mined from early times, has long figured in African history, as has copper. Africa also has major petroleum deposits and many other important minerals such as uranium, manganese, and chrome. There are some countries such as Tanzania, however, that have virtually no exploitable mineral deposits, so the distribution of the mineral resources is uneven.

The climate, vegetation, soils, and mineral resources of the continent have all contributed and posed obstacles to human endeavor on the African continent over the centuries. Disease is yet another dimension of the physical environment that has had tremendous consequences for human development. For a long time, the standard view has been that Africa is an intrinsically unhealthy continent. The argument runs that, while human groups have developed some biological defenses against the tropical diseases, there has nonetheless been an exceptionally high infant mortality rate that has led to underpopulation until recent times. It is clear that the African environment hosts certain tropical diseases such as malaria, yellow fever, onchocerciasis (river blindness), and trypanosomiasis (sleeping sickness) that have been highly detrimental to humankind. Yet, as some scholars are beginning to argue, the position that over the course of human history Africa has been intrinsically less healthy than other continents is an untestable proposition.

Indeed, another and more recent perspective on the African disease environment is that, instead of being intrinsically unhealthy, it has become *increasingly unhealthy* as a result of intensified contact with the rest of the world, in particular dating from the start of the trans-Atlantic slave trade, some five hundred years ago. Major epidemic diseases such as smallpox, venereal disease, influenza, and cholera entered Africa through the coastal ports and then spread into the interior along the trade routes. The colonial era continued the introduction and dispersal of diseases from outside the continent through intensified contact and increased population mobility within the continent. In recent decades, this process has increased even further with additional negative consequences for the health of the continent's population. Of special note is the AIDS pandemic, which has had a greater impact to date on the population of Africa than that of any other continent. Finally, and particularly in more recent times, changes within various ecosystems of the continent have altered disease patterns, but often with a varying impact on different segments of the affected population. An example of this can be seen in the spread of schistosomiasis in association with development projects involving dams and irrigation.

From *Sahelanthropus Tchadensis* to *Homo Sapiens*

For a number of decades, scientists have accepted Africa as the birthplace of humankind. This is due largely to the favorable environment of the African continent. Modern human beings (*Homo sapiens*) belong to the general branch of primates known as hominids, that is, creatures with brains larger than other primates and able to walk upright on two legs. Until very recently the search for human origins focused on the fossil remains of early hominids in the open savanna grasslands and woodlands of Eastern and Southern Africa. In 1925, based on the discovery of a skull 2.5 million years old, Professor Raymond Dart named these creatures, ape-like in appearance but with certain human characteristics, *Australopithecus*. The 1974 discovery in Ethiopia of a 3.18 million year-old skeleton, named "Lucy" by archaeologists (from the Beatles's song "Lucy in the Sky With Diamonds"), provided substantial new insights into the physical characteristics of these earliest hominids. Then, in 2002, scientists announced the discovery of a skull along with fragments of five other hominid specimens from Chad that belonged to a new genus and dated to between 6 and 7 million years ago. They named the genus *Sahelanthropus* and the species *Tchadensis,* with the nickname of Toumaï (meaning "hope of life" in the local Goran language). With this momentous discovery, the search for the point at which the human lineage separated from that of chimpanzees moved much further back in time and broadened out from its earlier eastern and southern Africa focus.

Other early hominid forms also emerged. In 1973, Louis and Mary Leakey announced the discovery of the 1.9 million year old *Homo habilis* species from their research at Tanzania's Olduvai Gorge. Then, about 1.6 million years ago, *Homo erectus*, appeared. They represented a more advanced hominid genus, which soon replaced the other hominid types. By this time, too, it was clear that hominids were engaged in hunting. It was also with *Homo erectus* that hominids began to move out of Africa, as discoveries of skeletal remains in France, dating back some 800,000 years, and in China and Indonesia, dated to some 700,000 years ago, demonstrate. The 1991 discovery of a hominid fossil jawbone in the former Soviet republic of Georgia, dating back perhaps as early as 1.6 million years ago, suggests that the migration of *Homo erectus* from Africa to other continents was much earlier than had been previously thought. In any event, *Homo erectus* was able to migrate out of Africa because of an ability to adapt to a far wider range of environmental conditions than had been the case for earlier hominids.

Well into the 1980s, the study of human evolution had been based on the discovery and dating of fossil remains and other evidence of human activity. In the late 1980s, however, scientists studying human origins began to utilize molecular biological evidence as well as fossil evidence and came to the conclusion that Africa was not only the place of origin of hominids, some 4 million years ago, but also of anatomically modern human beings (*Homo sapiens*), approximately 200,000 years ago. Specifically, through studying DNA evidence, these scientists have traced modern humans back to a common woman ancestor (who they named "Eve") living in Africa. Her genes seem to be in the blood of all currently living humans. Furthermore, sometime between 90,000 and 180,000 years ago, her descendants began to emigrate from Africa, gradually displacing other hominids such as the Neanderthals and eventually populating the entire world.

The Evolution of Cultures and Civilizations

The complex and diverse cultural patterns of contemporary human society are simply the current stage of a long process of cultural evolution that goes back to early hominids. The material evidence for the development of culture begins with the identification of the earliest stone tool technology. The *Homo habilis* species were seemingly the first hominids to use simple stone tools for cutting and scraping. With the appearance of *Homo erectus*, 1.6 million years ago, a much more sophisticated stone technology emerged, centered around the hand axe. There is also evidence of organized hunting and the use of fire.

The emergence of early *Homo sapiens* signaled a quickening pace of cultural change and growing sophistication of technology and social organization, often referred to as the Middle Stone Age. New techniques emerged in tool making, and the resulting products were more efficient and applicable to a wider range of tasks. Hunting skills seem to have advanced as well, fire was used more extensively, and rudimentary shelters were constructed from readily available materials. The earliest examples of modern human behavior also appear to date from

Africa, as exemplified by the discovery of engraving at Blombos Cave in South Africa in 2001. As of now, this is the earliest example of human artistry.

A yet more advanced stage of the Stone Age, known as the Later Stone Age, was in evidence by 40,000 years ago. People became even more skilled in working with stone and were able to make artifacts such as arrow heads (thus leading to the development of the bow and arrow, yet another significant advance in hunting and fighting techniques). Fine bone tools were also in evidence, as were artistic efforts such as beads made from eggshell and scenes painted and engraved on rocks and in caves. In contrast to earlier Stone Age developments, there was also greater regional variation in cultural patterns. Thus, the culture of the savanna grasslands differed from that of the rain forest and so forth.

As hominids evolved, so too did their skills at hunting and gathering. By 10,000 years ago, hunting and gathering societies had emerged on the African continent in their modern form—a form which has continued to exist in some regions of the continent. Anthropologists have extensively studied peoples such as the Khoisan speakers of the Kalahari Desert in Botswana and the BaMbuti of the Ituri forest of the Congo Basin to gain insights into the earlier era when all Africans sustained themselves through hunting and gathering. The fact that, even today, some few Africans still largely follow such a way of life is due primarily to the fact that the environments in which they live are more conducive to economies based on hunting and gathering than they are to food production. Indeed, while some societies rapidly adopted food production techniques once they were available, others persisted in utilizing hunting and gathering and only gradually shifted to food production. The primary explanation for these differences lay in the environmental conditions various societies faced.

The Shift to Food Production

The pace of human cultural development gradually picks up the closer one moves to the present. Yet, the transition from one major stage to the next required major new technological breakthroughs. Hunting and gathering societies ultimately reached an optimum level beyond which they could not move. No matter how refined, tools made from stone, bone, and wood could only accomplish so much. Similarly, hunting and gathering techniques could only be developed to sustain a certain level of population and social organization. They simply did not have the capability of providing an economic base for the increasingly complex and diverse human cultures and societies that have taken shape over the last several thousand years. Two developments were crucial in enabling human society to advance to more complex stages: food production, that is, the development of farming and pastoralism; and metallurgy, especially the development of an iron-based technology.

The beginning of food production has often been referred to as the "agricultural revolution" because of its implications for human society and the pace of change it introduced. In many ways, this revolution marks the beginning of history. History is, above all else, about change over time. Prior to the emergence of agriculture, change was so imperceptible that it was measured in the Late Stone Age in thousands of years, and prior to that in tens of thousands or even hundreds of thousands of years. With farming and, perhaps to a lesser extent, pastoralism, the process of change propelled itself forward at an ever increasing intensity. However, one should not envisage the pace of change being even remotely similar to that of the "communications revolution" of our own era or even that of the "industrial revolution" of the eighteenth century, when change came to be measured in decades and then in years or even shorter periods of time.

Africa was at the forefront of the agricultural revolution. Between 11,500 and 10,000 years ago people living in three widely separate areas of the world—the Middle East, southern East Asia, and the eastern Sahara region of Africa—began to grow crops. The Saharan Africans were also domesticating cattle, perhaps even before they grew crops. A second global wave of agricultural innovation emerged by 7,000 years ago, with two of the new centers in the Horn of Africa and a third in the wooded savanna region of West Africa. The principal crops developed in Africa during the early agricultural revolution were the grains sorghum, millet, rice, and teff, plus yams, cotton, and enset.

The key factor in food production, in terms of human existence, was the beginning of control over the environment. Human activity through planting, breeding, and the care of animals could begin to determine the level of food supply (the most basic of all economic factors)—something previously entirely at the whim of nature. Furthermore, in favorable environments (as was the case in the Nile Valley), food production could lead to food surpluses, sometimes in large quantities. On the other hand, where the environment was unfavorable to food production, human societies continued to adhere to a hunting and gathering existence. Hunting and gathering societies generally had to move with the food supply; farming communities mainly stayed put; and pastoralists, as they moved, took their food supply with them. Food production thus led to a concentration and growth of population. The existence of a food surplus enabled part of the population to move out of the tasks of food production and into other occupations, thus leading to both job specialization and social differentiation. The potential for the most far-reaching developments along these lines was greater for farming populations than it was for pastoralist societies. For instance, it was from the agricultural societies that the earliest states in Africa emerged.

Early African States

A number of factors influenced and determined the location of early states in Africa. None, however, were more important than an environment that was conducive to a highly productive agriculture. There were, of course, other factors. One of these was geographic location. The earliest states in Africa emerged in areas that could readily be in contact and communication with areas outside the continent going through similar processes of development. Another factor was trade, which was facilitated by geographic location. Trade not only involved an exchange of goods but also of ideas, thus facilitating the transfer of cultural and technological knowledge in a decidedly two-way process.

Bantu Expansion

It is within this context of cultural and economic diffusion that the great Bantu expansion, although occurring at a later date (between the early first millennium BCE and continuing into the eighteenth century), has significance. Bantu speakers, comprising most of the ethnic groups in Central, Eastern, and Southern Africa, are believed to have originated in the area now linking Nigeria and Cameroon, and to have spread out in search of new lands to settle and perhaps new peoples to conquer. They had two major advantages over the people they encountered: they had a long sedentary tradition as experienced farmers and by the mid first millennium BCE had mastered the use of iron. Consequently, not only did they possess superior technology over their new acquaintances but they also had a more advanced culture. This culture provided opportunities for more leisure time and higher accomplishments in the arts than that of their new counterparts, most of whom are said to have been either fruit-gatherers and hunters, pastorals, or both.

As the Bantu speakers pushed east and south, they mingled (peacefully or through war) with the indigenous populations, intermarrying and thus creating, over the centuries, new cultures, new kingdoms, new civilizations, and new languages. At times, the encounter resulted in clashes which may have forced the original inhabitants to seek a new but less hospitable environment, as presumably was the case of the BaMbuti who now inhabit the Ituri forest and the San who live in the Kalahari desert.

Although much has been written on the long and sustained expansion of the Bantu speakers, much of the evidence remains linguistic. Historians still question the precise origins, the path of migration (was it through the rainforest, skirting the rainforest, or otherwise?), and the nature of Bantu assimilation with the new people. However the Bantu expansion occurred, its impact on Sub-Saharan Africa prior to the conquest of the continent during the nineteenth century was significant. From Zaire to Uganda, from Angola to Kenya, and from Namibia to South Africa—the multitude of new communities and states and of languages with similar vocabulary and grammatic structures reflect the Bantu expansion.

It may be helpful at this point to clarify briefly the issue of languages in Africa. Linguists have identified at least 1,000 indigenous languages on the continent and have attempted to give a semblance of rationality to them for comparative purposes and to facilitate the study of human cultural evolution and diffusion on the continent. Joseph Greenberg and other modern linguistics have classified these African languages into four major families: 1) Afro-Asiatic, in the northern half of the continent, comprising ancient Egyptian, the Berber languages of the Maghrib, Chadic, which includes Hausa, the Cushitic languages of the Horn, and the Semitic branch that includes Arabic; 2) Niger-Congo, of which the Bantu (meaning humankind) sub-group is a part, spoken in parts of West, Central, East, and Southern Africa; 3) Nilo-Saharan, which includes the Shilluk and Dinka languages of Sudan, and some others along the Nile and in the Sahara (Chad, for example); and 4) Khoisan, comprising the languages spoken by the Hottentots, the Khoi, and the San in the Namib and Kalahari desert areas.

Egypt

The first states in Africa emerged in the Nile Valley and were ultimately to evolve into Egypt, one of the cornerstones of the ancient world. In discussing the nature of Egyptian civilization, it is well to keep several points in mind. The first is that Egypt rested on the rich agricultural potential and the natural unity of the Nile valley from the sea to the First Cataract (i.e., the border between modern-day Egypt and the Sudan). Second, the flowering and then the continuity of Egyptian civilization grew out of mastery of the Nile Valley's agricultural potential. Until the nineteenth century, the techniques of cultivation had not changed greatly from those utilized by the farmers who worked the fields some 5,000 years earlier. These early and rather remarkable accomplishments provided effective answers for the environmental problems which the valley's inhabitants faced and enabled them to establish an effective social and political system. Third, Egypt was, relatively speaking, geographically isolated from other civilizations at the time of its flowering. This isolation and its own successes with developing the potential of the Nile helped produce an innate conservatism. Once launched, this great civilization during its peak had little to fear and, due to its own accomplishments, little to learn from its neighbors. This view was reflected in the Egyptian outlook on the world. The Egyptians identified their own land with the organized world and other lands with the forces of chaos. With these points in mind, let us turn to a brief discussion of the Egyptian civilization.

The roots of Egyptian civilization lie in the development of agricultural production that appears to date from some 7,000 years ago. At this time, communities were organized on a small scale, and hunting and fishing, rather than agriculture, provided the basic economic subsistence. There was as yet no thought of public works or capital improvements such as the later irrigation system. However, a changing environment, brought about by the gradual desiccation of the Sahara, forced a change in the economic level of these early Egyptians.

The fourth millennium was a critical period, for as agriculture became impossible on the edge of the Nile Valley, the population moved into the valley itself, which was an area of greater agricultural potential. This move led to expanded agricultural productivity and consequently a growth in population. Other developments also began to take place. Permanently settled communities grew in size and complexity, and trade began to develop among these communities and with centers in the Aegean and the Middle East. The establishment of agriculture and the expansion of trade led to both job specialization and social stratification. People could now earn their livelihood as merchants or craftsmen. Some people also benefitted more from the changing economy than others, so that incipient inequalities in wealth came into evidence, suggesting the rise of a class structure.

Of course, there also emerged competition among the various communities in the Nile Valley for land resources and control of trade routes. In addition, by the third millennium, when most of the basic agricultural and industrial processes were in place, the peasant farmers were producing approximately three times as much food as they themselves could consume (a level rarely reached by any other pre-industrial society). This gave rise to the surplus needed to support an elaborate political structure. Between 3200 and 2900 BCE, the rulers of Upper (Southern) Egypt conquered Lower (Northern) Egypt and created a unified country, installing themselves as the absolute temporal and religious rulers of a strong and powerful centralized state. This led to the establishment of the First Dynasty about 3000, the first of thirty dynasties that made Egypt the "land of the Pharaohs" and which finally ended in 332 BCE with the Greek conquest.

The results of the political unification were momentous in a number of different areas. In the first place, it produced social and economic growth which in turn led to revolutionary changes that ensured ancient Egypt's place in world history as one of humankind's greatest cultural achievements. A demographic revolution transformed the size of the population from the thousands to the millions. The growth of the population and the development of the state served to produce even greater specialization and also a growing class structure. This meant that Egyptian society was increasingly complex and capable of producing and consuming a broadening range of goods and services. Out of the dynamics of this rapidly evolving society emerged the architecture, the writing, the accumulation of knowledge, the extensive trade, and the other related developments which were to be the hallmarks of Egyptian culture for the next 3,000 years. But there was also a tremendous social imbalance, for at the top of society was a ruling nobility and a god-king who lived off the productivity of a large serf population. This static hierarchy was to be yet another hallmark of ancient Egyptian civilization.

While cultural continuity was the hallmark of ancient Egyptian civilization, the Egyptian state during the era of the Pharaohs did have several distinct periods. The period prior to 3200 is known as the Predynastic Era and covers the time of political organization. By the onset of the Archaic Period (3200–2900 BCE) there were two states, Lower Egypt and Upper Egypt, which in turn became unified into a single state. In the Archaic Period, we see the evolution of a new dogma in which the king (or Pharaoh) came to be considered a god, not a human, who reigned over humans. Unification set the stage for the Old Kingdom (2900–2280 BCE), which witnessed the full flowering of Egyptian culture. The culture then, having established itself, stifled further innovation. For example, some of the most impressive pyramids of the entire 3,000 years of the Pharaonic era were built in the middle years of the Old Kingdom. The Old Kingdom also saw military expeditions and trade, especially to the upper Nile, although the first cataract marked the southernmost limit of the state's direct political control.

By the end of the Old Kingdom, however, impoverishment and disintegration set in. An explosion of feudal disorder, with anarchy, social chaos, and civil war, ushered in the First Intermediate Period (2280–2060 BCE). Ultimately, a new dynasty was able to gain control over the entire country and launch a new great period of national development known as the Middle Kingdom (2060–1785 BCE). Egyptian control now extended farther south along the Nile, coming to rest at the Second Cataract in Nubia. As shall be discussed further below, it was during this era that lower Nubia became, for a time, an integral part of Egypt as Egyptian activity outside its own borders increased.

The Middle Kingdom gave way to the Second Intermediate Period (1785–1580 BCE). This period was marked by the growing existence of a large Asiatic population in Lower Egypt, as can be seen in the names of some of the Pharaohs of the Thirteenth Dynasty. These Asiatic immigrants became known as the Hyksos. By 1700 BCE, they had conquered much of the Delta region. For the first time in their history, the Egyptians found themselves under foreign rulers. Such a humiliation challenged their long-standing belief in their supremacy over other peoples and their sense of security under their gods. The Egyptians ultimately rebounded, however, and undertook a 150-year war of liberation to free themselves from the Hyksos. Out of this struggle emerged the New Kingdom (1580–1085 BCE).

The era of the New Kingdom was a time of political and military expansion, as Egypt established a far-reaching empire. Egyptian armies moved into Asia as far as Lebanon and Syria and controlled the upper Nile as far as the Fourth Cataract. The Egyptian presence in Nubia, for instance, can be seen in the great rock-cut temples at Abu-Simbel in Lower Nubia which Pharaoh Ramses II built after 1300. Around 1250 BCE, however, the New Kingdom began a period of gradual decline due to external invaders and internal ills such as labor troubles and inflation.

About 1085 BCE, the dynasties again began to consist of foreign-born rulers who seized the Egyptian throne. One of them, the Twenty-Fifth, came from the thoroughly Egyptianized state of Kush to the South. When this dynasty seized control of Egypt in the mid-eighth century, it thus was foreign in terms of its origins but also very Egyptian in its outlook. Within sixty years, an Assyrian invasion forced the Kushite rulers back to Nubia, where they and their successors ruled for many centuries. The Assyrians were in turn driven from Egypt with the help of Lydia and Greek mercenaries, who established yet another dynasty (the Twenty-Sixth). Persian invaders founded another dynasty, which in turn was overthrown by a local dynasty which, with its successors, ruled Egypt free of foreign control for about sixty years. Another Persian invasion in 341 BCE, followed by that of Alexander the Great in 332 BCE, brought a final end to the era of the Pharaohs, an era that had begun nearly 3,000 years earlier. As a footnote, Egypt would not again be under indigenous rule until Col. Gamal Abdel Nasser and his colleagues established a new Egyptian government in 1952.[1]

The Middle Nile

To the south of Egypt in modern-day Sudan lay the Nubian or middle Nile, the area running north from the confluence of the White and Blue Niles to the First Cataract. This region came under the pervasive influence of Egypt, as the discussion of the Kushite Dynasty (the Twenty-fifth Dynasty) has already indicated. However, the middle Nile also stands out as a major landmark of its own in the history of ancient Africa. The institutions of sacral chiefship that were to blossom forth in the divine kingship of Egypt appear to have originated in the sudanic Nile before spreading northward into Egypt. Somewhat after the establishment of the Old Kingdom, the Kerma kingdom emerged along the Dongola Reach of the Nile and continued in existence until the New Kingdom established imperial control of the region. After the indigenous political hiatus of the New Kingdom era, Kush emerged. With its capital first at Napata then farther south at Meroë, it had a political history that stretched for nearly 1,500 years from approximately the tenth century BCE into the fourth century CE. The underlying cultural history is of even greater length, originating with the early agricultural developments in the region. Nubia, then, stands not simply as an offshoot of Egyptian civilization but as an ancient civilization in its own right that was developed by the indigenous middle Nile population.

---

1. On the scholarly controversy over Egypt and Afrocentricity, see chapter 2.

Geographical location and environmental factors shaped the history of the middle Nile as much as they did for Egypt. As with Egypt, Nubia could not have existed without the Nile, but in this instance it was not as bountiful as it was farther north. The series of rocky swift rapids that constituted the six Nile cataracts greatly hindered navigation, the river corridor was at places so narrow or rugged as to prevent farming, and the surrounding environment was one of the most extreme on earth. Thus, while it was the water and the soil of the middle Nile that brought and sustained the region's population, human settlement could not be as continuous or as dense as it was in Egypt, nor could river-borne communication be as continuous as in Egypt. In fact, the cataracts led to overland roads cutting off the bends, so that the middle Nile civilization was not as solely focused on the river for transportation as was the lower Nile. Indeed, a whole regional overland network emerged both within the Meroitic state and linking it with more distant regions. Such a development was lacking in Egypt because of the unsurpassed transportation system offered by the Nile.

Egypt heavily influenced Nubia, as has already been noted. By the middle of the Old Kingdom period, it had become the most important foreign field for Egypt, with the First Cataract as the boundary. Under the Middle Kingdom (2060–1785 BCE), lower Nubia to the Second Cataract became an integral part of Egypt. The occupation, though, seemed to be largely commercial and military in nature. The era of the New Kingdom (1580–1085 BCE) brought a new relationship between Egypt and the middle Nile. No longer was the middle Nile a trading zone beyond the frontier (as under the Old Kingdom), or a region of fortified trading posts denoting a permanent military as well as commercial presence (as under the Middle Kingdom). The Egyptian presence was now one that was overwhelmingly cultural as well. Egyptian control extended to Napata at the Fourth Cataract and perhaps as far south as Meroë. The boundary between Egypt and Nubia, to all practical purposes, was nearly obliterated. By the end of the New Kingdom, Nubia and Kush had developed as a base for the control of Egypt itself. And this was, indeed, what happened late in the eighth century B.C with the emergence of the Twenty-fifth Dynasty.

The collapse of the New Kingdom (1085 BCE) led to a retreat of Egyptian power from the area, but Egypt left behind a thoroughly Egyptianized society in its place. Indeed, Nubia now became one of the last strongholds of the old faith and culture of ancient Egypt. A process of unification of the middle Nile began which, by 750 BCE had united the region from the Second Cataract to beyond Meroë, forming the kingdom of Kush with its capital at Napata. Its Egyptianized kings then took over Egypt itself as the Twenty-Fifth Dynasty and tried to resurrect the older Egyptian traditions. Driven out of Egypt by the Assyrians in 663 BCE, and then defeated in 591 BCE by an Egyptian invasion which sacked the capital of Napata and established a garrison at the Second Cataract, the Kushite kings retreated farther up the Nile to establish a new capital at Meroë.

Meroë was located deep in the Sudan south of the Atbara-Nile confluence. Rainfall agriculture and pastoralism were possible outside the Nile Valley and contributed significantly to the subsistence base. Overland trade routes spread out from the main towns on the Nile, so that commerce no longer focused so exclusively on the river. Also, it was the site of one of Africa's early significant iron industries due to a plentiful supply of iron ore and of wood to make charcoal used in smelting. Meroë continued to thrive, with imposing buildings, large towns, and the like, and it was well-known far beyond its borders. Indeed, Herodotus, the "father of history," writing in the fifth century BCE , described it as a great city, and other Greeks and Romans were also to write of it.

For a while, Meroë's culture remained uncompromisingly Egyptian, but gradually isolation from the north and the earlier decline of the old Egyptian culture itself began to leave its mark. For instance, by 500 BCE or so, the written language began to shift away from Egyptian hieroglyphs. What was taking place was the steady displacement of Egyptian cultural influences by an indigenous culture at times tempered by contacts coming from other directions. In the early centuries of the Christian era, Kush entered into a final decline, sharing a fate that was also facing the Mediterranean world. Finally, in the early fourth century CE., the neighboring state of Axum, located in the northern Ethiopian highlands, conquered Kush and totally destroyed the kingdom that had once flourished at Meroë.

Other Early and Late African States

Egypt and Kush were but the earliest indigenous states on the African continent. Other significant states were to develop throughout much of the continent. For example, the origins of Axum, which defeated Meroë, went back at least as early as 500 BCE In the broad savanna regions, far to the west of the Nile Valley in the area of upper Senegal and upper Niger Rivers, major states began to emerge within the first few centuries CE. By 750, Ghana, known as far as Europe for its abundance of gold, was a powerful entity. It was to be succeeded by Mali around 1200, with Songhai supplanting it in turn in the fifteenth century. Mali and Songhai are remembered for their institutions of learning at Senkore (Timbuktu), Djenne, and Gao between the thirteenth and sixteenth centuries.

To the south, in the forested regions of what is now western Nigeria, urbanization and the development of states had their start among the Yoruba by the late first millennium CE. By the thirteenth century, the site of Benin, the center of a state that remained powerful until the late nineteenth century (known for its early experiments with republicanism, rotational monarchy, and primogeniture, and famous for its bronze sculpture) was already occupied. A series of cities which were the focal points of small states began to appear on the East African coast by the eighth century CE. As noted below, they reached a point of development by the 1330s such that the renown world traveller, Ibn Battuta, could describe the principal coastal town, Kilwa in southern Tanzania, as "one of the most beautiful and well-constructed towns in the world." South and west of Kilwa in the eastern highlands of modern-day Zimbabwe, a site known as Great Zimbabwe, which contained massive stone structures, was the capital of a major state from about 1250–1450.

The vast number of African states existing before the European arrival and conquest of the continent cannot be adequately covered in this limited space. However, brief mention of other significant states is warranted. Dahomey, which flourished in West Africa until it was conquered by the French during the nineteenth century, is remembered for the absolute power of its rulers and by the fact that women shared civilian and military responsibilities with men. The Ashanti Confederation, on the other hand, emerged during the seventeenth century out of the initiative of Osei Tutu who was able to loosely unify the Akan people of present Ghana, using the royal stool as the symbol of unity of the "nation" and the sacredness of its ruler. Before the British conquered it during the nineteenth century, the Ashanti Confederation successfully fought them on the battlefield.

The Bunyoro and Buganda kingdoms in Central and East Africa, which developed between the sixteenth and nineteenth centuries, were noted for their elaborate investiture rituals, for control of the ivory trade, and for patronizing the arts. There were other kingdoms scattered throughout Africa such as the Mossi kingdoms of Upper Volta (four kingdoms occupying 30,000 square miles, with more than 1 million inhabitants prior to European conquest) and the Fulani Muslim Kingdoms of Futa Toro and Futa Jalon in Senegal, governed by a council of elders (*alfas*) who elected a king. The Lunda empire in Zaire, which rose during the seventeenth century, had developed a complex but well structured system of popular representation and administration of justice and tax collection before European arrival. Kanem-Bornu, a Muslim state (800–1893) located between the Nile and the Niger, prospered from the trans-Saharan trade in salt, dried fish, gold, kola nut, and cloth, and survived many Fulani incursions.

One should note the Sokoto empire created in present Northern Nigeria by Usuman Dan Fodio at the start of the nineteenth century. Sokoto resulted from the unification of several Hausa states which had arisen during the fifteenth century—Kano, Zaria, Katsina, and Gobir—and survived the cultural onslaught of British imperialism, while the Yoruba Kingdoms of Oyo and Ile-Ife distinguished themselves in their trading skills, warfare, and artistic talent. In East Africa, the cosmopolitan city-states where the Swahili culture emerged became the envy of the Portuguese and other European powers following Vasco da Gama's voyage to India in 1497–1498. In Mogadishu, Zanzibar, Pemba, Brava, Mafia, Sofala, Mombasa, Malindi, and Mozambique Island, Africans, Persians, Arabs, Indians, and Europeans traded actively in items such as ivory, cloves, gold, silver, animal skins, carpets, cloth, guns and gun powder, incense, and myrrh. In Southern Africa, the Zulu kingdom which emerged in 1818 with Chaka as its first king has been well documented for its advanced military strategy and its resistance to British and Boer imperialism.

These kingdoms were, in most cases, societies that political scientists have labeled as "state societies." There were other societies, however, conveniently called "stateless societies," which had no chiefs or kings, no centralized structures or governments, and where decisions were made by groups of elders, by the entire community, or by a council specifically selected for that purpose. Among these stateless societies stood the BaMbuti, the Tiv, the Nuer, the Ibo, and the Amba.

The arrival of Europeans, beginning in the fifteenth century, and the subsequent introduction and rapid expansion of the trans-Atlantic slave trade and, later, European imperialism, ultimately resulted in the partition of Africa during the nineteenth century. Partition frustrated indigenous political and economic development, stifled initiative, and led to chaos and much suffering.

Summary

Only some of the more significant early African states have been mentioned. They clearly differed from one another as they also differed from the states in the Nile Valley, existing as they did in a wide range of environments, in different geographic locations on a vast continent, and spread across several millennia. Yet, they also shared important features in common. Above all else, they showed the potential of the people of Africa to take full advantage of the specific environments in which they lived. As such, they were a logical stage in human development on the continent. The examples of Egypt and Kush, which were examined in some detail, illustrate how human potential could work itself out in a specific context. When the environment was as highly favorable as that of the Egyptian Nile, then truly great achievements were possible. The environment of the middle Nile was not so favored, but there too human society and culture made significant advances.

In conclusion, this chapter stressed five major points: 1) that the physical environment always plays a crucial role in determining the course of human development, but that, over the course of time, humans (as in Africa) have, with increasing frequency, been able to alter both the physical environment and the way that it impacts on their societies; 2) that Africa is a vast continent of great human and geographic diversity, containing in turn a great diversity of human societies and cultures; 3) that the African continent was the cradle of humankind, not only for the earliest ancestors of humans but also of modern human beings, who began to emerge some 200,000 years ago; 4) that Africa was in the forefront of two developments that were crucial in enabling human society to advance to more complex stages—food production and metallurgy; and, finally, 5) that the early states in Africa were indigenous in origin and demonstrated the ability of Africans to develop and master the potential of the differing environments of the continent.

Study Questions and Activities

1. Discuss the ways the diversity of the African physical environment has affected the types of human societies that emerged on the continent.
2. What were the various stages in human evolution from their earliest origins on the African continent to their modern status?
3. Why did states not evolve in Africa out of hunting and gathering societies?
4. What were some of the basic features of the states that emerged in the Nile valley? How does one explain some of the differences that came to exist among them?
5. Having studied in some detail Egypt and Kush, what would be some of the questions one should expect to be answered if one were to study some of the other early African states in greater detail?

References

J. F. Ade Ajayi and Michael Crowder (eds.). *Historical Atlas of Africa*. Cambridge: Cambridge University Press, 1985.

Graham Connah. *African Civilizations: Precolonial Cities and States in Tropical Africa*. 2nd ed. New York: Cambridge University Press, 2001.

Christopher Ehret. *The Civilizations of Africa: A History to 1800*. Charlottesville: University of Virginia Press, 2002.

Toyin Falola, ed. *African History Before 1885*. Durham: Carolina Academic Press, 2000.

Ricardo René Laremont, Fouad Kalouche (eds.). *African and Other Civilizations: Conquest and Counter-Conquest*. Trenton, NJ: Africa World Press, 2002.

James L. Newman. *The Peopling of Africa: A Geographic Interpretation*. New Haven: Yale University Press, 1995.

Thurstan Shaw, Paul Sinclair, Bassey Andah, and Alex Okpoko, eds. *The Archaeology of Africa: Food, Metals and Towns*. New York: Routledge, 1993.

4

Legitimate Trade, Diplomacy, and the Slave Trade

M. Alpha Bah

Introduction

The initial African-European contact was a result of European expansion during the Age of the Renaissance. Nation-states had emerged in Europe, and each state was subsequently eager to expand beyond its borders using its newly implemented technological innovations. Soon, however, such contact produced one of the most unfortunate episodes in the history of mankind: the trans-Atlantic slave trade.

This chapter examines the nature of the early contact between Europeans and Africans, beginning with the Portuguese exploration of the coast of Africa during the fifteenth century. Curiosity, trading motives, and the desire to expand Christendom led the Portuguese to establish trading posts mainly dealing in gold, weapons, and agricultural commodities. Over time, legitimate trade (in goods) gave way to a trade in human beings as a response to the high demand for labor on the plantations of the New World which Christopher Columbus had reached in 1492. By necessity, the present discussion also focuses on the nature of the institution of slavery in Africa, the Middle Passage, abolition, and the effects of the trans-Atlantic slave trade on the continent, and highlights the major theoretical issues illustrated by the continuing debate among such scholars as Philip Curtin and J. E. Inikori.

Major terms and concepts: trade, "discoveries," slavery, the slave trade, servility, servitude, Middle Passage, *lançados*, plantation, Fulbe, New World, sea route to India, interlopers, abolition, Cape of Storms, *asiento*, diaspora, American Colonization Society, Sierra Leone, Liberia.

The Fatal Encounter

In the modern era, significant direct African-European contact began only with the Portuguese capture of the fortress of Ceuta from the Moroccans in 1415. It took the Portuguese over seven decades (from 1415 to the 1490s) to become the sole European traders along the western, southern, and eastern coasts of Africa. This penetration was a result of numerous objectives: Europeans in general wanted to find a way to reach the numerous gold mines of Western Africa and control the gold trade in Southern and Eastern Africa. They were also keenly interested in breaking the Islamic-Arab control of the trans-Saharan trade through maritime trade, and finding "Prester John," a mythical Christian king with whom they wished to make an alliance against the Moors (who had, for a long time, occupied part of the Iberian Peninsula). Finally, Europeans were eager to find a maritime route to the Far East, with the main aim of controlling the Asian trade in spices by getting to the source itself and eliminating the Arab or Indian middleman. In combination with these goals, the spread of Christianity, often in the minds of the royal family and the Catholic Church, assumed a prominent role in the early voyages.

With the Portuguese capture of Ceuta and the appointment of the young Prince Henry as governor of the territory, the exploration along the western coast of Africa intensified. Henry's commitment to the southward exploration of the Atlantic and his manning of the royal navigation school at Sagres earned him the name of "Prince Henry the Navigator." Thus, Portuguese navigators seized Madeira in 1419 and, in 1434, took over Cape Bojador and eventually occupied and colonized the Azores. In 1441, Nuno Tristão, a Portuguese explorer, "discovered" Cape Blanco. A group of Portuguese merchants used force to occupy the Arguin Islands in 1444, and later built a fort which served as a trading base there. By 1460, the Cape Verde Islands had been colonized by the Portuguese who also began laying claims to the Island of Goree as well as the ports along the coast of Senegal. Two years later, in 1462, Pedro da Sintra surveyed the coast of Sierra Leone, farther down the west coast of Africa, while other Portuguese explorers, such as Fernão Gomes, came across an impressive gold trade in the region between the upper Guinea coast and Sierra Leone. Consequently, by 1482, the Portuguese had established the important trading fort of Elmina, had subsequently built other commercial forts in the Gold Coast region, and continued their voyages down the west coast of Africa. A major break-through occurred in 1487, when Bartolomeu Dias reached the southern tip of the continent. Frightened by the storms and heavy currents at the Cape, but pleased by his daring feat, Dias returned to Lisbon and reported to his king that he had reached the frightening Cape of Storms (*Cabo das Tormentas*). Beginning his expedition to India in July 1497, Vasco da Gama, commissioned by King Manuel I, succeeded in sailing past the Cape of Good Hope (formerly the Cape of Storms) and continued his expedition along the East African coast, arriving in March 1498 in what would become Mozambique, and then sailing across the Indian Ocean, reaching India in May 1498.

It is important to reiterate here that a large part of this early European-African contact concentrated on the gold trade. The Portuguese set up numerous trading posts and ports (*feitorias*) along the coast sponsored directly by the Portuguese government. However, there also existed a very powerful private group of Portuguese traders known as *lançados*. As the *prazeros* did in Mozambique, this group settled permanently along the coast among the Africans and adopted African customs, even intermarrying with local African women. The *lançados* of the Guinea coast, for example, played a role similar to that of the *pombeiros* of Angola in facilitating trade between the official Portuguese traders and the

Africans, especially those in the interior. An interesting relationship developed between these resident Portuguese middlemen and the various segments of the African community. In many instances, the *lançados* enjoyed African rights and privileges as hosts, and their marriages with Africans produced a new breed of people sometimes referred to as an Afro-Portuguese community. Besides facilitating trade, these Africanized Portuguese played other roles such as encouraging the resolution of complaints or *palavras* in public hearings. As a result of the ensuing relationship, many local African rulers began to claim inheritance rights over the property of the *lançados* whenever they moved to other areas or returned to Portugal. A similar development occurred in Mozambique during the seventeenth century on the *prazos* (estates entrusted to Portuguese female inheritors for three consecutive generations), when the *prazeros* (estate renters) married and employed African women and slaves in every capacity, and became Africanized Portuguese lords, a condition well studied and documented by Allen Isaacman in *Mozambique: The Africanization of a European Institution* (1972).

It is unfortunate that the contact between Africans and Europeans—which began with the Portuguese settlements in upper Guinea, the Gold Coast, the Gulf of Guinea, Angola, and along the East African coasts, stretching from Mozambique to Sofala—ended with the forced transportation of Africans as slaves to the New World. This movement was preceded by other forced migrations of Africans engineered by Arab slave dealers across the Red Sea and the Indian Ocean into Asia, as well as across the Sahara Desert and the Mediterranean Sea into Southern Europe during the eighth century. Most of the slaves were prisoners captured in the *jihads* (holy wars) during the spread of Islam from the Arabian peninsula along the Persian Gulf, into North, West, and East Africa. Muslim slave traders used their religion and the *sharia* (law of Islam) to justify the enslavement of non-Muslims who served mainly in the army, in households, and in state administration. The supply area for this trade was primarily the savanna region of the continent and the Horn of Africa, making the inhabitants of Eastern and Central Africa the main victims of what can be called the oriental slave trade.

The external demand of this oriental slave trade focused on children and women. While males were often castrated and then trained as eunuchs to oversee harems, women and female children quite often became concubines of their masters. Within this context, Oromo, Ethiopian, and Nilotic women, for example, were the prey most sought after because of their reputed natural beauty, obedience, and fidelity. The demand for men came from the work in the farms of prominent Muslims, often within the African continent itself, as was the case of the clove and food plantations of Zanzibar and Pemba and along the Kenyan coast. Undoubtedly, the African regions affected experienced devastating raids (*razzias*) from slavers. Africans living in the proximity of Khartoum, Dar Fur, and Baguirmi, for example, including the Sara of Southern Chad, were victims of untold atrocities at the hands of seasonal raiders, as surviving elders in Chad have attested with horror.

Consequences of the oriental slave trade, however, were relatively less destructive than those of the occidental Atlantic slave trade. The number of those exported to Asia is believed to have been under five million. Emancipation within the Arab-Islamic slavery was achieved through a long term integration process that ultimately made people acceptable as members of the group. As a result, a slave community could not be identified easily and racism seems to have been less of a factor; and, unlike its occidental counterpart, the Arab slave trade failed to develop an economic system strictly based on slave labor.

Thus, strictly speaking, the infamous trans-Atlantic trafficking in human beings was not the first in Africa. Nevertheless, neither the trans-Saharan trade nor the slave trade across the Red Sea have received as much attention from scholars as the trans-Atlantic slave trade. Despite the frequent focus on the trans-Atlantic slave trade and its undisputed historicity, however, scholars continue to disagree over some major aspects of the trade itself. Paramount among these are the nature of the treatment of the captured Africans on their way to the New World and in the plantation system (in Portuguese-controlled versus Anglo-Saxon-run plantations, for example) and the impact of the trade on Africa, the Americas, and Europe. In order to fully understand not only the Atlantic slave trade but also the controversy surrounding it, one must examine the institution of slavery itself and the nature of the trade in Sub-Saharan Africa before the African-European contact.

African Internal "Slavery"

In light of its possible implications for the African continent and the Americas, an overview of the institution of slavery in Africa before European contact is necessary. The first difficulty facing experts, however, is defining intra-African slavery prior to the Atlantic slave trade, sometimes labelled as servitude or servility. Indeed, in some African societies, a slave did not fit the various models of servitude held by scholars, which tend to portray the institution as generally milder in nature and practically more uniform than its trans-Atlantic and oriental counterparts.

Among the Asante of Ghana, for instance, the term *akoa* denoted, as is the case in many African languages, different levels of servility some of which could be loosely translated to mean "servant" or "subject."[1] Similar problems of definition exist in other societies. Among the Fulbe of Futa Jallon, for example, the word for slave varies from *machudo* to *huwowoh*, meaning a worker, and to kaado, signifying someone different or an outsider. The word *machudo* (*machube*, plural) is sometimes ironically used with reference to *majudo*, meaning one who is lost, an unbeliever, or an ignorant person. The Fulbe definition was undoubtedly influenced by Islamic religious sentiment which provided a marked pretext for the perpetuation of an extensive slavery system among the Fulbe of Futa Jallon. Among the Anyungwe of Central Mozambique, *kapolo* meant a person of inferior status, forced to work without pay.

The foregoing discussion illustrates the difficulties involved in trying to equate African slavery with the concepts of slavery held in the West. By no means, however, is this discussion intended to exclude the major characteristics of slavery in general from the institution as it manifested itself in Africa. In fact, slavery in Africa was not devoid of exploitation; nonetheless, as Paul Lovejoy notes, the idea that slaves in African societies were absolute property or chattel of their owners or that they were denied their sexual rights, as was the norm within the trans-Atlantic

---

1. Edward Reynolds, *Stand the Storm: A History of the Atlantic Slave Trade* (New York: Allison & Busby, 1986), pp. 5–9.

slavery and slave trade, seems to have been foreign on the continent, although further studies are still needed before absolute statements can be made.

Recent studies confirm that the institution of slavery in Africa is as old as its counterparts in Asia and Europe. However, the recruiting of slaves on the continent was generally through warfare among states, towns, and villages. Most wars were concluded with the taking of large numbers of prisoners who became enslaved by the victorious states. Sometimes powerful states forced weaker societies to enter into a tributary arrangement, while crimes, harassments, indebtedness, threats, famine, and hunger, often led people to leave their homes and place themselves into voluntary slavery. Other times, criminals, such as murderers, lost their freedom and became slaves.

It is now generally accepted among scholars that slaves, even prior to European arrival, were in demand in Africa and that the trade existed before any recorded European involvement in it. Indeed, it appears that large numbers of Africans were enslaved and forced to work in the Gold Coast mines prior to European contact. The Portuguese became middlemen in this regional slave trade between the 1470s and the 1620s, supplying the needed labor force in the Akan gold mines with slaves from Angola, Congo, Arguin, Benin, and the Grain coast. The Akan gold miners and African authorities paid the Portuguese traders in gold in exchange for the slaves provided. Likewise, other Europeans, including the English, the Dutch, and the Danes, entered the trade and provided slaves in exchange for gold with the Akan people.

The Doula of West Africa, found in present day Côte d'Ivoire and Burkina Faso, also became involved in the trade when they needed workers in their gold mines, most of which belonged to kings, who fed, clothed, and sometimes married their slave women. It is also known that the rulers of the Western Sudanic empires of Ghana, Mali, and Songhai used slave labor on their royal plantations, while Songhai is said to have used significant slave labor in agricultural production. The Mali empire and other states such as Kanem-Bornu used slaves in the army and in administration. Thus, slavery became useful in the affairs of the state. In fact, slaves are said to have often intervened during succession crises. Among the Mossi of West Africa (in present-day Burkina Faso) slave soldiers played a significant role in the selection of a king. In other areas, slaves became trusted advisers and administrators to royal courts, and, at times, presided over religious rituals. Some Igbo clans, as Chinua Achebe writes in *Arrow of God*, had cult slaves who became known as *osu* and had a permanent low status. Recruitment into the *osu* society was generally voluntary, but some "volunteers" saw this as preferable to enforced slavery elsewhere. (Interestingly, records on the *osu* reveal that they were Nigeria's most unsympathetic tax collectors during the colonial era.)

Another important aspect of intra-African slavery was the use of slaves as domestic servants. In contrast to the trans-Atlantic slave trade, domestic slaves usually became part of the kinship group and the family of their masters. As a result, the mechanics of domestic servitude relationships, as they transpired between servants and the family of their masters, created an interesting social milieu. As expected, domestic slaves were entrusted with the household needs and chores, but some of the young females became wives to their masters or to some other free members of society. Interestingly, such relationships between descendants of former domestic slaves and families of their former masters lasted, in some parts of the continent, up to the mid-twentieth century. In Futa Jallon, Guinea, for example, the institution of domestic slavery was well established and persisted for a long period. New extended family settings became by-products of the relationship between domestic slaves and their masters' families. Over time, large numbers of descendants of domestic slaves even became family leaders of their former masters' households.

Apart from their other domestic obligations, female domestic slaves were also employed as babysitters or babytenders. A few examples of such domestic babysitters who are now regarded as the oldest living family heads remain in parts of Africa. A typical example of the above is a situation with which the writer is familiar in his own extended family. A lady (who must be between 95 and 98 years old, and has gone blind recently), was once the domestic babysitter (*kuurkaadu*, in Pular or Fulani) of one of Futa Jallon's royal families. Among those for whom she babysat was a prince who migrated to Sierra Leone around 1920, where he later became a leader within the traditional political power structure. In an interview, in April 1986, this writer had learned that this elderly woman had exclaimed in tears during the funeral ceremony held for the prince whom she once cared for as a child: "I saw him being born, circumcised, marrying his first wife, and now I am witnessing his burial. Allah wanted me to totally take charge of this prince, my master, my son and my grandson."

The woman is not only grandmother to her children's children but to those of the late prince, most of whom could not fully understand the nature of the relationship between their father and the old babysitter. Nonetheless, to everyone else, including the children of the prince, whose parents once owned her, she is still the grandmother and remains the symbolic head of both her own immediate family and the family of her late master. Similar examples exist within the Fulbe communities of Futa Jallon.

This Fulbe tradition underscores the diversity of what some still call African "slavery." It is, however, difficult to determine how long such a system had existed. Walter Rodney, the late Guyanese historian, believed that slavery was not in existence in the upper Guinea-Sierra Leone region until the introduction of the Atlantic slave trade. He argued that some type of political clientage existed which could not be classified as slavery. Rodney later claimed that this was true of the whole continent, but numerous scholars have disagreed with his sweeping conclusion. Nonetheless, Africans who became involved in the external slave trade across either the Red Sea or the Mediterranean, or even across the Atlantic, found it almost impossible to discontinue the practice, despite the changes forced by time.

The Trans-Atlantic Slave Trade

The issue of the trans-Atlantic slave trade is replete with contradictory theories, sweeping generalizations, and controversial arguments. For our purpose, however, one needs to highlight only two controversies: the "numbers game" and the impact of the slave trade itself on the African continent. Estimates of the total number of slaves taken out of Africa and of those who arrived in the New World has received much attention from scholars. Philip D. Curtin in his *Atlantic Slave Trade: A Census* (1969) sparked off an unprecedented debate on the topic when he estimated that about 11.5 million human beings were forced to leave Africa and that about 9.5 million reached the Americas. This number was considerably lower than any previous figure calculated by historical statisticians or suggested in any scholarly writing on the Atlantic slave trade. Fifteen million was the lowest number of slaves to reach their destination previously cited by such scholars as Edward Dunbar and R. R. Kuczynski. While J. Olivar Martins had estimated the number to have been 20 million, W. E. B. DuBois, J. D. Fage, and Basil Davidson argued for a much higher figure, close to 50 million. To many African scholars, Curtin's low estimate underlies a sinister motive on the part of some Caucasian scholars to minimize the impact of the slave trade on Africa.

One such scholar, J. E. Inikori, quickly challenged Curtin's methods and figures as not being based on primary data but on "Curtin's ingenious application of quantitative techniques to the figures in various published works." Inikori accused Curtin and his followers of intentionally underestimating the numbers of slaves transported to the New World, and challenged suggestions that the total number reached by Curtin was final, as was implied in the book.

Inikori likewise criticized both the formula and the quality of the data Curtin used. He rejected the book's data on the annual rates of the net natural decrease or increase among slave populations in the colonies and pointed out that Curtin's computations on the British West Indies not only excluded Jamaica, a major slave destination, but deliberately preferred quoting figures from the French West Indies and Spanish America. Inikori further noted that Philip Curtin had based his estimates on tax records, which had evidently underreported the actual figures on the importation of slaves into the Americas.

J. D. Fage, another highly regarded scholar in the discipline, argued, in *A History Of Africa* (1978), that the criticism against Curtin had little to do with scholarship, and that it was rather the shock many felt as a consequence of his unprecedented low figures. He, nonetheless contended that Curtin's total figure was still an estimate. Paul Lovejoy also expressed doubts about the figures used by Curtin to frame his global estimate and called for a revision. He agreed, however, that Curtin's estimate of 9.5 million Africans as the total was reasonable and unlikely to change.

Another major point most scholars have raised regarding Curtin's census is the emphasis on those slaves who landed in the Americas. Curtin's arguments pay little attention to the number of lives lost during wars and raids in the interior and the Middle Passage (or the long voyage from Africa to the New World). Both Patrick Manning and Joseph Miller have added some insight to the controversy about the numbers initiated by Curtin, but no one has come up with an estimate that does not elicit further questions. Patrick Manning's greatest contribution is his new model, based on statistics, which looks at the effects of the slave trade on the African population. He is critical of those who underestimate the economic and social damages of the slave trade. Joseph Miller, in *Way of Death* (1990), on the other hand, used his extensive knowledge of Angola to reach the conclusion that depopulation in Angola in particular, and Africa in general, was not just a consequence of the slave trade as much as a result of periodic droughts, natural disasters, famines, and epidemics.

Notwithstanding the controversy presented above, and irrespective of the sophistication of modern tools of research used to calculate the total number of Africans forcibly transported to the Americas, the suffering of the victims cannot be adequately described or understood, nor can their descendants expect any form of adequate physical or psychological compensation. Thus, in order to appreciate the complexity of the "peculiar institution," the sufferings of those who were enslaved and the extent of the consequences of the trade on Africa must be examined.

The notorious Atlantic slave trade, which began in Africa during the fifteenth century, lasted until the 1870s. The total number of those forcibly transported across the Atlantic to work in the plantations of North, Central and South America, and the Caribbean will never be known, as the numbers controversy has demonstrated. As a complex enterprise, the slave trade involved four continents: Europe, Africa, North America, and South America. While Europe provided the capital and the managers, and Africa the labor-force, the Americas provided a fertile soil that produced tobacco, cotton, and sugar cane. As such, therefore, the sordid traffic in human beings required an elaborate network of European slavers and African collaborators.

With positive feedback from the experimental plantations in São Tome e Principe, Madeira, and other Portuguese-occupied islands off the coast of West Africa, Africans were sought to work on similar undertakings in the Americas over Amerindians and immigrant Europeans because of their unique adaptability. As a result, the European-African contact, once dominated by the legitimate trade in gold, was replaced with a shameful commercial undertaking—the trade in slaves. By the middle of the fifteenth century, the Portuguese, soon joined by the Dutch and traders from other European nations, had become the major slavers along the coast of West Africa, acquiring large numbers of African slaves whom they transported to the Americas, particularly Brazil. In 1663, the British became formally involved in the trade when Parliament granted a monopoly on slave trading activities along the African Coast to the Company of Royal Adventurers of England.

Of course, European slavers needed and found African collaborators who became trusted middlemen in the trade. In this context, Walter Rodney claimed that Europeans initiated the trade by directly attacking coastal African inhabitants until Africans began to organize defense groups. The Portuguese realized that force alone could not succeed in maintaining a trade that would marginally also benefit the African middlemen. Thus, in general, the Europeans, who wanted slaves, gold, and other commodities, began to offer manufactured goods as a means of exchange. For the most part, African middlemen took up the responsibility of raiding, capturing, and transporting Africans from the interior to the coast where European slavers shipped them to the New World, an activity that, over time, became extremely profitable.

Walter Rodney blamed the success of the slave trade on ethnic rivalries or what he called "tribal conflicts" and European activities which deliberately chose to exploit them to suit the slave traders' interests. He accused the Europeans of having sown the seeds of hatred and hostility among Africans by supporting one ethnic group against another. Of course, the more vicious and widespread the conflict, the more "prisoners" of war were sold or exchanged as slaves to the Europeans. Although Rodney also claimed that divisions based on class were a major factor in the availability of slaves for foreigners, many scholars find it difficult to differentiate ethnic from class conflicts in Africa. It is easier to agree with Rodney, however, that those Africans with political, military, and economic power seemed to have been the allies of European slavers and that Europeans did, indeed, sow seeds of hatred among certain societies. In general, however, they seem to have exploited (rather than initiated) ethnic differences, some of which were already present in many parts of the continent.

Main Sources of Supply

West Africa is believed to have supplied about 60 percent of the slaves taken to the Americas, not only because of the proximity of its coast to the New World, but also due to the high population densities and the availability of experienced middlemen in the region. The nature of the trade between European slavers and West African middlemen has received considerable attention from various scholars, some of whom tend to overemphasize the bargaining skills of the African middlemen. In some instances, these exaggerations seem designed to underscore the willingness on the part of African middlemen, chiefs, and kings to exploit their own people. How was business conducted? One of the most common currencies in the transaction of slaves was an iron bar which became legal tender from Senegal to Côte d'Ivoire (Ivory Coast). Other popular means of exchange, especially in the region known as the Gold Coast, were gold dust, the "trade ounce" (half the value of a measured ounce of gold dust), the "manila" (a bracelet or horseshoe-shaped object made of brass and copper), cloth (a narrow strip of cloth, usually Indian), and cowrie shells. African middlemen also demanded gifts and certain fees, such as charges for anchorage, interpreters, wood, and water. Of course, currencies and commercial practices varied from location to location and from ethnic group to ethnic group. Following is a summary taken from Orlando Peterson's study *The Sociology of Slavery* (1967) on the regional sources of slaves in West Africa. Six areas of the West African coast have been identified as the major sources of the slaves who were eventually taken to North America, Brazil, Barbados, Jamaica, the Leeward Islands, and elsewhere.

First was the Senegambia area populated by four major ethnic groups: The Mandingo, the Fula, the Jallof or Wollof, and the Jola (or Feloop). According to the earliest accounts by the Portuguese and, later, by explorers such as Mungo Park, internal slavery was rampant here prior to European arrival. Mungo Park claims, although without convincing evidence, that only one-third of the population was free in the region and that, therefore, most of those enslaved by Europeans were already in bondage. Here, the slave catchers occasionally entered the hinterland from the coast, depending on availability. During the hey-day of the trans-Atlantic slave trade (the eighteenth and early nineteenth centuries), this area, comparatively speaking, provided a small number of slaves—perhaps 500 a year. Most of the slaves were either abducted through kidnapping or were debtors, criminals, starving destitutes, or war captives who were sold to slavers. Experts estimate that the Senegambia supplied one-fourth of the slaves to the New World prior to the seventeenth century. The decline and fall of the Jolof empire seems to have also contributed to a decline of the trade in the area. Subsequently, the Senegambia became a major route for rather than a source of slaves.

The second pool of slaves could be found along the Sierra Leone and the Windward Coast, extending, according to Patterson, from River Sherbro to Cape Palmas and down to River Ancober, near Axism, about two hundred leagues long. It included the so-called Grain and Ivory Coasts, which compromised the largest number of ethnic groups: Bakwe, Bassa, Belte, Dida, Greobo, Kru, Sapo, Wobe, Temne, Gola, Kissi, Bullom, Guru, Mende, and Kono. The Windward Coast was never a very attractive slave trading region, as the absence of good natural harbors prevented major slave trading companies from doing business. Private traders or interlopers were more frequent in the area. Thus, fewer people were snatched from here.

In Sierra Leone, however, the authorities insisted that the Europeans hire an African to "act as an agent for them in procuring slaves," whereas in the Ivory and the Grain Coasts, Africans prevented the Europeans from coming into the interior, restricting them to trading slaves only on the coast, where the Africans themselves went "instead to the anchored ships in their canoes to trade." As in Senegambia, most of the slaves here were kidnapped or captured at war or during raids. During the 1766-1785 period, this area seems to have provided between 2,500 and 3,000 slaves a year, two-thirds of whom went to the British and one-third to the French.

The third source of slaves was the Gold Coast, whose major ethnic groups were the Twi-speaking people—the Akan and Fanti, the Gae, the Guang, and the Adangme. From the time of the European arrival until the early eighteenth century, this was an area devastated by political turmoil and warfare culminating in the rise of the Ashanti Confederation, which created favorable conditions for the slave trade. However, the interior ethnic groups, including the Mamprusi, the Dagomba, the Nankanse, the Talense, the Isala, and the Lober, constituted the major slave reservoir. Here, European slaving activities and centers were so numerous and effective, particularly along the Gold Coast, that, at the beginning of the eighteenth century, twenty-four forts had been erected, eight British, twelve Dutch, two Brandenburger (German), and two Danish, while Cape Coast Castle and Elmina became the headquarters of the British and the Dutch slave traders respectively, as W. W. Claridge notes. During the seventeenth and eighteenth centuries, most of the slaves were prisoners from the large coastal area groups, but the situation changed when relative peace ensued thereafter: hinterland kidnapping became the norm. An estimated six thousand to eight thousand people were enslaved yearly here between 1778 and 1782, two-thirds of whom going to the British. One-fourth of this slave volume originated on the coast and three-fourths in the hinterland.

The Dahomey area, known as the Slave Coast and dominated by the Ewe, the Yoruba, and the Bini, was the fourth and busiest slave trading frontier. It was marred by constant warfare, particularly, as Patterson observes, when Dahomey attempted to eliminate all non-Dahomean state middlemen between the coast and the interior during the eighteenth century. Because the state had a monopoly on the slave operations, a European traveller described the area as "the greatest trading place on the coast of Guinea, selling as many slaves, as all the rest together,"—between 12,000 and 20,000 yearly, most of them going to French traders.

The next major slave trading area was Benin and the Niger Delta. As early as 1510, Benin seems to have been trading "exclusively in slaves with the Europeans," although on several occasions, the Oba of Benin refused to participate in the trade by refraining from trading activities altogether or by not allowing women and children to be taken as slaves. On this score, Patterson adds that "it was not until after 1818, with the final collapse of the Benin and Oyo empires due to civil wars, that vast numbers of slaves began once more to leave the area," going almost exclusively to Brazilian and Portuguese traders. The Niger and the Cross deltas, however, inhabited by the Ibo, the Ibibo, the Edo, the Ijo, the Atisia, the Ogony, and the Epie, developed three major slave trading centers: New Kalabar, Bonny, and Old Kalabar, the majority of the slaves here coming from the hinterland by river, "during which trips the average slave was sold about six times before reaching the European traders." An estimated number of 6,000 Ibo were sold yearly between 1800 and 1820, while other coastal societies lost their people from kidnapping activities. At first, the Dutch were the overlords here. From 1776 to 1784, this area had, indeed, become "the largest exporter of slaves in Africa:" about 14,000 slaves, annually, from Bonny and New Kalabar alone. The disintegration of Oyo, one of the last Yoruba kingdoms to supply the Americas with slaves during the nineteenth century, made that state the largest supplier on the eve of abolition.

The sixth major source of slaves was South-Western Africa—Cameroon, Congo, Angola, Gabon, the Democratic Republic of Congo, down to Cape Negro—supplying most of the slaves to Jamaica and the rest of the West Indies. Angola and the Congo seem to have provided from 13,000 to 14,000 slaves a year between 1776 and 1784. Angola became a major source of slaves to the Americas, particularly Brazil and Cuba. In general, however, the volume of slaves from this area remained relatively small until the end of the seventeenth century as a result of low demand and resistance by African authorities such as Queen Nzinga Mbande of Matamba in the Congo, who fought against Portuguese slave traders for over 20 years. It is important to note here, as Patterson does, that:

> No doubt a considerable number of slaves sold on the Nigerian coast came from a great distance inland, but it is known that almost all these inland slaves came from one basic ethnic stock, the Ibo, who despite their highly segmentary social structure and small area of political allegiance, nonetheless, spoke basically the same language and adhered to what amounts to a remarkably uniform pattern of values and behavior.

Altogether, West Africa seems to have provided as much as 60 percent of the slaves brought to the New World at different periods. East Africa also provided a steady flow of slaves, but, as mentioned earlier, this was often the Arab preserve, and those taken by Europeans ended up in the sugar plantations on the islands of the Indian Ocean or on Brazilian plantations.

The Middle Passage and Final Settlement

Before the final journey to the unknown land, slaves were usually organized in such a way as to allow their owners to identify them easily. Their bodies were usually branded with a hot iron with the initials of the company or owner. Some of the slavers baptized their human cargo before taking them on board to guarantee their salvation in case of a shipwreck. In fact, those carrying slaves into certain regions of the New World such as Brazil were subject to excommunication from the Catholic Church if they were Catholic but failed to baptize them.

Some ruthless captains and sailors treated their passengers as physical cargo throughout the journey from Africa to the New World. As expected, the majority of the slaves experienced distress and unhappiness throughout the Middle Passage, especially because they were not sure of the future. Angry and frustrated by the fact that they were being taken away from their families, many even feared that they would be cannibalized by their captors. At times, these helpless human beings, fearing those whom sometimes they called "devils"—the white slavers— would jump overboard rather than allow themselves to be taken away to the unknown. Thus, numerous slaves committed suicide during the Middle Passage.

On several occasions, slaves revolted violently against the crew on board the ships. The most remembered are the mutinies on board the *Little George*, in 1730, when 96 African slaves from the Guinea Coast successfully forced the crew to take refuge in the ship's cabinet, reversed the direction of the ship to the Sierra Leone River, and jumped inland as free men and women, after abandoning the *Little George*; the mutiny on the *Jolly Bachelor*, in 1740, when the ship, sailing with slaves on the Sierra Leone River, was attacked by free Africans, stripped, and abandoned after its human cargo was set free; and the *Amystad*, in 1839. On board, Joseph Cinque, an African prince, led a bloody slave revolt against the Spanish crew on the high seas, and forced the ship to sail back to Africa, but it was spotted and intercepted by the U.S. Navy and brought to shore. Cinque and his slave companions were tried in the U.S. and found not guilty and allowed to return as free people to Africa. The *Amystad* became the most celebrated of the slave ship mutinies, as it galvanized the zeal of the abolitionists who enlisted former U.S. President John Quincy Adams to argue successfully on behalf of the mutineers before the Supreme Court. Otherwise, captives, particularly adult males, were customarily chained and kept naked throughout the journey to prevent mutiny. Women and children were often treated a little better, except when suspected of disobedience or aggressive behavior. Often, many slaves fell ill from malnutrition, inadequate food and diseases (smallpox and seasickness, in particular), and most of the sick deteriorated because of bad ventilation, bad weather, unsanitary travelling conditions, brutal treatment, and the lack of proper medical care. Those who were suspected of serious sickness, and, therefore, deemed unprofitable, were frequently thrown overboard to the sharks.

Slave mortality rates during the Middle Passage fluctuated throughout the slave trade period. Because of the primitive conditions on board the ships, the lack of basic care, ill treatment, and the duration of the journey, which took from three to four weeks, the number of deaths during the early period of the slave trade was high. When captains and sailors finally realized that their jobs hinged greatly on the number and the health of their cargo, they began to improve the living conditions aboard the ships. Consequently, most ship crews were delighted to arrive in the New World with few deaths and a healthy batch of African slaves who were sold on arrival to private planters or to wholesaler merchants who in turn sold them to planters. Another method of sale was the rough public auction which was mostly for cheap and unprofitable sick slaves. Sugar, rhum, and the dollar, continued to serve as the form of payment for slaves. Later in the trade, bills of exchange or a combination of the latter, as referred to earlier, were adopted as acceptable forms of conducting slave business.

The labor needs of the New World increased the demand for African slaves. The Spaniards were among the first Europeans to demonstrate a greater need for labor in their settlements in Central and South America. Sugar production in large quantities demanded a regular and effective labor force. Unlike Portugal and Holland, however, Spain had no forts in Africa and began early to issue special licenses, or *asientos*, to citizens willing to participate in the lucrative slave trade. However, many traders from other nationalities acquired *asientos* as well and made good use of them until the Spanish government decided to stop granting them in 1773.

The Portuguese, the first to be involved in the African slave trade (some scholars say as early as 1441), after experimenting with the cultivation of sugar in the islands of Madeira, the Azores, Cape Verde, and São Tome (as briefly mentioned earlier), began their sugar production in Brazil during the sixteenth century. The Dutch soon replaced the Portuguese, however, both in Africa and in Brazil during the seventeenth century, and sugar production and gold mining lightened Brazil's demand for African slaves. Brazil seems to have imported about 38 percent of the slaves destined to the New World, while the Portuguese colonies, the British Caribbean, the Dutch West Indies, the French possessions, and the North American colonies, shared the remaining slaves imported from Africa.

By the late eighteenth century, however, the plantation system and slavery in the Americas, especially in the United States, had reached its climax. Religious opposition, slave revolts, and the economics of the Industrial Revolution in Europe and in the northern United States called for the abolition of the infamous trade.

The Abolition of the Atlantic Slave Trade in Africa

A combination of religious, philosophical, economic and revolutionary factors brought about the abolition of the slave trade. The religious and philosophical considerations combined to produce a group of English philanthropists including Granville Sharp, William Wilberforce, Thomas and William Clarkson, assisted by the Quakers who were the first major group in the West to condemn slavery and call for its abolition. John Wesley, the founder of Methodism, also a champion of the anti-slavery movement, called for the Christianization and subsequent emancipation of slaves.

Thus, in England, Granville Sharp and his brother helped Jonathan Strong go free after the brutal treatment he received from his master. The two brothers also supported James Somerset from the West Indies whose case became famous in 1772 when Lord Mansfield declared that Somerset's master could not forcibly take him back to the West Indies. With the help of Wilberforce, a member of the House of Commons, Sharp and his friends proceeded to raise the issue of slavery in Parliament. Sharp not only became chairman of the newly formed Abolition Committee but also spearheaded the establishment of a settlement in Sierra Leone for free blacks. With the assistance of the Clarkson brothers, the new settlement in Freetown served as the core of the future modern state of Sierra Leone and the base for a physical "assault" on the slave trade by British ships. From here, the British urged other nations to acknowledge the 1807 Parliamentary bill abolishing the traffic in humans.

Many analysts, however, consider economic factors to have been the major forces behind abolition. The Scottish economist Adam Smith agreed that slave labor was inefficient and that it was also counterproductive in a laissez-faire economic system. Thus, one of the best economic thinkers of the time went on record and declared that slavery was not important in the new economic system (capitalism) which placed more emphasis on commerce and industry. A century later, the late West Indian historian and once Prime Minister of Trinidad, Eric Williams, also advanced an economic interpretation of the slave trade in his book *Capitalism and Slavery* (1944). Among his many arguments stands one that contends that the slave trade greatly contributed to the development of Western capitalism and that it was abolished only when it became unprofitable.

Beyond the factors promoting abolition mentioned above, the slaves themselves constantly resisted the humiliating evils of slavery. The most significant slave rebellion that had an impact on the abolitionist movement occurred in Haiti in 1791. The island was well-known for its production of cotton, indigo, coffee, cocoa, and sugar cane. It also had a highly mixed population of blacks, whites, and mulattoes, all of whom welcomed the French Revolution, which began in Paris in 1789. While mulattoes hoped for equality with whites, blacks wanted to be free. Accordingly, a slave priest named Boukman called on his followers during a church service in 1791 to revolt against their masters and to ask for salaries and compensation for the work they performed. The rebel slaves also insisted that they be given three days of rest a week. On August 22, 1791, the rebels decided they would kill all white islanders and a bloody rebellion followed. By the end of the rebellion, they had actually killed about two thousand whites. The French army responded by jailing and punishing all mutineers including Boukman himself, but the revolutionary French government freed all slaves on the island in February 1794.

In the southern United States, slaves were also intensifying their effort to gain freedom. In Virginia, Gabriel Prosser led a foiled revolt in 1800, and, in 1822, Denmark Vesey planned the well-known rebellion in Charleston, South Carolina. These and other manifestations of slave dissatisfaction signalled the revitalization and formation of numerous abolitionist movements in many slave-holding areas and especially in the United States. The protests and ideas of well-known Quakers like Francis D. Pastorius, John Woolman, and Anthony Benezet, and the Methodist leader John Wesley led to the Congressional act that put an end to the slave trade and which was signed into law by President Jefferson in March 1807. Between 1807 and 1834, Britain formally abolished slavery in all of its colonies. Similarly, the United States moved toward the abolition of the institution, but the total emancipation of slaves occurred only after the Civil War (1861-1865), as discussed in the next chapter.

Britain's commitment to ending the slave trade led to the establishment of a Court of Mixed Commission in 1817, in the new West African colony of Sierra Leone. This Court was set up primarily to adjudicate cases of violation of the abolition law by slave captains and sailors of various nationalities. Freetown, the harbor capital of Sierra Leone, served as the port of trial for slavers and the reception center for those Africans freed on the high seas. Meanwhile, the Sierra Leone Company, organized by philanthropists responsible for the repatriation of numerous blacks from England and North America to Sierra Leone, was entrusted to those Africans rescued on the oceans.

In the United States, the American Colonization Society was formed in 1817 with the aim of sending freed blacks to Africa. It was mainly responsible for the founding of Liberia in 1822. Encouraged by Justice John Marshall, President James Monroe, and Senator Henry Clay, a relatively large number of blacks made their way to the new settlement. Thus, the abolition of the slave trade gave rise to the modern states of Sierra Leone and Liberia, a unique blend of citizenry comprising the returnees and the indigenous Africans.

Impact of the Atlantic Slave Trade on Africa

Although scholars of the Atlantic slave trade agree that the trade in human beings was immoral and indefensible, they have differences of opinion about the nature and degree of its demographic, economic, and political impact on Africa. Demographically, the slave trade seems to have had a devastating effect on Africa. Estimates of the number of Africans forcibly removed from the continent to the New World range from 10 million to 50 million, as mentioned earlier. The forced exile of 50 million would devastate any continent, especially if those taken away included many in the most productive age bracket, whose potential contribution to their own society was then lost.

The economic factor was closely tied to demography. Because of the large number of able-bodied men and women removed from the African work force, it is only reasonable to conclude that productivity decreased on the continent. A few African leaders and middlemen profited from the slave trade but their wealth seldom trickled down to the rest of society. On many occasions, African chiefs and merchants were only able to obtain certain European manufactured goods such as cloth and guns, in exchange for human beings. In fact, many Africanists, notably the late Walter Rodney, have advanced the theory that the major reason why Africa did not experience an industrial revolution was the negative impact of the slave trade. They argue that the continent was robbed of its best young minds, of its creativity in the arts, and of those who could have provided intellectual and positive commercial leadership. These scholars further contend that slavery gave way to another form of exploitation in the name of "legitimate" trade, namely, European imperialism and colonialism in Africa.

To comprehend the magnitude of the human loss to Africa and its families, due to the slave trade, one needs only to examine the importation of slaves from Angola to Brazil, subject of Joseph Miller's *Way of Death* (which won the Herskovits Award of the African Studies Association in 1989). Miller notes that:

> The losses, late in the history of the trade, are generously estimated at 10 percent fatalities in the process of capture, 25 percent of the remainder lost on the way to the coast, 10 to 15 percent in the port towns, another 10 percent at sea, and perhaps 5 percent during the process of sale in Brazil; the total would compound the deaths in excess of half the people originally captured in Africa. The first year of "seasoning" in America would have claimed 15 percent more of 100 people seized in Africa, 75 percent would have reached the market places in the interior; 85 percent of them, or about 64 of the original 100, would have arrived at the coast; after losses of 11 percent in the barracons, 57 or so would have boarded the ships; of those 57, 51 would have stepped onto Brazilian soil,

and 48 or 49 would have lived to behold their first master in the New World. The full "seasoning" period of 3-4 years would leave only 28 or 30 of the original 100 alive and working. A total "wastage" factor of about two-thirds may thus be estimated for the late eighteenth-century Angolan trade, higher earlier in the trade, probably a bit lower by the 1820s, with slaves from the wetter equatorial latitudes showing a lower mortality rate than those from Luanda to Benguela.

Undoubtedly, as a result of the slave trade, several areas of West and South-Western Africa were depopulated. In fact, Walter Rodney demonstrated by inference that, for three hundred years, while the population of the continent remained static, that of other continents increased dramatically. While Africa's population remained at 100 million in 1650, 1750, 1850 and 1900, that of Europe rose from 103 million to 144 million, to 274 million, and finally to 423 million respectively, while Asia's population rose from 257 to 437, to 656, and to 857 million during the same period.

The demographic instability, when viewed in light of other factors, such as disease, must have had a debilitating effect on the family. The fact that slave traders preferred productive men and young women meant that many villages were left with only women, children, and the elderly, making the economic situation extremely precarious. Basil Davidson observes that:

> As African production for exports became a mono-culture in human beings,…the nature of the payment for Africa itself was strictly non-productive; for African slave dealers, it was the sale of consumer goods for the raw material of slave labor.…There was no creative marriage of cultures, no passage of ideas, no sharing of wealth or achievement. To Europe, the trade with Africa was always an enrichment and this enrichment could and did lead Europe into new and more productive forms of society and government.

In Africa, slavery stifled initiative, relegating to oblivion the incipient manufactures in pottery, basketry, glass making, masonry, weaving, and mineral exploitation of gold, silver, and iron.

Using data on the price of slaves, the cost of corn and millet during the eighteenth century and later, records of slave food rations, and other relevant data, Henry Gemery and Jan Hogendorn have attempted to estimate the economic impact of slavery and the slave trade on West Africa. Their study concluded that, although depending essentially on subsistence agriculture, West Africans usually had a surplus output in food production, supplemented by trade over wide areas, and that "productivity loss between 1701 and 1800 from the slave trade exceeded the average amount of grain necessary for subsistence."

They further estimated that, in general, fifteen years was the average productive time of an able-bodied African during the mid-eighteenth century. Using Curtin's population figures of 4.67 million slaves taken during that period, factoring in a death rate of 20 percent, and estimating that each able-bodied African would have had a production output equivalent to £80 to £20, Gemery and Hogendorn concluded that the actual loss would have ranged from £54.5 million to £81.8 million, while the gains from slave imports could not have amounted to more than £79.8 million for the 1701-1800 period. They note that, no matter how one computes gain vs. economic loss using the available evidence, and that when all social and other factors are taken into account, the conclusion will always point to an enormous loss for Africa.

It is only natural that the slave traders always attempted to maximize their business and had definite opinions about which people would make the best slaves. Thus, Eric Williams points out, for example, that in slave traffickers' circles,

> An Angolan Negro was a proverb for worthlessness; Coromantes (Ashanti) from the Gold Coat were good workers but too rebellious; Mandingoes (from Senegal) were too prone to theft. The Ibo from Nigeria were timid and despondent although they were easy to catch; the Pawpaws or Whydahs from Dahomey were the most docile and best-disposed.

Williams further notes, that, "one Liverpool merchant cautioned against buying rupture slaves, idiots or any of old spider legged quality" and that a West Indian poet advised slave dealers to select a slave whose "tongue was red, with a broad chest, and non-prominent belly. Buy them young," he said, "them full grown fellers think it hard to work; never being brought up to it, they take it to hart and dye or is never good for anything."

Contrary to common, oversimplified accounts, slave traders were sophisticated and, even though they did not have modern computers and methods of communication, they sought to respond to changes in market prices by adjusting the composition of their cargo to maximize their profits. They designed complicated auctions to increase their revenues, developed an extensive network of credit financing, and devised institutional arrangements that allowed risk sharing, not only among partners, but also with employees and purchasers. Sophistication resulted in further interference with African development in other sectors of life. Indeed, common sense alone indicates that, for any productivity to occur, a society must have not only an able labor force but also long-lasting stable political conditions. Historians almost unanimously agree that the intermittent slave raids increased warfare in Africa. Curtin notes, for example, that, during the eighteenth century, warfare was an important determinant of the short-run rise and fall of the slave trade. European slave traffickers made sure that African attention was turned away not just from legitimate economic activities but directed toward the (violent) acquisition of slaves. It became a vicious cycle: guns for slaves and slaves for guns through warfare, all buttressed with liquor. Thus, according to Williams, rum became so popular in Africa that British merchants ran two distilleries at Liverpool in 1765, just to satisfy the African demand. In 1770, Africa imported four-fifths of the rum manufactured in New England, while Birmingham guns exchanged for slaves also became an important commodity for Africans during the eighteenth century, reaching the volume of 100,000-150,000 a year destined to Africa alone.

Warfare, however, was not the only violent curse of death among the slaves caught. Wars also spread epidemics such as smallpox, and exacerbated the impact of periodic droughts particularly in the fringes of the Sahara and in South-Western Africa. Miller observes that, in Angola,

> starvation and disease forced the expansion of the slave catching zones in part because they reduced populations near the coast so severely—one report claiming 50 percent losses east of Luanda on the occasion of the 1680s drought— that the coastal areas could no longer support existing levels of slave exports.

Ultimately, the political consequences of the trade encouraged the use of force and the militarization of African political institutions. The introduction of guns and gun powder created a new breed of African leaders whose legitimacy was based solely on force. New sets of rules for law and order were in place in most of Africa suggesting that "might made right." True justice was hardly preserved since those who occupied the centers of power had no legitimacy except that they possessed the machine gun, a new weapon in African interstate diplomacy.

Mention must be made of another consequence of the slave trade: the creation of large but suffering African communities in the diaspora. Africans who had been taken away from their homes eventually became citizens and compatriots of their former enslavers. Tragically, the descendants of the African slaves are still struggling to achieve full citizenship. One important aspect of the diaspora was the "back to Africa" movement. Many Africans in the diaspora opted to return to the continent of their ancestors, and established the modern states of Sierra Leone and Liberia. Unfortunately, these states were created to serve primarily as centers for the Christianization of Africans and the advancement of Western civilization. It was not surprising, therefore, that many of the new citizens of Sierra Leone took up the cross and sailed along the West African coast to spread Christianity, while others assisted the British colonial administration.[2] Ironically, these settlements (created to receive former slaves and their descendants) and other coastal areas where the British Navy "harassed" those who persisted in the illegal slave trade, eventually became headquarters for the conquest of West Africa and the imposition of colonialism.

Summary

European desire to control the African gold trade, break the Islamic-Arab control of the trans-Saharan trade, and find a route to the East for spices, as well the hope of establishing a "network" with the legendary "Prester John" (a mythical Christian king who ruled Ethiopia), and expanding Christendom, led the Portuguese and other Europeans to explore the coast of West Africa beginning in 1415. By 1497, Portuguese explorers had succeeded in establishing fortresses along the coast and penetrated as far as South-Western Africa, an effort which culminated in Vasco da Gama's expedition to India where he arrived in 1498.

At first, the relations between the Europeans and the Africans centered primarily on the trade of such items as gold, ivory, cloth and guns. Friendly relations led to an exchange in diplomatic missions. During the latter part of the fifteenth century and later, however, the African-European trade took a grim turn when human beings occupied center stage. Slavery and the slave trade involved millions of Africans, who were captured, chained, brought to the coast, transported across the hazardous Atlantic Ocean on a journey to the New World, and badly treated by their plantation masters in the Americas. Untold sufferings led to numerous slave rebellions in such places as Haiti in 1791, Virginia in 1800, Charleston in 1822, and on board ships—as was the case of the *Amystad* mutiny in 1839.

A combination of several factors, including economic changes, religious movements, philanthropic societies, and slave rebellions led to the eventual abolition of the slave trade and slavery. Ironically, some of the beneficiaries of the slave trade

---

2. This explains, at least partially, the synchronic spread of Krio, the Anglophone Sierra Leonean Creole, to such states as The Gambia, Nigeria, Ghana, and Cameroon.

became the champions of the abolitionist movement. Between 1807 and 1834, for example, Britain had abolished slavery in all of its formal and informal colonies, while its Navy intercepted ships from other European governments and companies that persisted in the exportation of slaves from Africa. In their effort to end the slave trade, resettle free blacks, and spread Christianity and "civilization," Britain established the modern West African state of Sierra Leone, while the Unites States spearheaded the creation of the state of Liberia which declared its independence in 1847.

Although Africa had experienced some form of internal slavery prior to the sixteenth century, the demographic, economic, and political impact of the trans-Atlantic slave trade seems to have been devastating to the continent, particularly in West Africa. Estimates of the number of Africans forcibly brought to the Americas range from 10 to 50 million and are far from being conclusive. Some scholars, such as the late Walter Rodney, have advanced the theory that the major reason why Africa did not experience an industrial revolution was the Atlantic slave trade. (Interestingly, based on this argument, General Ibrahim Babangida, President of Nigeria, has asked that Africa and the descendants of those who were enslaved be compensated by the beneficiaries of the slave trade, namely, the Europeans and the Americans.) One could justifiably say that one of the major consequences of almost four centuries of slavery and the slave trade in Africa was the European conquest of the continent and the imposition of colonialism during the late nineteenth century. It must also be said that, while many African authorities resisted the slave trade, particularly during its early days, others participated in its devastating impact in search of material profit. Some, however, remained powerless and their action neither assisted nor slowed the trafficking in human beings.

Overall, in both Africa and the diaspora, slavery had no redeeming value whatsoever. What started as an economic experiment soon developed into an entrenched institution whose sole objective was to exploit human labor for the development of Europe and the Americas. In the process, the peculiar institution forced the underdevelopment of a continent, destroyed viable political institutions, depopulated and devastated once fertile and densely populated areas, exacerbated racism, culturally uprooted millions of people, and dehumanized entire populations in Africa and the diaspora. Indeed, as John Hope Franklin notes:

> The expatriation of millions of Africans from the continent in less than four centuries constitutes one of the most far-reaching and drastic social revolutions in the annals of history....The removal of the flower of African manhood left the continent impotent, stultified, and dazed....The encouragement which Europeans gave Africans to fight among themselves, with explosive weapons donated by the Europeans, further debilitated them and removed the last vestige of opportunity to recover from the body blow which the slave trade had dealt them. Africa, that culturally was within some measurable distance from Europe at the beginning of the fifteenth century,...began a recession that in time was to be accelerated by the imperialist enslavement that was to be thrust upon her in the nineteenth century.

The humiliation suffered under slavery and the cultural and psychological deprivation at the hands of the slave traders have left a legacy of scars that have yet to be removed both in Africa and the vast diaspora.

Study Questions and Activities

1. Describe the nature of the early African-European contact.
2. Compare and contrast the institution of slavery in Africa and in the New World.
3. Describe the Middle Passage.
4. Identify and discuss reasons for the abolition of slavery and the slave trade.
5. Evaluate the impact of the Atlantic slave trade on Africa.
6. Do further research on the ship mutinies commonly known as the *Little George, the* Jolly Bachelor, and the *Amystad.*

References

W. W. Claridge. *A History of the Gold Coast.* London: F. Cass, 1964.

Philip Curtin. *The Atlantic Slave Trade: A Census.* Madison: The University of Wisconsin Press, 1969.

Basil Davidson. *The Atlantic Slave Trade.* Boston: Atlantic-Little Brown, 1961.

J. D. Fage. *A History of Africa.* London: Hutchinson University Library for Africa, 1978.

John Hope Franklin. *From Slavery to Freedom.* New York: Knopf Publishers, 1947.

Henry Gemery and Jan S. Hogendorn. *"The Economic Costs of West African Participation in the Atlantic Slave Trade: A Preliminary Sampling for the Eighteenth Century,"* in Henry Gemery and Jan S. Hogendorn. *The Uncommon Market: Essays in The Economic History of the Atlantic Slave Trade.* New York: Academic Press, 1979.

J. E. Inikori. "Measuring The Atlantic Slave Trade: An Assessment of Curtin and Anstey." *Journal Of African History*, XVII, 2(1976): 197-223.

Allen Isaacman. *Mozambique: The Africanization of a European Institution: The Zambezi Prazos, 1750-1902.* Madison: The University of Wisconsin Press, 1972.

Paul Lovejoy. *Transformation in Slavery.* Cambridge: Cambridge University Press, 1983.

Suzanne Miers and Igor Kopytoff (eds.). *Slavery in Africa.* Madison: The University of Wisconsin Press, 1977.

Suzanne Miers and Richard Roberts (eds.). *The End of Slavery in Africa.* Madison: The University of Wisconsin Press, 1988.

Joseph Miller. *Way of Death.* Madison: University of Wisconsin Press, 1988.

Orlando Patterson. *The Sociology of Slavery.* Rutherford, NJ: Fairleigh Dickinson Press, 1967.

Edward Reynolds. *Stand the Storm: A History of the Atlantic Slave Trade.* New York: Allison & Busby, 1986.

Walter Rodney. *How Europe Underdeveloped Africa.* Dar-es-Salaam: Dar-es-Salaam University Press, 1972.

———. *West Africa and the Atlantic Slave Trade.* Dar-es-Salaam: Tanzania Historical Association, 1967.

Eric Williams. *Capitalism and Slavery.* New York: Praeger Books, 1944.

5

Diaspora Africans and Slavery

Raymond Gavins

Introduction

Pioneer scholar W.E.B. DuBois gives us a compelling description of the modern black diaspora. "Raphael painted, Luther preached, Corneille wrote, and Milton sung; and through it all, for four hundred years, the dark captives wound to the sea amid the bleaching bones of the dead," he stated in *The Negro* (1915), "for four hundred years the sharks followed the scurrying ships; for four hundred years America was strewn with the living and dying millions of a transplanted race; for four hundred years Ethiopia stretched forth her hands unto God." In 1492, a half-century after the Portuguese began trading African slaves into nations of the Mediterranean basin, Christopher Columbus discovered America for Spain. In 1500, Pedro Alvares Cabral claimed Brazil for Portugal. Spanish explorer Juan de Ponce de León landed on the coast of North America in 1513, while Vasco Nuñez de Balboa crossed the Isthmus of Panama and reached the Pacific Ocean. By 1519, Hernán Cortés had disembarked in Mexico with an army and had overrun the Aztec empire. These events linked Africa, Europe, and the New World, the destination of more than 11 million captive Africans from 1441 to 1888. About 38% were shipped to Brazil, 42% to the Caribbean, 15% to Spanish America, and 5% to British North America.

Building on Africans' forced migration and bondage in the Western hemisphere, this chapter discusses the evolution, nature, and destruction of slavery in the emerging United States.

Major terms and concepts: African diaspora, Amerindians, indenture, "Black Codes," Maroon colony, "Seasoning," manumission, "money crops," proslavery clauses, Haitian Revolution, Cotton Kingdom, "task system," "Black Belt," "peculiar institution," First Emancipation, slave compensation, extended family, Africanisms, abolitionist movement, Underground Railroad, general emancipation.

The New World Slave System

Racial slavery spread with the white conquest of the New World, where mining and agriculture required a massive exploitation of laborers. The biggest portion of exploited labor came from the conquered Aztecs, Incas, and other indigenous peoples (Amerindians) who fell to European firearms. During the first century of white-red contact, these indigenous peoples were also decimated (from 80,000,000 to 10,000,000) by white-borne diseases like malaria, measles, or smallpox. They slaved in the gold and silver mines of South America, while often attacking their captors and escaping into familiar terrain. As the Amerindians perished in lowland and coastal centers, the conquerors brought "indentured servants" and black slaves to replace them. Servants earned their transportation by a contract of indenture to labor for a term of several years, routinely seven. By 1650, some 849,000 whites (Portuguese, Spanish, English, French, Dutch), compared to 384,000 blacks, inhabited the Americas. Better wages in England and Europe, however, reduced supplies of cheap servant workers, so colonies imported more and more slaves from Africa.

Colonists emphasized the advantages of doing so. For example, blacks could be held in perpetuity. Runaways, because of their black skin, would be recognizable among whites. Blacks were also considered cannibals and "pagans" (worshipers of ancestors or tribal gods). The rules of Christian conduct did not include these "heathens." Inferior in intelligence but superior in brawn, black slaves could be disciplined harshly. Furthermore, African populations not only were considered innately immune to tropical diseases and tolerant of inclement weather, but also inexhaustible.

Slavery anchored merchant capitalism; it coerced manpower for the colonies' economies. Sugar cane was the major crop of the Portuguese in Brazil. Regions of Bahia and Pernambuco in the north and Rio de Janeiro in the south produced the bulk of it. By the 1580s, Brazil was the chief sugar producer and in turn made the 1600s "the century of sugar." Tobacco and sugar cane were cultivated in the British Caribbean (Barbados, Jamaica), as were coffee and cotton. Such crops necessitated strong hands and Atlantic slavers supplied them. Slaves were abused and severely overworked. The historian Basil Davidson quotes a British eyewitness in the Dutch West Indian colony of Suriname whose comment applied to other places as well. "Plantation mortality was so high, he found, that the 'whole race of healthy slaves, consisting of 50,000, are totally extinct once every twenty years.'" Few slaveowners cared as long as they made money. Profit had become their sine qua non.

Even as it framed cultural exchanges between Europeans, Indians, and Africans, slavery was dehumanizing. Interracial sexual contacts generated groups of mestizos (European-Indian), mulattoes (European-African), and mustees (African-Indian) in all areas of the hemisphere. In the Spanish and Portuguese domains, the Catholic church sought "to mitigate the evils of slavery" by teaching the humanity of the slave. But slaves knew harsh realities—frequent flogging, unhealthy clothing, poor diet, and insufficient housing. Bondwomen were exposed to rape and, despite the hardships of childbirth and mothering, labored with men in the fields. In many colonies blacks outnumbered whites. "Black Codes" were adopted to restrict slaves' mobility (required passes), to crush rebellion (hanged insurgents), and to enforce white supremacy (forbade assaulting, disobeying whites).

Some slaves complied under threat of punishment, but many resisted. White laws revealed much angst about resistant slaves. These slaves ran away intermittently; some instigated insurrections. In 1620, Santo Domingo escapees created a Maroon colony (refuge for slave rebels) and staged three uprisings. When the British captured Jamaica from the Spanish in 1655, numerous slaves fled to the mountains. These slaves repeatedly attacked or robbed plantations and retreated to mountain refuges.

Slavery's development in the islands greatly shaped North American slavery. Both systems fed raw materials and capital into Britain's manufactures. The bulk of slaves transported to the thirteen seaboard colonies originated in the Caribbean, which provided the first ports of call for slave ships, and received a third of North America's agricultural produce until 1815. On island plantations, new or "salt water" Africans also underwent "Seasoning." "Seasoning" was done in two ways: by placing newcomers with slave veterans to learn work routines and by a "breaking in" regimen. The latter involved overwork, torture, and sometimes death. Bondmen and women succumbed to whipping and disease as well. Many were killed fleeing patrollers and in other freedom struggles.

Slavery in the United States

Black bondage spanned more than two and a half centuries (far surpassing the 140 years since the general emancipation of 1865). Slavery developed in the colonial period, emerged during the American Revolution, and expanded widely in the Old South, achieving its heyday between 1830 and 1860.

Long before the British established Jamestown, Virginia in 1607, Africans came to North America. In 1526, about 400 Spaniards with 100 slaves arrived on the coast of the Cape Fear River, but this settlement failed due to famine, internal strife, and a slave uprising. Survivors decamped for Santo Domingo, but the rebel blacks settled among the Amerindians. Slaves serviced subsequent Spanish expeditions, helping to settle St. Augustine, Florida in 1565. In 1584, the British planted a colony at Roanoke Island, but in 1591 rescuers found the site deserted. Sir Francis Drake's fleet, carrying 300 Amerindian and 200 African prisoners, rescued settlers around 1588, but in that rescue the Amerindians and Africans escaped.

Follwing generations of Africans would not escape. In 1619, white Virginians bought twenty slaves from a Dutch ship and gradually moved toward black enslavement. With no law defining a slave status before 1659, masters employed blacks as servants. Indentured whites customarily got freedom dues (clothes, a few acres) after completing their terms. They also assimilated, but this pattern eluded the "black indentured servants." Deemed sub-human, blacks met with harsher discipline and periodically served more years. White racism stigmatized blacks.

Virginia's pioneer Africans and their posterity thus faced a hard future. There were only 23 of them among 2,000 whites in 1623, as June Purcell Guild explains. The black population grew not only by births but by importation, totaling

300 in 1649. Statuses of "negroe" and "slave" overlapped, while Anglicans had begun to evangelize them. By 1662, Virginia ruled "that all children borne in this country shall be held bond or free only according to the condition of the mother." Freedom was denied to Christianized blacks in 1667: "It is enacted and declared by this grand assembly, and the authority thereof, that the conferring of baptism doth not alter the condition of the person as to his bondage or freedom..." Blacks comprised 2,000 taxables or 5% of inhabitants in 1671. Both in 1670 and 1682, the legislature authorized that "all persons of non-Christian nationalities thereafter coming into the colony, whether they came by sea or land and whether or not they had been converted to Christianity after capture...were slaves for life." Maryland passed a similar statute in 1663.

North America was a closed society. Some revisionist historians argue, as does Gary B. Nash, "that slavery in Spanish and Portuguese America was never as harsh as in Anglo-America nor were the doors to eventual freedom so tightly closed." Revisionists contend that Africans had religious protections and frequently commingled with whites in Brazil and Cuba. Slaves could achieve manumission (liberation from slavery) in Venezuela, form autonomous enclaves, and become valued members of the larger society. British American slaves, by contrast, "lost all of their rights" and were "treated as mere chattel property." Britons discouraged manumitting blacks, enacted anti-miscegenation statutes, and excluded free blacks as a despised caste.

The number of blacks in North America increased steadily in the 1600s. Slavery advanced through Virginia, Maryland, the Carolinas, and Georgia, into New York, Delaware, Pennsylvania, New Jersey, and New England—covering a broad landscape. By the century's end, there were nearly 25,000 slaves, largely male and perhaps a tenth of all colonists. Southern regions witnessed the largest proportion of the enslaved. Large plantations dotted the Chesapeake, Tidewater, and Low-Country. Producing "money crops," slaves worked on satellite farms or quarters in squads (tobacco) and by assigned tasks (rice, indigo). Owing to a warmer climate and willful neglect, masters' maintenance expenses were minimal. Fewer slaves were used in the middle colonies of New York, New Jersey, Pennsylvania, and Delaware. Farms were generally small, except in locations like those along the Hudson and Delaware rivers. Northerners utilized comparatively few slaves in business and commerce. Slaves were least numerous in New England, where family farming prevailed. In 1700, New Englanders had fewer than 1,000 slaves, many of them household servants of well-to-do merchants.

The black presence widened in the eighteenth century. The greatest numbers of Africans arrived between 1721 and 1780, when a decreasing male-female imbalance permitted them to build families and become self-reproducing. In 1708, Virginia counted 12,000 slaves and added over 1,000 a year. In 1743, the colony had 42,000; by 1756 it reported 120,000. The population was almost evenly divided between blacks and whites in 1775. South Carolina's white and black races were numerically even in 1708. Yet by 1765, South Carolina tabulated 40,000 whites and 90,000 blacks. The black majority endured brutal repression.

Bondage fueled the Atlantic slave trade. Between 1715 and 1750, some 2,500 slaves were imported annually. Annual importations averaged 7,500 in the 1760s. Economic expansion was clearly wedded to this trafficking. It persisted in spite of the Declaration of Independence, which defined liberty as an inalienable human right, and the Northwest Ordinance (1787), which banned slavery from an area where it would be unprofitable anyway. But the Constitution of the United States, by virtue of its proslavery clauses, legalized slavery where it existed. For example, Article IV, Section 2, granted masters' the right to reclaim any "person held to service or labor in one State...escaping into another." Slavery branched into the Lower South, the southwestern frontier, and the borderlands in the 1790s. The engine fueling it was the Industrial Revolution, especially its cotton market. Demand by overseas and New England textile industries, plus the invention of the cotton gin in 1792, secured the South's position as the leading supplier. This quickened slavery, which crisscrossed the Louisiana Purchase of 1803 and ushered in the Cotton Kingdom. It caused the removal of probably 1.5 million slaves from the Upper South to the Lower South by 1850. Soil exhaustion in Maryland and Virginia, alongside Federal outlawing of the slave trade in 1808, slowed slavery's rapid growth. But smuggling escalated, as did domestic trading.

Domestic traders clustered in Maryland and Virginia (sites of a slave surplus). After 1815 firms in Baltimore, Alexandria, or Richmond sold slaves at prices ranging from $350 in Virginia to over $500 in Louisiana. Prices averaged $1,000 in Virginia and $1,500 in Louisiana by 1860. Local newspapers advertised slave auctions, escapes, and arrests. Auction blocks, jails, pens, and coffles were universal sights. Some traffickers profited by hiring out or renting blacks. Others specialized in transport by coffle, flatboat, or wagon. Belying the stereotype of their docility, many slaves wore neck, hand, or foot irons lest they should abscond. Chastised and flogged for disobedience, they were sometimes maimed for resisting separation from kin.

Planters abetted "slave breeding." Some Virginians did so to offset losses from exhausted soil and falling prices. Thomas R. Dew, professor of Moral Philosophy at William and Mary College, described Virginia in 1832 as "a negro raising state." Between 1830 and 1860, it sold "nearly three hundred thousand [slaves]—almost the whole of her natural increase" (see Kenneth M. Stampp). One planter boasted to northern visitor Frederick Law Olmsted that his bondwomen were "uncommonly good breeders" and that slave babies were "worth two hundred dollars" the moment they "drew breath." Coaxed by rewards like extra rations and by being habitually raped, many female slaves "became mothers at thirteen and fourteen years of age."

Slaves shouldered the southern economy. Their population enlarged from about 700,000 in 1790 to 3.2 million in 1850 and reached 4 million by 1860. In 1850, approximately 500,000 slaves resided in towns and cities. Over 2 million were cotton cultivators. Many slaves cultivated corn, tobacco, rice, and sugar cane. Cotton and sugar cane gangs were ordered by whip-toting black drivers and white overseers. The ordinary slave toiled from daybreak until dark, typically on a farm. Rice producers adhered to a "task system." It set the slave's daily work (so many rows to hoe or drain) and rewarded its completion. For instance, a bondman could finish the task by mid-day then leave the field to tend his gardenplot or pursue other self-help. Besides shouldering the burdens of fieldwork, slaves did a plethora of manual jobs and services. They tended heavy industries— timber and construction; gold, coal, salt, iron, and lead mines; iron furnaces and tobacco factories; cotton presses and sawmills; road, railroad, and shipbuilding. Slaves also performed skilled crafts like blacksmithing and carpentry.

A white minority dominated slaveholding and traditionally in the "Black Belt." Known for its black soil, cotton, and black-majority counties, this vast region swept through parts of Virginia, the Carolinas, Georgia, Florida, Alabama, Mississippi, Tennessee, Louisiana, Arkansas, and Texas. One third of the region's white families owned slaves. Of all slave-owning whites, some 10,000 owned 50 or more slaves per family; 3,000 possessed 100 or more slaves per family. About three-fourths of whites had no familial or ownership ties to slavery. The "typical" white southerner was a yeoman farmer and a non-slaveholder. His whiteness accorded him the psychological benefit of white supremacy.

Slavery functioned principally: (1) to maintain a forced labor arrangement, using coercion and terror; (2) to perpetuate a caste hierarchy of masters, non-slaveholders, slaves, and free blacks; and (3) to regulate race and class relations, utilizing racist ideology to justify black subordination and white deference. Free blacks were allowed to own slaves. Many did so to ransom or provide protective custody to kinfolk. Some elite free people of color (a minuscule element) did so to accumulate wealth.

Masters called blacks natural slaves, but they knew the limits of such rhetoric. Blacks devised strategies to mask their feelings, survive, and fight back. So masters took steps to exert control. For example, by isolating the house servant from the field hand, the master attempted to weaken slaves politically. While the master's informant against field hands normally was a loyal domestic, it is also true that scores of plots were not given away by informants. Slaves suffered extreme privation, yet they shared resources to subsist. Their quarters consisted of a single or double row of cabins near the overseer's house. Ordinarily, a slave cabin was drafty, unfurnished, and overcrowded. Field hands went mostly barefooted and ragged even in the winter. Slaves' weekly ration consisted of hominy and cornmeal, irregularly with fatback bacon or salt pork.

Legally, the slave was a chattel. Slaves could not be parties in lawsuits, except indirectly when a free person sued on their behalf. They could offer testimony in court only against other blacks. Slaves were forbidden to enter agreements for exchanging goods and services. Nor could they own property by law. Their marriages had no legal standing. However, laws safeguarded the master's interests. States assessed serious penalties for the theft of slaves. When a slave was executed for a capital crime, states ordinarily paid the owner a fair price or slave compensation from tax revenues. Owners determined if and when to hire out or sell bondpeople. Used as collateral on a loan, slaves could be taken by creditors in lieu of payment. Often a master's will would break up slave families to liquidate his estate.

Southern planters dreaded the idea of black freedom. During the First Emancipation in the North (1780–1830), they decided to outlaw manumission. Lower South states such as Alabama and Georgia outlawed it in the early 1800s, declaring freedmen to be a menace to slaves. The border state of Maryland avoided such a declaration, though insisting that those manumitted could not be public charges when they were old or sick. In the Upper South, both Virginia and North Carolina mandated that released blacks migrate or risk re-enslavement. Owners could still manumit slaves and relocate them to a free state by their wills, but this privilege was repealed in the 1840s and 1850s. Dissenters were persecuted and usually expelled.

Slaves composed an oppressed lot. They were imprisoned on plantations, unless given permission to leave. Any white person could arrest a slave, particularly one traveling without a pass or "freedom papers." Forging papers and possessing a firearm were felonies. Nor should slaves visit whites and free blacks or receive them as visitors. It was unlawful to teach slaves to read and write. Blacks were never to strike whites, an offense punishable by lashing or worse. Humane masters let slaves worship on their own, travel, trade, hunt with guns, or hire out. Some enabled them to learn and to live in autonomy. Such benevolent acts were too few, overwhelmed by rampant inhumanity.

Force and proslavery reigned side by side. Every county maintained a patrol to prevent blacks from congregating, arming, or revolting. All adult white males had to serve. The patrols as a rule depended on the poorer whites, who resented wealthy masters and their slaves. States seldom regulated plantations and rarely convicted masters for abusing slaves. They were, announced the Chief Justice of the U.S. Supreme Court in 1857, "so far inferior that they had no rights that the white man was bound to respect" (see Henry Steele Commager).

The Response to Slavery

Culturally, slaves straddled two worlds. Torn from their motherland, described by the poet Countee Cullen as "Women from whose loins I sprang when the birds of Eden sang, "they remained strangers in America. Describing the estrangement, Cullen was "One three centuries removed from the scenes his fathers loved." Slaves were mainly of West African origin, mostly from the Gold Coast, Bight of Biafra, and Congo-Angola subregions. Yoruba, Akan, and Bokongo were just three of their myriad ethnic groups. Africans and Creoles (American-born slaves) built methods to communicate, cooperate, and resist. They braved oppression by means varying from accommodation and conformity to defiance and insurgence. Their resilience under adversity is hardly conceivable in contemporary America.

Slaves were complex, "a troublesome property." Masters bragged on childlike and obedient slaves. Masters also complained about slave arson, flight, malingering, poisoning, sabotage, and theft. Thus blacks both accommodated and opposed domination, indirectly and directly. Facing violent subjection, the mass of bondmen and women coped on "the middle ground, in which conformity is often a self-conscious strategy and resistance is a carefully hedged affair that avoids all-or-nothing confrontations" (see James C. Scott). Slaves calculated their risks.

Proslavery spokesmen insisted that slaves were contented. Nevertheless, we should ask: why was slaveholding America an armed camp? Why slave codes and compensations? The overreaction to rumors of insurrection? The suppression of freedom of thought? What an ex-slave termed "yearnings to be free" frightened and provoked slaveholders.

Africans yearned to break their chains. Largely war prisoners of better-armed tribes, they were traded to whites. Captives chanted songs expressing their sadness and suffering. They also fought openly, committed suicide, or otherwise rebelled. Their blood streaked the caravan routes from the interior to the coast. Rebellions broke out in holding pens or baracoons and in the dungeons of slave forts; at loading docks; aboard ships on the Gambia River and Atlantic Ocean. The transatlantic "'middle passage'" lasted three to four months, with 25–40% of slaves dying from illnesses, mutinies, and suicides. The survivors clung to their ancestral customs or Africanisms, like naming children by days of the week to mark a time or place. As in Columbia (1550) and Brazil (1630), they struggled heroically throughout the New World.

Mainland slaves drew on their heritage to affirm themselves. West African "feasts and burials" were common. After watching a slave funeral in colonial Virginia, one Briton observed: "They sing and dance and drink to the dead his new home, which some believe to be in old Guinea" (see June Purcell Guild). At this solemn ritual, they could share memories of home, plan to flee and hide among the Amerindians, or conspire to rise. In any case, black gatherings troubled whites. As soon as 1644, the Virginia assembly passed a resolution "concerning the riotous and rebellious conduct...of Negroes." It resolved in 1680 that "the frequent meeting of considerable numbers of negro slaves under pretense of feasts and burials is judged of dangerous consequence."

Freed blacks meantime aspired to get ahead. On Virginia's Eastern Shore some prospered as artisans, buying tracts of farmland and servants of both races. They were parties in contracts and lawsuits. Anthony Johnson owned 250 acres and therewith qualified to vote. Manumitted around 1635, Johnson acquired land and livestock in Northampton County. His herds multiplied and he had a dozen servants and slaves. His home and plantation burned in 1653, but Johnson petitioned the court for tax relief. Partly granting it, the justices excused Johnson's wife and two daughters "from paying 'Taxes and Charges in Northhampton County'...for 'their natural lives'" (see T. H. Breen and Stephen Innes). Other free black landowners included Benjamin Doyle, 300 acres in Surry County; John Harris, 50 acres in New Kent County; and Phillip Morgan, 20 acres in York County.

Bondpeople persevered. They forged an Afro-American "slave culture" grounded in an extended family. Parents, children, grandparents, other blood relatives, and fictive kinpeople formed help networks (see Herbert G. Gutman). Slaves hid their aspirations from whites. In candle-lit cabins Africans and Creoles agreed, disagreed, negotiated, and conspired to be free. They partnered in the fields, developing pidgin languages not understood by slaveholders. Slave communities afforded them sanctuary from auctions and toil, space in which to socialize. They chose leaders; practiced mutual support; taught job skills and coping strategies to the next generation. Through oral traditions (African trickster tales) and worksongs, they instilled values of pride, sharing, and solidarity (see Lawrence W. Levine).

Christianity was a vital source of affirmation and inspiration. Hundreds of slaves converted during the southern sweep of the "Second Great Awakening," a revival beginning in the 1790s. Methodists and Baptists, who welcomed poor folk, attracted large numbers of slave converts. Slaves worshiped in "hush harbors," secluded clearings in gullies, ravines, and woods. In towns they congregated in church houses. Revivals and Sunday services were "occasions for socializing, news gathering, and picnicking as well as for prayer" (see Albert J. Raboteau). Black exhorters and preachers told the faithful about a gospel of liberty. Worship featured testifying, ring shouts, and spirituals. The song "O Canaan, sweet Canaan, I am bound for the land of Canaan" not only meant deliverance in heaven. Freedom also must come on earth.

Learning, too, was a stepping-stone to liberation. The bondman and woman who could read and write were shining lights in the community. His master's wife taught the young Maryland slave Frederick Douglass. "The argument which he so warmly urged, against my learning to read, only served to inspire me with a desire and determination to learn," Douglass recalled in 1845. "In learning to read, I owe almost as much to the bitter opposition of my master, as to the kindly aid of my mistress. I acknowledge the benefit of both" (see Michael Meyer). Slaveholders never intended to educate blacks, but conceded that training could make them more profitable. Certain bondmen therefore learned crafts and industries, which augmented skills like metalworking and wood carving transmitted from Africa. Training also varied slaves' routines (many were hired out) and gave them a sense of autonomy.

Christian missions promoted slave literacy and salvation. In 1620, the English clergy pledged to ameliorate the plight of those "in bondage beyond the seas." This ministry was intact a century later when Thomas Bray founded the Society for the Propagation of the Gospel in Foreign Parts. An arm of the Anglican Church, the Society raised funds, trained teachers, and opened schools for Amerindians, slaves, and free blacks in Charleston, Savannah, and parts of Georgia. Quakers joined and energized this cause. Between 1764 and 1785, they launched a Virginia mission school and trusteeship to prepare blacks for manumission. Presbyterians took similar steps. They sponsored John Chavis, a free black Revolutionary War veteran, at Princeton Seminary in the 1790s. Chavis emerged to be a prominent minister and schoolmaster to whites and free blacks in North Carolina until 1831, when the state's slave code silenced black preachers.

Literacy and slavery were incompatible, of course. Education was denied to slaves because it portended their freedom. The educated slave contradicted whites' caricatures of a dissembling "Sambo" or "Mammy." Harriet Ann Jacobs, a literate North Carolina slave, personified the contradiction. Taught to read and sew by her mistress, she defied a licentious master by hiding from him for seven years before fleeing to the North. Her narrative, *Incidents in the Life of a Slave Girl, Written by Herself* (1861), echoed ideals of dignity and self-determination. Slavery intimidated and suppressed most slave dissidents, for whom there was no defense. Rape and murder of whites, arson, and conspiracy were punished by execution. From 1705 to 1865, Virginia sentenced thousands of bondpeople to whippings or other corporal punishment; deported at least 983; and put 1,237 to death (see Philip J. Schwarz). Owners of executed slaves were compensated.

Slaves authored an enduring legacy of struggle. Generations sang the spiritual "O Freedom, O Freedom over me; and before I'll be a slave I'll be buried in my grave and go home to my Lord and be free." In 1712, New York City authorities burned thirteen, hanged eighteen, and deported eighty slaves for torching buildings and killing nine whites. Fear prompted the assembly to impose a heavy tax on slave imports. South Carolina bondmen killed three whites in 1720. In 1730, a bondman informed on his brethren's plot to capture Charleston. Under pretense of holding a "dancing bout" in St. Paul's Parish, blacks gathered together, ready to seize arms, but the militia defended the armory. Most of the rebels were killed; a few got away. An outbreak at Stono, South Carolina, in 1739, incited white panic across the South. Led by Jemmy, about twenty slaves marched toward Spanish Florida, beating drums, burning houses, killing white people, and adding recruits. While camped out, the insurgents were ambushed and destroyed by a white posse.

The "inalienable rights" of the American Revolution forecast gradual emancipation in the North amidst widening slave unrest in the South. Slaves ran to the British lines. Patriot masters manumitted many. Probably 100,000 slaves of British Loyalists and American Patriots were freed by flight, manumission, and military evacuation at the war's end. Others bolted into Canada or Florida to live among Amerindians. Blacks also were buoyed by the revolution in the French colony of St. Domingue. Also known as the Haitian Revolution, it broke out in 1791. Led by Toussaint L'Ouverture, slaves won freedom in 1793 and independence by 1804. Scores of planters embarked for Cuba, New Orleans, Savannah, Charleston, and Baltimore. France abandoned her plans to reconquer St. Domingue (renamed Haiti) and thereafter consented to a U.S. purchase of Louisiana. The advent of an independent black nation, "the child of a revolt, had an emboldening effect on the slaves in the United States" (see Benjamin Quarles).

Nationally visible slave conspiracies were led by Gabriel Prosser in Richmond (1800), Denmark Vesey in Charleston (1822), and Nat Turner in Southampton County, Virginia (1831). Gabriel plotted in extreme secrecy on the plantation of Thomas Prosser, several miles from town. Inspired by the example of Haiti, he and 110 bondmen made a blood vow to fight until death. They planned to take the arsenal and other strategic sites. Then, they estimated that 50,000 slaves would join the battle. But someone betrayed the conspirators. A fierce storm arose on the target date and the Federal cavalry decimated them. After speedy trials, Gabriel and three dozen of his brethren died on the gallows. A free black Charlestonian, Vesey paid for his freedom in 1800 with money from a lottery prize. An exhorter in the local African Methodist Episcopal (AME) Church, he had once spent three months on St. Domingue and, like Toussaint, wanted to liberate his people. He prepared for a judgment day against slaveholders. Insurgents planned to takeover and torch Charleston. Seizing all ships, they would sail to the West Indies. But a spy disclosed the plot, causing a severe backlash. Authorities hanged thirty-five blacks and deported thirty-seven. Laws were enacted to ban free blacks from entering the state, to close Charleston's AME Church, to silence black preachers, and to prohibit slave importation. Turner's insurrection, occurring seventy miles from Richmond, incited widespread fear. A mystic and lay preacher, he had great power over his peers. So, on the divinely revealed night in 1831, he and his followers invaded plantations, killing about sixty whites before militias could respond. They killed more than a hundred blacks. Turner, thirteen other slaves, and three black freemen were hanged.

Resistance escalated as slaves purchased and stole freedom. Using earnings from hiring out, a trade, or vending, some satisfied their owners' asking price. Elizabeth Hobbs Keckley and Lunsford Lane, both North Carolina slaves, emancipated themselves and relatives by "bill of sale." Frederick Douglass, Harriet Jacobs, and Harriet Tubman absconded, like 100,000 others between 1810 and 1850. Some fugitives traveled on their own, but most had help from black and white conductors and stations on the fabled *Underground Railroad*. Perhaps 40,000 of them traveled through Ohio alone. Fugitive and narrator William Wells Brown saw them "running from under the stars and stripes, and taking refuge in the Canadas; . . . some leaving their wives, some their husbands, some leaving their children, some their brothers, and some their sisters" (see Paul Jefferson). They represented a loss of $30,000,000 to the slavocracy, which demanded stricter Federal enforcement of the Fugitive Slave Act (1850). Most bondmen, women, and children could not flee, but longed to break their shackles. Rumor of a Virginia slave conspiracy in 1856 anticipated John Brown's attempt to overthrow slavery at Harpers Ferry in 1859.

Antislavery and Emancipation

Accelerated by the activism of African Americans and their allies, events sweeping from the 1830s to 1861 sharpened conflict over the "peculiar institution." The outcomes were southern secession, the Civil War, the destruction of slavery, and the general emancipation of 4 million black folk, freeing "a larger number of slaves than lived in all other New World slave societies combined" (see Ira Berlin et al). Earlier attempts to ameliorate and contain slavery set the stage for these developments. Opposition was deep-rooted, with slaves and free blacks playing critical roles in organized antislavery.

Religious dissenters were crucial. As slaves hoped and masters armed, several church bodies condemned slavery as immoral. Quakers set the pace early on. With bold leadership, Friends ceased slave trading and, by the 1760s, slaveholding. Forming an abolition society in 1775, they encouraged free blacks' justice petitions and slaves' liberation battles during the war. In the North, where geography and ideology ill-suited a slave economy, the First Emancipation liberated 47,000 blacks by 1800. Vermont acted first in 1777. Then followed Massachusetts and Pennsylvania in 1780; New Hampshire in1783; Rhode Island and Connecticut in 1784; New York in 1799; and New Jersey in 1804 (see Arthur Zilversmit). Congress also barred slavery in territory north of the Ohio and east of the Mississippi rivers.

Antislavery societies seized the times. They publicized slavery's injustice and strengthened their ties with British abolitionists, notably Olaudah Equiano whose influential *Narrative* (1789) traced his journey from African abduction at age eleven and bondage in the Americas to self-paid freedom. "Tortures, murder, and every imaginable barbarity and iniquity, are practised upon the poor slaves with impunity," Equiano exclaimed. "I hope the slave trade will be abolished" (see Robert J. Allison). Societies assisted runaways, black schooling, and efforts to colonize freed blacks. Like women, freedpeople had their own organizations. They mobilized through churches, clubs, and fraternal associations. Like black shipbuilder Paul Cuffee, many were pro-colonizers. But sailmaker James Forten and others rejected colonization, arguing that it separated free and unfree African Americans.

Anti-colonizers comprised the larger and more militant group. Catching "the contagion of liberty" from the Haitian Revolution, antis championed black emancipation. They opposed the American Colonization Society (ACS). Founded in 1816, ACS listed slaveholders among its sponsors for ex-slave colonies in West Africa. Antis also monitored Congress' debates on the Missouri Compromise (1820), which admitted Missouri as a slave state and Maine as a free state, easing conflict even as abolitionism grew. By 1827 its advocates belonged to 154 affiliates, dozens of them black. Freedom and slavery were antithetical, they contended, pressing the sectional divide. They challenged the nation to insure liberty for all.

Abolitionists were increasingly outspoken. "Remember Americans, that we must and shall be free," warned David Walker, a North Carolina-born black Bostonian, in *Walker's Appeal* (1829), a pamphlet censored by southern legislatures (see Charles M. Wiltse). He denounced the ACS, contending "America is more our country than it is the whites'—we have enriched it with our blood." Invoking "a God of justice," he charged slaves to wage a collective revolt. African emigration and individual manumission were like telling "a man whose house is on fire to give a moderate alarm," declared William Lloyd Garrison, a white Bostonian and publisher of *The Liberator*, the leading abolitionist journal. "I do not wish to think, or speak, or write, with moderation" (see Truman Nelson). He vowed "no union with slaveholders." In 1833, two years after Nat Turner's rebellion and the year Parliament approved compensated emancipation in the British West Indies, Garrison and other radicals started the American Anti-Slavery Society (AAS). It not only accepted women and blacks into membership but also crusaded for immediate and uncompensated abolition. Within a decade, AAS distributed 1 million pieces of literature, chartered 1,350 branches, and recruited 250,000 members, Frederick Douglass being among the most outstanding.

The movement exacerbated sectional politics. If disagreements about moral suasion versus political action split Garrisonians, opponents dubbed them "abolition tyrants." Activists such as Douglass became the conscience of 1840s and 1850s third parties—Liberty, Free Soil, Republican—while the actions of a Sojourner Truth or slave litigant Dred Scott intensified the "irrepressible conflict." To southern planters, John Brown's raid and the 1860 election of a free-soil Republican president confirmed a northern scheme to dominate the Union. They chose to protect their slave property by seceding.

Secession, cornerstone of the Confederate States of America, ignited the Civil War. "One section of our country believes slavery is right, and ought to be extended, while the other believes it is wrong and ought not to be extended," asserted President Abraham Lincoln. He proposed to disturb neither existing slavery nor the domain of free labor but to preserve the Union. Abolitionists, as Douglass put it, envisioned "the complete and universal abolition of the whole slave system" (see Gary B. Nash et al). Slaves prayed that they were on the verge of "being free." One ex-slave woman recollected "the whisperings among the slaves—their talking of the possibility of freedom." Vindicating her, the Union defeated the Western world's most powerful planter class and hereby emancipated slaves.

Emancipation depicted the interplay of slave initiative and Union strategy. Many masters were disturbed when their allegedly docile slaves flocked to the Federal lines. These "contraband" blacks numbered almost 30,000 by 1862. Their activism helped pressure Lincoln and Congress to confiscate Confederates' slaves; to emancipate slaves in the District of Columbia and allocate funds for colonizing them; to authorize recruitment of black soldiers; to secure diplomatic recognition from England and France, each declining to recognize the Confederacy; and, with the Union's improving fortunes on the battlefield, to issue the Emancipation Proclamation (1863). Although the document exempted some 800,000 slaves of Unionists in border states, Lincoln justified it as "an act of justice, warranted by the Constitution upon military necessity." As the president's words "forever free" were proclaimed, slave defections rose. Black enlistments in the Union army and navy totaled 200,000. Still most blacks were not liberated until the final defeat of the Confederacy and adoption of the Thirteenth Amendment in 1865.

Freedpeople gave abundant evidence of their expectations. They undertook "a dress rehearsal for Reconstruction" in missionary and federally-sponsored experiments. In the Union-occupied Sea Islands of South Carolina and Georgia, as in other places, they embraced free labor arrangements. They grasped the opportunity to earn wages and acquire land; to attend schools and worship in their own churches; to reunite slave families and develop black institutions. These experiences deepened their commitment to self-empowerment. In 1865, they hailed General William T. Sherman's Field Order Number 15 distributing Confederate lands to 40,000 freedmen, women, and children in forty-acre tracts. Although the measure was rescinded, they fully expected "that, in short, we be dealt with as others are—in equity and justice" (see Thomas R. Frazier). With that hope, they began the quest for racial equality in Modern America.

Summary

Underlining this discussion is the importance of a theoretical approach emphasizing cultural encounter and fusion. New World slavery constructed a crucible of interaction between Amerindians, Europeans, and Africans. In the Caribbean and South America, as in the British North American colonies and eventual United States, red, white, and black peoples interacted in slave-based societies where whites exercised racial hegemony.

The hemispheric perspective considers Africans and African Americans' experience in and contribution to those multiracial interactions. Scholars continue to explore the encounters, but no longer in terms of whether Africans were stripped culturally and then acculturated. As illustrated in Joseph E. Holloway, ed., *Africanisms in American Culture* (1990), they focus on the provenance, retention, and fusion of African culture in the Americas. Portia K. Maultsby, Beverly J. Robinson, and Robert L. Hall trace West African music, folklore, and religions in slaves' history. John E. Philips demonstrates that African retentions influenced the making of white America's customs (like cooking) and institutions. *Slave Culture* (1987) by Sterling Stuckey traces Africans' resilient values and world view.

This chapter emphasizes the evolution, character, and destruction of black bondage in the colonies and states that became the United States. Prior to large-scale African importing, whites did not hesitate to enslave the New World's indigenous peoples. As the Amerindians battled and escaped from the white conquerors, millions died in European-borne epidemics of malaria, measles, and smallpox. White servants were too few to supply the mines and fields, so employers turned to Africa. Regarded as subhuman, easily identified by their black skin, Africans could be held in lifetime servitude. Uprooted from Africa and considered an inexhaustible source, they constituted the "final solution" to the labor problem in South America, in the West Indies, and in North America after 1619.

Slavery was a highly profitable institution in the American South. Enriching planters of cotton, tobacco, indigo, and sugar, it enthralled many generations of Africans. The number of blacks on the mainland slowly increased not only by natural birth rate but also by the slave trade: the trickle became a flood after

1650. There were nearly 25,000 slaves in British North America (approximately a tenth of the total population) within a half-century and more than 4 million by 1860. In northern colonies, including New York, New Jersey, Pennsylvania, and Delaware, farms were generally small and the numbers of slaves minimal. Indeed, businessmen viewed slave labor as an obstacle to commerce and industry. New Englanders in 1700 owned fewer than 1,000 bondpeople, many of them household servants. Plantations dominated the southern Chesapeake and Low-Country, enslaving tens of thousands. South Carolina slaves outnumbered whites 90,000 to 40,000 in 1765 alone. Enslaved blacks were deemed essential to the planters' wealth and to white supremacy.

Black captivity lasted in spite of the Declaration of Independence, which defined liberty as an inalienable human right, and the U.S. Constitution (three-fifths and three other clauses sanctioned slavery). Slaves were classified as chattels; legally, they could not sue, own property, make contracts, marry, or learn to read and write. They could travel only by permission. Slavery's cruelty was palpable in the courts: when a bondman was executed for a capital crime, the state compensated his master.

Denying the humanity of African Americans, slavery served three major functions: to maintain forced labor, commonly terrorizing the victims; to preserve a caste order of masters, nonslaveholders, slaves, and free blacks; to regulate race and class relations, using racism to justify black subordination and white deference. Slavery thus evolved through nearly 250 years as an economic, political, social superstructure to perpetuate planter domination, white supremacy, and black subjugation in the United States.

Culturally, slaves lived between two worlds. Torn from Africa, yet retaining many of their native traditions, they were subjugated and isolated in America. They responded to slavery by entwining African survivals and American realities. Their responses varied on a continuum from abject acquiescence and passive resistance to confrontation and insurgency.

Organized antislavery owed to individuals and organizations, white and black, from colonial times. It burgeoned during the American Revolution and First Emancipation, as well as in the national crisis attending southern secession, war, and the Emancipation Proclamation of 1863. But it was the Thirteenth Amendment that legislated slaves' general emancipation, laying the foundation for racial equality.

Study Questions and Activities

1. Forced displacement and isolation proved to be central mechanisms in New World enslavement of Africans. What are some other factors that explain why they were enslaved?
2. On the North American mainland, how and why did African slavery become so important in southern colonies and states?
3. By what means did African American slaves seek survival and liberation?
4. Slaves and free blacks' actions propelled the issues that culminated in the Civil Warm and Thirteenth Amendment. Do you agree or disagree? Provide evidence for your position.

5. Annually, thousands of Americans visit the African diaspora landmark on the Island of Gorée, Dakar, Senegal. Discuss the pros and cons of having a national slavery monument or museum in America.

Glossary

African Diaspora: Dispersion of Africans throughout the world from ancient to modern times, mainly by slave trading and slavery; emphasis on transatlantic trade and its consequences in the Western hemisphere (1441–1888).

Amerindians: Indigenous peoples of the Americas; their civilizations and kingdoms thrived before the arrival of white colonists.

Indenture: Servant's contract to work a fixed number of years for transportation and upkeep.

Black Codes: Laws regulating slaves and free blacks in slave colonies or states.

Maroon Colony: Rebel slave community, typically in a remote or hazardous area.

Seasoning: Practice of slave making on plantations; work routines, breaking the will of new slaves.

Manumission: Formal release of the slave by the slaveholder, usually in a deed or will.

Money Crops: Sugar, coffee, tobacco, corn, indigo, wheat, rice, and cotton were major ones; required intensive labor; marketing fueled servitude, slavery, and capitalism.

Proslavery Clauses: Article I, sections 2, 8, 9, Article IV, section 2 of the U.S. Constitution, legalizing slavery.

Haitian Revolution: The 1791 overthrow of slavery on French island of St. Domingue culminating independence (1804); fearful of its influence on slaves, the U.S. refused to recognize the black republic until1862.

Cotton Kingdom: Expansion of cotton cultivation and slavery in the Lower South (1800–1860) along with the U.S. textile industry.

Task System: Incentive-based labor practice started on rice plantations; slaves completing assigned tasks could leave the fields by mid-afternoon to help themselves.

Black Belt: Region stretching through densely black counties from Virginia to Texas; center of cotton production and the antebellum slave system.

Peculiar Institution: Moniker for slavery in the American South; enforcing unfree labor, caste, and master-class domination; also inspiring Afro-American culture, agency, and freedom struggle.

First Emancipation: Gradual freeing of slaves in northern states (1780–1830) by constitutional provisions, judicial decisions, and legislation.

Slave Compensation: Market price of an executed bondman or woman, payable to the master; allocated from tax revenues of the colony or state.

Africanisms: Beliefs and customs of African origin, enabling slaves to create Afro-American cultures and establish themselves as an integral part of a varied cultural mix in the Americas.

Extended Family: Adaptation of African kinship tradition; connecting nuclear slave family to blood and fictive kin (grandparents, aunts, uncles, cousins), to form a supportive network—resident and interplantation.

Abolitionist Movement: Biracial antislavery crusade (1831–65) seeking immediate abolition without compensation to masters.

Underground Railroad: South-to-North stream of runaway slaves aided by slave, free black, and white contacts; ex-slaves became narrators and abolitionist leaders.

General Emancipation: Thirteenth Amendment (1865) emancipating all slaves in U.S. states and territories.

References

Robert J. Allison (ed). *The Interesting Narrative of the Life of Olaudah Equiano Written by Himself*. Boston: Bedford Books of St. Martin's Press, 1995; orig. pub.1789.

Lerone Bennett, Jr. *Before the Mayflower*, 7th ed. Chicago: Johnson Pub., 2003.

Ira Berlin et al (eds). *Freedom: A Documenty History of Emancipation*, ser. 1, vol. 1. New York: Cambridge University Press, 1985.

Ira Berlin. *Many Thousand Gone: The First two Centuries of Slavery in North America*. Cambridge, MA: Harvard University Press, 1998.

John W. Blassingame. *The Slave Community: Plantation Life in the Antebellum South*, rev. & enl. New York: Oxford University Press, 1979.

T. H. Breen and Stephen Innes. *"Myne Owne Ground": Race and Freedom on Virginia's Eastern Shore, 1640–1676*. New York: Oxford University Press, 1980.

Mark C. Carnes and John A. Garraty. *The American Nation*, 11th ed. New York: Longman, 2003.

Henry Steele Commager (ed). *Documents of American History*, 10th ed., 2 vols. Englewood Cliffs, NJ: Prentice-Hall, 1988.

Wesley Frank Craven. *White, Red, and Black: The Seventeenth-Century Virginian*. New York: Norton, 1977.

Countee Cullen. *Color*. New York: Harper and Brothers, 1925.

Basil Davidson. *The African Slave Trade*, rev. & enl. Boston: Little, Brown, 1980.

Thomas R. Dew. *Review of the Debate in the Virginia Legislature of 1831 and 1832*. Richmond, VA: T.W. White, 1832.

W. E. Burghardt DuBois. *The Negro*. New York: Oxford University Press, 1970; orig. pub. 1915.

Stanley M. Elkins. *Slavery: A Problem in American Institutional and Intellectual Life*, 3d ed., rev. Chicago: University of Chicago Press, 1976.

David Eltis. *The Rise of African Slavery in the Americas*. Cambridge, UK: Cambridge University Press, 2000.

John Hope Franklin and Loren Schweninger. *Runaway Slaves: Rebels on the Plantation*. New York: Oxford University Press, 1999.

Thomas R. Frazier (ed). *Afro-American History: Primary Sources*, 2d ed. Chicago: Dorsey Press, 1988.

Larry Gara. *The Liberty Line: The Legend of the Underground Railroad*. Lexington: University Press of Kentucky, 1996.

June Purcell Guild. *Black Laws of Virginia*. Richmond, VA: Whittett and Shepperson, 1936.

Herbert G. Gutman. *The Black Family in Slavery and Freedom, 1750–1925*. New York: Vintage Books, 1977.

Vincent Harding. *There Is A River: The Black Struggle for Freedom in America*. Vintage ed. New York: Vintage Books, 1983.

Joseph E. Holloway (ed). *Africanisms in American Culture*. Bloomington, IN: Indiana University Press, 1990.

Nathan I. Huggins et al (eds). *Key Issues in the Afro-American Experience*. New York: Harcourt Brace Jovanovich, 1971.

Paul Jefferson (ed). *The Travels of William Wells Brown*. New York: M. Weiner, 1991.

Allan Kulikoff. *Tobacco and Slaves: The Development of Southern Cultures in the Chesapeake, 1680–1800*. Chapel Hill: University of North Carolina Press, 1986.

Lawrence W. Levine. *Black Culture and Black Consciousness: Afro-American Folk Thought from Slavery to Freedom*. New York: Oxford University Press, 1978.

Michael Meyer (ed). *Frederick Douglass: The Narrative and Selected Writings*. New York: Modern Library, 1984.

Philip D. Morgan. *Slave Counterpoint: Black Culture in the Eighteenth-Century Chesapeake and Lowcountry*. Chapel Hill: University of North Carolina Press, 1998.

Michael Mullin. *Africa in America: Slave Acculturation and Resistance in the American South and the British Caribbean, 1736–1831*. Urbana: University of Illinois Press, 1992.

Gary B. Nash et al. *The American People*, 4th ed. New York: Longman, 2003.

———. *Red, White, and Black: The Peoples of Early America*, 4th ed. Upper Saddle River, NJ: Prentice Hall, 2000.

Truman Nelson (ed). *Documents of Upheaval: Selections from William Lloyd Garrison's The Liberator, 1831–65*. New York: Hill and Wang, 1966.

Colin A. Palmer. *Passageways: An Interpretive History of Black America*, vol. 1. New York: Harcourt Brace, 1998.

Richard Price. *Maroon Societies: Rebel Slave Communities in the Americas*. Baltimore: Johns Hopkins University Press, 1979.

Benjamin Quarles. *The Negro in the Making of America*, rev. ed. New York: Collier Books, 1969.

Albert J. Raboteau. *Slave Religion: The "Invisible Institution" in the Antebellum South*. New York: Oxford University Press, 1978.

Philip J. Schwarz. *Twice Condemned: Slaves and the Criminal Laws of Virginia, 1705–1865*. Union, NJ: Lawbook Exchange, 1998.

James C. Scott. *Weapons of the Weak: Everyday Forms of Peasant Resistance*. New Haven: Yale University Press, 1985.

Archer H. Shaw (ed). *The Lincoln Encyclopedia*. New York: Macmillan, 1950.

Kenneth M. Stampp. *The Peculiar Institution: Slavery in the Ante-Bellum South*. New York: Vintage Books, 1989; orig. pub. 1956.

Sterling Stuckey. *Slave Culture: Nationalist Theory and the Foundations of Black America*. New York: Oxford University Press, 1987.

Deborah Gray White. *Ar'n't I a Woman? Female Slaves in the Plantation South*. New York: W. W. Norton, 1985.

Eric Williams. *Capitalism & Slavery*. Chapel Hill: University of North Carolina Press, 1994; orig. pub.1944.

Charles M. Wiltse (ed). *David Walker's Appeal, in Four Articles, Together with a Preamble*. New York: Hill and Wang, 1965; orig. pub.1829.

Jean Fagan Yellin (ed). *Incidents in the Life of a Slave Girl Written by Herself. By Harriet A. Jacobs*. Cambridge: Harvard University Press, 2000; orig. pub.1861.

Arthur Zilversmit. *First Emancipation*. Chicago: University of Chicago Press, 1967.

6

European Exploration and Conquest of Africa

Mario Azevedo

Introduction

The following chapter discusses the reasons why Europeans became interested in Africa in the aftermath of the slave trade, the strategies they used to divide and conquer the continent beginning in 1885, and how they managed to maintain an exploitative rule on the continent until the 1960s and 1970s. Although the historicity of colonial rule is indisputable, analysts' views about the motives that led the Europeans to conquer Africa by force during the nineteenth century differ. While some tend to stress only economic motives as a corollary to the industrial revolution in Europe, others point to the preponderance of nationalist reasons among the nation-states of Europe which regarded overseas empires as symbols of national greatness.

Some experts, including economist Joseph Schumpeter, have even viewed imperialism as an "atavism," or as an irrational but an irresistible historical tendency on the part of any state to attempt to conquer alien peoples and lands. Most scholars, however, claim that, to understand Western imperialism in Africa, one must analyze Europe, country by country, and that economic, nationalist, cultural, and religious factors, as well as "scientific" curiosity, all played a role. According to them, therefore, no single theory can adequately explain European activities in Africa during the 1885–1960 period.

On colonialism, Africanists are still debating the nature of direct and indirect rule, its policies, and effect upon the Africans. Most recent scholars, however, have shown more interest in the African response toward colonial rule and its policies, with the objective of perhaps rewriting or reinterpreting the history of the continent following the introduction of colonialism.

Major terms and concepts: Slavery, slave trade, colonialism, imperialism, exploration, Berlin Conference, effective control, indirect and direct rule, assimilation, association, paternalism, warrant chiefs, "scramble" for Africa, "mission civilisatrice," "burden of empire."

The Scramble for Africa and
African Response

[margin: Why?]

As the viability of the slave trade began to wane in European circles due to the abolitionist and evangelical movements, Europeans suddenly turned their attention to the geographical configurations of the continent: its rivers, lakes, mountains, fauna and game; its ethnography, and the state of its cultural advancement; as well as the wealth of its economic resources. The first impetus came in 1788 from the African Association, also known as the Association for Promoting the Discovery of the Interior Parts of Africa. This association, which survived until 1815, was created by wealthy Britishers precisely to achieve the goals outlined above. The Association sent several explorers to Africa, the most successful of whom was Mungo Park. The sensational accounts of his travels in the Gambia and Niger Rivers area in 1795 intrigued many other European adventurers and missionaries throughout Europe.

[margin: the story]

Detained in prison by Africans, Park was able to escape his captors and returned to Europe in 1797, relating stories that were generally uncomplimentary to the African authorities and their people whom he considered to be inferior to the Europeans. Subsequently, the British government itself became interested in his exploits and sponsored and protected with armed men his expedition to the same area, to solve the dispute over the mouth of the Niger. Taking with him gifts and enough food provisions, Park embarked for Africa in 1805. As he navigated the Niger River, the explorer was attacked by African warriors, and, to escape death, he allegedly jumped into the river at a narrow point and drowned on the rapids at Bussa. His death did not deter others, however, and a number of explorers crisscrossed the continent in search of similar sensational stories for European audiences, government bureaucrats, and business investors.

[margin: adventure/pioneers]

David Livingstone, a Scottish member of the London Missionary Society, humanitarian, and medical doctor, left England in 1840 (at the age of twenty-seven) and travelled across Southern and Central Africa three times from 1851 to his death in Africa in 1873, thus becoming the most celebrated European explorer. Unlike Park's accounts, Livingstone's writings show both great sensitivity toward African suffering and respect for African traditions. Between 1854 and 1855, British explorer Richard Burton, although seriously wounded, travelled through Somalia and Ethiopia to reach Lake Tanganyika, Dahomey, and the Cameroon coast. John Speke, Burton's companion at one time, travelled with James Grant, and proved, during a second expedition, in 1861-1863, that Victoria Nyanza was the major source of the White Nile. In 1864, Samuel White Baker happily reached Lake Albert. Other explorers followed these pioneers.

In 1871, Henry Morton Stanley, working for the *New York Herald* in search of Dr. Livingstone (who was presumed dead or lost), reached Ujiji, Tanganyika, where he found the missionary alive, but sick. In subsequent years, Stanley returned to Central Africa on behalf of King Leopold II of Belgium for whom he carved, often through fraudulent and forced treaties and war, the Belgian Congo (now the Democratic Republic of Congo), in 1876. He also visited Lake Victoria and Buganda, and followed the Zaire (Congo) River from its source to its mouth. In 1873, Verney Lovett Cameron became the first European to cross Africa from east to west. German explorer Henry Barth, working for Britain (1850-1852), explored Western and Central Sudan, while Gerhard Rohlfs crossed the Atlas Mountains in Morocco and eventually reached Libya, Chad, and Ethiopia.

Joseph Thompson visited Lakes Nyanza and Tanganyika in 1879-1889, crossed Masailand (1883-1884), reached Central Sudan, and Southern Morocco, and explored the Zambezi River basin. At the same time, German missionaries John Kraft and John Rebman, members of the Church Missionary Society, became the first Europeans to see the highest mountain in Africa, Kilimanjaro (19,000 feet high) in 1848, and recorded their encounter with the Chagga on the mountain's slopes. Present-day Northern Nigeria and Lake Chad were visited, among others, by Major Dixon Danham and Captain Hugh Clapperton (the only one to reach Kano and Sokoto, where he was received by Sultan Bello) between 1821 and 1825, after crossing the Sahara from Tripoli. Between 1820 and 1827, French explorer Rene Caillie, after learning to speak Arabic, travelled to Senegal and Sierra Leone disguised as an Egyptian, thus becoming the first European to reach Timbuktu, from where he proceeded, across the desert, to Morocco.

Many other adventurers such as Pierre Savorgnan de Brazza, who travelled to the Congo (later Congo-Brazzaville) under French auspices, and Portuguese Alexandre Serpa Pinto (who crossed Central Africa from Angola to Pretoria, South Africa, in 1877) scattered throughout the continent of Africa, most of them supported by European governments and scientific societies such as the Geographic Society of Paris, the Geographic Society of Lisbon, and Leopold II's International African Association. Overall, this proved to be a period of excitement and novelty for the Europeans (and not the Africans who knew their continent), as they established new contacts and satisfied their cultural curiosity.

Several conclusions can be made of the age of exploration, as the 1788-1885 period has been called. Although explorers such as Barth and Livingstone were humanitarian at heart, most had travelled to Africa for cultural and scientific curiosity as well as for profit. As Robert Rotberg puts it in *Africa and Its Explorers* (1973), most of the explorers were "infected to a great degree with the microbe of prejudice" and almost all posed as "explorers first, geographers second, natural scientists third, and humanists last." As a result of their strong ethnocentrism, their accounts were, by and large, derogatory to Africans—notwithstanding the fact that they could never have completed their assignments were it not for the hospitality of the Africans who provided them with the information they needed, housed, fed, and protected them, and showed them the route to their next destination.

Clearly, their adventures became sources for a wealth of information about Africa's geography, cultures, and the degree of African cultural advancement and technological conditions, as well the nature of the continent's resources (rubber, cotton, coffee, iron, gold, diamonds, palm and peanut oil, ivory, fish, animal skins), all of which could enhance the European "industrial revolution." Thus, through their activities, European explorers unwittingly paved the way for the eventual conquest of Africa, initiated formally at the Conference of Berlin in 1884-1885. Finally, it must be noted that most of the explorers alerted the European community to the continuation of slavery and the slave trade on the continent, practiced mainly by Arabs or Islamic African authorities in Western and Central Africa (at such places as Chad and Sudan) and in North Africa. This concern became part of the Act of the Berlin Conference which urged the colonial powers to eradicate the vestiges of the trade in human beings in newly acquired territories. Proving the dictum that knowledge is power, Europeans then embarked on subjugating the peoples they had just "discovered."

To the African, however, the explorers were non-entities and, by and large, they remained ignored in the places they visited. Indeed, they did very little to expand African knowledge of other parts of the continent and did not contribute significantly to the expansion of commerce which, at the time, was already quite extensive. Consequently, as Rotberg stresses, almost no explorer is remembered in oral traditions. Thus, Rotberg further notes of the African attitudes towards the new visitors:

> The explorers were worthy bearers of tribute and, conceivably, representatives of powerful monarchs, but, with one or two exceptions, they created no sensations and were received with (sometimes impolite) curiosity and affection of a kind usually reserved for visiting men of commerce. The least powerful were occasionally mistreated, robbed, and bullied. All were made to experience the sense of their inferiority.

In a sense, therefore, insofar as the Africans were concerned, the explorers were like a footnote in the history of their lives. In the long-run, however, the explorers made a difference.

Until 1884, Europeans had not formally divided Africa among themselves, although, as early as the sixteenth century, some governments had claimed spheres of influence and economic and political monopoly over certain areas. Thus, France, for example, as early as the eighteenth century, had considered Senegal, Gabon (1849), Algeria (1830), and Tunisia (1881), as her domain, while Britain claimed Sierra Leone (proclaimed a Crown Colony in 1808), the Cape Colony in South Africa, the Gambia area, Lagos (annexed in 1861), the Gold Coast (declared a colony in 1874 after long and fierce fighting with the Ashanti Confederation) and Egypt (made a protectorate by force in 1882). Whereas, on the one hand, Leopold II of Belgium had, since 1876, maintained brutal economic control over the Congo (recognized by other European powers in 1884 as the "Congo Free State"); the Portuguese, on the other, had all along claimed that Angola, Mozambique, Cape Verde, São Tomé e Principe, and Guinea-Bissau were part of their colonial empire as early as the fifteenth century. By 1884, several European powers became keenly interested in colonial acquisitions in Africa as sources of raw materials and cheap labor, as pawns of diplomacy, and as outlets for national frustrations. In an attempt to prevent conflicts that could eventually lead to war among themselves, European governments agreed to formalize their territorial wishes and to partition Africa at the Berlin Conference, hosted by the Chancellor of unified Germany, Otto von Bismarck, between November 1884 and February 1885.

Attending the Conference were delegates from fourteen nations who agreed on the following terms as guidelines for the peaceful division of Africa: 1) proof of effective control of a territory (through an army of occupation, demonstrable treaties with African kings and chiefs, or a proven administrative apparatus); 2) free trade and free navigation on the Congo and Niger basins (then contended areas for international trade); 3) a vigorous campaign to end slavery and the slave trade in one's territory; and 4) recognition of the right of all Christian denominations, regardless of origin, to open missionary outposts in colonial territories.

As a result of the Conference (at which Africans were not represented), from 1885 to 1905 Africa was divided into some fifty-five or so small colonies, quite often carved in European capitals without regard to cultural links among the people conquered. Instead, rivers, lakes, and mountains were used as boundaries, with the lion's share going to France and Britain, followed by Portugal (5 colonies), Germany (4), Spain (3), and Italy (Eritrea, Italian Somaliland, and Libya, the latter annexed in 1911–1912). Only Liberia, which remained protected by the United States, and Ethiopia (except for the 1935–1941 period, when it was annexed by Benito Mussolini), escaped colonial conquest.

Africans, learning of the impact of the Berlin Conference, violently opposed the loss of their sovereignty and land. Wars of resistance erupted in Dahomey, Chad, and Madagascar, against the French; in Angola, and Mozambique (until 1917), against the Portuguese; in Tanganyika (the Maji Maji Rebellion of 1905–1907 being a good example) and South-West Africa (the Herero revolts), against the Germans; in the Gold Coast, against the British; and in Northern and Southern Rhodesia (in the 1890s), against Cecil Rhodes's British South Africa Company. The Italians were defeated by the Abyssinians (Ethiopians) at Adowa in 1896, while Sudanese Muslim nationalists, known as Madhists, fought against the British and the Egyptians in the 1880s. During these wars of resistance, Europeans often suffered heavy casualties, but ultimately their superior military technology and a lack of concerted and sustained resistance proved fatal to Africa's independence. By the 1920s, Europeans had, for all practical purposes, "pacified" the whole continent.

The interesting question is: why did the "scramble" for Africa occur in the 1880s and later rather than during the earlier period of European contact with Africa? While some historians emphasize economic reasons, some stress nationalistic motives, and others refuse to advance a theory of a single cause to explain this unprecedented imperialist frenzy about Africa. Those who stress economic factors usually repeat a modified version of the thesis developed by John Hobson, derived mainly from his 1902 study of the Boer War (1899–1902). Hobson, a British laissez-faire economist, claimed that Europe had industrialized itself during the nineteenth century, through a process that required expanded raw materials, new markets for goods resulting from overproduction, and investment for the surplus capital accumulated by successful businesses and factories. The implied (hardly proven) assumption of most economic theorists has been that capitalism cannot regenerate itself, and that its profits tend to decline over the years, leading to its eventual demise. This is also essentially how the followers of Karl Marx tend to explain European imperialism. Hobson, however, maintained that, while capitalism was by nature democratic, imperialism was anti-democratic, and that the latter resulted from the former's "financial" problems (usually resolvable). V.I. Lenin, on the other hand, called imperialism "the highest stage of capitalism." He wrote:

> Imperialism is capitalism in that stage of development in which the dominance of monopolies and finance capital has established itself; in which the export of capital has acquired pronounced importance; in which the division of the world among the international trusts has begun; in which the division of all territories of the globe among the great capitalist powers has been completed.

Marxists and neo-Marxists have continued to blame bourgeois capitalists for the evils of imperialism, predicting the demise of capitalism and the political and economic take-over by the proletariat, a phase which would lead the world to socialism or to communism, the perfect stage in man's economic and social evolution.

Other analysts, on the contrary, note that economic motives for imperialism cannot apply to countries such as Portugal, Spain, and Italy which experienced very little industrialization at the time. These scholars prefer, therefore, to explain the European desire to build vast overseas empires as a way to ensure national greatness and survival in a competing world, as was the case of Portugal. Accordingly, France's major preoccupation was to regain its lost prestige resulting from the defeat of Emperor Napoleon III at the hands of the Germans in 1870, and the loss of Alsace-Lorraine. The unification of Germany in 1870–1871 worsened French fears that France would be reduced to a minor power as Spain was. This is the reason, these theorists note, why France was willing to annex even the poorest areas in Africa—Chad, Mali, Mauritania, Upper Volta (now Burkina Faso), and Oubangui-Chari (now Central African Republic).

This is also the argument presented by American historian Carlton J.H. Hays who, while not denying the influence of capitalists in the imperialist frenzy, maintained that "basically the new imperialism was a nationalistic phenomenon" and that "in the last analysis it was the nationalistic masses who made possible and who most vociferously applauded it and most constantly backed it." A similar thesis was held by Nicholas Mansergh, British historian, who wrote that "The rulers of Europe thought primarily in terms of political not economic advantage," preoccupied with a continental balance of power. Accordingly, those espousing the nationalistic theory like to trace imperialism back to the year 1870 (rather than 1884) which marks France's defeat and the beginning of German unification. While scholars advocating economic motives consider the second industrial revolution of the 1870s as the most important landmark, those stressing diplomacy see the Berlin Conference of 1884–1885 as crucial to the understanding of the phenomenon.

Harvard historian William Langer, skeptical of the claim that imperialism was a result of capitalism, argued, instead, that psychological factors must be taken into account. He noted, for example, that most European investment did not go to the colonies but to America and Australia, and that investment returns were not encouraging to those who invested in the colonies. Consequently, he praises economist Joseph Schumpter, mentioned earlier, who defined imperialism as "the objectless disposition on the part of a state to unlimited forcible expansion" and maintained that capitalism was intrinsically anti-imperialistic.

Recent analysts, however—political scientist Hanna Arendt being one of the most widely known exponents—tend to consider a combination of economic, nationalist, and religious factors, as well as (scientific and cultural) curiosity, as the reasons why Europe partitioned Africa at the time it did. This is also how D.K. Fieldhouse argues, for example, when he concludes in his *Problems and Perspectives in History: The Theory of Capitalist Imperialism* (1967) that "there is only one possible way to explain the phenomenon of imperialism: to begin by studying as fully as possible the general forces operating within Europe [the perimeter] and in other parts of the world [the periphery] to study each particular case of annexation as a special problem..." He goes on to say that:

> In some cases economic motives may seem to have predominated; in others political or idealistic motives. But the sum of these multiple investigators is the nearest the historian can come to achieving a general explanation of the tendency of Europe to expand after about 1870. Anything more comprehensive will almost certainly be misleading.

R. E. Robinson and J. A. Gallagher (both British historians) in their *Britain and the Partition of Africa* (1961), developed the periphery approach earlier and essentially argued that strategic reasons, particularly for Britain, played the major role. The importance of India and South Africa, they claimed, dictated British expansion in Northeast and East Africa, in spite of the fact that British businessmen favored West Africa. It appeared, at that time, that Egyptian and South African nationalism threatened British interests in Asia. This forced Britain to occupy Egypt in 1882, to fight the Boer War from 1899-1902, and to approve the annexation of the Rhodesias by Cecil Rhodes in the 1890s. To Robinson and Gallagher, therefore, capitalism was not in the forefront of the imperialist frenzy. In fact, they add, imperial expansion took place where expectations of profit were least, namely, in East Africa. The debate has underscored the complex nature of imperialism and exposed the shortcomings of unicausal explanations.

Interestingly enough, the partition of Africa occurred without causing a single war among the colonial powers—a credit to the Berlin Conference—at least insofar as the strategy of the planners and the participants of the Conference was concerned, namely, a need to divide the continent without resorting to force against one another. Two instances, however, brought some powers to the brink of war in their colonial disputes and are worth mentioning. One was the Fashoda incident that took place between September 18 and November 3, 1898, when a French expeditionary force (of 7 French and 120 African soldiers) under Captain Jean Baptiste Marchand and a sizeable Anglo-Egyptian force under General Sir Herbert Kitchener, fighting in Sudan (while building a railroad up the Nile simultaneously), under General Sir Herbert Kitchener, met and tensely faced each other on the banks of the Nile river near Fashoda (presently Kodok), and almost fired shots at one another. Both forces were vying for the control of the Nile and Sudan and influence in Egypt. Kitchener ordered Marchand to retreat, which the latter did, in humiliation, on November 3, 1898, both because the French government was not in a position to fight a war at the moment and Marchand's forces had no chance of winning a skirmish no matter how insignificant. Eventually, on March 21, 1899, the French renounced all claims over any territory along the Nile and settled, instead, for unproductive desert areas near present Chad.

The second incident resulted from a dispute between Portugal and Britain over Mashonaland and the Shire river in 1899, following the annexation of the Macololo people by Portuguese explorer Serpa Pinto. The British, who considered the area to be theirs, delivered a threatening ultimatum to Lisbon on January 11, 1899, to which the Portuguese capitulated immediately. In the end, the two colonial powers ratified a treaty settling the boundaries between Mozambique, Nyasaland, and Southern Rhodesia on June 11, 1891, but the capitulation, which brought down the government of Luciano Castro in Lisbon, was and still is viewed by the Portuguese as one of the worst humiliations they have ever suffered.

Diplomacy, therefore, along with the incipient colonial armies that were too small and thinly scattered throughout the continent of Africa contributed to the peaceful nature of the partition among the conquerors but not between the conquerors, the Europeans, and the conquered, the Africans.

Colonial Policies in Africa

Conquering and pacifying the Africans was one thing. Governing and thus transforming them, however, for the benefit of the European colonial powers, was another. Until 1884, Europeans had only maintained limited involvement (and had not interfered) in African traditional life and had secured only "informal rule," slightly felt in matters of religion and aspects of political life, regulated by mutual treaties or by limited wars sometimes won by Europeans and other times by Africans, the British and the Ashanti Confederation wars being a good example.

In order to achieve total control after 1884, Europeans attempted to devise the most appropriate colonial policies that civil servants and Africans in responsible positions in the territories would have to follow. British official policy, devised by Lord Frederick Lugard, Nigeria High Commissioner (1900–1907), became generally known as "indirect rule." Starting from the premise that African cultures were incompatible with British traditions, Britain believed that, unless African political structures and institutions were somewhat preserved and local Europeans acted as advisors to the African authorities, the colonial system could not work. The traditional chiefs and kings in power, therefore, should be maintained, ethnic loyalties and traditions governing marriage and land, for example, allowed to continue, and the use of African languages, even in the few Western schools in the colonies, permitted, all of which would guarantee the success of the colonial experiment, ensure everlasting peace, and require the use of fewer financial resources.

The French and the Portuguese, on the contrary, stressed the premise that all men are born equal and that what makes them different is education and nonsegregated living patterns. Both colonial powers held the view that Africans, as a matter of principle, should undergo "assimilation" and thus qualify to become French or Portuguese citizens. Hence, the Portuguese and the French divided the colonized population into assimilated (*assimilés*, in French, and *assimilados*, in Portuguese) and indigenous. This policy, if applied, however, would have required a great infusion of white administrators and civil servants to replace, whenever possible, African authorities, force the Africans to learn how to speak French or Portuguese, have a profession, and adopt European cultural traits. (Due to criticism, the French, prior to African independence, preferred to use the word "association"—a policy designed to attempt to fuse Africans and Frenchmen in a multiracial society, with much internal autonomy for the colonized. The basic notion of assimilation, however, remained the cornerstone of French policy throughout the colonial period in Africa.)

The other colonial powers vacillated between direct and indirect rule. The Belgians are known to have used a type of direct rule called "paternalism." They viewed Africans as children who had to be taught and told everything by the Europeans and, with the collaboration of the Roman Catholic Church, be given only the rudiments of primary education. Hard physical work, in the form of rubber and cotton collection for concessionaire companies in the Belgian Congo, government projects, cash crop cultivation, and porterage, were enforced by the colonial agents. The Germans also adopted direct rule whenever possible, with the sole purpose of making the Africans produce crops for the colonial master on large plantations and build roads and railroads. The Italians and the Spaniards had no clearly defined colonial policies but they, too, made the Africans work from dawn to sunset.

Thus, despite the apparent differences, colonial powers in Africa had the same objectives, adopted similar strategies, and achieved the same results: the exploitation of the Africans primarily for the benefit of the mother country and the European colonial settlers. All European powers were interested in "modernizing" the Africans and making them more Europeanized to facilitate the exploitation of the local resources. They all established an army, a police force, and a network of informants to maintain law and order and crush any possible rebellion. They all forced the Africans to pay taxes in cash (most often in the form of head or household taxes), which mostly benefited the European population. Considering the Africans to be naturally lazy, the French, the Portuguese, the Belgians, the Spaniards, and the Germans introduced forced labor. Although the British officially claimed to be against it, they indirectly forced the Africans to work to earn the cash that would enable them to pay taxes.

As a result of these policies, the educational levels of Africans under any of the colonial powers were not very different prior to 1945. Although the British encouraged maintenance of cultural traditions, educated Africans in their colonies were not very different from those from other colonies in their outlook, and most admired European culture and were eager to live abroad. In fact, indirect rule worked only where the Africans had strong governments prior to conquest, and mostly on the local level, because all colonies were under governors and civil servants appointed by the metropolitan colonial office. Consequently, recalcitrant kings and chiefs were always removed forcefully or assassinated, and replaced by more accommodating individuals. In the British colonies, the appointed authorities, known as "warrant chiefs," had no traditional legitimacy. In fact, British colonials were so obsessed with maintaining law and order along their ethnocentric tradition that they forced such people as the Ibo and the Maasai, who never had chiefs, to have them.

The official colonial policies, however, provided the Africans a differing status, at least on paper, within the colonial context. The British always considered the Africans "subjects" and never citizens of the empire who could have representation in Parliament. The French and the Portuguese considered the few assimilated Africans "citizens," enjoying all the rights of European citizens, who by law could not be discriminated against, and had representation in the metropolitan National Assembly (although, in Lisbon, the representatives of the colonial people remained white Portuguese citizens). The Belgians, on their part, wished neither to make the Africans "citizens" nor to educate them beyond primary school. Those who completed primary schooling were known as "evolués" (the evolved ones), who were neither European nor totally African. It would be inconceivable, however, that the Germans, who despised even other Europeans on the continent, would have attempted to make the Africans "citizens," lifting them from the inferior beings that they were in the eyes of the colonial administrators.

Overall, one ought to bear in mind that, throughout the colonial period, the losers were the African masses, regardless of the colonial system under which they lived. All colonial systems were meant to benefit the Europeans; they segregated and discriminated against the Africans; they exploited their subjects economically; and established, instead, small colonial "dictatorships"—a situation that continued until 1945. Thus, the French "mission civilisatrice" (civilizing mission) or the British "altruistic" claim of the "burden of empire" turned out to be nothing more than subjugation, exploitation, and oppression.

Impact of Colonial Rule in Africa

The overall political, economic, social, and cultural impact of colonialism on Africa is still being debated in academic circles. One can say, however, that the impact was profound. Politically, the traditional state systems were superseded forcibly by new political entities bringing together diverse ethnic and linguistic groups—the colonies—which later became the new states of Africa. Stateless societies were, at first, compelled, contrary to their tradition, to accept the authority of one man and later forced to be fused with the colonial state. Until the coming of independence, traditional authorities had either been kept in their positions, as was the tendency in the British colonies, or replaced, as was more customary in the French, Belgian, and Portuguese colonial territories. In most cases, however, African authorities, while deprived of their legitimacy before their own people, received further powers and were backed by their own police forces which made them extremely vulnerable in their own areas because they were seen as tools of colonialism. Their new responsibilities included collecting taxes, recruiting manpower for forced labor and the military, and enforcing the cultivation of certain cash crops in their region.

In every colony, political expressions of any kind against the colonial regime were strictly forbidden until the post-Second World War period. Although in the British colonies some Africans were appointed to the governor's legislative councils and, in the French colonies, chosen as delegates (*députés*) to represent their homelands, colonized people did not participate in the decision-making process prior to 1945. In the Portuguese colonies, for example, Europeans represented Africans in Lisbon, while in the Belgian, German, and Italian territories African representation was never a concern of the administrators.

The issue of taxes and cash crop cultivation has already been mentioned. By and large, however, taxes did not benefit the Africans, and the cash crops made the newly carved territories dependent on one or two commodities that, following independence, became a source of problems when Africans made an attempt to diversify the economy. Furthermore, international fluctuation of consumer needs and resulting prices made African economies vulnerable to external forces, and the emphasis on exports overlooked the real needs of the Africans. Major business enterprises (banks, commercial houses, shipping, and mining, for example) remained in the hands of Europeans or Asians (Lebanese, Syrians, Pakistanis, and Indians), a trend that continued even following independence. Before the 1960s, little capital was invested in Africa and the concessionaire companies such the Royal Nigeria Company, the Societé Comerciale de l'Ouest Africain (in French West Africa), and the Mozambique Company in Mozambique secured monopolies over the cultivation and export of products such as cotton, and did little to assist the Africans or develop the regions where they operated. Quite often, the concessionaires contributed little to local taxes.

It should also be noted that emphasis on exports favored the processing of products abroad, thus depriving the Africans of industrial plants. Railways and harbors were built but only to facilitate the export of goods from a productive area to European plants and markets. In general, until the 1940s, Africans remained a large reservoir of cheap labor for the government, the European companies, and the enterprises of Asian expatriates.

Socially, colonialism increased intercommunication and commercial links on the continent, established new cities and towns, and provided the first "modern" educational opportunities and health facilities. However, opportunities were available to only a few—to certain ethnic groups, to wealthy Africans, and to sons (and sometimes daughters) of traditional authorities—a process that resulted in the emergence of an elite that was more European than African in outlook. The migrations to the cities by young men and women deprived the villages of necessary work to sustain the family, imposing more responsibilities on village women. The lure of the city— education, health, jobs, and good living—was often an illusion which contributed to poverty, despair, slums and ghettos, prostitution, and crime. During this social transformation, individualism began to replace African communalistic traditions, although voluntary associations initiated by co-ethnic and co-regional African individuals emerged in many colonies, especially in West Africa.

By design as well as from adverse circumstances, colonial administrators did little to alleviate the suffering of the Africans, and, up until the 1940s, very few schools had been built to educate the colonial subjects or assimilable citizens. Invariably, emphasis was on primary education to train interpreters, auxiliaries or assistants, teachers, and catechists (for the Christian missions). Thus, for example, up until 1918, in French West Africa, only the Ecole Normale William Ponty (in Dakar) provided meaningful education to the few Africans selected to attend it and become teachers. In fact, by 1909, there were only 190 primary schools throughout French West Africa, with 1,000 students enrolled. The British did not do any better, although Fourah Bay College, in Sierra Leone, founded by missionaries in 1814, had become a teacher and missionary training college by 1827. (After 1918, some Fourah Bay College graduates received further academic training in England.)

In the health area, initially, health facilities were designed to serve the European population. This pattern changed after World War I, particularly in the French and British colonies. By 1936, for example, the French had trained 185 African doctors for their West African colonies, and, by 1938, Nigeria and Ghana, had fourteen and eight doctors respectively. Campaigns against sleeping sickness, leprosy, malaria, and other tropical diseases were underway particularly after World War I, and, in places such as Cameroon, Chad, and the Gambia, Africans did benefit from these efforts. Overall, however, the effort was too little and the problems enormous, and thus the majority of the Africans remained untouched by Western innovations.

Culturally, the introduction of Christianity resulted in thousands of converts and the further erosion of African traditional practices such as polygamy and the concept of the extended family, which were a protection against age, adverse social changes, and natural calamities. Christianity did, however, train many Africans in its schools, some of whom became the leaders of the new nationalist movements, but it also caused severe psychological and social dislocation, eloquently described by African literary men and women such as Chinua Achebe in his *Things Fall Apart* and *Arrow of God*.

Africans were never, of course, simple onlookers, who peacefully accepted colonial domination. Throughout Africa, prior to 1945, there were wars and revolts, strikes, and demonstrations, refusals to work for colonial administrators and to serve in the army, and several attempts at organizing parties to fight colonial oppression and repression. The National Congress of British West Africa (founded in the Gold Coast in 1920 with Casely Hayford as its first president) and the Young Kikuyu Association (founded by Harry Thuku in Nairobi in 1921) were two examples of such organizations. However, the power and the control of the colonial apparatus were overwhelming, and only in the aftermath of World War II did Africans begin to pose a greater threat to the very foundations of the colonial state.

Summary

The demise of the slave trade and slavery helped the Europeans to develop a new interest in the African continent, clearly manifested in geographical and cultural curiosity, which led to the age of exploration at the end of the eighteenth century. The travels and the resulting accounts by explorers such as Mungo Park, David Livingstone, Richard Burton, and Heinrich Barth removed most of the mystery about Africa, exposed its political weaknesses, but revealed the continent's hidden resources. As Europe experienced the industrial revolution (1760-1914), capitalists needed precious raw materials to feed their factories and machinery as well as new opportunities to invest surplus capital and new markets to sell their goods. The extreme nationalism of the European nation-states resulted in several wars during the nineteenth century, forcing countries such as France, defeated by the Germans in 1870 (who also took Alsace-Lorraine from France and made it a part of a new unified Germany), to look for empires overseas as a way to redress national humiliation.

Portugal, Italy, and Spain, which were not sufficiently industrialized and therefore remained weak powers, combined the economic and nationalistic factors (fearing a loss of their old empires), and looked for further opportunities overseas to restore or maintain their imaginary greatness and national pride. Pressure from businessmen, traders, and missionary societies (as was the case in Germany), as well as from humanitarians who wished to see Africans "civilized" and saved from their supposedly barbarous ways and "backward" governments, compelled European powers to agree to hold the Conference of Berlin in 1884, following which they divided the continent among themselves, initiating the period of formal empires. Whereas, until then, they had concentrated their settlements and activities along the coast, now they ventured into the hinterland of Africa, attempting to impose their colonial rule and policies everywhere, primarily to benefit their own metropolitan and settler populations.

Europe's desire to maintain colonial rule promoted the development of major colonial policies: indirect rule, officially applied by the British, whose aim was to rule Africans by using African institutions on the local level. (The truth of the matter, was that indirect rule was earnestly applied only in areas where African leaders had been strongest prior to conquest, such as in northern Nigeria and Buganda); and direct rule, which manifested itself as assimilation in the French and Portuguese colonies and as paternalism in the Belgian Congo (as well as in Rwanda and Burundi following World War I). Although the remaining colonial powers preferred direct rule, quite often circumstances forced them to use indirect rule, economic productivity always being their primary concern.

In spite of the existence of different colonial models, however, the fate of the Africans was not fundamentally different, particularly among the non-educated majority, which was miserably exploited through taxes, forced labor, military service, and cultivation of certain export crops. It is clear, however, that the greatest impact of colonial rule occurred along the coast, where Europeans, until the end of World War II, succeeded in introducing an administrative structure of their own and their flag, built administrative centers to conduct civil service, and a few schools, created a police force and an army of officers who played more than a military role and created strategic economic networks, eventually linked by road and rail leading to the ocean in order to facilitate the export of commodities to Europe.

In the hinterland, such as in Northern Nigeria, Northern Cameroon, Northern Chad, and Northern Mozambique, where Islamic states were well organized and strong, the European conqueror left the systems almost intact. The difficulty in travel, the hostile climate, and the fierce resistance of the Muslims to the "white infidels," as they used to call the Europeans, forced colonial agents to cooperate with the traditional authorities. It can be accurately said, therefore, that colonial rule had to "adapt" to political realities rather than "dictate" its own policies in the African upcountry.

Study Questions and Activities

1. What motivated European exploration of Africa during the nineteenth century and what was its impact upon Europe and Africa?
2. Why did the Conference of Berlin take place at the time it did and not earlier? What was its effect upon Europe and Africa?
3. How did Africans react to the partition of their continent?
4. Explain the various colonial policies in Africa and how they affected the African people.
5. If you had to choose one among the various colonial policies, which would you consider the worst of all? Explain.

References

Hanna Arendt. *Imperialism.* New York: Harcourt, 1968.

Adu Boahen. *Topics in West African History.* London: Longmans, 1969.

Paul Bohannan and Philip Curtin. *Africa and Africans.* Prospect Heights, IL: Waveland, 1988.

Basil Davidson. *Modern Africa.* London: Longmans, 1987.

D.K. Fieldhouse. *The Colonial Empires from the Eighteenth Century.* New York: Delta Book, 1965.

————. *Problems and Perspectives in History: The Theory of Capitalist Imperialism.* London: Longmans, 1967.

Murray Greene. "Schumpeter's Imperialism—A Critical Note." *Social Research, An International Quarterly of Political Science,* vol. XIX (December 1952): 453-463.

Carlton Hays. *A Generation of Materialism, 1871–1900*. New York: Harper and Brothers, 1941.

John Hobson. *Imperialism: A Study*. London: George Allen and Unwin, 1902.

John Iliff. The African Poor: A History. Cambridge: Cambridge University Press, 1987.

E. Jefferson. *History of African Civilization*. New York: Delta Book, 1972.

William Langer. "A Critique of Imperialism." *Foreign Affairs*, vol. XIV (October 1935): 102-115.

V. I. Lenin. *Imperialism: The Highest Stage of Capitalism*. New York: International Publishers Co., 1939.

Nicholas Mansergh. *The Coming of the First World War: A Study in the European Balance*. London: Longmans, Green, and Co., 1949.

R. E. Robinson and J. A. Gallagher. *Britain and the Partition of Africa*. London: Macmillan, 1961.

Walter Rodney. How Europe Underdeveloped Africa. Washington, DC: Howard University Press, 1972.

Robert Rotberg. *Africa and its Explorers: Motives, Methods, and Impact*. Cambridge, MA: Harvard University Press, 1973.

Harrison Wright. *The New Imperialism, Analysis of Late Nineteenth-Century Expansion*. Boston: D.C. Heath and Company, 1961.

7

Civil War to Civil Rights: The Quest for Freedom and Equality

Marsha Jean Darling

Introduction

This chapter explores the impetus, values, attitudes, behaviors, and achievements that have defined and focused African American progress from the period immediately following the Civil War—generally referred to as the Reconstruction era—to the years of the Civil Rights movement. African American efforts to promote economic, political and cultural self-reliance are identified and delineated as the cornerstone foundation of an evolving African American ethos. The chapter also identifies the ideology of white supremacy as a significant factor in the evolution of a white "race consciousness" that has, throughout the period of time under consideration in this chapter, generated opposition to African American progress and development. Consequently, the following analysis explores the emergence of a black protest tradition, dating from the earliest African resistance to enslavement to the contemporary continuation of efforts to realize civil rights.

Historians of the nineteenth and twentieth century differ in their perceptions of how to present black life and culture. Some scholarship of the period emphasizes the impact of white values, institutions, and actions on African American choices, attitudes, and behaviors. While scholarship in this tradition identifies many of the difficulties black Americans have encountered in their direct efforts at a meaningful and enfranchised citizenship, the perspective in these works often emphasizes white activity and black passivity. Blacks are depicted as static, passive, and totally victimized, while whites, though acting out views of white race supremacy, are seen as initiating, active, and totally in control. In contrast, other scholarship exists that emphasizes the positive attributes and endeavors that African Americans have pursued, even while indicating the obstacles and struggles that blacks confronted in their attempts to realize a first class citizenship. Much of the scholarship in this tradition explores the tensions that emerged and developed within African American communities to define strategies for change as well as the obstacles from outside the culture of being a black American.

This chapter places African Americans at the center of their own experience. Essentially, that is to say, that African American history from 1865 to the present is a narrative rendering of black struggle, progress, black creative initiative, black accommodation, black protest struggle, black militancy and black progress. Indeed, the complexity of black folks' lives must be understood to have entailed a long-standing commitment to self-help, mutual aid, and benevolence, initially against the backdrop of their involvement in a strident anti-slavery movement, and later against the backdrop of black peoples' struggles against racism, sexism, and other forms of oppression.

Major terms and concepts: Quest for self-determination, African American protest tradition, Emancipation, the betrayal of Reconstruction, Constitutional Amendments as reforms, forty acres and a mule, franchise and elective political participation, civil rights and a desire for literacy, white resistance to black progress, disfranchisement, landmark court decisions, articulation of black male and female leadership to serve post-emancipation needs, cashless debt peonage, migration, separate and unequal, state's complicity in undermining African American economic and political development, the Harlem Renaissance, blacks in the military, the Civil Rights movement, Affirmative Action.

Reconstruction: Education, Leadership, and the "Negro" Movement

Against the backdrop of the Civil War years, with its outcome of emancipation from enslavement, African Americans eagerly engaged in the pursuit of liberty, justice under the law, political equality, economic development, the acquisition of literacy, mutual self-help, and nation-building. The processes of developing self-reliant African American communities was and continues to be fraught with a number of complexities and challenges. Most notably, white racial opposition has, over time, generated significant opposition to African American self-reliance and self-determination. Although the evolution of a self-help consciousness pre-dates the Reconstruction years, emancipation from slavery served to expand the options and possibilities for African Americans to engage in activities on a scale unprecedented in the antebellum or pre-Civil War period. This chapter explores the African American quest for self-development by examining the goals, activities and setbacks that exist in the historical record.

By the end of 1865, three-fourths of the state legislatures had accepted the Thirteenth Amendment to the United States Constitution, making the abolition of slavery and emancipation national in scope and irreversible. The Thirteenth Amendment to the Constitution dramatically altered the Constitution and the prevailing understanding of the responsibility of the federal government to African American men and women living in individual states. Southern states had previously enjoyed unfettered privileges and rights with regard to the legal and political rights of their enslaved and free black populations, especially in their ability to shelter and justify chattel slavery, and further to arbitrate and enforce the absence of any rights and privileges not only for enslaved African Americans, but also, increasingly, for the populations of varying sizes of free blacks. With the Thirteenth Amendment, Congress mandated that the rights of African Americans to liberty was fundamentally more important than the rights of states to hold blacks in slavery. Thus, the abolition of slavery also brought about a sweeping reinterpretation of the relationship between individuals, states, and the national government.

While congressional and presidential changes on the national level were received with approval and appreciation, it was also true that African Americans had themselves long agitated for the demise of slavery. A long and persistent effort to abolish slavery characterized the efforts of both free blacks as well as those free and enslaved who labored to strengthen the effectiveness of the Underground Railroad. Indeed, in mentioning the anti-slavery movement, one should remember the existence of a rather substantial free black population, committed to slavery's demise, who lived in the South. According to historians of the period, as many as 250,000 free blacks lived and worked in the cities and towns of the antebellum South. The existence of productive and viable black communities that predated emancipation proved vital to anti-slavery efforts, as well as to efforts to facilitate the adjustments freed African American women and men undertook as they embraced their emancipation freedom.

Reconstruction, or the reconstitution of economic, political, and social relations in the South, proved a complex and complicated undertaking. White Southerners, having gone to war to preserve a way of life that included holding more than 4 million black people in chattel slavery, wanted to begin again, with as little deviation from the antebellum norm as possible. Whites had used chattel slavery to order and define the economic, political, and social relationships between the two races, principally in the South, but also, by extension, in those areas of the country where the negative treatment accorded free blacks often derived from the racism set into motion by white people's perceptions of black potential and status as a consequence of slavery. For white Southerners, eradicating slavery meant eliminating the justification basis for the disparate treatment of black men and women.

Almost all white Southerners strongly opposed accepting African Americans as equals. Almost overnight, white paramilitary terrorist groups like the Ku Klux Klan that operated outside the law sprang up to physically harass and persecute blacks and progressive whites. In addition to extra-legal attempts to intimidate and deny legal, political rights, and economic opportunities to African Americans, racist white Southerners persistently engaged efforts to further a racial definition of existence that cut across class and gender lines. For instance, where working class organizing to improve agricultural working conditions might have appeared a rational alternative to the absence of any organized self-interest efforts, white race supremacy propaganda in the South effectively distanced most working class whites from any willingness to see their class interests as similar to those of black agricultural workers, or tenant farmers.

African Americans had waited a long time for an end to slavery and for the opportunity to move toward citizenship, political participation, and economic development. Black newspapers and bulletins, letters, petitions, and testimony before congressional committees are only some of the primary sources that provide ample historical documentary to the intensity and commitment of African American thought and action. African Americans pressed and lobbied to obtain the same rights and opportunities accorded white Americans. As such, African Americans have been actively involved in promoting civil rights from the years following the Civil War right through to this day. Significantly, African American efforts and achievements in promoting civil rights reform have always benefitted all other Americans, even as the quest for justice, due process, protection under the law, liberty, and the pursuit of first class citizenship have emerged as the centerpiece of social protest movements moved along principally by black women and men.

African Americans actively sought involvement in influencing congressional decision making in the months preceding the Freedmen's Bureau Act of 1866, ratification of the Fourteenth and Fifteenth Amendments to the Constitution in 1867 and 1868, the Civil Rights Act of 1866 and 1873, and the anti-Clansmen Act. It is clear from primary sources and secondary accounts of the period that African Americans and progressive whites moved the Congress, the Republican Party and organizations like the Union League, to legislate and promote radical changes in the ordering of legal, political, economic, and social institutions in American society.

Where African Americans did not have legal and political rights, the Fourteenth Amendment defined citizenship, the rights, and responsibilities of states and the federal government in their respective relationships to individual rights. Where African Americans did not have meaningful legal protections from the excesses of vagrancy laws and black codes enacted by southern localities, Congress enacted a Civil Rights Act on March 14, 1866, and passed it over President Johnson's veto on April 6 and April 9. Where African Americans did not have the ability to involve themselves in political elections and legislative proceedings, the Fifteenth Amendment gave voting rights to half of African American adults by granting the franchise to black males. Where the Democratic Party in the South identified itself with the ideology of white supremacy, the Republican Party and the Union League reflected black political aspirations and interests.

It is important to note the activist efforts of African Americans and the advocacy efforts of those who worked on behalf of progress for freed persons and the nation using moral persuasion, appeals to democratic ideals, morality, and rational business sense in their appeals for assistance to the newly emancipated African Americans. Many were concerned that, without financial equity, land, the vote, legal rights and protections, African Americans would continue under the austere conditions imposed by angry Southern whites, who, having lost the institution of chattel slavery, sought to replace it with vagrancy laws, black codes, and, later, with grandfather clauses, restrictive state constitutions, poll taxes, requirements that black voters recite verbatim sections of the U.S. Constitution, and all-white primaries.

It bears placing African American activism and the work of advocates in the context that governed the day by remembering that the vast majority of African Americans were poor, landless, and illiterate. The primary goals of African American men and women was the acquisition of land—40 acres and a mule—and inclusion in racially segregated and exclusionary labor unions, as the basis for economic stability, the vote as a means to acquire political representation, and literacy as a vehicle for intellectual development and artistic achievement. While the promise and opportunity of Reconstruction was ripe for restitution to a people aggrieved by two hundred and forty-five years of enslavement, on compensation or restitution was awarded to African Americans. Indeed, in an economy driven by property relations as the basis for the acquisition of wealth, the absence of a homestead for black families severely restricted the ability of African Americans to pro-

[handwritten: "lack of Home ob problem"]

tect the freedoms granted through Emancipation. History makes clear that, without the land reform that was called for by many, African Americans called themselves free, but found themselves financially dependent on the very Southern whites who wanted to return the South as nearly as possible to slavery days.

Historians refer to the absence of an economic program to benefit African Americans and the resulting disfranchisement, physical violence—lynching, raping—against blacks, emergence of a debt peonage system called the crop-lien system, and the removal of federal troops and marshals (to enforce the constitutional amendments and statutory laws) from the South, as the betrayal of Reconstruction. Although revisionist American historiography asserts that African Americans were freed with little, if any financial resources, one ought to keep in mind that, for quite some time, historians sympathetic to the Old South and its racial credo argued that Reconstruction was a failure because blacks, northern white "carpetbaggers," and southern white "treasoners" nearly ruined the moral, financial, and political order that had shaped the South. These historians—Ulrich B. Phillips, for example—concluded that slavery had been good for blacks and the South, and furthermore, that the emergence of the legal and extralegal means to return the South to white control were justified means to bring about a resurgence of "white civilization." *[handwritten margin: "share cropp"]*

The disparity between the possibilities of the post-war years and the reality were quite stark reminders to African Americans that racism occupied a central place in American thought and action. While black Americans made steady progress toward employment, entrepreneurship, the acquisition of land, and institution building—churches, lodges, clubs, schools, colleges, and universities, sororal and fraternal orders, burial and life insurance companies, and philanthropic and mutual aid societies—the constraints imposed by a virulent racial segregation and exclusion from receiving those opportunities afforded to whites, limited black economic development, employment, access to education, the ballot, quality land, credit, and other financial options and opportunities. A noted historian has compared the process of racially segregating blacks from opportunities to participate in democracy and development as analogous to the creation of apartheid in South Africa. Although aggregate population statistics belie an important overall demographic difference in the two countries, Professor George Frederickson correctly identifies the role of white racism in establishing two separate societies, predicated on inequality, injustice, and lack of economic opportunities and financial options. *[handwritten margin: "limit"]*

According to the U.S. Census of 1870, there were approximately 4,880,009 African Americans, accounting for 12.7 percent of the total U.S. population. Importantly, there were many counties in the South where the concentration of enslaved blacks had far outstripped the numbers of whites in those counties during the antebellum period. A number of those counties remained predominantly black in the post-war period, and the physical intimidation and forced disfranchisement of large numbers of black men, foreclosed the potential for a democratically elected leadership that would have represented black as well as white interests.

History records a brief period of black male electoral participation in the Reconstruction period. Though not a product of black majority demographics, but rather a combination of eager black male voters and white males who voted for the Republican and not the Democratic Party, voter registration under the provisions of the Reconstruction Act of 1867 produced African American males as a

majority of the electors in South Carolina, Georgia, Florida, Alabama, Mississippi, and Louisiana. In addition, some counties and states were demographically
dominated by large numbers of African Americans. For instance, 78,982 African
American males and 46,346 white males registered to vote in South Carolina.
Likewise, 60,167 African American males and 46,636 white males registered to
vote in Mississippi. According to noted chronicler Peter Bergman, 10 counties in
South Carolina and 33 out of 61 counties in Mississippi had a majority of black
male voters.

   The preponderance of African American male voters in Mississippi elected then
Alderman Reverend Hiram R. Revels to the State Senate in 1870; in the same
year, Senator Revels was elected to fill an unexpired seat as a U.S. Senator. Likewise, majority black male voters in Mississippi counties elected U.S. Senator
Blanche K. Bruce (1874), who was the only black male during Reconstruction to
actually serve a regular term in the U.S. Senate. Finally, black voters from Adams
County Mississippi elected John R. Lynch to the State Legislature, where he became Speaker of the House. Active in the Republican Party, Lynch later served
terms in the U.S. House of Representatives from 1873–1877, and again from
1881–1883. While historians often refer to the voting conduct of African Americans and whites, it should be remembered that women were ineligible for suffrage
until the passage of the Nineteenth Amendment to the United States Constitution
in 1920.

   The gains accrued to African Americans during the years in which black men
exercised their right to the franchise included the institution of public schools,
often appearing for the first time in areas of the South. However, as eager as
African Americans were to participate in representing and furthering their own
development by participation in electoral politics, a virulent white racism, combined with growing indifference to violations of the law and the Constitution in
the South, swept away the progressive changes begun in the region. Within a few
years, the ideology of white supremacy again dominated the operation of state
and county development. In such a climate of white racial hysteria, African Americans were disfranchised from their rights under the law. White Southerners either
rewrote the law, ignored civil rights legislation, or denied that African Americans
were ever the subject of the law. The result was the complete segregation of white
and black society, with virtually all the resources for development maintained to
promote separate and unequal development favoring whites only.

   It is often said that law follows social custom. The Supreme Court in 1896 did
exactly as racist whites in the country wanted done. The opinion of the Court in
Plessy vs. Ferguson was that America consisted of two nations, separate in all matters. Mandating what racist whites were already instituting as racial segregation,
and unequal resource allocation and economic development, the Court insisted in
its written decision that blacks and whites would be *separate and equal*. Racism is
never equal, and so progressive people in the nation watched as African Americans
were systematically legally stripped of their right to a first-class citizenship. By the
turn of the century, large numbers of white Americans had repudiated and denied
the Civil Rights Act of 1866 and the Fourteenth and Fifteenth Amendments to the
Constitution, meaning that African American development was abandoned by
most of white America. Decades of African American self-determination and
protest had already preceded the *Plessy* decision; now, the institution of Jim Crow
segregation narrowly confined black expression and visibility.

African Americans were forced to do what no other group in America, except Amerindians, had been forced to do, namely, to aid and assist white development, while receiving little, if any, assistance in developing their own communities. Much of the economic development—that is, industrial, manufacturing, scientific and educational, as well as banking progress—and philanthropic assistance from wealthy white industrialists and financiers went directly to develop and assist white communities. In addition, all branches of government aided and assisted in creating "a white man's country," where tax revenues and government wage differentials and social welfare assistance was distributed in accordance with the prevailing acceptance of the ideology of white supremacy.

In essence, development in America has never been race neutral. From the earliest days of the Republic to the present, development has, with rare and short-lived exceptions, meant that the resources of local, state and federal systems of government, and the fruits of private industry, have always served and abetted white development. Other than the short-lived attempts to improve the opportunities and rights enjoyed by African Americans during the early years of the Reconstruction era, there has only recently (since the 1960s) been any attempt to pursue race-specific development policies and programs that emphasize the development of human potential in black, Amerindian, Hispanic/Latino(a), and Asian communities. The issue of sustainable development for people of color, therefore, is an underutilized development strategy for the country and an unrealized aspect of the expectations of citizenship for African Americans and other people of color. It is precisely because of the disparity between the historical evolution of development advantage and opportunity for whites and the under-development, disadvantage and exclusion from opportunity, that the African American protest tradition is so important a tool or measure for effective and sustainable social change.

Historically, with far fewer resources, and the disparate distribution of public funds, blacks in the South were locked into a cashless debt peonage system, denied their right to representative government—elected through the right to vote—and denied access to education. In classic studies of the development of education in the South, Louis R. Harlan's *Separate and Unequal* (1969), and James D. Anderson's *The Education of Blacks in the South*, 1860–1935 (1988), two noted historians examine the evolution of racial separation and inequality in schooling for African American children across the South, from the years following the Civil War until well into the twentieth century. Both scholars credit African American teachers and black and white philanthropic institutions and individuals with the achievements in acquiring literacy that were made by African Americans.

Literacy rates for African Americans showed steady and committed increase. According to census data, 18.6 percent of African Americans were literate in 1870; in 1880, African American literacy rose to 30 percent, and, by 1890, fully 42.9 percent of African Americans were literate. However, it is important to note that acquiring literacy for Southern blacks remained a serious challenge, and historically black colleges and universities, then as now, have served a vital role. Tuskegee Institute, organized by Booker Taliaferro Washington, Hampton Institute (now University), Fisk University, Howard University, Bennett College, Spelman College, Meharry Medical College, Morehouse College, and many others have, for decades provided both intellectual, philosophical, scientific, theological, agricultural, industrial, and medical training for African Americans. Institutions of higher learning functioned as both centers of teaching and research, and as centers for leadership training. Some of black America's most prominent leaders and thinkers have been the product of black colleges and universities.

Booker Taliaferro Washington was born to a black woman whose legal status also determined the status of all children born to her. As such, Booker T. was born enslaved on a plantation in Virginia in 1858. In his adult years, Booker T. Washington attended school at night while working in coal mines in West Virginia. Later, he enrolled at Hampton Institute, graduating in 1875. After some years of teaching at Wayland Seminary in Washington, D.C., and Hampton Institute, Booker T. Washington was asked to organize a school at Tuskegee, Alabama. Initially working with a $2,000 budget, Washington rapidly developed the new school, emphasizing industrial training which led Tuskegee students to construct forty of the Institute's buildings over the course of twenty years. In those years, Washington gathered a reputation for being a moderate on matters relating to African American involvement in the struggle for political and social rights. Indeed, Booker T. Washington made his position on the subject of black rights in America very clear in his speech in 1895 at the Cotton States Exposition, held in Atlanta, Georgia. Referring directly to his kinsfolk, Washington called for blacks to "...cast down your bucket where you are," and work to develop and build the South.

Seeing the intense poverty in which most Southern blacks lived, Washington's approach traded employment and the possibility of economic self-reliance against the pursuit of political and social rights. Washington was as aware as anyone that the white initiative to disfranchise large numbers, if not all, African Americans living in the South was well underway. In fact, historians believe that Washington's accommodationist position might have contributed to white perceptions that they would meet little organized resistance against their attempts to disfranchise blacks. It has also been suggested that the austere actions of the Supreme Court against Homer Plessy in its landmark decision to establish a racially segregated society, predicated on the very racial inequality that was already so evident, drew cover from Washington's Exposition Speech. In his vision of an economically self-reliant black population, Washington called on blacks to accept the conditions in the South, because, as he suggested in his speech, whites were friends to black people.

Washington's position as an educator and prominent spokesperson in the African American community was expanded to include his influence amongst whites because of his accommodationist posture which brought him immediate approval from whites around the country. Although a number of African American men and women—W. E. B. DuBois, scholar, activist, and editor of *Crisis* magazine; William Monroe Trotter, outspoken editor of the *Boston Guardian*; and anti-lynching crusader Ida B. Wells (and other black women) whose writing and public speaking was later responsible for the formation of the Black Women's Club Movement—disagreed with Washington's position, for still others, Washington's visibility identified him as the national black American leader.

Washington was very concerned about promoting economic self-reliance amongst African Americans and, in 1900, he organized the National Negro Business League. Beginning in about 1899, he embarked on an impressive career as a published writer, authoring a number of books: his autobiography, *Up From Slavery* (1901), *The Future of the American Negro* (c. 1899), *Character Building* (1902), *Working With the Hands* (1904), *Tuskegee and Its People* (1905), *Putting the Most into Life* (1906), *Life of Frederick Douglass* (1907), *The Negro in Busi-*

ness (1907), *The Story of the Negro* (1909), *My Larger Education* (1911), and *The Man Farthest Down: A Record of Observation and Study in Europe* (1912).

Throughout the decades, African Americans have expressed a strong desire to participate fully in economic, social, and cultural development in participatory democracy, giving rise to committed African American male and female leadership. Singular in their emphasis on progress for black people, African American leaders have differed not so much in their objectives or even goals, as much as on their strategies, methods and means. Frightful and threatening challenges faced those African American men and women who took the business of leadership seriously. Where Booker T. Washington identified himself with "accommodationism," one of his fiercest critics was an accomplished scholar, teacher, writer, activist, and statesman named W. E. B. DuBois.

In addition to being a contemporary of Booker T. Washington, and one of Washington's most articulate critics, DuBois rose to a level of national and even international leadership. Born in Great Barrington, Massachusetts in 1868, just after the demise of slavery, William Edward Burghardt DuBois later graduated from Fisk University, receiving a B.A. degree in 1888. Still later in his early adult years, DuBois is recognized as having been the first black American to receive a Ph.D. from Harvard University. To his credit, DuBois entitled his dissertation *The Suppression of the African Slave Trade to the U.S.A.: 1638–1870.* Not only would DuBois distinguish himself as a scholar and writer, undertaking the research for the highly regarded Atlanta Studies that emphasize black self-help and self reliance, but, over the course of many years, he would be seen developing his activism on behalf of African Americans. This occurred initially through the Niagara Movement (founded in 1905), later through his efforts to build and strengthen the NAACP, and still later, through his support for independence movements in Africa. Throughout his adult lifetime, W. E. B. DuBois was known to be an activist on behalf of full legal, political, economic, and social rights for African Americans. In addition, DuBois became identified with the theory of the "talented tenth," which related to the expectations that groups of African Americans who became accomplished and successful would accept the responsibility to provide financial and intellectual leadership for an emerging African American people.

If Booker T. Washington feared white reprisal to the point of avoiding public condemnations of lynching, Ida B. Wells became one of the nation's most outspoken and effective anti-lynching crusaders. Ms. Wells, raised in humble circumstances, would in her adult years work exceedingly hard to be able to buy an interest in *Free Speech*, a publication that she used to give voice to pressing social issues. Wells is perhaps best known for her willingness to use her position as a journalist to publicize the atrocities committed primarily against black men.

Ida B. Wells repeatedly called on the entire nation to demonstrate concern and outrage for the gross violation of human and civil rights practiced as mob violence, often with the consent, involvement or knowledge of law enforcement officials. Indeed, if Ms. Wells had any doubts about the dubious circumstances surrounding many reported as well as unreported lynchings, the lynching death of Thomas Moss, a hard-working Memphis businessman and long time personal associate of hers, crystallized for her an understanding of lynching as a means of white social control. For Ida B. Wells, Moss's brutal slaying reflected the degree to which many whites in Memphis were willing to sabotage black economic and institutional development by killing black entrepreneurs and leaders.

While highly respected by the African American community, Ms. Wells often encountered denial, justification, and ambiguity from whites she approached with a condemnation of lynching. Often the white press accused black men of raping white women, and such reports almost always linked the lynching of black men with allegations of white female rape. So accustomed were whites to viewing black men through racist stereotypes of bestiality established as one of several defenses of slavery, that it must have been nearly impossible to reckon the actual instances of black male violence against white women. According to the research that Wells published in a study that she authored on lynching, only about a third of the 728 black people lynched over the course of ten years had even been accused of rape. Black women's historian Paula Giddings notes that Wells discovered that most of the black men, women and children lynched were murdered for "incendiarism," "race prejudice," "quarreling with Whites," and "making threats."

Equally disturbing for Wells and other black women was the widespread stereotype of black women as promiscuous and immoral. The stereotype derived from the misogynist treatment of black women during slavery. Where allegations of rape against white women blurred the tendency of whites to murder prosperous or civic-minded black men, allegations of sexual immorality by black women blurred or obscured the rape of young black girls and black women by white men. So widespread was this practice that southern folklore recounts how white men were thought to have come of age if they had raped a black woman. Wells, often at risk of being physically harmed, or of becoming one of the black women raped or lynched by white men, continued a persistent activism against lynching and the rape of black females.

Just as Ida B. Wells distinguished herself in working to define a moral standard for humane conduct on the issue of human rights violations, there were other black women whose voices were raised on behalf of the black family, black children, and always on the place of women's issues in the formulation of African American efforts at race improvement and nation-building. The black women who wrote on pressing issues of the day and spoke publicly on a wide range of topics almost always concerned themselves with issues of racial *and* gender improvement. In reflecting on the work and writings of black women of the late nineteenth and early twentieth centuries like Anna Julia Cooper, it is clear that their words and actions were in keeping with the tradition of African American female activism and leadership embodied in women like Maria Stewart, Mary Ann Shadd Cary, Sojourner Truth, and Harriett Tubman from earlier in the nineteenth century.

The tradition of African American women's self-help and protest is well documented. Dating from the antislavery movement, African American women actively resisted and struggled against the institution of slavery. African American women were also actively involved in organizing and supporting the mutual aid and benevolent societies that were so crucial to familial and community survival and institutional growth in free black communities in the antebellum period. The demise of enslavement brought the promise of racial betterment to a new high, and African American women, long accustomed to hard work, sacrifice on behalf of others, and persistent protest against the violence that whites inflicted on black people, articulated an impassioned commitment to see black people become increasingly self-reliant. Throughout the first two decades of the twentieth century, they persistently struggled to acquire the franchise as a basic right of citizenship.

In addition to suffrage, access to education, civil and human rights, Mary Church Terrell, Josephine St. Pierre Ruffin, and Mary McLeod Bethune were among the black women who committed themselves to a self-help movement, the National Black Women's Club Movement, which they believed would empower black women, and, by so doing, increase the power of black people's self-reliance and self-development.

African Americans have a long tradition of raising and cultivating the leadership necessary to articulate issues and pose solutions and remedies. For as long as African Americans have trod the soil in America, they have created a leadership to articulate their aims and achievements. Historically, the black Church has served as a pivotal and unique institution in the United States, for it is a religious and spiritual institution, even as it is a social and political institution. The black Church has served the spiritual needs of African Americans and has been a major philanthropist in African American communities. It has also been one of the institutions most responsible for training and providing a haven for emerging African American leadership, particularly those men and women whose lives are documented testimonies to their insistence on struggling to improve human and civil rights for African Americans. In this manner, the black Church has facilitated the emergence of an African American protest tradition.

In addition to a protest tradition, an emphasis on acquiring literacy and formal education, exercise of the franchise, access to land ownership, emphasis on employment as a path to entrepreneurship, the development of mutual aid and benevolent assistance and philanthropic giving, and the development of the black Press, African Americans have developed an artistic tradition that reflects black history and culture. The Harlem Renaissance, an outpouring of African American artistic and literary achievement, encompassed the New "Negro" Movement of the 1920s. The Movement produced a heightened racial consciousness, and it visibly represented and depicted African Americans in humanistic ways.

In the introduction to his classic book, *The New Negro*, Dr. Alain Locke, described the New "Negro" Movement as having "inner objectives" and a "newness" that emphasized philosophical and aesthetic dimensions of black life and culture. Significantly, literary and artistic themes and images arose with a new fervor during the Harlem Renaissance against a backdrop of decades of the emergence and evolution of a distinctly black American nationalism. Alain Locke, Jean Toomer, Zora Neale Hurston, Langston Hughes, Countee P. Cullen, Claude McKay, Jessie Redmon Fauset, Angelina W. Grimke, Arna Bontemps, Arthur A. Schomburg, and Nella Larsen were among the writers who gave renewed significance to the ideals, aspirations and accomplishments of African Americans.

As images of racial pride and themes of racial solidarity served as a backdrop for the Harlem Renaissance, the persistence of efforts to further the progress of African Americans remained in the forefront of political action and economic growth and development during the decade of the twenties and beyond. The evolution of self-help strategies and efforts to promote self-reliance has remained a constant component of African American social, political, and economic movements to this day. Where the artistic community endeavored to portray a myriad of images that defined brownness in a creative and positive manner, Marcus Garvey's called on African Americans to recognize common shared goals. Born into a large family in Jamaica in 1887, Marcus Garvey was active as a political reformer from an early age. After apprenticing as a printer in Jamaica, Garvey turned his attention to political activism, founding the Universal Negro Improvement Association (UNIA) in 1911. After largely unsuccessful attempts to expand the UNIA in Jamaica, Marcus Garvey emigrated to the United States where the UNIA became tremendously successful, and, in 1917, he started *The Negro World*, a newspaper devoted to discussions of black self-help and self-reliance. Garvey's appeal to African Americans gained strength steadily, and the UNIA organized over thirty chapters. Most popular was Garvey's call for a "Back to Africa" movement, which steadily gained supporters, despite his untimely incarceration for two and one-half years for alleged mail fraud.

Garvey's and DuBois's popularity might be better viewed not only in the context of an increasingly visible cultural revival, and the continuation of an articulate black nationalism, but also against the backdrop of significant demographic changes underway throughout the first several decades of the twentieth century. Historians and demographers alike note the dramatic redistribution of African Americans, from the South to the North, as in large part responsible for many of the major shifts in black economic, social, and political behavior.

Migration, the Military, and the Courts

Economic recession, the boll weevil, white violence, disfranchisement, and the lack of legal rights and the near absence of educational and economic opportunities prompted widespread black emigration from the South. On the other hand, opportunities to earn a cash wage for factory jobs in the North, and to participate in the institutional, political, cultural, and social life of predominantly northern black communities, somewhat more sheltered from white violence, appealed to many African Americans.

Scholars characterize the mass exodus of African Americans from the South to the North in the early decades of the twentieth century as the Great Migrations. Although generally welcomed by blacks already living and working in urban cities, the arrival of large numbers of African Americans from the rural South was resisted by many northern whites. Beliefs about white supremacy that served to convince white workers that blacks had no right to jobs desired by whites served to prompt white physical violence. Frequent and destructive race riots almost always instigated by whites scarred the urban landscape.

The early decades of the century were characterized by African Americans having to confront legal segregation, political disfranchisement, escalating white violence, and unequal access to the nation's resources for business and employment development. African Americans responded to the oppression and limited options with protest, resistance, and self-help efforts in the form of black-run businesses—grocery and general merchandise stores, funeral homes, barber and beauty shops, doctor's and dentist offices, emotional and psychic healers, boarding houses, food preparation shops and restaurants, catering businesses, carpentry and masonry services—and parallel institutions such as schools, colleges and universities, churches, banks, insurance and realty companies, art galleries, music studios, and newspaper and book publishing companies.

At the same time that many sought their expressions of self-help in employment opportunities, and where possible, start-up businesses, African Americans consistently articulated a desire to participate in the rights and responsibilities of American citizenship. Nowhere is the paradox that confronted African American men and women more clearly evident than in the willingness to support and serve in active duty in America's wars for world democracy and peace. Indeed, for many decades African Americans often fought for liberties and freedoms seldom extended to them at home in America.

The fact of a civil war, two world wars, and four major military excursions dating from the mid-nineteenth century to the present has pressed first African American men, and then later African American women into military service on America's behalf. Despite a second-class legal, civil, political and social status, African Americans have fought in all of America's wars and displayed valor and a commitment to destroy the institution of slavery during the Civil War. The recent movie *Glory* celebrates the famed 54th and 55th Massachusetts Negro Regiments of the Union Army. In addition, one notes that the 1st and 3rd Louisiana Negro Regiments, 9th and 11th Louisiana, the 1st Mississippi, and the 1st North Carolina Negro Regiments, distinguished themselves in very difficult battles.

All total, 186,000 blacks fought as combat troops, and another 200,000 served in "service units." Of the blacks who served the Union Army, 93,000 were from the Confederate South, 45,000 came from the Border States, 34,000 joined from the New England area, and 12,000 came from the West. Noted for their courage, African American men fought in America's wars for expansion, or "manifest destiny," as it is called. Hardly were black men themselves freed from enslavement, but that patriotism called on them to fight against the indigenous peoples, whose treaties with white men were consistently broken or ignored.

The use of black soldiers in the 9th and 10th cavalry and the 24th and 25th infantry marked the escalation of military excursions against Amerindians. African American men found themselves fighting against other people of color, whose experience of racial and cultural oppression mirrored the extent to which the ideology of white supremacy dominated America's actions. Manifest destiny in the nineteenth and twentieth centuries has meant territorial expansion on behalf of capitalism and the ideology of white supremacy. Little wonder then that America's wars for expansion have brought relatively little change in the denial of civil rights that blacks and other Americans of color confront. If annihilating Amerindians on the frontier secured manifest destiny at home in America, then militarily overwhelming people fighting for their liberation in the Philippines and Cuba during the Spanish-American War (1898) secured imperialism abroad.

World War I began in 1914 in Europe, and the United States entered the war against Germany in 1917. Although blacks were 10.7 percent of the U.S. population, 13.1 percent, or 350,000 black men served in America's war effort. As before, black troops fought in segregated units of the military—in the 92nd and 93rd Divisions. Having won honors and medals for bravery, black troops returned to America to confront race riots, racism, lynching, Jim Crow, disfranchisement, and the other aspects of second class citizenship that had come to characterize the underdevelopment of black communities in the name of white supremacy.

Blacks enlisted in military service again for World War II (1941–1945) when fascism threatened to engulf Europe and the rest of the world, rendering the world unsafe for people of color. Paradoxically, while America's leadership called on the African American community to purchase war bonds and enlist in support of the war effort following the Japanese bombing of Pearl Harbor Naval Station, America's domestic policies of legalized segregation and the unequal distribution of the nation's public resources for community, business, and institutional development—separate and unequal—required persistent and vigilant opposition from civil rights activists and organizations. Despite questions and a concern for the treatment of blacks enlisting in the branches of the United States military, the majority of African Americans supported the war effort. By war's end (Harry Ploski and Ernest Kaiser observe in "Black Servicemen and the Military," in *The Negro Almanac*), 700,000 blacks had served in the Army, 77,592 in the Air Force, 165,000 in the Navy, 17,000 in the Marines, 5,000 in the Coast Guard, and 4,000 black women in the WACS and the WAVES.

Sensing the intensity of black disdain for "separate and unequal," longtime activist and organizer A. Philip Randolph challenged America's white leadership to remove the barriers that held segregation in the armed services in place. Threatening to mobilize a 300,000-person March on Washington in 1948, Randolph pressured President Truman to issue Executive Order 9981, which barred segregation in the armed services. Randolph and his supporters, acting in the tradition of direct action protest, moved the country forward decisively in the 1940s mounting an effective protest campaign against Jim Crow segregation and its accompanying exclusion of blacks from an equitable share in America's abundance. The work to advance civil rights for black Americans continued against the backdrop of the Korean War and later the Vietnam War, where by 1968, 44,867 blacks had served in the Army, 3,609 in the Navy, 8,883 in the Air Force, and 8,657 in the Marines.

While fighting wars abroad for freedom, African Americans have waged a struggle for civil and human rights at home in American cities, towns and countryside. Key black institutions have long spearheaded the ongoing efforts of many people to promote civil rights. At issue has been the enforcement of existing law and creation of new statutes and court precedents. The National Association for the Advancement of Colored People (NAACP) has for nearly eighty years been in the vanguard of efforts to use the law and the courts to affect positive reforms for African Americans. The National Urban League, organized in 1911, has been instrumental in providing leadership and innovation for black communities. The Brotherhood of Sleeping Car Porters, a black trade union organized by Asa Philip Randolph in 1925, promoted the interests of the thousands of black men who worked as pullman coach porters on the racially segregated trains in America.

However, by far, the most impressive effort to realize civil rights for black Americans came about as the result of the combined efforts of many individuals and organizations such as the NAACP, the Congress of Racial Equality (CORE), the Brotherhood of Sleeping Car Porters, the Universal Negro Improvement Association (UNIA), the Urban League, and the National Negro Women's Clubs. These activist groups organized around black people's insistence on producing a social protest movement aimed at establishing a new moral order, legitimized by the creation of new laws and statutes and buttressed by an insistence on legal and moral enforcement of existing laws and statutes and protection of civil and human rights in America.

Out of the struggles for civil and human rights, out of the tradition of social action and protest against inhumane treatment, and out of centuries of self-help business development, organization and institution building, and philanthropic giving to charitable causes, the recent Civil Rights movement emerged. The Civil Rights movement of the 1960s was not a "new movement," as some would suggest, but rather a part of an historical continuum, which has come to characterize those actions desirable, and most often necessary, for African Americans to realize some meaningful measure of participation in democracy. The measures of African American participation have almost always been linked with the nature of treatment accorded them as human beings and as citizens. The struggle to be accorded treatment as human beings was the struggle to end chattel slavery and its accompanying deprivation and denial of human rights, let alone civil rights. The antislavery and abolitionist efforts of the nineteenth century were effective in forcing Americans to confront the inhumanity of the enslavement of millions of Africans and their descendants.

The struggle to advance civil rights is inextricably linked with efforts to clarify and promote human rights. Even before the Civil War had irrevocably altered the status of enslaved Africans, a morally bankrupt ideological defense of slavery had ambitiously carved out intellectual territory that contributed to the diminution of civil rights for blacks. The emergence of pseudo-scientific dogma and propaganda in the nineteenth and twentieth century contributed significantly to the role that "scientific" racism would play in American society. Racism had, in fact, infiltrated all aspects of American society, from social relations to the evaluation of what constituted knowledge and science.

Decades of defending the economic interests of those men whose wealth and privilege had derived from the kidnapping and exploitation of millions of African men and women produced an intellectual and scientific climate in white America sharply divided on the issue of human rights for African Americans. There were white men of means who used their wealth and education to promote white supremacy against the presumption of African American inferiority. In their writings and speeches, concepts were presented as discourses on oppositions. Although in time these discourses would reveal far more about the evolution of dualist thought in European history than any innate truism about non-European peoples, African Americans and Amerindians were nonetheless debased and oppressed by white society's preoccupation with an emphasis on opposites, instead of cultural parallels or similarities.

Where Europeans were viewed as human, capable of sentience, intelligence, and divine guidance, African Americans and Amerindians were viewed and depicted by white society as inhuman, bestial, dumb, incapable of intelligence, cursed and ungodly. It is praiseworthy that such a dichotomy is now known to represent European images of the "other" or the opposite of self, instead of any genuine insight into the nature and true culture of Africans. While this insight is now clear, many people believed and internalized the racist teachings they were exposed to, including some of the very people who were victimized by it. Hence, lest the effort had to be unceasing to abolish slavery, an ongoing effort to expose the racism inherent in so much of the intellectual and pseudo-scientific discourse of the day has been underway throughout the past two centuries. Therefore, although there is a tendency in the current climate of discussion about the meaning of civil rights to associate the quest for civil rights with the acquisition and use of political rights and the social status that derives from utilizing political involvement and activity as the basis for economic and social advancement in the twentieth century, it is wise to remember that the struggle for civil rights has also entailed the challenge to confront and transform racist ideas and concepts, values, and teachings embedded in the humanities, social disciplines, and life sciences. Indeed, it has been the influence of racist dogma into the very portals of knowledge, religion, science, and the structures and operations of the state that has required such persistent attention to the eradication of racism and sexism and the elevation and reaffirmation of civil rights.

In this century, the large scale coalition movements on behalf of collective bargaining, civil rights, and Affirmative Action have also had to confront the tenacious beliefs that have for so long served as the biological justification for the racial and sexual advantages accorded males of European ancestry. Indeed, while the story of the labor movement entails a discussion of collective bargaining, it is also the case that, with few exceptions, it is replete with the racial exclusion of black men and women.

It is precisely because African Americans have been significantly responsible for raising a consciousness of principled action as it relates to concepts like equity, justice, fairness, equality, and freedom, that an agenda for social action in America has progressed forward. Significantly, their agenda has included an insistence that laws mirror principled concepts, that principled concepts be the basis for the actions of the state(s) toward citizens, and that citizens be responsible for fashioning the state into an entity that adheres to principles, laws, and a neoplatonic basis for moral conduct. Furthermore, because African Americans have sought to actualize participatory democracy, the ongoing nature of civil rights activism has characterized the conduct and behavior of key institutions and leadership in the black community. Perhaps more than anything else, African Americans have viewed participatory democracy as being about _inclusion_ in the structures and operations of government, societal institutions, and economic development. The inalienable right to inclusion was a fundamental issue in the emergence of the recent Civil Rights movement of the 1950s and 1960s.

Direct action campaigns assumed a pivotal significance in the efforts of African Americans to reform the separate and unequal doctrine that everywhere denied their civil rights. In the traditionalized with effectiveness by Asa Philip Randolph, Bayard Rustin and Marcus Garvey, James Farmer, the Race-Relations Secretary of the Quaker-Pacifist Fellowship of Reconciliation, joined by students from the University of Chicago, organized CORE in Chicago in 1942. The Congress of Racial Equality early on forged a coalition with progressive whites that helped bring about the non-violent integration of long racially segregated restaurants in Chicago. James Farmer was strongly influenced by Mahatma Gandhi's non-violence and passive resistance teachings. While CORE shared similar goals and objectives with the NAACP, it was among the critics of the NAACP's emphasis on legalism. As an alternative, CORE's strategies for affecting progressive social change included sit-ins, the standing line, and the Freedom Ride, as tactics to eradicate discrimination and racial segregation, and encourage the growth of cooperative communities.

In October, 1942, three CORE members were refused service at racially segregated Stoners Restaurant in Chicago's Loop. In the year that followed, CORE devised effective measures for breaking the stranglehold segregation held on people's lives. Initially, CORE sent interracial groups to Stoners seeking seating and service. When they were refused, CORE began leafletting patrons and moved to a strategy where 65 persons, including 16 blacks, undertook sit-ins, first outside, then inside Stoners. Finally, Stoners acquiesced and CORE celebrated a strategically well orchestrated non-violent demonstration for racial justice.

Two years after a black woman named Irene Morgan, with the assistance of the NAACP, successfully sued the state of Virginia in _Morgan vs. Commonwealth_

of Virginia (1946) for the treatment she received when she refused to move from the front of a Greyhound bus in Richmond, CORE organized and sent an interracial group on the First Freedom Ride. Significantly, the first Freedom Riders, unlike their successors—the Freedom Riders of 1961—bypassed the deep South, thereby avoiding the violent reactions of southern whites intent upon holding racial segregation (and its advantages to whites only) rigidly in place.

To be clear, racial segregation meant the exclusion of blacks from access to opportunities, goods, and services. Some historians, as pointed out earlier, have likened America's rigid system of racial segregation to South Africa's apartheid system. There are indeed many historic parallels, for certainly segregation in America had the same purposes and goals as apartheid in South Africa—that is, the use, expropriation, and exploitation of black resources, with the intention of giving as little as possible to assist blacks in their own development. In America, white people took the best of everything for themselves, usurped a disproportionate amount of public revenues for white institutions, wrote disparate and unjust laws based on the presumption of the inferiority of people of color, and interpreted and executed the letter of the law differently across racial lines.

However controversial its emphasis on legalism as a mechanism for social reform has been, the NAACP (particularly under the capable and adept leadership of Thurgood Marshall as the director of the NAACP Legal Defense Fund) persistently endeavored to bring about legal redress and reforms. Its efforts in the late 1930s and throughout the 1940s also helped pave the way for racial justice. Whether the NAACP was directly involved in arguing a case before the court, its commitment to legalism meant that people perceived the Legal Defense Fund as actively in support of legal redress and remedy. Cases in point include several major court victories in addition to *Morgan vs. Commonwealth of Virginia* that helped bring America closer to racial and sexual equality. In *Lloyd Gaines vs. University of Missouri* (1938), the court ruled that the State of Missouri was obligated to admit blacks to the all-white state university law school, if no all-black professional graduate school existed. Then, in *Congressmen Arthur Mitchell vs. U.S. Interstate Commerce* (1941), the court required that Pullman accommodations be provided for African Americans. Again, in a landmark case originating in Texas, *Smith vs. Allwright* (1944), the court ruled that "white primary" laws were a violation of the Fifteenth Amendment to the Constitution and, as such, white primaries were declared unconstitutional.

Following closely on the court's strike against white primaries was still another blow at segregation. In *Shelley vs. Kraemer* (1948), the court ruled that states could not enforce racially restrictive covenants in real estate. Again, in 1948, in *Perez vs. Lippold*, the court ruled that anti-miscegenation laws were a violation of the Fourteenth Amendment. In 1950, in *Sweatt vs. Painter*, the court required the all-white University of Texas Law School to admit Herman Marion Sweatt because the all-black law school, consisting of "…three small basement rooms in an office building eight blocks from the University of Texas Law School…," was unequal and inadequate. These are but a few of the landmark court cases that, along with advocacy and activist based social protest efforts, influenced the course of social reform in America, particularly in the 1940s.

Each of these court cases struck a death blow at the *Plessy vs. Ferguson* (1896) Supreme Court decision that legitimized an apartheid system in America and paved the way for the ideology of white supremacy to be codified in law as well as in social practice. By far the most far reaching of the Supreme Court decisions in this century, built on the success and progress of each previous progressive landmark court decision, was the watershed decision of *Oliver Brown et. al. vs. Board of Education of Topeka, Kansas*, in which the Supreme Court unanimously ruled school segregation unconstitutional, declaring that "separate educational facilities are inherently unequal." Without question, the Court's decision aided black Americans in their quest to realize equality of opportunity.

Direct Social Action and its Aftermath

Although Irene Morgan's treatment by Greyhound and her legal actions against the bus company that had demanded she move to the back of the bus did not mobilize a massive grass-roots level, direct-action social protest movement, Rosa Parks's treatment and actions in December 1955, effectively triggered a mobilization and grass-roots level activism for civil rights unparalleled in America's history. Beginning as a bus boycott in the wake of Rosa Parks's arrest for refusing to move to the back of the Cleveland Avenue bus in Montgomery, Alabama, the protests quickly grew. The efforts that produced the Montgomery Improvement Association and that propelled to leadership the young minister of Dexter Street Baptist Church, the Reverend Martin Luther King, Jr., went full circle in launching a 381-day bus boycott that was effective in eliminating segregated seating. Significantly, the boycott would transform the very nature of civil rights activism, even as a movement—arising out of a tradition of a self-help and protest continuum—pushed forward in pursuit of goals and objectives long cherished and long overdue.

If the ability of African Americans to gain the rights long denied them in law and social custom constitutes a Great Awakening for American society, then the Montgomery bus boycott produced a southern based protest movement and a civil rights leader who would indelibly change the course of African American and American history. In 1955, the Interstate Commerce Commission forbade segregated buses and waiting rooms for passengers travelling interstate in response to the NAACP's legal efforts. In the midst of the Montgomery bus boycott, in the winter of 1956, the Reverend King, the Reverend Ralph Abernathy, and 87 others were indicted on charges of conspiring to orchestrate a boycott. In the same year, the NAACP took the case to Federal court, and, in November 1956, the Supreme Court declared bus segregation ordinances unconstitutional. The effectiveness and success of the bus boycott and the visibility that accompanied judicial victories, press conferences, sermons, and speeches, increasingly focused attention on the movement's most forceful and enigmatic leader, Martin Luther King, Jr.

Martin Luther King, Jr. (1929–1968), was born in Atlanta, Georgia, and was educated at Morehouse College, Crozier Theological Seminary (ordained in 1947), and Boston University, where he earned his Ph.D. Martin Luther King, Jr. shared in common with James Farmer and Bayard Rustin (one of the founders along with Reverend King and Stanley Levinson of the Southern Christian Leadership Conference [SCLC]) a firm grounding in Mahatma Gandhi's teachings on non-violent direct action. During his years as the leader of the movement, King was thoroughly involved in all aspects of the movement. So clear was his commitment to the liberation of the human spirit from oppression that King was celebrated as an international spokesperson and awarded the Nobel Peace Prize on December 10, 1964.

As the civil rights activities of the movement expanded beyond Montgomery, the SCLC, an interracial organization committed to equality and full citizenship, sought to network and enhance civil rights protest actions around the country. The activities and actions of the movement's leadership captured the essence of non-violent philosophy and direct action protest. Ella Baker, previously a field secretary of the NAACP, joined SCLC at its inception in 1957 to mobilize and organize mass meetings. By 1958, she had established SCLC's Atlanta office, where she served as the executive secretary. King, Abernathy, Baker, and others noted the increasing involvement and militancy of college students in civil rights protest activities.

In February, 1960, four college students at North Carolina A & T College, in Greensboro, initiated a sit-in at a segregated Woolworth lunch counter. The students employed tactics CORE had used with success. Rapidly, the student-inspired sit-in movement spread through the South and was accompanied by read-ins, wade-ins, kneel-ins. Immediately after the start of sit-ins in Greensboro, 40 students from Fisk University initiated a sit-in at a Nashville, Tennessee Woolworth lunch counter. At a landmark meeting of students, held on the campus of Shaw University in Raleigh, North Carolina, in April 1960, the Student Non-Violent Coordinating Committee (SNCC) was created to give structure and provide support and coordination to the student movement for civil rights. Although Martin Luther King, Jr. and Ella Baker both attended the student meeting and the SCLC donated monies to help offset the cost of the meeting, the student membership of SNCC insisted on remaining an independent organization although they agreed to work with the SCLC. SNCC, under its first elected chair (the same Marion Barry who would later serve as mayor of the nation's capital city), set out to raise monies and coordinate student activities in the South. So ambitious and committed were student protest activities in the South that a chronicler of the student movement estimates that over 70,000 black and white students participated in sit-ins by 1961. Importantly, the jail-in movement began in 1961 when students arrested in Rock Hill, South Carolina, declined to pay fines and requested jail sentences.

The second Freedom Ride took place in 1961. Organized by James Farmer and other CORE members, and joined by the SNCC, an interracial group departed from the nation's capital en route to New Orleans to test the Interstate Commerce Commission's orders to integrate interstate travel facilities. For many Americans, the plight of the Freedom Riders emerged as a compelling issue when the media presented graphic, visual coverage of the brutal attack by white men and women at a bus station in Alabama. The intensity of the attack on the riders and the burning of the Greyhound bus they rode symbolized the white South's escalating resistance to written and interpreted law and moral persuasion. Nonetheless, the SNCC, the SCLC, and student and activist groups across the country continued the sit-ins, boycotts, and jail-ins, designed to challenge and eradicate separate and unequal segregation of public facilities.

Building on the legal strength and moral force of the sit-in movement and freedom rides, the SNCC, the SCLC, and others next moved to promote voter registration and voter participation in local, state, and federal elections. Civil rights advocates turned their attention to working in areas of the South where blacks had been prevented from exercising their constitutional right to vote. When black southerners attempted to register to vote, they were often met with economic or physical opposition. Civil rights activists learned that the reality of white violence victimized anyone intent upon changing racially maintained injustice. Three civil rights workers (Michael H. Schwerner and Andrew Goodman, both white men, and James E. Chaney, a black man) were brutalized and murdered by whites in Mississippi in 1964. In the very next year, 1965, more white volunteers were murdered: Viola Liuzzo, a housewife who had come South compelled by her conscience was shot in the head because she transported people who had come for the Selma March; Jonathan Daniels, a seminary student was killed while performing voter registration work; and the Reverend James Reeb was clubbed in the head and killed as he left a black-owned restaurant.

Yet, some would say that there had always been white violence aimed at intimidation, even against the young and harmless. In 1955, Emmett Till, age fourteen, was visiting Mississippi from Chicago on summer vacation. Till was abducted from his uncle's farm one night, brutally beaten, and shot through the head by white men who were then quickly acquitted in a trial that made a mockery of the judicial system. Still later, in 1963, white supremacists bombed the 16th Street Baptist Church in Birmingham, killing four African American children and injuring over 20 people.

It seemed as if each advance was met with pain—inflicted either by illegal white terrorist violence or by the betrayal and disappointment of the federal government's delayed or inadequate protection of citizens engaged in civil rights activities. Clearly, it must have been difficult for civil rights activists to maintain a commitment to non-violent social protest in the face of intense white violence. And yet, despite the killings, beatings, job firings, tenant evictions, and many other illegal and immoral violations, the movement continued pressing for enforcement of: a) existing constitutional provisions for black entitlement and enfranchisement, and b) existing and proposed civil rights legislation aimed at the protection of liberties and the eradication of discrimination and oppression.

Legislation and legal victories continued reinforcing the social transformation that was at hand in America's communities. Direct-action social protest and mass demonstrations were effective tactics for change. The march on Washington, organized by A. Philip Randolph and Bayard Rustin in August 1963, brought 250,000 people together in support of the movement. Martin Luther King, Jr. addressed the movement's supporters, from the steps of the Lincoln Memorial, with an impassioned speech that reflected his measure as the movement's visionary: "I have a dream that one day this nation will rise up and live out the true meaning of its creed: 'We hold these truths to be self-evident; that all men are created equal.'" Empowered by the movement's moral clarity, zeal, and effectiveness, civil rights activities intensified in the South. By the mid-1960s, an important shift was underway in the movement. When Stokley Carmichael, a student at Howard University and a field worker for the SNCC was elected chairperson of the SNCC in 1966, he began to call for "Black Power" within the SNCC and the movement. In the following year, H. Rap Brown, national chairperson of the SNCC, articulated and intensified Black Power activities.

Increasingly, African Americans outside the South also challenged decades of *de facto* and *de jure* segregation. Historians record the boycott of Chicago schools by 220,000 black children in 1963 to protest the segregationist policies of school Superintendent Benjamin C. Willis as symbolizing the movement's expansion into northern, midwestern, and west-coast cities. As African Americans in the South were seeking fundamental human and political rights, many others in urban areas like New York, Chicago, Washington, Detroit, Philadelphia, Oakland (CA), and Los Angeles had left the South behind in the earlier waves of migration North from the South. Though faring better than when they lived in the South, millions of blacks in northern cities remained poor and powerless, even when they exercised the civil rights they had struggled to effect in the North. Throughout the decades of the twentieth century, the expansion of black northern communities has created a leadership that addressed urban black issues.

Malcolm X (1925–1965) was born Malcolm Little in Omaha, Nebraska. Having completed only the eighth grade, Malcolm X was largely self-taught, later becoming a Black Muslim and joining the Nation of Islam. In 1964, Malcolm X, recognized as one of the most powerful spokespersons on behalf of empowerment for blacks, founded the Organization of Afro-American Unity, a nationalist organization. His speeches before thousands revealed the manner by which Western education and information distorted and denied the realities of African and African American history. He called for the creation of organizations, institutions, schools, programs, research, and scholarship that would redress the deliberate miseducation of African Americans as a first step toward self-acceptance, personal empowerment, and nation-building. Malcolm mirrored the sentiments of many who were strongly influenced by the nationalist liberation movements underway in Africa in his insistence that out of a black identified positive self-image would come the strength and cohesiveness to build new realities for black American progress.

Urban black communities intensified cultural and political activities, generating a leadership that reflected the many issues that needed articulation. The black militancy that emerged as the Black Power Movement promoted positive self-image and black input into the formulation of solutions for the many issues and problems confronting black communities. The Black Panthers, organized in October 1966 by Huey P. Newton and Bobby Seale in Oakland, developed a ten-point program that was strongly influenced by Stokely Carmichael's call for Black Power and by the effective organized mechanisms used by the SNCC. Other voices of militancy were Gloria Richardson of the Cambridge Non-Violent Coordinating Committee and Cecil Moore of the Philadelphia NAACP.

Urban inner city riots, arising from the despair, anger, and powerlessness that oppressed most blacks, erupted in scores of American cities in the 1960s. While the Civil Rights Act of 1964 was the most far reaching civil rights bill ever passed, the differences between the letter of the law and the time and persistence it would take to implement and enforce its measures was still unknown. The Act's eleven "Titles" dealt with: a) prohibiting discrimination in public accommodations—desegregating public facilities, b) strengthening voting rights and protecting citizen access to participation in federal elections, d) prohibiting discrimination in education, e) prohibiting discrimination in federally funded programs, and f) prohibiting discrimination in employment and establishment of the Equal Employment Opportunity Commission (in Blumberg, *Civil Rights: The 1960s Freedom Struggle*).

In addition, the Voting Rights Act of 1965 was ushered through a joint session of Congress by President Lyndon Johnson one week after the massive civil rights march of 40,000 people from Selma to Montgomery. The Act banished poll taxes and literacy tests, and required federal registers to register African American voters. The impact of legal and civil rights activism was clearly discernible; no court cases were needed. Within a year, over 50 percent of the population of the South registered to vote. As the movement peaked in the 1960s, activists continued civil rights activities by challenging the right of the right-wing of the Democratic Party to represent the Southern states, particularly because Southerners controlled eleven of the sixteen committees in the House of Representatives. In Mississippi, one of the movement's most forceful and eloquent leaders, Fannie Lou Hamer, articulated the Mississippi Freedom Democratic Party's challenge to the Democratic Party leadership at the National Democratic Party Convention.

It has been more than two decades since the movement's peak in the 1960s. The 1960s produced unprecedented advances. Civil rights activists and the law effectively dismantled racial segregation in public accommodations. The federal government expanded its powers to protect the civil rights of African Americans. African Americans, in unprecedented numbers exercised their right to enfranchisement by voting and developed a sophistication and assertiveness likely to sustain their continued efforts to remedy the still unfulfilled promises of equality and justice. To the extent possible, African Americans participated in the processes of legal enforcement of existing laws, and made gains in education, employment and housing.

However, the ill effects of 245 years of enslavement, discrimination, and disadvantage could not be resolved and remedied in so little time, and so much remained to be done. Enforcement resources at various federal agencies and offices charged with investigating violations and pursuing compliance sometimes faltered and did not match the enforcement mandate. Also, because residential segregation proved to be linked with school segregation, efforts to desegregate schools confronted an enormous challenge in dealing with strategies to effect school integration, and thereby dismantle separate and unequal education.

While the movement made it more difficult for political leaders to ignore civil rights, the white racial backlash that fueled conservative victories in the late 1960s put civil rights advocates on notice that liberal changes would be met with growing resistance. In the main, conservative federal administrations have given civil rights a low priority. The record of the Supreme Court since the 1960s has produced mixed results. In *Swann vs. Charlotte-Mecklenburg Board of Education* (1971), the Court approved of busing as a tool to achieve school integration. The Court's ruling on *Griggs vs. Duke Power Company* (1971) addressed the issue of workplace discrimination by placing the burden on employers to prove the relationship between hiring criteria and a job applicant's qualifications. In the 1970s, Affirmative Action programs emerged as the remedy for employment and workplace discrimination. The term "Affirmative Action" was developed in 1965 when President Johnson issued Executive Order 11246 which prohibited discrimination by firms doing business with the federal government. Johnson's order gave federal agencies, namely, the Labor Department, a directive to investigate and take "Affirmative Action."

Affirmative Action, initially an enforcement measure, also suggested standards and protocols, and was in time validated by federal courts. Most African Americans supported Affirmative Action efforts, because, in many cases, it represented a challenge to the protocols and practices established by decades of white male control over hiring criteria and employment qualifications. Affirmative Action was defended as a remedy for past discrimination and disadvantage experienced by racial minorities and women. Many African Americans benefitted from the Affirmative Action programs developed by government contracting and private industry. Clearly, political leadership at the national level, corporate interest in enlightened social responsibility, and the continued activism and advocacy of civil rights organizations contributed to the survival of Affirmative Action as a tool for social transformation.

Affirmative Action has had its detractors—those who have argued that Affirmative Action constitutes "reverse discrimination." Spurred on by the Supreme Court's decision, in *Regents of the University of California vs. Allen Bakke* (1978), that the University violated the equal protection clause of the Constitution and Bakke's civil rights, opponents of Affirmative Action celebrated. But many agreed with Justice Thurgood Marshall's assessment that the civil rights act and the equal protection clause had been designed to dismantle America's dualistic and separate racial caste system and to remedy the continuing effects of previous discrimination. Many rightly feared that the Equal Protection Clause would be used as a weapon to reinforce white supremacy, thereby blunting the short period of commitment that employers—and, in Bakke's case, a medical school—were willing to make to eradicating the systematic underdevelopment of African Americans caused by enslavement, disenfranchisement, separateness, and inequality.

The most ominous attack on Affirmative Action for both supporters and detractors was that of the University of Michigan (Gritz vs. Bollinger, Undergraduate Programs, 2000, and Grutter vs. Bollinger, Law School, 2002), brought to the High Court by conservatives supported by the Bush Administration, through white students who had been denied admission. By a decision of 5 to 4 on June 23, 2003, the Court rejected the institution's undergraduate admission policy, which used a point-system to diversify its student body, noting that the policy was not "narrowly tailored" to achieve the institution's diversity through its admission policy. Yet, invoking Bakke, the Court upheld the Law School's admission policy that considered race as one of the criteria for admission. Both sides claimed some type of victory. At this juncture, however, even though Affirmative Action has suffered serious setbacks over the years, it is still being applied under stricter guidelines that may consider race as part of the overall criteria such as economic circumstances and admission test scores.

Along with greater enforcement of existing federal statutes, revision of racially prescriptive state laws, and enactment of progressive and forward looking legislation designed to promote and protect human, civil and legal rights provided significant measures toward participatory democracy. Likewise, the bold and innovative measures embodied in Affirmative Action objectives and goals produced concrete, if not large-scale economic change. Many believed that several hundred years of enslavement, followed by legal, economic and political disenfranchisement, followed still by legalized and unequal segregation could be redressed in the few short years following the movement. Still many others understood that the progressive changes brought about by the movement created another opportunity for African Americans to assert self-help and self-determination, particularly in the political arena.

Between the passage and enforcement of the *Brown* decision and the emergence of Affirmative Action efforts to alter discrimination in the workplace, black Americans significantly altered their material, political and social standing in America. Unquestionably, by pulling the spectre of legalized segregation down,

African Americans spearheaded the removal of the greatest barrier to access, and hence participation in American society. At stake were concepts of significance, such as the right to an equitable share of society's bounty in exchange for the responsibilities of citizenship. But there were also economic, social and political matters of pressing importance, and material matters like the right to vote, the right to literacy and the economic and political payofffs those rights bring.

To be clear, much more needs to be done, as many African Americans, though now able to vote, remain locked in poverty, and, hence, in need of greater involvement in the nation's economic development. Unprecedented numbers of African Americans *can* now vote, and blacks elected as city council members, mayors, governors, senators, representatives, and other recognized public officials across the country attest to the increasing viability of black empowerment. The next challenge of forging business and economic development strategies is already at hand. As more African Americans use the access that has come with the victories of the civil rights movement to further their options and alternatives, it bears remembering that the black community as a whole needs to care for all its members. There is a mandate that has arisen out of the collective experiences of struggle for economic self-determination and human and civil rights, which requires that African Americans shape the individual experience so that commitment to a whole community as a collective entity sustains the ongoing struggle for inclusion and access.

Summary

In recent decades, scholars of African American studies have been challenged to reconsider the ideological perspectives that shaped much of the scholarship on African American history in this century. African Americans have insisted on the inclusion of perspectives that emphasize their efforts to promote self-help and self-reliance, instead of perspectives that deny or trivialize initiative and creativity. African American values, attitudes, behaviors and achievements more regularly serve as the focal point for a scholarship which offers an assessment of African American historiography. African American inspired institutions and organizations emerge as viable, useful efforts to promote self-determination and development. In such scholarship, African American resistance and antipathy to enslavement is clearly identified, as are attempts by African Americans to forge new opportunities and possibilities in the aftermath of the Civil War. Hence, a responsible rendering of African American history brings to light and explores both a black self-help heritage and a black protest tradition, even as it identifies white opposition to black progress and self-determination.

As African American activity, and not passivity is exposed, the enormity of what black Americans have accomplished becomes clearer. Significantly, African Americans have been principally responsible for their own empowerment. By so doing, they have been the catalyst for human and civil rights activism in the country at large. In essence, because the black protest tradition has focused on securing rights under the law, every positive gain for blacks has meant a positive gain for America's other ethnic/racial groups, and for participatory democracy. African American women and men have persistently struggled to achieve justice, inclusion in economic development, and political equality.

African Americans have faced tremendous challenges in their quest to realize a first-class citizenship. The betrayal of the Reconstruction era made the acquisition of post-Civil War goals virtually impossible. Nearly 4.5 million African American men and women were emancipated with no compensation for their or their ancestors' 245 years of unpaid laboring. Without money, education, land, or access to unions and jobs, African Americans confronted unparalleled obstacles; only Amerindians confronted a more destitute reality. The ideology of white supremacy dominated many white people's thinking in the South, and in many places in the North as well. The emergence of white terrorist hate groups like the Ku Klux Klan threatened the livelihood and life blood of individual blacks. Between the 1800s and 1960s over 5,000 black men, women, and children were lynched in America. Black men were systematically excluded and disenfranchised from the right to exercise their Fifteenth Amendment right to vote. It took nearly 100 years of protest and struggle to bring the Voting Rights Act and federal enforcement of that law into existence.

By far, the most pervasive and destructive oppression black people experienced in the aftermath of enslavement was the legally sanctioned creation of an apartheid system of racial segregation and subordination in the form of racially separate and unequal nations of people on one soil. Segregation meant that white people expropriated only for themselves quality education, technology, union industrial and manufacturing jobs, health care innovations, philanthropic giving, segregated religious worship services, status and rank in the military, elected enfranchisement as the basis for democratic participation, paths to entrepreneurial growth via access to bank credit, and legal and civil rights protection under the law.

Even as African Americans have pressed for human and civil rights, they have consistently fought in America's military excursions. Indeed, as black Americans helped make the world safe for democracy, they were often unsafe at home. Even what had been home underwent a transformation as the great migrations of African Americans from rural areas of the South to the urban areas of the North and Southwest changed the demographic racial landscape of America. Since earlier this century, the black experience, as it is sometimes called, has increasingly become an urban experience. The southern-based Civil Rights movement, one of the "great awakenings" of the twentieth century, effectively used massive direct action protest to bring down *de jure* segregation and to call attention to gross violations of the civil rights of black Americans. The movement forced the country to confront the reality of legalized economic, political, social, and cultural disparity in the richest nation on Earth.

The Civil Rights movement served as a catalyst for other ethnic/racial movements for civil rights, and many women later active in the women's movement, learned how to effectively challenge unequal treatment while activists in the broad-based coalition fashioned during the movement. Unprecedented numbers of African Americans now vote, and interventions like Affirmative Action have made a positive difference when and where they have been welcomed as remedy for past and even continuing racial discrimination and disadvantage. Urban social movements have also challenged the *de facto* segregation that characterized life in northern cities. And, in the tradition of enigmatic African American leadership, elected black leaders have tried with varied success to implement measures that strengthen black business development, as the next necessary step toward black economic development is furthered. African Americans have accomplished significant progress in just over 100 years since enslavement. While there is still a long road ahead, and many obstacles, much that is empowering and good has been attained and should be remembered and celebrated.

Study Questions and Activities

1. What issues were important to African Americans during Reconstruction?
2. Trace the significance of Court rulings and legislation in effecting changes in the status of African Americans.
3. Define and trace African American efforts to promote self-reliance and self-help initiatives.
4. Identify and discuss African American male and female leadership since the late nineteenth century.
5. Discuss the impact of white opposition to participatory democracy for African Americans.
6. Identify the contributions African Americans have made to military wars, and discuss the paradox of fighting for democracy abroad but being deprived of civil rights at home in the United States.
7. Identify the role of black people in creating and sustaining the recent civil rights movement.
8. Identify key black institutions that have fostered self-help, mutual assistance, charitable giving, and black nationalism.
9. Assess the changes that have taken place in the collective experience of African Americans since Emancipation.

References

James D. Anderson. *The Education of Blacks in the South, 1860–1935*. Chapel Hill, NC: University of North Carolina Press, 1988.

Peter M. Bergman. *A Chronological History of the Negro in America*. New York: Harper & Row, 1969.

Rhoda Lois Blumberg. *Civil Rights: The 1960s Freedom Struggle*. Boston: Twayne Publishers, 1984.

Clayborne Carson et al. (eds.). *A Reader and Guide: Eyes on the Prize: America's Civil Rights Years*. New York: Penguin Books, 1987.

Carl Cohen. *Affirmative Action and Racial preference: A Debate*. New York: Oxford University Press, 2003.

Bell Derrick A. *Silent Covenants: Brown v. Board of Education and the Unfulfilled Hopes for Racial Reform*. New York: Oxford University Press, 2004.

W. E. B. DuBois. *Black Reconstruction in America*. New York: Atheneum Books, 1970.

John Hope Franklin and Alfred A. Moss, Jr. *From Slavery to Freedom: A History of Negro Americans*. 6th ed. New York: McGraw-Hill, 1988.

George W. Frederickson. *White Supremacy: A Comparative Study in American and South African History*. New York: Oxford University Press, 1981.

Paula Giddings. *When and Where I Enter: The Impact of Black Women on Race and Sex in America*. New York: Wm. Morrow & Co., 1984.

Louis R. Harlan. *Separate and Unequal*. New York: Atheneum, 1969.

Gerald David Jaynes and Robin M. Williams, Jr. (eds.). *A Common Destiny: Blacks and American Society*. Washington: National Academy Press, 1989.

Steven F. Lawson. *Running for Freedom: Civil Rights and Black Politics in America Since 1941*. New York: McGraw-Hill, 1991.

Leon Litwack and August Meier (eds.). *Black Leaders of the Nineteenth Century*. Chicago: University of Illinois Press, 1988.

Alain Locke. *The New Negro*. New York: Atheneum Books, 1968.

Bert James Loewenberg and Ruth Bogin (eds.). *Black Women in Nineteenth-Century American Life*. University Park, PA: Pennsylvania State University Press, 1976.

Gunnar Myrdal. *An American Dilemma: The Negro Problem and Modern Democracy*. 2 vols. New York: Harper & Row, 1944.

Donald G. Nieman. *Promises to Keep: African-Americans and the Constitutional Order, 1776*. New York: Oxford University Press, 1991.

Harry A. Ploski and Ernest Kaiser (eds.). "Black Servicemen and the Military Establishment," in *The Negro Almanac*, 2nd ed. New York: Bellweather, 1971.

Ida B. Wells. *U.S. Atrocities*. London, 1892.

8

The Caribbean: From Emancipation to Independence

Nikongo Ba'Nikongo

Introduction

Understanding the Caribbean today, particularly the English-speaking Caribbean, demands good insight into its societal development, the dynamism of human interaction, and the place different groups occupy in it. The sociocultural and politico-economic structure today reflect the evolution of societies from the post-Columbian (1492 onwards) period to the present. The student is advised to pay particular attention to the genesis of class formation, the development of political participation, and the nature of race relations in what one could refer to as post-colonial states, i.e. states which were once colonies of Europe and are now at least politically independent.

The importance or relevance of Caribbean Studies to the student of African American Studies lies in the fact that the Caribbean occupies an equal place in the triad of the discipline along with the experience of Africans in Africa and the United States. It is also a major region of settlement for Africans outside of the African continent itself. A significant number of African Americans can and increasingly will trace their immediate parental roots to Jamaica, Trinidad/Tobago, Barbados, Guyana, and other islands in the archipelago. Moreover, if the strength of groups rests in their members' ability to identify with and relate to their diverse elements, then it becomes doubly important to understand this region. Finally, the student of Afro-American Studies will find that much similarity exists in the experience of Africans in the Caribbean, in Africa and elsewhere in the diaspora. This chapter focuses on three aspects of that experience: 1) colonialism and the drive to independence; 2) contemporary society and culture; and 3) political economy and economic strains.

Major terms and concepts: Class formation, political participation, race relations, diaspora, colonialism, imperialism, federation, underdevelopment, neocolonialism, dependence, unequal exchange, nationalization, import substitution, debt crisis, Caribbean Basin Initiative, comprador, industrialization by invitation.

Slavery and Emancipation

The colonization of the Caribbean region had as its basis the expanding economic opportunities of European states. If the European arrival on the continent of Africa was in search of new routes of trade, new areas of investment, and new lands to conquer, clearly the exploration of the Americas and the Caribbean archipelago was not without similar motivations. But the idea of imperialism (the expansion of a nation beyond its borders to manage and control the territory of another), the early twentieth-century writer J.A. Hobson tells us, had an added importance to Europe. It was, he says, a safety valve for a stagnant economy needing new areas to invest, new markets to trade, and a means to displace unemployed labor. The occupation of Caribbean lands provided all of the above for the Portuguese, the Spanish, the French, and the English.

The Caribbean islands provided an additional bonus—agriculture, land to till—so much land to till that the need for affordable labor became important. It must be understood that the problem was not a shortage of labor, but rather a shortage of labor at an economically viable price. This then explains the importation of human cargo from the continent of Africa to these islands to complement and later substitute the existing laboring force which was either overly-expensive, inadequate, or unwilling to meet the demands. Why, the question emerges, was African unpaid labor sought?

Perhaps, the fact that Europeans already had ownership and control of much of Africa made it a natural reservoir of workers. Perhaps, too, their ability to obtain unpaid labor from their own people simply could not fit into the legal and sociological structure of the time. The historian Eric Williams in *Capitalism and Slavery* tells us that enslavement was not a result of racism but rather racism was a result of enslavement. It seems a plausible enough analysis. However, it is also true that, in order to justify and legitimize the enslavement of Africans, it was necessary to devalue and dehumanize them both in practice and in the philosophy of the time.

The system of slavery in the Caribbean was organized, sanctioned, and administered by the particular European governments in the particular periods. Although the cases in which we have an immediate interest would have been, for the most part, administered by the British government, the colonial ownership did periodically change hands among different European states. All economic activity was geared toward the good of the colonial government and colonial land holders, many of whom were absentee landlords. Since the landlords wished to extract as much wealth as possible, the work was laborious for the slaves; since they wished to extract the wealth in as little time as possible, the hours of work were long. Long periods of rest and relaxation were luxuries which plantation society did not afford; the harsh treatment that was meted out to slaves cannot be overstated.

It is that dehumanization and cruel treatment of Africans in the Caribbean islands as, indeed, elsewhere, which would come to characterize their slave experience. Some writers have argued that slavery in Spanish and Portuguese territories was more benevolent than that in English territories. Certainly, to the slave, this would have mattered little because the nature of the experience—whether at the hands of the English, Spanish, or French—was unjust, rigid, and inhumane.

Williams, in another essay, "Massa Day Done," explains the rigors of plantation life for the African slave. He points out that the horrors of physical work were only equalled by the horrors of corporal punishment, while the colonial slave master enjoyed a life of luxury, excess, and ingratitude. Says Williams, "massa was an uncultured man with an illiberal outlook." For slaves in the Caribbean, then, the gradual crawl toward emancipation could not have come too soon.

The genesis and processes of the emancipation effort should not be misunderstood. One could say that it all had to do with the awakening of consciousness with regard to the inhumanity of slavery on the part of European governments and plantation owners in the late eighteenth century, but one would be wrong. One could say that it derived from the humane concerns and Judeo-Christian ideals of the abolitionists in Europe, but again we would be incorrect. One would need to understand that the push toward abolition and, hence, emancipation and independence, had its driving force firstly in the struggles of the slaves themselves who seized every opportunity to free themselves and secondly in the economic transformations of the day. This does not imply that the efforts of abolitionists were insignificant, but rather that the impetus for change and the momentum for metamorphosis of the slave order/economy had their own dynamic.

In Haiti, the activities of Toussaint L'Ouverture, Dessalines, and Henri Christophe led the way. In Jamaica, the Maroons (rebel slaves) defied the system by establishing run-away societies of their own and, in Trinidad and elsewhere, sporadic uprisings against the yoke of enslavement were evident. But the abolition of slavery and the emancipation of slaves did not immediately change the nature of relationships because new categories of workers were introduced.

As this chapter will demonstrate, the introduction of East Indians and Chinese as indentured laborers would later have a tremendous effect on the emergence of Caribbean societies after independence and the nature of party politics. The quest for independence itself was extremely dynamic.

The decline of slavery in the English Caribbean set the stage for the anti-colonialist and pre-independence sentiments. The end of both the First and Second World Wars (1914–1919 and 1939–1945, respectively), would have an impact on this process, especially in the demands of securing the self-government of peoples. By the 1920s, the signs of discontent were clear particularly among island elites whose cultural ties to Europe were becoming increasingly weak and whose economic interests were more and more at variance with the mother country. Something had to be done to create a government more representative of island interests.

The establishment of Crown Colony governments in these islands fell far short of the islands' objectives. Indeed, the nature and structure of administration were such as to preserve Europe's economic interest in these territories. As much as the European business and administrative classes in the Caribbean wished for greater autonomy from Europe, they wished to preserve for themselves the recluse of political life.

The 1930s, however, would witness significant challenges to the established order. Between 1934 and 1939, social disturbances in the form of strikes and riots were widespread and represented the just demands of the former enslaved and indentured. The Afro-Caribbean working classes demonstrated their dissatisfaction with working conditions and became increasingly mobilized and politicized, while trade union activity, as a means of organizing labor, provided an active role for the yearnings of the masses.

Like workers elsewhere, the working classes in these island territories provided the physical force for political changes if even the intellectual direction was later superseded by an educated vanguard. The movement of workers, joined by sectors of the middle classes who would come to identify more and more with their objectives, was cataclysmic in its impact. And, it is interesting that the agenda as defined went beyond what may be considered simple working-man's issues. Among the workers demands and objectives of the movement were the following: 1) higher wages, 2) better working conditions, 3) constitutional reform, 4) universal suffrage, and 5) electoral reform.

The political movements of workers and intellectuals alike in the 1930s had an even more important dimension. The internationalization or regionalization of the movement provided coordination and uniformity as the movement pushed for a Federation of States and established communication among laborers in the various islands. Despite London's attempt to truncate and pacify the movement offering little in the way of reform, the winds of change could not adequately be suppressed. By 1944, limited self-government, with an entirely elected House of Representatives, was achieved in Jamaica. This process was quickly followed by Barbados in 1947; Trinidad and Tobago, in 1950; Grenada, St. Vincent, St. Lucia, Dominica, Antigua, St. Kitts-Nevis, Monserrat, Leeward Islands in 1951; Guyana in 1953 with some variations; British Honduras, and British Virgin Islands in 1954. These developments, along with the rise of universal suffrage and the removal of property and income qualification for candidates, would usher in major changes by 1960.

In a real sense, the political transformations of the 1930s through the 1960s allowed for the transference of political power to the Afro-Caribbeans or at least provided them the opportunity to share more equally in it. Yet, other constitutional changes needed to take place if power was actually to be exercised by the people. Control of the legislature was one thing, control of the executive branch another, for it remained the prerogative of the executive to initiate, frame, and enact public policy. How was this to be achieved? The answer was found in making the Chief Executive answerable to the Legislature and nominated by it. (Prior to this, the Executive was answerable to the Crown.) Once full internal self-government was achieved, the drive toward independence was made all the more easy, helped along by the slogans of the struggles of 1939–1945, the decline of European supremacy, and the rivalry between the United States and the Soviet Union after the war.

Independence was intertwined with the issue of federation. Federation was the attempt to bring the various English-Speaking Caribbean states into a common union for the greater good of them all. Whether or not that union should be loose or tight, encompassing all or some of their activities, was the source of much debate. The dominant members in the federation effort were Trinidad/Tobago, Jamaica, and Barbados.

Those who supported federation argued on the basis of political and economic strength that would accrue and the cost of going it alone, that is, each individual state being independent. The skeptics were concerned with the loss of identity, and sovereignty and domination by stronger members. Historians suggest that, during the days leading up to the start of the proposed federation, in 1947–1958, "more time was spent bickering" among the islands than ironing out problems. Most historians point to Jamaica as being principally responsible for the failure of this effort. Certainly, Jamaica had a keen interest in seeking to limit the powers of the Federal government and was not as strong an advocate of the idea as was Trinidad/Tobago, for instance. To a large extent, the disposition of the particular states reflected not so much the leanings of their people but rather the outlook of individual leaders. In any event, Jamaica voted to exclude itself in 1961, setting in motion a chain reaction and leaving Barbados with the smaller Windward and Leeward Islands in what Lewis called, "The Agony of The Eight." The road to independence proved more attractive than the highway of federation. Jamaica, Trinidad/Tobago, Guyana, and Barbados quickly achieved independence, establishing separate societies but with similar problems.

In the Caribbean, the dynamism of political interaction among ethnic groups reflected the historiography and social-transformation of the place. Colonialism had a definite impact on the ethnic structure of these societies giving rise to multiethnicity and, in turn, the multi-ethnicity of these societies had an impact on the nature of politics and political development. In a real sense, therefore, the rise of party politics would reflect the politics of ethnic groups in many of these areas. The dominant groups here were Africans, East Indians, Europeans and Chinese, but not all of them would play the same role in each of the islands.

Independence and Social Structure

European desires to explore, exploit, and export the wealth of foreign lands established populations of strangers in strange lands. The needs and requirements of plantation society in the "West Indies," particularly what is now the English-Speaking Caribbean, were no less responsible for this situation. The merger of African, Indian, Chinese, and European populations was nothing short of an accident of history which, while fulfilling the demands of European capitalism, was to have a major sociological impact upon them, once some semblance of independence was achieved. Thus, the nature of Caribbean society and the cultural heritage which exists must be understood in the context of that development.

The role of European nations notwithstanding (and it was significant), suffice it to say that the achievement of political independence witnessed the jockeying of groups to position themselves in as enviable a place as possible in the new order. Yet, their place in the new society would reflect their prior role in the productive sphere (i.e., the work they performed) as earlier determined by the demands of colonial production and the logic of colonial governance. Hence, while on the one hand, some categories of the African population, along with groups primarily phenotypically European, were better poised to assume the mantle and burden of governing in the newly independent states and determine in large measure the structure, organization, and functioning of the new society. On the other hand, groups such as East Indians, Chinese, and Europeans for the most part monopolized the market activities and retained for themselves the realm of entrepreneurship, industry and merchandising. (One needs to be extremely guarded in this assessment, however, since the social-organizations of post-colonial societies are as much determined by their existence within the global organization of labor as by any factor internal to their development.)

The sociocultural evolution of these societies was demonstrative of the ethnic diversity present. More importantly, however, is the fact that one's place in society did not altogether change with the coming of independence. In Jamaica and elsewhere, the minority Caucasian population managed to retain political control, as

Jamaica demonstrated more a politics of class than race. For these reasons, throughout the islands, Caucasian populations, despite their small size, continue to enjoy a disproportionately superior place in these polities today helped along in part by a culture of inferiority which persists in treating them as such.

In Trinidad and Guyana, particularly, East Indians have succeeded in wresting the comprador sector of the economy and have secured for themselves a middle ground in the society. Their demonstration of upward social mobility has been consistent, experiencing a lull only in times of general economic downturn or social disturbance. In addition, in both Guyana and Trinidad/Tobago, East Indians are increasingly poised to dominate the political sphere.

In places where the Chinese were well represented, they tended to be shopkeepers and grocers. In Jamaica, they moved into larger industrial holdings, but they distinguished themselves in most places by their ability to maintain a guarded distance from every sphere of societal intercourse save the economic.

Africans, by far the largest group in these islands, remain at the bottom of the social hierarchy. In most of these places, they have managed to harness the reins of politics. Yet, on close inspection, one finds that political rulership has had little spillover effects for them and has not translated into significant and meaningful change in ways that one might expect. In Trinidad, Jamaica, and Barbados, where economies are strongest, their social existence stands in stark contrast to that of other groups. In Grenada and Haiti, for much of their twentieth century experience, they have had governments not necessarily dedicated to improving their situation. In the smaller islands, Africans have been busy trying to escape first to larger islands and then to North America or Europe. In the Caribbean, therefore, they might be proud of themselves but they cannot be enviable of their social standing.

In fact, the Africans in the Caribbean, it seems, have emerged last in everything. The casual observer to these islands may be tempted into thinking that there is no authentic indigenous culture there, considering the degree of cultural imperialism particularly from North America. Although the region is well known for its "reggae" and "calypso," American and British "pop" is still likely to dominate the airwaves. More than 90 percent of the television shows are imported, and there is hardly a fad or fashion emanating from the United States, however inappropriate to weather or environment, in which the Caribbean resident is not a full participant. Consequently, in the Caribbean, a culture has evolved which is somewhat hybrid, somewhat fused, and in that limited sense, indigenous.

In Trinidad, for example, the Chinese have continued to celebrate the festival of "double ten" (10th of October). East Indian Muslims and Hindus remain faithful to such religious observances as Ramadan (Muslim month of fasting) and Divali (Hindu festival of lights). Europeans, on the other hand, have their Christmas; meanwhile, Africans curiously participate in every group's festivity. In very few places does there exist any celebration of specific cultural significance to Africans. And, having nothing of their own may well explain why they are part of everything. The writer Lloyd Best, in an essay entitled "The February Revolution," remarked: "I don't know what kind of society each of you wanted to build in the Caribbean, but I know that all of us...have dreamt of something different from the order which has existed there since the days that Columbus launched the Enterprise of the Indies." These remarks were made thirty years ago in 1970; not much has changed since then.

Caribbean culture and society in the English-speaking islands have always been and remain something of a curiosity. Political independence gave rise to new leadership but not new policies. Establishing governments proved to be much less difficult than establishing nations. Yet, the Caribbean has been relatively free of cultural turbulence and ethnic fighting. In most places, there appears to be relative calm. The cultural environment has bred some form of peaceful coexistence in part because the economic elites have isolated themselves from the rest of society. In some respects, it has been achieved because ethnic social intercourse exists without disturbing ethnic boundaries. The point here is that while Africans, Indians, Chinese, and Caucasians work and celebrate together, most have managed to retain a barrier of identifiers around their in-group to which group members could recognize and relate. This has, however, been less true of the African population.

The Caribbean sociocultural environment evolved in such a way as to establish an atmosphere wherein Anglophone and Francophone values still dominate, where, the more one could display these alien idiosyncrasies the more social respect one would likely enjoy, and where the potential for employment and social mobility remains tied to these anachronistic values. In this regard, Africans and Indians have suffered unjustly, and it is here where the roots of revolutionary activity have been observed.

Political and social events in the United States and Europe did not go unnoticed in the Caribbean islands. Indeed Caribbean citizens were often in the vanguard of revolutionary activity in the United States, in Canada, and in the United Kingdom. Major cultural and revolutionary movements of the Afro-diaspora in the twentieth century such as Garveyism, the Harlem Renaissance, and the Black Power movements in the United States and the United Kingdom all had Caribbean citizens in the forefront. The spillover effect to the islands themselves and its impact on society and culture was significant, if not immediate.

In Jamaica, Rastafarianism came to symbolize the revolt of the culturally and economically suppressed and was an attempt to redefine or to define a culture for the African masses. As a movement, it could not be confined to national boundaries despite attempts at suppression. In Jamaica, too, revolt against what was viewed as the miseducation of the people gained full expression in the Walter Rodney Riots of 1968 which followed the historian's assassination. Again, these winds of change blew across the entire archipelago as Rodney himself was to emerge as champion of the revolutionary intellectual elite in his vivid descriptions of the commercial exploitation of Africa and Africans by European nations.

In Trinidad, Africans and Indians teamed their energies to demand a restructuring of the society in 1970. Whether or not they succeeded remains an open question, but they did succeed in releasing a host of problems to fester throughout the region. Reverberations from these events, including the transition to socialism in Grenada in 1979, were felt island-wide in the following years.

Today, Caribbean societies remain marked by inequality and unevenness. As in most other nations, there is significant poverty amidst wealth. It is not unusual to see homes that approximate great manors not more than half an hour's drive from near shacks. It is commonplace to find the most sophisticated gadgetry, devices, instrumentation, and machinery in societies where physical infrastructure is still fifty to one hundred years behind time; where waste water still runs in open canals in the heart of capitals and neighborhoods; where electricity often is not available for long periods during the day; where one could wait months to obtain telephone service; and where living on a hill (and many people do) means coming down to bathe and fetch water at a standpipe. And the contradictions do not end here. In the Caribbean, it is not at all unusual to find residents living in sloping wooden dwellings enjoying an evening of "Lifestyles of the Rich and Famous" on a color television set sent to them by their relatives abroad.

Africans in Caribbean society see governments that are phenotypically reflective of themselves; that is where the resemblance ends. In most places, stores and other businesses are owned by Europeans, Chinese, or Indians. In many areas, too, the professional elite such as medical doctors and lawyers are disproportionately non-African, and some fields such as banking and manufacturing are almost exclusively Caucasian. There is no doubt that Africans in the Caribbean occupy a lower place in the social ladder, and that they are mere workers trying their best to emigrate, even while they sing "Trinidad Is My Land," "Sweet Island In The Sun" or "Grenada Me Come From." Alas, for the African in the Caribbean, as for the African everywhere in the diaspora, even though centuries have passed, time seems to have stood still.

Political Economy and Economic Strains

To understand the political economy of the Caribbean today is to understand the history of its development and underdevelopment. The writer, W. Arthur Lewis, in his book, *The Evolution of the International Economic Order*, explains the rise of European powers and European peoples as producers of manufactured/finished products, whereas Africa and Africans emerged as producers of agricultural/primary products. He explains also the rise of dependence of the developing world on the developed for finance and growth incentives. This particular development was neither accidental, incidental, nor natural to the nations involved, rather, it was planned, contrived, and administered.

If Europe, North America, Australia, New Zealand and other temperate regions entered the twentieth century as economically viable nations, and they did, it was precisely because they capitalized on the wealth of the African world for the rise of their industrial and military superiority. In the process of colonization, Walter Rodney explains in his text *How Europe Underdeveloped Africa*, the wealth of Africans which should have formed the basis of their entry into the modernized, productive world was denied them. Hence, unlike Europe, which started from a state of underdevelopment and moved to a state of development, African nations had to initiate the process without the requisite resources, without control of what resources were left, and without equality in the global market. The process of exploration, exploitation, and exportation of the wealth of these nations, then, determined their position vis-à-vis others and defined the lives of their citizens. This was true of Africa and certainly true of the Afro-Caribbean.

The rise of independence granted superficially and *de jure* economic control to Caribbean governments but did not in a *de facto* sense allow for autonomy in decision making, in strategies or in the determination of product prices. The Ghanaian statesman and liberator Kwame Nkrumah refers to this as neo-colonialism or a new form of colonialism. Caribbean economies today are dependent economies in the sense that they are tied to the economic performance of Europe and North

America (the center) in such a way that any negativism (recessions, depressions, inflations) in the center have direct and immediate repercussions in the periphery. The terms center and periphery are used to suggest the central role of North America and Europe in relation to Caribbean economies which merely revolve around them.

The economic outlook of the Caribbean today is one marked by high inflation rates (15% to 21%), high unemployment rates (10% to 20%), and twin deficits. On the one hand, the Caribbean nations experience significant international trade deficits and external indebtedness, while, on the other hand, they have large internal budget deficits, that is, greater expenditure than income. In these nations, generally speaking, productivity is low and not geared toward the needs and requirements of the local market. The consumption of foreign goods and products is disproportionately high so that spending on imports is extreme but reflective of the fact that these are economies which "produce what they do not consume and consume what they do not produce."

Caribbean economies, despite the existence of light manufacturing in some regions, remain for the most part agriculturally based plantation economies. The major products and thus the majority of exports are sugar cane, rice, bananas and spices. In Guyana and Jamaica, the presence of bauxite allowed for the development and export of iron ore, aluminum and related products. In Trinidad/Tobago, and to a lesser extent, Barbados, oil reserves have played an important part in the economy. For a long time, however, these mineral reserves were fully in foreign hands and remain significantly so as far as control, exploration, marketing and shipping are concerned. Moreover, the determination of prices are almost completely outside the influence of these nations.

Tourism remains a mainstay of Caribbean economies. In some regions such as the Bahamas, it constitutes the backbone of the economy and for each country it is an important source of foreign exchange. It is clear that the performance of a tourist-based economy is tied to the disposable income of would-be tourists at any given time.

If the bulk of production is agricultural, then it follows that most manufactured and finished products must be imported. It is not that Caribbean states import few foodstuffs, rather, in addition to their growing appetite for foreign goods for which locally produced items might be substituted, there is a need for products for which they have not developed industries. Such products as electronics, motorized vehicles, telecommunication devices, home furnishings and general usage items are among the necessary imports.

Since Caribbean states do not exert influence in the working processes of the global market, they suffer from all the disadvantages of being insignificant players. Their ratio of income from exports to expenditure on imports is severely skewed so that their import bill far exceeds their export intake. This is possible for two reasons. Firstly, the prices of their agricultural products are relatively cheap, while the prices of manufactured imports are relatively high. Secondly, the determination of product prices are not necessarily a result of negotiations in which they are significant actors. In their trade relations with metropolitan countries, therefore, the Caribbean suffers from both "unfair trade practices" and "unequal exchange."

Most all of the Caribbean island states have adopted or rather continued in the capitalist mode of production. Indeed, the post-colonial order left them as part and parcel of the world system of capitalism. In select cases, governments have officially declared socialism as the preferred system (Guyana), while in others there have been intermittent flirtations with a mixed economic model (Jamaica). The fact of the matter, however, is that any attempt to deviate from the basic capitalist mode meets with strangulation or other forms of outward and clandestine sabotage from the advanced industrial states, particularly the United States.

Caribbean states have experimented with several economic strategies. In the immediate post-independence period, there was a major drive toward nationalization and localization of key industries. Since they were former British colonies, public utilities and mass communications were already in government hands. Nationalization was that attempt to remove ownership of major assets from foreign domination and control often by locals owning at least 51 percent of the entity; not always did this practice succeed in wresting control from foreign hands. Attempts at forging regional economic cooperation have had mixed results. The Caribbean Free Trade Association (CARIFTA) was superseded by the present Caribbean Community (CARICOM). These were organizations designed to remove or reduce tariffs and other barriers to inter-island trade. While the principle was a sound one, the similarity of products undermined the basis for inter-island trade as well as increased competitiveness among the several islands for external trade.

Recently, the push has been to establish a Common External Tariff (CET) with regard to international trade. The need for this type of cooperation is becoming more imperative as Europe, a major market for Caribbean products, moves toward economic integration. Economic hardship may result from reducing or eliminating once profitable markets.

As with many other Third World nations, major emphasis was placed, in the period from the 1960s to the 1980s, upon industrialization. In the Caribbean, this was done by offering major incentives such as free lands, tax shelters and the like, to multi-national companies. This "industrialization by invitation," as it has been termed, characterized the modernization process in the region. The idea of local production of manufactured goods to replace imports, otherwise called "import substitution," suffered from the absence of "economies of scale," that is, sufficient market size, and also from the fact that the metropolitan centers enjoyed a monopoly of production, so that in most instances it was less expensive to import a product than to produce it locally.

Other attempts were made to obtain some transfer of technology, investments, and greater financial assistance in international fora. The New International Economic Order (NIEO) was one such proposal in the 1970s which achieved very little. Later, in 1982, the United States announced the Caribbean Basin Initiative which promised a secured and guaranteed market for certain products. Its many stipulations, however, limited the ability of the Caribbean states from fully taking advantage of the program, and in its design, it facilitated American enterprise in the region more than Caribbean trade.

Perhaps the most severe economic situation these islands have faced is external indebtedness. The rise of international credit from foreign governments and from international private lending agencies has left many Caribbean states in a debt crisis. Guyana, for example, had a $1.8 billion debt to the United States alone in 1991. The ability to repay loans at high rates of interest have proven unmanageable. It has also created fiscal crises within countries and forced them to undertake measures which have had deleterious effects economically, politically, and socially.

Many Caribbean governments have found it necessary to reduce public spending and social services to their populations. In some instances, massive devaluations of their currencies (70% in Guyana) have reduced the purchasing power of citizens overnight. Cost of Living Adjustments (COLA) have had to be suspended or postponed, and it is not uncommon for public sector workers to be asked to take significant pay-cuts or not to obtain their salaries on time. The political-economic outlook in the Caribbean, therefore, remains characterized by negative terms of trade, foreign capital domination, external indebtedness, and populations lacking in basic needs. In short, the economic picture of the Caribbean, as it now stands, with unremarkable exceptions here and there, remains bleak.

Summary

The end of the colonial era in the Afro-Caribbean left intact a sociological order of peoples and institutions. The privileges and opportunities enjoyed by groups, then, were defined and determined by these realities. In every walk of life—the parliamentary structure, the structure of jurisprudence, the social hierarchy, and the social relationships—the colonial system remained influential.

The drive for political change was dynamic as it forged new alliances, displaced old powers and created some tensions. In many ways, the process here was far less volatile than in other parts of the post-colonial world. It did, however, have some tensions as jockeying for political dominance assumed racial, class, or ideological overtones.

Political metamorphoses did not take place, however, in such a way as to create social transformations which totally displaced heretofore powerful groups. There still emerged societies in which Caucasians and Chinese retained top strata in the social hierarchy with Indians and Africans following. Indeed this manifested itself in different ways consistent with the population mix of the colonial era. The cultural topology which emerged is often difficult to define save to say that it has been heavily imbued by Anglo-American influence. Economically, the Caribbean remains a collection of dependent states whose development is tied to the fluctuations and reverberations of the global economic market; the evolution of the international economic order has seen to that. Caribbean states have started as independent nations for evolution just over thirty years now, still relatively young in the lives of nations. The problem, however, is that, in the foreseeable future, there does not appear to be any potential for these states ever catching up with the advanced industrial states economically, making autonomous decisions politically, or enjoying equal status, internationally. Indeed, emancipation has led to a severely limited and debilitating independence.

Study Questions and Activities

1. Why did African labor emerge as the labor of choice in the colonies? What was the nature of plantation life in the Caribbean colonies?

2. What factors led to the decline of slavery and the emancipation effort in the Caribbean?
3. Describe the social forces, issues, conditions and processes at work in the independence movement.
4. Explain the process of political reform in the shift from Crown Colony to full self-government. What is understood by federation and how did it evolve and die in the Caribbean?
5. What determined the structure, organization and functioning of the newly-independent societies in the Caribbean and how have Africans fared in the sociocultural evolution of the region?
6. What factors determined the place of Caribbean states economically in the global order?
7. What forms have the economic modernization processes taken in the Caribbean since 1960 and how can one characterize the politico-economic outlook in the Caribbean today?

References

Nikongo Ba'Nikongo. *Debt and Development in the Third World: Trends and Strategies*. Washington: IAAS Publishers, Inc., 1991.

George Beckford. *Persistent Poverty*. New York: Oxford University Press, 1972.

Lloyd Best. "The February Revolution." Tunapuna, Trinidad: Tapia House Publishing Co., Tapia #12, December 20, 1970.

———. "Outlines of a Model of Pure Plantation Economy." *Social and Economic Studies*, 17 (September 1968).

J. A. Hobson. *Imperialism: A Study*. Ann Arbor, MI: University of Michigan Press, 1965.

Gordon K. Lewis. *The Growth of the Modern West Indies*. New York: Monthly Review Press, 1968.

W. Arthur Lewis. *The Industrialization of the British West Indies*. Bridgetown: Advocate Printers, 1958.

David Lowenthal and Lambros Comitas. *The Aftermath of Sovereignty: West Indian Perspectives*. New York: Anchor Books, 1973.

Angus Madison (ed.). *Latin America, the Caribbean and the OECD*. Paris: OECD Development Center, 1986.

Walter Rodney. *How Europe Underdeveloped Africa*. Dar-es-Salaam: University of Dar-es-Salaam Press, 1972.

Thomas Swartz and Frank Bonello. *Clashing Views on Controversial Economic Issues*. Guilford, CT: The Dushkin Publishing Group, 1990.

Eric E. Williams. *Capitalism and Slavery*. New York: Capricorn Books, 1966.

———. *From Columbus to Castro*. New York: Harper & Row, 1971.

———. *British Historians and the West Indies*. New York: Africana Publishing Corporation, 1966.

9

Africa's Road to Independence (1945–1960)

Julius E. Nyang'oro

Introduction

For the last thirty years or so, the debate on African decolonization has been informed by several contending positions. The first position is that African independence was achieved because European colonial powers no longer felt it necessary to have formal control of colonies in order to continue with their economic exploitation and control of African natural resources. This school of thought is generally known as the neo-colonial school and is associated with a dependency theory of writers such as Walter Rodney. A second position is one advocated by African "nationalists" who contend that political agitation by nationalists in Africa galvanized world opinion against colonialism in general and European colonial powers could no longer morally defend their role in Africa and inevitably had to give up their colonies. This school of thought can be found in the writings of nationalist leaders such as Julius Nyerere of Tanzania and Kenneth Kaunda of Zambia.

A third position is advocated by authors such as Basil Davidson who make connections between global developments and Africa's decolonization. Here the emphasis is on, among other factors, the emergence of the United States as a global superpower representing western interests against the Soviet Union and its allies after World War II. Support for Africa's decolonization by either the "West" or "East" is thus seen as a function of the "Cold War."

Certainly more positions on decolonization exist, but in one way or another they reflect aspects of the three positions stated above. This presentation of some of the main currents in the decolonization process will center around the political, social, and economic factors influencing the decolonization process; the principal figures in Africa's move toward independence; and the policy of various colonial powers which influenced the decolonization process on the continent.

Major terms and concepts: Colonialism, neo-colonialism, nationalism, underdevelopment, political independence, mass party, elite party, League of Nations, economic independence, trusteeship/mandate territories, guerrilla war, United Nations, assimilado, cold war, civil disobedience, socialism, marxism, Leninism and capitalism.

Background to Decolonization

As chapter 6 has shown, large portions of Africa were formally colonized by European powers in the aftermath of "the Scramble" and the Berlin Conference of 1884–1885. Prior to 1884, European contact with Africa was mostly of a commercial nature, with "free trade" as the operational concept not only between Europe and Africa, but also among European powers themselves. The Berlin Conference changed all that; from then on, African territories became exclusive preserves of their respective colonial powers, as the latter proceeded to establish their authority and forms of administration in their respective colonies. By far, Britain and France had the largest number of colonies, followed by Germany, Portugal, Italy, and Spain.

Africans never accepted colonialism lying down. Even as the Berlin Conference was in session, Africans in different parts of the continent were fighting wars to maintain their independence. For instance, Samori Toure of the West African Guinea Coast fought the French for sixteen years (1882–1898) in defense of his empire. He used both conventional and guerrilla war tactics to wage his military campaign against the intruders. He was eventually defeated. However, in Ethiopia, King Menelik II fought successfully to keep Europeans out of Ethiopia. After the Italians had manipulated and misrepresented the terms of a May 2, 1889 treaty, which had recognized Italian sovereignty over Eritrea and Ethiopian sovereignty under Menelik II, the two countries went to war. The background to the Italo-Ethiopian conflict in many ways is an illustration of the manipulation by European powers in their dealings with African societies which culminated in these societies losing their independence. Thus, in the case of Ethiopia, on October 11, 1889, Italy, in violation of the May 2, 1889 treaty, had submitted to other European imperial powers a treaty which purported to establish Italian control over Ethiopia. In order to enforce its sovereignty over Ethiopia, Italy launched an attack against Menelik II. The war culminated in the battle of Adowa in January 1896 where Menelik II's forces soundly defeated Italian forces, making Ethiopia one of only two countries not to fall under direct colonialism (the other one being Liberia).

Other examples of military resistance to European rule were the Maji Maji revolt in Tanzania, 1905–1907, and the Shona/Ndebele wars in Zimbabwe, 1896–1897. But military resistance was not the only means utilized by Africans. King Jaja of Opobo used diplomacy to resist British encroachment on his territory in the Niger Delta (Nigeria). But in the process of negotiations on board a British vessel, he was kidnapped and exiled to the West Indies by British Vice-Consul Harry Johnson in 1887. Jaja never saw his native land again. He died en route home from exile.

Examples given above reflect the fact that the colonization process should not be seen as a simple exercise of European peaceful occupation of the African continent. These examples also show that anti-colonial forces within Africa were not an exclusive phenomenon of the post-World War II period. Thus, the movement toward independence in Africa should be seen as a process that began simultaneously with African societies' loss of their independence. But it is also clear that, after 1900, Africa was effectively brought under European colonial rule, making the period 1900–1939 the heyday of colonial rule on the continent. Although

Germany lost the African colonies of Tanganyika, South-West Africa (Namibia), Cameroon, Togo, Rwanda, and Burundi as a consequence of her defeat in World War I, these territories were subsequently administered by Britain, South Africa, and France on behalf of the League of Nations. This arrangement caused many legal and political problems, especially in the case of Namibia which did not regain its independence until March 1990.

Post-World War II Developments

The people who organized opposition to colonial authority between the two world wars were primarily professionals who had been educated in missionary schools. These professionals were interested in the improvement of working conditions for Africans within the context of the colonial government, but they were also overtly political. Thus, for instance, the Tanganyika African Association (TAA) was established in 1929 purporting to represent the interest of all Africans in Tanganyika. The immediate stimulus for the formation of TAA was controversy over the proposed closer union of Tanganyika with Kenya and Uganda under British tutelage. Although Tanganyika was under British rule, technically it was a League of Nations mandate territory which would eventually become self-governing. Tanganyika's legal status was therefore significantly different from the colonial situation in both Kenya and Uganda. A closer union between Tanganyika and the two other territories would have undermined this advantageous legal position. As John Iliffe has shown in his book *A Modern History of Tanganyika*, TAA was the first territorial organization in Tanganyika with aspirations of national unity and self-determination. The views of TAA were expressed in its publication, *Kwetu*.

Similarly, in West Africa, the National Congress of British West Africa (NCBWA) was formed in 1919 as a result of a meeting called in Accra, Ghana, by J.E. Casely-Hayford, a leading attorney in the then Gold Coast. The first NCBWA Congress was held in 1920, attracting delegates from many parts of West Africa. Casely-Hayford and his colleagues in NCBW, Ofori Atta and R.A. Savage, envisaged a larger and united nationalist forum for all territories under British rule. NCBWA demanded the introduction of universal adult suffrage, equal employment and promotion for both Europeans and Africans in the civil service, higher educational opportunities for Africans, and a clearer separation of the judiciary from the colonial administration. These demands fell on deaf ears, however, as the British showed no inclination to allow more African participation, despite the NCBWA sending a delegation to London for talks with the British government. By 1930, the Congress had run out of steam as it exhibited the usual strain of lack of leadership when its leader Casely-Hayford died.

Both TAA and NCBWA had been organized and run by the African elites who may not have had direct contact with the masses and lacked the capacity and vision for long range planning. Therefore, it was to be expected that a new group of leadership would emerge to supplant the existing one. During and after World War II, charismatic leaders such as Kwame Nkrumah of Ghana, Sekou Toure of Guinea, Nnamdi Azikiwe and Obafemi Awolowo of Nigeria, Jomo Kenyatta of Kenya, and Julius Nyerere of Tanzania took the leading role in the agitation against colonialism. A little background to World War II is necessary here in order to understand the significance of the war in wider political terms and the emergence of the new dynamic African leadership during this period.

It was noted earlier that Ethiopia was one of two countries not to come under direct colonial rule. But Ethiopia's history is much more complicated than that, especially in the 1935–1941 period, a time which saw the transformation of world politics and nationalism in Africa. Although Italy had been defeated by Ethiopia at the battle of Adowa in 1896, she did not abandon her quest to colonize Ethiopia. Thus, while Europe was busy trying to avoid and/or prevent war at home, Italy seized the opportunity to invade Ethiopia, a fellow member of the League of Nations. In the pretext of avoiding conflict, European members of the League failed to come to the rescue of Ethiopia. The Italian invasion and occupation of Ethiopia and the manner in which European powers sacrificed the symbol of African independence to appease Italy outraged African nationalists and other people of African descent throughout the world. This experience convinced African nationalists that they had to fend for themselves and that any thought of a "progressive" colonialism was but an illusion. Colonialism had to be defeated in all its aspects and independence for Africa restored.

Within four years of the invasion of Ethiopia, European powers were at war with each other, the appeasement posture toward Hitler (and Mussolini) having failed miserably. European colonial powers immediately embarked on a massive program of drafting Africans to fight the war, as they had done in World War I. Many Africans saw action in Europe, the Middle East, and Asia, as the British and French sought to counter the fascist menace globally. But there was something missing in this struggle against the Axis powers. The war cry by Britain and France was the restoration of freedom and justice. Africans were fighting for those ideals, yet, in reality those ideals were absent in their daily lives as colonial subjects. Thus, it is significant that as Africans were contributing to the war effort, President Franklin D. Roosevelt of the United States and Prime Minister Winston Churchill of Britain met and issued the Atlantic Charter (in 1940). The Atlantic Charter was a complicated agreement between the US and Britain over collaboration in the war, but of importance to Africans was a provision in the Charter which stated, inter alia, that, after the war, independence would be granted to non-self-governing territories. Of course, Churchill protested that he had not become the King's First Minister in order to preside over the dissolution of the British Empire, but he had little choice as the U.S. insisted on that provision. After the war, African colonies were not granted independence at a speed which was satisfactory to the Africans, and this increased their agitation, especially for those who had participated in the war against Hitler and his allies and had seen their fellow Africans die for freedom.

Why was the United States eager to support independence for colonial possessions of European powers? One line of thought suggests that the U.S. has had a long history of anti-colonialism, beginning with her own struggle against British colonialism in America. This may be so, but one also must remember that the U.S. has participated in forms of rule that qualified it to be called a colonial power. The Philippines is a case in point. A much more plausible reason for U.S. insistence on the ending of colonialism in Africa and elsewhere would be the changing nature of global politics and economics after the war. By 1940, France, one of the major colonial powers, had been effectively overrun by Germany. Not until the U.S.-led invasion towards the end of the war was France liberated. Britain likewise had been under constant German threat militarily—which in turn undermined both its global political and economic power. Thus, the U.S. was poised to fill this vacuum created by the disintegration of the old order. With the emergence of the Soviet Union as a legitimate competitor for global power and influence, it was only the U.S. which could serve as a counterforce to this new power. Furthermore, with British and French power undermined by the war, it became apparent to the nationalists in Africa that continued political agitation would bear results. It was not uncommon for African nationalist leaders to appeal to the U.S. for support. Among those who travelled to the U.S. to seek support for the nationalist cause were Tom Mboya of Kenya and Nnamdi Azikiwe of Nigeria.

It is fair to say, therefore, that, although the 1920s and 1930s, particularly in North Africa, experienced some political activity on the part of the Africans, it was not until the post-World War II period that African political boldness became evident. Throughout the continent, the "winds of change" created conditions which defied the status quo. Africans, especially through the formation of political parties, were posed to wrestle power from their European oppressors: Nigeria saw the emergence of the National Council for Nigeria and Cameroons (NCNC) in 1944; J.B. Danquah's United Gold Convention (UGCC) was formed in Ghana in 1947; Kwame Nkrumah's Convention People's Party (CPP) formed in 1949 and agitated for self-government; and Kenyan nationalists under Jomo Kenyatta created the Kenya African Union (KAU) which became the Kenya National Union (KANU) in 1960.

Although the French colonies tended to prefer to remain "autonomous republics" within the French Union, after the war political activity increased, demanding an end to discriminatory practices and forced labor (abolished in 1946) and urging the creation of political conditions as free as those enjoyed by metropolitan Frenchmen. General Charles de Gaulle saw himself as indebted to the Africans who rallied to the Resistance following the leadership of Felix Eboue, black Governor of Chad and Governor-General of French Equatorial Africa (1940–1944). After becoming President of the Fifth Republic in 1958, de Gaulle conducted a referendum on independence in the colonies and the result was pleasing to the French. Under the initiative of Felix Houphouet-Boigny of Côte d'Ivoire, the Rassemblement Democratique Africain (African Democratic Rally), with branches in the former French colonies (such as the Parti Democratique de Côte d'Ivoire, Parti Democratique de la Guinee), saw its birth at Bamako (Mali) in 1946. In Cameroon, Ruben Um Nyobe, a trade unionist, organized the Union of the Populations of Cameroon (UPC), in 1948. Kenneth Kaunda, in 1959, formed the United National Independence Party (UNIP) in Zambia, then known as Northern Rhodesia. In Malawi (former Nyasaland), the nationalists founded the Nyasaland African National Congress, later known as the Malawi National Congress, in 1944, which, in 1958, came under the leadership of Dr. Hastings Kamuzu Banda, who had just returned from England. By 1960, following the independence of Ghana in 1957, the demand for independence had spread even to the French colonies which, as mentioned earlier, in a 1958 referendum had voted (with the exception of Guinea) to remain within the French Union. The Belgian Congo and Somalia, as well as many other colonies, including the mandated territories, voiced one demand: independence.

Throughout this exciting period, the most powerful agents for mobilization were the mass parties, which appealed to all segments of the population and had no membership restrictions. There were also other political organizations, commonly known as elite parties, which catered to certain interest groups, such as lawyers, religious and traditional authorities, the educated, and the workers. Most of the examples given above were mass parties, which tended to stand for radical and immediate changes, as was the case with Nkrumah's Convention People's Party. Among the elite parties, which often advocated gradual and moderate change in the colonies, stood the Whig Party in Liberia, the Congolese Workers Party in Congo-Brazzaville, the Comité d'Action Musulmane in Mauritius, and the Royal Party in Swaziland. As demonstrated later in this chapter, the Portuguese colonies, due to the extreme nature of the Portuguese policies and the high rate of illiteracy and poverty, were slow in embracing the slogans of independence. In due time, however, they did forcefully remove the shackles of colonialism.

The end of World War II also ushered a new era in international organization, which helped the African nationalist movement. After World War I, international organization had been characterized by the League of Nations—a weak organization whose ineffectiveness was demonstrated by its inaction on the Ethiopian question in 1935. Still in its isolationist mood, the U.S. had refused to join the League even though President Woodrow Wilson was in favor of it. With the collapse of the League, a new organization—the United Nations Organization (UN)—was established in 1945. The U.S. and the Soviet Union, the two most powerful nations in the world, became founding members, and the credibility of the UN was immediately established. The UN began at the outset to champion the doctrine of national self-determination, a doctrine which holds that individual nationality groups have the right to determine the sovereign state to which they want to belong and the form of government under which they want to live. The concept of self-determination has remained a powerful force in world politics as the events in Eastern Europe have demonstrated in recent years as the Baltic states of Lithuania, Latvia, and Estonia broke away from the Soviet Union and joined the United Nations as independent states.

With the acceptance of the principle of self-determination by the United Nations, a Decolonization Committee within the UN system was established to ensure the smooth transfer of power from colonial to independent governments throughout the world—especially in Africa where the majority of colonial possessions were held. As a result, the UN became the principal forum for galvanizing international opinion against colonialism. Nationalist leaders in Africa began to make trips to New York, the seat of the UN, to make their cause more visible. One such trip was taken in 1955 by Julius Nyerere, the leader of Tanganyika African National Union (TANU), a successor organization to TAA, which by now was openly agitating for political independence, having transformed itself into a political party in 1954. It is generally acknowledged that Nyerere's eloquent defense of Tanganyika as a trusteeship territory of the UN—as a successor of the League—made the British withdrawal from Tanganyika inevitable.

In many ways, India served as an example of what concerted effort against colonialism could yield. Like many territories in the Third World, India had fallen under colonial rule as a result of European expansion abroad. Specifically, India had become a British colony. But from the early years of the twentieth century, India had shown the capacity to resist colonialism by employing a variety of peaceful political methods. Opposition to the British in India in the latter years of colonial rule was led by Mohandas Gandhi who developed the philosophy of civil disobedience. In the 1920s, Gandhi led the movement against apartheid laws in

South Africa as a young lawyer. His tactics, however, proved to be more effective after his return to India. In 1947, India gained independence although Gandhi was murdered as a result of the conflict between Hindus and Muslims in India, culminating in the split between India and Pakistan. But the larger impact of India's independence remained, especially for Africans who saw India's triumph over British colonialism as the beginning of a wave of independence for colonial territories. Many African leaders adopted elements of the Gandhian philosophy of civil disobedience. (It is significant to note that, in the Civil Rights campaigns in the United States in the 1950s and 1960s, Gandhian principles of civil disobedience were widely applied.)

While it is true that the principle of self-determination was accepted even by European colonial powers, on many occasions they showed reluctance to let the colonies go. As a result, in some cases, the use of violence by nationalists became necessary in order to dislodge colonialism. This was the case, for example, in Kenya where the Mau Mau war of independence was waged against the British from 1952 to 1958; in Algeria, guerrilla warfare against the French lasted from 1954 to 1962. Although there was no clear-cut winner militarily in these two examples, the war initiated by African nationalists speeded up the decolonization process. The British reacted by proposing changes in colonial administration in Kenya which led to independence. In the case of France, the emergence of Charles de Gaulle as an effective leader under the Fifth Republic became a strong counter force to entrenched French settler interests in Algeria.

The fiercest military conflict to end colonialism in Africa took place in the Portuguese colonies of Angola, Mozambique, and Guinea-Bissau. Although Britain and France had accepted the principle of self-determination for their colonies and were making plans for the independence of Africa, the Portuguese government was making no preparations to leave the continent. Indeed, the Antonio Salazar government in Portugal never intended to promote independence in its colonies, which, in 1951, were formally declared to be overseas provinces of Portugal. The Portuguese government resisted pressure to begin transfer of power to African hands, whether originating from moderate (elite) reform groups led by African *assimilados* or even from the United States and the UN. By holding fast to colonial control, the Portuguese government inevitably radicalized the resistance of nationalist groups in its colonies. Thus, the Movimento Popular de Libertaçao de Angola (MPLA) was established on December 10, 1956, to fight the Portuguese. Armed conflict broke out in February of 1961. In Mozambique, the Frente de Libertaçao de Moçambique (FRELIMO) was formed in June 1962 and began operations in the colony in September 1964.

Finally, in Guinea-Bissau and Cape Verde, the Partido Africano da Independencia da Guiné Cabo Verde (PAIGC) was formed in September 1956 and armed conflict began in July 1963. MPLA, FRELIMO, and PAIGC eventually led their respective countries to independence: Angola in 1975, Mozambique in 1975, and Guinea Bissau/Cape Verde in 1974. Although these parties became the ruling parties after independence, other organizations had in one way or another participated in the struggle against Portuguese colonialism in their respective, albeit less effective ways. Such was the case in Angola with the Frente Nacional de Libertaçao de Angola (FNLA) and the União Nacional pela Independencia Total de Angola (UNITA) and, in Mozambique, with the Comité Revolucionário de Moçambique (COREMO).

At this point, the political and social/moral reasons for decolonization should be clear. However, economic reasons for decolonization also deserve mention. First, as the strain of war became obvious to the European economies, colonies were quickly pressed into service to provide raw materials for the war effort. This meant that the colonial economies were made more efficient in producing whatever was necessary in the execution of the war, essentially transforming the production structure of the colonies. Second, as metropolitan industries failed to meet demands from the colonies, colonial governments proceeded to establish and/or encourage local production. The earliest of the Import Substitution Industries (ISI) in Africa owe their origin to this necessity. The changing nature of production meant that Africans assumed new and enlarged roles in the economy, allowing them to have access to more money, knowledge and education. The new production structure also led to the formation of trade unions which became important vehicles for nationalists organizing against colonial rule. Indeed, some of the leadership within the trade union movement assumed prominence in the nationalist struggle. Such was the case of Tom Mboya in Kenya, Sekou Toure in Guinea, and Rashid Kawawa in Tanzania.

The most important period for nationalist struggle in Africa is probably the decade of the 1950s. The majority of African countries gained their independence in 1960, with sixteen of them being admitted to the UN as independent nations in one day. Although most of the discussion on colonial powers referred to France and Britain, and, to a lesser extent, Portugal, other colonial powers in Africa also faced opposition by Africans. One such colonial power was Belgium which controlled Zaire (as a colony), and Rwanda and Burundi (as trust territories of the UN). Although Belgium had only one true colony, it nonetheless controlled a substantial part of Africa because Zaire is approximately one million square miles— equivalent in size to the U.S. east of the Mississippi. Zaire became independent in June 1960, but the country has experienced political turmoil ever since. The post-independence political turmoil in Zaire can, in part, be explained by Belgium's colonial policy which never prepared the territory for independence.

Political Independence and Challenges

One principal characteristic of Africa is that it has an underdeveloped economy. The history of African underdevelopment is a controversial subject which has given rise to several schools of thought, a subject beyond the scope of this essay. Here one can simply point to the theorization by scholars such as Walter Rodney and Immanuel Wallerstein who have connected Africa's underdevelopment to the expansion of European capitalism, of which colonialism was only one of its many manifestations. But since colonialism in Africa is a relatively recent phenomenon (1884/85–), the understanding of underdevelopment requires a more thorough analysis that not only addresses the issue of the relationship between colonialism and African underdevelopment but also examines the structural relationship between Europe and Africa before colonialism (slavery and mercantilism) and after colonialism (the post-1960 period). The post-independence structural relationship between Africa and the developed world has been called a structure of neo-colonialism, for it reflects structural similarity with the colonial era except that African countries are now politically independent. This suggests that the nationalist struggle was only the first phase in the struggle against external control. The second phase must be that of economic independence.

In their attempt to implement the second phase of the nationalist struggle, African leaders adopted several ideologies as guiding principles in their quest to attain their goal. Broadly speaking, three ideological frameworks seem to have guided African leaders in this quest: socialism; Marxism/Leninism; and capitalism. It would be a mistake, however, to suggest that these categories and the practice by African leaders were sharply divided. Indeed, in all African countries, the government has always played an important role in planning for economic development and has participated in economic activities through the formation of state-run agencies (parastatals). The post-independence economies of African countries have been a mixed bag of successes and failures, and more needs to be done to pull the continent out of economic difficulties. A few statistics will demonstrate this point.

In a 1989 publication, *Sub-Saharan Africa: From Crisis to Sustainable Growth*, the World Bank stated that the majority of Africans are poorer today than they were thirty years ago—at the time of independence. The GNP of the sub-Saharan region was equivalent to that of Belgium, a country with a population 40 times less. The World Bank has suggested that part of Africa's problems are caused by excessive government participation in the economy which kills individual initiative. This criticism by the World Bank applies across the board to countries theoretically tied to socialism, Marxism, or capitalism. Thus, government participation in economic activities may require better understanding than simply a zeal by government bureaucrats to run the economy of their respective countries. It is not clear, however, at least at the moment, how African countries can begin to tackle the problems of economic independence, the second phase of the nationalist struggle.

Summary

This chapter began with a discussion of the colonization process and the resistance by Africans to European encroachment. Africans did not simply accept colonial rule, but effectively fought foreign domination. Samori Toure and the Shona/Ndebele provide examples of such resistance. However, only two countries—Ethiopia and Liberia—managed to retain their independence. This background suggests that the period after World War II, which is the main period for decolonization, was not the beginning of the movement toward independence. Decolonization must be viewed as a process which began at the instant of colonialism.

Leadership of the nationalist movement went through changes from an emphasis on elite opposition to mass action after World War II. Forces that were taking place on the ground in Africa were related to forces occurring elsewhere in the world, such as in India and at the United Nations, and to the changing structure of power relations in the world. Finally, the movement toward independence must be seen as only the first step in the nationalist struggle—economic independence probably presents a much more difficult task.

Study Questions and Activities

1. What was the importance of the Italian invasion of Ethiopia in the decolonization process?
2. What distinguished the Portuguese from the other colonial powers in Africa on the issue of African independence?
3. What were the main phases in Africa's decolonization?
4. What was the United Nations' role in Africa's decolonization? What were trusteeship territories?
5. Name at least five African nationalist leaders and contrast their role in the movement toward independence.

References

George B. N. Ayittey. *Africa Unchained: The Blueprint for Africa's Future.* New York, NY: Palgrave Macmillan, 2005.

Basil Davidson. *Let Freedom Come: Africa in Modern History.* Boston: Little, Brown, 1978.

John Hargraves. *Decolonization in Africa.* London: Longman, 1988.

Arslan Humbaraci and Nicole Muchnik. *Portugal's African Wars.* New York: The Third Press, 1974.

John Iliffe. *A Modern History of Tanganyika.* Cambridge: Cambridge University Press, 1979.

Ali Mazrui and Michael Tidy. *Nationalism and New States in Africa: From About 1935 to the Present.* London: Heinemann, 1984.

Julius Nyerere. *Freedom and Unity.* Dar es Salaam: Oxford University Press, 1967.

Patricia Palumbo (ed.). *A Place in the Sun: Africa in Italian Colonial Culture from Post-Unification to the Present.* Berkeley: University of California Press, 2003.

Walter Rodney. *How Europe Underdeveloped Africa.* Dar-es-Salaam: Tanzania Publishing House, 1972.

Robert I. Rotberg. *Ending Autocracy, Enabling Democracy: The Tribulations of Southern Africa, 1960–2000.* Washington, D.C.: Brookings Institution Press, 2002.

Sub-Saharan Africa: From Crisis to Sustainable Growth. Washington, DC: World Bank, 1989.

Immmanuel Wallerstein. *The Modern World System*, 3 vols. New York: Academic Press, 1974.

10

The Pan-African Movement

Michael Williams

Introduction

Pan-Africanism has been one of the most fundamental experiences within the history of the African world community. Before analyzing the historical evolution of this movement, it is first necessary to discuss its meaning. There is enough consensus among scholars and consistency within the movement itself to argue that Pan-Africanism has been and continues to be the cooperative movement among peoples of African origin to unite their efforts in the struggle to liberate Africa and its scattered and suffering people. More specifically, Pan-Africanism can be understood as the movement among African peoples in different parts of the world to unite Africa and its people in an effort to liberate them from oppression and exploitation associated with European hegemony and the international expansionism of the capitalist system. Furthermore, Pan-Africanism has always manifested a multi-dimensional character, which has included the use of political, economic, religious, and cultural approaches in the struggle to rehabilitate Africa and its people. In short, Pan-Africanism can be defined as the multifaceted movement for transnational solidarity among African people with the purpose of liberating and unifying Africa and peoples of African descent.

However, during most of the twentieth century, because of its entanglement with Western expansionism, Pan-Africanism has evolved into a variant of the socialist movement as well. In fact, the leading advocates of Pan-Africanism during the twentieth century espoused some form of socialism. Hence, the broadest definition of Pan-Africanism includes both unity (of Africa and peoples of African descent) and socialism.

Major terms and concepts: Pan-Africanism, diaspora, repatriation, African World, Berlin Conference, Garveyism, Nkrumaism, imperialism, Eurocentrism, assimilation, self-determination.

Origins and Early Emigration Efforts

Contrary to the conventional wisdom of most historians of the Pan-African experience, there is sufficient reason to argue that the origins of Pan-Africanism can be traced to experiences on the African mainland during the period of the European-dominated, triangular slave trade. This is because the sentiments and desires for Pan-African unity have been an integral part of the movement. And clearly, those mainland Africans who lost family, clan, and ethnic members to the slave trade manifested a pristine desire for Pan-African unity by grieving for their relatives' safe return to Africa. Similarly, the minority of leaders in Africa who led their people in battle against the European slave trade were putting original Pan-African sentiments into practice.

Instead, the standard approach to analyzing the origins of Pan-Africanism is characterized by a solitary focus on the efforts of African descendants in the Western Hemisphere who responded to the injustices of slavery by seeking to return to Africa or fighting for self-determination in the diaspora. Perhaps the most balanced approach to this question, for now, is to argue that the origin of Pan-Africanism was characterized by a form of mutual duality, thus recognizing the genuine sentiments and concrete efforts of the struggle for Pan-Africanism in Africa and in the African diaspora. It can be plausibly argued that Pan-Africanism originated in the dispersion of Africans and not necessarily just among those who were dispersed.

The struggle of Africans who had been (or whose forebears had been) forcibly removed from their homes to reunite with Africa began in earnest during the earliest years of slavery in the Western Hemisphere. Not only did the lyrics of songs sung by Africans during slavery, in both North America and the Caribbean, indicate a strong desire to reunite with Africa, but even attempted suicides often reflected their longing to return home. This rudimentary manifestation of Pan-Africanism among enslaved Africans and their emancipated descendants continued throughout the slavery period and for many years thereafter, albeit at different levels of momentum and with different degrees of success.

As would be expected, the interest among Africans in North America in physically returning to Africa was greater among those who were most oppressed and most excluded from American institutions. And since lower class Africans in North America experienced a far greater number of injustices than their middle class brethren, the desire to physically reunite with Africa was always greater among the former. This pattern of interest toward Pan-Africanism paralleled experiences in different parts of the Caribbean as well.

The repatriation experience of Africans in the diaspora, who returned to West Africa during the nineteenth century and established Sierra Leone and Liberia, is often included as part of the historical development of Pan-Africanism. However, this experience was more anomalous than congruent with the historical evolution of the Pan-African movement. Both states became, in effect, colonies of the West. And with the use of a class of educated, privileged or financially advantaged African descendants from abroad, the indigenous African population was compelled to provide exploitable labor for European capitalist investments. Still, the willingness of thousands of Africans in North America and the Caribbean to return to Africa, as arranged under white tutelage, is an indication of the sentiments for Pan-African unity among the scattered descendants of Africa at that time. Moreover, many emigration movements, organizations, and the leaders that emerged after the founding of Sierra Leone and Liberia often centered their efforts around the existence and symbolic nature of these two states.

Contrary to the white-dominated emigration schemes of groups such as the American Colonization Society, which transported thousands of Africans in

North America to Liberia, there were many black-controlled efforts to reunite with Africa. This activity also represented a genuine sentiment and burgeoning struggle for Pan-African unity. As early as 1773, slaves petitioned the colonial legislatures of North America to be emancipated in order that they may return to Africa. Around this same time, Africans from Jamaica who were exiled by Great Britain to Canada were making identical requests to their European captors. Also in the Caribbean, men such as Cinque in Cuba and Daaga in Trinidad led movements in the 1830s to reunite with Africa. However, throughout most of the nineteenth century, in general, the efforts by African descendants in the diaspora to reunite with Africa were better financed and organized than the attempts just cited.

The New Englander, Paul Cuffe, is often credited for organizing the first serious attempt to return Africans in the diaspora back to Africa. Driven by almost as much missionary zeal as a genuine thirst for freedom, Cuffe, had he not died unexpectedly in 1817, might have succeeded partially in his objective given the enthusiasm he received from fellow blacks interested in his plans.

By 1859, Robert Campbell of Jamaica and Martin Delaney of the U.S. travelled together in Africa in search for land for resettlement purposes and succeeded in signing an agreement with a Yoruba King that gave them and their followers the rights to uncultivated land. The advent of the Civil War in the U.S., however, was among other factors that prevented Delaney and Campbell from realizing their Pan-African goals.

One year before Delaney and Campbell travelled to Africa, Henry Highland Garnet founded the African Civilization Society, of which he became president. While this organization, like others before it, had ambitions that reflected the Eurocentric biases of the nineteenth and twentieth centuries—which sought to "civilize" Africa with Euro-Christianity—it also had aims that were both militant and Pan-African. In addition to seeking to "strike the deathblow to American slavery," one of its major objectives in Africa was "to establish a grand centre of negro nationality, from which shall flow the streams of commercial, intellectual, and political power which shall make colored people respected everywhere." Despite his occasional vacillation, Garnet succeeded in keeping alive the notion of reunification with Africa; still, he was unable to implement his plans effectively, partly because of the hostility he received from men such as Frederick Douglass in the United States who adamantly opposed any efforts that were inconsistent with his aspirations for black assimilation into the North American mainstream.

During this same period, in the Caribbean and in Latin America, there were many African descendants who sought and advocated a return to Africa in order to assist in Africa's development. Although they mostly came as Christian missionaries, these black missionaries had motives that were often significantly different from their European counterparts, the latter of whom often worked in concert with European explorers and colonizers. One of the groups responsible for organizing this trek of black missionaries from the Caribbean to Africa was the West Indian Church Association, formed in the 1850s. One of the most successful products of this effort was Edward Blyden from St. Thomas, in the Virgin Islands, who began his evolution into Pan-Africanism as a Christian missionary. After dropping this pursuit, Blyden soon became one of the leading Pan-African intellectuals in the African world. Throughout the last quarter of the nineteenth century, he worked laboriously for African descendants in the diaspora to return home. Due largely to his encouragement, many other African descendants in the Caribbean sought to return to Africa.

During the last decade of the nineteenth century, no one better embodied the notion that oppressed descendants from Africa, especially in the United States, should return to Africa in order to liberate Africa and Africans everywhere than Bishop Henry McNeal Turner. He was a leader in the African Methodist Episcopal Church in the United States and organized many efforts to realize his Pan-African goals. Turner made frequent trips to Africa and constantly promoted the idea of African emigration which nourished the growing disenchantment among the poorer segments of the African American population in the United States. Poor black peasants were especially receptive to Turner's message. Although he never succeeded in transporting any significant number of people back to Africa, he did make a significant contribution towards keeping alive certain fundamental Pan-African ideals. Foremost among these was the notion that the only hope for scattered African descendants was in building a powerful and independent nation of their own in Africa.

While there were many other emigration efforts that took place throughout the African world that have not been covered in this brief summary, a genuine appreciation of this dimension of the historical evolution of Pan-Africanism requires an understanding of several key points. First, the black controlled efforts never made claims on land outside or inside of Africa that required the eventual expulsion or political and economic subjugation of indigenous inhabitants. Second, the majority of followers of these movements belonged to the poorer segments of the African world population, as the more economically mobile African descendants observed with disdain. Third, in relative terms, the number of African descendants who actually returned to Africa was never that large, although the figures can belie the actual support that emigration schemes received from the masses of scattered Africans. Fourth, these movements, although never really anti-capitalist in their ideological orientation, were clearly manifestations of a resistance to the consolidation of black suffering and white supremacy under the growing domination of the international capitalist system. Fifth, the movements were very influential in the historical development of Pan-Africanism, as they became effectively interwoven with similar movements and events that occurred in the struggle for Pan-African unity throughout the twentieth century.

Twentieth and Twenty-First Centuries Developments

Pan-African activity geared towards physically reuniting African descendants abroad with their ancestral homeland did not stop after the turn of the century. Bishop Turner continued to lead the emigration movement in the United States during the first decade of the new century. Replacing the void left by Turner after his death was Chief Alfred Charles Sam of the Gold Coast in West Africa. Chief Sam generated considerable enthusiasm for his emigration plans by travelling extensively, forming emigration clubs and selling shares of stock in his emigration company, the Akim Trading Company. He received his greatest support from all-black communities in Oklahoma in 1914. Although Chief Sam succeeded in re-turning a small amount of followers back to the Gold Coast, conditions in Africa—the result of British lack of cooperation and African underdevelop-ment—led to disenchantment among the emigrants.

The evangelical dimension of the Pan-African struggle to return African de-scendants to Africa also continued. These efforts contributed in no small way to the radicalization of the religious leadership and laity in Africa. As a consequence, by 1926, white missionaries—the religious embodiment of European expansion-ism—grew so disquieted from the growing Africanization and radicalization of Euro-Christian doctrines, that they organized, in Le Zoute, Belgium, an interna-tional conference of missionaries concerned with Africa. One of its main purposes was to prevent the return of black missionaries whose teachings resulted in "seri-ous disturbances" in Africa.

Although the European partitioning and colonization of Africa began nearly two decades before the beginning of the new century (formalized at the infamous Berlin Conference of 1884–1885), it was not completed until two decades into the twentieth century. The Pan-African response to this bold initiative on the part of the European capitalist powers was significant. Given the considerable amount of communication and interaction that had already taken place prior to the twen-tieth century between Africans on the mainland and their brethren scattered abroad, it is no wonder that African descendants in different parts of the world were able to engage themselves effectively in Pan-African cooperation against the injustices of European hegemony during the first quarter of the twentieth century. Several conferences, congresses, and conventions were organized by African de-scendants, some even before the twentieth century, to address the common misery and suffering experienced by Africans under European colonial rule in Africa and African descendants living in the Caribbean and within the colonial metropolitan governments in Europe and the United States. Some of the most important meet-ings of this type included the Chicago Congress on Africa of 1895; the Atlanta Congress on Africa of 1895; the Pan-African Conference of 1900 in London; the First Universal Race Congress of 1911 in London; the Pan-African Congresses or-ganized or inspired by W. E. B. DuBois in 1919, 1921, 1923, and 1927; and Mar-cus Garvey's Universal Negro Improvement Association conventions that met in the United States between 1920 and 1925.

These meetings were organized and attended by outstanding Pan-African pro-ponents as well as other notable intellectuals, businessmen, bureaucrats, and roy-alty within the African world. Although reformist in nature, the resolutions drafted at these meetings were consistent and demonstrated an anti-imperialist awareness; a strong desire for greater Pan-African unity and cooperation between peoples of African descent; an aim of industrializing and advancing Africa in par-ticular and all African peoples in general; an effort to preserve and regenerate Africa's most worthy cultural traditions; and a responsibility to protect the sover-eignty of Ethiopia, Liberia and Haiti against the attacks of European imperialist domination. It is interesting to note that, due to the political, economic and mili-tary hegemony of the West, all of these meetings were held outside of Africa, de-spite attempts by DuBois and others to hold such meetings inside.

In 1914, Marcus Garvey founded the Universal Negro Improvement Associa-tion and African Communities League (UNIA-ACL) in Jamaica. He did so, ac-cording to his own account, in order to address the wretched condition of the

African World at that time—which he observed, firsthand, throughout his travels. Furthermore, Garvey benefitted from, and was deeply influenced by, the Pan-African efforts of his nineteenth-century and early twentieth-century predecessors. The impact that Garvey and the UNIA-ACL had on the African World in general, and the Pan-African movement in particular, was monumental. Their influence is still being felt today, in large part because of the tremendous organizational success that characterized the Garvey movement. With chapters and divisions of the UNIA-ACL in almost every corner of the African World, Garveyites could boast a membership of nearly six million. That Garveyism had a profound impact on the thinking and behavior of millions of African descendants struggling to be free during the 1920s and 1930s is unquestionable. Even Garvey's detractors had to admit that he "was undoubtedly one of the greatest Negroes since Emancipation, a visionary who inspired his race in its upward struggle from the degradation of centuries of slavery."

With great organizational skill and oratorical mastery, Garvey took advantage of the frustration and disillusionment that peoples of African descent were feeling after the First World War in which they had fought and died, supposedly, to make the world safe for democracy and to ensure the right to self-determination. Having been denied these basic human rights for so long and experiencing greater levels of economic penury, African people around the world, especially those in the United States who had migrated to either southern or northern cities with the false expectation that life would be better, placed unparalleled faith in the Pan-Africanism of Garvey and the UNIA-ACL. And while Garvey's program, despite its limitations, did address, concretely, many of the basic problems that confronted the African World community, most historians and other commentators have consistently and mistakenly reduced Garveyism to simply a "Back to Africa Movement." However, although emigration plans were undoubtedly a part of the UNIA-ACL's overall strategy, its primary and ultimate objective was to liberate and reconstruct Africa into a nation powerful enough to liberate Africans around the world. On behalf of the UNIA-ACL, Garvey declared:

> We are determined to solve our own problem, by redeeming our Motherland Africa from the hands of alien exploiters and found there a Government, a nation of our own, strong enough to lend protection to the members of our race scattered all over the world, and to compel the respect of the nations and races of the earth.

In short, the contribution of Garvey and the UNIA-ACL to the struggle for Pan-Africanism was unrivaled, and explains the keen interest the imperialist powers had in seeing Garvey fail. As a movement staunchly opposed to European imperialism, the Garvey movement lionized the fundamental ideals of Pan-Africanism in a way never before done in the long history of the movement.

In addition to the Garvey movement, at the end of the First World War, there emerged a number of other activities centered in Western Europe, that were significant expressions of Pan-African struggle. While some of them received their initial impetus from the Garvey movement, these efforts, in the main, were also a product of increased disenchantment with colonial rule that resulted from the hundreds of thousands of black troops who returned from the war effort and were denied the basic human rights that they had been told they were risking their lives to defend. These expressions were manifested in the creation of several organizations dedicated to the realization of Pan-African aims. In London, Africans from West Africa and the Caribbean formed the Union for Students of African descent in 1917. A year later, also in London, the African Progress Union (APU) was formed, with the famous Egyptian Pan-Africanist, Duse Muhammed Ali, as one of its members. The APU's declared aim was to promote the social and economic welfare of African peoples throughout the world. By the mid 1920s, the influential West African Student's Union (WASU) was established, including in its membership, despite its name, Africans from other parts of Africa besides West Africa. Moreover, it was concerned with other issues besides student-related ones, such as the future advancement of Africa and African peoples throughout the world.

France, as the colonial power that had expropriated more of Africa's land than any other European nation, was not devoid of Pan-African activity after the First World War. In addition to its capital serving as the location of the 1919 Pan-African Congress, the Paris Peace Conference at Versailles was the target of further Pan-African efforts. DuBois, along with others, sought to arrange for Africa to have a voice at this Conference. Besides advocating the establishment of a Charter of Human Rights to guide the colonial powers in their relations with mainland Africa, they sought to affect the impending redivision of Africa by the victorious Allied Powers along lines consistent with their Pan-African goals. That the European powers chose to ignore these concerns and continue pursuing their imperialist interests in Africa should not overshadow the significance of this Pan-African attempt. Indeed, subsequent to this, not only did DuBois make similar requests to the newly-formed League of Nations, but Marcus Garvey and the UNIA-ACL made identical demands to this same body.

The French-speaking African community in France created several Pan-African organizations in Paris. Men such as Marc Kojo Tovalou Houenou of Dahomey, founder and president of the Ligue Universelle pour la Defense de la Race Noire, challenged the assimilationist policies of French colonialism between the years of 1924 to 1936. Interestingly, Houenou was invited to the 1924 UNIA-ACL Convention in New York City. With the production of its journal, *Les Continents*, the Ligue Universelle pursued aims that were fundamentally Pan-African.

Also important during this period was the Comité de la Défense de la Race Nàegre, led by Lamine Senghor from Senegal, and the Ligue de la Defense de la Race Nàegre, led by Tiemoho Garon Koyate from the Sudan. These organizations, built by French-speaking African descendants from Africa and the Caribbean, showed great interest in the plight of the African diaspora in the United States, and were particularly impressed with the rise of Garveyism. Moreover, they were more radical than the Ligue Universelle, since they understood, and vehemently criticized, the collaboration between the rulers of French colonialism and the French-speaking African middle class. Consequently, they earned a considerable amount of hostility from French governmental authorities.

The ideological radicalization of the Pan-African movement continued during the 1930s. Led by African descendants from the Caribbean located primarily in Great Britain, numerous Pan-African organizations were established by committed socialists such as George Padmore and C.L.R. James—friends from childhood in Trinidad. During the mid 1930s, James formed the International African Friends of Abyssinia (IAFA). Shortly afterwards, Padmore created the International African Service Bureau (IASB), which was replaced by the Pan-African Federation in 1944. James and Padmore, along with other West Indians, were joined by other notable figures from different parts of Africa, such as Jomo Kenyatta of Kenya and I. T. A. Wallace-Johnson of Sierra Leone. Collectively, through the convening of several meetings and the dissemination of anti-colonial writings, they were essentially responsible for maintaining the only significant Pan-African opposition to imperialist plunder throughout the African World. While the ideological persuasion of this group of Pan-Africanists was diverse, they were practically all heavily influenced by the writings of Marx and Lenin.

In 1935, the Italian invasion of Ethiopia intensified the growing anti-imperialist orientation of the Pan-African movement. As chairman of the IAFA, James's reaction to this crisis reflected the views of many Pan-Africanists during this period when he wrote:

> Africans and people of African descent, especially those who have been poisoned by British Imperialist education, needed a lesson. They have got it. Every succeeding day shows exactly the real motives which move Imperialism in its contact with Africa, shows the incredible savagery and duplicity of European Imperialism in its quest for markets and raw materials.

The Italian invasion also served to galvanize the seemingly latent Pan-African aspirations of African descendants around the world. For instance, in different countries they organized Ethiopian support groups, raised funds for weapons and medical supplies, boycotted Italian-produced goods, wrote articles condemning Italy and admonishing the League of Nations, petitioned European colonial powers to deny Italy loans and weapons, held prayer meetings, staged violent riots against colonial governments, and sought to join the Ethiopian military effort against the Italian invaders. However, despite the groundswell of popular support this movement received from countless black communities around the world, African peoples were still unorganized. Hence, they lacked any significant amount of power to save Ethiopia from the clutches of European imperialism or to achieve any other meaningful Pan-African objective.

Post-World War II Trends

The end of World War II, a decade after the Italian invasion of Ethiopia, meant the beginning of the end for colonialism proper in Africa. Factors associated with this development had a profound impact on the Pan-African movement. Like the Italian invasion, factors related to the end of the Second World War stimulated the growth and development of Pan-Africanism significantly, contributing further to its radicalization. One of the most stimulating factors during this period was the international espousal of the right of all people to independence and self-determination contained in the Atlantic Charter, a document created by Great Britain and the United States. No less significant was the fact that, once again, hundreds of thousands of black troops from North America and the colonial dependencies in Africa and the Caribbean had participated in this war that was supposedly fought for the democratic ideals extolled in the Atlantic Charter. Hence, these circumstances contributed significantly to the growing unwillingness to tolerate inequality and oppression throughout the African World. Unlike the period following the First World War, during the post-World War II period the imperialist powers would not succeed in denying, at least in principle, the right of African peoples on the continent, and soon afterwards in the Caribbean, to govern themselves. After the wreckage of World War II, the weakened European victors were in no position to reverse the anti-colonial movement that was gaining in strength, especially in light of the growing socialist threat in parts of Asia and Eastern Europe. And so it was in the context of these opportunities that the Pan-African movement, during and after the Second World War, became stronger and more militant.

This development culminated, to a large extent, in the Fifth Pan-African Congress of 1945 in Manchester, England. Organized by George Padmore, Kwame Nkrumah and other important figures associated with the Pan-African Federation in Great Britain, this Congress symbolized in many ways the coming-of-age of Pan-Africanism. It differed significantly from other Pan-African meetings, conventions and congresses in that: 1) the numerical participation of native-born Africans was greater; 2) there was a greater ratio of delegates who represented the organized labor of African workers and farmers; 3) the socialist world view clearly dominated in the discussions on the solution to the problems facing Africa and its people; 4) the more passive and reformist resolutions passed in previous Pan-African meetings were replaced with more radical resolutions (one of which did not rule out the use of force to achieve Pan-African objectives); and 5) a strategy to liberate Africa, in Africa, became the primary focus for the new, revolutionary Pan-African agenda.

Specifically, the Manchester Congress condemned the partition of Africa and the economic exploitation of the continent and the lack of industrial development, advocated a stronger stand against settler colonialism, demanded an end to illiteracy and malnutrition, and supported the independence of Algeria, Tunisia, and Morocco. It further requested the recognition of the rights of syndicates and cooperatives by colonial powers, and approved the demand for independence by West African delegates present at the Congress, and embraced the UN Charter. That many of the participants at this historic Congress made quite notable contributions to the defeat of colonialism proper in Africa a decade or so later only indicates the importance of the Manchester meeting.

One such contribution was the pivotal role Kwame Nkrumah played in the struggle to wrest political control from the British in Ghana (in what was then called the Gold Coast). From 1947 until Ghanaian independence in 1957, Nkrumah led his countrymen in a Positive Action campaign of mass strikes, boycotts and demonstrations. The strategy used in Ghana by Nkrumah was heavily influenced by the Manchester Congress. The British were left with no other choice but to relinquish political power. The implications of this event for the rest of Africa and the entire African World were astounding. With practically every part of the African World experiencing, in some form or another, political subjugation at the hands of powerful white nations, Ghana's independence in 1957 symbolized, at least in the hearts and minds of countless African descendants around the world, the beginning of a new world order. Understanding the significance of this emerging sentiment, Nkrumah made his famous declaration that the independence of Ghana was meaningless without the total liberation of Africa.

It was at this juncture in the historical development of Pan-Africanism that Nkrumah became the leading embodiment of the movement. As such, he wasted no time in making Ghana the major citadel of the Pan-African movement. In 1958, Nkrumah, with the critical assistance of George Padmore (his African Af-

fairs advisor), convened two conferences in Ghana that were historical mile-
stones in the struggle for Pan-Africanism. The first was a conference of Independent African states, held in April of 1958. The second was the All-African
People's Conference in December of the same year. While there were many important resolutions passed at these conferences, their real significance lay in the fact
that they were held on African soil. These conferences inspired the convening of
other similar conferences later held in Tunis in 1960, in Cairo in 1961, and again,
in Ghana, in subsequent years. Even the formation of the Organization of African
Unity in 1963 can be traced to the efforts of Nkrumah to achieve his Pan-African
goals for Africa. In short, until his death in 1972 (even after the 1966 coup d'etat
that toppled his government), Nkrumah's theoretical and practical efforts to realize the goals of Pan-Africanism had a tremendous impact on the world in general
and the African World in particular.

The OAU is one example of this, for, although it has never measured up to the
radical demands and expectations of Nkrumah and other revolutionary Pan-
Africanists, it has provided some assistance to the Pan-African movement in
Africa over the past three decades. The OAU's mild successes have included its
contribution to conflict management, the struggle against colonial and settler
colonial rule, and economic development and cooperation. However, because of
its lack of genuine authority and control over its member states, and the ideological disunity of Africa's leadership, its resolutions and decisions have not been always adhered to and implemented.

In fact, the OAU, whose Charter was signed by thirty African States on May 25,
1963, in Addis Ababa, was a compromise between those States which advocated
outright unification of the continent, comprising Morocco, Mali, Ghana, Guinea,
Algeria, and Libya (with delegates from Ceylon), known as the Casablanca Group
(so named after their conference in Morocco, in January 1961) and those who favored a gradual approach to unification and regional associations or groupings.
The latter have been commonly known as the Monrovia Group (which had met in
Monrovia, the capital of Liberia, in May 1961.) Included in the Group were Somalia, Liberia, Nigeria, Sierra Leone, Congo-Brazzaville, Tunisia, and Ethiopia,
joined by the Brazzaville Group, made up of several of the former French colonies,
such as Côte d'Ivoire, Gabon, Chad, Senegal, Madagascar, and Cameroon.

In reality, the moderates, led by Felix Houphouet-Boigny (of Côte d'Ivoire) and
Lepold Senghor (of Senegal), prevailed over Kwame Nkrumah (of Ghana), Mod-
ibo Keita (of Mali), and Sekou Toure (of Guinea). Thus, the objectives of the
OAU were to:

> Promote unity and solidarity of the African States; coordinate and intensify
> their cooperation and efforts to achieve a better life for the peoples of Africa;
> defend their sovereignty, their territorial integrity, and independence; eradicate
> all forms of colonialism from Africa; and promote international co-operation
> having due regard to the Charter of the United Nations and the Universal Dec-
> laration of Human Rights.

The OAU Charter made Addis-Ababa the headquarters for the Secretariat-Gen-
eral, and provided for a yearly meeting of the Heads of State and a biannual gathering of the Foreign Ministers to prepare for the meeting of the Heads of State.

The civil war in Chad, for which the Organization dispatched a peace-keeping
force in 1981, the Eritrean war, the protracted fighting in former Spanish (Western)

Sahara, the Somali-Ethiopian war of 1977–1978, and the dispute following the assumption of power by the MPLA in 1975 demonstrated clearly the powerlessness of the OAU and the ideological divisions, as well as the personal ambitions of the African Heads of State—all underscored by the lack of action by this august body during the recent civil war in Liberia (which saw the intervention, not by a OAU force but by that of the Economic Council of West African States [ECOWAS] entirely dominated by Nigeria). Hence, since 1963, the OAU has failed to solve many of the major problems confronting the African continent, despite the fact that, by 1990, its membership had risen to fifty-one countries. (The OAU's problems have been compounded by a low turnout at the meetings of the Heads of State, personal and ideological differences, external pressures, particularly from France and the United States, and inconsistency in the payment of membership dues). No matter its successes or failures, the OAU has not turned out to be the kind of a unifying vehicle or the real aim of the founders of Pan-Africanism.

The 1966 coup in Ghana was a major setback to the Pan-African movement. However, the emergence of the Black Power movement that same year in the United States, and later in other parts of the African diaspora, represented the continuation and spread of the Pan-African idea. Personified best by Caribbean-born Kwame Toure (formerly Stokely Carmichael), this radical movement was strongly influenced by the nationalist uprisings in Africa and the work of Pan-Africanists such as Nkrumah, Sekou Toure, Frantz Fanon, and Malcolm X (whose courageous efforts, especially during 1964, played a tremendous role in shaping the consciousness of young activists towards a Pan-African orientation). After exhausting all reformist means possible (during the Civil Rights movement) to end the economic exploitation and political subjugation experienced by African descendants in the United States, a large sector of activists began seeing their plight as indistinguishable from other African peoples in the Caribbean, Europe and Africa. Hence, as early as 1968, Black Power activists in the United States, as they were encouraged by Nkrumah and Malcolm, began advocating that all peoples of African descent were African, and that Pan-Africanism was the solution to the problems facing the entire African World. By the 1970s, the Black Power movement was clearly manifested in the ideological and organizational development of young black radicals in the Caribbean, Western Europe, and South Africa. As in the United States, it soon transformed itself into a variant of Pan-Africanism.

In the United States, the generative effect of the Black Power movement continued unabated, with several Pan-African formations established during the early 1970s. The African Liberation Support Committee (ALSC) was one important formation during this time. However, the most significant of these was the founding of the All-African People's Revolutionary Party (A-APRP) in 1972, shortly after Nkrumah's death. The A-APRP was created by African descendants from different parts of the world who were committed to practicing the Pan-African ideas of Nkrumah, i.e., Nkrumaism (since Nkrumah himself had called for the formation of an A-APRP in 1968). Its original founders included, among others, Black Power advocates such as Kwame Toure and Willie Ricks, and Nkrumah loyalists such as Lamin Jangha of the Gambia.

During the 1980s, several events, some of them tragic, have had a significant impact on the Pan-African movement. Before the tragedies began, the birth of the Pan-African Revolutionary Socialist Party (PRSP), which split from the AAPRP in 1983, represented the further development of Pan-Africanism in the creation of another Nkrumaist organization. Its newspaper, *The Nkrumaist*, is one of the few Pan-African publications, since Garvey's *The Negro World*, fifty years ago, that attempts to speak to and for the entire African World. However, Sekou Toure's sudden death in 1984 and the subsequent right-wing coup in Guinea, have meant a significant loss to the movement because of the late President's dedication to the Pan-African cause. Other similar and decisive events that have damaged the Pan-African movement have been the assassinations of presidents Maurice Bishop of Grenada (and the dismantling of the Grenadian Revolution) in 1983 and Thomas Sankara of Burkina Faso in 1987. As committed Pan-Africanists, their deaths have deprived the Pan-African movement of potential and badly needed land bases on which the Pan-African movement could be better coordinated and consolidated. In the 1990s, other centers and sources of Pan-African activity emerged in different parts of the African World. The heightened level of struggle to end apartheid in South Africa is perhaps one of the most fertile locations for the development of Pan-Africanism today.

At the dawn of the 21st century, new Pan-African developments began to take shape in the face of the continued inefficiency of the OAU. Spearheaded by Libya's Mummar Al Qaddafi, and influenced by the growing strength of the European Union, a call for the creation of an African Union (AU) was made at the 36th meeting of the OAU in Lome, Togo, in July of 2000. By July 2002, in Durban, South Africa, the AU was formally launched. Designed to respond to the challenges faced by globalization and to enhance the pace of African development, African Heads of State and Government have formalized their effort to speed-up the process of African continental integration. Some of the main features of the AU will include the establishment of an African Central Bank, an African Monetary Union, an African Court of Justice, and a Pan-African Parliament.

However, while the AU seems to be an improvement from the erstwhile OAU, problems remain. There has been, for instance, very little effort to educate the masses of African farmers, workers, and youth about the imperative of African unity. In short, in the villages, towns, cities, and campuses where the concept of African unity must take root, nothing is being done to foster its development amongst the millions of people who must bring it into fruition. Furthermore, certain internal flaws in the constitutional structure of the African Union serve to detract from the realization of genuine African unity. For example, Article 3b of the AU constitution lists as one of its objectives "to defend the sovereignty, territorial integrity and independence of its member states." Hence, like the OAU before it, the AU is in some ways serving to reify the bulkanization of Africa.

Furthermore, despite the constant challenges of the AU to contribute to Africa's security, stability, and development, it continues to remain ineffective in the face of ever-increasing problems around the continent. Recent conflicts in the Democratic Republic of the Congo, Cote d'Ivoire, and Liberia reinforce this fact—with foreign troops, including American, French, and British, still being relied upon to settle intra-African disputes. In fact, even a small army in the tiny Republic of Sao Tome e Principe can—as the recent coup makers there have proven—defy the existence of the AU. So far, the modalities for an African Union's intervention force are nonexistent and so is the mechanism for the election and seating of a continental (Pan-African) Parliament. Ambiguity also remains vis-à-vis a common front against international terrorism (usually defined in terms of violent, anti-West Islamic fundamentalism), some member states, such as

Kenya, favoring the US Administration's preemptive war to topple governments that are unilaterally declared the "axis of evil" and the assassination or "elimination" of their leaders. Others maintain a defiant stance but are unable to voice it openly, making their statements and policy on terrorism and the appropriate approach to deal with it utterly ineffective. Therefore, the new AU fervor notwithstanding, the jury is still out and Pan-African advocates should not be surprised if the new organ turns out to be just the old OAU in disguise.

Summary

In sum, Pan-Africanism has been a multifaceted movement that has undergone many changes and has experienced much development. However, it has not yet met its ultimate objective of unifying and liberating Africa and its people along the path of socialist reconstruction. There are a number of reasons that account for this fact, not least of which includes the manipulations and intransigence of imperialist domination, especially in its neo-colonial phase of development. Another significant and related factor is the failure of Pan-African organizations to build the type of unity among themselves that is necessary to achieve the objectives of Pan-Africanism. In other words, the Pan-African movement has always been poorly coordinated, with no umbrella organization having ever been created to consolidate it transnationally. This partly explains why so many Pan-African organizations have been created, only soon to be disbanded after a few years of existence. Thus, while the motive for Pan-African resistance seems strong and consistent, there still exists no institutionalized mechanism within the African World to ensure its continued growth and development.

Study Questions and Activities

1. Discuss the meaning of Pan-Africanism.
2. What were some of the characteristics of the early emigration efforts of Pan-Africanists prior to the twentieth century?
3. Who were some of the major figures in the Pan-African movement, and what were some of the contributions they made?
4. In what way has the Pan-African movement been influenced by major world events?
5. Discuss some of the more recent developments in the Pan African movement that have occurred since the 1980s.

References

Yassin El-Ayouty (ed.). *The Organization of African Unity After Thirty Years.* Westport, Conn.: Praeger, 1994.

Olisanwuche Esedebe. *Pan-Africanism: The Idea and Movement, 1776–1963.* Washington: Howard University Press, 1982.

Marcus Garvey. Editorial in *Blackman*, Dec. 30, 1939.

Imanuel Geiss. *The Pan-African Movement: A History of Pan-Africanism in America, Europe and Africa.* New York: Africana, 1972.

Tony Martin. *The Pan-African Connection: From Slavery to Garvey and Beyond.* Cambridge, MA: Schenkman, 1982.

John Mukum Mbaku and Suresh Chandra Saxena (eds.). *Africa at the Crossroads: Between Regionalism and Globalization.* Westport, CT: Praeger, 2004.

Kwame Nkrumah. *Africa Must Unite.* New York: International, 1963.

W. Ofuatey-Kodjoe (ed.). *Pan-Africanism: New Directions in Strategy.* New York: University Press, 1987.

George Padmore. *Pan-Africanism or Communism.* Garden City, NY: Doubleday, 1971.

Vincent Bakpetu Thompson. *Africa and Unity: The Evolution of Pan-Africanism.* London: Longmans, 1969.

Robert G. Weisbord. *Ebony Kinship: Africa, Africans, and the Afro-American.* Westport, CT: Greenwood, 1973.

PART III

THE PRESENT AND THE FUTURE OF THE BLACK WORLD

11

The Contemporary African World

Luis B. Serapiao

Introduction

Chapter 9 outlined Africa's struggle towards political independence. As a logical follow-up, this chapter focuses on the major problems of post-colonial Africa and identifies some of the solutions proposed by government officials as well as scholars. It is obvious that some of Africa's problems have their origins in the natural process of colonies becoming nations. Scholars have identified them as problems of nation building. Similarly, Africa has had to establish and maintain relationships with the outside world, which most scholars have characterized as relationships of dependency. Thus, the assessment of the performance of African governments in the post-colonial era has produced two major types of theoretical framework. One is based on general theories of nation-building or what some call theories on development. The second type, which attempts to explain the nature of Africa's relationship with the outside world, includes the entire approach to the understanding of dependency. It is not the object of this chapter to discuss the theories in detail, but only to such an extent as to provide to students simple tools of analysis of the achievements and failures of post-colonial Africa.

Major terms and concepts: National integration, new economic order, revolution of rising expectations, hegemony, apartheid, dependency, non-alignment, homeland, ethnicity, irredentism, secession, colonialism, macro-nation, micro-nation, per capita GNP, Group of 77, UNCTAD, trade deficit, ANC, neo-colonialism, LDC's, Cold War, ECOWAS, SADCC (now SADC), marginalization, demarginalization, and conditionalities.

Nation-Building and Economic Development

Africa's decolonization process has been marked by three main periods or waves of independence: the 1950s, the 1960s, and the 1970s. Prior to 1950, only

Liberia, which became independent in 1847, Egypt in 1922, and Ethiopia, for centuries an independent state (except for the brief interlude between 1935 and 1941 under Italy), were independent states. During the 1950s, three colonies in Sub-Saharan Africa, Sudan (1956), Guinea (1958) and Ghana (1957), achieved independence, joining the already independent states of Libya (1951), Morocco (1956), and Tunisia (1956). The majority of the African colonies (some thirty-one of them) joined the rank of independent nations during the 1960s. During the 1970s, the five Lusophone former colonies, Mozambique, Angola, Guinea-Bissau, Cape Verde, and Sao Tome e Principe, achieved their independence in 1974–1975, followed by Comoros (1975), Seychelles (1975), and Djibouti (1977). Zimbabwe, Namibia, and Eritrea became the last to join the community of independent African states in 1980, 1990, 1993, respectively.

The achievement of independence in Africa elicited many hopes within the leadership and among the African masses. For some leaders, such as Kwame Nkrumah, first President of Ghana, political independence became a key for the solution of all problems related to socioeconomic development. "Seek, ye, first the political kingdom," said Nkrumah, and all Africa's problems will be resolved. Many other political leaders at the time of independence shared the same philosophy. For the common people, political independence meant the opening of doors to those opportunities which were closed to them during the colonial era. In summary, the euphoria of independence created what Africanists have called a "revolution of rising expectations." Strategies to achieve these expectations became part of the main process of nation-building.

Forging national unity has been the major political problem of every independent African state. The process of achieving this objective falls under the strategy commonly known by scholars as national integration. Colonial boundaries and ethnicity (identification with one's ethnic origin) have been singled out as two major sources of the problem. Most ethnic groups in Africa form what may be considered mini-nations, or groups of people with a common culture and language and shared historical experience, usually living in or originating from a specific geographical area. As a result, they exhibit close affinity and bond, and find it difficult to transfer allegiance to a state or the "macro-nation," which was artificially created by outsiders with no regard for cultural boundaries. Scholars and politicians alike in Africa have argued that the success of national integration depends on the subordination of these ethnic micro-nations to the macro-nation. The resistance of the micro-nations has created two main problems, commonly known as irredentism and secession.

Irredentism usually emerges out of a situation where one ethnic group was split by colonial boundaries, resulting on two or three sometimes antagonistic countries sharing parts of that group, as it happened with the Makonde in Tanzania and Mozambique, the Dan in Sierra Leone and Cote d'Ivoire, and the Somali in Somalia, Ethiopia, and Kenya. It has happened at times that an ethnic group, enjoying the support of one of the macro-nation, has sought the unification of its members. When the process of seeking this unity is violent, it is often called irredentism, and can cause border conflicts and even wars. A typical example of this kind of conflict occurred between Somalia and its neighbors, Ethiopia and Kenya. During the 1970s and 1980s, the government of Somalia, in pursuit of the unification of the Somali, demanded the political and territorial unification of its people. Obviously, its neighbors would not go along with the demand. This led to a war between Somalia and

WAR

Ethiopia during 1977–1978 and clashes in 1986 (Somalia having lost that contest), while Kenya and Somalia maintained extremely tense relations throughout that period (Somalia and Ethiopia signed a treaty ending hostilities in April 1988; Kenya and Somalia had signed one in November 1984.) At times, ethnic allegiance has resulted in internal political turmoil and even civil war, as has been the case, at least in part, in Liberia, Sudan, Mozambique, Rwanda, and Burundi.

Another aspect of micro-national or ethnic loyalty over nationwide or macro-national loyalty has taken the form of secessionist movements. Some ethnic groups have attempted to form their own government and become independent from the present macro-nation, as defined by the colonial boundaries. Typical examples of these attempts are the cases of Katanga (the present Shaba Province) in the Democratic Republic of Congo (DRC), the former Belgian Congo, Congo-Leopoldville, or Zaire, in 1944, and of the Ibo of Biafra, (1967–1970). In DRC, a civil war broke out in 1960, partly as a result of secessionist tendencies which ended temporarily with the assumption of power by Joseph Mobutu in 1965. (Political rivalries and foreign interests, particularly Belgian mineral companies, heightened and compounded the national problem.) During 1977 and 1978, Mobutu had to request the assistance of Belgian, French, and Moroccan troops to quell the resurgence of the rebellion, while the Ibo of Eastern Nigeria fought unsuccessfully against the federal government of General Iakubu Gowan from 1967 to 1970. None of these ethnic groups, however, ever succeeded in breaking away from the nation-states. In 1991, the Eritrean ethnic group declared independence from the rest of Ethiopia. This event became historic, not only because it violated the principle of the Organization of African Unity (OAU) on national integration, but also because it challenged the whole notion that the principle of self-determination was not applicable to post-colonial Africa.

It was mentioned earlier that independence was perceived by many as a panacea to all problems, as an "engine" which would totally eradicate poverty on the continent. Unfortunately, the expectations did not materialize. In fact, according to Roel Van der Veen, Africa failed to break free of poverty after gaining independence. Today, Africa is the poorest continent. The concept of poverty, here, includes three main approaches. The first one, which is influenced mainly by economists, analyses Africa from a financial perspective. It emphasizes one dollar per person a day as a criterion for the definition of poverty. Anyone living below one dollar a day will fall in the category of a poor person. In 2004, when U.S. former President Jimmy Carter was observer of the presidential election campaign in Mozambique, he considered Mozambique one of the poorest countries on earth because most people were living below one dollar a day. There are other scholars who argue that the dollar yard-stick cannot be used in all social environments. For example, what one can buy with one dollar in a country could differ in another. Thus, this writer suggests the inclusion of other factors in the definition of poverty, namely, social, economic, political, and psychological considerations. The argument is that we must pay attention to inadequate control over productive facilities, lack of political influence, and poor access to such services as health care, education, water, and sanitation. Additionally, the concept ought to include the lack of information and awareness of the public services that are available to individuals. These two last criteria are necessary to prevent the marginalization or exclusion that has been linked to poverty. The model emphasizes the human poverty approach which is much closer to reality than the one-dollar a day approach. Amartya Sen, the Indian Nobel Laureate, advocates the choice theory. For him, poverty is a lack of opportunity, a lack of choice. Indeed, he equates poverty with a lack of choice. In the case of Africa, the logic will dictate that the entire continent is not free. It has no choice.

How many people, then, have been losing their freedom, or how many people in Africa are living without a choice? The World Bank, in the late 1990s, provided statistics which shows that the population of Africa would rise by over 300 million in 2000 and by 345 million by 2015. Obviously, the preceding statistics cause concern to many responsible African leaders. The problem demands a solution. Scholars on poverty in Africa agree that there is no single cause that can explain these grim statistics. Also, there are those who insist that the shortage of skilled people contributes greatly to the impoverishment of the continent. The painful situation, however, is that Africa rather than maintaining its own skilled people, is losing them to the Western world, to the USA, in particular. For example, according to UN statistics, from 1985 to1990, Africa lost 60,000 professionals, among them doctors, lecturers, and engineers. Since, then, Africa has been losing 20,000 professionals annually. For every 1000 professionals sent abroad for training, 35 do not return home. As mentioned earlier, most of them go to the U.S.A. The International Organization for Migration statistics show that there are more African scientists and engineers working in the U.S.A. than in all of Africa. A few years ago, Zambia had 1,600 doctors, now only 400 work there. More than 21,000 Nigerians are working in the U.S.A. In Zimbabwe, two-thirds of the professionals left the country during the past five years. Unfortunately, the exodus of such skilled workforce is causing a heavy financial burden on the African governments. The continent spends an estimated $4 billion annually for the recruitment of some 100,000 expatriates.

The international economic system has also had a negative impact on African development. Mention was made of Africa's staggering foreign debt, the terms of which have almost bankrupted some African states. The acquisition of capital for the colonies and, later, for independent Africa, depended partly on the exportation of Africa's minerals, oil, and cash crops to the Western industrialized world. Yet, not the African governments but European and North American governments and multinational corporations have continued to determine and control the prices of these commodities on the one hand—prices which, in most cases, have not been favorable to the Africans. On the other hand, both during and after the colonial period, Africans have been compelled to pay for finished manufactured goods from overseas and finance their economic development using so-called hard currencies (the dollar, the franc, the British pound, or the Deutsche mark). This economic relationship with the industrialized world, particularly in the trading sector, has been and continues to be detrimental to Africa and underscores its state of dependency. It is an unfair and exploitative relationship. Unfortunately, in a true sense, the colonial legacy, adverse natural geo-physical factors, and the international economic system can be seen as problems that are beyond the immediate control of the African governments.

The root of Africa's socioeconomic stagnation, however, is the direct consequence of policy formulation by the African leaders, who must themselves bear the responsibility for much of what is going wrong in Africa today. In most cases, the wrong policies have been the outcome of well-intentioned development strategies, which can be characterized as poor planning. Yet, in the case of some

African leaders, policies or ideologies of personal aggrandizement, misguided ambitions, and corruption have ruined any chances of development which might make a difference in the lives of the people. Following independence, Africans adopted different ideologies as guiding principles to deal with their problems and sometimes spelled out their priorities. Instead of food sufficiency, for example, their most common priority was law and order as a prerequisite to any development. In other words, political order took precedence over economic policies, instead of having both as partners of concomitant approaches.

In the name of political order and unity, for example, many African leaders advocated a one-party state or military rule. Paul E. Sigmund, in *The Ideologies of Developing Nations* (1963), noted that Julius Nyerere of Tanzania, one of the most respected leaders on the continent, used to say that foreign nations would take advantage of a country with an opposition and a multi-party system, confuse people, and create chaos. "Who does not know," he asked, "any stooge who will dance to their political tune?" For Nyerere and other leaders at the time (such as Joseph Mobutu), opposition political parties were not concerned with the welfare of the nation. African leaders have also argued that political maturity did not exist yet in Africa. In fact, Nyerere once said that "mature opposition is rare in a newly independent state. Usually, the irresponsible individuals I have mentioned have neither sincerity, conviction, nor any policy at all, save that of self-aggrandizement." For many leaders in Africa, therefore, a one-party state was the only viable strategy for development, because, they claimed, countries, with the exception of Senegal, The Gambia, and Botswana, adopted a one-party system immediately after independence. Unfortunately, the system did not result in socioeconomic improvement in the lives of the people. Instead, it gave rise to a new wave of opportunism in African politics: the military, which, during the mid-sixties and seventies, toppled civilian governments left and right. In 1966, for example, six army coups took place in Africa and, by April 1985, 24 countries were under military regimes, while only 21 still maintained civilian rule. Interestingly enough, the main arguments of law and order and nation-building advocated by the military were not different from those put forth by civilian single-party advocates. In order to maintain themselves in power, both military and civilian leaders have often squandered the resources of the nation by apportioning a greater part of the national budget to procure arms and satisfy the military that are a threat that can topple most governments as they please.

Most recent analysts, particularly Samuel Decalo, insist that personal power and self-aggrandizement are the major reasons for the intervention of the military in African politics. Indeed, reality has shown that *coups d'etat* have not been aimed at radically changing Africa's basic socioeconomic and political structures. Most leaders of both regimes have continued to support a capitalist path toward development, even though a few have advocated, as early as the sixties, socialism as an alternative to capitalism. The promoters of this new approach included the late Kwame Nkrumah of Ghana, Sekou Toure of Guinea, Modibo Keita of Mali, Gama Abdel Nasser of Egypt, Ahmed Ben Bella of Algeria, and Julius Nyerere of Tanzania. In general, their brand of socialism was still influenced by the ideology of anti-colonialism; it was nationalist socialism. In 1975, particularly with the independence of the five Lusophone former colonies, a new type of socialism, namely, Afro-Marxism, emerged, with Mozambique, Angola, and Ethiopia becoming its leading practitioners. As an ideology, Afro-Marxism represented a rad-

ical departure from a pure one-party state system, such as the one adopted in
Cote d'Ivoire a few years ago, and from a military regime, such as the one prevalent in the DRC (formerly Zaire), because these countries still pursued a capitalist
model of development. At the same time, however, Afro-Marxists distanced themselves from any type of nationalist socialism, as they insisted that the other brands
of socialism in Africa lacked the ingredient of "scientific socialism."

Afro-Marxism upholds the classic theory of class struggle, emphasizing that
African governments are ruled by a bourgeoisie elite class which maintains strong
ties with the bourgeois classes in Western capitalist states. Domestically, while it
calls for the elimination of the bourgeoisie and the abolition of private ownership
of the means of production, it advocates democratic centralism and the establishment of state-directed economic institutions. As for relations with the capitalist
world, Afro-Marxism favors restricting linkages (trade relationships), avoids active participation in world economic organizations (such as the World Bank and
the International Monetary Fund), and it used to call for strong ties with the Soviet Union and its ideological allies, such as China and Cuba. Unfortunately, none
of these ideologies succeeded in solving the socioeconomic malaise in Africa. In
effect, wherever these ideologies existed, they shared a common "value" of an authoritarian system. They emphasized government control and monopoly over the
sociopolitical and economic activities of the country and remained anti-democratic by nature. Violations of human rights, including the suppression of dissenting
opinion, incarceration and death sentences without trial, and restriction of freedom of movement within and outside the country, became part of the dominant
style in African politics. Yet, even though the dream of those who aspired and
fought for the true independence of Africa remained illusive, it was alive, as the
latest changes on the continent have demonstrated.

This section would be incomplete without taking note of the phenomenon of
political change which began in the 1980s and 1990s, which is now sweeping
through the African continent. The Afro-Marxist states of Mozambique, Angola,
and Ethiopia, for example, have caved in to domestic and international pressure.
They have renounced their "Afro-Marxism-Leninism" (Ethiopia, having been the
most radical of the states, in this camp) in exchange for a multi-party system and
privatization. Military dictatorships (such as the one in former Zaire), as well as
civilian dictatorships of one-party rule (as evidenced in Cote d'Ivoire, Zambia,
Cape Verde, Sao Tome e Principe, Kenya, Cameroon, and Gabon) are either being
dismantled or have already been dismantled, as is the case in Zambia and Togo.
Yet, not all African countries were victims of authoritarian rule. Those which enjoyed a modicum of democracy such as Botswana and The Gambia, are the leading examples in Africa, while, more recently, Namibia has been hailed as a model
other countries on the continent should emulate. One should likewise point out
that independence brought some social gains to the continent. The most frequently cited example falls in the areas of education, health, water, feeder roads,
and energy. However, an assessment of the balance sheet on the development of
post-colonial Africa indicates that the losses outweigh the gains, as the following
statistics show.

In education, African leaders today have been eager to promote a peace-building education. The obvious reason for the new emphasis is that, during the last
past two decades, almost half of Africa has been devastated by armed conflict.
The wars affected universal access to primary education whose enrolment fell by

30 to 40 percent. African governments reacted by calling a conference on conflict and education in Africa, which took place in Mombasa, Kenya, on June 2–4, 2004. The conference paid most of its attention to three main points: prevention of conflict, education in emergence situation, and post-conflict reconstruction of the educational system. The main argument here is that, in this era of so many conflicts, the scope of education should include not only cognitive issues but ought to capitalize on policies and models that promote values, attitudes, and socially appropriate behavior. Accordingly, in their classrooms, teachers should introduce syllabi whose content reflects the values noted above. Thus, they urge, one of the strongest components of the syllabi should emphasize inter-group skills, since conflict analysis identifies inter-group confrontation as the main characteristic of Africa's contemporary conflicts.

In addition to conflicts, another "curse" plaguing the continent is the HIV/AIDS crisis. In some countries, education, especially health education, has been contributing greatly to limiting an escalation of the crisis. For instance, South Africa, in conjunction with the Southern African Development Community (SADC), launched *The Higher Education HIV\AIDS Programme, in November 2001*. The program involves the partnership of three educational organizations: The South African Vice-Chancellors Association (SAUVCA), the Committee of Technikon Principals (CTP), and the National Department of Education (DoE). It is designed to provide support to all public universities, technikons, and SADC partners. One should note that, on February 21, 2005, the University Vice-Chancellors from SADC launched the Southern African Regional University Association (SARUA). SARUA members will coordinate efforts to combat the HIV/AIDS in the Southern African region where the population has tripled since the 1960s, while the population of African capital cities has increased ten times. During the 1960s, most African capitals had approximately 50,000 inhabitants. But, by year 2000, virtually half of those capitals reached a population of half a million. Three major factors contributed to the mass migration to the urban centers, particularly the capital cities. Natural disasters, such as drought, the first factor, pushed the population to the cities were food was still available. The second factor has been internal conflict, civil wars and all kinds of armed violence, which forced people to seek security in the urban areas. Capitals that experienced heavy population due to civil war include Maputo (Mozambique), Luanda (Angola), Khartoum (Sudan), and Freetown (Sierra Leone). Job opportunities and freedom attracted particular young people. Fall in this category Johannesburg (South Africa), Addis Ababa (Ethiopia), Lagos (Nigeria), and Kinshasa (DRC).

Africa in World Affairs

It was noted earlier that the international environment has played a relevant role in the performance of independent Africa. When Africa became independent, it entered a world divided politically and militarily into two camps: the Eastern bloc, led by the Soviet Union, and the Western bloc, led by the United States. Economically, however, the world was dominated and controlled by the Western industrialized countries, with the United States as the leading giant. Thus, Africa had to find political and economic strategies which would enable her to survive in this "alien" and ever-competing international environment. While in the field of politics the major obstacle was the Cold War, trade became the stumbling block in the economic arena. At this juncture, two aspects of Africa's international relations are worth exploring briefly.

Politically, the two antagonistic blocs of East and West were competing for politico-military hegemony in world affairs. Both were eager to secure spheres of influence, establish military bases in allied countries, and control votes in international organizations. Toward this end, they were prepared to deliver political and economic favors to the newly-independent African states: economic aid, educational assistance, and support for the total decolonization of Africa, the Portuguese colonies and Namibia included. Because it had no colonies in Africa and no colonialist allies, the Soviet Union championed decolonization openly. Accordingly, at the United Nations, it supported every resolution against colonialism, imperialism, and Zionism. In fact, it went so far as to provide military assistance to anti-colonial movements in the Portuguese colonies, Namibia, Ethiopia, and Zimbabwe. Although, on one hand, Africans welcomed this special military assistance from the Soviet Union and its allies, on the other hand, they refused to allow foreign military bases on their soil. The United States and other Western countries, aware of the financial difficulties the newly independent African states were facing, pledged to provide economic and technical aid. Africans, of course, welcomed this help, but their policy on foreign military bases on their soils adopted vis-à-vis the Soviet Union did not change in their relations with the West.

The policy of refusal to establish a military alliance with either bloc became known as non-alignment. Although non-alignment turned out to be the guiding principle of African states in world affairs, it did not exclude special relationships. For example, the former French colonies maintained a tight relationship, which included military pacts, with France after they achieved their independence. Also, as Africa became deeply divided ideologically during the 1970s, the socialist-oriented countries, with Afro-Marxists at the center, developed stronger socioeconomic and even military ties with the Soviet bloc, while the pro-Western states cultivated similar relations with the United States and its allies, making non-alignment an empty word. From a guiding principle, non-alignment became a movement (a movement may shift emphasis and goal in midstream), capitalizing instead on the solidarity of Afro-Asian countries with the objective of extracting concessions from the West in some specific socioeconomic and political areas. Starting with the Banding Conference in 1955, by mid-1960 the non-aligned bandwagon was joined by the Latin American countries and referred to as the "Group of 77." During the first phase of the new movement (1950–1970), which covers the period leading to the Lusaka Conference, most of the demands from non-aligned countries were political, particularly in regard to the decolonization process, which it hastened through its bloc voting in the United Nations.

During its second phase, the non-alignment movement shifted its emphasis from political to economic matters. During the 1970s, African leaders and experts realized clearly that the continent's colonial role of providing raw materials to the west had not changed drastically. As was the case during the colonial period, Angola, Congo, Nigeria, and Gabon, for example, continued to export oil to the West; Liberia, Mauritania, Niger; Sierra Leone, Togo, Zaire, and Zambia still shipped minerals, such as copper and iron (at a loss), to the West; Ghana, Cote d'Ivoire, Kenya, and Malawi exported such agricultural products as cocoa, coffee, tea, and tobacco; while Mozambique, Lesotho, Swaziland, and Botswana continued to provide their human resources (manpower) to the mining industry in South Africa. Yet, Africans neither dictated nor controlled the prices of the resources provided to the world market. The prices of their commodities often fluctuated according to the perceived needs and demands of the Western countries. A typical example of this fluctuation was that of Ghana's cocoa in the 1980s and Zambia's copper in the 1970s. This situation has not been altered today.

Another problematic aspect of Africa's persistent colonial (or neo-colonial) position in the world economy is the need to import manufactured goods. Colonial powers were not interested in building manufacturing industries in the colonies or improving the local African economy in order to benefit the Africans — indeed, one of the major objectives of imperialism was the accelerated exploitation of raw materials to feed European industries. Since African industrial development has lagged, the continent had little choice after independence but to export its raw materials to the West and buy back the processed materials in the form of tractors, clothing, cars, tires, coffee, cigarettes, etc. The price Africans pay for these finished goods includes the wages of the Western industrial workers who process the raw materials and the profits of manufacturing companies. If African countries had their own manufacturing industries, the money spent on imported manufactured goods would be paying African workers and nourishing African economies, rather than draining them for the benefit of the former colonial powers and other industrialized countries.

In an effort to solve the dilemma of Africa's powerlessness, leaders and scholars have advocated three major approaches. The first, which is prevalent among "core conservative" leaders and scholars, advocates keeping the status quo in trade relationships, with minor changes. Countries perceived to lean toward such an approach included Malawi, Kenya, Cote d'Ivoire, Lesotho, and perhaps Cameroon. The second approach has been articulated by "radical" leaders and scholars such as Samir Amin and A. Babu, and it emphasizes what has come to be called "delinkage." According to the proponents of this theory, Africans and no one else ought to determine the nature of their trading relationships, which should result in either Africa not having any relationships at all or in reducing it to a minimum. Countries advocating this approach included the Afro-Marxist states of Angola, Mozambique, and Ethiopia. This explains why, for example, for approximately 10 years, Mozambique did not open its doors to international cooperation and refused to join the International Monetary Fund and the World Bank.

The third theoretical approach has been advanced by the majority of the African states and scholars, and it calls for the reevaluation of this historically distorted trade system. It seeks dialogue between Africa (and all developing countries, including those in Latin America) and the Western industrialized nations. The dialogue has essentially taken place within the United Nations Conference on Trade and Development (UNCTAD). African demands have been articulated by the Solidarity Group or the Group of 77, comprising every developing country, sometimes called the less developed countries (LDCs). The argument of the developing countries is that the terms of trade between them, particularly Africa, and the industrialized countries have been one-sided, to the detriment of those who provide the raw materials.

Three major factors contributed to the unfavorable trade balance between Africa and the western world. The first was the result of Israel-Palestinian war in which Arabs lost miserably. The OPEC, which was dominated by Arab nations, decided to use oil as a weapon against the West because of the help it provided to Israel. It raised the oil price, and African countries were the most affected by it. They now had to pay not only for the high price of oil, but for other needed products as well. The terms of difference in the trade of primary commodities, namely, agricultural products and minerals, shifted in favor of the Western world. For instance, in mid-980s, Zambia's copper price fell by almost half from the price it used to sell it in world market. Also, Western countries began to reduce their imports, including those from Africa. As a result, African exports began to decline, while the import level continued to be relatively high. The second major factor that affected unfavorably the balance between Africa and the West was the collapse of the Eastern Bloc. The Western world was now eager to invest and to trade with the former communist countries. As a result, such primary products, as uranium from Niger and manganese from South Africa, lost their former communist buyers. Consequently, the price of Niger's uranium and South Africa's manganese dropped. These incidents prove the loss of strategic importance of Africa to the Western countries.

Finally, the appearance of the former communist countries in the international market at the end of the Cold War reinforced globalization, which became linked with the economic marginalization of Africa. Currently, the open market in the former communist bloc attracts multinational corporations, which are quick to invest and initiate trade wherever favorable economic opportunities present themselves. Unfortunately, Africa will not compete successfully with these new comers. As for debts, fortunately, Africa will have some degree of relief. Following the creation of the African Unity (July 2002) and the Agreement on the New Economic Partnership for African Development (NEPAD), NEPAD member states—Nigeria, South Africa, Senegal, and Algeria—met leaders of the G-8 nations to seek support for NEPAD. Obviously, the meeting had positive results. In 2004, British Prime Minster Tony Blair brought together 17 experts and concerned citizens to form a Commission for Africa. The objective of the Commission was *to define the challenges facing Africa and to provide clear recommendation on how to support the changes needed to reduce poverty*. Tony Blair has been lobbying the G-8 members to gain support for this program aimed at the eradication of poverty in Africa. Surprisingly, on June 11, 2005, Finance ministers of G-8 announced a 100 percent debt cancellation of 18 developing countries, of which twelve are African.

In 1963, African nations banded together and formed the Organization of African Unity. Developed to assure Africans a voice in both political and economic matters on the continent, the OAU struggled for decades to establish its position of authority on the continent. While in theory it was supposed to function much like an African version of the United Nations assisting to stabilize and develop the continent, the OAU often faltered in its scope, and failed to provide any lasting impact. Recognizing the ineffectiveness of the OAU, and desiring to see an African body which would serve the continent's varied needs and goals, African leaders opted to disband the Organization of African Union and replace it with the African Union (AU). In July 2002, the African Union was established as a new incarnation of the OAU. Like the OAU, the African Union is a unifying body of African nations dedicated to the advancement of African nations and peoples and seeking new alternatives to combat Africa's many social, economic, and political problems. Unlike the OAU, the AU has an expanded role and a more detailed focus, one which will be put forth by its various operating organs and legislative bodies. Currently, the African Union is comprised of fifty-three member states. Each member state plays a valuable role in representing its country's interests to the entire body while also helping to formulate policy and plans for a united Africa.

The structure of the African Union is similar in many ways to other multinational organizations, including the United Nations and the European Union. The assembly is the chief organ of the AU, comprised of heads of state and government from member nations. The Executive Council is made up of the Ministers of Foreign Affairs from member countries, while the Permanent Representative Committee is made up of various representative and ambassadorial positions. There are a variety of specialized technical committees charged with addressing various aspects of Africa's development—political, social, environmental, and economic. The Pan-African Parliament, a new body of the African Union being organized, but one that has not yet been ratified, seeks to bring unity to the continent through the fostering of Pan-African ideals and encouraging member states to act together to tap into Africa's potential. Other bodies within the AU include the Economic Social and Cultural Council (ECOSOCC) the Court of Justice and African financial institutions including the African Bank, the African Monetary Bank, and the African Investment Bank.

The goals of the African Union are multi-faceted and varied, but encompass broad efforts at development, and ambitious plans for monitoring civil and regional unrest, social and cultural marginalization, education, protecting the environment, and a host of other issues. More specifically, the AU has endeavored to work towards a peaceful, unified Africa through the enforcement of the African Charter on Human and Peoples' Rights, encouraging all African peoples to respect the rights and self-determination of others, fostering economic growth and building Africa's capacity for involvement in the global marketplace, and promoting better health and education initiatives throughout the continent. A Peace and Security Council of the AU is garnering considerable attention as of late, largely due to the ever-present conflicts on the continent and the need for a pan-African consensus on how to handle the conflicts as a continent. At a meeting in Maputo, Mozambique, bolstered by support from the United Nations Development Program (UNDP), the AU established the Peace and Security Council which functions somewhat like the UN Security Council. The Peace and Security Council is made up of 15 member states, but, unlike the Security Council of the UN, none has veto power. The Council will be supported by a "Council of the Wise," made up of five respected African dignitaries appointed for three-year terms. In an attempt to dissuade countries from conflict and encourage a stabilizing presence on the continent, the Peace and Security Council will have the power to dispatch troops from stand-by African armies, and will assist in peace-building efforts. In addition to the UN, certain Scandinavian organizations have been involved in capacity training and funding of the council.

Additionally, a recent outgrowth of the African Union is working to develop the economic interests of Africans and ensure the continent a successful future outside the Western sphere of influence. This new approach to demarginalize the continent and work towards a better future for Africa has been substantiated by the New Economic Partnership for African Development. The New Economic Partnership for African Development is a recent agreement of the African Union aimed at addressing the problems plaguing the African continent with regard to deficits in economic development and integration into the world economy. Beginning with the broad concept of economic development, the initiative seeks to raise awareness of how the lack of development (and by extension bad development practices) affects a myriad of issues, including the position of women and children on the continent, political progress, health, and technology and environmental concerns.

The New Economic Partnership for African Development (NEPAD) is a program of the African Union, in essence a vehicle for development with the full support of the AU. Thabo Mbeki, current president of South Africa, is widely considered to be the driving force behind the NEPAD program and has worked to empower NEPAD to replace former initiatives for development such as the failed Lagos Plan of Action developed in 1980. The major impetus for NEPAD is an understanding by African leaders that, in order to develop, African nations must be able to take care of themselves, to develop outside of Western involvement and to begin to provide goods and services by Africans for Africans. Recognizing that financial assistance provided by Western nations often carries controlling stipulations, African leaders are concerned that Africans extricate themselves from Western control, through working to develop their own resources and dedicating themselves to building capacity for development. However, while NEPAD seeks to free African nations from the control of developed nations, it recognizes that African nations do not possess the financial resources necessary to accomplish its goals. NEPAD, therefore, seeks to procure Western financial contribution to Africa's development through the encouragement of equitable industry investments, partnerships, and ventures that will contribute to the advancement of the African economy.

NEPAD's program attempts to set up a formula for African development. Its core documents analyze the many development roadblocks that African countries face, most notably, lack of technological know how due to widespread education and training deficiencies, political instability and governmental corruption, the marginalization of women and certain ethnic groups, and environmental problems that threaten the eco-stability of Africa's future. It appears that the major problem with NEPAD is similar to the major problem of the African Union. It has not been around long enough to determine whether or not it is actually a viable mechanism for development. The NEPAD structure is organized, coherent, competent and widely supported, but it is not necessarily implementable if African nations do not seriously approach it in terms of its practical applicability. Concerns as to the future of NEPAD seem to be that it will fall by the wayside much as other development programs have, as currently African nations lack the united front necessary to make the initiative effective. Still, the African Union hopes that African nations and leaders will be drawn to the possibilities of NEPAD and, in the hopes of bettering their own countries, they will be willing to band together with others to make it work.

In short, while there are, as one writer put it, "laudable goals" associated with NEPAD, it remains to be seen if NEPAD will, in fact, be effective in its approach. However, the documents produced by the NEPAD commission describing its goals and intents include very perceptive and seemingly accurate assessments of Africa's current development dilemmas, from social and political, to economic and environmental. If it receives the necessary support from the international community and is given concerted attention from African nations, it might have the potential for successful and sustainable growth and development on the continent.

Southern Africa

The independence of Africa, which was technically completed with the successful decolonization of Namibia in 1990 and the recognition of Eritrea's independence in 1993, left behind some 34 million blacks under the apartheid system in the Republic of South Africa. The Nationalist Party seized power in 1948 and has since then controlled the lives of its non-white population. Known as Afrikaners (derived from Afrikaans, the language they speak) or as Boers (descendants of Dutch farmers and sailors who arrived in the Cape beginning in 1652), the white minority (which includes another minority of British descendants) constitutes a tiny proportion of the 39,549,941 people living in the country, as the following percentages show: 73.8% black; 14.3% white; 9.1% colored (of mixed white and other ancestry); and 2.8% Indian. In their effort to secure political and economic power as well as "cultural identity," the Boers had adopted a policy of racial separation, euphemistically known as "separate development," targeting four areas: legal classification of the population according to race; designation of specific areas for a determined race; interdiction on interracial marriages; and prohibition of sexual relations between whites and the other races. The laws governing these aspects of civic life were enshrined, respectively, in the so-called Population Registration Act, the Group Areas Act, the Prohibition of Marriages Act, and the Immorality Act.

Given that the laws were inhumane, their implementation made South Africa a police state. Individuals sixteen years of age or older had to carry a pass card featuring a photo, race, residence, and employment of the carrier. The cards likewise controlled the movement of blacks as "domestic visas" required for them to enter and exit the white man's towns. In the past, signs separating the people according to race were displayed on mobile and immobile facilities. This was also an attempt to enforce the Immorality Act. Understandably, African resistance to apartheid was inevitable, and resulted in the creation, over the decades, of several resistance groups: the African National Congress (ANC), the Pan-African Congress (PAC), the Black Consciousness Movement, the Azania People's Organization (AZAPO), the United Democratic Front (UDF), and the predominately Zulu Inkhata Movement. At present, the ANC is the most active political organization whose leader, Nelson Mandela, South Africa's first black President, released in 1990 from state prison where he was detained since 1964, is internationally known. Other major figures have included the late Steve Biko, leader of the Student Consciousness Movement of the mid-1970s, who was murdered in jail by the police in 1977; the Anglican Archbishop Desmond Tutu; and Chief Gatsha Buthelezi, leader of the separatist Inkhata Movement.

During the early stages of the struggle, most of the organizations listed above, including the ANC, limited their strategies for majority rule to non-violent action. This changed, however, following the 1960 Sharpville Massacre, when 69 peaceful apartheid demonstrators were shot and killed by the police. Since then, internal as well as external pressure on the apartheid system increased, with the Organization of African Unity and the United Nations playing a major role in isolating and punishing South Africa. The United Nations General Assembly, for example, adopted several resolutions over the years, some of which included the following provisions to be enforced by the member states: The breaking off of diplomatic relations with the apartheid regime; prohibition of ships from entering South African ports; a boycott of all South African goods and refrain from exporting goods, including arms and ammunition to South Africa; and refusal of landing and passage facilities to all aircraft belonging to that regime and all companies registered under its laws.

As a counter-offensive, South Africa adopted several strategies, some of which are discussed here. One was an attempt to win the sympathy of the West by capitalizing on its anti-communist stand as the bastion of Western civilization in Africa and on its strategic position. This approach had some success, as South Africa is an important source of several strategic minerals such as chromium, manganese, cobalt, and platinum. The strategic minerals are, of course, not limited to South Africa, as the following figures demonstrate, but the apartheid regime controlled the important quantities of them, as Buts and Thomas remind us. South Africa has 91% of world chromium reserves (7% owned by Zimbabwe and 2% by others); 41% of the manganese (37% owned by the former USSR, 11% by Gabon, and 11% by others); and 79% of the platinum (19% owned by the former USSR, 1% by Canada, and 1% by others). Cobalt reserves are more widespread, with 40% being owned by DRC, 15% by Zambia, 8% by Caledonia, 7% by Cuba, and 32% by others, including South Africa. The country is, indeed, strategically located, with the Cape of Good Hope serving as a conduit of oil imports to Europe and as a trade link between the Middle East (and the Far East) and Western Europe.

South Africa's second approach to maintaining its racist policy internally was structured within its regional foreign policy. Militarily, South Africa is the regional superpower, while economically it is the giant of the region, two assets the government has used successfully in the past. Thus, economically, most Southern African countries, most of which are landlocked, depend greatly on South Africa's good will for access to the sea. Furthermore, mining industries in South Africa employ thousands of workers from the neighboring states, particularly Lesotho, Mozambique, Malawi, and Swaziland. Mozambique, for example, as a result of colonial agreements, used to export to South Africa at least 150,000 workers a year prior to 1975. (The number was reduced to 45,000 a year during the past decade.)

Many of the neighboring states have been humiliated by South Africa through military strikes undertaken to prevent them from harboring nationalists, such as guerrillas from the ANC, especially during the 1970s and 1980s (three strikes against Mozambique; three against Zimbabwe; two against Zambia; several against Angola, with an actual battle at Cuito Cuanavale, and three against Botswana). In some instances, destabilization of the regimes took place in the form of military and financial assistance to resistance movements, as is the case with the Mozambique Resistance Movement (RENAMO) in Mozambique and the Uniao Nacional para a Independencia Total de Angola (UNITA) in Angola.

In order to counteract South Africa's economic and military stranglehold, the Southern African states (Angola, Botswana, Lesotho, Mozambique, Swaziland, Tanzania, Zambia, Malawi, and Zimbabwe), formed the Southern African Development Coordinating Conference in 1979 (SADCC), now called the Southern African Development Community (SADC), which attempts to coordinate regional projects (roads, harbors, railways), agricultural activities, technical training, and energy. However, because the Community has depended heavily on Western donors such as the United States, Britain, and France, SADC has met with mixed results. Of course, the effort was greeted with scorn and anger by the South African government which retaliated, whenever possible, against the member states, as it did against Mozambique by reducing the amount of cargo allowed to pass through Maputo harbor and the number of workers recruited for the South African mines.

Internally, South Africa propped up its strategy with the establishment of the Bantustans, or separate homelands, for each of the nine major ethnic groups in the country, promising them independence. Bophuthatswana, Transkei, Ciskei, and Venda were supposed to be independent states. However, the world community refused to recognize these homelands as such. In addition to the homelands, the regime introduced a plan of cosmetic constitutional changes providing seats for coloreds and Indians within the white parliament. The main objective of the "liberalization" policy was, of course, to gain international credibility, while at the same time keeping intact the system of apartheid. Ultimately, however, South Africa's strategies failed to stop the tide of internal and international opposition to its regime, particularly during the late 1980s, when the Western powers finally decided to impose trade and financial sanctions, the impact of which seems to have extracted the hoped-for concessions from the government: The repeal of all apartheid laws and negotiations toward majority rule, both initiated after Nelson Mandela's release from prison in 1990.

On May 10, 1994, South Africa adopted a new constitution that has granted majority rule to blacks. Since then, one may say that South Africa became the most powerful black state on earth. It inherited the best economic infrastructure and the strongest military of any post-colonial country in Africa. Nelson Mandela, the first President of post-Apartheid South Africa (1994–1999), replaced in 1999 by Thebo Mbeki—a less charismatic although articulate leader—became the most powerful black leader in the world. Indeed, South Africa is now in a position of selling military armament outside the continent. In early 1997 a reporter insinuated that the government of the United States of America was unhappy because South Africa was now selling armament to Israel's nemesis, Syria. The economic and military strength of South Africa does not necessarily guarantee future socio-political stability. Like all African states, South Africa still faces the problem of nation-building, transparency in governance, and equitable redistribution of mineral and agricultural resources, such as land.

Summary

The independence of Africa gave rise to high expectations among the African masses. Indeed, to most, independence meant the end of taxation (with or without representation) and the elimination of poverty and illiteracy. The task of nation-building, however, was formidable, and African leaders struggled to adopt the appropriate strategies. Unfortunately, the policies they adopted most often reminded Africans of the colonial oppression from which they had just freed themselves. The one-party state became the symbol of the new authoritarian rule and a reminder of the past as well. Leaders also saw ethnic loyalties as the major obstacle to nationhood and development. Because members of ethnic groups shared common historical experiences and values and perceived themselves to be "nations," the efforts of the leaders were directed, above all, toward thwarting ethnic loyalty or what was then called "tribalism." In part, the leaders were right, as some countries' ethnic loyalties lead to irredentism and in others to secession and civil wars. However, African leaders often abused their powers by justifying every action in the name of law and unity or national integration.

As elsewhere on the globe, Africa has had to overcome economic woes such as food production shortages and the international debt. For example, almost one-third of the African states were not be able to feed their own populations in 1995, and the foreign debt has continued to rise above the 1991 figure of $272 billion to over $500 billion. Africa's problems are, of course, compounded by the fact that they stem from several factors, including colonial legacy, adverse geographical factors, and the international economic system (all outside the control of African leaders), and from bad policies and poor planning. The international economic system, or the external economic environment, affected Africans adversely immediately following independence. At the root of the problem lies, of course, the lack of capital on the continent and Africa's inability to improve its capital formation. Thus, one of the strategies adopted by African leaders has centered on generating capital through export. The setback, however, comes from the fact that Africa does not control the prices of the raw materials she sells in the world market, nor does she control the prices of the manufactured goods which she buys from the Western world. As a result, Africans have been demanding, through the "new international economic order," a change in these one-sided practices which perpetuate established unfair patterns of trade.

In the political arena, on the other hand, Africans have adopted the principle of non-alignment, and, for the most part, stayed away from the Cold War between East and West, as dramatized, for example, by their refusal to provide military bases on their soil to either of the superpowers. In the post-cold war era Africans have adopted the strategy of demarginalization in the hope that, by meeting the conditionalities imposed on them by the West, they will secure economic development on the continent. While the rest of the continent was achieving independence, however, the South African government was intent on perpetuating the system of apartheid by capitalizing on its country's strategic international importance to the west, and by adopting economic and military strategies designed to destabilize the southern part of the continent and maintain its hegemony. Fortunately, apartheid is history now but South Africa, as many other African countries, is facing similar problems, especially in health and equitable distribution of resources, including land and business opportunities for all.

African leaders are now acutely aware of the magnitude of the task ahead and have vowed to take the necessary steps to stimulate development. At the 1991 OAU summit at Abuja, Nigeria, the 34 attending Heads of State signed a treaty to establish, by the year 2025 an African Economic Community. They pledged to work immediately towards a "phased removal of barriers to intra-African trade, the strengthening of the existing regional economic groupings," and the enhancement of "economic cooperation and integration" as a response to their own 1980 Lagos Plan of Action, which was adopted but not seriously implemented. Whether their actions are a result of a new resoluteness on their part to tackle Africa's difficult situation is something Africans and the world are waiting to see.

Beyond economic and political problems and apart from potential crises in education, health, and urbanization, stands a milliard of other concerns, such as the issues of women, who are often treated as secondary citizens. Also pressing is the state of the environment. The U.N. reports that Africa loses some 23 million hectares of "open woodland yearly, compared to 3.8 million hectares world-wide." The AIDS epidemic is also a major threat, infecting tens of millions of Africans. It is clear, therefore that the continent's problems, issues, and concerns require well thought out policies and programs and demand bold action from those at the helm as well as sacrifice, at least in the short-run, from the African masses. The issues of democratization, transparency, and trade have been bol-stered by the creation of the African Union replacing the ineffective OAU, as well as by the objectives and goals set in NEPAD.

Study Questions and Activities

1. When did independence occur in Africa and what did it mean to the majority of the African people?
2. Identify and analyze four major roots of Africa's economic problems. What are some of the major solutions proposed by African leaders and scholars to re-solve such problems?
3. Identify the major ideological approaches adopted by African leaders to solve Africa's social and political problems.
4. Discuss the origin and the focus of the "new international economic order."
5. Discuss the impact of South Africa's policies and strategies in Southern Africa and how the new changes have affected the region.

References

Commission for Africa, *Our Common Interest: Report of the Commission for Africa*. London: Commission for Africa, March 2005.

Role Van Deer Veen. *What Went Wrong With Africa; A Contemporary History*, Amsterdam: KIT Publisher, 2004 (English version), 2002 (Dutch).

Africa: South of the Sahara London: Europa Publishers. 1992

Samir Amin. "Underdevelopment and Dependence in Black Africa: Origins and Contemporary Forms." *Journal of Modern African Studies*, 10, 4(1972): 503–24.

A.M. Babu. *African Socialism or Socialist Africa?* London: Zed Books, 1981.

Kent H. Buts and Paul R. Thomas. *The Geopolitics of Southern Africa: South Africa as Regional Superpower*. Boulder, CO: Westview Press, 1986.

Naomi Chazam et al. *Politics and Society in Contemporary Africa*. Boulder, GO: Westview Press, 1988.

D.K. Fieldhouse. *Black Africa 1945–1980 Economic Decolonization and Ar-rested Development*. London: Allen and Unwin, 1986.

Phyliss Johnson and David Martin. *Apartheid Terrorism: The Destabilization Report*. Bloomington, IN: Indiana University Press, 1989.

Martin Minogue and Judith Muijoy. *African Aims and Attitudes: Selected Docu-ments*. London: Cambridge University Press, 1974.

Paul E. Sigmund. *The Ideologies of the Developing Nations*. New York: Praeger 1963.

United Nations. *Africa Recovery*, vol. 4, 3–4 (Oct. 1990): 1–52; *Africa Recovery*, vol. 5, 3 (April 1991): 1–12; *Africa Recovery*, vol. 5, 22–3 (September 1991): 1–56.

12

Contemporary Diaspora and the Future

Alphine W. Jefferson

Introduction

Blacks in the African diaspora beamed with pride as the 1960s opened with Patrice Lumumba wrenching independence for Zaire from the Belgian government; and, in the 1990s, blacks watch with anticipation Nelson Mandela's heroic crusade to eradicate the last vestige of European control on the African continent as he seeks to built a multiracial South Africa. Indeed, the two leaders symbolize both the continuity and change which has characterized the struggle of people of African descent all around the world over the last forty years. Gaining freedom and safeguarding equality has been a constant battle. While former African colonies became free and independent nations during the 1960s, little by little, the children of Mother Africa, scattered throughout its diaspora, came to new levels of consciousness and power in the economic, political, and social spheres of their lives in North America, Central and South America, as well as the Caribbean Islands and in a host of other countries in Europe. In the three decades which spanned from 1960 to 1990, the African diaspora has moved from isolated self-absorption to Pan-Africanist consciousness and a global identity. While this has been an age of enormous change, it has also been a time of constant struggle. In many ways, the history of the Americas is the history of the African diaspora and its interaction with different groups of people and cultures in the New World. Blacks in the Americas, from those who first went to Nova Scotia to escape slavery and find freedom four hundred years ago, to those who have lived on the coasts of Latin America for centuries, from those still living in free and autonomous "Maroon" communities in the Caribbean and South America to those living in North America, all have come to a new level of local self-consciousness and international solidarity with Africans on the continent and people who claim African ancestry anywhere in the world. While diaspora blacks derive a great deal of psychological comfort, racial pride, and cultural identity from Africa's success and progress, Africa has benefited a great deal from the technical skill and education of her new world sons and daughters who return "home" for various periods of time. This link between Africans and African descendants in the New World has been recently highlighted.

When L. Douglas Wilder, of Virginia, the only elected black governor in the United States in the twentieth century, went on a trade mission to seven African nations in June 1992, he was startled by the high-level reception and overwhelming homecoming he received from Senegal to South Africa. He was treated more like a head of state and an international leader than the governor of a single state. Hence, Wilder's trip is illustrative of the symbiotic relationship—in terms of both culture and politics—that blacks have established and maintained worldwide. He was greeted by tens of thousands in city after city and was viewed as a symbol that black people cannot only endure but also prosper against incredible odds. Moreover, this connection between Africans at home and abroad extends into and defines the very nature of the Western Hemisphere. No part of the New World escaped the black presence; and, in many places, from the 1 million blacks and "coloreds" in Canada to the 30 million in the United States to the millions living on islands in the Caribbean and the more than 100 million people of African descent in the United States of Brazil (the official name of Brazil), people of the African diaspora have been central to each nation's history and its collective destiny. (Sources disagree on the number of Afro-Brazilians in Brazil. Further discussion of Brazil is found later in the chapter.)

From the urban centers of Rio, Kingston, Port-au-Prince, Watts, Harlem, and Toronto, blacks have been instrumental in not only conquering but also shaping the life and culture of the Americas. Hence, many of the struggles of blacks and "people of color" in Europe are being played out in the same way and through the same lenses that the struggle for freedom and equality have developed in North America. Indeed, it seems that the struggle of blacks in the United States of America has not only been the most advanced but also the most articulate in analyzing the legitimacy of the place of black people in the Western Hemisphere. Although their struggle has been on-going since the first Africans arrived in the New World, it took on a greater urgency and a new direction in the economic, political, and social arena during the militancy of the 1960s. Thus, though many advances were achieved, and while some blacks were allowed to advance in American society, too many were allowed to slip further away from claiming that illusive "American dream" as a part of their birthright.

Major terms and concepts: Emergence and development of an African diaspora identity, racial progress and setbacks in the United States, the myth of racial democracy in Central and Latin America, branqueamento, mestizaje, Negritude, miscegenation, Maroon societies, Afro-Caribbeans, American racism, global context.

African Americans

As the flames from the rebellion in south central Los Angeles smoldered in April of 1992, few commentators recalled the saliency of W. E. B. DuBois's surprisingly accurate and amazingly prophetic comment that "the problem of the twentieth century is the problem of the color line." Indeed, in Los Angeles and elsewhere, African Americans, Asians, Latinos, and Hispanics, as well as large numbers of Euro-Americans, took to the streets to show their displeasure with a system which promises to deliver the goods and services of the world's greatest democracy but often fails to do so for the vast majority of its population. Hence, the anger over the Rodney King verdict became a symbolic metaphor for the pent-up anger that millions of American citizens felt at the grossest miscarriage of justice from a system which neither "serves nor protects" its basic interests. Thus, the "dream" of Martin Luther King's stirring speech in August of 1963 resonates as a nightmare forty years later for most of black America. Although his exaltations were not in vain, the daily lives of African Americans in the economic political, and social spheres give grim testimony to the inconclusive struggles of the militants in the 1960s, the moderates of the 1970s, and the entrepreneurs of the 1980s. Indeed, the life and times of most blacks in the 1990s reflect both a mythical paradise lost and the omnipresent feeling that progress has come to a standstill.

From 1960 through 1990, the African diaspora in the United States developed both a sense of its own unique position in the world and a consciousness of its connection to people of African descent everywhere. In some ways, what happens in the United States determines the social, economic, and political plight of Africans around the world. Whereas the actions and activities of a small but growing black elite is exaggerated by conservative and right-wing politicians in order to blame the poor for their plight, there have been both gains and losses in the struggle for liberation. Realistically, there are two African-Americas emerging: one prosperous, middle-class and fully participating in every aspect of American life and culture (as much as overt and covert racism will allow); and a second black America—poor and unskilled, inadequately educated, cut-off from the mainstream of society, alienated, and incapable of even imagining its way out of poverty and despair. Therefore, whereas about two-thirds of black America is generally described as working and middle-class, a large segment of the population, about one-third, has been labeled "the underclass." These blacks are not only caught up in a rising cycle of poverty but also they are victims of the changing social context of a post-industrial society. This has left them physically and socially isolated as well as unable to interpret or negotiate the changing social terrain.

Socially, black Americans have made significant gains and suffered some incredible losses in the last forty years in both education and in the legal sphere. The laws and progressive social action, started in the 1960s to end overt racial discrimination and ensure equality, were effective in erasing the most blatant and socially offensive forms of racism. They succeeded in tearing down the noxious "colored" and "white" signs of yesteryear, yet they were ineffective in changing racist attitudes and behaviors by whites as well as the lack of black empowerment. From 1960 to 1990, the civil rights of African Americans were expanded; yet, a progressive commitment to furthering those rights was halted in 1980. Indifference, inaction, and ineptitude on the part of the national government gave overt signals to those people in positions of power who complied with equal opportunity laws out of coercion rather than conviction. This told them that they could relax their efforts because the federal government was not going to aggressively push for an egalitarian society. The conservative credo, which "blames the victim," confirms white ignorance of the negative impact that racism and discrimination have upon the quality of life, health, and happiness that most blacks endure. Though profound changes have occurred in American society in the last forty years, the reality of racism can be most clearly seen in the field of education.

Education remains one of the nation's most controversial social problems because most people think that the opportunity for equal education exists for all children. Yet, the American belief that education can create social, economic, and political equality has never been adequately tested in Afro-America. Indeed, soon after the Supreme Court's ruling in *Brown vs. Board of Education of Topeka, Kansas*, outlawing segregation and the "separate but equal" provision in education, large numbers of whites, from every social strata, pulled their children from public schools. Contemporary calls for a voucher system are nothing more than sophisticated attempts to end what little racial integration in public education remains in most large cities. In fact, *de facto* segregation has achieved monoracial schools as effectively as the *de jure* policies before *Brown*. Residential patterns in the North, which are characterized by racism, housing discrimination, and racial steering, have created more segregated schools in northern cities than in the traditional southern states. Any change in levels of integration in urban education has to be first accompanied by a change in residential patterns. Busing has emerged as a divisive social issue because it seeks to redress on wheels what a segment of the white population does not want to achieve in fact—integrated communities.

Racism in housing is the country's most serious social problem. Surveys of housing patterns in America's largest cities reveal continuing white-flight and out-migration as well as the increased social, economic, and educational isolation of blacks in the central city. A change in urban housing patterns would give African Americans increased access to the better educational and economic opportunities which exist in racially and commercially integrated areas. The emergence of a distinct African American subculture among urban youth is the direct result of the social, economic, cultural, and political distance which segregated housing perpetuates. Moreover, over the last forty years, some blacks have moved into middle-class integrated areas; however, most African Americans live in inner-city areas without daily contact with people—black, white, and other—who observe a different cultural norm. In some ways, this is a dichotomous tragedy. Blacks are isolated in ghettos because historically a powerful faction of whites have wanted them there. Yet, middle-class blacks are forced to remain in some of those areas because housing discrimination, which is based on fear, mythology, and stereotype, conspires to keep blacks and whites apart. Therefore, until it is clearly understood that blacks are not the creators of ghettos, but their inheritors, then the fear, mythology, and stereotype which surrounds housing discrimination and residential segregation will remain. Moreover, laws and regulations must be changed to eliminate the enormous profits reaped by those who create, maintain, and manipulate the "dual housing" market. Hence, this issue will never be resolved until the silent conspiracy which exists between the financial institutions, legal services, and real estate agencies is exposed. America's social ills can be eradicated if its housing allocation systems are reformed. Residential occupancy determines both educational opportunity and occupational exposure. In many ways, it creates the future. Segregation negates the early opportunity for black youth to find gainful employment and to learn the skills necessary to compete in a rapidly changing world.

The employment picture of most of African-America is very bleak. For too many African Americans nothing has changed in their employment profile or chance to obtain decent employment at a livable wage since Lyndon Johnson called for a "Great Society" program in order to launch a war on poverty. Indeed, not only has the war on poverty been lost but also the limited victories in long-fought battles have been repudiated. Los Angeles burned because of racism and poverty; poverty remains because the economic system in America is structurally designed to keep most of its citizens underemployed, burdened by large personal debts, and manipulated to spend and consume by Madison Avenue advertising firms. The promises of change, hope, and upward mobility articulated in the 1960s, gave way, in the 1990s, to calls for industrial restructuring, corporate downsizing, and business efficiency. Of course, those changes are being wrought on the backs of the working poor and the chronically unemployed.

Despite the much touted rhetoric of Affirmative Action, very few ordinary blacks have had their employment chances affirmed in any significant way. Moreover, in reality, Affirmative Action has accelerated the separation of a once fairly heterogeneous black community by allowing some of its most talented and highly educated members to move away from the centers of largest black concentration and into all-black or integrated suburban enclaves. In actuality, the rhetoric surrounding Affirmative Action has created far more of a backlash and charges of reverse discrimination than actually ameliorating black un-, under-, and subemployment. Hence, the reality of this issue is so charged with racist emotion that the facts are obscured. For example, in 1990, the number of black physicians in the United States seems capped at approximately 3 percent. This figure is only slightly higher than the figure for 1960. Hence, the illusion of tremendous progress is challenged by the reality of a crucial lack of progress for the largest portion of black America. This dichotomy is having disastrous consequences for both intra- and inter-racial relations in America. As class differences emerge in response to the economic segmentation inherent in a post-industrial economy, middle-class blacks are leaving traditional black communities without the leadership and expertise needed to continue to direct and mobilize a people only a few generations removed from slavery. Some upper income blacks are as isolated from and uncomfortable with the black underclass as middle-class whites. Some major social theorists are arguing that race has declined as a significant variable in determining life chances and that class has become the most potent factor in creating or denying opportunity. Thus, there is a failure to assist the people who need the most help by the people who could provide them with the greatest guidance.

The universally held notion that blacks do not want to work is regularly contradicted by the reality that thousands of people show up to interview for low-skill, low-wage and dead-end jobs. Few people link black unemployment to the fundamental structural changes which have occurred in American society since the 1960s. Indeed, there was no black unemployment during slavery; obviously, each slave performed a task vital to the South's economy. Thus, it is necessary to conclude that there is no place for black workers, particularly black men, in a society where large numbers of white men, historically blue-collar but most recently, skilled craftsmen and white-collar, have seen their jobs shipped overseas or eliminated through technology, rampant corporate merges, and pernicious rationalizations to cut overhead and improve profit margins by the corporate elite. Consequently, the competition for scarce jobs at the lower end of the employment spectrum pits black workers against rural whites migrating to the city, recently arrived immigrants, countless undocumented workers from all over the world and women of all races. The American tendency to "blame the victim" or to assign individual responsibility to personal failure, therefore, fails to explain an unemployment profile which has the official rate for blacks frozen at 20 percent and notes that more than 76 percent of black youth cannot find stable employment. Thus, blacks are forced to participate in the labor market as occasional, part-time, and seasonal workers, receiving inequitable and poverty-level pay. Certainly, racial discrimination as well as a changing economic structure account for the high levels of black unemployment and low levels of black capital accumulation.

In an era of stagnant economic growth and diminishing employment options, Afro-America has become the scapegoat for an economic system which is showing signs of collapse. Indeed, as the large amounts of wealth and money acquired during the last few years attest, there is an affirmative action of privilege; there is a quota of influence; and there seems to be a system in place which protects and rewards those who have accumulated great wealth, while punishing those who are barely meeting their basic needs. Political challenges to this system prove ineffective because they are undermined by a "conspiracy of color." Even though the white working class and the white poor are victims of an inequitable economic system also, they fail to join progressive groups and organizations which challenge the status quo because they are socialized and taught to see themselves first as white and only incidentally as workers and members of the exploited classes. This silent conspiracy of race becomes audible, albeit, in code words and slogans when politicians speak, and it makes itself manifest in massive resistance to change.

Undeniably, blacks have made significant gains in the political arena since 1960. Indeed, by 1990, the elections of Douglas Wilder, as Governor of Virginia and David Dinkins, as Mayor of New York, represent a political maturation of blacks in American politics that would have been unthinkable forty years ago. In both of these cases, blacks won what amounts to national victories in local elections in a state and a city where blacks are in a minority. Blacks have made massive strides in politics over the last three decades. From token representation in a few cities and state houses and minimal representation in Congress, blacks now head many of America's largest cities, and scores of smaller ones. Blacks are in Congress, are present at every level in the judicial system, represent millions of people in hundreds of state and local legislatures and distinguished members of Presidential Administrations, state and municipal governments, and serve as high ranking officials in the military. Indeed, the nation beamed as General Colin Powell, a diasporan black of immigrant parents, conducted the Persian Gulf War as the nation's Chairman of the Joint Chiefs of Staff, one of the most important positions in the country. Yet, despite all of these gains, politically, blacks do not exercise the might and power of their numbers, and politicians—black and white—are far less responsive to black demands after the election than they are to those of white middle-class citizens. Moreover, many black officials are hampered in their efforts to create true reform by the entrenched bureaucratic business and political interests of the organizations they head. Therefore, most of these officials cannot effect the kind of meaningful change which would have a significant impact on the lives of the black poor. Black elected officials are usually the only blacks in various offices with real power; but they are forced constantly to confront and compromise with hostile administrations, scandal-ridden, insolvent, and indifferent banks and financial institutions as well as reactionary police and fire departments, in addition to angry whites wanting their "turf" back, as they seek to reclaim some mythical past which was "fair" where they could pass their jobs on to their children and grandchildren. The black politician has a very difficult time trying to realize his inflated campaign promises and the realities of "democratic" politics in contemporary America. Ultimately, black politicians are symbols and cannot contain or control those corporate and financial leaders who hold "real" power in every facet of American life and culture. They represent the hope of what is possible in a "democracy" and at some level they do articulate the hopes, fears, and aspirations of those yearning to be free; yet, they cannot fully accomplish the liberation of their people because "true freedom" remains an illusion for most Americans, black and white.

The African diaspora in the United States, though approximately 30 million strong, is still basically mired in poverty and despair as a result of both continuing racism and racial discrimination as well as structural impediments inherent in American capitalism. Despite all of its problems and its disappointments, America is still seen as the preeminent leader in the world; and thus, black America has become the center of the African diaspora. From black leaders going to and convening meetings in the Caribbean and Central and Latin America, to the continuation of W. E. B. DuBois's Pan-African Congresses, the link between the United States and the rest of the African diaspora is stronger now than ever before. Given the internal migrations among various Caribbean people and Caribbean immigration to the United States, firm links have always existed between the various regions. Indeed, much of Panama's predominantly black population can trace its legacy directly to hundreds of thousands of contract workers from Barbados and Jamaica. The vital Panama Canal owes its existence to these capable and hard-working laborers. The impact of Afro-Caribbeans on the continental United States has been enormous. When Marcus Garvey left Jamaica for America in 1916, he was but one of many who would fuel the rise of black consciousness among America's black urban masses.

Afro-Caribbeans

Direct connections between African Americans and Afro-Caribbeans have existed for a long time. Indeed, the Afro-Caribbean community in the United States is so large that it contains millions of blacks who trace their ancestry to Jamaica, the Dominican Republic, Panama, Haiti, Puerto Rico, Cuba, and the other West Indian Islands. Moreover, Afro-America traces much of its own political and cultural history to the interaction of these two areas and their people. Indeed, several noted black leaders in the United States are from "The Islands," as they are affectionately and nostalgically called. These leaders include such noted figures as Malcolm X (first-generation American), Marcus Garvey, Kwame Toure (Stokely Carmichael), Harry Belafonte, Sidney Poitier, and Shirley Chisholm. The diasporan link was recently reaffirmed when the well-known dancer Katherine Dunham fasted to protest George Bush's treatment of Haitian refugees. Indeed, the problems in Haiti, Jamaica, and Cuba are illustrative of the historic link which remains between people of African descent in North America and elsewhere in the Caribbean.

From the time of its burst upon the world stage as a free and independent nation, Haiti has been an international symbol of black pride and progress. When Toussaint L'Ouverture overthrew the shackles of French colonial rule in 1804, he

announced to the world that black people were not only capable of self-government but also that they had both the ability and the will to defeat a major European power. However, contemporary Haiti defies both the substance and spirit of
that nation's earlier revolutionaries. From 1960 to 1990, Haiti has experienced
the exhilaration of overthrowing the two-generation Duvalier regime to the democratic election of a President to the contemporary realization that the current
military government can be just as repressive as any dictator. Indeed, Haiti seems
to be an extreme example of the ambiguous status of many of the nations of the
African diaspora. They are caught up in a historical cycle of producing for and responding to the demands of an international market which can basically dictate
the price of its goods. In addition to being among the poorest nations in the "New
World," Haiti has to contend with a large scale AIDS epidemic.

In some ways, Jamaica has become the center of a major black cultural redefinition of both Africa and the African diaspora. In actuality, Jamaica has one of the
most interesting histories of any nation in the New World because of its Maroon
societies, which exist to this day. As soon as Africans were brought to Jamaica,
many rebelled and fled to the mountains. There, they established independent and
self-sufficient communities (called Maroon societies) and continued to live out
their lives recreating traditional African forms, transforming their environment,
engaging in small farming operations, and selling their goods in town. Like other
Maroon communities from the southeastern coast of North America to the highlands of Central America and Brazil, the Jamaicans were able to defend themselves against attempts to capture and re-enslave those who fled to freedom.
Moreover, some Maroon societies continue to exist after four hundred years.
Suriname fought a bloody civil war in the 1980s to eradicate its last Maroon
colony. Other governments have sought to dismantle these autonomous regions.
Yet, the spirit of independence lives on in Jamaica, as it remains one of the New
World's most revolutionary and political nations.

When Jamaica gained independence from Britain in 1962, it adopted the slogan: "Out of many, one people." However, the substance of this motto suggests a

This small country seems incapable of solving its own problems and fails to get
the attention of any world leader because it has no strategic or economic importance. Moreover, even though Haiti is more than 90 percent black, there are major
class and racial divisions as a mulatto middle-class elite governs for its own profit
and enjoyment. In addition, Haiti has become one of the "dumping grounds" for
American companies to pick up extremely cheap labor for light manufacturing;
thus, one group of diasporan blacks is pitted against another as each seeks to en-
tice multinational corporations to come and exploit its large, vulnerable, and low-
wage labor supply. Yet, despite these problems, Haiti has the ability to claim its
rightful proud place among the nations of the new world. In fact, Haiti has not
only contributed great men and women to world civilization but it has also preserved many African cultural and religious traditions. Hence, Voodoo, usually
mentioned in jest and derision, is emerging as a serious religion to be both practiced and studied. Movies such as "The Believers" and "The Serpent and the Rainbow" give ample testimony to the diverse group of people interested in *Vudun*.
One of the biggest tourist attractions in New Orleans is getting to attend an illegal
Voodoo rite, meeting a Voodoo priest or priestess, or visiting the grave of famed
Voodoo "saint" Marie Laveau. In addition, on-going medicinal and botanical research is evidence of the importance of Haiti to the future of the New World.

basic problem with much of the African diaspora: conceiving of itself along historical and colonial rather than racial and ancestral lines. Thus, while more than 90 percent of Jamaicans have distinct amounts of African blood, it was not until the Rastafarians, drawing inspiration from Marcus Garvey and his call for the creation of an African identity, that most Jamaicans came to see themselves as black. Indeed, this sentiment is much more prevalent among the poor and the destitute than among the educated middle class of whatever skin color. (Famed scholar-teacher Walter Rodney was exiled from Jamaica and later killed in his homeland of Guyana for his unabashed calls for the liberation of African people through a racially based cultural and economic fusion.)

Recently, Jamaica has moved between conservative capitalist-oriented governments and progressive socialist ones. Yet, the plight and problems of the average Jamaican remains as pressing as ever. It, too, like so many new world nations, is caught in a cycle of poverty and depravation created in response to the needs of international capitalism and neo-colonialism. Although, Jamaica possesses tremendous wealth, its economic policies are much more directed by the World Bank and the International Monetary Fund (IMF) than by the elected Prime Minister. Indeed, when Michael Manley sought to move the nation toward a progressive socialist state, his efforts were actively hampered by a host of regulations, stipulations, and conditions set by the American-controlled lending agencies. Despite this, Jamaicans continue to press forward and to have hope that, one day, their nationhood can be realized. Jamaica's place in the world's consciousness is secure because of the increasing interest being paid to the Rastafarians—their religion, philosophy and beliefs—as well as the indigenous music which comes out of Jamaica—reggae. Moreover, reggae has become so popular that its impact is felt worldwide. In addition, Jamaican arts and crafts as well as its cuisine are beginning to get international notice.

In spite of its constant international attention, Cuba remains an enigma among New World nations. Cuba is central to the African diaspora because its population is more than 60 percent black and its socialist government has sought to actively wipe-out both racial prejudice and color consciousness. Cubans enjoy one of the highest literary rates in the world as well as one of the most efficient health care systems. Despite outright terrorism, embargoes, sanctions, and censure, contemporary Cuba offers a model of positive benefits of nationalistic self-determination. Castro's revolution in 1959 started Cubans on the path away from outright domination by the United States. Interestingly enough, it was large numbers of "white Cubans" that America admitted on the heels of the revolution. Those with money, status, and power, following the traditional New World model, were those of lighter skin. Thus, America's hatred and determination to destroy Cuba's government can be looked at as both outright racism and hypocrisy. America refuses to countenance the existence of a very small (approximately 10 million people) democratic socialist nation, while maintaining and supporting threatening communist societies and repressive right-wing dictatorships around the globe. Hence, American policy toward Cuba can be seen as a threat to all of the African diaspora. Its unlawful invasions of both Grenada and Panama indicate to some that the United States will commit illegal acts to subvert the self-determination of "people of color" around the globe. In some ways, what happens in Cuba after Castro portends for the treatment of progressive black regimes elsewhere. Indeed, this policy is already clearly evident in America's support of repressive governments throughout the Caribbean and Latin America as long as they follow American dictates by swearing allegiance to the so-called "free-market" principles, oppose communism and dissent, and unrest. Consequently, the place of the African diaspora in South and Central America is related to the degree to which the nations define themselves as "white" and European.

Afro-Latinos and Afro-Europeans

The African diaspora in Latin America contains the largest concentration of blacks outside of Africa. In some ways, Latin American nations have sustained the greatest cultural miscegenation and racial intermixture anywhere in the New World. Afro-Latinos speak Spanish, Portuguese, French, Dutch, English, a host of Amerindian languages, Creoles, and patoises. The most striking feature about Afro-Latinos is a conscious and unconscious attempt, on the part of millions there, to deny, outright, any connection to Africa. The twin myths in much of Latin American history of flourishing racial democracies and continuing color-blind societies function effectively to render more than 150 million members of the African diaspora invisible. Yet, it has been during the last three decades that the black consciousness movement has begun; and, to varying degrees, some people are reclaiming their black heritage as a way to organize and fight against racial discrimination and prejudice in Central and South America. Indeed, it is difficult to get an accurate count on the number of "blacks," as the term is used in the United States, in Latin America, and the Caribbean, because there is no uniform criteria for racial classification. The pervasive practice of using a host of undifferentiated terms in several different languages and cultural contexts, as well as historical time periods to identify people, make an accurate count of the African diaspora even more challenging. In addition, the terms "black" and "white" exist in a very fluid, highly ambiguous, and deliberately manipulated set of economic, political, and social contexts. An extreme example of this is Brazil.

Brazil officially lists its black population at approximately 6 percent. (The *Report on the Americas* recently recorded Brazil's total population at 160 million and United Nations' estimates suggest that by 1995, Brazil will reach a population of 165 million.) A recent *Britannica Yearbook* survey places Brazil's black population at 33 percent, or over 50 million people. However, a special issue of *Crisis* dealing with blacks in South America claims that Brazil has more than 100 million people with African ancestry within its borders. Another problem in numbering diasporan blacks is that of identity. The United States and Brazil each determine "blacks" differently, and so does much of the rest of the Caribbean and Latin America. For example, Venezuela, like most of Central and Latin America, is considered a *cafe con leche* (coffee with milk or *cafe au lait* in French) society because of the intense interracial mixture of its inhabitants; yet, success is determined by degree of "physical whiteness," affinity for Europeanization cultural affectations and a denial of any African heritage. Thus, few of Venezuela's 60 to 70 percent black population will claim any African identity. It is common practice for lighter-skinned Afro-Latinos to classify themselves as whites in the official census, while blacks will label themselves as mulatto or *mestizo*. In most cases, the designation of *mestizo* simply means mixture, usually of white and

Amerindian, and basically denies the inter-marriage and miscegenation of millions of Africans. This process of "whitening" or "whitenization" (*branqueamento* in Brazilian Portuguese) is endemic throughout Latin and Central America. In this process, "whiteness" is determined by both color and status. Hence, in many societies, "money whitens"; thus, a dark-skinned man is considered mulatto or *mestizo* if he has status through education, family, or employment.

This desire to be white is so pervasive that most societies suffer collective amnesia. For instance, the official census of contemporary Argentina lists no black residents; however, in the 1850s, the population of Buenos Aires was one-third African. In some cases, the denial of an African past is so strong that some blacks have created a mythical autogenic past. Indeed, members of the African diaspora of the Pacific lowlands of Columbia, Ecuador, Panama, and elsewhere claim no connection to Africa at all. They assert that their history begins when they established their own independent communities and created a new culture and became a new people. These sentiments are echoed in parts of French Guiana and Suriname as well as other parts of Latin and Central America and in contemporary Maroon communities, some established 400 years ago. Despite these gross denials of and the attempts to "bleach" Africa out of both bloodlines and history, the African diaspora is slowly, if reluctantly, in some cases, coming to terms with both the positive cultural value and the historical reality of its African connection. The dynamic power and assertive nature of the Civil Rights movement in the United States has influenced a generation of activists and is beginning to culturally reclaim some parts of the rest of the African diaspora in the New World.

Since the mid-fifteenth century, European hegemony of the world's economic, political, and social systems have made most non-Europeans value and revere both white skin and European traditions. Most indigenous people came to accept the European definition of white as superior and black as inferior. Therefore, any color in between has come to be regarded as better than the assumed wretchedness of abject darkness. These views were firmly planted in Latin American society, and explain why so many blacks minimize their African ancestry. Many Afro-Latins (Spanish or Portuguese Africans) have accepted Europe's racist hierarchy. Therefore, African heritage is denied; European heritage is embellished; Amerindian ancestry is manipulated depending on location, and any "color" is valued, if it is not black. Thus, racism is so entrenched in most people's psyche that anything white is treasured and desired; and, consequently, anything black is despised and rejected. Though these attitudes, beliefs, and practices are prevalent in most of Latin America and the Caribbean, they are most developed and institutionalized in Brazil.

Certainly, as the country with the largest concentration of black people outside of Africa, and as the second largest "black nation" in the world (Nigeria is larger), Brazil deserves special attention. Yet, most Brazilians would deny their special place in the African diaspora. The word *negro* (black in Spanish and Portuguese) has such a negative connotation in Brazil that its usage is usually considered a racial slur. Instead, most people use the terms mulatto (mixed) or (*moreno*, brown) as complimentary ascriptions. The official census of Brazil records less than 6 percent blacks; however, if judged by North American standards and using the American definition of race, then there are more than 100 million "blacks" in Brazil. However, Brazil has reversed the North American model of racial classification where one drop of black blood makes a person black, to any white blood makes a person not-black. Thus, in Brazilian Portuguese, there are more than 100 formal and informal terms to describe people on a vast somatic (physical) continuum from the whitest of whites to the blackest of blacks. Indeed, blackness is such a potent psychological force in Brazil that to call someone *preto* (black) is an insult. This national retreat from blackness has powerful implications for the economic, political, and social life of the African diaspora in the country.

Economically speaking, black Brazilians have not benefited from the global prosperity of the last 30 years, and the historic correlation between color and wealth in Brazil continues. Generally, the poor and powerless are black, while the rich and powerful are white. Wealth and status exist on a continuum based on color and "refinement," as an approximation for closeness to "white" or visible levels of European acculturation. An example from Bahia, called "the capital of Black Brazil," shows how these considerations work to the economic disadvantage of blacks and create racial divisions in a nonracial society. A restaurant in Bahia advertised for a "blond receptionist." Obviously, this is more than simple employment discrimination. It is both racial and cultural imperialism. As a consequence of this racial and cultural imperialism, even in areas where they predominate, blacks cannot even secure low-wage, low-status occupations. Another arena in which the economic place blacks occupy can be seen is access to education, which in turn leads to skilled and professional employment. As late as 1988, 100 years after the abolition of slavery, blacks constitute less than 1 percent of the students enrolled in Brazilian universities. Moreover, of the 7,000 faculty members employed in two of the nation's most important universities, only 9 are black. The economic statistics suggest that Brazil has become two societies: one modern, rich, technologically advanced, and white, while the other is black, poor, undeveloped, subemployed, and uneducated. Despite Brazil's myths of racial democracy, blacks and mulattoes have limited access to education, employment, and decent housing. Afro-Brazilians have not benefited from the prosperity of the last three decades. Black males continue to congregate in the lowest economic strata and are paid about half the mean monthly income of white males. Black women in Brazil are concentrated in the traditional service and private-duty home occupations which pay low wages, offer no security, and consume large amounts of time at work and in travel. Brazil's shantytowns are overwhelming black, just as the millions of street children who eke out an existence "by any means necessary." It is the economic crisis and the slowly emerging black consciousness movement that have fomented political action in Brazil.

Brazil's black consciousness movement has taken on both a cultural and a political agenda. In politics, Afro-Brazilians are using some of the same tactics and actions of the North American Civil Rights movement. Thus, on May 11, 1988, two days before the centennial of the abolition of slavery, thousands of Brazilians marched in Rio de Janeiro to demand an end to a new slavery, and for an admission that racial democracy is a pathetic illusion. Political organization in Brazil is generally subsumed under the black consciousness movement, of which there are more than 6,000 different organizations operating in most of the nation's 26 states. Their aims range from the fostering of racial pride and the development of a positive black identity to preserving and encouraging traditional cultural expressions in the arts, music, and crafts, to demanding economic development and political empowerment. Although each group has a different agenda, all seek to help Afro-Brazilians claim their rightful place in a land their ancestors helped to build. Politically speaking, black Brazilians have a great deal of work to do in order to achieve even a modicum of success.

In Salvador, capital city of Bahia, which is more than 80 percent black, the mayor and 32 of the 35 members of the City Council are white. Attempts by political groups to make this city of 2.5 million people, which has grown from 300,000 in the last 30 years, integrated, seem to go unheeded. Indeed, one white political leader noted that poor Brazilians will not vote for their own people because of fear and low self-esteem. Some political organizations say that few Brazilian authorities take note of or even respond to charges of racism and racial discrimination. Indeed, most of the country's preoccupation with race tends to focus on the southern part of the nation where there is a very large European and Asian immigrant presence. In some ways, race relations in Brazil are where they were in the southern United States in the 1950s. Black newspapers report racist advertisements, sports clubs segregating pools, and black visitors being told to use service elevators in some buildings. The political movements of Brazil will therefore grow, expand, and increase as more Afro-Brazilians develop a wider racial as well as political consciousness. Many believe that the best way to expand and develop consciousness is to reclaim the positive attributes of a cultural ancestry and a historical legacy universally denied.

People in Brazil express themselves socially in as many different ways as they identify themselves. Given the diversity of their institutions and practices in religion, music, and dance, Brazilians have no peers. Ostensibly a Catholic country, Brazil has most major religions represented among its population. Even though the nation is 90 percent Roman Catholic, Brazil remains a religious enigma. Brazilians are involved, to some degree, in one of the many variations of traditional African religions that exist presently. Catholicism, with its many saints and rituals, allowed African slaves to continue to observe their own religious practices in disguise. The average Afro-Brazilian, as well as many whites, will attend both a formal service in the Catholic Church and one of many non-traditional services in a host of religious traditions which are holdovers from African spiritual practices. The variety of religious activity in Brazil ranges from non-Vatican sanctioned Catholic rituals to *Candomble* and *Santeria*, from *Umbanda* to Pentecostalism, from Spiritualism to Voodoo (*Vudun*). It is in this religious pantheon that many Afro-Brazilians find both psychological and personal comfort. Many view this religious smorgasbord as both heresy and satanism; yet, Brazilians continue to expand and define their own religious heritage through a variety of media, including music and movement.

It is in music and dance that Afro-Brazilians converge the sacred and the profane. Taking their cues from the continued secularization of music in the United States in the 1960s and 1970s, Afro-Brazilians rejected the mainstreaming of both the *samba* and *capoeira* (which is a traditional African martial arts form that Afro-Brazilian men recreated and enacted as a dance in order to be allowed to practice and not alarm whites) and pioneered new forms of musical expression using standard instruments and others of their own creation. It is typical to see young men gathered at bars singing, drumming, and practicing for inclusion in larger groups known as a "*samba* schools," which will display and parade during Carnival. Millions of men belong to these schools, and their constant rehearsal is symptomatic of the seriousness with which they take their presentations during the week before Lent, when all Brazil indulges in a week of parties, frivolity, and decadence, when roles and status are less important than merriment. The contributions of blacks to mainstream Brazilian culture are so deep and so profound that they tend to go unrecognized.

While Afro-Brazilians are indistinguishable from the music of the nation, a new celebrity has emerged combining an ideal persona. Indeed, Brazil's most famous celebrity is a native-born woman, Xuxu, of German immigrant parents with blond hair and blue eyes. She has modeled herself after popular American music groups and, since beginning as a very successful singer, has transformed herself into a popular talk-show host and cultural icon. She has a line of dolls, clothes, and a huge following among Brazilians of all colors. Children who are sick in the hospital swear that they will get better if she visits. In some ways, she is a model Brazilian, combining the most "pleasing" nordic (white looks) with an appealing Brazilian (black) sound. Yet, the danger of this singer is that millions of Afro-Brazilian children look upon her as representing an ideal to which they should aspire. The desire to be white is so intense that one of Brazil's richest men is a plastic surgeon whose specialty is "whitening." Despite all of the contradictions in culture, however, Brazil remains central to any discussion of diasporan blacks.

The importance of Brazil to the African diaspora was validated in 1992, 500 years after Columbus "discovered" America, when the 6 Lusophonic nations agreed to adopt Brazilian Portuguese as the international standard for textbook production, language teaching, and spoken instruction. This measure, vetoed in 1988 by the Portuguese Academy of Arts and Sciences, was finally passed when the former mother country and colonial power was forced to concede that it had been surpassed by its most exotic, and significantly larger, former colony. Indeed, the five most famous celebrities in film and television in mainland Portugal are Brazilian, as is the most famous designer. Apparently, the European Portuguese are looking to Brazil to infuse both drama and sensuality into their staid cultural traditions. Thus, the role of the African diaspora in renewing and redefining Europe continues to occur and cannot be denied.

The impact of people of African descent has been felt in Europe for centuries. A significant part of the African diaspora had its origins in the interaction between blacks and whites where the African coast meets Europe and Asia at the Mediterranean. Hence, a recorded black presence in Europe dates as far black as 711 when African soldiers invaded Spain and Portugal. A Viking raid on Spain and North Africa saw the capture of black soldiers in 862, and Irish records reveal that these men were carried to Dublin and dubbed "blue men." Africans fought with the Moors in the conquering armies of the Iberian peninsula in the tenth century, while large numbers of slaves were imported to Europe during the slave trade. Obviously, there was some intermixture because there exists among the Irish a group called "the Black Irish" due to their slightly darker hair and skin.

Thus, blacks have had both a glorious and despised history on the European continent. Many of these connections were beginning to be made in the 1960s as the emerging black consciousness movement began to take hold in Britain, France, Germany and elsewhere. Yet, as blacks were beginning to claim their place in Europe, certain groups were emerging to demand the outright expulsion and elimination of "foreigners" from their respective countries. The activities of the German youth in black jackets who call themselves neo-Nazis, French youth attacking Arabs and Africans, and British youth assaulting British subjects from the Indian sub-continent, Africa, and the Caribbean, all signal a rise in racism in Europe and suggest that the issues have not been resolved. Forty years ago, Britain sought to deal with these problems by imposing immigration restrictions.

Just as the black consciousness movement was in its embryonic stage, the British Parliament proposed the Commonwealth Immigrants Act in 1962 limiting the number of "blacks" from its former colonies. In Europe, the term "coloured" is used to refer to all "people of color" from India, Pakistan, the Caribbean, Africa, and elsewhere. Given some of the recent racist tensions, the term "black" has been appropriated by some racist whites as an insult to all of these people; on the other hand, the term is now being appropriated by several groups of militants (claiming Malcolm X as their inspiration) within each of these subgroups as a banner of both identification and pride. As a result, "white" has come to mean British, and "black" has come to refer to "the other." (Obviously, all blacks and "coloureds" do not subscribe to or accept this designation.) The Act is significant in that it marked the emergence of race as an issue in British politics, and it signified a new understanding of the place of blacks in British society.

The "place" of the African diaspora in Britain was always complicated by the presence of large numbers of dark-skinned Indians and Pakistanis. Some Britons have come to despise these "coloureds" even more than both Jamaicans and Africans. The Act, therefore, delineated a major change in British race relations and ushered in a period where black Britons began to reject the condescending notions of the acculturation and civilizing influences of British culture; instead, they demanded direct integration on equal terms and the validation of Afro-West Indian culture and contributions to British civilization. Whereas blacks had been welcomed into Britain in the 1940s and 1950s to fulfill a labor shortage caused by World War II, by the 1960s, unrest and racism among unemployed Britons forced Parliament to link immigration to the likelihood of immediate employment.

The rise of much of the racism in contemporary Europe can be linked directly to the earlier British youth practice of "Paki-Bashing." That is, British youth, usually males, would assault and sometimes kill, Pakistanis and Indians who performed public-sector jobs and thereby engendering the rage of the unemployed who believe that jobs should be reserved for white Britons. Indeed, many activists and civil rights workers in Britain agree that the place of blacks has deteriorated and patterns of discrimination are emerging similar to those in the United States. The link between the rise in racist activity and the economy is firmly proven as is certainly the case in Germany. The emergence of "skin-heads" in West Germany and increased racist activity in former East Germany are linked to several factors: a younger generation coming to terms with some of the contradictions of its past; a rise in xenophobia; new levels of German nationalism; high youth unemployment caused by the merger of the two nations; and the belief, on the part of many German youth, that Turks and other minorities are unfairly limiting their economic opportunity. The African diaspora in Germany is small, mainly from Mozambique, Namibia, and Cuba. As a result of the acceleration of racist activity, however, more than half of the African diaspora has left Germany in deadly fear in recent years. Indeed, German nationalism and an uncomfortable accommodation with the nation's almost 2 million Turks have made the German public less tolerant of other foreigners, particularly those who are "visible" minorities.

Racial visibility seems to be the most prominent cause of racist and ethnic violence in France. Welcomed as laborers in the 1960s and 1970s, 3 million West and North Africans seem to no longer have a place in France, once considered the most non-racist country in Europe. Jean-Marie Le Pen and other conservative leaders claim that France is going to explode if immigration is not halted and Africans and

Afro-Caribbeans are not deported. Most of the racism seems focused on younger Africans, the descendants of the original migrants, who are having a difficult time finding their place in France, even though they are citizens by virtue of birth. Economic and cultural issues both seem to fuel the fire of racism. In a period of declining employment opportunities, many French youth resent the employed blacks, while others question the nature of French society as its character changes through the impact of racial and cultural diversity. Like France, Italy and the other nations of Europe, are having to adjust to a world where the former colonial models are no longer possible and the former colonial powers must absorb some of the members of their former colonies. Consequently, this reality, along with the growing independence and declining infatuation for the "superior" culture of Europe, is causing the place of the African diaspora to assume center stage.

Summary

Over the last forty years, the African diaspora has come to see itself as part of a world-wide vanguard seeking to create a new world order out of one which began in racist chains and economic exploitation. From local and independent national struggles to the broad-based Pan-Africanist concept, the African diaspora has become much more conscious of both its collective identity and history. Between 1960 and 1990, the African diaspora saw an increase in its effective use of political power; it became more aware of its economic might; and it came to understand its impact on both society and culture. Indeed, many of the most important musical and cultural influences during the last forty years have come out of various facets of the African diaspora. Yet, despite all of its contributions to world civilization, the African diaspora is mired in poverty, low-levels of political power, and still reflecting the impact of European cultural hegemony. Though many advances have been achieved, the lack of a coherent global program limits the ultimate power of the African diaspora, although the potential of that power is clearly and universally understood.

At the Sixth Pan-African Congress in 1958, Kwame Nkrumah proclaimed the African continental and diasporan connection when he affirmed that it was New World blacks who lobbied for the liberation of the motherland from colonial rule. That relationship continues as American blacks seek their own liberation from the confines of an oppressive capitalistic and individualistic society. They are calling for not only a new global definition of diasporan contributions to Western civilization but also a fundamental restructuring of the economic system so that the face of poverty is not so black. Indeed, the African diaspora could be a potent force to shape a world seeking to develop a more rational and coherent "new world order."

Study Questions and Activities

1. Why did North and South America, as well as the Caribbean and Central America, develop very different conceptions of race? Whose interests does this difference serve?

2. Despite forty years of struggle and change, why are most blacks in the United States still marginalized and underdeveloped?
3. Is the "African diaspora" a legitimate concept in the social, economic, and political spheres? If so, what are the connections and how are they related?
4. What specific factors, at home and abroad, have contributed to a rise in the level and the development of new forms of racism and discrimination in Europe? How have the victims of discrimination attempted to overcome the adversity?
5. Suggest a set of concrete actions and strategies to liberate people of African descent in the Americas. How would you implement your plan and deal with opposition?

References

"The Black Americas, 1492–1992." *Report on the Americas*. New York: North American Congress on Latin America, Inc., vol. XXV, 4 (February 1992).

"Brazil and the Blacks of South America" and "The Blacks of Central America." *The Crisis*. New York: The National Association for the Advancement of Colored People, vol. 93, 6(June/July 1986).

Theodore Cross. *The Black Power Imperative: Racial Inequality and the Politics of Nonviolence*. New York: Faulkner, 1984.

John Hope Franklin. *Racial Equality in America*. Chicago: University of Chicago Press, 1976.

Gerald D. Jaynes and Robin M. Williams (eds.). *A Common Destiny: Blacks and American Society*. Committee on the Status of Black Americans, Commissions on Behavioral and Social Sciences and Education, National Research Council. Washington, DC: National Academy Press, 1989.

Manning Marable. *How Capitalism Underdeveloped Black America*. Boston: South End Press, 1983.

Waldo E. Martin. *No Coward Soldiers: Black Cultural Politics and Postwar America*. Cambridge, MA: Harvard University Press, 2005.

13

Continental Africans and Africans in America: The Progression of a Relationship

F. Ugboaja Ohaegbulam

Introduction

The relationship between continental Africans and Africans in the American diaspora is a complex and multifaceted one. At the same time, there exists between the two kin groups a close relationship with deep historical and cultural roots; a relationship of relative mutual prejudice and mistrust; a not-so-easily bridgeable gulf; and, yet, a common world view and a shared experience of oppression and degradation that points to a common destiny. It is a relationship that, on the one hand, has been cultivated by the kin groups and fostered by external forces and, on the other hand, has been neglected over the years. Yet, it has weathered internal and external storms that dared to break it apart. Thus, there abound ups and downs, paradoxes, and inconsistencies in the history of the relationship.

Until recently, masses of continental Africans were largely ignorant of their kin in America while, on the other hand, because of stereotypes of incredible longevity, masses of Africans in America historically developed negative feelings about Africa and frequently refused to identify with the continent. Even the small number of the elites of both groups, who were aware of each other, had their mutual misperceptions and a definite need to understand each other better, a need that was part of the driving force of racial pan-Africanism.

Now that there is a greater awareness of each other (a consequence of the post-World War II revolution in mass communications which brought members of both groups into closer proximity and of political changes that occurred in both Africa and America), the relationship is one of cooperation on a relatively small scale. But still, the relationship is complicated by tensions, imagined or perceived superiority complexes, mutual jealousies, and lingering stereotypes about each group. These complications are, among others, a function of the depth of experience, for example, with racism, changes over centuries of separation and of living in different psychological, economic, and ideological environments. They also reflect the influence of white supremacist values which frequently shaped the behavior of the elites of both groups. The continental African's understanding of the African American's experience and the realities of his existence in America is frequently superficial. Hence, continental Africans do not seem to fully appreciate the dilemmas of African Americans and their feelings of paranoia, hatred, and hostility toward white Americans. For their part, African Americans do not realize the scope of the limitations of their continental African kin group. Externally invented myths and stereotypes about both groups, just as external control by forces of colonialism, have historically tended to limit their mutual understanding and prohibited effective cooperation between them.

In this chapter, we have limited ourselves to a survey of the progression of the more positive aspects of the relationship as it has existed especially between continental Africans and African Americans, the largest and, certainly, the most powerful group of Africans in the diaspora in North America. We have excluded the story of how Africans came to the Americas, since that story is a well-known one. We have concentrated on the relationship from the beginning of the African presence in what became the United States of America to the present, as the following concepts in the survey indicate.

Major terms and concepts: diaspora, overseas Africans, pan-Africanism, double-consciousness, race conservation, "the talented tenth" of the Race, "the advance guard" of the race, Ethiopianism, Eurocentric perspective, Afrocentric or African-centered perspective, collective security, globalization.

Naming the Race in Diaspora

Throughout the centuries that they have been domiciled in America, black people have referred to themselves, at one time or another, as Africans, Afro-Americans, black, colored, and negroes. Their earliest known designation of themselves is the name African. Earliest extant documents about them, including letters, poems, pamphlets and autobiographies bear such designation. Similarly, practically all their earliest schools, churches, and social organizations were also christened African or, at times, Ethiopian, a generic synonym for African. Having been stripped of their national and ethnic group identities and renamed by their enslavers, they found it natural and necessary for themselves and their descendants to designate themselves and their organizations as African. The nomenclature served them as a communal and unifying symbol of shared suffering, a rallying point for developing pride, and an indication of their separate identity and vital ancestral roots. Thus, there is no period of black peoples' presence in America when there was not clear and definite evidence of their sentimental attachment to and nostalgia for Africa.

As a result of widespread stereotypes and myths about Africa during the nineteenth and much of the twentieth century, some black people in the United States began to stress their birth in America and to criticize and reject the designation "African" as well as its derivatives "Afro-American" and "black." W.E.B. DuBois, and Henry Highland Garnet before him, wrote that, because of the constant campaigns in American churches and society to discredit Africa, its culture and history, black people in America "shrunk from any ties with Africa and accepted the color line." The terms "colored" and "negro," by which Europeans and their descendants in America referred to black people, also began to be used by black people in referring to themselves. Some insisted that they were bona fide citizens of the United States and espoused the notion of a complete cultural break with Africa because they surely did not care to be known as resembling in any way those "terrible" Africans. A dissociation from Africa and its fabricated negative and primitive images, which had become an argument for the alleged inferiority of black people and a justification for their enforced lower social status in America appeared to be the acceptable antidote to the black American's low status and poor self-esteem. However, both appellations—"colored" and "negro"—although widely used, were criticized by elements of the black population as vague. They had neither geographical nor political locus or significance. They were simply a device by the enemies of black people designed to make them contemptible in the eyes of the world and to deny them the "true, vital, and honorable connection" with their ancestral or present land, history, and culture. The dissociation from Africa which they sought to convey was impossible. The pervasive fact of the physical characteristics of Africa stamped on black people in America remained indelible. And so, their rejection of Africa was, at bottom, a rejection of themselves.

Therefore, the designations "colored" and "negro" did not enhance the dignity of black people in America or ameliorate their sense of alienation and rejection. On the contrary, the terms may have accentuated that double-consciousness of being "an American, a Negro; two souls, two thoughts, two unreconciled strivings; two warring ideals in one dark body, whose dogged strength alone keeps it from being torn asunder" which, W.E.B. DuBois wrote, was felt generally by black people in America. "The history of the American Negro," DuBois wrote in *The Souls of Black Folk*,

> is the history of this strife—this longing to attain self-conscious manhood, to merge his double self into a better and truer self. In this merging he wishes neither of the older selves to be lost. He would not Africanize America, for America has too much to teach the world and Africa. He would not bleach his Negro soul in a flood of white Americanism, for he knows that Negro blood has a message for the world. He simply wishes to make it possible for a man to be both a Negro and an American without being cursed and spit upon by his fellows, without having the doors of opportunity closed roughly in his face.

The double-consciousness notwithstanding, the nomenclatures "African" and "black" survived the other names by which black people in America were referred to. They symbolized a psychological return to and a continuing connection between the descendants of Africa in America and their ancestral homeland. They helped to maintain the peoples' continued cultural and spiritual identity with their ancestors. For DuBois, who articulated the feeling of two-ness, they meant not just psychological but also physical return to his land of ancestry where, in Ghana, he now rests eternally with his ancestors.

The independence revolution in Africa elevated the continent and black skin pigmentation to new heights of appreciation and respectability. It certainly changed, in varying degrees, not only the self-image of increasing numbers of black people in America, but also their vision of their place in America and the world generally. After that independence revolution, black was seen as beautiful and black people in the diaspora in America began to see Africa in a new light and to take pride in being black and Afro-American, in taking African names for themselves and their children, in wearing "Afro" and "natural" hairstyles and African clothing styles, and in learning to speak an African language. Thus, as they began once again to identify with their African roots, "black" and "Afro-American" became the most popular appellations of black people in America after the emergence of sovereign nation-states in Sub-Saharan Africa. In December 1988, the Reverend Jesse Jackson and other black leaders espoused the belief that people of African descent in America should be designated as African Americans. This, they held, would embellish their cultural anchor such as other ethnic Americans enjoy, as well as reflect their double heritage. About four years after their demand, black people in America became officially so designated. Today the vast majority of them refer to themselves as Africans and demonstrate their nascent identity with renewed interest in Africa and African cultures. That identity with the continent and its cultures is shown in a variety of ways, including personal names, sojourns, extended academic study programs, group and individual contributions to the economic, social, and political development of the continent.

Pre- and Post-Garvey Emigration Schemes

The interest of African Americans in Africa is not new. It began from the inception of black peoples' enforced domicile in America. Their songs, especially the spirituals, expressed their longing for their people and fatherland. As already noted, they gave the name "African" to their churches and social organizations: The African Union Society of Newport, Rhode Island (1780), The Free African Society of Philadelphia (1787), New York African Free Society (1787), The Free African Society of Newport (1789), The African Benevolent Society of Newport (1827), The Anglo-African Magazine (1859), Bethel African Methodist Episcopal Church (1794).

Between 1773 and 1790, groups of black and Free African societies in New England, Rhode Island and Massachusetts especially, expressed their desire to emigrate to Africa in petitions to New England legislatures. Prince Hall, a Methodist preacher, and 74 other blacks sought assistance from the Massachusetts legislature in 1787 to return to Africa. They referred to Africa as their native "country" where they would live among equals and be more comfortable than they were at the time in the United States. Interest in emigration to Africa, collectively or individually, continued in varying degrees from the eighteenth century to the last years of the twentieth century and, to some degree, to the early years of the current millennium.

Emigration schemes that developed during the entire period had three related motives. The major driving force of all the early emigration or back-to-Africa schemes was the belief by leaders and participants alike that only by leaving America, a nation they believed to be dedicated to their suppression and degradation, and returning to their peoples in Africa could they ever free themselves and their brethren still under the bondage of slavery in America from further oppression and achieve happiness and prosperity. The realities of the black condition in the United States had taught them that blacks, even as legally free individuals, could never achieve real freedom, equality, and dignity in the land. Had Africans in the diaspora in America enjoyed the freedom, the dignity, the civil and political rights, and the economic opportunities enjoyed and shared by other ethnic Americans from Europe, for instance, there probably would have been no organized back-to-Africa movements. On the contrary, like other ethnic Americans, they would have employed their liberties and opportunities to do good for and advance their ancestral homeland.

A related motive of the back-to-Africa movements was that of service to their brethren in Africa by the participants. By emigrating to Africa, the emigrants hoped to carry the Christian Gospel and the fruits of Western civilization to the continent, which was generally believed to be primitive and heathen. Christian education would eradicate "heathenism, ignorance, and barbarism" by which Africa had been stigmatized by Europeans. Profitable commerce would develop between enlightened Africa and the Western world and, in turn, undermine slavery in the American South.

A third motive for back-to-Africa movements was nationalism. A newly established black nation outside the United States could aggressively strive to improve the well-being of black people in America. A black nation outside the U.S. could become closely allied with other black people in Africa and throughout its diaspora and incorporate their resources. Early nationalist emigrationism champions hoped that the political and commercial strength of such a black nation would speedily lead to the destruction of American slavery as well as European and American notions of black inferiority. Similar hopes were entertained in the late nineteenth and early twentieth centuries for a black nationality in Africa which would attack and destroy European imperial occupation and economic exploitation of Africa. It was believed that the elite of the Africans in the diaspora in the Americas were destined to lead the black nation and their "backward" African kin groups along the path of political, economic, and spiritual emancipation.

To the motives discussed above must be added the fact that the persistence of the interest and sentimental attachment of black people in America to Africa cannot be dismissed as merely a corollary or consequence of the ebbs in black fortunes in America. The cultural pull of Africa must be factored into the equation and recognized as central to the struggle for freedom by overseas Africans. Finally, emigrationism was also a reflection of confidence in the capacity of black people to create and control their own reality without the fetters and corrupting influences of the white man's culture.

In 1789, a contingent of Newport free blacks conducted preliminary inquiries about resettlement in West Africa. In 1808, Paul Cuffe, a wealthy New England shipbuilder and owner, called for the establishment of a colony in West Africa and received the support of other New England blacks. After an exploratory trip to Sierra Leone in 1811 and a petition for assistance to the U.S. Congress in January 1814, Cuffe took, at his own expense, 38 blacks to the West African country in 1815. He planned to send missionaries to Africa and to establish a single organization to represent the "African Nation" in America. His death in 1817 ended his evangelical, mercantile, and other plans for both West Africa and his "African Nation" in America. His activities may have inspired the formation of a racist organization called the American Colonization Society by Henry Clay and other white

Americans. Created in 1816, the Society sought to serve as a vehicle for deporting free blacks to Africa, thereby removing the problem they represented for slavery. In 1822, the Society founded Liberia and dispatched ninety initial repatriates.

In 1820, Daniel Coker, an ordained minister from Baltimore, traveled with a group of ninety blacks to Sierra Leone with the support of the American Colonization Society. Coker, like Paul Cuffe, sought to evangelize Africa and to promote the freedom of his black brethren in the United States. Another early black colonizing missionary to go to Africa was Lott Cary of Virginia. Cary went to West Africa in 1821 to preach the Gospel of Jesus Christ to Africans, to escape from racism in America, and to live within a country where he would be judged by the merits of his character and ability and not by his complexion. The Reverend Edward Jones, educated at Amherst College, Boston, migrated to Sierra Leone where he served as the Principal of Fourah Bay College in the 1850s. From there, he led an expedition to Igboland in what is now Nigeria in 1853.

John B. Russwurm, a graduate of Bowdoin College and one of the first black people to earn a degree from an American college, initially opposed the idea of a return to Africa. But, by 1824, he became the first of such opponents to change his mind and migrated to Liberia. There, he served as the Superintendent of Schools and as editor and owner of the *Liberia Herald*. He was convinced, he wrote, that there was "no other home for the man of color, of republican principles, than Africa."

Frederick Douglass, a leading black abolitionist, was perhaps the preeminent opponent of emigration to Africa. Henry Highland Garnet was another prominent opponent of emigration. These two and other opponents of the idea believed that blacks were in America to stay; that their destiny was tied for better or for worse with that of white Americans; and that to withdraw to Africa after their sweat and blood had built up America would signify complicity with the racist American Colonization Society and a surrender to bigotry.

In the meantime, the condition of black people in America worsened, especially after the passage of the Fugitive Slave Act of 1850 and the Dred Scott Decision of the U.S. Supreme Court in 1857. By the former, whose enforcement procedure was biased against free blacks, persons accused of being fugitive were denied trial by jury and were readily re-enslaved. The latter, the Dred Scott Decision, excluded blacks from protection under the U.S. Constitution and asserted that blacks had no rights which the white man was obligated to respect.

As a consequence of these, a number of opponents of emigration to Africa began to re-evaluate their position on the issue. One such individual was the Rev. Henry Highland Garnet. A preacher and militant abolitionist, Garnet abandoned his earlier stand and began to advocate emigration as a path to economic and political advancement. Another opponent of emigration, who reversed his position on the issue, was Martin R. Delany, a Harvard trained physician. Again, the reversal of his position on the emigration question was brought about by the worsening condition of blacks in America. Delany was one of those small but vocal number of black people in America who, after the increasing voice of the slave interest in U.S. national affairs, the passage of the Fugitive Slave Act, and the consequent deterioration of the civil position of the free blacks in the northern United States, believed that there was no future for Africans in the United States.

In 1852, Delany wrote *The Condition, Elevation, and Destiny of the Colored People of the United States"* (published in book form by Arno Press and *The New*

York Times in 1969.) Delany examined the true position of black people in the United States and articulated the causes and cure of that position. His objective was to induce black people to act upon the remedy. Delany's major argument was that color prejudice had become so deeply imbedded in the American society that the black man was not and could never be politically included in the American body politic. The only way to remove the color prejudice, he said, was the complete destruction of the identity of the black man. Since this was not desirable, for the black man to remain in America, he said, was to consign himself to perpetual vassalage. The only remedy to the black condition in America, as he saw it, therefore, was emigration to or resettlement in a country where there was no color prejudice and where black people could, as worthy citizens, elevate themselves above the status and condition of a race of servants. He considered Central and South America as possible sites, then, East Africa, and, eventually, West Africa, excluding Liberia which he regarded as a tool of slavery created by the racist American Colonization Society.

In August 1854, Delany helped to organize a National Emigration Convention in Cleveland, Ohio. In 1859, he led the Niger Valley Exploration Party as a commissioner of the National Emigration Convention. Besides its scientific objective, the mission was to promote the cultivation of sugar and cotton in the West African region by black emigrants as a means of undermining slavery in Southern United States, to evangelize and "civilize" Africans, and to establish a homeland where black people could fully develop their abilities and function as a nation. He believed that blacks in America already comprised "a nation within a nation."

Delany remained in Yorubaland in what is now Western Nigeria for one year negotiating treaties for land for the settlement of blacks in keeping with the goals of his mission. In his *Official Report of the Niger Valley Exploration Party*, Delany asserted that "Africa is our fatherland" and that "our policy must be Africa for the African race, and black men to rule it." Black men he defined as "men of African descent who claim an identity with the race." The Civil War, which began upon his return, and the hope that the war would bring complete liberation and equality for black folks in America, prevented the implementation of Delany's plans to establish a black nationality in West Africa. Delany himself served in the Union army and, after the war, participated in politics in South Carolina during Radical Reconstruction.

The Civil War brought about emancipation and constitutional rights but not equality and, certainly, not economic advancement for black people. The Compromise of 1877 and the collapse of Radical Reconstruction had the effect of consolidating white supremacy and vitiating whatever civil and political rights and economic opportunities black people had shared after the end of the Civil War. Black hopes were dashed. New interest developed in emigration to Africa.

This new interest received the endorsement and encouragement of Edward Wilmot Blyden. Born of Igbo parents in the Virgin Islands, Blyden voluntarily emigrated to Liberia in 1850 after his encounters with racism in America. Blyden consistently maintained that "outside Africa, the fatherland, dignity and respectability were beyond the reach of blacks"; that Africa required its children in diaspora in the Americas for its redemption and regeneration as much as those children "needed the land of their ancestors for their spiritual salvation" and the full development of their manhood. He reiterated in his speeches before black audiences in the United States that, collectively, black people would never be respected by other groups of human beings until they established a powerful nationality. He appealed to those he described as "pure blacks" to emigrate to Liberia which, he said, needed the skills and wisdom of overseas Africans in its strivings to build a powerful black nation.

Despite the black condition in the United States and these appeals and schemes for emigration to Africa, it is estimated that the number of African Americans who actually emigrated permanently to Africa between the end of the Reconstruction in 1877 and 1910 was about two thousand, a far cry from the number of those who migrated from the southern United States to the urban centers of the north. The explanation is not far to seek. The vast majority of the Africans in the United States were too poverty-stricken to emigrate to Africa. Collectively, blacks could not afford the capital to operate a steamship line to transport willing and mobile blacks to Africa during the period when few merchant vessels plied between the United States and West Africa. Very few of the blacks who had the means to emigrate to Africa were willing to do so. Powerful capitalist forces and state, local, and national forces in America put road blocks to emigration schemes to conserve black labor essential for profit and to avoid the embarrassment and humiliation a mass departure of African Americans would cause America. Also, fearful that contact between African Americans and their colonial wards could exacerbate colonial revolts, European powers in Africa discouraged immigration into their colonial territories. Imperial policy was to prevent the entry of black nationalist visitors and expatriates viewed as potential subversives.

Interest in emigration to Africa was revived after World War I by Marcus Garvey who, encouraged by Booker T. Washington, had traveled from his native Jamaica to America in the hope of gathering support for a proposed school in Jamaica patterned after Booker T. Washington's Tuskegee Institute. Arriving after Washington's death, Garvey settled in Harlem, New York, where he established an unprecedented mass nationalist emigration scheme, the Universal Negro Improvement Association (UNIA), that had more than two million members. The black condition after World War I—the climate of disillusionment and hopelessness amidst unprecedented interracial strife—provided Garvey the opportune moment to launch his back-to-Africa movement. Garvey fully exploited the prevailing climate. He effectively preached race pride, the glorification of black skin, the glories of the African past, and the possibilities of a great nation in Africa that black people could call their own, and one which could speak and act for them and at the same time redeem Africa for Africans at home and abroad. From these and other activities, Garvey developed into one of the foremost advocates of a reclamation of Africa as a way of enhancing the tarnished image of black people and their opportunity for advancement.

In 1921, Garvey formally proclaimed the existence of a black empire in Africa with himself as the provisional president. He planned to use Liberia as the base of his African empire, but the plan fell through and the land for which he had negotiated was leased instead to Firestone, an American rubber company. Garvey's scheme included elaborate plans for black psychological, religious, and political independence, economic self-determination by blacks, a national liberation army, and a propaganda organ, the *Negro World*. Also included in his plan was a return, albeit not a wholesale exodus from America, to Africa. He boldly articulated his vision of a united Africa under the rule and control of black people.

While Garvey's back-to-Africa scheme was never implemented in the form of a physical return of Africans in America to the African continent, his speeches and activities had profound political and psychological impact on the black world. They inspired nationalists in Western, Eastern and Southern Africa, including those who thought that his schemes were grandiose and such continental Africans as Kwame Nkrumah, of Ghana, Nnamdi Azikiwe, of Nigeria, both of whom studied in the United States. The colonial powers in Africa were so frightened by Garvey's activities that they monitored the movements of those among their colonial wards who dared to communicate with him, and either banned or strictly regulated the circulation of his *Negro World* in their colonial domains. Representatives of the British Government in the United States went further to assist in financing a new magazine — *The British West Indian Review* — to offset the impact of UNIA's *Negro World*. In America, Garvey increased black people's consciousness of their African roots and identity and at the same time struck at the heart of the race problem in America by instilling pride and a spirit of militancy in black people.

Garvey was not without his American and continental African critics who saw him as a pretentious and impractical upstart. DuBois was his severest American critic. Blaise Diagne of Senegal, West Africa, who served as a deputy in the French National Assembly, believed that Garvey had unilaterally arrogated too much power to himself when he proclaimed himself the provisional president of Africa, and that he and his fellow citizens and subjects of France were satisfied with the work the French were doing in Africa and wished to remain under French sovereignty. Other African critics, like Prince Madarikan Deniyi of Nigeria and Mokete Manoedi of Lesotho (then Basutoland), mounted vigorous campaigns to discredit Garvey in the United States.

Garvey's nationalist emigration scheme collapsed for reasons similar to those that caused the failure of the earlier ones. It attracted masses of poor blacks who were caricatured as "monkey chasers" and "race fanatics" by more affluent blacks who, in the first place, disliked Garvey because he was a foreigner. The latter had accepted and internalized the widely disseminated stereotypes about Africa and Africans as primitive and jungle-dwelling brutes and savages. Having grown up learning that Africa was black and that black was bad and dirty, they cringed upon hearing the word Africa or African. Therefore, they would have nothing to do with the source of their hated physical characteristics and lowered social status in America. Furthermore, the movement had no solid political support in America or base of operation in Africa occupied by European imperial powers who saw it as a threat to their imperial interests. The glue that held it together was lost when its leader was deported to his native Jamaica by the U.S. Government in 1927, after a brief imprisonment on the conviction of using the U.S. post office to defraud shareholders in his failed Black Star Steamship Line.

Following the eclipse of UNIA, after the deportation of Garvey in December 1927, no other emigration scheme of comparable size developed. Because of factionalism within the UNIA after Garvey's deportation and the ravages of the Great Depression of 1929 to 1932, and the continuing impact of overt and institutional racism on black people in America, the former Garveyites could not promote or implement a scheme of mass exodus to Africa. However, the idea of back-to-Africa did not die. On the contrary, the hopes and aspirations of a few were directed towards Africa. Hence, since that time, individuals or small groups, without much publicity, have physically returned to or sought refuge in Africa.

The Nationalist-Negro Movement was one group that directed its efforts towards resettlement in Africa. It petitioned the League of Nations for land for settlement in the Cameroons, lost by Germany during World War I and controlled by Britain and France under the League's mandate. Nothing came of the petition to the League. Another group, known as the Pacific Movement, based in Chicago, appealed directly to the King of England for assistance for repatriation from the United States back to their home and native land, Africa. The appeal was treated with silence. A third group, the Peace Movement of Ethiopia, based also in Chicago, petitioned President Franklin D. Roosevelt to use relief monies earmarked for blacks during the Depression to subsidize repatriation of African Americans to West Africa. The petition was rejected as impractical. The group's persistent desire for resettlement in West Africa was supported by a leading racist senator from Mississippi, Theodore G. Bilbo, who introduced a bill in the U.S. Senate to that effect. But the U.S. Congress flatly refused to enact such legislation.

Additional efforts to emigrate to Africa were sparked by the emergence of independent nations in Sub-Saharan Africa after 1956. The best known is the emigration of about 175 black Jews in 1967 to Liberia. Some of the emigres left Liberia for Israel after two years. Again, since the emergence of sovereign nations in Africa, a number of individuals have emigrated physically to the continent and others, spiritually. In a conference, in 1970, at Howard University, in Washington, D.C., PASO (Pan African Students Organization) and the Student Organization for Black Unity called for a treaty between the United States and African states to guarantee human rights to Africans born in the United States and to grant automatic citizenship in African states to all diaspora Africans. Similarly, the Rev. Jesse Jackson proposed the granting of dual citizenship to Liberia and U.S. blacks. None of these propositions has thus far been implemented. However, in the 1990s, the Nigerian government provided that citizens of Nigeria could become naturalized citizens of the United States and still retain their Nigerian citizenship, while Jerry Rawlings of Ghana invited African Americans to become naturalized citizens of Ghana.

Although he did not repudiate the idea of resettlement in Africa as a long-term solution to black people's problem in America, Malcolm X stressed the restoration of cultural and spiritual bonds between African Americans and continental Africans. He saw such restoration as the immediate priority. He shared the belief that black people had a duty to stay in the land of their birth and citizenship to wage their struggle for freedom and justice by any means necessary. They could not, in his view, abandon the nation they had built and for which they were still making sacrifices. Malcolm also urged black people in America to recognize that they are essentially Africans in America. He traveled extensively in Africa, mingling with the masses, university students, and political leaders, and urging his hosts to recognize that Africans in America are their children. In Ghana, where he had been provided the opportunity to address the Parliament, Malcolm pleaded with the members of that body to show their support for "our black people in America who are being bitten by dogs and beaten with clubs." At the Organization of African Unity (OAU) Summit held in Cairo, in July 1964, Malcolm entreated the OAU states to assist their long lost brothers and sisters in placing their problems and the U.S. Government before the United Nations. His travels and reception in Africa convinced him that there was, undoubtedly, a reservoir of sympathy and concern in Africa for the dilemmas and tribulations of black people in America. Thenceforth, Malcolm became an articulate exponent of "establishing direct brotherhood lines of communication between the independent nations of Africa" and Africans in America. To that end, he established the Organization of Afro-American Unity (OAAU) by which he planned to unite Africans in the diaspora in the Americas and then these overseas Africans with continental Africans. His assassination in February 1965 prevented full implementation of the program.

Kwame Ture, formerly Stokely Carmichael, a pan-Africanist and black power advocate, resettled in Guinea, West Africa where he eventually diied. He believed that continental Africans and Africans in the diaspora comprise a single African nation. Regardless of their particular domicile in the world, African peoples, Ture asserted, share a common oppressor and common problems—racism and imperialism—and a common destiny. The final solution to the oppression and exploitation is the complete liberation of Africa which then becomes a land base from which black people, he held, would work out their destiny.

For their part, leaders of independent African states generally have been receptive to the idea of immigration of Africans in the diaspora to Africa, although an October 1968 motion to bestow automatic Kenyan citizenship upon all African Americans was rejected after debate in the Kenya legislature. Given the economic and social realities of their embryonic states—their citizens' needs for employment, education, and housing, for example—and the potential problems and difficulties wholesale immigration would pose, African leaders have a particular preference for the immigration of skilled and highly educated African Americans into their countries. Historically, this has been the group most reluctant to and unwilling to emigrate. However, some leaders saw no harm in mass immigration into their territories provided the immigrants would work hard, adapt to local conditions and not serve as subversives. Other leaders, best represented by the late Tom Mboya of Kenya, believed that the African American's battle for justice, equality, and human dignity had to be fought in America and could not be won by emigration. This stance is part of the general belief that Africans—all black people—cannot be fully free if there remains any part of the globe where a black person is denied his or her rights, and that Africans in the diaspora in America should look for opportunities in Africa to give and to receive guidance for the collective good of the African world.

The above positions notwithstanding, the economic and political condition of Africa since the 1980s, especially, has not been conducive to immigration into the continent. Economic and political difficulties and acts of nature have marginalized the continent, causing a brain drain from the ancestral homeland to America, Europe, and Asia. This continental African situation is completely different from the cause of the African American interest in emigration. It is economic, not racial. The African American emigrationism is a reflection of the black American's utter despair over racism and ever achieving first class citizenship, justice, and full humanity in the United States.

Historically, any aggravation of this despair and black condition in America heightens black people's consciousness of Africa and a longing for emigration to the continent. The greatest obstacle to that emigrationism is, perhaps, not the series of measures and roadblocks imposed by external forces to impede it, nor merely the poverty-stricken condition of black people in America, but the fact that the vast majority of African Americans, naturally, seem to love the United States, their native land, more than their ancestral homeland. Those, for example, who resettled in Liberia never stopped being Americans. They totally refused to turn their backs to America and their faces to Africa. Their ideal was to transplant the United States to Africa where they could live as a white man rather than integrating themselves into African society. Thus, their flag and constitution were patterned after those of the United States; and they referred to themselves as Americo-Liberians, while those in Sierra Leone called themselves Creoles.

What we have witnessed, especially since the 1980s, is a reverse migration of continental Africans into the United States. This recent development is not just a function of globalization feeding global migration. Rather, it is more the result of individuals seeking greener pastures and better opportunities for self improvement, and refuge from internal wars and political repression. The reverse migration is transferring most highly skilled and educated continental Africans to America. Undoubtedly, the African immigrants and their offsprings are leaving an indelible mark on America's social, political, religious, and economic development. One very conspicuous example is Barack Obama (whose Kenyan father had been such an immigrant) who was elected in November 2004 by the state of Illinois to serve as Democratic senator in the U.S. Congress. Earlier, Obama had contributed to his state and nation in a variety of ways. He taught constitutional law at the University of Chicago Law School, worked as a community activist, pushing for voter registration and better public housing, and served as a senator in the Illinois State Senate.

Africa and African American Institutions and Scholars

The interests of African Americans in Africa were not confined to physical and spiritual return to the continent. They were manifested in various other ways. Black colleges and universities — Xavier, Tuskegee, Hampton, Lincoln, Livingston, Wilberforce, Bethune-Cookman, Fisk — opened their doors to African students and provided them the material, spiritual, and intellectual support and nourishment that prepared them for their future missions in Africa. John Chilembwe and Hastings Banda of Malawi (formerly Nyasaland), Nnamdi Azikiwe of Nigeria, Kwame Nkrumah of Ghana, and Eduardo Mondlane of Mozambique, became nationalist leaders either after their studies in black colleges in America or following extensive contacts with black people in America . Mondlane, who attended Oberlin College and Northwestern University and later taught at Syracuse University, led a determined Mozambique liberation struggle against imperial Portugal which arranged his death by a letter bomb in his office in Tanzania in 1969.

Black churches, for their part, supported Christian evangelism, missionary activities, and education in various parts of Africa. The Rev. Alexander Crummell, one of the earliest black missionaries to West Africa, served as the principal of an Episcopal school at Cape Palmas. Crummell strongly believed that New World blacks had a duty to assist the Christian and commercial elevation of Liberia which he regarded as the center of an emerging black nationality in West Africa. In his view, the Great Ruler of all things assured the regeneration of Africa by working through black missionaries. The Rev. Edward Jones, as we have already noted, served as the principal of Fourah Bay College, Sierra Leone, in the 1850s. Bishop Henry M. Turner, of the African Methodist Episcopal Church, and the leading emigrationist of the late nineteenth and early twentieth centuries, toured Africa in the 1890s. He consciously sought to promote the emigration of poor black sharecroppers and itinerant laborers in Africa. Bishop Alexander Walters of the African Methodist Episcopal Zion Church participated actively in the first racial Pan-African Conference held in London in 1900 to promote black solidarity and the elevation of the race.

Earlier, in 1895, black religious leaders had met in Atlanta, Georgia, to discuss contemporary developments in Africa and produced a report—*Africa and the American Negro*—that included the largest body of accurate information on Africa then available anywhere. African American missionaries serving in various parts of Africa flatly refused to maintain silence about civil and political injustices meted out to Africans by European imperial administrators. The missionary William Sheppard helped to expose to the outside world the atrocities of Leopold II of Belgium in the Congo during the 1890s and early 1900s. The resulting opprobrium forced the Belgian monarch to surrender the territory to the Belgian government in 1908. Collaboration between the black missionaries and continental African Christian churches encouraged the formation of separatist African Christian churches under African leadership. Such churches frequently served as centers of opposition to both European colonial rule and the ecclesiastical paternalism of the white clergy in Africa. Consequently, African American missionaries in Africa were suspected by the colonial powers and white missionaries as subversive to the colonial order and the ecclesiastical status quo.

The Italian invasion of Ethiopia, in October 1935, roused pan-Africanist passions in the African community in America. To members of that community, Ethiopia was a symbol of African independence and evidence of African civilization. Frequently, Ethiopia was used as a synonym for the entire African continent, and Ethiopianism as a manifestation of African religious, cultural, and political nationalism. Hence, the Italian invasion and consequent conquest and occupation of Ethiopia constituted a dastardly attack upon Africa and peoples of African descent and their heritage. The invasion sparked off anti-Italian sentiments and support rallies for Ethiopia in several black communities in America. Concerted efforts were made to raise funds, to purchase medical supplies for Ethiopia, and to boycott Italian products. Black newspapers, such as the *Chicago Defender*, the *Pittsburgh Courier, Amsterdam News*, the *Afro-American*, and the *Crisis Magazine* provided extensive and passionate coverage of the conflict. They implored the League of Nations to support Ethiopia on the basis of justice and the international organization's basic principle of collective security—that an attack on one member constituted an attack on all. J.A. Rogers, who had been dispatched to the war zone by the *Pittsburgh Courier*, wrote several pieces on both the war and on Ethiopian history, while DuBois wrote a series of articles in *Foreign Affairs* on the conflict, including one on its inter-racial implications. Prayers were offered across the United States in support of Ethiopia in its hour of need. Volunteers offered their services but were discouraged by the U.S. Department of State. Clearly, the whole unfortunate episode, which really marked the beginning of World War II, demonstrated the oneness and racial solidarity of Africans in the diaspora in America with the land and people of their ancestry.

A venerable number of African American scholars and writers took pride in their African roots and demonstrated their concern for and appreciation of the continent's past and the possibilities of its future. J.A. Rogers, in his numerous writings, including *The World's Great Men of Color*, in two volumes, documented the contributions Africans at home and overseas made to world civilization. Arthur Schomburg, a Harlem Renaissance essayist, accumulated an extraordinary collection of books, periodicals and newspapers by and about black people worldwide. The Schomburg Center for Research in Black Culture, the New York Public Library, stands as a monument to his efforts. Chancellor Williams produced *The Destruction of Black Civilization: Great Issues of a Race from 4500 B.C. to 2000 A.D.* in which he provides a comprehensive analysis of the African past and a perceptive illumination of the present condition of black people. William Leo Hansberry wrote and taught African history and civilization from 1922 to 1959 at Howard University. *Pillars in Ethiopian History* and *Africans As Seen by Classical Writers*, both edited by Professor Joseph Harris and published posthumously, are collections from Hansberry's *African History Notes* which he prepared and used as lecture notes at Howard University. It is no wonder that one of his students and founder of the University of Nigeria at Nsukka, Nnamdi Azikiwe, honored him by naming that university's library after him.

The most prolific writer of his time on the world of black people was W.E.B. DuBois. DuBois provides us a rich and insightful historical narrative of the black race in his published works which include *The Negro, The Gift of Black Folk, Black Folk Then and Now, Africa: Its Place in Modern History, Color and Democracy: Colonies and Peace, The World and Africa: An Inquiry into the Part Africa Has Played in World History.* In *The World and Africa*, for example, DuBois attempted to reconstruct the mutilated story of the African past, emphasized the historic presence, achievements, artistic and social history of Africa, and refuted with a masterful marshaling of facts the misinformation of Eurocentric scholarship that Africa had no history prior to its imperial occupation by European nations. DuBois also is regarded as the intellectual "father of Pan-Africanism" (a topic discussed in an earlier chapter), the belief by certain individuals of African descent that the continent of Africa is a national homeland for Africans at home and abroad which should be independent and free under African leadership; that African peoples should unite in a collective effort for mutual understanding, liberation, and advancement.

The reality of race and race prejudice in the black experience in America and the world, generally, persuaded DuBois to believe that the conservation of the black race was a critical part of the only way out for black people and for making their full, complete contribution to the world. Years of experience taught him, he wrote, in *Dusk of Dawn: An Essay Towards an Autobiography of a Race Concept*, "that the whole set of the white world in America, in Europe, and in the world was too determinedly against racial equality to give power and persuasiveness" to the agitation of black people. Therefore, he believed that only black people, "bound and welded together" as a race and "inspired by one great ideal" can develop the black genius and "work out in its fullness the great message they have for humanity." DuBois believed that African Americans could never solve their problem by focusing entirely on the American context. The source of their difficulties, in his view, lay in the weakness of Africa and could not be solved apart from the liberation of the continent.

DuBois, at first, regarded the "Talented Tenth" of black people in America as "the advance guard" of the black race who should provide the leadership for the conservation, solidarity, and regeneration of the race. By the 1950s, however, he conceded that role to continental Africans. He was then appalled by what he had perceived was the apparent apathy and aloofness of African Americans from their ancestral homeland, while their continental African brothers had intensified their struggle against European colonial rule.

Along with historians and sociologists, several African American creative writers manifested deep interest in and warm sentiment for Africa. Their works explored the meaning and significance of Africa and African heritage to their art and for black people in America. In "The Negro Speaks of Rivers," Langston Hughes illustrates the African American's search for his African roots and identity in the 1920s. Similar sentiments were expressed in "Georgia Dusk" by Jean Toomer; "Heritage" and "What is Africa to Me" by Countee Cullen; and "Stars of Ethiopia" by Lucian Watkins. Also, writing in the *New York Age*, (12 May 1923), James Weldon Johnson articulated the feeling and the wish that "it may be that the day is not far off when the new Negroes of Africa will be demanding that their brothers in the United States [should] be treated with absolute fairness and justice." The entire tradition and sentiment were continued by African American writers and intellectuals who, in 1956, organized an American branch of the Society for African Culture—AMSAC—to assess their African roots and to educate other Americans about Africa.

In 1977, the late Alex Haley sparked off a great interest in the African roots of African Americans when he traced his own to West Africa and condensed the saga of that effort into a book, *Roots*, and a television mini-series that caught and occupied the attention of the entire nation over a period of time. Collectively, African American writers, whose sampling we have provided above, fostered the interest of their readers in Africa as well as continuing ties between African communities in America and those in Africa.

In addition to black colleges, religious bodies, missionaries, and writers, several other African American organizations have demonstrated in various ways their solidarity with African countries. Examples include:

1. The Council on African Affairs. The Council was founded in New York in January 1937 by Paul Robeson who, at that time was, perhaps, the most famous and controversial individual of African descent in the world. Inter-racial but under black leadership, the Council had other prominent members, including Ralph Bunche who later became Under Secretary-General of the United Nations and who had ensured in Francisco in 1945 that provisions for decolonization were included in the Charter of the UN, Mordecai W. Johnson, president of Howard University, Raymond Leslie Buell, a Harvard University political science professor specializing in African affairs, and the Reverend Adam Clayton Powell of Harlem's Abyssinia Baptist Church. The Council sought and promoted four specific objectives: provision of concrete assistance to African nationalist struggles; dissemination of accurate information on Africa and peoples of African descent; exertion of pressure on the U.S. government to adopt policies favorable to the independence of African descent; mobilization of of public opinion to foster the above goals. The Council ran into trouble

with the Harry Truman administration when it denounced the Marshall Plan, the North Atlantic treaty, and the creation of the North Atlantic Treaty Organization (NATO). It saw these as mechanisms that would guarantee that colonial peoples under Western European imperial domination would not regain their freedom and independence. It became defunct in 1955 partly because of internal leadership rift but mainly due to the communist witch hunting of Senator Joseph McCarthy.

2. Operation Crossroads Africa, created in 1957 to aid African development. The organization was founded by the Rev. James H. Robinson. It is interracial, volunteer, and youth-oriented. It sends young American volunteers to different parts of Africa every summer to work in various aspects of rural development. It became the model on which the U.S. Peace Corps was established in 1961 by the John F. Kennedy Administration.

3. The American Negro Leadership Conference on Africa (ANLCA), formed in 1962 to promote civil rights in the United States and independence and development in Africa. Its membership included such prominent African Americans as Roy Wilkins, president of the National Association for the Advancement of Colored Peoples, the Reverend Martin Luther King, Junior, Whitney Young, leader of the National Urban League. During the first of its series of biennial meetings, the ANLCA expressed delight over the success of African peoples who had recently regained their political freedom. It urged African Americans to pressure the U.S. government to formulate African policy designed to promote the independence of the remaining colonial and white-dominated territories. It urged for greater participation by African Americans in American public and private programs in Africa. In its second biennial meeting, ANLCA urged America's historically black colleges and universities to institute African studies courses and to initiate exchange programs for faculties of African universities and their African American counterparts. In 1964 its leaders appealed to the Lyndon B. Johnson administration to prohibit future American investment in South Africa and to support UN endorsed embargo against the republic as part of the pressures on its government to abandon its policy of apartheid. In 1967 its executive director, Theodore E. Brown, visited Africa twice in a futile attempt to mediate the Nigerian civil war. The Conference became defunct in 1968 when it was learned that its leadership had received funds from the U.S. Central Intelligence Agency (CIA).

4. Congressional Black Caucus (CBC). CBC was established in 1972 to improve the effectiveness of black members of the U.S. Congress as a group in the performance of their duties to their domestic constituencies. It was active in seeking relief and solution to various problems, such as drought and famine, civil war in Angola, the struggle for independence in Namibia, the end of apartheid in the Republic of South Africa, that afflicted Africa in the 1980s and 1990s. A late member from Texas, George "Mickey" Leland, had been instrumental in the passage of an African Famine Relief bill in the U.S. Congress. He died in a tragic air crash with his team in 1989 in Ethiopia in the course of providing assistance to vic-

tims of war, drought, and famine in the Horn of Africa. In 1998, members of CBC exerted pressure on the Bill Clinton administration and the U.S. Immigration and Naturalization service to increase the number of African refugees granted asylum in the United States. It was also very effective in congressional passage of the Africa Growth and Opportunity Act (AGOA) in 2000. AGOA institutionalized a process for strengthening U.S. relations with sub-Saharan African states and provides incentives for the countries to achieve political and economic reform and growth. It established a U.S.-sub-Saharan Africa Trade and Economic Cooperation Forum to facilitate, among others, regular trade and investment policy discussions between the countries and the United States.

5. TransAfrica, Inc., established by the Congressional Black Caucus in 1977 to lobby the U.S. Congress and government in the interest of African and Caribbean nations. TransAfrica has was very active on the problems of Southern Africa, especially the total elimination of apartheid. It organized a Free South Africa Movement in the 1980s and worked closely with the Congressional Black Caucus and other cooperating members of Congress to foster the passage of the U.S. Comprehensive Anti-Apartheid Sanctions Act of 1986 over President Reagan's veto. The Act contributed to the process of dismantling apartheid and to the negotiations that culminated in a non-racial democratic Republic of South Africa. (TransAfrica publishes *TransAfrica Forum*, a quarterly journal focusing on various aspects of the problems of African national communities.) It holds an annual colloquium to examine U.S. relations with African and Caribbean nations and the role of African Americans in determining and influencing the relations.

So far, this survey has focused largely on the activities of African Americans. Part of the explanation is that we have more available documentary evidence of the activities of the Africans in the diaspora than we have of those of the communities in Africa itself. People plucked from the roots from which they require nourishment and obtain ministration in order to fulfill themselves completely have a fundamental need to re-establish connection with their roots. Africans in the diaspora, unlike the economic and religious refugees from Europe and Asia who emigrated to America, started to do this from the moment they were forcibly uprooted from Africa. The degraded condition of their existence in America reinforced this activity perennially.

The fundamental explanation for more focus on the activities of African Americans, however, lies beyond the availability of evidence of those activities. It may be found in the circumstances which permitted and fostered the dispersal of Africans to the Americas. The circumstances include the organization of Africa as a mosaic of small states and communities which frequently, as in other human societies, fought each other and enslaved the victims of those wars. Since those enslavements occurred within the African geographical context, the plight of the enslaved, even though he was an outsider, a stranger, was relatively benign. He could be fully absorbed into his new domicile as a full-fledged member with equal rights, privileges and obligations as other members; or he could be freed or ransomed to return to his original community. Because of this and other practices in Africa's domestic servility, a bonded individual slave could succeed in life, even to the extent of becoming a king, depending on his ability, regardless of his prior condition of servitude.

The trans-Atlantic slave trade, which brought about the dispersal of Africans to the Americas, was an entirely different phenomenon. It enlarged the scope and frequency of the wars and transformed them from wars of self-protection to slaving wars among African communities that were already smaller than the contemporary European states and so unable to protect their members or to ensure that victims dispersed overseas received humane treatment. Furthermore, throughout the years of the trans-Atlantic slave trade, the African communities were too preoccupied with the task of ensuring their own survival and preventing their enslavement to engage in any concrete plans to re-establish connections with their uprooted and dispersed children in the Americas. Although we are not aware of any written records of any plans or activities, it does not mean that there was no desire on their part for the return of the exiles or that the exiles were entirely forgotten. There was always deep sorrow for their loss and hope that they might return.

The powerlessness inherent in Africa's misfortune of comprising a mosaic of small states and communities was a factor in the continent's conquest and occupation by larger and better armed European nations as soon as the trans-Atlantic slave trade was abolished. The powerlessness was perpetuated by the European imperial occupation and control of Africa for about one hundred years, a control which was certainly another form of slavery. During those years, continental Africans could organize no activities either to re-establish meaningful relations with Africa's overseas communities or to advance the well-being of those communities. Instead, the communities in the diaspora were the ones which continued to seek to re-establish links and to attempt to liberate their ancestral homeland.

As expected, the European imperial powers frowned upon contacts between the two groups and were suspicious of subversive African American influences on their imperial wards. The British, in particular, discouraged Africans in their colonies from studying in America. The alleged reason was that American education was inferior. Contact, however, was never completely severed, and, in collaboration with other forces, bore fruit in the fullness of time.

The political independence of African states in the 1950s and 1960s marked the beginning of the fullness of time. Its timing during the era of the Cold War and a bi-polar world, was, racially speaking, propitious for black people's drive for full political equality with their former oppressors. It provided continental Africans leverage and forums they had lacked which now, as sovereign states, they began to utilize to promote the interest, well-being and dignity of all peoples of African descent. African leaders began to demand justice and fairer treatment for all peoples of African descent by their national governments. Independent Nigeria's first foreign minister, Jaja Wachuku, whose government had already declared that it could not be neutral on any issue affecting the destiny of peoples of African descent, reiterated that declaration before the UN General Assembly on December 13, 1960, when he said: "any body who is not prepared to eradicate that humiliation that had been meted out to people of African descent or people of our racial stock cannot claim to love us."

Individually and collectively, African leaders registered loud and clear protests to U.S. officials during the 1960s against the degrading Hollywood images of black people. Milton Obote of Uganda sent President John F. Kennedy a letter in 1963 protesting the racial oppression and police brutality meted out to black people in Alabama. The OAU cabled Kennedy in the same year its resolution expressing concern over racial discrimination and brutalities committed against

African Americans in Alabama and other parts of the southern United States. The Organization's resolution in its Cairo Summit Conference in 1964 expressed the disturbance of African states over continuing manifestations of racial bigotry and oppression against black people in America. In 1968, African diplomats at the UN, in New York, offered Julian Bond their vocal support and a luncheon when the Georgia legislature denied him his elected seat because of his criticism of American policy in Vietnam. In the era of the ideological struggle between the United States and the Soviet Union for world hegemony, these protests had salutary effects on official position on the race problem in America.

As DuBois and other pan-Africanists had foresightedly stated that an improvement in the future status of black people in America would result from a victory against colonialism in Africa, the political victory in Africa now began indeed to contribute to the improvement of the black condition in America. The respected African American professor and historian, John Hope Franklin, has suggested in *From Slavery to Freedom* (1988) that it was critical international factors, among them the political evolution of Africa, and not merely either the U.S. presidential advocacy or the mounting pressure of Civil Rights movements, that induced the U.S. Congress to enact the Civil and Voting Rights Acts of 1964 and 1965. Franklin affirms:

> The emergence into independence of the sub-Saharan nations enormously changed the world-wide significance of the American race problem and provided a considerable stimulus to the movement for racial equality in the United States. As Congress began to debate the proposed civil rights bill in the summer of 1957, the diplomatic representatives from Ghana had taken up residence at the United Nations and in Washington. This important fact could not be ignored by responsible members of Congress. It seemed that black men from the Old World had arrived just in time to help redress the racial balance in the New.

The Civil and Voting Rights Acts, to which Franklin referred, empowered African Americans to elect representatives to the U.S. Congress. Two products of that empowerment to which we have already referred include the Congressional Black Caucus and TransAfrica. The same empowerment that produced these results contributed to the election of African Americans in several high offices in the land, for example, as Governor of Virginia, as mayors of such major American cities as New York, Los Angeles, Atlanta, Chicago at one time, Detroit, New Orleans, and Philadelphia and as members of practically every state legislature and judiciary, the U.S. Supreme Court and in the Constabulary of American cities.

While racism, overt and institutional, remains alive and well in the United States, there is no doubt that the independence of African states helped to minimize its scope and effect on African Americans. The influx of African students, diplomats, and businessmen into America contributed to sending the walls of segregation tumbling down in American restaurants, hotels, and other places of public accommodation.

The ethnicity of African Americans came into vogue after the emergence of sovereign nation-states in Africa. The phenomenon of independence helped blacks in America to redefine themselves in relationship to Africa, to question and, eventually, to reject the assimilationist assumptions and goals of the Civil

Rights movement of the 1950s. It inspired an African American African renaissance, an unprecedented interest in African culture, in blackness and in African names and history. The Black Studies revolution and the demand for a multicultural curriculum and holistic approach to education not just from the traditional Eurocentric perspective but from the African or Afrocentric perspective also are all aspects of the African American's new interest in Africa.

As evidence of the continuing interest in Africa, the African American National Black Arts Festival was inaugurated in 1988 as a national showcase for black artists. The biennial festival reaches far and wide to draw talents from Africa, Latin America, the Caribbean, and the United States in its efforts to disseminate knowledge about the influence that people of African descent have had on major cultures throughout the world. An observer, Don Winbush, writes (in *Upscale: The Successful Black Magazine*, August/September 1992) that "few events can match the festival's ability to teach broad and powerful lessons about the heritage and culture of people of African descent and how the world is influenced by them."

Tensions in African and African American Relations

The new image of Africa in a politically changing world and the consequent African American African renaissance have not prevented tensions between the new generation of both kin groups, especially since the 1960s when increasing numbers of continental Africans came to the United States. The tensions could be traced to a variety of sources. Elliott P. Skinner, Franz Boas Professor of Anthropology at Columbia University, attributes part of the source to white Americans who sought "to frustrate any solidarity between Africans in the diaspora and those in the continent for a radical improvement of [the] status of Afro-Americans." He notes how frequently continental Africans were accorded treatment, rights, and privileges denied their African American cousins, and how both groups were often manipulated into believing that they were different and had nothing in common. Other members of the black community believe also that both groups have often manifested superiority complexes towards each other because of stereotypical images created by white people to hinder black solidarity. Decades after the assassination of Malcolm X in 1965, the belief is still strong among several members of the black community in America that the black nationalist leader was killed because of his efforts to forge links with the leaders of African states to indict the United States before the United Nations for the violation of the human rights of Africans in America.

Mutual resentment is another source of tension. This, often, is a function of a sense of frustration that each group, consciously or unconsciously, takes out on the other as the real or imagined source of its discomforts or because of relative powerlessness to effect real changes in the local or global dilemmas that confront black people. Despite the passage of time, many African Americans still feel that historically they have been victimized because of Africa's alleged inglorious past and the role of Africans in the trans-Atlantic slave trade. They feel the injustice and bitterness of their condition at the fond attention given continental Africans in their midst. Often, similarly, continental Africans domiciled in the United States feel a sense of rejection by their African American kin. Such rejection was manifested by statements made by three prominent African Americans in 2004. First, in January of that year two senior African American professors at Harvard University made a divisive statement about the makeup of black students enrolled at that university. They claimed, critically, that the majority of black students enrolled at the university "were not true African Americans but West Indian and African immigrants or their children." The second statement was made later by Alan Keyes, a former Republican presidential candidate recruited by Republicans in the state of Illinois to oppose the popular Democratic candidate, Barack Obama, in the 2004 election for the U.S. Senate. Keyes claimed that Obama was not "a true enough African American." He went on:

> Barack Obama claims an African-American heritage. [He] and I have the same race—that is, physical characteristics. We are not from the same heritage. My ancestors toiled in slavery in this country. My consciousness, who I am as a person, has been shaped by my struggles, deeply emotional and painful, with the reality of that heritage.

Keyes' attempt to disown Obama is not typical of prominent African American leaders. Nor is the attempt by the two senior African American professors at Harvard University to create a wedge between African students and their diaspora cousins.

Due to cultural and historical differences, both continental and overseas Africans tend to define their common problems in terms of their distinctive histories. Continental Africans tend to stress the system of exploitation, while African Americans tend to define the enemy in terms of skin pigmentation. This tendency of both poses a problem for developing a strategy towards the attainment of a common goal.

Many African Americans accepted and internalized the false images of Africa and Africans as barbarous and primitive and so tend to feel superior to continental Africans. This is not new. Many of the African American emigres to Africa felt the same way. They were frequently paternalistic and condescending to and exploitative of Africans when they proposed or implemented their remedies for the economic and spiritual ills of Africa. The notion of a mission to Africa impelled them to believe that Africa was there for them to civilize and save with little or no reference at all to the local people and their culture. Garvey's vision of Africa typifies the situation. It was patronizing and deficient of continental African involvement. The image of Africa as a primitive land inhibits the desire of some African Americans to visit Africa or resettle there. Some would rather visit Europe. The loss of their ethnic or nationality group identity compounds the problem of resettling or adjustment in African societies where ethnicity remains a major force in political, economic, and social life.

Finally, the unscrupulous behavior of the great powers, including the United States, creates an atmosphere that causes African states great concern that African Americans might take advantage of their African links to subvert African states and their leaders as agents of neo-colonialism. Therefore, whether as a Peace Corps volunteer or as a diplomat or a visitor, the African American is frequently suspect as a possible agent of the U.S. Central Intelligence Agency (CIA) who might work to promote the interest of America as a superpower to the detriment of Africa.

The situation delineated above is not entirely unique to African peoples. It has neither created a wedge between Africans and their overseas cousins, nor has it impeded their solidarity. The need today is to expand cooperation between the two. FESTAC, the Festival of Black and African Arts and Culture, held in Lagos, Nigeria, in 1977, is an example of a past measure in that direction. FESTAC provided a magnificent opportunity for cooperation, solidarity, and display of the connections between continental Africans and Africans in the Americas. On a personal level, the fair employment guidelines introduced in 1977 by the Rev. Leon Sullivan, the African American board member of General Motors Corporation, a definite step towards ethical and morally responsible policies for U.S. companies operating in South Africa is another example. Known as the Sullivan Principles, the guidelines comprised part of the general offensive by black people against apartheid or legalized racism in the Republic of South Africa. The ongoing series of performances by African artists in various American cities and the Africana Studies revolution are additional measures. We have already mentioned the activities of the Congressional Black Caucus and TransAfrica. It is appropriate also to include here the ongoing activity by an individual African American scholar in southern Africa and in Ethiopia in the Horn of Africa. Since 1992 Julius Wayne Dudley, a native of Atlanta, Georgia, history professor at Salem State College, Massachuset, and subsequently Vice President of the Phelps-Stokes Fund, New York, has made several trips to these regions of Africa, specifically Angola, the Republic of South Africa, and Ethiopia to help build a culture of reading in rural schools. He has donated over 3.1 million books and other educational materials to disadvantaged schools in South Africa through a nonprofit enterprise — Collaborative Education With South Africans (CEWA) and has spent more than $33,000 of his own personal income on the philanthropic project. He initiated similar projects in Angola and Ethiopia in a spirit of practical "pan-Africanism."

Finally, there is increasing communication between African American leaders and leaders of African states for the mobilization of the energies and talents necessary to deal with the problems of African peoples and the development of Africa. The First African and African-African Summit was organized and co-chaired by Rev. Sullivan and President Felix Houphouet-Boigny and was attended by 1,500 delegates from Africa and the diaspora and by 5 African presidents. Held April 16–19, 1991 in Abidjan, Côte d'Ivoire, the conference was an outward manifestation of the efforts toward that end. Subsequent summits have been held in Libreville, Gabon, Accra, Ghana, Harare, Zimbabwe, Dakar, Senegal and Abuja, Nigeria. The African Society of the National Summit on Africa organizes forums on U.S. policy towards Africa. Collaborative efforts spearheaded by the kin groups have produced actions, first on the part of the United Nations, to build a memorial at Goree, Senegal, West Africa, to honor all the sons and daughters of Africa who had fallen victim to the Atlantic slave trade and who never returned to the continent. Secondly, the kin groups in Africa and the Americas in general are demanding for themselves world wide reparations, including acknowledgment of past abuses, as part of the remedy for years of subjection of their ancestors to servitude, racist oppression and colonial exploitation. These demands were part of the issues discussed and debated at the 31 August to 7 September UN World

Conference Against Racism held at Durban, South Africa. Before and since then, the issue has received increased attention although it remains doubtful whether the goal will be accomplished.

Summary

In a survey of this type it is impossible to exhaust the many issues involved in the relations between Africans at home and those in the diaspora in America. Thus, the survey has touched upon various aspects of the relationship which may lead to in-depth research on those aspects or to the investigation of other related aspects not directly touched upon by it. The problems of powerlessness and stereotypical images created by outside forces which, for example, have adversely affected the relationship are still with us and deserve urgent attention. For some black people in America the issue of name designation of Africans in the diaspora has not been completely resolved. In their view, they are not Africans. Yet, after globalization, worldwide political and mass communication changes helped to foster greater mutual awareness and appreciation among peoples of African descent, the bonds between continental Africans and Africans in America are stronger than ever, and continue to grow. The tumultuous and heartwarming reception accorded to Nelson Mandela by Americans, especially by African Americans, during his tour of the United States in 1990 following his release from jail, and Reverend Sullivan's delegates' triumphant landing in Abidjan in 1992, amidst dances and a great outpouring of emotions by their African brothers and sisters, are partial evidence of the fact. There is now greater awareness by the elite of African peoples of the pan-Africanist concept that African peoples are much stronger together than separate. There is now a sure political base in Africa which all African people, in the words of DuBois, "bound and welded together" as a race and "inspired by one great ideal," can use to develop the black genius, to promote the well-being and dignity of all Africans and "the great message [they] still have for humanity."

Study Questions and Activities

1. Discuss the pros and cons of the claim that generally speaking, the interest of African Americans in Africa is merely a side effect of the ebbs in black fortunes in America.
2. The Jews, taken captive to Babylon by King Nebuchadnezzar, refused to sing the "Lord's songs" in a strange land. Instead, they sat and wept when they remembered Zion. Why do you think that the African exiles in America, on the contrary, sang to the Lord's melodies known as "spirituals" in their land of exile?
3. "Not Yet Uhuru." Is this an accurate characterization of the conditions of Africans in America and in Africa?
4. Do you agree that W.E.B. DuBois was essentially correct when he said that an improvement in the future condition of Afro-Americans would be conditioned by developments in Africa?

5. What do you consider to be the major sources of tension between African
    Americans and continental Africans? How, beneficially, may these sources be
    eliminated or reduced?

References

Howard Bell. *Search for a Place: Black Separatism and Africa*. Ann Arbor: Uni-
    versity of Michigan Press, 1969.
J.W.E. Bowen (ed.). *Africa and the American Negro*. Atlanta, GA: Atlanta Uni-
    versity, 1896.
James S. Coleman, *Nigeria: Background to Nationalism*, Berkeley: University of
    California, 1958.
David Cronon. *Black Moses: Marcus Garvey and the Universal Negro Improve-
    ment Association*. Madison: University of Wisconsin Press, 1955.
John P. Davis (ed.). *Africa As Seen by American Negroes*. Paris: Presence
    Africaine, 1958.
———(ed.). *The American Negro Reference Book*. Englewood Cliffs, NJ: Pren-
    tice Hall, 1966.
Martin R. Delany. *The Condition, Elevation, and Destiny of the Colored People
    of the United States*. New York: Arno Press and *The New York Times*, 1969.
———. "Official Report of the Niger Valley Exploration Party," in Howard
    Brotz (ed.). *Negro Social and Political Thought: 1850–1920*. New York:
    Basic Books, 1966.
W.E.B. DuBois. *Dusk of Dawn: An Essay Towards an Autobiography of a Race
    Concept*. New York: Schocken Books, 1960.
———. "The Inter-Racial Implications of the Ethiopian Crisis." *Foreign Affairs*,
    vol. 14, 1 (October 1935).
———. *The Souls of Black Folk*. New York: Penguin Books, 1989.
———. *The World and Africa: An Inquiry Into the Part Africa Has Played in
    World History*. New York: International Publishers, 1965.
John Hope Franklin. *From Slavery to Freedom*. New York: Knopf Publishers,
    1988.
Joseph E. Harris (ed.). *Global Dimensions of the African Diaspora*. Washington,
    DC: Howard University Press, 1982.
———(ed.). *Pillars in Ethiopian History: The William Hansberry African His-
    tory Notebook*, vol. 1. Washington, DC: Howard University Press, 1987.
Adelaide C. Hill and Martin Kilson (eds.). *Apropos of Africa: Afro-American
    Leaders and the Romance of Africa*. New York: Doubleday, 1971.
Robert A. Hill and Barbara Bair (eds.). *Marcus Garvey: Life and Lessons*. Berke-
    ley: University of California Press, 1987.
Henry F. Jackson, *From The Congo to Soweto: U.S. Foreign Policy Toward
    Africa Since 1960*. New York: William Morrow and Company, Inc., 1982.
Martin Kilson and Daniel Fox (eds.). *Key Issues In Afro-American Experience*, 2
    vols. New York: Harcourt Brace, 1971.
Floyd J. Miller. *The Search for A Black Nationality: Black Emigration and Colo-
    nization 1787–1863*. Chicago: University of Illinois Press, 1975.
John N. Paden and Edward W. Soja (eds.). *The African Experience, Vol. 1: Es-
    says*. Evanston, IL: Northwestern University Press, 1970.
Edwin Redkey. *Black Exodus*. New Haven, CT: Yale University Press, 1969.
J.A. Rogers. *The World's Great Men of Color*. New York: Macmillan, 1972.

Elliot Skinner (ed.). *Peoples and Cultures of Africa*. Stanford, CA: Stanford University Press, 1964.

Okon Uya. *Black Brotherhood: Afro-Americans & Africa*. Boston: D.C. Heath & Co., 1971.

Robert G. Weisbord. *Ebony Kinship: Africa, Africans, and the Afro-American*. Westport, CT: Greenwood Press, 1973.

Chancellor Williams. *The Destruction of Black Civilization*. Chicago: Third World Press, 1974.

Carter G. Woodson. *The African Background Outlined*. Washington, DC: Negro Universities Press, 1968.

———. *The Miseducation of the Negro*. Washington, DC: The Associated Press, 1933.

PART IV

CONTRIBUTIONS OF THE BLACK WORLD

14

Music in Africa and the Caribbean

Roderic Knight
Kenneth Bilby

Introduction

Bring up a map of the world on your computer. Cut and paste the United States over the continent of Africa. It will take three such moves to cover the continent. From the Mediterranean to the tip of South Africa, the land stretches from one temperate zone to the other, encompassing the Sahara desert, lush tropical forests, and towering peaks in between. Nearly one thousand languages are spoken there. How can the music of this vast place be characterized in a few pages? Fortunately, despite the diversity of cultures and terrain, there are common features that link the continent, especially when focusing, as this book does, on Black Africa — Africa south of the Sahara. Certain types of instruments are distributed widely in this large area; playing styles, singing styles and song content, and the roles of musicians in their respective societies can all be broadly stated, and illustrated with some relatively familiar examples.

Today anyone listening to popular music with the least bit of international content has heard at least one African musician. A generation ago, it was Miriam Makeba, Hugh Masekela, or Olatunji. Today Angelique Kidjo, Habib Koité, Thomas Mapfumo and Joseph Shabalala are familiar and beloved by many. Several books have been written on African popular music. Although popular music blends features from Africa and the West, the African traditions have come to dominate more and more as the styles have developed. In this chapter, the focus will be on African traditional music rather than the popular styles. Of interest are the cultural contexts for music, the instruments and vocal styles that typify Africa, and some of the stylistic features of performance.

Major Terms and Concepts: personal music, griot, group music, listener's music, polyphony, *balafon, mbira, kora, goge, donso koni, mvet, toke, djembe, inanga, towa,* hemiola, offset alignment, call-and-response, antiphony, polyrhythm, *reggae, calypso, salsa, soka, meringue, merengue,* inter-African syncretism, creolization, highlife, maroon, metronome sense, polymusicality, stylistic continuum, "nation," collective participation, improvisation.

Music in Africa

Cultural Context and Genres

Hundreds of commercial recordings of traditional music have been issued, beginning with 78 rpm records early in the 20th century, spanning the era of the LP, and continuing today with CDs. These recordings represent well the diversity of settings in which music is performed in Africa. Writings on traditional music from any part of the world are plagued with problems in assigning names to types of music. The long-used terms classical or art music, popular, folk, and tribal music, have all come under fire recently, and with good reason, because each has been applied to too many dissimilar styles. For Africa, I propose three terms that have meaning both musically and socially to encompass all the traditional styles. With more emphasis on the social than the musical, these terms identify the recipient of the music: *personal* music, *group* music, and *listener's* music.

Briefly, *personal* music is performed for one's personal enjoyment. It is performed by a single individual, singing, playing an instrument, or doing both at once. There is a large and varied body of such music in Africa: a woman sings a lullaby, accompanying herself with a rattle made of a large empty land snail shell which she also slaps against her palm for a deep resonance; a boy sitting on a platform in a rice field to scare birds from the ripening crop plays a small ocarina-type flute of unfired clay; a man walking from one village to the next plays his *mbira,* plucking the metal tongues for a soft melody; a girl twirls two dried fruit pods on a string—they rattle and click together in a catchy rhythm.

Group music is music performed by a group, and *for* that group. More often than not, dancing is an essential component. The performance may comprise a wide range of participation, from virtuoso drumming or singing to simply repeating a vocal refrain or hand-clapping, but the overriding feature is that everyone present takes part in some way. Group music events span a wide range: children playing a singing game, women dancing for recreation to the music of a traveling drum troupe; men or women singing as they work a field; family members dancing and singing at a wedding or child-naming; entire communities taking part in a ritual observance, a funeral, or a festival celebrating a successful hunt or harvest.

Listener's music is music performed by professionals, in some societies defined as distinct from the rest of society *because* they are musicians. In other societies no such distinction is made. Rather than stumbling over definitions of professional, semi-professional, or any other terms that might be used to describe the status of the musicians, I prefer to simply define listener's music as music that is performed for a clearly discernible audience that is listening to the music. For example, an East African player of the *inanga* trough zither whisper-sings an epic tale; a troupe of young Chopi men dance a tightly choreographed virile dance to the accompaniment of a huge *timbila* xylophone orchestra in Mozambique; a West African *xalam* plucked lute player and his wife entertain a patron family in their home; or newly initiated girls perform songs and dances unique to their coming-out festival.

Clearly, much crossing over between these categories is possible: a personal song with a chorus added becomes a group song (the concept of personal *ownership* of a song, familiar in some American Indian cultures, is not common in Africa); group music may become listener's music when a village flute ensemble plays at the king's court (this was common in the former kingdom of Buganda). Even though the choice of a label rests primarily on the social use, and even though the musical variety within each type is potentially large, there are certain predictabilities: a single performer playing personal music is limited in what he or she can do; the numerous performers in group music (in Africa, at least) invariably define a multipart or polyphonic style; listener's music, springing ultimately from either personal or group music, usually displays an added degree of polish or professionalism, or perhaps only an added social importance.

It appears that group music predominates in Africa, for observers and researchers frequently note the absence of a clearly-defined audience. Instead, everyone is taking part. In certain contexts, however, most notably in the many West African cultures where a hereditary professional (often known by the generic term *griot*) provides much of the music, listener's music is more the rule, and monetary gain is an important factor. Of the three categories, personal music is the sort that suffers most under urbanization and the electronic invasion of radio, television, and cassette industries, but historically personal music has been a vital part of most African cultures. All traditional music in Africa is transmitted aurally, with neither words nor music being written down.

Dance has been mentioned in several instances above. Focusing on music in this chapter will put dance in the background, but it must be noted that if people are dancing, the event is by definition a dance, not just a musical event. Most African cultures have some dances that are gender-specific, and others that can involve both men and women, though usually not as couples. Some events call for group dancing with predetermined and synchronized steps as noted above, but in many cultures the more common style is one that emphasizes spontaneous interaction between individual dancers and the instrumentalists: drummers play invitational signals, dancers enter and dance to the beat or initiate another by their steps, and the instrumentalists follow. Dance postures range from erect to deeply bent, with strong foot stamping and angular arm motions more common than side-stepping, graceful arcs, or turns. The familiar wooden masks in African art collections are part of the elaborate costume for some dances.

Musical Instruments: An Overview

Musical instruments provide a handle for comprehending the enormous variety of African music. Often visually striking as well as appealing in sound, instruments catch our attention first. The instrument that everyone seems to have noticed first in Africa is the drum, often leading to the unfortunate impression that this is Africa's *only* instrument. Drum ensembles and solo drumming are indisputably important in many African cultures, but in some they play no part. Among other types of instruments played widely on the continent, two deserve special note: the xylophone and the *mbira* (the latter is known technically as a lamellophone, an instrument with springy tongues plucked with the thumbs or fingers; the word *mbira*, from Zimbabwe, has become a generic term). The xylophone in Mali, known as the *bala* or *balafon,* with gourd resonators under the keys, was described as early as the fourteenth century by the Arab geographer Ibn Battuta. Similarly, the *mbira* drew the attention of the earliest European visitors to East Africa. Flutes, in all the varieties known in the West—transverse, vertical,

oblique, and the "panpipe"—are also played widely, as are stringed instruments, in variety of shape and type equaling any other place in the world.

Some stringed instruments, known well from 20th century recordings, are nearly extinct today (the many varieties of musical bow in South Africa, for example) but others flourish, such as the *goge* monochord fiddle, played across the savanna belt of West Africa. Still others, such as the *kora*, 21-string double-row bridge harp of the Mandinka of West Africa, have become internationally familiar. Reed instruments (oboe or clarinet types) are rare, as are trumpets, except for ensembles of single-note trumpets of antelope horn, elephant tusk or wood that are unique to Africa and the Caribbean diaspora. Instruments of the "rhythm section"—rattles, clapperless bells, *claves*, scrapers—instruments that in their African form have in large part *defined* the rhythm section in Western popular music, are widespread, both geographically and across genres.

Singing Styles and Content

There are very few purely instrumental genres in Africa. Singing is a part of every music tradition, even if people are not singing. Beneath the surface of an instrumental piece one typically finds a song; the musician might be humming it, or at the very least, it will be revealed as essential to learning how to play the piece. Complicated multi-part pieces involving many players, such as the horn ensembles noted above, or the same idea applied to single-note flutes, where each player has only one note to play and must do so in a precise rhythm, are held together by a song in the players' heads. Verbal expression, if not singing, applies to drum playing as well. Drummers talk with their drums, not only the well-known "talking drums," whose hourglass shape allows squeezing the cords between the heads for infinite pitch variation, but any drums. Drummers play greetings to the town square before a dance begins, greetings to the host of the dance, praise and thanks to prominent members of the community, praise for good dancing. These are not just signals, but replications of the rhythm and tonal pattern of spoken phrases. Proverbs or praise names are often spoken in this way on other types of instruments as well.

Thus, it is not quite accurate to describe vocal music as distinct from instrumental music, but rather to talk about the vocal parts. A feature known to many, and indeed widespread, is the African responsorial style of singing, known popularly as "call and response," in which a soloist sings a line, answered by a chorus. Variations are manifold: the soloist may utter a word or two followed by a long choral response, or the solo part may be long and elaborate with a short response; both parts may be equal in length and identical in melody or vastly different; sometimes the parts overlap, with one coming in before the other is finished.

Singing in Africa tends to be extrovert and forceful; it is rarely timid or plaintive. Soloists achieve their leadership role not necessarily because they are endowed with a beautiful voice (a concept that *is* valid in many African cultures), but because they are unashamed to sing and adept at extemporization. Even though African women rarely play melodic instruments or drums, their roles as singers, dancers, and handclappers or players of various rhythm instruments mark them as absolutely vital to the music. On the subject of handclapping, it is worthy of note that multipart handclapping is typical in many African genres. We tend to take handclapping for granted, because it is a component of Western folk and popular music as well, but the question is: Where did it come from? Hand-clapping is not a cultural universal, and perhaps the West learned it from Africa.

Choral singing, with two, three, or four different parts spanning the bass to soprano range is not common in Africa as a whole, even though it is a mainstay of the *mbube* style of groups like Ladysmith Black Mambazo in South Africa. Rather, African women tend to sing in the alto range and men in the tenor, in what might be called a unisex voice range. In some cultures, especially where listener's music predominates and vocal soloists are specialists (such as the famous soloists Baaba Maal and Youssou N'Dour from Mali and Senegal), voice quality tends to be stylized, much in the way Western operatic or *bel canto* singing is stylized. Western-trained singers, hearing this African-trained voice quality, identify it immediately as the sound of a high larynx. But in a large majority of African cultures, singers sing with what we call the "natural" or open-throated voice. The familiarity of this sound contributes to the affinity Westerners feel for African music.

The content of songs in Africa is noticeably different from the West. Love songs as we know them, expressing desire, lament, pleasure or tragedy, are virtually non-existent. Protest songs and ballads, arguing a point or telling a story verse by verse are also rare, although several cultures have an epic narrative tradition: Fang players of the *mvet* harp-zither in Gabon narrate battles from mythic times, and Mande players of the *donso koni* hunter's harp in West Africa tell of animals cleverly eluding experienced hunters. In both, rapid declamatory singing is punctuated by short choral songs at appropriate points. By far the most common song type continent-wide is the praise song. In East Africa, cattle nomads praise their cows; where kings ruled in earlier days, descendants of court musicians praise today's government leaders; soloists in group singing all over Africa extemporize greetings and praise for anyone who should appear at an event, to be echoed immediately by the chorus. The genre can be turned around as well: if someone is more deserving of scorn or criticism than praise, an oblique statement, often in the form of a proverb, can be incorporated into a song. Praise takes on a lighter air in topical songs, commonly sung at recreational dances in many cultures: song leaders "praise" their friends with extemporized lines such as "Her groundnut stew is the best in town!" or poke fun in jocular ways.

Work songs are also an important genre, usually of the work-synchronizing variety. This genre is not unique to Africa—other well-known examples are European sea shanties and many Japanese folk songs—but the African expression is most familiar in America Work songs were still being sung in southern black prisons in the late 1960s before integration. Still today, Jola farmers in Senegal line up across a field in two groups with long-handled shovels to turn over the earth, trading verses back and forth as they work. Mandinka women in Gambia sing as they hoe a field. Gabra men drawing water from cavernous wells in Kenya keep the rhythm of passing buckets from hand to hand by singing as they work.

Naturally there are many celebratory songs linked to events or festivals, such as weddings, child-namings, harvest time and other calendrical events, and initiation into age-grades, secret societies, or adulthood. A special celebration in many African cultures is the funeral, which, in addition to providing formalized mourning, is an occasion for upbeat music, often on the xylophone, with the purpose of celebrating the greatness of the deceased and giving the soul a rousing send-off to the realm of the ancestors.

Stylistic Features of Ensemble Performance

Singers call and respond, dancers move to a drumbeat. Without delving too deeply into musical terminology, it is possible to note some general features of multipart performance in Africa. The most pervasive feature is polyrhythm, in which individual parts (instrumental or vocal) are intertwined to form a composite whole. Drum ensembles of the Ewe of Ghana are typical: four barrel drums of different sizes, two types of iron bells (one looking like a taco held in the open palm and called *toke*, the other, paired cowbells on a single handle), and one or two gourd rattles in a net of beads, each play a short, assigned rhythm, establishing a steady composite rhythm, or "groove." Variation is minimal and the tempo is rigid. Each part has an identity of its own—a succession of tones and tone colors in a particular rhythm. The composite sound, a variegated mix of simultaneous strokes by several instruments, individual strokes on single instruments, and momentary silences, identifies the rhythm as belonging to a particular dance. Over this a lead drummer controls the group with a more sporadic and constantly changing part, signaling changes for the ensemble and dancers alike. A smaller ensemble is the *djembe* ensemble of the Malinke of Guinea. Minimally, only two drums are needed: the cylindrical *sangba* for the basic rhythm, and the goblet-shaped *djembe* in the solo role. More typically, two other cylindrical drums, *kenkeni* and *dundun*, complete the ensemble, with two of these players also playing an iron bell mounted on their drum.

Western percussionists, masters of counting, are always amazed to learn that African musicians do not count. Instead, they keep their complicated polyrhythms in tight synchrony by the mere physicality of playing and by knowing how their part fits with another part playing simultaneously. Despite the musicians' disdain for counting, we may apply the Western concept of pulse to quantify what they are doing. With very few exceptions across the continent, rhythms may be perceived as strings of six or eight pulses (or their multiples, 12, 16, 24). Rhythms in 6, 12, and 24 are especially suited to juxtapositions of duple and triple patterns ("two against three"), known as hemiola in the West, and familiar to most people in the song "America" from *West Side Story*. African musicians, listening to the resultant sound of their rhythm and another player's rhythm and watching dancers' footsteps, know perfectly well where they are in the music. But Westerners can become confused, hearing "multiple downbeats" or strong accents coming at the "wrong" place. These perceptions only serve to emphasize a crucial feature of African polyrhythm: the parts are offset in their alignment with each other, whether applied to the starting points, accents, or entire rhythmic patterns.

Polyrhythm does not require an ensemble, nor is it restricted to drums and bells. Melodic instruments played by a single player, such as the *kora*, various arched harps of Central Africa, most xylophones, the *mbira*, and other two-handed instruments are typically played in a polyrhythmic manner. Even a solo song is likely to be sung to an independent rhythm played on a resonant object, such as the *shantu*: Hausa women in Nigeria play this tubular gourd as they sing, tapping the surface and striking the open end for an almost drumlike sound.

Melodically and harmonically, African music has much in common with the West. The earliest European visitors noted that singers in many parts of Africa sang in parallel thirds (a sound familiar to most Westerners from singing the round *Frère Jacques*). This coincidental similarity to Western music made the early introduction of church-style hymn singing comparatively easy. Today numerous hybrid styles can be traced to this blending of traditions; an early success was the *Missa Luba*, a mass in Luba style from Zaire, released in the 1950s. Instruments are typically tuned to pentatonic (5-tone) or heptatonic (7-tone) scales. Western versions of these scales may be played on the piano keyboard (black keys/white keys respectively), illustrating a close similarity, but subtle differences in intonation define the African versions. Although western instruments and their tuning (keyboards, for example) are taking over the popular music today, the African scales that sound western were not borrowed from the West but coexisted all along, as evidenced by early travelers' reports of familiar sounds, such as singing in thirds, even on first contact.

Vocal polyphony (i.e., multipart singing) reaches a height of complexity and appeal in the music of the Pygmies of Central Africa. The best known are the Babenzele and the Bambuti or Aka. Singing as they gather honey or edible plants, or as they dance in celebration of a successful hunt, a group may have as many parts as there are performers. Each man, woman, or child sings a partially improvised melody, usually wordless, and all conforming to the same scale. Some may sing one or two tones, others may sing the full range of five or six. The resultant sound is a sustained tone-cluster, such as the notes B-D-F-G-A, static in harmony but varying in texture (thickening/thinning) as singers begin and end their parts at different points and as one melody or another comes to the fore. This style of performance, built on a few fixed melodies with leeway granted to each performer in how to sing them, plus the possibility of participation by all present, typifies in many ways the African approach to music.

Today, the lure of urban life draws many people away from traditional music. Coinciding with the emergence of the recording industry in the 20th century, the guitar gained a permanent foothold in Africa. Today it attracts young players away from the instruments of their ancestors, such as the *towa*, a soft-toned V-shaped zither once played by Kissi men in Sierra Leone and Liberia. Famed virtuosos such as Sekou Diabaté of Guinea's Bembeya Jazz, or the Congolese masters of *soukous* Franco and Rochereau are the idols of many young players today.

On the other hand, some traditional music thrives in the urban or international setting: upon independence in the 1960s many countries formed national ensembles, establishing a "trademark sound" based on existing music. Among the best known are the Ensemble Instrumental du Mali, incorporating instruments of many ethnic groups with the Mande dominating, and the Royal Drummers of Burundi—a massed drum ensemble whose powerful non-polyrhythmic unison sound attracts a wide audience today. Whether creating an international-style spectacle, as in the Royal Drummers, or adding dignity and musical depth to state affairs, as in the Mali Ensemble, these new directions represent the trends that will endure and form the future of traditional African music.

The Music of the Caribbean

For centuries the Caribbean region has provided Europe and other parts of the world with much-desired commodities, such as sugar, coffee, and rum. The wealth of more than one European empire was built in considerable part on a system of exploitation consecrated to the production of such goods. The Caribbean, more than most areas of the world, bore the brunt of this enterprise and was shaped by its demands.

The millions of human beings who were pressed into the service of this system were drawn from nearly every continent. Whether indentured Europeans, enslaved native Americans or Africans, or post-emancipation African and Asian contract laborers, their primary reason for being there was—like that of the Europeans in control—to contribute to the machinery of production. Indeed, the plantation-based Caribbean societies of the slavery era have been characterized by some authors as little more than artificially created industrial complexes, held together only by the threat or use of force. Given such a history, dominated so singularly by bare economic considerations and populated by such a diversity of individuals thrown so suddenly together, one might be led to assume that little in the way of a cultural life could have developed in the Caribbean. In fact, such a view has been common in the past, and many people continue today to see the Caribbean as a "cultureless" region, or a region where the only culture that exists consists of fragmentary or corrupt versions of transplanted European traditions. Even in the Caribbean itself, Eurocentric ideologies have penetrated at every level, and in spite of growing nationalism, this attitude is still held by many.

The great irony is that, during this century, even as this ideology has continued to hold sway, the Caribbean region has become a major exporter of culture. The material products exported in previous centuries have more recently been joined by a succession of musical forms, born and bred in the Caribbean. Not only Europe, but much of the rest of the world as well, has developed a steadily growing appetite for the indigenous musical creations of Caribbean peoples. This process has unfolded gradually, one wave of musical exportation following on another, and practically every major linguistic sub-region of the Caribbean (hispanophone, francophone, and anglophone) has been represented. Afro-Cuban and Dominican music, Haitian *meringue*, and Trinidadian *calypso* have all had international success. More recently, Jamaican *reggae* has had the widest, and perhaps the most significant, impact of any Caribbean form to date.

The remainder of this chapter is intended as a synthesis of much of what has already been published on Caribbean music, which will provide the reader with some idea of the variety of musical forms to be found in the region, their essential characteristics, their social significance, and the wider impact that some of them have achieved.

Most Caribbean musical forms, like Caribbean language forms and other aspects of culture, are characterized by a simultaneous newness and oldness, the heritage of a historical process that has come to be known as creolization. That is, most Caribbean musical forms are the relatively recent products of a meeting and blending of two or more older traditions on new soil, and a subsequent elaboration of form. This creative process appears to have been set in motion during the earliest years of the European settlement of the area. Although the contributing peoples and their traditions varied from one part of the Caribbean to the next, the results were similar in many ways. One reason for this is that almost everywhere in the region the creolization process brought a variety of European and African musical traditions into contact.

There were, of course, exceptions to this rule. In places where large-scale plantation systems did not take root, and where the population included few persons of African descent, the process of creolization took a rather different shape. In the rural interior of Puerto Rico, for example, where small farms predominated and settlement was more limited to Europeans and their descendants (the native population having been decimated and/or assimilated early on), musical forms tend to be almost exclusively Hispanic-derived. In addition, there remain a few Caribbean areas (such as the coastal strip of South America that includes Guyana, Suriname, and French Guiana) where Amerindian populations have until recently remained relatively isolated and have maintained purely native musical traditions.

The process of blending began very early on. There exist numerous reports of slaves dancing, sometimes encouraged or forced by Europeans, on board ship while en route to the Caribbean. These impromptu musical events were sometimes backed by European instruments, such as concertina or fiddle, sometimes by African percussion, and sometimes by a combination of the two. On the plantations, the initial process of creolization took several directions. Blending occurred not only between European and African traditions, but also between the varied traditions of the multitude of African ethnic groups, whose cultures and languages often differed from each other at least as much as did those of the various European colonizers. This blending of distinct African traditions, which occurred throughout the Caribbean, has sometimes been referred to as "inter-African syncretism." The new musical creations that resulted sometimes owed a particularly heavy debt to one or more specific African ethnic groups; but even when this was not the case, they often remained predominantly African, in that they displayed very little European musical influence.

At the same time, there existed everywhere in the Caribbean purely European musical forms, stemming from both folk and art traditions, performed at first by Europeans on European musical instruments. As slave musicians were exposed to these forms and were increasingly integrated into the social contexts in which they occurred, a host of new and strikingly different musical forms began to emerge. In many cases these new creations were neither predominantly European nor predominantly African in form and style but rather represented a thorough fusion of the two.

In most parts of the Caribbean, then, there developed out of this creolization process a broad spectrum of musical forms, ranging from purely European-derived examples at one extreme to what have sometimes been called neo-African styles at the other. Each colony evolved its own version of such a spectrum, a fact that now makes it possible, in spite of tremendous local variation, to treat the Caribbean as a single region.

Music constituted only one aspect of the creole slave cultures that flourished throughout the Caribbean region, but it was an important one. The historical literature leaves no doubt that music loomed very large in the lives of the slaves. Nearly everywhere in the Caribbean, for instance, slaves regularly held their own dances—both on the plantations and in towns—accompanied by drumming and singing. These dramatic musical events (referred to as "fetes," "plays," and so on) often took place on holidays or "off days" when slaves were not required to work, and they sometimes continued without interruption for several days and nights. It is clear from the existing descriptions of these ceremonies that they sometimes had religious significance; they were commonly tied to slave funerals, and they often involved spirit possession. (There is also evidence that they were sometimes tied to well-organized cults.) The slaves' owners felts obliged to allow these periodic "entertainments," even though they feared that they provided opportunities for the planning of revolts, for they viewed them as "pressure" valves that helped to discharge the pent-up resentment of the slaves before it could reach the point of explosion.

The daily work regimen also had an important musical component. Field gangs often carried out their tasks to the accompaniment of work songs, performed in call-and-response style by a leader and chorus. These songs, most of them sung in the local creole language, often served—as did many songs at slave dances—as satirical vehicles, commenting on, and often ridiculing, the behavior of local personages. No one was immune to this form of social criticism, including Europeans, who frequently found themselves the butts of slave humor.

In most parts of the Caribbean, a grand theater of cultural and musical blending was to be found in local carnival traditions. These island-wide celebrations often began as traditional observances of European religious holidays but over time became increasingly dominated by slaves and free blacks, who incorporated many of their own innovations. A typical Caribbean carnival during the slavery period included participation by both blacks and whites and involved colorful troops of costumed and masked dancers (sometimes organized in competing "teams" or "sets") who paraded through the streets and lanes to the accompaniment of singing and music, which was played on a variety of African and European instruments. In many cases, such festivities coincided with brief periods of general license, during which slaves were temporarily allowed to violate certain rules of plantation regime with impunity.

Survey of Caribbean Music

It is difficult to find a major island or other territory in the Caribbean where African-derived traditions showing only very slight European musical influence do not continue to exist. Whether religious or secular, these traditions are distinguished by their fundamentally African instrumentation, consisting of a variety of drums (usually of African design, and most often played in ensembles of two or more) and other percussion instruments, such as rattles, scrapers, sticks, and bells (or bell-like metallic objects). Almost always, drumming is based on a principle of interlocking leading and supporting parts. In most cases, these traditions, in their general outlines, harken back clearly to the "plays," or slave dances, held so often on the plantations in previous centuries.

Not only the centrality of drumming and percussion, but also a number of stylistic features—such as the close interaction and communications between musicians and dancers, as well as the presence of a "metronomic sense," overlapping call-and-response singing, off-beat phrasing of melodic accents, and occasionally polymeter—reveal the African origins of these traditions, it is usually limited to the language and melodic shape of songs. One of the most interesting things about these neo-African traditions is that, although they remain essentially African in every respect, most of them must be seen as syncretic (blended) New World creations, for with few exceptions they are not traceable in their entirety to any specific region or ethnic group in Africa. And this is the case even with traditions that bear the names of specific African places or peoples. That such syncretic styles flowered so consistently throughout the Caribbean gives eminent testimony to the fundamental affinity—and easy compatibility—of African musical traditions south of the Sahara.

Beginning with the anglophone Caribbean, we note the presence of an African-based drumming tradition in the Bahamas, where two- or three-drum ensembles, accompanied by a saw scraped with a knife, are used to provide music for a variety of dances such as the "jumping dance" and "jook dance."

Farther south, Jamaica displays a rich variety of musical traditions clustering around the African end of the stylistic continuum. The various communities of Jamaican Maroons (descendants of slaves who fled the plantations in the seventeenth and eighteenth centuries to form their own societies in the forest) possess a religious tradition known as "*Kromanti* dance" or *Kromanti* play," in which ceremonies revolve around the possession of participants by ancestral spirits who use their powers to help the living solve various problems. The Maroons also have a large repertoire of complex drumming traditions (most often played on an ensemble of two drums) used to invoke and entertain the ancestors. Among the several musical categories employed in *Kromanti* ceremonies—each of which is associated with a particular dance, and songs, sung both in Jamaican Creole and a number of African-derived languages—are *prapa, mandinga, ibo, dokose* (said to be the names of "nations"), and *saleone, tambu,* and *jawbone* (recreational styles).

In the western part of the island, there is a religious tradition known as *gumbe.* Similar in many ways to Maroon ceremonies, *gumbe* dances include musically induced spirit possession, ritual healing, and complex drumming. Also in the western area are the *nago* and *etu* traditions, said to be practiced by the descendants of post-emancipation indentured African immigrants, many of whom were Yoruba. The ceremonies of both groups make use of songs in Yoruba and Jamaican Creole, accompanied by distinctive styles of drumming that are found nowhere else on the island. *Tambo* (or *tambu*), found primarily in the parish of Trelawny, is a Kongo-related drumming tradition, used mainly for entertainment, that may also have been introduced by post-emancipation immigrants; here, a single drummer produces subtle and complex rhythmic variations by applying the heel of his foot to the head of the drum to change pitch. (He is often accompanied by another musician, who beats the back of the drum with two sticks.)

In the central part of Jamaica, there is a tradition known as *buru* (a word used elsewhere on the island to refer to any African-derived dancing or drumming; *buru,* played on an ensemble of three drums, along with scrapers, rattles, and other percussion instruments, is associated in some areas with secular masquerade dances and is said to derive from work songs stemming from the slavery period. When this music was carried by rural migrants to the ghettos of West Kingston several decades ago, it played an important role in the development of a new kind of drum ensemble music, called *nyabingi*, created by adherents of the Rastafari religion.

Still in Jamaica, but farther to the east, we find the *kumina* cults, whose members possess a vital dance-drumming tradition that is largely Kongo-derived. Specific drum rhythms (usually played on a battery of two drums, though sometimes three or more are used) and "African county" songs are used to summon the spirits of deceased cult members so that they may possess devotees and maintain contact with the living. *Kumina*, like a number of other African-based traditions, is thought to have evolved shortly after emancipation, primarily among recently arrived indentured African immigrants. The Afro-Christian religious tradition known as *convince* or *bongo,* limited to the eastern part of the island, also makes use of a clearly African-derived style of music. Although drums are generally not used in *convince* ceremonies, songs are backed by polyrhythmic clapping (sometimes reinforced by percussive sticks) and are performed in typically African call-and-response style. Ceremonies almost always involve possession by ancestral spirits.

The Virgin Islands, which have been under the control of various colonial powers in the past, possess an interesting dance-drumming tradition called *bamboula*, which is thought to go back at least to the eighteenth century. The *bamboula* is danced during wakes, in carnival celebrations, and on other socially important occasions. Usually played on a single drum known as the *ka* (found historically in many parts of the Caribbean), the music may incorporate a second player who beats the back of the drum with percussive sticks. The drummer, as in Jamaican *tambo* and *kumina*, and a large number of other Caribbean traditions, skillfully uses the heel of the foot in order to vary the pitch of the drum.

In the chain of islands that make up the Lesser Antilles, most of the English-speaking islands have at one time or another either been French possessions or received substantial numbers of French immigrants; the populations of some of these remain largely bilingual (in English and French-based creoles), and their musical traditions—even those closer to the African end of the continuum—continue to show varying degrees of French influence. But in some of these traditions this is seen only in the existence of songs sung in French Creole and, as in other areas of the Caribbean, there are some musical styles that display almost no French influence. This is true, for instance, of the *kutuma* and *kele* ceremonies of St. Lucia (the former associated primarily with wakes and the latter with memorial rites for the ancestors). These two traditions are practiced by people who claim descent from a number of African "nations," and the songs, dances, and drumming that form an essential part of all their ceremonies are, for the most part, unmistakably African-based.

African influence is also central in the "big drum dance" of Carriacou, a tiny island off the cost of Grenada, whose neo-African musical traditions are some of the best documented in the Caribbean. Big drum ceremonies are held for a wide variety of purposes, ranging from weddings to ancestral memorials, and although they do not involve spirit possession, the dead are nonetheless invoked and given offerings. Like the *Kromanti* play of the Jamaican Maroons, and a number of other African-based traditions in Cuba, Haiti, and other parts of the Caribbean, the big drum tradition encompasses a large repertoire of distinctive singing, drumming, and dance styles, all of which belong to the African end of the island's musical spectrum. Some of these are associated with particular African "nations" and carry religious significance; others are primarily recreational.

Trinidad is particularly rich in African-based traditions. One of the more notorious, because of its connections with social unrest and riots at several points in the island's history, is known as *kalinda*. (The dance carrying the same name in Carriacou is said to have been brought there from Trinidad.) Dances called *kalina* or *calenda* have been noted as well in several other parts of the Caribbean in the past. The Trinidad tradition centers on intricately choreographed stick-fighting, accompanied by music played on two or three drums, and sometimes also by *tamboo bamboo*, a type of stamping tube that is beaten rhythmical against the ground. *Kalinda* bands and stick-fighters once competed for regional championships but, after being banned by the authorities, were forced to go underground.

The *bongo* is a dance found in several parts of the island, traditionally performed at wakes for the purpose of placating ancestral spirits. The *bongo* dance is backed by drumming, and sometimes the *tamboo bamboo* as well. Sung in call-and-response styles, *bongo* songs often include humorous social commentary.

Trinidad also boasts a number of musical traditions that seem to have been introduced by post-emancipation African immigrants. The *congo* (or *kongo*) dance, held by people who claim Kongo descent, occurs in conjunction with weddings and christening ceremonies. Songs sung by a leader and chorus are backed by a three-drum ensemble. The *rada* tradition (whose name is derived from Allada, a major port on the coast of what was once Dahomey) incorporates music played by a three-drum ensemble, to which are added a rattle and a piece of iron used as a percussion instrument. The drumming, as well as call-and-response singing, is used to bring on spirit possession. The *shango* or *arisha* religion (also known as *yarraba*), largely of Yoruba origin, makes use of three or four drums, along with rattles, and a wide repertoire of songs, to invoke a number of deities (known as "powers") to come and take possession of dancers. Minor ceremonies are held throughout the year for a variety of purposes, and once a year a major four-day ceremony takes place.

Yet farther to the south and east, Guyana is the home of several predominant African-derived traditions. *Cumfa* and *kwe-kwe* (or *queh-queh*) are two of the better known ones; sometimes the two are combined in a single ceremony. These furnish us with yet another example of the sort of syncretic tradition that has over time integrated a varied selection of "nation dances" into a single complex. *Cumfa* and *kwe-kwe*, both of which center on ancestor veneration, include typically neo-African call-and-response singing, dancing, and drumming (played on two or more drums).

The Spanish-speaking Caribbean is no less rich in fundamentally African-derived musical traditions. Cuba, in particular, possesses some of the most purely African music in the entire Caribbean. Perhaps the best known of these traditions is that tied to the *lucumi* religion, which is derived primarily from religious traditions of the Yoruba people of West Africa, but which also contains influences from Catholicism. *Lucumi* worship centers on the invocation of a large number of deities (known as *orisha*) and a complicated system of divination known as *ifa*. There is a large repertoire of different songs and drumming styles associated with specific deities, such as *Ogun* (god of war and iron), *Ochun* (goddess of the rivers), and *Chango* (god of thunder). The hourglass-shaped drums used in *lucumi*, called *bata*, are essentially the same as those used in certain types of Yoruba music in Nigeria today. Also represented at the African end of Cuba's musical continuum is the music of several *congo* cults, such as *mayombe, kinfuite*, and *palo-monte*. All of these cults or sects are concerned with the tapping of *nganga*, a sort of magical or spiritual force that pervades the universe; but each has its own dances and songs, accompanied by several different kinds of drum ensembles.

Another Caribbean tradition, the *abakua*, must not go without mention. The *abakua*, a secret society with an all-male membership, is derived largely from the traditions of the Efik people of the Calabar region of Nigeria. The society is said to have emerged during the slavery period among the free blacks, who organized themselves and pooled resources in order to help buy the freedom of slaves, who were then admitted to the society. *Abakua* music is based on a percussion ensemble, at the center of which are two or three drums, and it is distinguished by its association with a unique masked dance, performed by a character known as *ireme* or *diablito* (Spanish, "little devil").

The Dominican Republic also possesses a number of African-derived musical forms, most notably those belonging to the *congo* ensembles. Although songs are in Spanish, the drums used to back them (known as *congos* or *palos*), the call-and-response form, and the wide variety of complex drumming styles, produce a music whose resemblance to African forms is as strong as any in the Caribbean. The groups that play this sort of music are found primarily in the southern part of the island, where much of the black population is concentrated.

Puerto Rico, which has a predominantly Spanish-derived population, also has a neo-African tradition, known as the *bomba*. A recreational dance dating back to the period of slavery and documented in the historical literature, the dance is a sort of contest between the leading drummer and a particular dancer. The dancer challenges the drummer by improvising steps that the latter must try to match on his instrument. If the drummer is unable to follow the steps, he loses; if the dancer runs out of improvisations, he or she loses. The traditional form of the *bomba* is confined primarily, if not exclusively, to the former plantation region of the island.

In the francophone Caribbean, the most famous African-derived musical traditions are associated with the Haitian religion known to outsiders as *voodoo*, *vodun*, or *vaudou*. (Although these names have been used by outside observers to refer to the entire ceremonial complex, the rural Haitian equivalent denotes only a kind of dance that may or may not be performed in religious contexts.) This religious system is present both in the capital of Port-au-Prince and throughout the countryside, and there is marked regional variation from one area to the next. Although the theological system of Haitian voodoo represents a syncretic blend, combining beliefs derived from a number of West and Central African religions with influences from Catholicism, the bulk of Haitian ritual music and dance styles are overwhelmingly African-derived. Throughout the country, particular categories of music are connected with different "nations" and/or *lwa* (or *loa*-possessing deities); in some areas these deities are divided into two major pantheons, known as *rada* and *petro*, each with its own type of drum and percussion ensemble and its own cycle of dance-drumming styles. Among the more widespread styles of Haitian ritual music and dance are *banda, nago, congo, yanvalou*, and *ibo*.

Farther to the east, in Guadeloupe, we find a tradition called *gwoka* (or *groska — ka* being the name of the type of drum on which the music is played. Essentially a recreational music, *gwoka* is associated celebrations of several sorts, sporting events, weekend parties, and other social events. Three or four drums, as well as rattles, percussive sticks, and sometimes tambourines, are used to back topical songs performed in call-and-response style.

French Guiana, located on the northeastern coast of South America, also has its neo-African tradition, known as *casse-co* (said to be derived from French casser-corps, "to break the body"). This is the traditional dance music of the African-descended creole population, which lives primarily in the coastal region. Played on two or three drums, along with a bench-like instrument beaten with two sticks, French Guianese neo-African music includes several distinct substyles, such as *grage, le role, belia*, and *camougue*, each of which has its own dance movements.

Finally, we come to the Dutch Caribbean. The islands of Curaçao, Aruba, and Bonaire (part of the Netherlands Antilles) possess in common a musical tradition known as *tambu*, usually making use of a single drum accompanied by a piece of iron struck with a stick or another piece of metal. The call-and-response songs, most often topical, are usually sung in the local creole language, *Papiamentu*, and show a certain degree of European melodic influence; but the drumming itself, often involving virtuoso displays and complex cross-rhythmic play against the patterns of the percussive iron, is quite clearly African-derived.

Suriname, the South American republic that gained its independence from the Dutch in 1975, is so well represented by musical traditions belonging to the African end of the spectrum that only the most summary mention can be made of them. The African-descended segment of the population divides roughly between the Creoles (living in the coastal region) and the Maroons (descended from slaves who escaped from the coastal plantations during the seventeenth and eighteenth centuries and, at least until recently, living primarily in the interior (forest). Because many of their original ancestors were slaves on the same plantations, the present-day Creoles and Maroons are culturally related in many ways.

The Suriname Creole religion known as *winti* incorporates a music and dance tradition much like many of the others already mentioned. Centering on the invocation of a large number of deities belonging to different categories, each with its own domain of concerns (and some connected with specific "nations"), *winti* ceremonies contain a corresponding diversity of styles.

The Maroons, on the other had, can be divided into six different ethnic groups (Kwinti, Saramaka, Matawai, Ndjuka, Paramaka, and Aluku, the last being the only Maroon group located primarily across the border in French Guiana), which are separated by both linguistic and cultural differences. But all of the Maroon groups are historically and culturally closely related, and they share a number of ritual music and dance traditions that, in their general outlines, resemble those of the Creoles. Thus, each Maroon group has its own version of a *kumanit/komanti, ampuku/apuku, papa*, and so on, all of them involving a variety of broadly similar styles of drumming , dance, and song, ministering to similar gods, and occurring in similar social context s (funerals, rites honoring deities, and so forth). But there are important regional variations as well, fostered by continual stylistic innovation; and a number of music and dance forms are associated with specific groups. The dances *susa* and *agankoi*, for instance, are considered to be specifically Ndjuka, while *tjeke* and *bandammba* belong to the Saramaka.

Before moving on to a discussion of Caribbean music forms located toward the middle of the African-European spectrum, I wish to mention one unique tradition found in the coastal Central American county of Belize. This is the ritual music of the Black Carib (also known as *Garifuna*). (The Black Carib are descended from African slaves who were shipwrecked off the coast of St. Vincent in the seventeenth century and merged with the Amerindians of that island to form a new society, which was later transported by the British to British Honduras—now called Belize.) What makes the ritual music of the Black Carib particularly interesting is that it has clearly blended African and Amerindian features and at the same time displays virtually no European influence.

Just as each part of the Caribbean has its neo-African music, each also has its European-African hybrids, These are forms that have their feet planted, as it were, in both musical worlds and yet belong to neither; and they occur throughout the Caribbean. The various European traditions involved in their formation were more homogeneous than the varied African traditions that contributed to

Caribbean music. For this reason, pan-Caribbean comparisons and generalizations are easier to make for these hybrid forms than they are for neo-African ones.

Perhaps the most ubiquitous musical traditions of this kind are those that grew out of the European social dance music of an earlier era. This music was pan-European, in the sense that it was shared—with local variations, of course—by all of the European countries involved in the colonization of the Caribbean. Not only did this sort of music everywhere make use of the same kinds of instrumental ensembles (including, for instance, violins, guitars, flutes, and concertinas), but it was also based on the same repertoire of pan-European popular ballroom dances.

Today, the direct descendants of these ballroom dance styles are still found in every part of the Caribbean, with names that differ slightly according to area, as part of the repertoires of local village bands. Whether in Haiti or Puerto Rico, Jamaica or Curaçao, Martinique or the Virgin Islands, one can find rural bands that continue to play their own versions of dances such as the *quadrille*, the *contredanse*, the lancer's dance, the polka, and the mazurka.

Some Caribbean village bands continue to be capable of producing less creolized renditions of these dance tunes, versions that sound very European and remain quite close to the originals. But what one hears much more often is a thoroughly Caribbean adaptation that could never be mistaken for European dance music. Many bands make use of non-European instruments, such as the *banjo* (an Afro-American instrument found in many parts of the New World), the *"rhumba box"* or *marimbula* (a large, bass version of the African instrument known as *sanza*, *mbira*, or thumb piano), and various kinds of drums, rattles, and other percussion. But it is the modification of style and form, even more than the instrumentation, that sets these Caribbean creations off from their European precursors.

The Caribbean village bands that play this sort of music—a music of irrepressible vitality, combining the best of both worlds—tend to be associated with purely secular recreational dances. However, there exist a few intriguing examples of musical traditions stemming from these same ballroom dances that have been wedded to ritual contexts. In Trinidad and Tobago, for instance, as well as some of the smaller islands of the Lesser Antilles, one finds versions of the reel and the *jig* performed in the context of *"jumbie dances"*—rites involving the invocation of the spirits of celebrated *obeah*-men (ritual specialists) of the past, who come to take possession of the dancers. The music of these dances fuses clearly British-based violin playing with African-influenced rhythmic accompaniment played on an ensemble of tambourines or drums, along with a triangle.

In most parts of the Caribbean, the repertoires of village bands are not limited to European-derived ballroom dances. After all, it was rural ensembles much like the contemporary village bands—with their predominantly European instrumentation and their fundamentally European harmonic underpinnings—that played an important part in the development and proliferation throughout the Caribbean of other, completely original song and dance styles (ones that have no direct European antecedents). Virtually every country or island in the Caribbean has its own version of such indigenous style, displaying its unique blend of African-derived and European-derived features, culled from the local corpus of folk traditions. In spite of the many ways in which they differ from one another, such "national" styles as the Dominican *merengue*, the Jamaican *mento*, the Puerto Rican *plena*, the Cuban *son* and *danzon*, and the Martiniquan *biguine*, all owe a great deal to the syncretic music first played by rural ensembles of the village band sort; all of them are rooted, ultimately, in creole forms developed during the slavery era. And all of them continue to grace the repertoire of present-day village bands.

Another widespread Caribbean genre deserving mention is that of the work song. In many places, cooperative labor gangs continue to coordinate their work to the rhythm of special songs, often performed in call-and-response styles by a leader and chorus. Most commonly these work songs are associated with agricultural tasks (such as the clearing and preparation of fields for planting), but their applications range from house building to rowing, and from food pounding to the cutting and hauling of lumber. A clear precedent for such musical forms is to be found in the historical descriptions of the work songs once employed by slaves on the plantations. It should come as no surprise, then, that many of the work songs heard in the Caribbean are closer to the African end of the African-European stylistic continuum (for example, in their melodic shape and in their short, repeating responsorial phrases).

Throughout the Caribbean, another important context for music making is the wake. Wake traditions such as the Puerto Rican *baquine*, the Haitian *gage*, or the Jamaican "nine-night" (or dinky-minny) display similarities. Among other things, they share an association with a number of similar musical genres. A typical Caribbean wake might include , at different points through the night, the music of a village band, the performance of game songs, and the singing of European hymns or other religious choral music. The game songs—which have a special association with wakes but often occur independently—are of particular interest. Performed usually in call-and-response style (the form often being dictated by the structure of the particular game), these songs also vary in style along an African-European continuum; examples range from those clearly related to specific songs of European origin to others that can only be considered indigenous and that show all of the more common African-derived stylistic features found in other kinds of Caribbean music.

The influence of European religious music has been felt in nearly all parts of the Caribbean. In the hispanophone areas, one still finds religious "brotherhoods," or *cofradias*, whose members perform ancient Spanish-derived religious chants. In Haiti, Catholic *cantiques* (hymns) have been integrated into *voodoo* ceremonies. In the anglophone Caribbean, where large-scale missionization among slaves tended to take place somewhat later than in other areas, a number of independent Afro-Protestant cults or sects sprang up during the nineteenth century. Their present-day descendants, including groups such as the Spiritual Baptists (Shouters) of Trinidad, and the Revival Zionists and *pocomania (pukkumina)* practitioners of Jamaica, possess particularly interesting musical traditions. Blending Protestant devotional songs (many taken from nineteenth-century British and American hymnals) with polyrhythmic clapping and, in the case of the Revival Zionists, forceful drumming, these groups have invented an entirely new musical form—once again, neither European nor African—which displays a certain kinship with North American gospel music.

Finally, we come to the great street celebrations or carnivals of the Caribbean where animated music and dance have always been central elements. Today, as in the past, virtually every island or territory observes its own annual calendar of outdoor festivities. During designated periods—usually coinciding with major holidays such as Christmas, the New Year, Mardi Gras, Easter, and a number of Saints' days—celebrants don festive apparel and take to the streets, adding their voices and movements to a folk drama in which performers and audience are one and the same. These communal manifestations have long served as meeting grounds where different musical forms normally occurring in other settings mingle and give birth to new styles.

Just a few examples from different parts of the Caribbean will suffice to show the variety and richness of these carnival traditions. The Cuban *comparsas*, or street processions, tied to the celebration of traditional religious holidays, have been a point of convergence for some of the most vital Afro-Cuban musical forms. Among the musical traditions having a special relationship with these festivities is the *rumba*. The traditional carnival music known by this name (to be distinguished from the popular styles known as *rumba* in North America, which was actually based on another Cuban form, the *son*), in fact, encompasses a variety of different dance-drumming styles, such as the *guaguanco, yambu*, and *columbia*. All of these must be placed close to the African end of Cuba's musical continuum.

In Haiti, the beginning of carnival (shortly before Easter) signals the arrival of the *rara* bands. Winding through the roads and lanes from village to village, the musicians pick up crowds of dancers, signers, and spectators as they go. The *rara* bands produce some of Haiti's most compelling music. *Rara* bands use a wide variety of instruments. Particularly noteworthy are the vaccines (long, hollow trumpet like tubes that are blown to produce single pitches); when played in ensembles of two or more, the vaccines produce complex interlocking melodic patterns, each instrument interjecting its own note at specific time intervals. This technique, known as "hocketing," is shared by traditional horn ensembles throughout West and Central Africa. Various kinds of drums are also employed, as well as rattles and other percussion.

The most famous of Caribbean carnivals is that of Trinidad, which draws thousands of tourists every year. The close relationship between *calypso* music and the Trinidad carnival—with its *calypso* "tents" (makeshift theaters where contenders compete for the *calypso* crown), steel bands, and annual "road march" (procession)—is generally well known. But most of the smaller islands in the Lesser Antilles also have vigorous (if less famous) carnival traditions that have borrowed elements from Trinidad, such as the steel band, while retaining their own distinctive features. Almost all of the islands have *mumming* traditions, derived in part from European folk plays, that have been integrated into the festivities. Masked dancers parade through the streets, pausing occasionally to recite passages from Shakespeare or medieval *mumming* plays or, in the French-influenced islands, to sing carnival songs in French patois.

A similar carnival tradition is found, in somewhat attenuated form, in the "John Canoe," or *jonkonnu*, in St. Kitts and Nevis. (A transplanted version of the latter is also found in San Pedro de Macoris in the Dominican Republic, brought there by immigrants from St. Kitts and Nevis.) These last examples deserve special mention because of the unique form of music they use: a type of fife and drum music that was born out of a blending of European military drumming traditions with the music of West African flute and drum ensembles. This exciting music is paralleled by similar traditions in Haiti and other parts of the Caribbean, as well as by Afro-American fife and drum traditions found in certain parts of the southern United States, and it is thought to bear a close relationship to the sort of drumming that was used in the very earliest forms of jazz.

Traveling along the Caribbean musical continuum yet farther, we arrive at the European extreme—musical forms showing little or no African influence. As should be evident by now, many of the African-European hybrid traditions already discussed contain occasional examples of specific songs or instrumental pieces that are primarily of European derivation. Some Caribbean village bands play versions of ballroom dances that sound purely European; and it is not difficult to find particular work songs or ring play tunes whose melodies can be traced to specific European folk songs.

Having finished our journey from the African end of Caribbean music to the European, it is necessary to mention that there are certain parts of the Caribbean where a strong Asian presence has also left its mark on local musical life. In countries such as Trinidad and Tobago, Guyana, and Suriname—where people of Indian descent are either in the majority or constitute a very substantial minority—there exist thriving musical subcultures based on both Hindu and Muslim traditions. Indian traditions such as the *hosse (hosein)* festival of Trinidad—with its *tassa* (kettle-drum) ensembles—are attended by people of all ethnic backgrounds, and drummers of African descent are not uncommon. So it seems more than likely that these Asian-derived musical forms, in spite of having arrived later than most others and remained more or less separate, will contribute more and more to the development of Caribbean music as time goes by.

Most writers on Caribbean music have noticed the extent to which musical traditions are closely integrated with social and religious activities. Music as an autonomous art form, pursued for its own sake, and divorced from every day social life—as in the Western classical tradition (or at least a large part of it)—is a concept foreign to all but the Eurocentric elite sectors of Caribbean societies. As should be evident from the preceding description of specific musical traditions, Caribbean folk music is almost always embedded in some larger social context, whether this be a religious ceremony, an afternoon of communal labor, or a weekend dance where young men and women seek out prospective lovers. Music is more than mere accompaniment to such activities; in many cases, it is central to them, and their successful completion depends upon it.

The use of song for social commentary has been so widely reported in the Caribbean that one must consider this a pan-Caribbean phenomenon. The topical song, relying for its effect on such devices as double entendre, irony, and veiled allusions, is a Caribbean specialty that cuts across many musical genres. Virtually anyone or anything can be made a target of such songs, and thus several writers have surmised that this sort of sung criticism functions as a means of social control. Attempts have been made, as well, to link these songs to the widespread West African tradition of "songs of derision." But not all Caribbean topical songs fit this mold; while some are used to ridicule human foibles, others are more neutral and serve simply to channel information on local current events through the community.

One of the most salient features of Caribbean musical life is the collective nature of most music and dance performances. In most traditional settings, there is no division of participants into passive audience and active performers. To be sure, there are specialized roles; specifically gifted instrumentalists, singers, or dancers are given recognition for their abilities. And individual performances, or segments of performances, may be dominated temporarily by one or more central performers. But all participants have the opportunity to contribute in some capacity. Indeed, a performance that does not inspire enthusiastic collective participation—and thus does not became "hot"—is a failed performance. What determines the success of a musical performance, then, is not only the technical skill with which it is executed, but also the degree to which it engages others in active participation; the process is circular, for the higher the level of participation, the more the leading players and dancers will be spurred on. The quality of communication and *interaction generated*—interaction between the listeners and watchers clapping and offering encouragements and the players and dancers receiving them—is what makes or breaks a musical performance. This general criterion of collective participation is something that Caribbean musical traditions share with African and Afro-American music in general, and it constitutes one of the most powerful reminders of the depth of the African contribution to Caribbean musical life. It is an aesthetic canon, a sensibility, that permeates nearly all Caribbean music.

At the same time, within this collective framework, there is a strong emphasis on individuality. Performers who wish to occupy the limelight must cultivate a personalized touch—an individual "flash" or *elan*—that distinguishes their performances from those of others. Originality and flamboyant individualism are encouraged. In all but the most conservative traditions (most of which are tied to religious contexts), improvisation—within limits, of course—is a normal and expected part of performance behavior. Variation and novelty are consciously sought, rather than standardization and accurate reduplication, as is generally the case in the Western classical performance tradition. This stress on individualized expression applies not only to musical performances, but also to much of the social interaction characterizing daily life in the Caribbean. It can perhaps be said that this is part of what lends Caribbean social life in general its particularly "dramatic" quality. But it must be emphasized once again that, in musical spheres, an individual's flare for performance cannot stand on its own, for the power of any individual performance flows in very large part from the context within which it unfolds.

Finally, it is necessary to assess the significance of the tremendous diversity marking most Caribbean societies for the musicality of the individual. The sheer diversity of the Caribbean individual's musical world is paralleled in few other parts of the globe. A tiny island such as Carriacou (seven and a half miles long by three and a half miles wide, with a population of roughly six thousand) can lay claim to as many as ten or fifteen distinct "types" of folk music, ranging from predominantly African-derived traditions such as the big drum dance, on the one hand, to British balladry, on the other. On many of the larger islands, internal regional variation creates an even more complex situation. So the individual Caribbean musician is confronted with an unusually wide variety of musical choices.

This has led to the development in many areas of a phenomenon that may be referred to as polymusicality. In a musical environment in which its possible for one to encounter virtually back to back the buoyant strains of string bands and the complex drumming of possession cults, the call-and-response of field gangs and the layered harmony of a Bach chorale, it is not surprising that many individuals acquire competence in more than one tradition. In the Caribbean, the individual musician who specializes in a single form or style to the exclusion of all others is a rarity; just as the instrumentalist who limits himself to a single instrument is an exception. This polymusicality of the individual Caribbean musician can be illustrated with an example drawn from my own field experience in Jamaica. One Jamaican musician whom I once trailed for a period of several days moved through the following succession of very different kinds of musical performances, never showing the least difficulty in switching from one style to another. Starting one morning by playing guitar in a coastal *mento* band for tourists, he returned later that day to his rural village to join in a fife and drum performance, playing the leading drum, and then, in the evening, added his voice to a Revival church chorus. The next day he treated a group of friends to an impromptu performance of British ballads, accompanying himself on guitar, and late that night, played guitar and led a number of religious songs at a "nine night" (wake). On the afternoon of the third day, I found him jamming on electric bass with a local *reggae* band, and by the early evening, he was contributing some excellent banjo playing to a village *quadrille* dance. The next morning found him on the coast entertaining the tourists again, this time on harmonica, and, when I left him that evening, he was on his way to a *Kumina* ceremony, where he intended to sit in on the supporting drum. While his musical schedule during these few days may have been more fully packed than usual, the easy movement between styles was not unusual for this man; nor was the wide scope of his musicianship extraordinary for a rural Jamaican musician.

There is a temptation to see Caribbean musical life, because of its great diversity, as being made up of a rich but incoherent patchwork of different traditions. However, Caribbean musical cultures—like Caribbean languages and Caribbean cultures more generally—are perhaps better represented as integrated wholes than as jumbled assortments of separate and competing cultural traditions. The African-European musical spectrum displayed by each Caribbean country of the islands belongs to its entire population, with the exception perhaps of small European-oriented elites. The polymusical individual—and almost all individuals are polymusical to at least some degree—moves across the stylistic continuum with no sense of discomfort or disjointedness.

The polymusicality of individual Caribbean folk musicians—who sample freely from the musical spectrum, without regard for the historical provenance of specific styles—provides the strongest evidence of the integration of Caribbean musical cultures. I offer another example from my own experience. When making a study of music of the Jamaican Maroons, who have a reputation for being the most culturally African of all Jamaicans, I discovered that one of the most knowledgeable and respected *Kromanti* drummers was also the best harmonica player in the area. His lively performances of jigs, reels, and the various figures of the *quadrille* were without equal and would have stood up to the best that the British Isles themselves have to offer. To suggest to this man that this music, in which he took such pleasure, was any less "his" than were the *Kromanti* drumming styles that he had also mastered would have been a patent absurdity. There was nothing in the least "schizoid" or incongruous about the way this individual had lent his talents to the whole range of Jamaican music. The two traditions, though tied to very different social contexts, belonged in equal measure to the integrated creole culture that had been handed down to him. Although he might divide his musical world into parts, he would have no doubt that his musicianship was equal to the demands of all of them.

With its wealth of coexisting musical styles, its history of blending and adaptation, and its polymusical citizenry, the Caribbean region has produced a series of particularly "open" musical cultures. Polymusical individuals in the Caribbean most often have no scruples about using what they have learned from one musical tradition to add something new to another. Moreover, the "typical" Caribbean citizen—regardless of class or level of formal education—shows a degree of musical sophistication and an appreciation for musical variety and innovation that are rare among North American and European audiences. Caribbean musical cultures, with their emphases on individual expressiveness, collective interaction, improvisation, and experimentation, are distinguished by their receptivity to new combinations of ideas and influences. Borrowing and blending between traditions, after all, has been occurring for several centuries; it is a part of the Caribbean heritage. Whatever else may be said about Caribbean music, it remains always ripe for change.

Popular Music and Its Links with Tradition

When speaking of Caribbean popular music, one thinks of contemporary, "modern" styles such as Jamaican *reggae*, Trinidadian *soca* (or *soka*), or the modern *konpa* of Haiti and the cadence (or *kadans*) of the French Creole-speaking islands of the Lesser Antilles. These are the sounds of the "new Caribbean," the Caribbean of oversized urban sprawls and rampant migration, of transistor radios and electrified sound systems. They are the sounds of music businesses, with recording studios and professional musicians. But one must be careful not to make too sharp a distinction between popular and folk music. In the Caribbean, the two have never really been severed. In spite of commercialization, Caribbean popular music styles can be considered urban folk traditions. Still largely orally transmitted, they continue to display many of the essential features of the rural traditions that have long fed into them.

It was inevitable that such popular styles should have sprung up throughout the Caribbean under the stimulus of urbanization, large-scale migration, and the spread of new technologies. The Caribbean penchant for musical experimentation and the receptivity to new ideas ensured that individual musicians would take full advantage of the new musical opportunities and influences to which these forces increasingly exposed them. The age-old process of blending and adaptation continued to give birth to new forms, which have since been further modified to create still other varieties. Yet, through all these changes, popular styles have remained firmly rooted in folk traditions, often passing through phases in which contributions from older, rural forms have surfaced (or resurfaced) with particular vigor. The basic outlines of this process can be traced for several of the better-known popular music forms, although the evolutionary paths of most styles have yet to be documented in detail.

Take, for instance, Trinidad. The island's first urban popular music form, the famous *calypso*. (or *kaiso*), grew up primarily in and around the capital of Port-of-Spain, where the variegated folk traditions of the countryside had long been converging. It is impossible to pinpoint exactly when the musical style today recognized as *calypso* emerged. But one thing that is clear is that it went through a steady succession of transformations before taking on its present-day form. It appears that the origins of *calypso* are to be found in a number of folk traditions, such as the *bamboula* and *bealir* (or *bele*), which go back to the nineteenth century or before making it one of the oldest Caribbean popular music styles. Apparently, the earliest songs were primarily in French Creole, but English was in use by the beginning of this century. Early on, a relationship was forged with the annual carnival, and so *calypso* acquired an association with the drum rhythms of the *kalinda* stick-fighting tradition. But it was not long before stringed instruments (such as guitar and cuatro) were adopted, and along with these, a number of stylistic influences from the dance music of nearby Venezuela. By the 1920s and 1930s, when *calypso* began to be commercialized and to achieve its first international exposure, the music of the *calypso* tents (where calypsonians preformed and competed during carnival) was being played on guitars, bass, trumpets, saxophones, clarinets, and a number of other instruments. At the same time, there was also the *calypso* dancing of the streets, the parades or "road marches," that was backed by the rhythms of *kalinda* and *tamboo-bamboo*. When the *tamboo-bamboo* (stamping tubes made of lengths of *bamboo*) were prohibited as dangerous weapons during the 1930s, urban musicians responded by coming up with an entirely new instrument to replace them: the tuned steel pan, fashioned from discarded oil drums. This new instrument, in turn, sired a profusion of new techniques and sub-styles, which continued to feed into the larger *calypso* tradition.

The innovations that have figured so greatly in the development of Trinidadian popular music have not always been the result of new inventions of new introductions from outside. Trinidad's own folk musical continuum still furnishes studio musicians—many of whom are conversant with the older musical forms—with a well-stocked reservoir of local styles into which they continue to dip from time to time. The currently reigning offshoot of the *calypso* tradition, a style known as *soca*, provides a good example of this. According to several of the musicians involved in its popularization, the *soca* "beat" was first developed during the 1960s by studio musicians who, while experimenting, used the trap drums to fuse a number of rhythmic patters derived from the *shango* cults and the *hosse* drumming tradition with the current *kaiso/calypso* style (by then played on amplified instruments, such as electric piano, guitar, bass, organ, and so forth). Elements of North American funk were added as well. The result was at first called the "rotto beat" or "rooto beat," and for some time it received little attention. During the 1970s, however, it resurfaced as the "*soca* beat" and contributed to the production of some of Trinidad's most vital music to date. Today, it continues to flourish.

Jamaican popular music, though much younger, has an equally convoluted history. As early as the 1940s and 1950s, a tiny recording industry had already begun to operate in Kingston. Local *mento* compositions, often influenced by the then popular Trinidadian *calypso*, were pressed and distributed on a small scale. This urbanized form of the *mento* achieved some popularity for a number of years, but it was not until the late 1950s and early 1960s that a completely original new style known as *ska* burst upon the scene. *Ska* was born when urban Jamaican musicians began to play North American rhythm and blues, a style that had penetrated the island via imported records and radio broadcasts from Miami and other parts of the southern United States. Whether consciously or not, these musicians began to graft certain rhythmic patterns derived from the music of the Revival cults and other traditional forms onto the basic rhythm and blues framework, and a completely new form of music gradually emerged. Within a few years, the *ska* had slowed down its tempo and absorbed a number of further influences from North American "soul" music and other sources; in its new incarnation, it was known as "rock-steady." Shortly after this, yet another new style known as *reggae* cropped up. *Reggae* retained the basic rhythmic structure of the previous popular styles but showed the influence of both *mento* and the Rastafarian drumming tradition known as *nyabingi*. (The liaison between popular musicians and the Rastafarian movement had actually begun back during the *ska* era.)

Since the late 1960s, *reggae* has remained the dominant popular style in Jamaica, but it has passed through countless trends and absorbed numerous new influences. *Reggae* covers of the latest North American popular hits coexist alongside traditional Rastafarian religious chants set to a *reggae* beat. Romantic ballads alternate with message songs, some earnest and some humorous, dealing with the latest local and international political events. A profusion of sub-styles — "rockers," "lover's rock," "militant," "dancehall," "*ragga*," and so forth — continue to pop up and to lead to further innovations. And the Caribbean penchant for variation and experimentation has been canonized in the Jamaican concept of "version": the practice of including on the flip side of a record a modified mix (often with vocal tracks removed) of the same song featured on the A side. This practice developed during the 1960s, when local disk jockeys began to "toast" — to improvise extended "raps" — over the sounds of the latest hits (thus the need for "versions" of these tunes minus the vocal tracks). Many North American and European record buyers interpreted this custom negatively, assuming that it was motivated solely by a desire among produces to take in as much money as possible by delivering a final product that cost less to produce. However, this practice helped spawn not only vital and still thriving deejaying tradition, but also a very important new sub-style known as "dub," in which local recording engineers and studio musicians used "version" sides to experiment with new sound recording technologies.

Some of the most important Caribbean music has grown up outside of the Caribbean, among immigrant communities in Europe and North America. Large-scale emigration has long been a feature of Caribbean life. For several centuries, movements of people from one part of the region to another have been resulting in inter-island musical cross-fertilization. But the last few decades have seen emigration — particularly to urban centers to the north — on an unprecedented scale. Sizeable Caribbean minority populations now exist in cities such as London, Paris, Amsterdam, Toronto, New York, and Miami, to name just a few. Caribbean music remains as important as ever in the lives of these immigrant communities. And so the creolization process continues both at home and abroad. In London, young Jamaicans, Guyanese, Trinidadians, Grenadians — as well as British-born children of immigrants from these and other parts of the Caribbean — have joined forces to create a new, and still evolving, style of "Brit *reggae*," reflecting their experiences in the metropole. In Paris, French Antilleans and their children have begun to cross *reggae* with their own styles of dance music. In London, New York, Toronto, and other cities, there are huge annual Caribbean carnivals rivaling those occurring in the Caribbean itself. The constant flow of people back and forth between the islands and the metropolitan immigrant communities ensures that the latest musical developments on either side of the ocean are rapidly circulated to all parts of the diaspora and added to the larger pool of musical resources.

New York's very large Latin community has made that city one of the great world centers of Caribbean music. So-called *salsa* — the name began to be applied to "hot" New York Afro-Latin dance music in the late 1960s/early 1970s — is but one of the more recent developments in a long line of musical innovations stretching back several decades. Several volumes could be dedicated to this branch of

Caribbean popular music by itself. In typically Caribbean fashion, New York Latin musicians have made use of the full range of musical resources available to them. Although much of New York Latin music is strongly based on Cuban folk and popular traditions (from all points on the spectrum), influences from Puerto Rican, Dominican, Panamanian, Colombian, and other varieties of music have surfaced time and again in the many stylistic permutations that the New York scene has produced.

And so Caribbean music can no longer be defined by geographical boundaries. Yet, wherever it is produced, it continues to be resolutely Caribbean, not only in its approach to structuring sound but also in its social dimensions. Collective participation remains a cornerstone of popular music performances. Although the line between performers and audience has become much more sharply drawn than in traditional contexts, a contemporary concert or dance is still not considered really satisfying unless it manages to elicit lively interaction between musicians, dancers, and listeners. Even Jamaican *reggae*—which until recently has been primarily a studio music, with performances by live bands being the exception rather than the rule—has always had its deejay tradition, in which the recorded output of the studios is reclaimed by live performers and made the basis of huge collective manifestations ("sound system" dances).

The genre of topical song—so important in Caribbean folk music—has never been healthier. The bustle and stepped-up pace of urban life and the experience of emigration have added new grist to the songwriter's mill. The frustrations, fears, hopes, and joys of life in the contemporary Caribbean—as well as in the diaspora—are given voice more clearly than anywhere else in popular song. Much of the recent popular music issuing from Haiti is dominated by images of New York City, Miami, and *laja* (l'argent). Jamaican *reggae* songs continue to protest as strongly as ever against injustice and to document the grinding poverty, overcrowding, and political violence that plague the lives of the urban ghetto dwellers. Trinidadian *soca* numbers persist in subjecting the latest political and social developments to the incisive critiques and save wit of the "Kaisonians." And the revolution in Grenada was chronicled by local *calypsos*. Indeed, the contemporary topical song provides much of the Caribbean with its most effective news medium. (This takes on special significance when it is recalled that levels of literacy vary a great deal from one part of the Caribbean to the next.) Few of those current events that matter most to the man in the street escape the scrutiny of popular songwriters. In many Caribbean societies, then, the pulse of contemporary life can best be captured in local popular music. No one understands this better than Caribbean politicians, who have often felt compelled to monitor closely the latest sounds, and who have not always been above dabbling in the local genre and attempting to manipulate it for their own ends.

Caribbean popular musicians continue to be distinguished by their polymusicality. Many of the top *salsa* musicians are devotees of *santeria* and double as drummers, percussionists, and singers in religious ceremonies. The names of top Jamaican *reggae* musicians can often be found in small print on the jackets of local Revivalist-tinged gospel recordings (this in spite of the fact that many of them are Rastafarians and are vocal in their rejection of Christianity). Some of the leading Trinidadian *soca* musicians are familiar with the drumming styles of the *shango* and *rada* cults. And many French Antillean popular musicians are regular participants in *gwoka* drumming performances.

One does not have to search very hard to find examples of the resurfacing of traditional influences in popular music. New York Latin music, for example, has gone through several periods dominated by new introductions from traditional sources. The *mambo*, which grew up in the 1940s and became a fad in the 1950s, stemmed in part from Afro-Cuban religious traditions. Around the same time, traditional *charanga* music—an older, less African-sounding form of Cuban music played by ensembles characteristically consisting of flute, fiddles, bass, and piano—experienced renewed popularity, with the introduction of the *cha-cha-cha*. The *pachanga* rage the followed a few years later came about as the result of the fusing of rhythmic elements taken from an Afro-Cuban dance celebration known as the *bembe* with current popular dance styles. More recently, a number of *salsa* musicians have begun to introduce the sacred *bata* drums of the Afro-Cuban *lucumi* religion, along with their distinctive rhythms, into popular music recordings. And in Haiti, popular musicians have drawn on the neo-African music of *voodoo* and *rara*, creating a new genre known as *mizik rasin* (meaning "roots music").

Borrowing from traditional sources, however, is not limited to such spectacular examples as these; it occurs continually, on a more modest scale, as a result of the input of polymusical popular artists who, whether intentionally or not, bring their familiarity with folk traditions to bear in the recording studio. And so subtle references to traditional music forms—stylistic quotations—are a regular feature of contemporary popular forms. In the latest Jamaican *reggae, dancehall*, and "dub" pieces, the attuned ear can occasionally separate out *mento*-style guitar strumming, "John Canoe"-influenced drum rolls, and Revival-like voicings.

Then there is the other side of Caribbean popular music; that which is outward-looking, which thrives on novelty, experimentation, freshness, and innovation; the side that remains always open to new influences from outside. One might even go so far as to say that many popular musicians subscribe to a "mingling ethic"—a conviction that to absorb new, external influences and create new blends is in itself normal and good, part of a natural process of musical growth. The record abounds with examples of new musical forms that have come into being when this attitude has been put into action. North American readers may recall, for instance, the "Latin *bugalu*," a blend of the New York Cuban *mambo* with black rhythm and blues, which managed to find a place on the AM radio play lists during a brief period in the 1960s. Or there is the *spouge* of Barbados, a new style that arose during the late 1960s and early 1970s, when local musicians began to remake Jamaican *ska* by merging it with their own traditions, Jamaican *reggae* is itself a product of such fusion, resulting from the blending of North American rhythm and blues with indigenous influences. The process continues in all parts of the Caribbean. Musicians in Martinique and Guadeloupe continue to build upon the new Antillean fusing called *zouk*, which achieved great popularity in the Caribbean and beyond during the 1980s. And at this moment, Trinidad "kaisonians" and popular musicians in the Lesser Antilles are in the process of breathing life into new musical varieties blending *soca, zouk,* and *reggae*. Some French Antillean musicians have been heavily influenced by *salsa*, one can sometimes detect Afro-Cuban-style *guajeos* (repeating melodic riffs providing a base for instrumental soloing) in popular *cadence* and *zouk* recordings. These few examples represent only the tip of an enormous iceberg. In fact, all of the older popular styles that are still in use—such as the Trinidadian *calypso*, the Cuban *son*, the Suriname *kaseko*, the Haitian *meringue*, and the Dominican *merengue*—are in their modern incarnations very different from what they used to be only a few decades ago, largely because they have been open to outside influences (changes in instrumentation, amplification, new stylistic introductions, and so forth).

Musical blending and cross-fertilization are of course not unique to the Caribbean. But there are few other regions where such a multiplicity of diverse musical currents have been packed into such close quarters; few other areas have been swept by such a whirlwind of musical interaction, or have given rise to so many fresh and original local musical expressions. Long before "fusion" became a self-conscious jazz fad in the 1970s, all that this term implies had already been successfully achieved a thousand times over in the Caribbean. And yet, in spite of its openness to currents originating elsewhere, Caribbean popular music remains anchored to local life; it continues to express the essential concerns of those by whom and for whom it is made. No matter how often they are temporarily co-opted by commercial or other interests, the various branches of the Caribbean musical family always manage, in the end, to stay in close touch with their constituencies. This is one of the great strengths of Caribbean popular music and part of what ensures its continuing vitality: it remains everywhere, in the truest sense, a people's music.

Caribbean Music and the Rest of the World

As much as Caribbean popular musical forms remain tied to the societies that gave birth to them, many of them have nevertheless proven—thanks to the spread of modern communications media—capable of transcending local context and of winning over foreign audiences solely on the basis of their musical appeal. Numerous Caribbean styles have managed to break through ethnic and geographical barriers. Some have succeeded in attracting substantial international followings indeed and have inspired important new musical developments by non-Caribbean musicians. In the history of Caribbean popular music, the phenomenon that has come to be called "crossover" (in the jargon of the popular music industry) goes back farther than one might think.

As early as the 1920s, there already existed a market for Trinidadian *calypso* in the United States. (It was during this period that North American record companies first began to release *calypso* recordings.) Not long after this, calypsonians were making appearances in New York nightclubs. But it was not until several years later that *calypso* reached its peak of international popularity, during the "calypso craze" of 1956–1957 (at which time *calypsos* or *calypso*-influenced recordings represented a reported one-fourth of United States record sales).

Then there was the Cuban *rumba*, which swept North America and Europe during the 1920s and 1930s; or the Cuban-derived dance known as the *conga*, which followed upon its heels. The 1940s saw a great deal of interaction between Latin and black American musicians in New York, culminating in the emergence and flowering of the "*Cubop*" movement—which was responsible for some of the earliest successful fusions between Afro-Cuban music and North American jazz. Shortly after this, North American rhythm and blues, from New Orleans to New York, began to show subtle but important Latin influences, and by the mid-1950s, Latin dance styles such as the *bugalu* were being played by both Latin and North American musicians. In their heyday, during the 1940s and 1950s, Latin dance styles such as the *meringue*, the *mambo*, and the *cha-cha-cha*, and the *pachanga* spread beyond the borders of the United States, conquering audiences in Japan, Europe, and several parts of South America. In the 1970s, a new fusion, "Latin rock," had an international impact, and by the end of the decade, a substantial market for *salsa* had grown up in Europe, Japan, and several other parts of the world.

The most recent success story is of course that of Jamaican *reggae*. As early as the 1960s, *reggae* began to make major inroads in Great Britain, thanks to the presence there of a large West Indian community; in the United States, the impact was much less marked, but significant nonetheless. By the mid-1970s, it was becoming a truly international music. Through a combination of economics, politics, favorable promotion and distribution, and sheer musical attraction, *reggae* music has, as of this moment, succeeded in penetrating virtually every part of the planet. The ongoing association between the Rastafarian movement and *reggae*—which led to its being thrust in the spotlight as a major vehicle of Third World protest—has been partly responsible for the music's dispersion. Active Rastafarian *reggae* bands can now be found in almost all parts of the Caribbean—as well as among Caribbean immigrant communities in Canada, the United States, Britain, the Netherlands, and France—and in South Africa and many West African and Central African countries. But the internationalization of *reggae* had not been totally dependent on this sort of cultural and political base. Today, *reggae* is being produced by local musicians in such unlikely places as Sweden, Germany, Japan, and Java. There is even an Austrian Aboriginal *reggae* band. In England, moreover, *reggae* strongly influenced a good deal of the punk rock and new wave music of the late 1970s ; and a short-lived but influential craze in British popular music at the end of the decade—the so-called Two Tone movement—was based almost entirely on a blend of rock-and-roll and Jamaican popular music styles. Since the late 1980s, the new style of *dancehall reggae* has had a major impact on urban African American styles such as hip-hop. And the last few years have seen the emergence of a new generation of *ska* bands in the United States, whose music fuses Jamaican styles with punk and other varieties of hard-core rock. Through channels such as these, *reggae* influences have finally entered the European mainstream in a big way. The point has been reached where *reggae*-tinged hits are now sold in massive quantities to European and American record buyers who—in many cases—have no idea of their debt to Jamaican popular music.

The place where Caribbean popular music has had its most significant international impact is Africa. In anglophone West Africa, the West Indian *calypso* contributed to the development of the hardy local style known as "highlife," which—after several decades of growth and change—is still going strong, from Nigeria to Sierra Leone. Beginning in the 1930s, popular Cuban recordings began to make their way into several parts of Central Africa, and ever since, Afro-Cuban music has remained tremendously popular in this part of the continent. More recently, *salsa* has experienced a growing wave of popularity in West Africa. And, since the late 1970s, *reggae* has enjoyed increasing popularity in almost every African country south of the Sahara (once again, thanks to the wide distribution of Jamaican recordings). Finally, during the 1980s, the new French Antillean style called *zouk* took much of the African continent by storm.

These new introductions, whose African-derived components are immediately grasped by an African ear, have often played a central role in the development of major new musical fusions. African popular music, like that of the Caribbean, has been marked by an openness to new ideas from the outside, a positive stress on innovation, an attitude supporting blending between different traditions, and a continual fluctuation between new introductions and traditional influences. The Afro-Cuban music that was so popular in Central Africa during the 1930s and 1940s paved the way for one of the greatest bursts of creative activity in African popular music to date. African musicians began experimenting with Cuban musical forms almost as soon as these reached their shores. By the late 1950s, popular musicians—particularly Congolese artists—had begun to develop a new style in which musical phrasings inspired by Cuban-style horn arrangements were being played on guitar. Before long, the new guitar style picked up other influences from traditional sources and was being adapted to local techniques used in playing traditional stringed instruments. Over time, the Cuban-based music of the Congolese guitar bands was radically transformed—one stylistic innovation following on another—and by the 1970s, there existed a vital new Congolese musical genre. It was wholly original musical form, with its lovely, fluid guitar work (three or four guitars being played simultaneously to create a rhythmically complex interlocking weave), and, although Cuban influences continued to be incorporated, there was no way of confusing this new style with its Afro-Cuban ancestors.

The "Congolese sound" (nowadays known as (soukous) is but one, albeit the most famous, of an untold number of Caribbean-inspired musical fusions in Africa. The biguine, meringue, calypso, and other older Caribbean popular styles have also attracted the attention of popular musicians in several parts of the continent. More recently, soca and salsa have been finding increasing numbers of admirers in Africa, and local salsa recordings from countries such as the Ivory coast and Guinea are beginning to show more and more indigenous influences. The explosion of interest in reggae has also led to a good deal of experimentation in the studies. Indigenized reggae recordings, sung in local languages—and sometimes transformed so thoroughly that they are hardly recognizable any longer as reggae—have been produced in such countries as Nigeria, Ivory Coast, Ghana, Zaire, and South Africa. The themes of black consciousness and pan-Africanism, that continue to dominate so many Jamaican reggae songs, ring with a special resonance in modern Africa, and so it seems likely that the popularity of reggae will do nothing but grow in this part of the world during the coming years. It would not be surprising, then, if experiments in blending reggae with indigenous influences were to lead in the future to a durable new fusion that, like the "Congolese sound," could take the entire continent by storm. For reggae, like much Afro-Cuban music, rests on a generalized African musical base that appeals to listeners in virtually all parts of Sub-Saharan Africa.

Meanwhile, back in the Caribbean, local musicians, largely oblivious to recent musical developments in Africa, continue to push forward with new innovations of their own. Caribbean popular musical remains in as close touch as ever with its local audiences. There has been some initial contact and cooperation between far-sighted Caribbean and African popular musicians, and the growing musical dialogue between continents promises to lead to some of the most exciting music of the future. Whatever may happen to Caribbean music in the coming years, two things seem certain: it will remain a people's music; and it will not stay still for long.

The story of Caribbean music is a remarkable one. For this relatively small geographical region, ravaged by centuries of European colonial domination and long looked upon as a region of "colonial backwaters," "deracinated" peoples, and societies that had supposedly produced nothing indigenous of any value, has over and over brought forth unique and vibrant musical creations to which the entire world can dance. That the story is far from finished means that the lives of music lovers in both the Caribbean and other parts of the world will be that much richer in the years ahead.

Summary

Traditional music in Africa fills many roles, which may be generalized into three broad types: personal music, performed by individuals for their own enjoyment; group music, performed by and for groups, rather than for an audience as such, and listener's music, performed by professionals for the enjoyment of an audience and for monetary gain. All music is transmitted aurally. Within each of these types, music may be only vocal or only instrumental, but more commonly the two are mixed, songs being accompanied by instruments, instrumental pieces having a song at their root.

In Africa, instruments include virtually every sound-producing mechanism devised by humankind: drums, xylophones, flutes, and the *mbira* are spread widely, as are lutes (both plucked and bowed), harps, and zithers. The musical bow in many varieties was formerly common. Ensembles of single-note horns or flutes are an African specialty. Rattles, iron bells, and wooden instruments both struck and scraped are widespread. Vocality (singing or speaking) permeates the instrumental realm: drums and other instruments can "talk" by imitating the rhythm and tones of speech, while multipart instrumental pieces are modeled after a song in the players' heads.

The call and response form is most common for vocal music, with a soloist leading, a chorus answering. Women's roles focus on singing and dancing, while drums and melodic instruments are typically played by men. Love songs and ballads are uncommon, but epic narratives and praise songs are widespread. Song leaders excel at extemporizing topical words to fit individual occasions, while at the same time, celebratory and ritual songs for important life events are retained unchanged. Polyrhythm, based on offset alignment of the parts and often incorporating hemiola, is a pervasive but not universal feature of the music. Melodies are pentatonic or heptatonic, and thirds-harmony is common. Today the guitar and popular music displace some traditions, while other traditions are bolstered by their use in national ensembles.

Study Questions and Activities

1. In what ways might a participant in a performance of group music take part? When might such a performance be considered listener's music instead?
2. What connections can be seen between the various environments in which Africans live and the types of instruments they play?

3. Comment on the interaction of speech and music, and the interaction be-tween vocal and instrumental music in Africa.
4. Focusing on song content, what types or styles of American music might be traceable to African antecedents? In what ways do the songs of the two continents differ widely?
5. Identify the characteristic features of multi-part performance in Africa: How is group singing typically organized? What are the essential components of polyrhythmic ensembles?
6. How do urbanization and other modern developments affect traditional musical styles? what might be the factors that cause one to languish, another to flourish?

References

Berliner, Paul F. *The Soul of Mbira*. Berkeley: University of California Press, 1978. Recordings with notes by the same author: *The Soul of Mbira*, Nonesuch CD 79704-2; *Africa: The Shona Mbira*, Nonesuch CD 79710-2.

Knight, Roderic C. "Music in Africa: The Manding Contexts," in G. Behague (ed.), *Performance Practice: Ethnomusicological Perspectives*. Westport, Conn: Greenwood Press, 1984, 53–90. Compact disc with notes by the same author: Gambie: L'art de la kora—Jali Nyama Suso. Ocora Radio France, C-580027.

Kisliuk, Michelle. *Seize the Dance! BaAka Musical Life and the Ethnography of Performance*. Oxford, 1998 (includes two CDs).

Locke, David, with Godwin Agbeli. *Kpegisu—A War Drum of the Ewe* (pron. "Peggy Sue"). Crown Point, Indiana: White Cliffs Media, 1992. Book with instructional and documentary videotapes.

Merriam, Alan P. *African Music in Perspective*. New York: Garland, 1982. A collection of nineteen articles by this pioneering writer.

Turnbull, Colin. *The Forest People*. New York: Simon & Schuster, 1961 (latest edition 1988). Recording with notes by the same author: *Mbuti Pygmies of the Ituri Rainforest*, Smithsonian Folkways SF CD 40401.

15

African American Music

Eddie S. Meadows

Introduction

It is widely acknowledged that music is the most significant contribution of African Americans to world culture. Within this context, several musical genres, sacred and secular, have evolved from African American experiences in North America, including jazz, blues, spirituals and Gospels, and are characterized by diversity within unity, creativity, rather than stagnation, and continuity, spiced with change. They reflect the attitudes and concerns of both the performer(s) and their culture at a specific time and place in history. In the following essay, ethnomusicological rather than historical musicological, principles and concepts are used to discuss selected African American musical genres: jazz, blues, spirituals, and Gospels. (Historical musicologists study the evolution of music in time.)

Major terms and concepts: Jazz, gospel, blues, spirituals, polyphony, African retentions, ethnomusicology, call-response, improvisation, genre, tempo, Bebop, swing, Hardbop, "jungle style," Funky Style, pentatonic, avant garde, instrumentation, scat singer.

Ethnomusicologists espouse the generally accepted view that music is more fully explained and understood relative to the culture of which it is an outgrowth—that, without understanding the cultural significance of the event in which music is performed, one cannot expect to understand the meaning of the performance by analyzing the music alone. In a paper that deals with the crucial immediacy that the concept of musical culture has for ethnomusicological analysis, Kwabena Nketia[1] described musical culture as:

> The aggregate of cultural traditions associated with music which become evident at the juncture of the social and the musical traditions that are learned in the social process or in special learning situations. Traditions that are cultivated, practiced, and recreated by members of a society in the different roles they assume as music makers, instrument makers, and audiences in different contexts of the situation.

---

1. J.H.K. Nketia. "The Juncture of the Social and Musical: The Methodology of Cultural Analysis," unpublished manuscript, 1980, p. 3.

Nketia adds that a musical culture maintains distinct identity not only through the musical but also the social sphere of culture, for the socio-musical juncture admits only forms of behavior, status and structural relationships, expressions and roles which are idiomatic to it.

Another tenet of ethnomusicology is that music varies drastically as culture varies. Moreover, the variation of musical styles between cultures and culture areas is clearly greater than between the styles of the individual or groups that compose cultures. If, as some scholars advocate, music is a communication system that lives in and varies by culture, it must be, somehow, a communication about culture rather than about other things, and its variation must symbolize specific differences between cultures. This chapter provides a concise introduction to jazz, blues, spirituals, and Gospels as cultural expressions of the African American community.

African Retentions in Blues and Jazz

Scholars interested in "Africanisms" retained in African American music, especially blues and jazz, date to the nineteenth century. Since the publication of Jeannette Murphy's "The Survival of African Music in America," one of the first articles to address the issue, a plethora of ethnomusicologists have published on the topic. Included are Ernest Brown, David Evans, Portia Maultsby, Eddie S. Meadows, Alan Merriam, and John Storm Roberts. African retentions in African American musical genres vary in both breath and depth, transformation, and reinterpretation, depending upon the traceable contact between cultures.

In the published research of the aforementioned scholars, one can find discussion detailing the difficulty of tracing and documenting African retentions, as well as a list of specific African musical elements and practices found in African American genres. In the Mississippi Delta Blues of Robert Johnson and Charley Patton, one can find descending melodic lines, shifting rhythms, pentatonic-hexatonic, and heptatonic scales with altered tones, polyrhythms, and call and response patterns. Among the transformed or reinterpreted African retentions in jazz are call-and-response patterns, repetition (especially riffs), polyrhythms, use of cowbells on early drum sets and the melodic use of rhythm by drummers like Baby Dodds. In addition, one can hear African influences (tonality, rhythms, instruments) in the jazz of Herbie Hancock (the Foday Suso recordings), Yusuf Lateef, and Randy Weston; in the classical works of minimalist composers Phillip Glass and Steve Reich; and in contemporary composers like Roy Travis and Olly Wilson.

Jazz Styles

Before discussing the evolution of jazz, one must realize that jazz is not a single, monolithic genre, but one whose documented history dates as far back as the late nineteenth century. Some scholars believe that jazz might have existed in antebellum America because its essence, particularly improvisation, was an important part of the music-making process. Jazz, which originated in the African American community, can be defined as a musical genre that incorporates improvisation, swing, phrasing, and articulation into one individual performance. While improvisation is, arguably, the most salient feature of jazz, improvisation alone does not make one a jazz musician. In addition to improvisation, swing, phrasing, and articulating, one must develop his or her individual sound and approach to performance, an approach that distinguishes one's sound performance from other performers of the same genre. Without diversity within unity, one is an imitator rather than an originator, because jazz expects and encourages individual interpretation of specific musical compositions to a much greater degree than Euro-American classical music.

Throughout its history, jazz has been dominated by African American musicians. Whether big bands, small groups, or vocalists, the greatest exponents of jazz, past and present, have been and continue to be African Americans. Typically, pre-1950 jazz musicians learned to play by emulating the masters that had preceded them, after which they developed their individual approach to sound, technique, and style phrasing. The field was dominated by males, with women relegated primarily to vocals. The few exceptions have included, among others, Lil Hardin Armstrong (the first wife of Louis Armstrong), piano; Dorothy Donegan, piano; Vi Redd, alto saxophone; Clora Bryant, trumpet; and Mary Lou Williams, piano. Most pre-1950 jazz musicians had excellent "ears": they could hear harmonies and, as a result, could improvise without knowing the technical term for a specific harmony. After 1950, some jazz musicians continued to espouse pre-1950 ways and means of learning to play jazz. Others, however, began to emphasize academic training as a vehicle to learning both the technical and subtle ways and means of playing jazz.

While no credible evidence has been presented to prove that jazz originated in New Orleans, there is little debate that New Orleans has always been a Mecca of jazz activity and innovation. Musicians who have performed or continue to perform New Orleans jazz include: Louis Armstrong, Sidney Bechet, Buddy Bolden, Joe "King" Oliver, Kid Ory, Baby and Johnny Dodds, Jelly Roll Morton, Wynton and Branford Marsalis, Terence Blanchard, and Donald Harrison. New Orleans, before and around the turn of the century, was an exciting city for both cultural and musical reasons. In the African American community, brass bands were an important part of the culture; they played in funeral parades and for business advertisements, especially in Storyville, a red light district that opened in 1897 and closed in 1917. Brass bands consisted of cornets, clarinets, trombones, a sousaphone (tuba), and, occasionally, tenor saxophones. Brass bands also played for funerals; they played slow dirges on the way to the funeral, such as "Didn't He Ramble: Till the Butcher Cut Him Down," and up-tempo, joyful compositions, such as "When the Saints Go Marching In," after the burial. Brass bands were hired by secret societies and religious organizations which emerged in earnest after a series of Black Codes were passed (beginning in 1724) to outlaw all religious worship except Roman Catholicism. Brass bands actualized, through music, an African American philosophy which espoused that one should cry at birth and rejoice at death— a philosophy that dates to slave times. This philosophy was of central importance to African American culture and brass bands are, perhaps, the primary reason why such thinking has survived from the nineteenth century until today.

In the brass band, the tempo was set by the drummers, alternating between the bass drum and the cymbal. The trumpets usually sounded the first phrases of the tune and doubled the reeds, with a clarinet obbligato added. The melody passes from trumpets to reeds, to trombones with subsequent repetitions of the chord pattern. On the final or "out" choruses, a trumpet player often improvises a solo, using high notes, and creating a euphoric, swinging ending to a song. Among the most famous brass bands stand The Excelsior Brass Band (1880-1931); The On-ward Brass Band (1885-1930); The Reliance Brass Band (1892-1918); and The Tuxedo Brass Band (1917-1925). These bands were important to the develop-ment of early New Orleans jazz because many of the early jazz stars were also members of brass bands, including Louis Armstrong, Buddy Bolden, Joe "King" Oliver, Bunk Johnson, and Kid Ory. The turn-of-the-century New Orleans jazz bands featured cornets, clarinets, trombones, drums, and a sousaphone. It was common to hear both five- and seven-man groups. A five-man group usually con-sisted of a cornet, clarinet, trombone, sousaphone (tuba), and drums. A second cornet and a banjo were usually added to convert a five-man into a seven-man group. The role of the instruments was as follows:

5-Man Group
Cornet—played the melody, was allowed to decorate the melody but not to the extent that one could not recognize the melody
Clarinet—had three roles: 1) played obbligato parts to complement the melody, 2) played the harmony above the melody, and 3) doubled the melody on occasion
Trombone—outlined the most important notes in a chord
Sousaphone/tuba—played background, two tones, "um-pah" parts
Drums—kept the tempo

7-Man Group
The 7-man group added the following instruments:
2nd Cornet—played counter melodies (counterpoint) to the main melody; would double melody on occasion
Banjo—strummed the harmony four beats per measure; could also vary the beat

All "front line" musicians (cornet, clarinet, trombone) and, on specific occa-sions, the drummer, were expected to improvise, if the situation warranted it. King Oliver's creole jazz band, Louis Armstrong's "Hot Five" and "Hot Seven" Groups (with a piano instead of a sousaphone or tuba), and groups led by Kid Ory, Baby and Johnny Dodds, Bunk Johnson, and Kid "Punch" Miller, espoused the aforementioned concepts. At least two additional New Orleans jazz musi-cians, Jelly Roll Morton and Louis Armstrong, should be mentioned. As Gunther Schuller notes, Morton might have been the first musician to clearly delineate be-tween blues, jazz, and ragtime. He believed that "blues was either a 12- or 16-bar single theme composition with a predetermined chord progression; that "jazz" should contain musical contrast (dynamics, form, thematic materials, and timbre); and that "ragtime" was a multi-thematic form. Louis Armstrong was also a leading exponent of New Orleans jazz. In addition to his expertise as a "scat" singer (the art of using voice as a musical instrument), Armstrong was known for high note playing (for his time), a strong vibrato and swing phrasing techniques.

Beginning around 1914, and especially after the closing of Storyville in 1917, New Orleans musicians began to migrate to cities throughout the United States.

Several moved to Chicago, where, by the mid-twenties, Louis Armstrong, Johnny and Baby Dodds, Kid Ory, and King Oliver were performing. Soon following their arrival, a debate ensued whether there was a "Chicago style jazz," or whether Chicago jazz, in reality, was nothing but "New Orleans jazz in Chicago." Both styles existed, however. Chicago style jazz was led by Bix Beiderbecke and the Wolverines, and featured a strong 2/4 rhythm, a tenor saxophone, and a guitar. New Orleans jazz featured the clarinet, a banjo, and preferred a flat four beat per measure. Both featured cornet or trumpet players, trombones, drummers, and occasionally a piano. Whereas small groups (five or seven) proliferated in pre-1925 jazz, big bands also began to appear more frequently in the mid-twenties.

Swing

Not all big bands were swing bands. "Swing," however, featured melodic lines that were written to be played in unison by the whole band or by a section of the band. Call-and-response patterns between the brass and reed instruments, known as "riffs," were also featured. To this, the band would add outstanding soloists, with one or more sections playing a suitably arranged background. Fletcher Henderson and Don Redman are credited with devising the "swing" formula. Henderson became the chief arranger for Benny Goodman around 1932-1933, and by 1934 Goodman had 36 of Henderson's arrangements/compositions in his repertoire. The first known recording of a swing composition was "The Stampede" done by Fletcher Henderson, in 1926.

Although there were several "Kings of Swing," such as (Jimmy Lunceford, Luis Russell, Andy Kirk, and Chick Webb), Count Basie and Duke Ellington seem to have been the best. Basie became leader of the Benny Moten Band following the death of Moten in 1935. Basie was known for a hard-driving, swinging band that featured short thematic melodies, shout brass courses, tight ensemble phrasing and articulation, and strong soloists. In addition, until his death in 1984, he used a "shouting" blues vocalist. Basie's appeal can be traced to his predictable style, rooted in communication rather than complexity, and a style that featured the strong rhythm guitar playing of Freddie Green. Basie realized that a swinging band that featured tight ensemble phrasing and strong soloists was more important than one featuring complex compositions for the sake of complexity, thus the reason why his band attained and retained its popularity among both jazz enthusiasts and musicians, from the time he assumed the leadership, in 1935. Whereas Basie's approach was musically monolithic, Ellington was very musically eclectic. Born in Washington, D.C., and exposed to both eastern and southern jazz styles, in his youth, Ellington moved to New York in 1922. Over the next few years, he worked with Wilbur Sweatman, Elmer Snowden, and his band, The Washingtonians. His first major break occurred when he accepted an invitation to perform at the Cotton Club (1928-1931). Ellington's acceptance of the Cotton Club engagement confronted him with a major obstacle: producing music for different acts and actors (dancers, arrangements for vocalists, dance music, and, of course, big band jazz), on short notice. With some help from Bubber Miley, he met this challenge, which helped to refine his compositional skills, and, eventually, catapulted him into jazz stardom. Miley co-wrote several of Ellington's most popular early compositions, including "East St. Louis Toodle-Oo" (his first theme song), "Black and Tan Fantasy," and "Creole Love Call."

In addition, Bubber Miley and Joe Nanton gave Ellington's band the grass roots and blues feeling needed to make his "Jungle Music" style sound authentic; his "jungle style" featured flutter tonguing, growls, and bending-of-notes. The music was used to accompany stereotypical scenes of jungle life, including an African American woman lying in a hammock, while men and other women were fanning her with palm leaves. Since the Cotton Club's clientele consisted primarily of gangsters and affluent whites, "jungle style" fed their negative and inaccurate perceptions of both Africans and African Americans. Ellington's most significant contributions to jazz included: his experimentation with musical forms (he wrote a fourteen bar blues titled "Diminuendo in Blue" and several extended compositions (concertos, suites) like "Black, Brown and Beige," and "Reminiscing in Tempo." His compositions also featured the abilities of his musicians ("Barney's concerto" for Barney Bigard; "Yearning for Love" for Lawrence Brown, and "Echoes of Harlem" for Cootie Williams). He also featured Harry Carney, his baritone saxophonist as a soloist on several compositions, unusual in jazz history. In addition, his big band, which performed from the late twenties to his death in 1974, was one of the most stable in pre-1950 jazz history. He wrote several instrumental pieces to which a text was later added like "In A Sentimental Mood," "Mood Indigo," and "Sophisticated Lady," and he pioneered sacred jazz concerts (setting biblical or religious text to jazz). Ellington was one of the most significant jazz musicians of all time not only because he refused to be stereotyped but also because he had an unyielding thirst for musical creativity.

Big bands, including swing bands, were popular at the time because they played music to which people could dance. They performed at movie theatres, and their music was easy to follow. They also promoted the star system, and, due to the influence of radio, persons of all ages throughout the United States knew their names, and, as a result, often idolized stars like Basie, Ellington, Goodman, Lunceford, Henderson, and Webb. Although swing enjoyed immense popularity, a growing number of jazz musicians grew tired of the cliché-filled compositions and improvisations and, consequently, began to advocate a return to small groups, with the emphasis on improvisation.

Bebop—Hardbop—Funky Style

This new style was labeled "Bebop," and it was in full force by the early forties, championed by several musicians who conceived of themselves as being creative artists rather than "moldy figs" (entertainers and musicians, out-of-touch with modern jazz). The new style emerged and flourished in the strong Harlem nationalistic environment of the early forties, which dates back to the UNIA (Universal Negro Improvement Association) Movement of the 1910s and early 1920s, headed by Marcus Garvey. UNIA was strong in Harlem and, arguably, planted the revolutionary seeds of the forties. Bebop was the antithesis to existing jazz styles, and became the subject of controversy among both jazz musicians and their fans. While some jazz musicians felt the music was dissonant and, thus, too difficult to perform or to enjoy, some of their jazz fans thought the music was dissonant yet enjoyable and that the musicians' reactions were too strong. Some

Bebop musicians were either Muslims or sympathetic to Islam and occasionally would stop a performance, spread their prayer rug, kneel, and pray toward the east. In addition, Beboppers did not cater to dancers or to popular entertainment venues because they felt they were creative artists, not entertainers.

What was Bebop? Bebop was a jazz style that featured primarily quartets and quintets (trumpet, alto or tenor saxophone, drums, bass, and piano), championed by musicians such as Dizzy Gillespie, Thelonious Monk, Charles Parker, and Max Roach. The compositions featured disjunct melodies, sometimes short introductions and endings, compositions based on the harmonies of other songs, (such as "I've Got Rhythm," "What is This Thing Called Love," "How High The Moon," "Cherokee"), and several more, extended harmonies, comping (short chord statements situated strategically between silences played by the pianist), and the dropping of "bombs" (loud explosions by the drummer).

Monk, a pianist, was known primarily as a composer, and his most famous compositions were: "'Round About Midnight," "Straight No Chaser," "Blue Monk," and "Mysterioso." Gillespie (trumpet), and Parker (alto saxophone), formed one of the greatest jazz quintets of all time in the early forties. Gillespie is known for playing long, fluid improvisational lines, and for possessing a great sense of both harmony and rhythm. He also composed several jazz standards, including "Salt Peanuts" and "Night in Tunisia." In his short life (he died at 34), Parker became the guru of the alto saxophone. His incredible technique, sense of rhythm, and ability to improvise has influenced jazz players, especially saxophonists, since his death in 1955. He also composed numerous jazz standards such as "KoKo," "Confirmation," "Moose the Mooch," "Anthropology," and "Warmin' Up A Riff." These musicians influenced numerous jazz musicians who followed them. In the fifties, especially after the death of Parker, other jazz stars and styles began to emerge.

Although big bands were around, they were both fewer in numbers and in popularity, when compared to those of 1930s and 1940s. Small groups, featuring outstanding soloists, began to permeate the jazz landscape, led by Clifford Brown, Sonny Rollins, Max Roach, Miles Davis, Cannonball Adderley, and John Coltrane. Within this context, a style coined "Hardbop" emerged, with the Max Roach—Clifford Brown quintet, featuring Sonny Rollins, and the Miles Davis sextet, with Cannonball Adderley and John Coltrane, setting the standard for excellence. "Hardbop" was an aggressive affirmation of Bebop musical concepts: harmonies, melodies, improvisations, and polyrhythmic drumming techniques. Pianists like Junior Mance, Richie Powell, and Billy Taylor played horn-like melodic lines, often slower than those heard in Bebop. The style was hard driving, and featured, in addition to the previously mentioned soloists, Benny Golson, Kenny Dorham, Paul Chambers, Art Blakey, Lee Morgan, and Horace Silver.

Concurrent to "Hardbop," a style that advocated a return to the blues and Gospel roots of jazz also evolved in the fifties. "Funky Style" performers played improvisations based on the harmonies of blues and Gospels. Blues and Gospel melodic inflections could also be heard, and the music was geared to grass roots audiences. Funky Style performers did not attempt to impress either audiences or other musicians with their technique. Instead, they chose to improvise within the context of the tune. Horace Silver, Stanley Turrentine, and the Jazz Crusaders are among the best performers of this style. Silver composed several pieces that have become jazz standards, including "Song For My Father," "Doodlin'," "Señor Blues," and "Sister Sadie." Silver's "Funky Style" is permeated with melodies played a fourth apart by the tenor and trumpet, occasionally unison lines between the bass and piano, atypical musical forms, and excellent soloists that play close to the harmonic structure. In addition, Silver's compositions are filled with both blues and Gospel musical characteristics, including harmonies and scales. With a deliberate return to the roots of jazz, Silver helped to reverse a trend that saw jazz becoming more esoteric and more removed from the average listener. The return to the roots movement also influenced a separate tract of jazz development (since the 1950s):

Jazz Since the Fifties

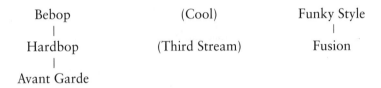

Bebop	(Cool)	Funky Style
Hardbop	(Third Stream)	Fusion
Avant Garde		

Funky Style ushered in the fusion styles (jazz-rock, and soul-jazz) and, to a lesser degree, what is called "third stream." At present, both jazz-rock and soul-jazz are receiving mass media exposure (radio and television) and, to the uninitiated, have become the only true jazz. The result is that fusion jazz has not only become today's most popular jazz style but also the most lucrative in record sales. Since the 1950s, the economic potential of fusion has had the effect of forcing some jazz artists and companies to record fusion albums.

Third Stream, Soul-Jazz, Fusion, Jazz-Rock

"Third stream" is a term coined by Gunther Schuller, and is defined as music which lies between jazz and classical music and embodies musical elements of both. It is a style that advocates the use of classical performance techniques (straight tone quality, phrase structures, and dynamics), and forms (canons, fugues, theme and variations) in jazz performances. The Modern Jazz Quartet (MJQ), Organized in 1952, and semi-disbanded since the early 1980s, is the foremost exponent of "third stream." The group consists of Connie Kay (drums), Percy Heath (bass), Milt Jackson (vibes), and John Lewis (piano and leader). Its style consists of Euro-American classical music performance techniques and forms, formal musical arrangements—each note precisely determined and performed—use of wire brushes in rhythmic accompaniments, less improvisational freedom (bending notes), and less freedom to perform extended solos. These concepts can be heard on *Third Stream* (1960, Atlantic SD1345) and *Blues on Bach* (1974, Atlantic 1962).

Soul-jazz fusion is characterized by the musical characteristics found in Funky Style, plus a penchant to record music originally recorded by a soul artist like

Marvin Gaye or Stevie Wonder. In the seventies, George Benson, The Crusaders, Stanley Turrentine, and Grover Washington, Jr., were stalwarts of this style, that eschewed complex and dissonant compositions and improvisations, choosing instead to espouse conjunct musical compositions with improvisations closely related to the harmonies. Unlike Bebop or Hardbop, soul—jazz is geared to entertainment, especially party settings, hence its popularity among party goers. From its beginnings in the 1950s, soul-jazz has set the stage for the styles of artists like David Sanborn, Earl Klugh, and George Howard.

Jazz-rock, on the other hand, with the exception of Miles Davis and Herbie Hancock, is a style that has been dominated by Anglo-Americans. Some of its most prominent exponents were former members of Miles Davis's groups of the late 1960s/early 1970s. These included Josef Zawinul and Wayne Shorter, co-leaders of Weather Report; Herbie Hancock's Head Hunters; John McLaughlin's Mahavishnu Orchestra; and Tony Williams's Lifetime. Since the early 1970s, jazz—rock groups have proliferated and influenced such groups as Fattburger and Spyro Gyra. Jazz-rock is characterized by the use of electronic instruments and devices, of multi-layered rhythm ostinatos (percussion and keyboard), solo/group improvisations, and of high volume levels with added musical abstraction. However, not all jazz—rock soloists or groups espouse high volume. Kenny G and Spyro Gyra, for example, lean more toward soft dynamics and soft volume.

Jazz-rock also appears to be entertainment focused (concerts and parties), and, along with soul—jazz, receive tremendous media exposure, and today is a billion-dollar business. Both styles have developed large followings because the styles are hybrids, thus attracting fans from rock, soul, and jazz. For these fans, it was easier to make the transition via a hybrid from rather than from one style to the other.

Free/Avant Garde

Concurrent with the development of fusion, the Bebop-Hardbop continuum evolved into a style termed "free" or "avant garde," because jazz musicians felt they had exhausted their creative potentials within the confines of specific predetermined harmonies, melodies, rhythms, and forms. The style espoused freedom of musical expression (melodies and improvisations), specifically, the freedom to perform extended improvisations and melodies, freely flowing between tonal and atonal concepts. In true "free" or "avant garde" jazz, compositions were never played the same way twice, and the music was difficult, if not impossible to notate. "Free" or "avant garde" musicians disdained performing only tonal music, harmonies, melodies, and forms; hence, it was not well received by large audiences in both the jazz and non-jazz communities. The music was spontaneous and difficult to follow; it was also permeated with grunts, screams, moans, groans, thereby creating a quantum leap from previous jazz styles enjoyed and performed by jazz musicians and listeners. The champions of this movement, dating from the 1960s, were John Coltrane, Ornette Coleman, Cecil Taylor, and their proteges.

Although exponents of "free" or "avant garde" concepts, both Coltrane and Taylor often featured tonal compositions, spiced with atonal sections. In fact, some of Coltrane's extended compositions, like "Out Of This World," would begin in a specific key or mode, proceed to an atonal section, and end with the melody (stated in the original key/mode), announced at the beginning. In turn,

Coleman expanded "free" or "avant garde" jazz principles further to incorporate his theory of jazz performance, "harmolodics," which espouses the simultaneous sounding of a specific melody or theme. Coleman believes Euro-American concepts like intonation and tonal centers are irrelevant. His music also features phrase pick-ups and unresolved melodic and improvisational ideas. Coleman's ideas and musical practices have allowed jazz musicians to experiment freely with ideas that until then had been considered to be outside of both jazz composition and performance.

In addition to Coltrane, Coleman, and Taylor, Sun Ra, Anthony Braxton, Donald and Albert Ayler, Don Cherry, and Archie Shepp have been some of the prime exponents of "free" or "avant-garde" jazz ideas. Whereas some of these musicians continue to be active, "free" or "avant garde" jazz does not presently enjoy a large following, because media exposure of fusion has overshadowed it, and it is too difficult for some musicians and most jazz enthusiasts to follow. In addition, "avant garde" music does not fit comfortably in either concert or entertainment (parties) venues. "Free" or "avant garde" jazz was jazz for its own sake and the logical extension for musicians who were tired of Bebop and Hardbop and wanted to continue to expand their own creative endeavors. Since it is not a commercially viable genre, this type of jazz is seldom heard on jazz radio stations, hence the culture shock and subsequent rejection a person feels upon first hearing the music.

Recent Trends

In recent years, a cadre of young jazz musicians, led by Wynton Marsalis, Roy Hargrove, Terence Blanchard, and Marcus Roberts have initiated a return to traditional jazz. Their music is marked by tonal melodies and improvisations, and they tend to pay homage to both past and present jazz masters. These musicians are both very articulate and serious about catapulting jazz into its rightful place as America's most significant, original contribution to world music. In addition to the return to tradition, one can find several additional trends in jazz since the 1950s: longer recordings (Coltrane, Davis), use of electronic instruments and devices, incorporation of world music influences into jazz (African and Brazilian), and a significant interest in both the number of academic institutions offering degrees in jazz and scholarly theses and dissertations on the subject.

In conclusion, jazz has remained one of the most significant contributions to world music. Born and nurtured in the African American experience, it is a genre that continues to develop, to expand, and to welcome new ideas, musically and technologically, from all sources.

Blues: Country, Classic, Early Urban, Urban

Like all African American musical genres, it is impossible to give a specific date and place of origin for blues. Some scholars believe blues originated in the post-civil war period. This writer, however, after examining the relationship between blues and spiritual texts, believes it existed in slavery, perhaps not by name, and that the word "blues" emerged after slavery, as the following illustrates.

Spiritual: I want to see my *Lord* one day
Blues:I want to see my *Baby (Mother/Father)* one day

By changing a word or symbol, one can change the meaning of a text: in this case, from sacred to secular. It is assumed that African Americans sang some of the aforementioned secular songs in the antebellum period because the context for such songs existed. Since all antebellum African American music, including work songs, field hollers and cries, and spirituals, evolved out of sociocultural conditions, and, since the conditions for blues existed, there is a logical reason to believe that blues were performed in antebellum America. In addition to text, call-and-response patterns, bending tones, textual improvisation, and complex rhythmic structures are common in both blues and spirituals, as well as work songs.

Blues is a genre that is defined by its harmonic structure. A blues piece can be performed fast or slow, and may be sad, melancholic, or euphoric. In its rawest, non-substitute harmonic structure, blues can be outlined as follows:

Harmony:	I	IV	I	V	I
	C maj.	F maj.	C maj.	G maj.	C maj.

Although multiple blues can be found, including 8, 12, or 16 bars, the most common blues structure is 12 bars. The harmonic and bars can be combined as follows:

Harmony:	I	IV	I	V	I
Bars:	1-2-3-4	5-6	7-8	9-10	11-12

The most common early blues form, especially Country Blues, is AAB; early blues harmony, bars, and form can be combined as follows:

Harmony:	I	IV	I	V	I
Bars:	1-2-3-4	5-6	7-8	9-10	11-12
Form:	A	A		B	

An AAB form text is as follows:

> A = when you see me comin' raise your window high
> A = when you see me comin' raise your window high
> B = when you see me goin' hang your head and cry

In AAB form, the first two lines were identical. However, early country bluesmen such as Son House, Robert Johnson, and Willie McTell might add a short introductory statement like "I said," before singing the second "A" line. The short introductory statement helped to increase the tension. Line "B" provided the release for the tension created in line "A." In addition, the last word of line "A" often rhymed with the last word of line "B." The blues structure was common to all early Country Blues, regardless of geographical location. Among the most discussed geographical Country Blues are the Mississippi Delta, and Texas, with the following selected characteristics:

Mississippi Delta. The blues here are characterized by the use of a harmonica, acoustical guitar, and, on some occasions, a piano; Bottleneck or a ring to actualize the slide guitar technique; Use of pentatonic, hexatonic, and heptatonic scales; use of melodic repetition moans and groans; use of harmonica tremolos; shifting rhythms (linear) and polyrhythms (vertical); descending melodic lines; borrowed material (melodies and text), musician to musician; and call-and-response patterns (often between a vocalist and his guitar). Exponents of Mississippi Delta country blues include Son House, Charley Patton, Robert Johnson, Willie McTell, and others.

Texas. Blues musicians here used acoustical and steel guitar; emphasis on single string melodies; used pentatonic, hexatonic, and heptatonic scales; some descending melodies; high nasal voice quality (cowboy influenced); borrowed material (melodies and text); and call-and-response (vocalist and his guitar). An exponent of this style is Blind Lemon Jefferson.

The characteristics outlined above, combined with Country Blues structure, harmony, bars, and form, were the sum total of the two geographical blues styles. The musicians—guitarists, composers, and vocalists—were predominantly African American males who were often transient, but excellent, musicians. They performed at barbecues, picnics, and in very small clubs—for little economic remuneration. The musicians played by ear and were basically self-taught. The music, created primarily for rural audiences, was performed in rural settings by musicians who were products of rural cultures.

Before the 1920s, African Americans began to migrate to major metropolitan areas like Chicago, Los Angeles, and New York. Concurrent with this migratory movement, major record companies began to notice the economic potential offered by these new immigrants and "race labels" were created to exploit the new market. The labels included Okeh, Paramount, Vocallion, and, according to some scholars, Blue Note. These labels specialized solely in African American musical genres, especially blues, Gospel, jazz, and spirituals, because the major record labels would not record African Americans. Within this context, the first blues was recorded in 1921 by Mamie Smith, although Country Blues had been around longer. Because the first blues was not recorded until 1921 (and a female recorded it), at least one question should be posed: Why was the first blues recording made by Mamie Smith when male Country Blues singers had been around since at least the turn of the century? In this writer's opinion, African American females were recorded before males because they were considered to be less of a sexual threat. Record executives felt an African American male singing text permeated with double entendre (double meanings), especially sexual metaphors, was a threat to the perceived superior masculinity of Euro-American males. Concurrently, allowing females to sing a text permeated with double entendres reinforced negative stereotypes of African American women as loose, available, and promiscuous. Both were antebellum racist attitudes.

As African Americans migrated from the South, especially the rural South, one also began to witness a transfer of culture to many metropolitan areas throughout the United States. The migrations transpired for many reasons including the opportunity to secure better jobs, educational opportunities, better living conditions, and to escape racism. Soon, Chicago, Los Angeles, New York, and Washington, D.C., became meccas of African American culture, hence the reason why blues, jazz, and Gospel became strong expressions in these cities. Concurrently, a new type of blues—called "classic"—became vogue in these and other cities.

Classic Blues

This music was called "Classic Blues," for two reasons: it contained all of the musical elements of the blues that had preceded it and it was the first blues (African American and Euro-American) to be accepted as public entertainment. It was also the first blues to be recorded, and to reap substantial economic benefits, and the first to benefit from marketing. Some of its performers were marketed as stars, especially Ma Rainey, Mamie Smith, Ida Cox, Alberta Hunter, and Bessie Smith. Arguably, Bessie Smith was both the best and most recognized of these performers. She was known for her clear diction, strong voice, good intonation, and ability to stage her performances professionally. The characteristics of Classic Blues include: a style dominated by African American females; many lyrics containing sexual overtones; variations on the AAB form; notated musical arrangements; instrumentation expansion to include trumpets, saxophones, trombones and rhythm section instruments (piano, bass, drums, and guitar); and harmony both changing and becoming stabilized because of notated arrangements and recording requirements. Note the following progression:

Harmony:	I	IV	I	V-IV	I
Bars/Measures:	1-2-3-4	5-6	7-8	9-10	11-12

In the 1920s and 1930s, Bessie Smith sold numerous records and became a popular club/cabaret performer and the symbol of Classic Blues in both the African American and Euro-American communities. She also made several thousand dollars a week—a lot of money in the late twenties. However, not all "Classic Blues" singers enjoyed the same economic success, and some, including Mamie Smith, who made only three recordings, received few recording opportunities. The success of a blues performer was directly related to both recordings and marketing. Thus, while some became economically successful, others faded into economic ruin.

Early Urban and Urban Blues

Classic Blues was not the only style to become popular in major metropolitan areas. Simultaneous to the popularity of Classic Blues, a style of blues flourished (especially in Chicago, New York, and Washington, D.C.) which this writer has termed "Early Urban." Because blues musicians were included in the migrations, some continued to espouse new influences while retaining some of the old. In particular, Mississippi Delta musicians, like Otis Spann, Muddy Waters (McKinley Morganfield), James Cotton, and bluesman John Lee Hooker, fit this classification. Early Urban is a style that contained selected country and Urban Blues musical elements including the AAB form; singers doubled as guitarists; call-and-response patterns; I-IV-I-V-I harmonic progressions (although these characteristics could also vary); amplified guitars; microphones; and text with country and urban metaphors. Audiences tended to be recent immigrants with limited economic means who wished to maintain contact with their indigenous culture. They, too, were caught half-way between two cultures. Early Urban Blues was prominent in the 1940s and 1950s. As time passed and urban culture became both internalized and actualized, a more culturally bound urban bluesman began to emerge.

In Urban Blues, one can hear four-line verses, followed by two line refrains; the use of amplified guitars and microphones; and big bands and lyrics more reflective of urban life and concerns, with both males and females represented. The style is also reflective of a closer alliance between blues and jazz in instrumentation, arrangements, sophisticated substitute harmonies, and improvisations. Urban Blues vocalists were not necessarily instrumentalists as they were in Country Blues.

Finally, in Urban Blues, one seldom hears the basic harmonic structure, lyrics that focus on rural concerns, or head arrangements. Instead, the Urban Blues is a polished, sophisticated genre, one that is reflective of the totality of the African American experience. Although it is seldom programmed on either radio or television, today blues enjoys a limited but dedicated audience throughout the world.

Spirituals and Gospel

Today, the meaning of the term "spiritual" is clouded by both its misapplication to another African American religious music—Gospel—and the mystery surrounding its origin. (Differences between "spirituals" and "Gospel" will be discussed later in this chapter). The term "spiritual" has come to mean any antebellum African American religious composition, although prior to 1909, it was mentioned in very few sources. (The only writers who used the term prior to 1909 were those who collected most of their songs in South Carolina and Georgia.) The expressions "slave hymns," "plantation hymns," and "cabin songs" were often used in different geographical regions to denote the same religious music commonly known as "spirituals" in South Carolina and Georgia. For example, collections such as Hampton's *Cabin and Plantation Songs* made no mention of "spiritual" in editions prior to 1909 (see Mary Frances Armstong and Helen Ludlow, *Hampton and Its Students*). Instead, the expression "slave hymns" is used. In addition, William E. Barton does not mention the term in "Old Plantation Hymns" nor does John Mason Brown refer to the term in his article "Songs of the Slave," published in 1868.

Perhaps, one of the most important questions one should ask is: Why was the term "spiritual" known and used in some geographical areas and not in others? At least two possible answers come to mind: 1) perhaps there was little or no contact between South Carolina and Georgia slaves and those in other geographical regions. Even if limited contact did take place (through the sale of a slave, for example), there is no evidence to suggest the new slave could or would supplant the terminology and practices already in place; and 2) perhaps, if contact did occur, the new arrival might not have felt a need to suggest new terminology, because the actual music performance was more important than the term used to identify it. It is also logical to assume that the new arrivals had a hierarchy of concerns about their new situation, and labels to identify musical genres were not as important to them as were issues related to family, work, and slave discipline.

Nevertheless, "spirituals" have taken on a life of their own. A thorough analysis of their text and other religious text, reveals that "spirituals" functioned in both secular and sacred contexts. Specifically, "spirituals" were often used as a way and means of conveying secret messages, as escape songs demonstrate. The desire to escape to freedom constituted a major theme in spirituals, and can be heard in the following: "Swing Low, Sweet Chariot" (sung when the great liberator Harriet Tubman was in the vicinity to lead slaves to freedom); "Follow the North Star" (directions to escape to freedom); "Goin' to Canaan" (escape to Canada) and "Steal Away" (also sung to indicate the presence of Harriet Tubman).

In addition to escape themes and meanings, spirituals were used for other secular reasons. The spiritual, "Couldn't Hear Nobody Pray," for example, was sung by a house slave to appraise others that neither the slave master, overseer, or driver heard the prayer meeting that transpired the night before. (Since open oral communication was not allowed in work situations, slaves used whatever means they had to communicate their feelings and messages—the reason why non-religious messages were coded in spirituals.)

Spirituals were sung and composed by leaders who possessed a melodic gift, talent for poetry, strong voice, good memory, and creativity. Since the leader had the ability to improvise, the text could change each time a song was sung. It is believed that slaves, who were either sold or had contact with other plantations, might have contributed to the music of their new situations, because the same text appears in several spirituals.

Antebellum spirituals contained vivid lyrics and were permeated with truisms like "no more whips cracking," and aspirations for freedom camouflaged in biblical text like "I will be free when I cross the ribber [river] Jordan." The songs could be sung either syllabic or melismatic, and were permeated with both syncopation and body rhythms (swinging of head and body and patting of hands and feet). They also featured hocketing (breaking the melody up among the group), and heterophony (straying away from the melodic line), from unison to harmony, as in the spiritual "Steal Away." The melodies were constructed on 3 to 7 tones, and prominently featured pentatonic, hexatonic, and heptatonic scales, which were permeated with lowered, raised, and bent tones. Several forms can be found, most often with leader and response, leader-response-leader, and chorus followed by the leader.

The controversy surrounding the origin of spirituals is worth discussing (see John Lovell, *Black Song, the Forge and the Flame*). After the Fisk Jubilee Singers' successful European tour made the spiritual famous, a debate over its origin ensued. Writers such as George Pullen Jackson and Newman White believed the African American spiritual evolved from the Anglo-American hymn tradition. Others, however, including John Work, Frederick Hall, and William Fisher, disagreed. Work disagreed with Jackson on three points. First, on form, Work observed that two-thirds of African American spirituals are call-and-response. He challenged Jackson and White to cite a single indigenous Anglo-American song in this form. Second, concerning scales, Work noted that the two groups of songs differ radically in the employment of scales. Finally, on text, although Work accepted the Bible as a common source of some text, he insisted that the metaphors used in African American spirituals were unique to that culture and that frequent references were made to freedom ("Goin' to Canaan," "Over the River Jordan"). Work also argued that, because Jackson found 15 or 20 song resemblances between the two groups, he was naive to conclude that 600 or 700 songs were imitations.

One can take Work's conclusions further because most spirituals were passed down orally from generation to generation, and their composers were unknown. It would seem likewise naive to assume that African Americans would adapt an entire religious repertoire from their oppressors rather than create songs to fit their specific concerns. This point is significant because few African Americans were baptized into Christianity during the antebellum period, although biblical teachings were often used to imbue both obedience and submission to slave owners. (Significant numbers of African Americans were not baptized because both the clergy and slave owners felt that baptizing them would put them on the same level as the slave owners, thereby raising serious moral and religious questions.)

Among the most prominent composers and performers of spirituals are the Fisk Jubilee Singers, the Hampton Institute Singers, the Tuskegee Institute Singers, Nathaniel Dett, John Work, Harry T. Burleigh, Marian Anderson, Paul Robeson, James Rosamond, and James Weldon Johnson. It is commonly accepted that spirituals rank second in popularity to Gospel music in many of today's African American Churches.

The roots of "Gospel music" (good news) date as far back as the nineteenth century. Today, Gospel music is a genre permeated with modern text and instrumentation, including electronic instruments, complex polyrhythms, and energetic, vibrant, and creative soloists and choirs. In musical terms, today's Gospel music dates to the "Jubilees," a religious song which became popular before the emancipation, and to the "Church Songs" heard during the late nineteenth century. Church Songs contained four lines of poetry, the second and fourth lines being the same or nearly the same. They contained few words, limited melodic range, and very complex rhythms. At the turn of the century, however, Rev. Charles A. Tindley introduced a novelty to Church Songs by setting hymn-like verse to the melodies and rhythms. From the synthesis, three famous Gospel songs emerged: "When the Storm of Life is Raging," "Stand By Me," and "I'll Overcome Some Day" (the predecessor of the Civil Rights anthem "We Shall Overcome").

Gospel music roots can clearly be dated to 1885, the year the Holiness Church (closed to outsiders until 1940) was organized. From 1885-1940, the musical practices of the church became permeated with improvisation, body rhythm, call-and-response patterns, and some instruments (especially drums, and tambourines, and, later, the organ, and the piano). Today, African American Gospel music is a specific body of religious music that reflects the past and present social, political, and cultural traditions of African Americans. Following is a concise chronology of Gospel since 1900 (limited primarily to the midwest):

1900-1930

Fueled by African American migrations from the South, a plethora of store front and other small churches in several northeastern and midwestern cities (including Washington, D.C., New York City, St. Louis, and Chicago) emerged. Indigenous musical traditions were maintained in the fundamentalist-type churches, which were not geared to traditional liturgy and formality of worship (Baptist, Pentecostal, and Holiness).

1930s

A period characterized by excellent Gospel composers: Thomas A. Dorsey, Lillian Bowles, Lucie Campbell, Theodore Frye, Sallie and Roberta Martin. Among these, Thomas A. Dorsey was labeled "Father of Gospel Music," although the title is better suited to Rev. Charles Tindley. Dorsey's compositions combined the style of Tindley with the praise songs and the contemporary popular style of the period. Among his most popular compositions are "Precious Lord Take My Hand," "When I've Done The Best I Can," and "Peace In The Valley." In addition to composed Gospel songs, both rural southern and urban metropolitan congregations continued to utilize improvisations in some of their songs. The preacher, song leader and congregation, all shared equally in the music making process.

1940s

This era was characterized by a continuation of composed Gospel songs, an increase in Gospel recordings, and the emergence of numerous Gospel quartets and ensembles. To the continued excellence of Thomas Dorsey, Sallie and Roberta Martin, and Lucie Campbell, one can add the name of Rev. W. Herbert Brewster, a Memphis preacher. Two of his most popular compositions are "Move On Up A Little Higher," and "Surely God Is Able." By 1940, Gospel music (not just its prominent composers) was known throughout the United States. Its spread was enhanced by the "race records" devoted to recording African American music (labels which recorded only African American music). The labels included "Apollo," "Savoy," and "Specialty." This was also the era that the Hammond organ was added to Gospel instrumentation. The 1940s were also characterized by the quantity and quality of Gospel groups, especially quartets, which were very popular and traveled throughout the country. They appealed to all segments of the community, and sang songs with text ranging from social to sacred. Their music served as a contrast to the more church-oriented arrangements sung by other Gospel communities.

1950s

This decade was characterized by a continuing proliferation of Gospel quartets and ensembles. Gospel ensembles, commonly referred to as "groups," could be either all female, male or mixed, and were accompanied by Hammond organ or piano and on some occasions by a tambourine. The groups featured call-and-response patterns, close harmonies, and improvisation by the lead singers. The 1950s also witnessed greater distribution of Gospel music, from its natural habitat in the church to more concert settings in large concert halls in limited situations, and social venues like Las Vegas, and on radio. In short, some Gospel performers felt they should take their music to all venues, social or sacred, in order to convert persons to Christianity. Within this context, the Clara Ward Singers performed on both the Ed Sullivan television variety show and in Las Vegas. In addition, they recorded the first million-copy seller Gospel record, "Surely God Is Able," composed by Rev. W. Herbert Brewster. This era also witnessed the birth of other great Gospel groups and soloists. The Staple Singers introduced a style that was characterized by a measured rhythm, unlike the fast-moving, highly syncopated styling of groups like the Clara Ward Singers. Mahalia Jackson introduced a full-throated style with a wide vocal range, permeated with emotional fervor and bending of tones.

1960s

The 1960s were characterized by the fame of Gospel groups like the Staple Singers and the Edwin Hawkins Singers. By then, Gospel music was permeated with rock, soul, and jazz influences, instrumentation, and musical characteristics. The Hawkins Singers produced a stunning success which produced the commercial cross-over recording "Oh Happy Day." The recording was successful in both popular and religious communities, and achieved a number one rating on both popular and religious music charts. The Hawkins's style represented a synthesis of religious text and contemporary rock, soul, and jazz musical characteristics, and instrumentation. Both the Fender Rhodes bass and bongo drums were used by

Edwin Hawkins, along with traditional Gospel instruments like the Hammond organ, the piano, and the tambourine. In addition to these developments, the success of composers/Gospel choir directors like the Voices of Tabernacle (James Cleveland), The Abyssinian Choir (Professor Alex Bradford), and the Chicago Community Choir (Jessy Dixon) was remarkable. Experimentation with "classical" music idioms was also evident, as classically trained musicians like Myrna Summers and Horace Boyer began to make significant contributions to Gospel music. Gospel soloists also continued to proliferate during the era.

1970-90

Since 1970, Gospel music has taken a quantum leap into the musical spotlight. The music is no longer characterized by a soloist or group primarily in sacred settings. During this era, Gospel performers became more commercially oriented (instrumentation and music). Both soloists and groups were more open to crossover to other musical genres: Johnny Taylor, from the Soul Stirrers to soul music; The Staple Singers, from Gospel music to soul; Andre Crouch, billed as a Gospel singer, appears to sing a synthesis of Gospel—soul music; and Aretha Franklin, from soul to some Gospel singing. In addition, one witnessed the birth of groups like Take Six, a Gospel group that uses sophisticated harmonies and a cappella singing to perform Gospel music in both sacred and secular settings throughout the world. Gospel groups and soloists continued to proliferate in churches throughout the country. One even saw the expansion of Gospel music into academic settings. It has become common to hear both high school and college/university Gospel choirs throughout the country. This has led to a rise in scholarly research devoted to Gospel music, including theses and dissertations by institutions and individual scholars such as Mellonee Burnim (Indiana University), Horace Boyer (University of Massachusetts), and Jacqueline DjeDje (UCLA). Thus, during the 1970-1990 era, it became common to hear both traditional and contemporary instrumentation, including electronic instruments.

Summary

This chapter attempted to introduce the student to the musical experiences of the African American community: jazz, the blues, spirituals, and Gospel music. Jazz is a diverse musical genre whose origins date as far back as the late nineteenth century. Although most scholars cite the late nineteenth century as a possible time of origin, some, including this writer, believe jazz existed in the antebellum period and that the descriptive term "jazz" was coined to identify this unnamed genre sometime during the late nineteenth century.

Both geographical and collective jazz styles can be traced, which include the New Orleans, Chicago, Swing, Bebop, Hardbop, Third Stream, and a plethora of fusion styles. The origin of blues is also clouded in controversy. While most scholars cite the late nineteenth century as a possible time of origin, evidence exists to trace its origins to the antebellum period. Blues is a musical genre defined by its harmonic structure, not by its mood or tempo. It, too, underwent an evolutionary process. Whereas Country Blues performers used acoustical guitars, harmonicas, and, occasionally, a piano, their Classic and Urban Blues counterparts used trumpets, saxophones and trombones, a varied harmonic pattern and form, and, from the vocalist, a text that espoused urban concerns. (The first blues, "Crazy Blues," was recorded by Mamie Smith on August 10, 1920.)

The African American experience, certainly incorporating the African experience, has given birth to two religious musical genres, spirituals and Gospel music. Spirituals date to the antebellum period. While prior to 1909, the term spiritual, was used primarily in Georgia and South Carolina, other terms like "slave hymns," "plantation hymns," and "cabin songs," were also common and referred to the same musical repertoire. Although most spirituals were religious in context, some were also used in escape songs, especially in situations where open communication was either dangerous or forbidden. Antebellum spirituals were sung a cappella and featured vivid texts, melodies based on three to seven tones, including pentatonic, hexatonic, and heptatonic scales, call-and-response patterns, as well as several additional musical characteristics and performance practices. Among the most significant nineteenth century exponents of spirituals were the Fisk Jubilee Singers, the Hampton Institute Singers, and the Tuskegee Institute Singers. One should not fail to note both the controversy surrounding the origin of the spiritual and the rebuttals presented against unproven claims. Specifically, George P. Jackson and Newman White advocated that the African American spiritual was copied from Anglo-American religious songs. Scholars such as John Work, however, refuted this theory on three levels: form, scales, and text. The popularity of spirituals has been supplanted by the preference for Gospel music in many African American Churches and religious settings.

Unlike the a cappella performance of spirituals, Gospel should be performed with instruments, including organs, pianos, guitars, bass, and drums. They vividly reflect the contemporary religious concerns of African Americans, and date as far back as the Church Songs of the nineteenth century and the turn-of-the-century arrangements/compositions of Rev. Charles A. Tindley. Since its documented history, around 1885, America has witnessed the creation, expansion, and development of Gospel compositions and groups. In addition to Reverend Charles A. Tindley, Thomas Dorsey, W. Herbert Brewster, Sallie and Roberta Martin, Edwin Hawkins, and Reverend James Cleveland have written numerous Gospel compositions which have become standards in the repertories of both Gospel soloists and choir/ensembles. Since around 1900, instrumentation has evolved from piano and drums to bass, organ, and electronic instruments and devices, including synthesizers. Today, Gospel music performers can be seen on television (as is the case of Bobby Jones) and can be heard or seen in large concert halls, or at jazz festivals—unlike in its early history when it was heard primarily in churches. Gospel music choirs are also common in both high schools, colleges, and universities. Today, Gospel music is reflective of the diversity of social, political, and religious attitudes of the African American community and continues to evolve and to incorporate new musical text and ideas, while maintaining close religious ties to its audience.

Study Questions and Activities

1. Define the role of the instruments in 5-man and 7-man New Orleans Jazz groups.

2. Discuss the musical difference between seeing and Bebop.
3. What are the differences between Country, Classic, and Urban Blues?
4. Analyze the three arguments that John Work gave to rebut Newman White's contention that the African American spiritual evolved from the Anglo-American spiritual.
5. Discuss the history of Gospel music from 1885-1990, mentioning composers, performers, styles, and innovations.

References

African Origins, Retentions, Transformations, and Reinterpretation

Jason Berry. "African Cultural Memory in New Orleans Music." *Black Music Research Journal*, vol. 8, 1(1988).
Lazarus Ekwueme. "African Music Retention in the New World." *The Black Perspective in Music*, vol. 2, 2(Fall 1984).
David Evans. "African and the Blues (A critique of Paul Oliver's *Savannah Syncopators: African Retention in the Blues)." Living Blues*, no. 10, 1972.
———. "African Elements in Twentieth Century Black Folk Music." *Jazzforschung*, no. 10, 1978.
Portia K. Maultsby. "Africanisms in African-American Music", in Joseph E. Holloway (ed.). *Africanisms in American Culture*. Bloomington, IN: Indiana University Press, 1990.
Eddie S. Meadows. "African Retentions in Blues and Jazz," in Talmadge Anderson (ed.). *Black Studies: Theory, Method, and Cultural Perspectives*. Pullman, WA: Washington State University Press, 1990.
Jeannette R. Murphy. "The Survival of African Music in America," in Bruce Jackson (ed.). *The Negro and His Folklore*. Austin, TX: University of Texas Press, 1967. [Reprinted from *Popular Science Monthly*, 55 (New York, 1899), pp. 660-672.]
Paul Oliver. *Savannah Syncopations: African Retentions in the Blues*. New York: Stein and Day, 1970.
John Storm Roberts. *Black Music of Two Worlds*. New York: Praeger, 1972.
Gunther Schuller. *Early Jazz: Its Roots and Musical Development*. New York: Oxford University Press, 1968.
Olly W. Wilson. "The Significance of the Relationship Between Afro-American and West African Music." *The Black Perspective in Music*, vol. 2, 1(Spring 1974).
The reader should also consult the writings of Ernest Brown, Dena Epstein, Portia Maultsby, Eddie S. Meadows, and J. H. Kwabena Nketia.

General

Maurice Peress. *Dvořák to Duke Ellington: A Conductor Explores America's Music and Its African American Roots*. New York: Oxford University Press, 2004.
Gwendolyn D. Pough. *Check It While I Wreck It: Black Womanhood, Hip Hop Culture, and the Public Sphere*. Boston: Northeastern University Press, 2004.

Hildred Roach. *Black American Music: Past and Present*. New York: Crescendo, 1973.

Margaret R. Simmons and Jeanine Wagner (eds.). *A New Anthology of Art Songs by African American Composers*. Carbondale, IL: Southern Illinois University Press, 2004.

Eileen Southern. *The Music of Black Americans: A History*, 2nd ed. New York: W. W. Norton and Company, 1983.

———. (ed.). *Readings in Black American Music*, 2nd ed. New York: W. W. Norton and Company, 1983

Jazz (text and reference)

Eddie S. Meadows. *Jazz Reference and Research Materials*. New York: Garland, 1981.

Gunther Schuller. *Early Jazz: Its Roots and Musical Development*. New York: Oxford University Press, 1968.

———. *The Swing Era: The Development of Jazz 1930-1945*. New York: Oxford University Press, 1990.

Billy Taylor. *Jazz Piano: History and Development*. Dubuque: William C. Brown, 1982.

The reader should also consult the writings of Douglas Daniels, Eddie S. Meadows, Thomas Owens, Gunther Schuller and Dempsey Travis.

Blues

David Evans. *Big Road Blues*. Berkeley, CA: University of California Press, 1982.

William Ferris. *Blues From the Delta: An Illustrated Documentary on the Music and Musicians of the Mississippi*. Garden City, NJ: Anchor Press/Doubleday, 1978.

Charles Keil. *Urban Blues*. Chicago: The University of Chicago Press, 1966.

Paul Oliver. *Savannah Syncopations: African Retentions in the Blues*. New York: Stein and Day, 1970.

———. *Story of the Blues*. Philadelphia: Chilton Book Company, 1969.

Harry Oster. *Living Country Blues*. Detroit: Folklore Associates, 1969.

Jeff Titon. *Early Downhome Blues: A Musical and Cultural Analysis*. Urbana, IL: University of Illinois Press, 1977.

Spirituals

Mary Frances Armstrong and Helen Ludlow. *Hampton and Its Students: By Two of Its Teachers with 50 Cabin and Plantation Songs*, arranged by Thomas P. Fenner. New York: G. P. Putnam's Sons, 1874.

William E. Barton. "Old Plantation Hymns." *New England Magazine*, December 1898.

John Mason Brown. "Songs of the Slave." *Lippincott's Magazine*, Philadelphia, December 1868.

W. E. B DuBois. *The Souls of Black Folk*. Millwood, NY: Kraus-Thompson Organization, 1973 (reprint of 1903 book).

Dena Epstein. *Sinful Tunes and Spirituals: Black Folk Music to the Civil War*. Urbana, IL: University of Illinois Press, 1977.

Miles Fisher. *Negro Slave Songs in the United States*. New York: American His-
   torical Association, 1953.
Cabin and Plantation Songs. John Lovell. *Black Song, The Forge and The Flame:
   The Story of How the Afro-American Spiritual Was Hammered Out*. New
   York: Paragon House Publishers, 1972.
The reader should also consult the writings of Nathaniel Dett, Frederick Hall,
   Portia Maultsby, Hall Johnson, James Weldon and J. Rosamond Johnson,
   and John Work.

Gospel

Jacqueline DjeDje. *Black Religious Music from South Georgia*. Birmingham, AL:
   Alabama Center for Higher Education, 1979.
Tony Heilbut. *The Gospel Sound: Good News and Bad Times*. New York: Simon
   & Shuster, 1971.
George Robinson Ricks. *Some Aspects of the Religious Music of The United
   States Negro: An Ethnomusicological Study With Emphasis on the Gospel
   Tradition*. New York: Arno Press, 1977.
The reader should also consult the writing of Mellonee Burnim, Horace Boyer,
   Jacqueline DjeDje, Irene Jackson, and Pearl Williams-Jones.

16

The Art of Africa and the Diaspora

Sharon Pruitt

Introduction

Although survey books on world art are beginning to provide discussions on the art produced by persons of African descent, the majority of the focus is on traditional Sub-Saharan African art. For other areas of the African disapora, such as the art by contemporary Africans, African Americans, and Caribbeans, the information is either scant or none existent. In the search for the original art of the world, survey studies place the civilizations of Egypt and Mesopotamia (both Neolithic) at the forefront. Much too often, Egypt is dealt with as an ancient Near Eastern culture while failing to identify its African component. In so doing, a two-fold problem exists: 1) the geographical progression of development of cultures moves from the ancient Near East (including Egypt, Anatolia [or present-day Turkey], Jordan, Syria, Israel, Iraq, and Iran) to Crete, Greece, Rome, other parts of Europe, and finally to America; this progression downplays the achievements made in many African cultures and 2) connections between Egypt and other African cultures are ignored, which not only misrepresents Egypt's "Africanness" but further inhibits a continuum in the broader study of African art history which could be more inclusive.

This chapter concentrates on the significant linkages between traditional African, contemporary African, African American, and Caribbean art. It begins with a method of approaching art from various regions of Africa in a manner which is not normally addressed in a survey book on world art. It continues with an examination of changes made in the practice and stylistic concerns in contemporary African art. This is followed by analyses of the contributions made by both African American and Caribbean artists. Because of the magnitude of the geographic areas and time periods covered in this chapter, the information presented here is obviously incomplete; however, its intention is to recognize the accomplishments of the numerous uncelebrated art and artists in Africa and in the diaspora as well as to generate encouragement for the pursuit of continuing research and study on the visual art produced by these individuals.

Major terms and concepts: Africanism, traditional, Caribbean, Limner style, art, curio, painting, sculpture, apprenticeship, stylization, art medium, terra-cotta, Nok culture, masquerader, conventionalism, Renaissance.

Toward an Approach to Understanding African Art

Africa's past and present art manifests ideologies of tradition and change. In its transformation over time, the art reflects both external influences and internal nuances of cultural dynamics which led to expressions of alterations made in style, techniques, media, and function. The intermingling of traditional practices with the modern developments in today's society indicates that an appropriate manner in which to study the art is to classify it under two categories: traditional and contemporary.[1]

The majority of African art exhibited in fine arts and anthropology museums in the United States and Europe may be categorized under traditional. Its purpose for creation and meaning are steeped in traditional values and belief systems. The art object requires understanding and appreciation based on its own cultural context. However, by its mere placement in foreign museums, African art is not only presented devoid of its original cultural context but is presented as an object evoking aesthetic responses within a Western connotation.

Despite its displacement in a foreign arena, African art withstands critical scrutiny and meets or sometimes exceeds its expected aesthetic impulses. For indeed, some of its forms of smooth, shiny surfaces and skillfully sculpted angular and rotund shapes are pleasing constructs even to the uninformed Western viewer. But frequently, the presentation of the object without contextual information places African art in a position subordinate to Western art. The reasons for this relates to our aesthetic education. Grounded in a Western artistic perception which favors realistic representations of images and a tradition of illusionism, our conventional and initial response to African art may evoke terms such as simple, crude, or "primitive." When this same art is examined within its own cultural setting, we realize the need to abandon terminology which fosters derogatory concepts and acknowledge findings which point to the art's sophistication, complexity, and mystery. An example of the manner in which art is misjudged and misinterpreted when viewed out of context may be observed in masks in museums. In their original context, they are not seen as static objects in museums but are worn by masqueraders in rhythmic dance movements. It may be argued that one of the museum's functions is to preserve artifacts from various parts of the world; in its new locale, the artwork is frequently viewed in an entirely different contextual framework. For example, a medieval painting intended to be revered as an altarpiece in its original environment is presented in the museum setting not

---

1. While some Africanists such as Salah Hassan and Ola Oloidi feel an appropriate substitution for the rubric contemporary art would be modern art, others such as Susan Vogel argue for further subdivision of this twentieth century art into categories which are more inclusive.

in situ but as a wall painting. Therefore, African art is not unique in its contextual transformation within the milieu of a museum. However, dissimilar cultural references which require understanding of the object's original context becomes an anomaly to the uninformed viewer in the West. Whereas a medieval altarpiece, because of its Christian religious overtones, may provide more relevance and comprehension to a Western viewer's cultural experience, the African artwork does not offer him the same familiarity. Because of the metamorphosis in meaning, the cultural displacement of an African artwork in a Western museum is more crucial. Perhaps, the cultural distortion of African artworks is less the fault and perception of museum personnel, who in some exhibitions today attempt to provide contextual information by including photographs and videos of artists or masqueraders, and may rest more in years of professed superior attitudes of Westerners reflected in their literature and training.

Westerners' interest in African art dates as far back as the thirteenth century. However, collecting objects as curios by European travelers began in earnest in the fifteenth century. During this period, recorded information revealed the existence of an overwhelming array of objects and riches. This material was subsequently altered, falsified, or held from publication until the seventeenth century. For two centuries, fears abounded among profiteering merchants who sought to reduce the number of potential competitors by advertising scant and erroneous information regarding Africa's resources. However, in the seventeenth century, when the economic interest turned to trading in slaves, public knowledge of Africa's riches no longer posed a threat to the merchants. European travelers did not actively turn their attention to collecting African art as curios again until the nineteenth century after the demise of the slave trade. At the turn of the century, European ethnologists and anthropologists began to systematically collect and study African objects as important artifacts of material culture and preserved them in ethnological museums.

During the fifteenth century, Westerners' economic strategy of falsifying documents was not the only factor which had a detrimental effect on perceptions of African art. It was during this period that a taxonomy was instituted in the European artistic community. Leonardo da Vinci, an Italian Renaissance artist, established a classification system which elevated the media of painting to the highest level of artistic achievement, while simultaneously relegating sculpture and other fine arts media to a subordinate status. Since sculpture was abundant in African societies and painting was believed to be nonexistent by Western scholars, African art was considered inferior to Western art. This perception has persisted despite acknowledgement of African paintings such as the paintings on rock surfaces in Mozambique, East Africa, which were reported as early as the eighteenth century, or those discovered later in Namibia, South Africa, dating to 27,000 B.C., or Africans' traditional custom of painting on the human body, masks, and architecture.

During the early part of the twentieth century, the modern European artists' interest in African art served as a catalyst for approaching African art from an aesthetic perception and distinguishing its validity as worthy of further inquiry. They recognized the vitality of its unnaturalistic forms during a period when anthropologists were still debating the primal evolution and "primitiveness" of its structure. Rejecting the Western tradition of illusionism and realistic representation, modern European artists admired the unique, distorted forms of African art and derived inspiration from it to create new styles of abstraction which changed the course of European art. Artists such as Maurice Vlaminck, André Derain, Pablo Picasso, George Braque, Henri Matisse, Ernest Ludwig Kirchner, and Emile Nolde observed examples of African art in curio shops, ethnological museums, or in their own or other artists' private collections. As a result of their fascination with interfacing African art forms into modern expressions, these artists sparked public interest and curiosity to the extent that fine art museums began to include African artworks in their collections.

Regardless of these developments, African art is still omitted from or downplayed in introductory courses on world art. A thorough study of the art is often plagued by obscure or non-extant material such as the artist's name, the location, dates, function, and other contextual information; this information was frequently not collected by or of little interest to early traders and anthropologists. Therefore, a huge gap exists in acquiring discernible facts, and our complete understanding of African art is hampered. Nevertheless, the literature available allows us to begin to appreciate African art and become fascinated with its aesthetically pleasing forms. And if we are willing to take the challenge further, we will find writings by anthropologists and art historians in the late twentieth century which provide us with a quest for the meaning, purpose, and stylistic achievements of African art within its own cultural milieu.

The Study of Traditional African Art

Traditional African art consists of a variety of media. Besides sculpture and painting, it includes textile, pottery, jewelry, household objects, and architecture. The traditional African art, which is frequently suspended in a web of spiritual essence, is produced to enhance the cycle of life experienced by members of the society. It portrays and embodies themes of fertility, rites-of-passage (e.g., transition from youth to adulthood or passing from the realm of life to death), and the constant permeation of vital, spiritual forces, including powers of deceased ancestors, in the lives of the present inhabitants of the society. The art supports the collective community's philosophical ideas and reaffirms its social, religious, political, and economic values. The artwork represents humankind's commitment to integrate himself with other animate beings and nature into the cosmology of the universe.

The predominance of the appearance of this art in wood results from its local availability. Heavily forested regions exist in West and Central Africa. These regions provided many of the traditional wood sculptures housed in Western museums. The nearby forest offered a vast supply from which the artist, assisted by the counseling of a diviner, could select. Before cutting down a tree for sculpting, the artist and diviner engaged in pouring libations around the tree and holding a ritual ceremony; these activities were performed in order to appease the spirits believed to be embodied in the tree. For the traditional African, vital, spiritual forces permeate all aspects of life and nature, including rocks, hills, and animals.

Since wood sculpture comes from tropical climates, the date of creation of many pieces is believed to be no more than 100 years prior to the date of its discovery by Westerners. Therefore, much of the traditional wood sculpture dates to the nine-

proto

teenth and twentieth centuries. Other destructive elements which wood faces include infestations caused by termites, or other insects and encrustations formed from the frequent application of substances used in ritual libations, such as animal blood, palm oil, or millet used to heighten the spiritual powers of the object.

However, wood is not the only material which is used for sculpture. Terra-cotta and various alloys of metal compose the sculpture which offers the best datable material from West Africa. Art such as Nok, Igbo-Ukwu, Ife, and Benin fall within this category and exist in Nigeria, the only country in Africa where a history of datable material has been established for non-wood sculpture. There are major gaps in the time span between these early cultures, and we can only hope that future research will provide a more cohesive chronology.

Nok culture (500 B.C.–200 A.D.) was located near the Jos Plateau in northern Nigeria. It is characterized by terra-cotta human heads, measuring from 3–14 inches in height, with expressive, large eyes, slightly opened mouths, and cascading hairstyles. Not much is known about the Nok culture; the purpose for these heads is uncertain but they are believed to have served a religious function and indicate a sophisticated clay production and firing technique.

From the burial site of Igbo-Ukwu (ninth to tenth century) in southeastern Nigeria, lead bronze vessels and staves with intricate geometric and zoomorphic designs were found. These objects were probably used in activities for the king, who ruled by divine right. A sophisticated casting technique known as *cire perdue* (lost wax) was used in the production of the bronze work by this culture.

Like the art of Nok, the art of the Ife kingdom (eleventh to fifteenth century) of southwestern Nigeria is characterized by human heads. However, the heads are not only done in an additive technique using terra-cotta but are also cast in brass. Unlike the Nok examples, the Ife forms are naturalistic and may have served as symbolic portraits of the ruler, or Oni.

Benin kingdom's art (fifteenth century to 1897) from central Nigeria, consists primarily of brass and ivory sculpture. Here brass heads are more stylized than Ife heads and portray strands of coral beads, reserved for royalty and worn as necklaces and crowns. The brass heads of the king, or Oba, were surmounted by an ivory tusk with low-relief images narrating the reign of the king. These heads were placed on the altars in the royal palace. Other art created during the Benin period includes brass plaques depicting royal activities, often the king's military entourage, brass musicians, brass equestrian figures, ivory leopard aquamaniles, and ivory bracelets. During the late fifteenth and early sixteenth centuries, the Benin kings traded heavily with the Portuguese. Slaves, ivory, pepper, and salt were traded for Portuguese brass manillas. Ivory saltcellars produced by Benin sculptors were created specifically for the Portuguese market.

Three of the cultures—Nok, Ife, and Benin—have a preponderant number of images portraying human heads. Placing emphasis on the head is also prevalent in the style of wood figural sculpture from various parts of Sub-Saharan Africa. The significance of the head is that it is the physical location of intellectual and spiritual powers; it is this part of the human body which defines the identity and the character of the individual. In figural sculpture, the emphasis on the head is portrayed in terms of its enlarged scale and its decorative coiffure or headgear. In comparison to the rest of the body, the head is often expressed in a numerical ratio of 1:3 or 1:4. Other qualities typically found in African sculpture, even Old Kingdom Egyptian stone sculpture, are a rigid, erect posture, frontal presentation, symmetrical composition, and placement of the hands alongside the body. This conventionalism in form reflects the numerous years of training by the artist in an apprenticeship program, which promoted the established canons of representing traditional styles. It also relates to the seriousness of the art's function. Figural sculptures and masks often embody the vital, spiritual forces of the community, nature, and the cosmos. In traditional societies, the figural sculpture, often displayed on altars or shrines, served as a mediator between humankind and the spirit world. The masquerader, attired in a mask and costume, also served as a medium through whom members of the society communicated with the spirit world for social control. The severe, abstract style expresses an anthropomorphic form, which does not imitate human likeness but instead represents a concrete idea of a spiritual force.

The attention paid to African art by Western scholars is not geographically balanced. For example, studies in North Africa focus on Egyptian art and rock art in Tassili n'Ajjer, dating as far back as 6000 B.C. and located in present-day Algeria. In Sub-Saharan African art, scholarly research on the art produced by West African ethnic groups outweighs available sources on the art of Central Africa. Unfortunately, the traditional arts of East and South Africa are too infrequently examined. As was mentioned earlier, West and Central African regions offer the most extensive amounts of wood sculpture where local supply of available resources is sustained by an ecology which yields thriving forested areas. Contrary to this phenomenon, regions in other parts of Africa are not as fertile with vegetation. For example, in East Africa, the climate is arid, and forested and savannah regions are sparsely scattered throughout. Many traditional ethnic groups, such as the Maasai of Kenya, are nomadic pastoralists and therefore create art objects which are light-weight, small in scale, and portable. Rather than focusing on figural sculpture, Maasai art is characterized by an abundance of beaded jewelry, paint applied to the body, and brightly colored textiles.

Personal adornment satisfies the artistic urge in many nomadic cultures. The human body is perceived as a sculptural three-dimensional form; it is transformed into an artistic expression by carefully applied colored pigment and ornate jewelry which, when active and in motion as in a dance performance, possesses a vital force of its own. The seriousness associated with this art form is evinced by the numerous hours spent by both men and women in its production. The manner in which the body is embellished indicates the individual's social position within the society. For example, an initiated male is identified by long hair accentuated with reddish clay. A warrior wears beaded earrings and necklaces given to him by his mother or girlfriend. A married woman wears beadwork and clothing different from that of a single woman.

Many of the traditional arts of Africa are not practiced today. Reasons for their termination rest with the changes in the societies. The intervention of two religious doctrines contributed to this decline of traditional arts: Islam, with its strong advocacy to denounce graven images; and Christianity, whose adherents believed that traditional African religions and art were heathen and therefore should be abandoned and destroyed. However, with African colonies' independence from European powers and continuous contact with the West, new techniques, training programs, and materials were introduced which led to the creation and production of art forms with innovative expressions that compete with other contemporary art on the international scene.

Contemporary Art in Africa

Of all the African countries, the largest number of practicing contemporary artists have historically emanated from Nigeria. This phenomenon is relatively recent dating to the early 1960s and includes sculptors, painters, and graphic artists. Two factors served as catalysts for inspiring new trends in contemporary Nigerian artistic development: the Nigerian heritage and Western training. First, Nigeria's known traditional artistic heritage is strong, dating as far back as 500 B.C., while contemporary artistic development takes root in the early twenties. Unlike contemporary Western artists who derive inspiration from their past heritage through research, publications, or museum and gallery visits, the contemporary Nigerian's knowledge of a past artistic legacy stems from oral traditions or traditional ceremonies and festivals. Even today in Nigeria, a minimum amount of artifacts are on view in the country's museums, which opened in the early fifties.

The numerous art training programs offer another stimulus for the occurrence of the abundant growth of artistic production in Nigeria. An artist trains in a program based on the traditional apprenticeship method or the Western studio system; the latter includes workshop programs and fine arts programs in academic institutions. Even though the majority of artists are trained in African art schools, many, often as recipients of government scholarships, studied in Europe or America where, in some cases, they were exposed to Western contemporary and historical art trends. Regardless of where they trained, many pioneering contemporary Nigerian artists, such as Chief Aina Onabolu and Ben Enwonwu, received instruction not from their own countrymen but from foreign teachers. Since independence in 1960, the number of Nigerian art teachers within the country has increased. After receiving their education abroad, many artists returned to the universities and polytechnic schools in their own country to teach. As a result, the present university art students have more in common with their art teachers than their predecessors had. Their Nigerian teachers have a better understanding of the culture and are equally versed in world art.

Although to some extent the traditional apprenticeship program is still utilized in some areas of Nigeria, its practice in large part has been supplanted by academic or Western forms of art education. In Nigeria, the most notable contemporary pioneering fine arts programs are the following three, two of which are associated with prominent individuals: 1) Aina Onabolu, 2) Kenneth Crosswraithe Murray, and 3) Ahmadu Bello University, formerly the Nigeria College of Art, Science and Technology.

The Western method of drawing directly from a model is a technique that is foreign to the traditional Nigerian artistic practices. When Western education was introduced to Nigeria by Christian missionaries in the early nineteenth century, the prospect of adding art to schools' curricula was held suspect and adamantly resisted. Because art education was viewed as insignificant for inclusion, fine art programs developed slowly, and the rapid emergence of contemporary art and artists was thwarted.

In the early 1920s, the successful addition of art programs to the curricula of Nigeria's secondary schools and colleges may be attributed to the relentless pursuits of Chief Aina Onabolu, a Yoruba painter and art educator. Onabolu coerced colonial government officials to implement art programs into the school systems all over Nigeria. His proposal was approved, and, in 1922, he was the first art education teacher in Nigeria. Simultaneously, Onabolu embarked upon a rigorous campaign to hire experienced, western-trained art teachers. The early art teachers, such as Kenneth C. Murray, came from England and obviously were well versed in Western aesthetics. Throughout his career, Onabolu was also a proponent of the Western aesthetic tradition. Having taught himself the technique of creating spatial illusions of depth and perspective on a two-dimensional surface by manipulating light-and-dark areas, Onabolu produced realistic paintings and drawings for two decades before studying art abroad. From 1920 to 1922, he trained at the academies of London and Paris and pursued courses in drawing, painting, and design. He is revered as the first African to study art in England and is the first known African artist to produce illusionistic portraits; his paintings and drawings captured the features of prominent Nigerian and British personalities. Thus, in his own artwork, Onabolu neither incorporated the abstract style of traditional arts from his heritage nor the new stylistic trends prevalent in modern European art of the time. Instead, his efforts were devoted to proving the outstanding ability of contemporary African artists to produce an illusionistic aesthetic tantamount to the achievements made by their European counterparts.

After the Nigerian Civil War, changes in curricula were made in the nation's institutions of higher learning to abandon the model used in the British educational system. Nigeria's oldest university fine arts program is that initiated at Ahmadu Bello University (ABU) in Zaria. Originally it was founded under the name of Nigeria College of Art, Science and Technology in Ibadan in 1953, and was part of the Department of Education. In its new location, the fine arts program became a separate school, offering courses in painting, sculpture, graphic design, textile design, and art history.

Many of Nigeria's leading contemporary artists received their diplomas from Zaria and, after completion, some continued their education abroad. Dissatisfied with the British art lecturers' Western orientation and heavily influenced by current discourse emanating from major cultural and political centers on "the African personality," the students professed to rediscover their heritage and recognize their African identity. Organized under the rubric of the Zaria Art Society in 1958, some of its earliest members included presently eminent Nigerian artists as Uche Okeke, Yusuf Grillo, Demas Nwoko, Simon Okeke, Bruce Onobrakpeya, Oseloka Osadebe, and Emmanuel Okechukwu Odita. In the creation of their artworks, the members vowed to follow the Society's manifesto, which involved an appreciation and willingness to promote natural syntheses of the aesthetics of traditional African art, the aesthetics of Western art, and contemporary African cultural experiences.

Workshop programs in Nigeria offered alternative art training for promising artists who could neither afford nor had the proper credentials to enroll in the university program. Unlike the fine arts program but similar to the traditional apprenticeship program, the workshop does not require students to take examinations or earn a degree or certificate. In addition, completion of the program is not set according to a prescribed schedule; the participating student elects to participate as long as he or she chooses.

Of all the art workshop programs in Nigeria, the Oshogbo workshop called "Mbari Mbayo" which was formed in 1962, has received the most international recognition. It was modeled after the summer art workshops which were part of the Mbari Writers' and Artists' Club, established in Ibadan in 1961. Unlike the group of intellectuals who comprised the Ibadan Mbari Writers' and Artists' Club, the Oshogbo workshop attracted individuals who were either primary school dropouts or had not receive any formal Western training. Its founder, Ulli Beier, an Austrian living in Nigeria at the time, fostered a philosophy that sought to nurture the fresh, untainted imagination and ability of promising, uneducated artists. It was his attempt to promote the African essence in the artworks of the students.

Like the original fine arts programs in the university, the workshop was organized and run by Westerners. Beier selected and invited the teachers. Even though most of the teachers were from Europe, two non-Europeans, Dennis Williams (a West Indian artist) and Jacob Lawrence (an African American painter) led programs during the tenure of the workshop.

The approach used to train students in the workshop was very informal. Students were not introduced to art theories. They were given very inexpensive materials, such as hardboard and emulsion, and were allowed considerable freedom to experiment on their own. Nevertheless, the students' artworks were judged and critiqued; at the end of each day, the teacher hung what was considered the best works and offered suggestions for improvement.

Although the Oshogbo workshop became defunct because of lack of funding in the late sixties, it had produced a wealth of students who are prominent artists today. Artists, such as Jacob Afolabi, Rufus Ogundele, Twins Seven, Muraina Oyleami, Adebesi Fabunmi, and Jimoh Buraimoh, have had works exhibited in Africa, Europe, and America. They have spawned interest among younger artists and have an impressive following of students, whose artworks have also been included in international exhibitions.

Africanisms and Pioneers in African American Art

The occurrence of Africanisms or African retention in African American arts are more prevalent in music, dance, literature, and drama than in the visual arts. The early art produced by slaves offers us some artistic links to Africa's traditional heritage. Artistic retention survived in regions of South Carolina and Georgia and include utilitarian objects of personal use. Traditional African motifs and techniques occur in textiles, baskets, wood canes, clay jugs, wrought ironwork, wood cabinet designs, musical instruments, and architecture. For example, the appliqué technique used in American quilts, in which cut-out pieces of cloth are sewn onto a cloth backing, is derived from appliquéd textiles produced by traditional artists in West Africa, such as the Fon in the Republic of Benin (formerly Dahomey).

Africans imported to the Americas were forced to adjust to a new lifestyle that involved the loss of freedom, religion, and family. The communal and kinship systems which were fostered in their African homeland were replaced by separations of the familiar group, strict confinement, and lack of mobility, which were adopted into America's Slave Codes. This adverse lifestyle was completely contrary to the African communal system which prompted the production of the figural sculptures, masks, and other arts. For the African slave in America, social changes, denial from practicing traditional African religions, and total absence of political and economic power, resulted in the dissipation of traditional African art and the development of new art forms, sometimes with African features, which catered to a new patron—the white slave master.

American art, whether created by African Americans or white Americans developed slowly. In colonial days, all artistic endeavors were adjusted to the needs of the new environment. White Americans had strong cultural ties to their mother countries, and yearned for personal possessions which both they and their forefathers had been accustomed to in their old homeland. Wealthy white southerners produced few of their own personal belongings and depended on the importation of necessary commodities from Europe. However, this venture proved to be ineffective because foreign merchandise was expensive and the transportation of these goods from Europe was too infrequent. Eventually, skilled European craftsmen were transported to America to establish apprenticeship programs for local artisans. Both white and slave artisans participated in these program, especially in the eighteenth century. They were trained as goldsmiths, silversmiths, dressmakers, cabinetmakers, printers, engravers, and portrait painters. These artisans' skills proved profitable for their slave masters who would hire them out for service. Sometimes, a white artisan would even buy, train, and then sell a slave artisan for profit. An alternative to apprenticed artisans was self-taught artists and artisans. Art programs were not officially incorporated into the schools' curricula until the mid-nineteenth century.

African American artists are outstanding when judged by their own epochs and restrictive opportunities. During the eighteenth and nineteenth centuries, a few African American artists achieved personal recognition. They were mostly in the Northern cities where white abolitionists funded and supported their profession. The African American artists acculturated Western techniques and aesthetic concepts in an attempt to merge with mainstream artists.

Some of the earliest African American professional artists were printmakers. Scipio Moorhead, a slave active around 1773, is among the most notable. He resided in Boston with Rev. John Moorhead, his slavemaster and a minister who allowed Scipio to receive training in art from his wife, Sarah Moorhead, an art teacher. Although art works by Scipio Moorehead do not survive today, it is believed that he was a favorite artist of Phyllis Wheatley, a renowned African American poet, who dedicated one of her poems to him; speculations abound that the unsigned portrait engraving of Wheatley which appears in several of her publications is by Moorhead.

Joshua Johnston, who was active from 1796 to 1824, is an eminent African American artist, who in the past has been included in survey books dealing with American limner painters without identifying him as a mulatto. He was the first African American artist to gain recognition as a portrait painter in oil. Most of the known limner portrait painters are white Americans. The procedure for painting in the limner style entails that the artist first paints the background, which includes props such as furniture, pet dogs, and books; then, he carries his rolled-up canvases around with him and paints patrons upon request. As Johnston moved around Baltimore where he resided, he was commissioned to do portraits of wealthy slaveholders and other aristocrats, a subject matter which was also popular among white artists. Although his background is obscure, it is believed that he was a slave who was self-trained and had the privilege of seeing works by white limner painters in Baltimore, particularly those of Charles Peale Polk, Charles Wilson Peale, and Rembrandt Peale.

None of Johnston's artworks are signed or dated; they are only known by his distinctive style. He portrays figures as stiff, rigid, and expressionless with pudgy hands. The sitter is depicted from a three-quarters viewpoint with taut lips and eyes gazing directly out at the viewer. The representation of space is sometimes awkward and indicates limited knowledge of linear perspective.

During the eighteenth and nineteenth centuries, African American artists who were offsprings of whites enjoyed special privileges in terms of free mobility, as Johnston experienced, and formal education, as Julien Hudson received. Hudson, the son of a wealthy slaveholder, was a free man living in New Orleans in the nineteenth century. He was exposed to the French tradition both in New Orleans and in Paris, where he visited briefly. Hudson became a teacher and painted miniature portraits in oil. His portrayals were more realistically and accurately rendered than those of Johnston.

Besides portraits, other subjects which African American artists represented were landscape scenes, again echoing the major concerns of their white counterparts. In the nineteenth century, both Robert Duncanson and Edward Bannister expressed the adored American land and nature in their oil paintings. Duncanson was a mulatto from New York State who was educated in Canada and traveled to Europe. He settled in Cincinnati where he received many commissions for portraits and landscape murals from prominent families but never did portraits of blacks. He studied the "classical tradition" in Italy and demonstrated a keen understanding of the Romantic sensibility used in the style of American Hudson River School painters who expressed the awesome vastness of nature. Duncanson is reputed to be the first African American artist to be recognized internationally.

Edward Bannister was born of mixed heritage—the son of a West Indian father and a Canadian mother—and studied art at Lowell Institute in Boston. Associated with the Barbizon School of American Regionalist Painters, he received national recognition for his work and was awarded a bronze medal in the Philadelphia Centennial of 1876 for his painting entitled *Under the Oaks*; at the time, this work sold for $1,500 but its present location is unknown.

Another African American artist who exhibited in the Centennial Exposition of 1876 was Edmonia Lewis, an internationally celebrated sculptress. Born of a mixture of Chippewa Indian and black, Lewis was always considered to be free-spirited and had a yearning to sculpt since childhood. She studied at Oberlin College in Ohio for three years, pursuing course work in the classics, until she encountered a racial incident which forced her to leave the city. She fled to Boston and trained under Edmund Brackett, a local sculptor. There, she modeled clay sculpture and designed a medallion of John Brown, an abolitionist associated with Harpers Ferry, as well as a bust head of Colonel Robert Shaw, a Civil War hero. The latter was purchased by members of the Shaw family and exhibited at the Boston Fair for Soldiers' Fund. Copies of Lewis's work were sold with the proceeds and with additional financial backing from other Boston patrons, Lewis was able to accumulate enough funds to travel to Rome in 1865. There, she was influenced by white American expatriates—Harriet Hosmer and Hiram Powers—which reflected her interest to conceive sculptural forms in the neo-classical style. Her artwork displays characteristics similar to Greco-Roman sculpture. Proportionately, the figures are accurately rendered. Their smooth, polished marble surfaces reveal a concern for fleshy illusionism.

Lewis's subject matter was diverse. It ranged from political themes, such as *Forever Free* (1867), which depicts a couple celebrating their freedom and was inspired by the Thirteenth Amendment to the U.S. Constitution forbidding slavery, to more gentle, whimsical themes such as the playful, cherub-like infants portrayed in *Awake* (1972) and *Asleep* (1971). Lewis represented her own Indian heritage in *The Old Indian Arrow Maker and his Daughter* (1876?) and biblical themes in *Hagar in the Wilderness* (1892). Despite a seemingly emotional subject matter, the marble sculptures exude expressions of calmness and serenity. This may be attributed to the Neoclassical style which they imitate; for this style is characterized by clarity of form, stoic and expressionless features, order, and, a complete sense of harmony. However, to these traits, Lewis added a sense of grace, elegance, beauty, and extreme naturalism to her sculptural figures. Even though Lewis had received both national and international honors for her artwork, she was still chided by American journalists as not being equal in ability and sculptural skill to her white American counterparts.

Henry Ossawa Tanner, a prominent painter during the nineteenth century, attended the Centennial Exposition of 1876. After viewing works produced by two African American artists—Bannister's painting *Under the Oaks* and Edmonia Lewis's sculpture *Cleopatra*—Tanner reaffirmed his belief that his people could achieve major accomplishments in art. Born in Pittsburgh to the son of a bishop in an African Methodist Church, Tanner attended the Pennsylvania Academy of Fine Arts and trained under Thomas Eakins, an esteemed American realist painter and teacher. From Eakins, Tanner learned to concentrate even more than he had before on the world around him and to focus on the psychological nature of man. His aim was to integrate movements and gestures with psychological expressions of figures.

Tanner began his career portraying blacks in his own portrait studio in Atlanta, Georgia. He was an avid photographer of the regional environment and rendered sketches of local residents. Although he taught at Clark College (presently Clark-Atlanta University), he was supported by patrons to go to Paris to study. For five years, he studied at the Académie Julien where his style matured. He was able to synthesize clarity of form which he had constantly explored under the tutelage of Eakins with color theories, paint applications, and the manipulation of light-and-dark which illuminated the works of European masters.

Even though Tanner felt at ease in France, the effects of the uncomfortable environment full of racial discrimination which he experienced upon his return trips to America, frequently plagued him throughout his career. At the beginning, he produced genre paintings depicting African Americans but eventually turned to religious subjects using Caucasian images, including those of his own white American wife, who often posed as his model. Tanner was continuously criticized by his own people for abandoning the black subjects in his works; but, this did not dissuade him from persisting in producing the religious works with non-black images which seemed to win recognition for him in the American mainstream and abroad. For example, his painting entitled *The Raising of Lazarus* (1896) won that year's Paris Salon's Gold Medal; in addition, it was purchased by the French Government and hung in the Luxembourg Palace.

The Harlem Renaissance heralded a campaign for artists to look to their African past for inspiration rather than to European models. As a result of this movement,

African American artists such as Aaron Douglas began to research and portray both African and African American images in their works. Douglas used a flat, silhouetted style for his forms which represented the African and African American milieu, but their abstract shapes were reminiscent of traditional African stylizations. His colorful four-paneled murals entitled *Aspects of Negro Life* (1934) reflect dancing figures pulsating to the melodic rhythm of African music.

Jacob Lawrence, one of America's most renowned contemporary African American artists, met many of the Harlem Renaissance visual and literary artists. Born in Atlantic City, New Jersey, he studied at community workshops in Harlem. As a Works Progress Administration (WPA) project recipient, Lawrence received instruction at the Harlem Art Workshop from Charles Alston, an African American painter who represented the human conditions of African Americans. Lawrence attributes his artistic development throughout much of his early career to the continuous support of Augusta Savage, an African American sculptress who was very influential among the Harlem art community in the 1930s and offered guidance to many African American artists.

By the time Lawrence was twenty-one years old, he was already recognized as a serious painter; his series of panel paintings about the Black Haitian General Toussaint L'Ouverture was shown along with works by other African American artists in an exhibition which was co-sponsored by the Harmon Foundation and the Baltimore Museum of Art. Later, he painted a series depicting the achievements of Frederick Douglass, an African American abolitionist, and Harriet Tubman, a leader in the Underground Railroad movement.

Perhaps, Lawrence's most publicly acclaimed series at the beginning of his career was *The Migration of the Negro* (1940–1941)—tempera paintings that represented the relocation of African Americans from the South to the North during the early part of this century. In sixty panels, he depicted their degrading social plight in both parts of the country and their dreams and frustrating attempts to obtain a better economic and educational status in the urban North. In short, Lawrence's interest was to portray the toils, the hopes, the disappointments, and the achievements of his people. His paintings reveal an intense understanding of and a sincere commitment to preserving African American social history, which he researched at the Schomburg Library (presently, the Schomburg Center for Research in Black Culture).

Although his figures are stylized—bordering on abstraction—and are reduced to their minimum essences, Lawrence's paintings are didactic, easy to read and understand. The images are flat, distorted silhouettes that are sometimes placed within complex compositions. Linear thrusts (especially of diagonal lines) throughout his paintings create intriguing patterns and sometimes suggest an interplay of tension between two-dimensional and three-dimensional spatial planes. As a result of Lawrence's style, his delicate treatment of the atrocities and sufferings experienced by blacks throughout their history results in an artistic exercise which stresses design, the dynamics of the picture plane, color, shape, and space.

Over the years, Lawrence's style has maintained its basic components but has become more sophisticated. His painting style reflects a background of artistic exposure which is varied, including experiences such as: teaching, during the summer of 1946, at Black Mountain College (a small avant garde school in North Carolina) where he was the only African American teacher; reaffirming his commitment to portraying the social conditions of the downtrodden by observing paintings by revolutionary artists such as José Clemente Orozco, a Mexican muralist; and teaching at the Oshogbo workshop in Nigeria. Besides this aggregate of experiences, Lawrence is further distinguished as belonging to the first generation of African American artists who received early formative training in the fine arts from African American teachers and was nurtured by the African American artistic community in Harlem.

Presently, the works of African American artists cover a gamut of styles; they are realistic, abstract, or non-representational without identifiable objects. Both subjects and themes traverse a variety of concepts. Some artists chose to stay in the mainstream so that their works will be accepted by established patrons through exhibition or purchased. Others rebut the need for this type of recognition and profess to produce art for the pure enjoyment of expressing their creative urges. Therefore, similar to the consequences resulting from the contemporary developments made in the art in Africa, contemporary African American artists are abundant in number and need to be documented for posterity.

Some Aspects of Caribbean Art

Caribbean art is full of vitality and vigor. Each region's art is slightly different based on the culture of the original inhabitants, the impact of the Western colonial powers that settled there, and the importation of slaves from various parts of Africa. Therefore, artistic, religious and other cultural ideas merge to form new nuances of expressive liveliness.

For example, the Haitians had their own religion, oral history, and other cultural idioms prior to the arrival of Columbus in 1492. After this date, the Spaniards ruled Haiti and its Indian population. As early as 1503, African slaves were brought to work in the mines in Haiti. Part of Haiti was acquired by France in a 1697 treaty with the Spaniards.

Many of Haiti's present inhabitants have ancestors from Africa—the Congo, Angola, Mali, Nigeria, and the Republic of Benin (formerly Dahomey). The creole culture evolved out of the merging of the various religions of these regions. For example, Dahomean influences on Haitian religion may be observed in examples such as the war and iron deity, Gū. Merged with Ogáun, the Yoruba (Nigerian) god of iron, from which it derives, Gū became Papa Ogáun, who is identified with the warrior saints of the Roman Catholic Church. The Church provided prints of the saints to the slaves. These materials served as teaching references.

African retentive objects which survived in Haiti include drums, ironwork, sculpture in cloth and wood, painted calabashes, and textiles. Many of the modern works reflect an interest in the abstraction of the figural form similar to African art and vivid colors which is apparent in the bright textiles that are part of the heritage of West African people.

Dynamism is present in works by Haitian artists. The Haitian artist combines the knowledge of Haiti's cultural pluralism with observations of nature and produces a painting tradition which is not illusionistic like Western art but maintains the integrity of a non-Western aesthetic tradition. Images are represented in vibrant colors, distorted shapes, often flat forms, and multiple viewpoints. The artists work directly on the surface, without preliminary sketches. This type of uninhibited approach to art and the candid representations which stem from it are accepted by Western observers who have become tempered by a style and approach that is reminiscent of the concerns of modern European artists who lauded and derived inspirations from traditional art of Africa and Oceanic cultures. Exhibitions and purchases of Haitian art have tended to come more from external than internal sources. Critics contend that this outside support has encouraged commercialism in the art. Despite this phenomenon, Haitian art maintains its variety, excitement, and spontaneous genre scenes of everyday activities. The old masters of Haitian art, including such personalities as Hector Hyppolite, Benoît, and Wilson Bigaud, have managed to inspire younger generations of promising artists.

Haitian art is closely interwoven into the belief system of *vodun*, which is a socioreligious custom that reflects a mixture of African and West Indian religions. In secular art, symbols associated with religion such as flowers, birds, and animals are frequently used. For religious art, Robert Farris Thompson acknowledges the links between the African and West Indian cultures and indicates that wrought iron crosses used for Baron Samedi, the graveyard deity, echo the patterns of ground paintings of *vodun—vàevàe*. To Thompson, both traditions appear connected to the Congo cosmogram drawn on the earth to signify "the boundary between two worlds and the moral watchfulness of God and the dead." He further states that the complete symbolism was lost in its transformation in Haiti.[2]

In the literature on Caribbean art, Haitian art dominates. Research on other islands' art is limited because interests are devoted elsewhere or political restraints deny access to artists and their work. Few publications portray the life of an individual Caribbean artist, especially a non-Haitian. One exception is Geoffrey MacLean's (1994) catalog on Boscoe Holder, a Trinidadian artist who painted portraits and nudes.

Finally, Middle America art impacted upon the art of the African Diaspora. During the nineteenth century, Mexico had a flourishing group of artists in landscape, portraiture, and religious paintings. However, the academically trained Spanish artists had a powerful influence upon these artists' development. Politically inspired artists such as Diego Rivera, José Clemente Orozco, and David Alfaro Siqueiros produced works with messages that dealt with human and class sufferings. Their mural paintings served as poignant reminders of the decadence of their culture. They also functioned as didactic tools to reprimand the wealthy and powerful about their greed as well as to evoke empathy for the poor, destitute, and illiterate who deserve better social conditions. By doing so, these artists were considered revolutionary. Their works had a profound effect upon African American artists such as Jacob Lawrence.

---

2. Robert Farris Thompson, "The Flash of the Spirit: Haiti's Africanizing Vodun," in Ute Stebich, *Haitian Art*. New York: Brooklyn Museum, 1978.

Summary

The art produced by the traditional Africans, the contemporary Africans, African Americans, and the Caribbeans may be difficult to discern in its entirety because the artists in the latter three categories assimilated Western cultures. This phenomenon does not suggest a need for exclusion of these artists from study but rather points to a crucial necessity for their inclusion. However, despite their Western connection, they have limited or no status in studies on world art. Our paucity of understanding and resources on the subject requires that we delve deeper to maintain our awareness and inspire documentation of cultural productions, such as art, to enhance our own self-worth as human beings.

Furthermore, even though the artistic connections between blacks in Africa and in the diaspora may appear to be shrouded in obscurity, clarity will only be achieved through exposure and discussion of these cultural expressions. Perhaps, of all the artists, the artistic union between African Americans and their African ancestors appears most grim. Nevertheless, many African American artists are making a concerted appeal to acknowledge African retention in their artworks through the suggestion of forms, colors, and compositions endemic to African stylistic idioms. For them, the continuities exist more so than a delineated breach in the aesthetic tradition of their African ancestors. Whether the representation of the artists' philosophies is achieved or even expressed here may be debated. However, the overall attempt of this chapter was to be inclusive of black artists from various parts of the world, who are too seldom celebrated as a collective group.

Study Questions and Activities

1. Discuss some of the past and present misconceptions about African Art.
2. What are some of the problems in the study of African Art?
3. Discuss reasons which contributed to changes in African Art which led to contemporary forms of expressions.
4. What considerations should be given when judging African American art?
5. Name some of the most prominent African American artists and discuss their artistic contributions.
6. What are some African retentions which exist in both African American and Caribbean art?

References

Ulli Beier. *Introduction: Contemporary Art in Africa*. New York: F.A. Praeger, 1968.

Tonya Bolden. *Wake Up Our Souls: A Celebration of Black American Artist*. New York: H.N. Abrams: Published in association with the Smithsonian American Art Museum, 2004.

Evelyn Brown. *Africa's Contemporary Art and Artists*. New York: The Harmon Foundation, 1966.

Judith Wragg Chase. *Afro-American Art and Craft*. New York: Van Nostrand Reinhold, 1971.

Donald J. Cosentino, ed. *Sacred Arts of Haitian Vodou*. Los Angeles: UCLA Fowler Museum of Cultural History, 1995.

Ekpo Eyo and Frank Willett. *Treasures of Ancient Nigeria*. New York: Alfred A. Knopf, 1982.

Lisa E. Farrington. *Creating Their Own Image: The History of African-American Women Artists*. Oxford; New York: Oxford University Press, 2005.

William Ferris. *Afro-American Folk Art and Crafts*. Jackson and London: University Press of Mississippi, 1983.

Salah Hassan. "Review on 'Africa Explores: 20th Century African Art.'" *African Arts*, vol. 25 2(January 1992): 36–37, 95–96, 100.

Grant Hill. *Something All Our Own: The Grant Hill Collection of African American Art*. Durham: Duke University Press, 2004.

H.W. Janson and Anthony Janson. *History of Art*, 6th ed. 2 vols. Upper Saddle River, N. J.: Prentice-Hall, Inc., 2004.

Kleiner, Fred S. and Christin J. Mamiya..*Gardner's Art through the Ages*, 11th ed. Belmont, CA.: Thomson/Wadsworth Learning, 2005.

Jean Kennedy. *New Currents, Ancient Rivers: Contemporary African Artists in a Generation of Change*. Washington, DC: Smithsonian Institution Press, 1992.

Alisa LaGamma. *Echoing Images: Couples in African Sculpture*. New Haven: Yale University Press, 2004.

Jean Laude. *The Arts of Black Africa*. Berkeley: University of California Press, 1971.

Samella Lewis. *African American Art and Artists*, 3rd ed. Berkeley, Los Angeles, and London: University of Califronia Press, 2003.

———, Floyd Coleman, and Mary Jane Hewitt (eds.). *African American Art and Artists*. Berkeley: University of California Press, 2003.

Geoffrey MacLean. *Boscoe Holder*. Trinidad and Tobago: MacLean Publishing Limited, 1994.

Lisa Mintz Messinger, Lisa Gail Collins, and Rachel Mustalish (eds.). *African-American Artists, 1929–1945: Prints, Drawings, and Paintings in The Metropolitan Museum of Art*. New York: Yale University Press, 2003.

Sharon F. Patton. *African-American Art*. Oxford and New York: Oxford University Press, 1998.

Warren Robbins and Nancy Nooter. *African Art in American Collections*. Washington, DC: Smithsonian Institution Press, 1989.

Roy Sieber and Roslyn Adele Walker. *African Art in the Cycle of Life*. Washington, DC: Smithsonian Institution Press, 1987.

James Edward Smethurst. *The Black Arts Movement: Literary Nationalism in the 1960s and 1970s*. Chapel Hill: University of North Carolina Press, 2005.

Ute Stebich. *Haitian Art*. New York: The Brooklyn Museum, 1978.

Robert Farris Thompson. *Flash of the Spirit: African and Afro-American Art and Philosophy*. New York: Vintage Books, 1983.

———. "The Flash of the Spirit: Haiti's Africanizing Vodun," in Ute Stebich (ed.). *Haitian Art*. New York: Brooklyn Museum, 1978.

John Michael Vlach. *The Afro-American Tradition in Decorative Arts*. Cleveland, OH: The Cleveland Museum of Art, 1978.

Susan M. Vogel. *Art/Artifact*. New York: The Center for African Art, 1988.

———. *Africa Explores: 20th Century African Art*. New York: The Center for African Art, 1991.

Frank Willett. *African Art: An Introduction*, Reprinted. New York: Thames and Hudson, 1985.

17

Literature in Africa and the Caribbean

Tanure Ojaide

Introduction

Literature is a major art form through which people exhibit their culture. In modern times, literature has become one of Africa's major contributions to the intellectual world. Oral or written, African literature has gained recognition worldwide with such classics as the Mandingo epic *Sundiata*, Chinua Achebe's *Things Fall Apart*, Ngugi wa Thiongo's *Weep Not Child*, and Wole Soyinka's *Death and the King's Horseman*. The winning of the Nobel Prize for Literature by Nigeria's Wole Soynka in 1986 and Egypt's Naguib Mahfouz in 1988 and both Nadine Gordimer and J.M. Coetzee of South Africa in 1991 and 2003 respectively has drawn further attention to the nature and the role of African literature on the continent of Africa and other parts of the world.

In Africa, two types of literature have flourished simultaneously: traditional oral literature and modern written literature. Traditional African literature is as old as the African people themselves. From the beginning of their history, Africans have always tried to understand their environment and interpret natural phenomena through myths. They sing about their experiences and teach the younger generations about morality, ethics, culture, and history with tales, myths, and legends, all of which have become part of a literary repertoire. With the general acceptance of oral literature by Western scholars as valid during the 1950s, the field of African literature has recently become so vast and complex that the following discussion is designed to provide the beginning student with only a general understanding of the nature of African literature—the genres, major developments over the past decades, the uses, the themes, and future prospects.

Major terms and concepts: written and oral literature, orality, folklore, myth, legend, didactic, fairy tale, epic, proverb, riddle, improvisation, poetry, prose, Negritude, literature, Caribbean, Afro-Caribbean, patois, Creole, black consciousness, anthology, novel, poem, expatriate.

Definition

The literary scholar Abiola Irele once said that there was "no satisfactory definition" of African literature. He noted that:

> The term 'Africa' appears to correspond to a geographical notion but we know that, in practical terms, it also takes in those other areas of collective awareness that have been determined by ethnic, historical and sociological factors, all these factors, as they affect and express themselves in our literature, marking off for it a broad area of reference. Within this area of reference then, and related to certain aspects that are intrinsic to the literature, the problem of definition involves as well a consideration of *aesthetic modes in their intimate correlation to the cultural and social structures which determine and define the expressive schemes of African peoples and societies.* [author's emphasis]

This definition of literature takes note of place and people with their "aesthetic modes" and "cultural and social structures." Language, Irele adds, is not the prime focus in his definition of literature, whose "essential force" is its "reference to the historical and the experiential." One other attempt at defining African literature is made by Chinweizu, Onwuchekwa Jemie and Ihechukwu Madubuike. It is quite clear to them that:

> Works done for African audiences, by Africans, and in African languages, whether these works are oral or written, constitute the historically indisputable core of African literature. Works done by Africans but in non-African languages, and works done by non-Africans in African languages, would be among those for which some legitimate doubt might be raised about their inclusion or exclusion from the canon of works of African literature.

Their definition recognizes the primary audience of a literature as defining that literature. Thus, if African countries adopt English, French, Portuguese, or Arabic as official languages, Africans writing in these alien languages primarily for Africans are African writers and their works are part of African literature. Whatever definition one adopts, however, there is agreement that African literature is that which is written by Africans for Africans who share the same sensibility, consciousness, world-view, and other aspects of cultural experience. In short, the writer must share in the values and experiences of African people for the writing to be classified as African.

The body of African literature, written in indigenous African and non-African languages, is rapidly growing. For example, there is a relatively large body of Yoruba, Hausa, Ibo, Swahili, Kikuyu, and Zulu literary works. Writers such as Mazisi Kunene, Ngugi wa Thiongo, and the late Okot p'Bitek have produced poems, plays, and novels in African languages before they were translated into English. At the same time, most modern African writers have used primarily English, French, Portuguese, and Arabic to express their ideas and feelings. While the attempts to express one's inner feelings and thoughts in a foreign language will remain a perennial problem for African writers, writing in a vernacular, which most readers are not trained to read, will equally continue to hinder their effectiveness. In addition, writing in African languages does cause the writer to lose not only other African readers but also Western audiences and readership entirely, and precludes financial reward for those authors who write for profit and to make a living, as many do.

Traditional Oral and
Written Literature in Africa

Prior to colonialism, traditional Africa was predominantly made up of non-literate societies among which orality was the major means of expression and communication. Songs were sung and tales told, and were orally passed from one generation to another. Because of its orality, therefore, traditional African literature depended heavily on memory for its transmission from person to person, from place to place, and from generation to generation. Yet, such literature always had an important function to perform in society. Indeed, African literature has, by and large, remained didactic over the centuries, and is used by the elders in teaching social mores and ethics and in the community's transmission of its most important traditions. In the days when there were no schools of the Western type, parents gathered their children by the fireside after the day's hard work, in the evening, and told them different types of tales: folktales, fairy tales, myths, legends, and epics. For instance, tales of the greedy tortoise are meant to teach children about selflessness, while those of the trickster Anansi (spider, in West Africa) and the rabbit (in East Africa) are designed to tell youngsters that cleverness is not a substitute for honesty and caring for others. Though many African tales have animal characters, their experiences are human, and everyone learns from them how to live and behave in a communal society.

The forest or grassland setting is the world in which many Africans live, and tales are meant to teach how one must treat others and the environment. The tales, especially the myths and epics, likewise inculcate the values and mores of the group into young ones, who imbibe the consciousness and sensibility of the race. Myths, for instance, explain natural phenomena. In African folklore, there are tales explaining why pigs always look downward, why the sky is so high from the earth, why man and woman cause each other problems but cannot do without one another, and why people must die. While legends and epics are told to inspire youngsters into heroic deeds, proverbs, riddles, and other rhetorical forms are learned to enhance verbal communication, sometimes to make one an orator, and to sharpen one's thinking skills.

Music is also an important part of African traditional literature. There is music or song for almost all daily activities and rites of passage, from birth to adulthood, and from marriage to death. There are lullabies to put children to sleep, work songs, play songs, initiation songs, and religious songs. Within each category, such as in work songs, there are some that are sung when men clear the farm and some which are sung by women weeding the field. In addition, some songs are for planting and harvesting, for paddling the canoe to fish, grazing cattle, and others for shelling groundnuts, grating cassava, and pounding yams. In short, song permeates the entire life of the African.

In contrast to Western tradition, African oral literature is a live art. It is performed, and each moment of performance is a "text" of its own. The narrator or the poet must simultaneously be an expert performer, which is not always the case in the West. In oral literature, memory is the most important medium of transmission of messages. However, because memory wears out with the passing of time, there is an inherent problem with oral literature. Thus, the same oral tale or song might have different versions or variants, as each performer tries to embellish or fill up the work to suit a particular audience and his own talent. Consequently, improvisation is very important in oral literature, as the performer introduces new elements and stamps his or her own mark on the tale. As a live art, oral literature maintains a symbiotic relationship between the performer and the audience. The audience participates in the songs in a tale, sings the refrain, and claps hands as an accompaniment, elements that are not always present in Western tradition, as when the poet is on the stage reading his work to the sitting audience.

Equally significant in oral literature is the very thin line in generic differentiation. A folktale may have songs (which are poems) at various sections, have narration and description, and much drama, as the performer mimics the action of animals or any other characters in the tale. Poetry and prose, on the one hand, are almost inseparable in the proverbs, axioms, riddles, and other rhetorical figures. Oratory, on the other hand, is highly cherished by the audience in Africa. The syncretic nature of traditional African oral literature is best expressed by festivals, which are theatrical, dramatic, ritualistic, and poetic re-enactments of the people's myths and legends, accompanied by music, artistic expressions and use of artifacts, and dance. One may say, therefore, that traditional African literature is generically inclusive, unlike Western literature, which is compartmentalized.

There are other important, often denied, qualities of traditional African literature in the poets and the singers of tales. For example, contrary to common misinformed impressions, the traditional artist in literature (or art) has an identity, and his or her work is not anonymous in the community. People are able to identify, for example, the person who produced a song. Thus, in the African oral tradition, individual oral artists exist with their unique compositions, which may have been edited in a communal "workshop," as in the case of *udje* dance songs among the Urhobo people of Nigeria's Delta State. It is not true, therefore, as Ruth Finnegan notes, that "the poetry of non-literate peoples" in Africa arises "directly and communally from the undifferentiated folk." The author's experience confirms the fact that each song bears the signature of its poet not only in its formulas and themes but also in the role and mission of its creator.

As Janheinz Jahn observed, the history of African literature corresponds with the history of the continent, a claim which has been reinforced by studies done by scholars such as Romanus Egudu on the writers' reflection of the historical reality of their people. Modern African literature started with the introduction of the script and the adoption of European languages by Africans in colonial times, notably during the nineteenth century. *The Life of Olaudah Equiano*, published in 1789, can be considered the first work of written African literature. It describes the traditional life and customs of the Ibo people and Equiano's capture, sale into slavery in Barbados, and subsequent travels to the United States, Britain, and Africa, among other places. However, since it was written by an expatriate, in some circles it may not earn the honor of having been the first.

Amos Tutuola's *The Palm-Wine Drinkard* (1952) is one of the early works of fiction to come out of Africa. It tells the story of a palm-wine drinker who searches for his dead palm-wine tapster into the "Deads' Town," where he finds him but cannot bring him back to life because the dead are dead. It is with the publication of Chinua Achebe's *Things Fall Apart* in 1958, however, that written African literature became recognized worldwide. In the novel, Achebe tells, in a masterly way, the tragic story of how the distinguished Okwonko and his Ibo village of Umuofia were destroyed by the arrival of the Europeans into the village. Like many educated Africans of the 1950s, Achebe had been bothered by such European writers as Joseph Conrad in *Heart of Darkness* and Joyce Cary in *Mister Johnson*, who, as a result of their deep-rooted prejudices, distorted the true African cultural image, and justified European colonialism as an agent of enlightenment rather than the economic exploitation that it was. Achebe thus wrote *Things Fall Apart* to show that "African peoples did not hear of culture for the first time from Europeans; that their societies were not mindless but frequently had a philosophy of great depth and value and beauty; that they had poetry and, above all, they had dignity." Achebe realistically exposes African culture to Europeans and to those who are ignorant of it, and asserts the dignity of the African past.

Although most of the examples provided above refer to Anglophone Africa, French-speaking Africa was no less prolific, beyond the Negritude writers discussed below. Among the early most known works are Camara Laye's novel *The African Child*, published as early as 1952, which tells Laye's life as a son of a goldsmith in his Muslim village and society, and Cheik Hamidou Kane's novel *Ambiguous Adventure* (1962), an account of the dilemma of a young Muslim student who faces the secular temptations of Western education and culture in Paris. There were others in South Africa, in North Africa, and lesser known writers in Lusophone Africa during the 1950s who should be counted among the pioneers of modern written African literature.

Within the context of exposing and restoring the dignity of African culture was Negritude, a literary movement started by Francophone African and Caribbean students, including Leopold Senghor of Senegal, Leon Damas of French Guyana, and Aime Cesaire of Martinique, in Paris, in 1934. Sustained by its journal *L'Etudiant Noir*, Negritude was a popular movement in Francophone Africa and the West Indies during the 1940s and 1950s. Abiola Irele describes Negritude as "the literary and ideological movement of French-speaking black intellectuals, which took form as a distinctive and significant aspect of the comprehensive reaction of the black man to the colonial situation, a situation that was felt and perceived by black people in Africa and in the New World as a state of global subjection to the political, social, and moral domination of the West." Though Negritude has been defined in different ways, essentially it means "the expression of blackness." In this sense, it is similar to the expression of the African personality in Anglophone Africa. It is generally acknowledged, furthermore, that Negritude was a move away from the themes of colonial oppression common among English-speaking African writers of the time.

In fact, Negritude brought forth African traditional culture vividly, exposed colonial exploitation and oppression, especially on the cultural level, and celebrated black dignity. Leopold Sedar Senghor (former President of Senegal), in particular, expounded the concept in various collections of poems and essays. While many Anglophone Africans, including South African Ezekiel Mphahlele, Malawian David Rubadiri, and Nigerian Wole Soyinka, have condemned Negritude ("a tiger does not proclaim its tigritude; it pounces," Soyinka once wrote sarcastically), it has historical validity as it afforded Africans in colonial times the opportunity to assert their Africanness. Indeed, in both Anglophone and Francophone Africa, literature was a vehicle of cultural nationalism in the colonial period and the years following independence.

To the extent that modern African literature is defined as the written literature started during the colonial times, when Africans who had gone to Western schools began writing poems, novels, short stories, and plays, it is expressed in two important forms: one in foreign European languages and the other in indigenous languages. The latter is not well exposed yet, and appears in languages such as Yoruba, Zulu, Hausa, and Ibo, which are almost unknown outside their geographical frontiers. In any case, the written literature of Africa is new compared to the indigenous oral literary tradition, which has always been on the continent, and is still very much alive today. Although modern African literature started as derivative and imitative of European forms, it has, over the past several decades, grown to be, in a true sense, very African.

The nature of the origin of modern African literature has often succumbed to the Eurocentric temptation of seeing the literature from the continent as a part of European literature. However, as this author has had a chance to observe, in the aftermath of

> ...modern imperialism, language alone cannot be the definer of a literature. A people must share common cultural and historical experiences, a value system, and aspirations, which condition their responses to reality. These considerations bear a distinctive imprint on their literature.

In many ways, however, modern African literature is a blending of traditional African "literary" techniques and borrowed European writing styles. Thus, the works of most of the best known African writers such as Chinua Achebe, Wole Soynka, and Ngugi wa Thiongo, have effectively combined the two worlds to bring out something which is simultaneously distinctively new and reflective of modern Africa.

Most African countries became independent between 1957 and 1963. Following the euphoria of independence, however, Africans realized that most of their rulers were politically corrupt and incompetent and generally failed to meet the expectations of their people. Embezzlement of government funds, ethnic favoritism, nepotism, and the rulers' dictatorial tendencies led to the African writers' preoccupation with expressing their views through biting satire. Ayi Kwei Armah's *The Beautyful Ones Are Not Yet Born*, Soyinka's *The Interpreters*, Achebe's *Man of the People*, and Ngugi's *Petals of Blood* reflect this period of promise, on the one hand, and disappointment, on the other.

The 1970s and later years witnessed a shift from cultural and political issues to socio-economic concerns among most African writers. With African economies on the downturn since the global oil crisis of 1973, a new breed of African writers, more radical in perspective, began writing about the conditions of the common people. Thus, the poor, the underprivileged, and the socially marginalized became the focus of poetry, fiction, and drama. As Ojaide noted (1990), what is said of the new poetry is true of all the genres in contemporary African literature, for:

> Contemporary African poetry is marked by a shift from culture, nature, individualism and lyricism of the late 1950s and the early 1960s to the national

socio-economic, political and class awareness of the 1970s and 1980s....There is movement away from Western modernist influences of fragmentation, allusiveness and difficulty to the traditional African oratorical clarity and simplicity. The poetry is gradually "decolonized" in the shedding of the poetical in diction and syntax. There is also movement from the private self, the individualistic and the universal to the public and socially relevant. This by itself is movement from a non-political conservative stance to a radical ideological posture. There is a new nation-oriented, audience-conscious rhetorical and didactic poetry.

The best-known works which represent the new direction of African literature include Festus Iyayi's novel *Violence*, Femi Osofisan's *Morountodun and Other Plays*, Jared Angira's poems *Cascades*, Niyi Osundare's poems in *The Eye of the Earth*, and Tanure Ojaide's *The Fate of Vultures and Other Poems*. It is clear, therefore, that, as elsewhere, African literary writing reflects the period of history and the stage of development in which the people find themselves. Within such a context, although modern African literature is written in foreign languages, it strongly mirrors traditional indigenous culture and is "marked by teaching and satire." Since the writer in Africa has been nurtured in a communalistic society (one which gives prominence to the community rather than the individual, where sharing is more cherished than owning and enjoying property privately), African literature is very socialized.

From the mid-1990s there appears to be a resurgence of African literary creativity across the continent. Many prize-winning and other great works have raised the profile of the African novel. South Africa Zakes Mda has two of his novels—*Ways of Dying* and *The Redness of the Hearth*—highly praised. Similarly, the Ethiopian's *The God Who Begat a Jackal* is a novel of epic proportion. Moses Isegawa's *Abyssynian Chronicles* received high commendations. In West Africa, the Nigerian Chimamanda Ngozi Adichie's *Purple Hibiscus* and Sefi Atta's *Everything Good Will Come* have raised the profile of the African female writer. Yvonne Vera of Zimbabwe produced fine works before her untimely death in 2005.

Though fiction appears to have overshadowed both poetry and drama, the latter two genres are still vibrant. In the poetry, there is diversification of themes as never before. The times of racial/cultural conflicts have passed. The ideological edge of the 1980s seems to have waned and poets express an array of themes as seen in works as diverse as Uche Nduka, Reesom Haile, Lupenga Mphande, Chimalum Nwankwo, and Ogaga Ifowodo. There is emphasis on performance techniques and a balanced attention paid to form and content. There is a combination of public and private/individual experiences and taken from different perspectives that reflect the complexity of modern African experience.

This discussion could not be complete without mention of the expanding role of African women writers in modern literature. Long disadvantaged by European colonial preference for the education of males as well as the tendency of African societies to promote boys over girls, African women's writing is promising and will likely go beyond the current brand of feminism and focus on family problems such as male marital infidelity, wife-abuse, and male-female relationships, and forcefully embrace other themes based on women's rich experience and the woes and the positive qualities of their societies.

Indeed, at present, most women's writing seems generally caught up with domestic themes. Mariama Ba, Aminata Sow Fall, Flora Nwapa, Zainab Alkali,

Buchi Emecheta, and Ama Ata Aidoo, in one way or the other fall in this category, of course, with degrees of treatment of this major theme, ranging from the more vitriolic Emecheta and Mariama Ba to the more subtle but equally critical and poignant Fall and Nwapa. However, there is already a slow movement away from this penchant, exemplified by Kenyan writers Marjorie Oludhe Macgoye (in *Street Life*, 1978) and Grace Ogot (in *Land Without Thunder*, 1988), whose works in the short story and other forms reflect more general themes based on Kenyan society. Aidoo's *Our Sister Killjoy* and Abena Busia's *Testimonies of Exile*, for example, are moving in this new direction.

The future of African women's writing is bright in output and quality. However, worsening economies will affect publication outlets in scaled-down magazine and book media. As the African world realizes, more than ever before, women's and men's contributions are equally essential and women writers are rapidly occupying and will continue to occupy their due place in African written (and oral) literature.

Undoubtedly, African literature, both oral and written, has come a long way, to use a common expression. Nonetheless, African writers have yet to overcome several obstacles, from the constraints of the medium of expression (European languages) to denial of the freedom of expression by African rulers (several have been incarcerated), and from the paucity of publishing houses on the continent and their lack of adequate resources to the continued control of the field of literature by Western scholars.

Literary Trends in the English-Speaking Caribbean

Afro-Caribbean writers have, in modern times, produced some of the best literary works in English. Wilson Harris, George Lamming, Michael Anthony, Derek Walcott, and Edward Kamau Brathwaite, among others, have established themselves internationally as classic writers in their respective fields. Yet, what Bruce King said of Caribbean literature as a whole is true of Afro-Caribbean literature in English: "not until the early part of this century that authors of real ability began to appear." Thus Caribbean literature is relatively young and is basically "the product of a society descended from European landlords...African slaves, and indentured Indians." Unlike African literature, which has individual national characteristics—one speaks of Nigerian, Ghanaian, Malawian, and South African literature, for example—Caribbean literature is regional, the reason being that the island-states, generally tiny, have not been able to forge a literary identity of their own. The small output of each of the islands has also reinforced regional rather than national identity.

This section intends to bring out only the major features of Afro-Caribbean literature in English, especially those related to history, place, and people, and briefly outline its evolution from an imitative literature to one which has found its own regional identity. The history of the Caribbean is a complex one, but the experiences of the Afro-Caribbean islands are essentially the same, reflected vividly in their literature. As. G.R. Coulthard observes, they have all experienced European conquest and colonialism, exploitation, poverty, racism, and cultural subjugation, coupled with the extermination of Indians whose labor on sugar plantations and estates was replaced with that of Africans, before emancipation and independence during the nineteenth and twentieth centuries respectively.

From the time of the so-called discovery by Columbus, toward the end of the fifteenth century, through slavery and the arrival of East Indians, to the present "post-colonial" state, the Caribbean region has had a painful history. The multicultural nature of the place and the white-black relations in particular have caused what Wilson Harris (quoted in William Walsh, *Commonwealth Literature*) has described as a "victor-victim stasis."

Bruce King in *West Indian Literature* notes that in the 1950s and 1960s Caribbean literature reflected the "growing nationalism, hopes of a regional federation, feelings of anti-colonialism, and interest in local culture." Roger Mais and Martin Carter were examples. However, by the early 1970s, King tells us once again:

> Many writers had become involved in the debates concerning ideology, neo-colonialism, black consciousness, folk traditions and an African heritage which resulted from the failure of independence to bring into being social justice and authentic national culture.

The physical environment has been a strong factor in the literature of the Caribbean. The sense of place, which the island condition affirms, gives its literature a spatial setting which is uniquely concrete. Living in tiny islands in the Atlantic and heirs to the slave past, Afro-Caribbeans look to Africa for their roots, to their erstwhile European colonial metropolis for education, and to the United States for better economic opportunities. While they also look to themselves, especially to Cuba and Brazil for pride and inspiration, Afro-Caribbeans generally look outward for their identity.

Perched on volcanoes and coral reefs rising from the Atlantic, life on these islands is closely related to the sea. Whether it is the poetry of Derek Walcott, as in *The Castaway and Other Poems* (1965), *The Gulf* (1970), *Sea Grapes* (1976), *The Star-Apple Kingdom* (1979), *The Fortunate Traveller* (1981) and *Omeros* (1991), or his play *Dream on Monkey Mountain* (1970), sea imagery constantly recurs. Similarly, in Brathwaite's *The Arrivants* and George Lamming's *In the Castle of My Skin*, the physical environment is an important factor. Images of islands, the sea and water, fish, plants, and occupations, such as fishing and sailing, are common. Fiction, in particular, has a picturesque quality, as characters move from place to place.

As elsewhere in the world, Afro-Caribbean literature is a reflection of the people and their lifestyles. The small size of each of the island-nations provides few resources. Tourism brings in some capital, but the people here are generally poor. Thus, emigration, necessarily a common phenomenon, is also reflected in the literature. Whether working in the building of the Panama Canal or in North America and Europe, Afro-Caribbeans have expatriated themselves considerably. With Claude McKay, George Lamming, Edward Brathwaite, Paule Marshall, and John Berry, among many others, one can understand why the theme of exile is common in local literature. As Walsh puts it, "in many ways the literature of the West Indies is, with notable exceptions, an expatriate literature." In Lamming's *In the Castle of My Skin*, the young boys look to America. In *The Arrivants*, Brathwaite writes of blacks of the region leaving for the United States, Canada, Britain, and Switzerland where they face racism and hostility. Though Samuel Selvon is of Indian origin, his black characters in *The Lonely Londoners* have emigrated to London in search of economic opportunities.

The migration of men for economic reasons has compelled Afro-Caribbean women to stay at home and take care of the children. This condition, together with the resilient practices of the slave days, has created a matriarchal social structure in the region. In recent years, women writers, in particular Grace Nichols, Michelle Cliff, and Lorna Goodison have been addressing this issue in their poems. In Lamming's *In the Castle of My Skin* and Michael Anthony's *The Year In San Fernando* mothers are more visible and dominant in the upbringing of children than fathers, who tend to travel abroad and make money to send home to their families. This persistent absence of men from home explains in part the abundance of novels with themes of childhood. *In the Castle of My Skin* and *The Year in San Fernando* are good examples of novels expounding this theme. Indeed, the black people of the Caribbean and their lifestyle have always formed the core material for the regional literature. History and environment, therefore, act themselves out in the people's way of life. Walsh appropriately comments that:

> The crackling life of the people, their nimbleness of wit, their great and disillusioned tolerance, their response to rhythm, their riddling uncertainties, and the one splendid instrument they developed for ordering a sad, comic, muddled universe, the language, all inform and shape the fiction of such West Indian novelists as George Lamming himself, Andrew Salkey, and Samuel Selvon.

In general, writers have attempted to capture the Afro-Caribbean reality in their works by portraying, for example, the folk-peasant life with its poverty, superstitions, love of cricket, and color discrimination. Brathwaite encompasses the tourism, calypso music, rum, emigrants, and the patois, which are significant features of Afro-Caribbean life. While Walcott treats the poor folk theme in his *Dream on Monkey Mountain,* where the sick and poor are exploited by Makak's men, George Lamming, Michael Anthony, and Samuel Selvon depict the poor peasants in their novels.

Closely related to the folk theme in Afro-Caribbean literature in English is the use of the Creole dialect. Arising from the multiplicity of peoples from different parts of the world with their own cultures and languages, the masses of the Caribbean have tried to survive in this cultural melee by developing a dialect in English and French which is a conglomeration of their ethnic origins in Africa, together with absorptions from languages of their new neighbors. With their indigenous African languages suppressed by the white masters in slave times, Africans had to use English, but, in Ashcroft's words, "found that psychic survival depended on their facility for a kind of double entendre." Creole is a product of a mixture of African languages, English, French, Portuguese, and Spanish. Brathwaite, Walcott, Lamming, Selvon, and others use Creole or patois in their literary work to reflect the true conditions of the peasants, the poor, and the common people.

Two major cultural trends which have caused much debate are also reflected in Afro-Caribbean literature and are linked to the compulsive quest for identity among the Afro-Caribbeans. One trend affirms African culture, as in the works of Edward Kamau Brathwaite, and the other, expounded by both Wilson Harris and Derek Walcott, portrays a hybrid Caribbean culture. The common themes of alienation and uprootedness arise from the slave origins of Afro-Caribbeans, who were forcibly brought to a new environment. Along with assuming an identity which gives meaning to their lives, many Afro-Caribbeans also wish to live an African cultural lifestyle.

Thus, Brathwaite of Barbados, who lived among the Akan people in Ghana, West Africa, for some eight years, preaches immersion in traditional African ways. Like most Africans, he attempts to forge a relationship between the individual and the spiritual world of the community through African symbols and images of masks and drums. He likewise uses African myths, legends, music, language, and ritualistic patterns. It is for his acceptance of Africa that he is identified with the mother continent and, in King's view, he "is perhaps the finest poet in English to express the 'black consciousness' of the sixties and seventies through sophisticated literary techniques."

Taking a different position is the poet and dramatist Derek Walcott, who, perhaps because he is a mulatto, expounds a Caribbean identity, a multicultural potpourri made up of the different races and cultures of the region. In Walcott's poetry, the African and the European are brought together. As Bill Ashcroft and others in their study of the post-colonial era put it,

> The present-day population of the West Indies consists of a variety of racial groups all more or less in ancestral exile, and all still subject to the hegemonic pressures of their former European owners, and, more recently, to that exercised in the region by the USA.

The reality of this "cultural heterogeneity," as Ashcroft adds, has made black writers like Wilson Harris and Derek Walcott to accept "cross-culturality, Creolization, hybridization, and catalysis" as the Caribbean historical reality.

No matter the writer's individual choice, the "African theme" appears frequently in the literature. Walcott's *Dream on Monkey Mountain* deals copiously with the identity issue which involves, in its exaggerated way, a return to Africa. In the play, the protagonist—Makak—looks toward going back to Africa, but, since he cannot cross the ocean on his own, he goes home. Home in Afro-Caribbean literature is both Africa and the Caribbean.

Summary

With the writer in modern-day Africa assuming the role of the conscience of his or her society, many works of African literature satirize the corruption and incompetence of modern governments, reminding readers and the entire society of the high cultural ethos that must be upheld. Because the literature is functional, modern African literature is the repository of the cultural life of the people and is a major source of education for the young everywhere as well as many urban people who have lost touch with their roots. Consequently, African writers consider themselves to be the cultural standard-bearers of their people, and use the medium of literature to assert and preserve "cultural independence."

Oral and written African literatures have flourished simultaneously on the continent. Despite the fact that the modern literature is written, the contemporary writer is carrying out the timeless mission of the oral artist of defending the cultural ethos of the people. Within this context, therefore, modern African literature informed by African culture is utilitarian, more socialized than based on individual psychology; it is community-oriented, didactic, and ethically and morally instructive; it is mystical, land-based, and rich in folkloric forms and rhythms; and it is peculiar as a linguistic mode. On another important level, modern African literature is a reflection of the profound reality of the African people. Even when written in foreign-derived languages which are now extra-territorial, as is the case with English, African literature is richer for its cultural uniqueness.

Unfortunately, the problems facing African writers are still many. Although African writers have excelled in their fields and have mastered the former colonial languages, both the European and indigenous African languages limit their ability to express themselves comfortably and reach the widest audience possible respectively. The restraints on the freedom of expression and the press in most African countries, on the one hand, present a dilemma for them: they are constantly threatened if they bring out the truth in whatever genre they might be writing. This dilemma is compounded, on the other hand, by the fact that the field of literature is still controlled by Western scholars who also exercise control over the publishing houses.

Afro-Caribbean literature in English, on the other hand, is relatively young. Recently, however, new significant voices like Andrew Salkey, Tony McNeil, Grace Nichols, and Lorna Goodison have appeared. Women writers, including Michelle Cliff, Audre Lorde, Grace Nichols, and Lorna Goodison are also becoming more visible. New anthologies and individual works of poetry and fiction in the West Indies itself, the United States, and Britain, put out by such publishers as Heinemann and Longman, presage a vigorous literary future which will continue to reflect the history, the place, and the people of the Caribbean. Expatriation, loneliness, and longing for home, the quest for self-identity, the attention by mainly middle-class writers to the poor, and the attempt to capture African roots to enhance the Caribbean reality will continue to appear as common themes, making Caribbean literature unique. Writers such as Harris, Brathwaite, and Walcott have achieved worldwide renown in their field. Walcott won the Nobel Prize for Literature in 1992. However, their pan-African links become clear when their work is compared with that of Africans and African Americans. In short, Afro-Caribbean literature in English, which is a part of the black literary heritage, is deeply rooted in and passionately expresses the condition of black Caribbeans in vivid, concrete images, and in diversified artistic forms.

Study Questions and Activities

1. How has the African writer reflected the realities of the community over the centuries?
2. Compare and contrast African oral literature and written literature on the continent.
3. Do research on three African writers who write in English and French and outline their major themes from the 1960s to the present.
4. Do further reading on Negritude, define it, and determine the major reason why it has been downplayed by some scholars.

5. Discuss one Afro-Caribbean writer whose work has dealt with the African origin of the Caribbean people.
6. What factors have influenced Afro-Caribbean literature to date?
7. How has Afro-Caribbean literature reflected the Caribbean experience?

References

Chinua Achebe. A Man of the People. London: Heinemann, 1966.
———. Things Fall Apart. London: Heinemann, 1958.
Michael Anthony. The Year in San Fernando. London: Longman, 1953.
Jared Angira. Cascades. Burnt Mill, Harlow: Longman, 1979.
Kwei Ayi Armah. The Beautiful Ones Are Not Yet Born. London: Heinemann, 1975.
Bill Ashcroft, with Gareth Griffiths and Helen Tiffin. The Empire Writes Back: Theory and Practice in Post-Colonial Literatures. London: Routledge, 1989.
Bill Ashcroft and others, eds. The Post-Colonial Studies Reader. London and New York: Routledge, 1995.
Edward Kamau Brathwaite. The Arrivants. London: Oxford University Press, 1973.
Laurence A. Breiner. An Introduction to West Indian Poetry. Cambridge, UK & New York: Cambridge UP, 1998.
Joyce Cary. Mister Johnson. New York: Time, Inc., 1962.
Mbye B. Cham. Ex-Iles: Essays on Caribbean Cinema. Trenton, NJ: Africa World Press,
Patrick Chamoisseau. Texaco. New York: Pantheon Books, 1997.
Chinweizu, Onwuchekwu Jamie and Ihechukwu Madubuike. Toward the Decolonization of African Literature, vol. I. Enugu: Fourth Dimension, 1980.
Mary Conde and Thorunn Lonsdale, eds. Caribbean Women Writers: Fiction in English. New York: St. Martin's Press, 1999.
Joseph Conrad. Heart of Darkness. New York: Norton, 1971.
O.R. Dathorne. African Literature in the Twentieth Century. London: Heinemann, 1975.
Carole Boyce Davis and Elaine Fido, eds. Out of the Kumbla: Caribbean Women and Literature. Trenton, NJ: Africa World Press, 1990.
Romanus Egudu. The Life of Olaudah Equiano. Burnt Mill, Harlow: Longman, 1970.
John Figueroa (ed.). Caribbean Voices. Washington: R.B. & Luce Co,, 1973.
Ruth Finnegan. Oral Literature in Africa. Nairobi: Oxford University Press, 1976.
C.L. Innes and Bernth Lindfors (eds.). Critical Perspectives on Chinua Achebe. London: Heinemann, 1979.
Abiola Irele. The African Experience in Literature and Ideology. London: Heinemann, 1981.
———. The African Imagination: Literature in Africa and the Black Diaspora. New York: Oxford University Press. 2001.
Festus Iyayi. Violence. Burnt Mill, Harlow: Longman, 1979.
Janheinz Jahn. A History of Neo-African Literature. London: Faber and Faber, 1968.
Cheik Hamidou Kane. Ambiguous Adventure. New York: Farrar, Strauss and Giroux, 1954.
Bruce King (ed.). West Indian Literature. Hamden, CT: Archon Books, 1979.

George Lamming. *In the Castle of My Skin*. London: Longman, 1953.

Camara Laye. *The African Child*. New York: Walker and Co., 1962.

Tanure Ojaide. "African Literature and Cultural Identity." *African Studies Review*, 1992.

———. *The Fate of Vultures and Other Poems*. Lagos: Malthouse, 1990.

———. *Poetic Imagination in Black Africa*. Unpublished Manuscript, 1990.

Femi Osofisan. *Morountodun and Other Plays*. Burnt Mill, Harlow: Longman, 1984.

Niyi Osundare. *The Eye of the Earth*. Ibadan: Heinemann Nigeria, 1986.

Kirsten Holst Peterson and Anna Rutherford, eds. *A Double Colonization*. Denmark: Dangaroo Press, 1986.

Kenneth Ramchand. *The West Indian Novel and its Background*. London: Heinemann, 1983.

Andrew Salkey. *Breaklight: The Poetry of the Caribbean*. Garden City, NY: Anchor/Doubleday, 1973.

Samuel Selvon. *The Lonely Londoner*. London: Longman, 1956.

Wole Soyinka. *The Interpreters*. London: Heinemann, 1965.

Henry Schwarz and Sangeeta Ray. *A Companion to Postcolonial Studies*. London: Blackwell Publishedrs, .

Ngugi wa Thiongo. *Petals of Blood*. London: Heinemann, 1977.

———. *Weep Not Child*. London: Heinemann, 1964.

Derek Walcott. *Collected Poems: 1948–1984*. New York: Farrar, Straus & Giroux, 1986.

———. *Dream on Monkey Mountain*. New York: Farrar, Straus & Giroux, 1970.

———. *Omeros*. New York: Farrar, Straus & Giroux, 1990.

William Walsh. *Commonwealth Literature*. London: Oxford University Press, 1973.

18

African American Literature: A Survey

Trudier Harris

Introduction

In order to understand African American literature, it is first necessary to understand the roles that the oral culture and the slave narrative had in its formation. This chapter examines those traditions in relation to the written literature and surveys the development of each genre (poetry, fiction, drama). Issues central to the literature begin with the role of the African American writer in relation to his or her community. Should a literate black individual devote a career to trying to improve the condition of the group, or should that person feel free to write out of individual desires and wishes?

This intersection of politics and art dominated discussions of African American literature well into the twentieth century. Issues include the representation of black characters: Should they always be complimentary or should they be realistic, even when they run the risk of damaging the group socially? In what language should literature be composed—black English or standard English? What of nationalism (the Black Aesthetic)? Who should teach the literature? African Americans? White Americans? Others? Where it should be taught? English Departments? Black Studies Departments? Others? To whom should black writers address their works? The problem of ghettoizing the African American creative effort was also raised in the twentieth century; black writers complained that critics discussed them only in connection with other black writers, not with the larger traditions of literary creativity. And today, the issue of the relevance of current critical theories to discussions of African American literature dominate the energies of many scholars.

Major terms and concepts: The role of writers in their communities, influences on literary creativity, racism, slavery, slave narratives, folklore, oral tradition, Harlem Renaissance, protest literature, Black Aesthetic, Black Arts Movement.

Oral Tradition and Slave Narrative

A study of African American literature naturally begins with the African American oral tradition and with the slave narrative. Africans brought to the United States and enslaved were obviously not brought here to produce poems, plays, short stories, and novels. Nor were they here with any consideration of perpetuating their own cultural traditions. Thus thrown into circumstances where their bodies were emphasized over their minds, and where the usual bonds of language were absent, enslaved Africans adapted the English language and used it to communicate as best they could. Through this hybrid, they passed on what they remembered of their own cultures, combined it with what they witnessed on new soil, or created something totally new. What they communicated in the patterned forms known as folklore reflected the best of the values they wished to pass on.

Their narratives, legends, jokes, songs, rhymes, and sayings recorded a world in which they reacted to their circumstances as an enslaved group and in which they passed on imaginative ways on interacting within that world. Early tales reveal, for example, the discrepancies in the economic conditions of slaves and masters. In 1853 in *Clotel; or, The President's Daughter*, the first novel by an African American, William Wells Brown recorded one of the earliest documented folk rhymes:

> The big bee flies high,
> The little bee make the honey;
> The black folks makes the cotton
> And the white folks gets the money.

It captures the thematic essence of the protest tradition that Richard Wright and other writers of the twentieth century would advocate so fervently. In a land so rich in resources and which professed to believe so strongly in democracy, it was unconscionable, these folk artists and literary writers would argue, for an entire group of people to be excluded from those resources, especially when those individuals had played a key role in the building of the country.

The song tradition, whether in spirituals, blues, or Gospel, similarly portrayed a people on the lower echelon of the social stratum who hoped for resolution of their plight in the afterlife if not in this world. Spirituals frequently suggested being done with "de troubles of the world" and going home to live with Jesus. While writers may not have advocated a literal interpretation of that tradition, the general tenet of the need for rectification of social conditions became a common theme in the literature. Music as an expression of the ability to deal with the troubles of the world similarly informs the literature, whether it is a Richard Wright character soothing her worries by singing in a short story like "Bright and Morning Star" (1938) or a character in James Baldwin's "Sonny's Blues" (1964) similarly singing to ease the burden of bearing her troubles. Music captured the general *weltschmerz* (pessimism at the state of the world; literally, "world pain") of being African and American in a country where simply being American was preferable.

Not only were the themes common to the written literature passed on in the oral tradition, but the structures as well. In the 1920s, Langston Hughes, in addition to adapting the themes of the blues, would adapt the AAB rhyme scheme of the genre as one of his primary literary structures. Thus compositions such as the following one from his "Miss Blues'es Child" became common:

> If the blues would let me,
> Lord knows I would smile.
> If the blues would let me,
> I would smile, smile, smile.
> Instead of that I'm cryin'—
> I must be Miss Blues'es child.

In addition to the blues, folk narratives also provided the shaping force for literary creativity. The structure of Ralph Ellison's *Invisible Man* (1952) is based on an African American folktale.

Numerous writers drew upon the African American folk tradition for characters and concepts. "Badman" heroes, for example, pervade the literature from Charles W. Chesnutt's Josh Green in *The Marrow of Tradition* (1901) to Appalachee Red in Raymond Andrews's *Appalachee Red* (1978). Conjure women and other healers modeled on characters from the folk tradition make their debut in Brown's *Clotel*, continue through Chesnutt's *The Conjure Woman* (1899), get transformed in Alice Walker's "The Revenge of Hannah Kemhuff" (1970), and emerge with true supernatural powers in Toni Morrison's *Beloved* (1987) as well as in Gloria Naylor's *Mama Day* (1988). Other writers and works that draw upon this tradition of characterization include Charles R. Johnson, *Faith and the Good Thing* (1974); Toni Cade Bambara, *The Salt Eaters* (1980); and Tina McElroy Ansa, *Baby of the Family* (1989). Traveling bluesmen are the subject of Langston Hughes's *Not Without Laughter* (1930) and Albert Murray's *Train Whistle Guitar* (1974). The man-of-words tradition, as exemplified in Muhammad Ali's rhymes such as "Float like a butterfly/sting like a bee/That's why they call me/Muhammed Ali," joins the preaching tradition as the focus of such works as Ellison's *Invisible Man* (1952), where mastery of language is the measure of reputation and effectiveness in the society. Other writers simply saturate their works with an aura of the folk tradition; these include Zora Neale Hurston, *Their Eyes Were Watching God* (1937), Ernest Gaines, *The Autobiography of Miss Jane Pittman* (1974), and Charles R. Johnson, *Middle Passage* (1990).

The slave narrative tradition, in which the protagonist documents (in the first person) his or her movement from slavery to freedom and from South to North, defines the autobiographical tradition that so informs the literature as well as the archetypal pattern of movement for literary characters, that is, from the South to the North. Perhaps the most exemplary of the slave narratives is Frederick Douglass's *Narrative of the Life of Frederick Douglass: An American Slave, Written by Himself* (1845), though Harriet Wilson's *Our Nig* (1859) and Harriet Jacobs's *Incidents in the Life of A Slave Girl* (1860) have gained prominence in recent years. Although it is technically classified as the first novel written by an African American woman, Wilson's *Our Nig* nonetheless documents the atrocities of enslavement; since the action is set in the Boston area, the book is especially interesting for providing a look at bondage on other than southern soil.

Douglass and Jacobs fit the tradition of documenting atrocities during slavery, the process by which they learned to read and write, how they became dissatisfied with their dehumanizing conditions, the aid they enlisted in planning and executing escapes, and the free existences that awaited them on northern soil. Douglass's work is as much literary as it is historical, for he is an effective storyteller who molds characters and circumstances to best advantage in making his points about slavery. He is also a master of figurative language usually identified with poetry and other consciously created imaginative works. Jacobs's narrative is particularly important for documenting the creation of a female self against the backdrop of sexual abuses during slavery. It, like Douglass's narrative, also recounts the process of literary creation, the assistance these early writers received in structuring their works and in getting them published.

The major theme of slave narratives, therefore, found a counterpart in the consciously created literary works. The progression from slavery or restriction (the South) to freedom and opportunity (the North) provides a prevailing pattern in the literature. The Great Migration that led to the tripling and quadrupling of African American populations in various northern cities between 1900 and 1930 illustrates the historical pattern as well. Writers who have their characters leave the South for presumed opportunities in the North include Wright in "Big Boy Leaves Home" (1938); Ellison in *Invisible Man* (1952); John Oliver Killens in *Youngblood* (1954), and a host of others.

Folklore and slave narratives, therefore, addressed the basic condition of black existence in the United States, of the discrepancy between a theoretical democracy and the reality of the failure of democratic principles. As the genres of the written tradition developed, they in turn were conceptualized, especially in the early years of development, with the larger issues of black life and culture in mind. Brown's *Clotel*, for example, is as much a treatise against slavery as it is a novel; it includes advertisements for runaways, accounts of dogs chasing slaves, abolitionist discussions, and characters who espouse one side of the slavery issue or the other. When Brown completed *The Escape; or, A Leap for Freedom* in 1858, that first drama by an African American also found its subject in slavery. Frances Ellen Watkins Harper, who published *Poems on Miscellaneous Subjects* in 1854, became a popular abolitionist lecturer, as did Brown. Her poems, such as "Bury Me in a Free Land" and "The Mother," depict the consequences of slavery on the family life of African Americans.

African American Poetry

Although the poetry in the latter part of the nineteenth century would be engaged with political issues, that was less true of the first verses composed by African Americans. Lucy Terry, who is credited with composing the first poem by an African American in 1746, centered her composition upon an Indian raid in Deerfield, Massachusetts. As a slave in a Deerfield home, she naturally identified more with the whites than with the "savage" Indians; the poem, "Bars Fight," reflects her identification. It was not published, however, until 1895. The first African American poet to publish a work in the United States was Jupiter Hammon, whose broadside entitled *An Evening Thought: Salvation by Christ, with Penitential Cries*, appeared on Christmas day in 1760. Phillis Wheatley, perhaps the best known of the early poets, published her *Poems on Various Subjects, Religious and Moral* in 1773. Brought as a child to the United States, Phillis grew up learning English and being encouraged to compose poetry in the Wheatley house in Boston. Her poems treat subjects as diverse as Africans being brought to America, the antics of students at Harvard, the military successes of George Washington, and the reception she received from the Countess of Huntington when she traveled to England. George Moses Horton, a slave poet in the country near Chapel Hill, North Carolina, put his talents to use in the service of the students at the University of North Carolina. He composed love poems and other sentiments at their requests. His first volume, *The Hope of Liberty*, appeared in 1829; a second volume, *The Poetical Works of George M. Horton, The Colored Bard of North Carolina*, appeared in 1845, the same year as Douglass's narrative.

It was Frances Harper, however, who retained the reputation as America's best-known African American poet until Paul Laurence Dunbar's reputation overshadowed hers in the last few years of the nineteenth century. Dunbar, born in Dayton, Ohio, in 1872, began publishing poems in 1893, when his *Oak and Ivy* appeared. A combination of standard English and dialect poems, the volume was well received and was followed thereafter by *Majors and Minors* (1896), *Lyrics of Lowly Life* (1896), and a host of others. He also wrote novels, the most famous of which is *The Sport of the Gods* (1902), which appeared just four years before his death in 1906.

African American poetry in the twentieth century has varied widely. It began with the dialect tradition that Dunbar institutionalized, the remnants of which were around well into the Harlem Renaissance of the 1920s. James Weldon Johnson, whom Dunbar knew well, included dialect poems such as "Sence You Went Away" in his first compositions at the turn of the century, yet he recognized the limitations of the medium. James David Corrothers and James Whitfield Campbell also wrote dialect poetry. The tradition finally led Johnson to complain in the introduction to *The Book of American Negro Poetry* (1922), which he edited, that dialect had "but two full stops, humor and pathos." He longed for the day when African American poets would be able to represent the complexity of black life and experience without resorting to "the mere mutilation of English spelling and pronunciation."

Certainly Langston Hughes's blues poetry in the 1920s was a move in a new direction, as was the folk poetry of Sterling Brown in the 1930s. Although Brown resorted to folk patterns of speech in *Southern Road* (1932), he did not rely on caricature and phonetic distortion. His characters, like those of Hughes in poems such as "Mother to Son," were able to retain a certain dignity and garner the respect of readers. Brown's successes in being more expansive in capturing the nuances of black language and life led Johnson to write a brief introduction to *Southern Road*. Another trend in poetry during the Harlem Renaissance was reflected in the works of Claude McKay, perhaps one of the most militant voices of the era. McKay's militancy derives not only from the sentiments he expresses but from his transformation of the traditional forms in which he writes. Using the Shakespearean sonnet, a form usually reserved for lofty sentiments of love, McKay documented the failures of democracy, painted the violence of societally-sanctioned crimes such as lynching, and called upon African Americans to take up arms against all who would seek to destroy them. In his signature poem, "If We Must Die," he urges oppressed people to "meet the common foe" and to "deal one deathblow!" for the thousand blows of the enemy. He concludes the poem with this couplet: "Like men we'll face the murderous, cowardly pack,/Pressed to the wall, dying, but fighting back!" His poetry certainly did not distort African American experience in the way that Johnson believed dialect poetry did.

Perhaps Johnson's call for a different kind of poetry was more fully realized in the academic verses of Robert Hayden and Gwendolyn Brooks in the 1940s. These poets, steeped in the western traditions of verse, structure, composition, and density of language, were judged to be successful by the more literary poetic establishments in the country. Hayden published *Heart-Shape in the Dust* in 1940, which picks up some of the themes of the writers of the Harlem Renaissance, especially questions of identity. By 1948 and his publication of *The Lion and the Archer*, however, he had dramatically altered his style to reflect the influence of such poets as Gerald Manley Hopkins, Stephen Spender, C. Day Lewis, and Rainer Maria Rilke; the result was six poems generally judged to be "baroque" in structure and execution. These include "A Ballad of Remembrance" and "Homage to the Empress of the Blues" (Bessie Smith). A later poem, "Middle Passage," which describes the transportation of Africans to the West Indies and other parts of the New World for purposes of enslavement, is one of the most anthologized of Hayden's works. Like Hayden, Brooks preferred the density and structure of poetry that reflected white western influences upon her. Her subjects are certainly those of African American life and experience, but they are shrouded in styles that appear at times to be antithetical to the very experiences she records. Her first volume, *A Street in Bronzeville* (1945), focuses on black people on the South side of Chicago and recounts occurrences in their everyday lives; narrative is the major technique she employs. She won the Pulitzer Prize for *Annie Allen* (1949), which is loosely based on the *Aeneid*; it follows a young girl growing up in a Chicago tenement. Although the volume was judged to be difficult and self conscious, it nonetheless received more praise than not.

The New Black Aesthetic movement of the 1960s brought a poetic revolution in its wake. It introduced a group of poets who are still publishing today. Nikki Giovanni, Haki Madhubuti (formerly Don L. Lee), Amiri Baraka (formerly LeRoi Jones), Sonia Sanchez, and others fashioned the poets' response to social change during this period. Advocating a nationalistic approach to literature, they called upon black people to take an active role in freeing themselves from a racist, undemocratic society. They also provided the path by which blacks were to arrive at being a nation of African Americans. They were to change their hair and clothing styles, their patterns of behavior, and even their names; it became the age of dashikis and afros. The nationalistic bent was reflected in the language of the poetry itself; it attempted to imitate speech patterns and colloquialisms of common black folk, and it consciously sought to dissociate itself with the conventions of western poetry. New words were created ("blkpoets," "nationbuilding," "u," "bes"), and structures were designed to resemble African American cultural forms such as jazz, not traditional sonnets or free verse.

There were still poets during this period who continued in the more traditional veins, including Robert Hayden and Michael Harper. Like Madhubuti and others, however, Harper did give attention to African American themes and structures, including adapting stanzaic forms based on compositions by jazz great John Coltrane. The difference is that Harper did not alter his poetry as radically as did some of the younger poets; nor was he as consciously militant. Brooks joined the younger poets in reevaluating her role in relation to the black community as well as in modifying her stanzaic forms. She published several small volumes for children in the 1960s and 1970s and wrote a poem on the occasion of Harold Washington being elected major of Chicago, a first for a black politician.

Brooks's success in winning the Pulitzer Prize in 1950 for *Annie Allen* (1949) was matched in the mid-1980s when newcomer Rita Dove won the Pulitzer Prize for her volume, *Thomas and Beulah* (1986). Focusing on the relationship between a man and his wife over an extended period of time, the volume alternates voices between Thomas and Beulah, allowing them to recount and record their own perceptions. The collection illustrated that less self-conscious structures and themes in poetry could be equally appealing to a panel of judges for one of the most prestigious literary prizes currently available.

African American Fiction and Drama

Fiction moved from its dual function as slave narrative and literature in the mid-nineteenth century, to romance and imitation of white writers in the late nineteenth century, to the autobiographical mode and more consciously designed protest novels in the twentieth century. Chesnutt explored the color problem in *The House Behind the Cedars* (1900), a novel focusing on a light-skinned black woman whose brief attempt to pass for white ends in disaster. He also reflects social concerns in *The Marrow of Tradition* (1901), a novel about the Wilmington, North Carolina, riot of 1898. On that occasion, black people who tried to vote were attacked and many of them killed by the whites who were intent upon preserving white supremacy.

The influence of the slave narrative upon the novel form can be seen in the autobiographical mode of *The Autobiography of An Ex-Colored Man* (1912), which James Weldon Johnson published anonymously. Johnson executed the first-person narrative device so well that readers believed the novel was indeed the historical life story of its author. The novel follows the life of a talented mulatto musician who is caught between the opportunities his talent offers and the limitations his classification as a Negro ultimately brings. He finally opts to deny his black ancestry and "pass" for white. It was only when Johnson acknowledged authorship of the book in 1927 that tales of its authenticity abated. Indeed, Johnson recounted attending a party prior to 1927 in which one of the guests "confided" to the gathering that he was the author of *The Autobiography of An Ex-Colored Man*.

Fiction published by writers of the Harlem Renaissance ranged from Jean Toomer's *Cane* (1923), which (to a degree) romanticizes black life in Georgia, to Claude McKay's *Home to Harlem* (1929), an account of the adventures of a fun-loving world traveler. It also included the genteel tradition of fiction writing represented by Nella Larsen's *Quicksand* (1928) and *Passing* (1929), and Jessie Fauset's *Plum Bun* (1924). Fauset, who assisted W. E. B. DuBois in editing the *Crisis* magazine in which many of the Renaissance writers were published, held *salons* at her Harlem apartment at which invited guests were expected to hold conversations in French about the latest developments in literature or world affairs.

One problem with these early novels was that very seldom were African Americans represented realistically in them. Indeed, there was a general movement in the first three decades of the twentieth century that might be referred to as "the best foot forward" tradition; writers were encouraged to portray complimentary images of African Americans. Characters should be engaged in pursuits that were in keeping with the objectives of the larger society. Therefore, general principles of democracy were to be upheld and education was a goal to be valued, as were habits of morality and cleanliness. "Bad niggers," whether male or female, were best left out of the literature. The belief that such positive images were important led in 1926 to a forum in *Crisis* magazine. It was entitled "The Negro in Art: How Shall He Be Portrayed? A Symposium." The forum received responses from Sherwood Anderson, Benjamin Brawley, Charles W. Chesnutt, Countee Cullen, W. E. B. DuBois, Jessie Fauset, Langston Hughes, Georgia Douglas Johnson, Alfred A. Knopf, Sinclair Lewis, Vachel Lindsay, H. L. Mencken, Joel Spingarn, and Walter White.

Fictional portraits of African Americans began to be more realistic in the decade of the 1930s. Zora Neale Hurston depicted a black preacher in *Jonah's Gourd Vine* (1934) that any reader would recognize. Her portrait of Janie Crawford Logan Starks Killicks in *The Eyes Were Watching God* (1937) brought a new dimension in realism to portraits of African American female characters. Janie is a working class woman who prefers spiritual fulfillment to gentility. After two disastrous marriages, she finally finds happiness with an itinerant laborer who takes her to pick beans in the Florida muck. The novel does not raise large political issues, although the social issues of woman's place in the society and what sacrifices she must make to find personal happiness are certainly important ones.

Hurston's more individually focused issues gave way to the politics of Richard Wright, who dismissed her work because she did not write as consciously in the protest tradition as he would have expected. For Wright, any black author should use his or her pen to point out the hypocrisies in American democracy, how black people were ground under the heels of white privilege and prejudice. He began such depictions in his first collection of short stories, *Uncle Tom's Children*, which was published in 1938. Almost all the stories are violent, and at least two of them embrace the communist philosophy to which Wright was becoming attracted at this time; he believed that African Americans had a better chance of obtaining democracy in America through that philosophy. His stories document black people being lynched and shot, denied medical services or the sympathy that should attend them, beaten by mobs, and burned alive. The few who decide to fight back, such as Silas in "Long Black Song," only end up being killed more dramatically. However, in "Fire and Cloud," one of the stories that embraces communist philosophy, Reverend Taylor is able to gather white and black working-class people together to put pressure on a city government to provide food during the Depression. Before that possible hope, though, characters such as Big Boy in "Big Boy Leaves Home" and Mann in "Down by the Riverside" are simply buffeted by the misfortunes of the societies in which they live. They must either escape to the North or die in the attempt.

Wright's hard-hitting approach to fiction continued in 1940 with the publication of *Native Son*, his most famous work in the protest tradition. It posits that black men in America are so confined physically and psychologically that the fear they sometimes experience can drive them to kill almost instinctively. Bigger Thomas does just that when he is found in the bedroom of his white employer's daughter, whom he has helped there because she was in a drunken stupor. Smothering Mary Dalton to death gives him a feeling of horror, but also one of exhilaration, for it is the first time in his life that he has acted against the wishes of the white power structure.

Other novels from the forties that fit into the protest tradition include Chester Himes's *If He Hollers Let Him Go* (1945), about a black man forced to join the military or be sent to prison because he was accused of raping a white woman, and Ann Petry's *The Street* (1946), about a black woman who suffers the stings of poverty and sexual politics when she tries to rear her son alone in Harlem. Such literary voices did not portend a particularly inviting future for African Americans. It would be the next decade before writers could assert with authority that the promise of American democracy did indeed apply to African Americans.

That authoritative voice belonged to Ralph Ellison, who asserted in *Invisible Man* (1952) that blacks should "affirm the principles on which the country was founded"—even when the day-to-day execution of those principles seemed to leave them out of the great American experiment. His optimistic voice for the larger nationalist agenda led into the cultural nationalism that would inform the fiction of the 1960s, such as John A. Williams's *The Man Who Cried I Am* (1967), which asserts that blacks must fight as best they can against the forces of repression.

More focus on the black community tended to occupy fiction writers in the 1970s, which began with Toni Morrison's publication of *The Bluest Eye*. That novel indicts the entire society for judging little black girls by standards of beauty that are culturally antithetical to them, but it especially places the blame on unthinking, unfeeling members of the black middle class. The pattern of focusing on black communities continued in the 1980s with Toni Cade Bambara's *The Salt Eaters* (1980), Alice Walker's *The Color Purple* (1982), Terry McMillan's *Mama*(1987) and *Disappearing Acts* (1989), and Tina McElroy Ansa's *Baby of the Family* (1989).

The last couple of decades have also witnessed an outpouring of dramas by African Americans. The dramatic scene is a far cry from where it started in 1858 with Brown's *The Escape; or, A Leap for Freedom*. Brown's play was written to be read rather than produced; it was not until the musical comedy era of the 1880s and 1890s that black playwrights saw their works on the stage. One of the earliest such achievements was a collaboration between James Weldon Johnson and Paul Laurence Dunbar. They wrote music and lyrics for *Clorindy, or the Origin of the Cakewalk* (1898). In 1900 Dunbar collaborated with black composer Will Marion Cook in the production of *Uncle Eph's Christmas*.

The first three decades of the twentieth century did not see much development in traditional dramas by black Americans, although the musical comedy tradition was popular until well into the 1920s. The year 1920 saw the publication of Angelina Weld Grimké's *Rachel: A Play in Three Acts* (produced in 1916), but it would be well into the 1930s before a black writer completed a drama that would have a successful run on Broadway. That distinction belonged to Langston Hughes, whose *Mulatto*, a dramatic rewrite of his short story, "Father and Son," ran on Broadway from 1935 to 1936, as well as for an additional two years on tour.

In the 1930s and 1940s, several black theatre companies were formed; most of their productions, however, were reworkings of plays by continental and white American playwrights. Alice Childress, whose *Trouble in Mind* was optioned for Broadway in the mid-1950s, worked closely with one of these companies. Other plays by African Americans that were produced during this period include *St. Louis Woman* (1946), a collaboration by Arna Bontemps and Countee Cullen in which Bontemps's novel, *God Sends Sunday* (1931), was adapted for stage; Louis Peterson's *Take a Giant Step* (1953); and Hughes's *Simply Heavenly* (1957).

Perhaps the most dramatic event in the history of the production of plays by black Americans occurred in 1959, when Lorraine Hansberry's *A Raisin in the Sun* opened in Philadelphia. It was the first time, James Baldwin asserts, that black people truly recognized themselves on the American stage. Blacks flocked to see the play because they saw accurate reflections of themselves, and they recognized Hansberry as a witness to their blackness and their aspirations in American society. That event was followed in 1964 by LeRoi Jones's *Dutchman*, which, in its depiction of the sexual tempting of a black man by a white woman and her eventual killing of him, had an equally profound effect on the American theatre as well as on black viewing audiences. Playwrights such as Ossie Davis (*Purlie Victorius*, 1961), James Baldwin (*The Amen Corner*, 1965), Ed Bullins (*In the Wine Time*, 1968), and Charles Gordone all had plays produced in the very successful decade of the 1960s. Gordone became the first black playwright to win the Pulitzer Prize for drama, for his *No Place to Be Somebody* (1969).

The shocker for the next decade would be Ntozake Shange's *For Colored Girls Who Have Considered Suicide When the Rainbow is Enuf* (1976), which focused critical attention on the problematic relationships between black males and black females. In 1981, Charles Fuller's *A Soldier's Play* opened on Broadway; the next year it followed the path of *No Place to Be Somebody* by winning the Pulitzer Prize for drama. The most publicized dramatic successes of the 1980s belonged to August Wilson, whose *Fences*, the story of an embittered player from the Negro Baseball League, won the Pulitzer Prize for drama in 1987. His other works include *Ma Rainey's Black Bottom* (1986), *The Piano Lesson* (1987), and *Joe Turner's Come and Gone* (1988).

Summary

In recent years, there has been a reevaluation of what southern territory means in African American literature, and writers have set their works on that soil and allowed their characters to define themselves and their world in that previously restricting territory. Such writers and works include Toni Morrison's *Song of Solomon* (1977), in which a spoiled middle-class black Michiganer returns to Virginia to uncover the meaning of personal history and ancestry; Alice Walker's *The Color Purple* (1982), in which a black woman who has been abused physically and psychologically overcomes these debilitations to become an entrepreneur in Memphis; and Gloria Naylor's *Mama Day* (1988), in which a descendant of slaves controls not only her family's destiny but the very elements of the universe. For these writers, the South is no longer forbidden territory, no longer a place of death, but a place where African Americans can choose reasonably well under what circumstances they will live in the world.

Its roots in the oral tradition and in the African American slave narrative have enabled African American literature to come of age in the twentieth century. From a literature that made obeisances to white reading audiences, as was the case with Charles W. Chesnutt, it has grown to insist, as Toni Morrison does, that readers come to meet it wherever it starts and agree to go wherever it takes them. Forms that were initially rooted in politics, such as Frances Harper's lyrics, gave way to the mythologically sophisticated verses of poets such as Jay Wright. And dramas that were initially intended for living room consumption serve as the origins of works that have won several Pulitzer Prizes.

The publishing industry has kept pace with audiences for African American literature, and today novels, poems, and plays by black writers are available for use in courses in American Studies, African American Studies, Religious Studies, History, and Sociology, as well as in the traditional English Department classes. Readership has transcended languages and national boundaries; Morrison's works, for example, are available in German and Japanese, among other languages, and she won Italy's highest prize for a creative writer in 1990. Doctoral students in India, Spain, Germany, Japan, and the Netherlands routinely come to the United States to study with specialists in African American literature, and they regularly write dissertations on African American writers. From a creative effort with a purpose, African American literature has grown to be recognized internationally as a richly complex area of study that will sustain many generations of students, teachers, and scholars.

Study Questions and Activities

1. How has the portrayal of African American characters changed in literary works from the nineteenth to the twentieth centuries?
2. What are some of the influences of the African American oral tradition upon the literature?
3. What would have been the consequences for an African American writer who ignored the fact of his or her race during the nineteenth century?
4. What are the social, cultural, and political implications of writing in a language you grew up speaking as opposed to one you have been taught?
5. In what ways was the New Black Aesthetic movement purely literary? In what ways was it political?

References

William L. Andrews. *To Tell A Free Story: The First Century of Afro-American Autobiography, 1760–1865*. Urbana, IL: University of Illinois Press, 1986.

Houston A. Baker, Jr. *Blues, Ideology, and Afro-American Literature, A Vernacular Theory*. Chicago: University of Chicago Press, 1984.

Bernard Bell. *The Afro-American Novel and Its Tradition*. Amherst, MA: University of Massachusetts Press, 1987.

Tony Bolden. *Afro-Blue: Improvisations in African American Poetry and Culture*. Urbana: University of Illinois Press, 2004.

Hazel V. Carby. *Reconstructing Womanhood: The Emergence of the Afro-American Woman Novelist*. New York: Oxford University Press, 1987.

Barbara Christian. *Black Women Novelists: The Development of a Tradition, 1892–1976*. Westport, CT: Greenwood Press, 1980.

Joanne V. Gabbin (ed.). *Furious Flower: African American Poetry from the Black Arts Movement to the Present*. Charlottesville: University of Virginia Press, 2004.

Henry Louis Gates, Jr. *The Signifying Monkey: A Theory of Afro-American Literary Criticism*. New York: Oxford University Press, 1988.

Stephen Henderson. *Understanding the New Black Poetry: Black Speech and Black Music as Poetic References*. New York: William Morrow & Company, 1973.

James Weldon Johnson (ed.). *The Book of American Negro Poetry*. New York: Harcourt, Brace and World, 1922.

Lawrence Levine. *Black Culture and Black Consciousness: Afro-American Folk Thought From Slavery to Freedom*. New York: Oxford University Press, 1977.

Stacy I. Morgan. *Rethinking Social Realism: African American Art and Literature, 1930–1953*. Athens: University of Georgia Press, 2004.

Loften Mitchell. *Black Drama: The Story of the American Negro in the Theatre*. New York: Hawthorn Books, 1967.

Joan R. Sherman. *Invisible Poets: Afro-Americans of the Nineteenth Century*. Urbana, IL: University of Illinois Press, 1974.

Jean Wagner. *Black Poets of the United States: From Paul Laurence Dunbar to Langston Hughes*. Urbana, IL: University of Illinois Press, 1973.

19

Contributions in Science, Business, Film, and Sports

Mario Azevedo
Jeffrey Sammons

Introduction

It is crucial that the work of black American scientists be given its proper place in the history of the development of the United States of America, not only because it is fair, but also because it provides role models for young African Americans as well as young Africans on the continent. For example, on the continent, what most African youngsters know is that African Americans were enslaved and that they continue to be discriminated against. They have only a superficial knowledge of famous personalities such as Jesse Jackson, Michael Jackson, and Thurgood Marshall. The accomplishments of blacks in this country, most notably in the sciences, are generally unknown in Africa. In this country, both black and white students show an equally appalling ignorance of the contributions of black Americans, particularly in the hard sciences.

Following is a brief summary of the contributions of black American scientists who have had a significant impact in their fields and in American society.[1] For complete details, we refer the reader to the *Negro Almanac* (1989 edition), compiled and edited by Harry A. Ploski and James Williams, from which most of the following information comes. The remainder of the chapter is devoted to the role of African Americans in business, in the film industry, and in sports.

Major terms and concepts: business, competition, finance, entrepreneurship, stocks, bonds, blaxploitation, "action" movies, "set-asides," sport, discrimination, patriotism, Americanism, class, race, gender, culture, stereotypes, self-help, parallel institutions, social control, empowerment, resistance, economics, politics, education, character, pseudo-science, social Darwinism, and misplaced values.

---

1. The sections on science, business, and motion pictures were written by Mario Azevedo. Jeffrey Sammons authored the section on sports.

Patenting by African Americans

At present, patents by African Americans exceed 3,000 and are ever increasing. Following the enactment of the Fourteenth Amendment in 1867, African Americans were finally allowed to register their inventions with the government. Earlier, as Ploski and Williams note, African Americans could not have their inventions registered, because, "since slaves were not citizens they could not enter into contracts with their owners or the government." Thus, several works by African Americans before emancipation and the Fourteenth Amendment were either lost or were stolen by masters who claimed them as theirs. In the case of free blacks, some of their inventions were patented.

For example, in 1832, a slave, Augustus Jackson of Philadelphia, was credited with inventing the process of making ice cream but his invention was not patented, while Henry Blair's seed planter was patented in 1834, because he was a free man. Thereafter, patents by black Americans ballooned, as the following individuals, presented alphabetically (and not chronologically), illustrate. This method is also borrowed from Ploski and Williams, referred to above.

George Alcorn, with eight patents, has distinguished himself with his work on missiles, amino acids, planets, and molecular and atomic physics. Architect Archie Alexander (d. 1958) is remembered for his construction of a major plant for the University of Iowa, which required several tunnels under the Iowa River. Benjamin Banneker (d. 1806) is famous for being the first American to make a wood clock, for his astonishing knowledge of mathematics and the solar system, and for publishing his own almanac. Banneker was also one of the six surveyor-architects who laid the foundations for the nation's capital. Andrew Beard (d. 1910) is credited with the invention of the Jenny Coupler, an "automatic device which secured two [train] cars by merely bumping them together." Henry Blair (d. 1860), currently considered to be the first black inventor to secure a patent (in 1834 and 1836), developed two corn- and cotton-planting machines. Otis Boykin has invented electronic gadgets for computers, radios, television sets; "a control unit for artificial heart stimulators"; resistors for computers; a burglar-proof register; and a chemical air filter—just to mention a few. John A. Burr (a lawyer) invented a lawnmower in 1899. And the list goes on.

George Carruthers, a physicist, is well known for having made his own telescope at the age of ten, and for coming up with an ultraviolet camera/spectrograph for NASA. George Washington Carver (d. 1943) had three patents on cosmetics and paint beyond his hundreds of purposely non-patented inventions related to peanuts, corn, and sweet potatoes—all of which revolutionized the economies of Alabama and other southern states. Engineer David N. Crosthwaith, Jr. (d. 1976) patented the automatic water feeder, the automobile indicator, the thermostat-setting device, the vacuum-heating system, and the vacuum pump. Dr. Charles Drew, who died in a car accident in 1950, perfected the process of blood preservation, to the extent that the British government asked him to organize the first blood bank in Great Britain. His process saved thousands of lives in World War II.

Meredith Gourdine, a physicist, has contributed to the principles related to the conversion of gas to electricity, while chemist Henry A. Hill (d. 1977) is recognized for his research in polymer chemistry and "fabric flammability." Lloyd Augustus Hall has invented a method of "curing" salts for meat preservation and processing, and owns over 100 patents related to food and baked goods. William A. Hinton developed the first reliable method of detecting syphilis—the Hinton test. Mention must also be made of Frederick McKinley Jones (d. 1961) who invented the first automatic refrigerator for long-haul trucks. Percy Julian (d. 1975), a chemist, had 86 patents, some of which are related to a drug used against arthritis pain.

Ernest E. Just (d. 1941) is known as the pioneer in the study of egg fertilization, artificial parthenogenesis, and cell division. Samuel L. Kountz (d. 1981) remains one of the country's most famous surgeons since he performed more than 500 kidney transplants, one of which was a transplant from a mother to a daughter—"the first [kidney] transplant between humans who were not identical twins." Lewis Howard Latimer (d. 1928) worked for himself and for Alexander Bell and patented a process to make carbon filaments for the Maxim electric incandescent lamp. Jan Matzinger (d. 1889) invented the shoe-lasting machine, while Walter McAfee is known for his work on radar detection and range, antennas, the effects of nuclear weapons, and quantum optics.

Elijah McCoy (d. 1928) invented the automatic lubrication process for moving machinery such as trains. Since the 1960s, W. Delano Meriwether has experimented with a potential cure for young leukemia patients. A. Miles is credited with the 1887 invention of the elevator. Garrett A. Morgan (d. 1963) invented the gas inhalator which is widely used today by fire fighters and mine workers and for the life-saving and indispensable traffic light. (He sold this last patent to General Electric for $40,000!) Norbert Rillieux (d. 1894) invented a vacuum evaporating pan used for sugar refinery, for condensing milk, and for soap making. Daniel Hale Williams (d. 1931) is remembered as a pioneer in heart surgery, who saved, almost miraculously, a patient who had a knife wound in an artery "lying a fraction of an inch from the heart."

Granville T. Woods (d. 1910) had accumulated fifty patents before his death, one of which was for an incubator in which large quantities of eggs could hatch. He also developed the induction telegraph system, which today allows communication between moving trains as well as between trains and stations. Last but not least (for our purposes), Louis T. Wright (d. 1952) is known for his successful analysis of the intradermal method of smallpox vaccination.

It must be pointed out, in conclusion, that many of these scientists and inventors had to struggle to obtain their patents simply because they were black and some were given credit only posthumously. In some cases, as with Granville Woods, employed by Thomas Edison, company owners attempted to steal inventions by blacks. Many other inventors, as is still the case in our own time, fell by the sidelines, after deciding that having their names in books and government registers was not worth the personal pain. African American scientists have also left an indelible mark in the development of the NASA program, and some have even served as astronauts, including Guion S. Bluford, Ronald McNair (killed in space), Frederick D. Gregory, and Charles F. Bolden, Jr.

African Americans and Business Ownership

In any society, one crucial power base is the ability to influence the country's economy through ownership and management of resources. Evidently, in most cases, ownership and management presuppose capital already accumulated either through inheritance (or sometimes gambling and lottery) or individual initiative, knowledge of the workings of the business sector, necessary skills for entrepreneurship, favorable economic climate and conditions, and a network of acquaintances and associates. For several reasons, however—racism being the most basic one—most of these prerequisites have been missing within the black community, making it extremely difficult for African Americans to advance economically.[2]

Although the situation seemed to improve during the 1960s and early 1970s, the African American share of the national "pie" continues to be dismal and is getting even smaller as other minorities—Hispanics and Asians (the Koreans in particular recently)—settle in America and enter the economic market. Since the issue of economic conditions for African Americans has been referred to in the chapters on the family and the diaspora, the following only briefly outlines the state of African Americans in business, including the movie industry.

The disadvantage African Americans experience in business today cannot be understood without examining their history in America. As we know, for some three hundred years, African Americans were held in bondage and, when finally freed, they were not provided with the necessary intellectual and material tools to become economically independent. While the federal government attempted, through its Freedmen's Bureau, to provide land, jobs, and education, most states (especially in the deep South, where most of the black community found itself) did nothing to make emancipation and Reconstruction meaningful. This neglect forced many ex-slaves to remain on the plantations as workers, renters, or as sharecroppers, without the advantage of ownership of the land they tilled or lived on. Destitute, therefore, the greatest majority of them had nothing of value to pass on to succeeding generations of freeborn men and women. Thus, practically every African American who has succeeded in the business world has had to start from scratch and rely on his or her own resourcefulness or entrepreneurship and not on inherited family income and wealth.

Economic destitution has also been a result of continuing institutional racism and the denial of opportunities for black Americans who, because of the past, are an already disadvantaged minority in a European-American (white) majority. Yet, against all odds, a tiny percentage of African Americans has been able to succeed, although the vast majority has lagged behind in poverty, unable to own and control the means of production which, in a competitive capitalist system, should lead to self-sufficiency.

To be sure, even during slavery, some free black men and women in the North as well as in the South (when allowed) did own small, family or individually run businesses. A classic example of a successful man was Paul Cuffe (1759-1817), a

2. The author wishes to thank Dr. Bennie Nunnally, Jr., Chair of Finance and Business Law at the University of North Carolina at Charlotte, for his assistance on the final draft of this section.

shipper and a merchant in New England. At times, even in the South, business ownership allowed some to buy their freedom. By and large, however, until the end of Reconstruction (1865-1877), African American-owned businesses were extremely small and invariably restricted to inn management, tailoring, catering, furniture, shoe-repairing, farming, shoeblacking, barbering, undertaking, hairstyling, and furniture distribution.

Only at the turn of the century did African American entrepreneurship begin to encompass such businesses as insurance, banking, construction, publishing, carpentry, masonry, and expanded janitorial services as well as the management of large restaurants, food stores, and gas stations. During the eighteenth and mid-nineteenth centuries, black entrepreneurship was spurred mainly by the black Church through the Free African Society (founded by Richard Allen and Absalom Jones in 1787), and several mutual aid societies (funeral associations having been prominent). Following emancipation, during the 1890s and later, the initiatives and efforts of Booker T. Washington became an inspiration for many business-minded African American men and women. On several occasions, representatives of mutual aid societies and those interested in business and economic independence met to find the formula for success and pull their resources together. Thus, a meeting of 2,000 fledgling insurance representatives took place in Baltimore in 1884, which led to the creation of the Southern Aid Society in 1893, and to others such as Liberty Life of Chicago subsequently.

Moreover, under Booker T. Washington's initiative, the National Negro Business League was created in 1900, which inspired the establishment of the National Bar Association, the National Banking Association, and the National Insurance Association during the 1900-1925 period. The first black millionaire, C. J. Walker, who owned and operated hair style salons during the early 1900s, was definitely a product of this new intellectual and business environment. The third factor which indirectly promoted black entrepreneurship, as W. A. Low and V. A. Clift point out in their *Encyclopedia of Black America* (1981), was the offering of courses and degrees in business at most of the six black colleges beginning in 1924. By 1940, twenty colleges had courses and by the 1970s practically all schools offered business courses. Education and inspiration led some African Americans to venture even into the sectors of the economy which seemed to be barred from them, including the banking industry.

Indeed, although there were "informal banks" owned and managed by free blacks as far back as the 1830s in places such as Philadelphia, New Orleans, Chicago, and New York, formal banks emerged only at the turn of the century and thereafter. These were operated independently from the black Churches, as was the case of the True Reformers Bank, founded in Virginia in 1889. (Prior to this time, many black financial institutions were associated with the black Church.)

During the past 75 years or so, however, any gains in business ownership and management by blacks, have been offset by negative business cycles in the country, such as the Panic and Depression of 1873, the 1929 Great Depression, and the periodic recessions the American economy has experienced during the past quarter-century. Securing capital has also remained a perennial problem for aspiring business-minded men and women.

Strides were made in the 1960s and 1970s due to the Civil Rights movement, the programs of the Great Society, and the Small Business Administration introduced by the Nixon Administration (which embraced the concept of "black capi-talism"). The gains were strengthened by executive Affirmative Action in busi-ness-bidding and contracts ("set-asides") for minorities during the Carter Admin-istration. Such strides, however, have been skewed or eliminated by negative economic changes such as inflation, high unemployment, and cutbacks in social and economic programs during the Reagan Administration, as well as by the heightened racial polarization of the 1980s. What are the facts?

While in 1950 there were 42,000 self-employed African Americans, their num-ber shrank to 32,000 by 1960, but rose to 163,000 by 1969 and to 195,000 by 1972. Yet, 182,000 of them (93.6 percent) were sole proprietorships, accounting for 57.8 percent of the gross receipts from all black business establishments. In 1982, the number of black-owned firms stood at 300,608, with aggregate receipts totalling $12.4 billion, up from $6.0 billion in 1977 (and $5.6 billion in 1972). A breakdown of the 1982 receipts (i.e., $12.4 billion) shows the inroads black busi-nesses have made in that time, namely: retail trade: $4.1 billion; service: $3.2 bil-lion; construction: $995 million; manufacturing: $998 million; wholesale: $859 million; transportation: $795 million; finance: $748 million; agriculture: $129 million; and mining: $37 million.

The number of black firms has continued to increase, however, reaching 424,000 by 1987 out of a total of 17,526,000 firms in the United States. Unfortu-nately, even at present, about 89 percent of black-owned businesses have no paid employees—the majority of them with receipts of less than $50,000—are of sole proprietorship, and invest mainly in the service sector geared toward the black community and not in finance or heavy industry. Those that have workers employ an average of three to four people only. In 1989, the total number of employees in black-owned businesses was 165,765 out of the total number of 70,000,000 busi-ness employees in the United States. In spite of the odds, some businesses have done well, as *Black Enterprise* magazine reports. In 1987, for example, TIC Beat-rice International Holdings, Inc., had receipts amounting to $1.8 billion, while Johnson Publishing Company had sales totalling $205.5 million, and Philadelphia Coca Cola Bottling, Inc., boasted sales of $160 million. At present, there are 36 black-owned banks (down from 39 in 1986) with aggregate assets of $1.6 billion, the most successful top three being Seaway National Bank of Chicago, Freedom National Bank of New York, and Industrial Bank of Washington. There are also some 32 insurance companies (from 34 in 1986), whose assets total $234 million (the best three being North Carolina Mutual Life Insurance Company, Atlanta Life Insurance Company, and Golden State Mutual Life Insurance Company, in Los Angeles). However, unlike white businesses, which are almost ubiquitous, most black businesses have been limited to the southern Atlantic states and some major cities and have invested most of their capital in filling stations, food stores, and restaurants.

David Swinton notes in *The State of Black America, 1989*, that there is a great "disparity" between black and white ownership in financial holdings (stocks and bonds, U.S. government savings bonds, IRAs, KEOGHs, etc.) with black house-hold ownership amounting to a mere 5 percent, compared to white household ownership of 22 percent. (The gap, Swinton adds, reflects an average of $3,077 for the black household, contrasted with an average of $30,293 for white house-hold ownership). Ownership of and income from farms are also minimal within the black community. While at the turn of the century blacks owned some

240,000 farms, black-owned farms presently represent less than three percent of the privately-owned farms in the United States. In 1980, the number of blacks living on farms was estimated at 242,000. By 1990 that number had plummeted to a mere 69,000. To prevent further deterioration, African American farmers have asked for more loans from the Farmers Home Administration and elimination of discrimination in federal agriculture programs.

Overall, while blacks represent about 12 percent of the total American population, African Americans own less than one percent of the businesses in this country. (Tables I and II, presented by Swinton, underscore the magnitude of ownership inequalities prevalent in the United States.) What is the solution? Opinions differ. Swinton believes that, since Affirmative Action has failed, and a separate state for African Americans is an impractical alternative, reparations to the black community are the only way to address the inequality problem fairly. He writes:

> Thus the only viable option is a program of reparations. A constructive and well-designed program of reparations will bring an end once and for all to racial inequality. No other strategy can work unless it eliminates the inherited disadvantages of ownership and power. Any strategy that accomplishes this without creating a separate black nation would have to be a form of reparations.

It is clear, however, that reparations also appear to be a nonviable solution because the Euro-American majority will never find it acceptable. Education, full employment, and the elimination of gross racist behavior and attitudes, as advocated by others, may be the only long-range realistic solution to the problem of black ownership and wealth accumulation. One should point out, however, that African American entrepreneurial skills are needed and often appreciated in the developing world, particularly Africa. There is no reason why African Americans should not follow the example of Reverend Leon Sullivan's successful and expanding Opportunities Industrialization Centers (OIC) in West and East Africa.

Evidently, lack of meaningful ownership in business does not mean that African Americans have been totally excluded from the executive boards of white companies and corporations. In fact, trained blacks who show leadership potential are constantly sought throughout the nation, and, once found, they are immediately recruited and co-opted as top executives—not as tokens of Affirmative Action goals but as acknowledged, talented individuals.

It is interesting to note that African Americans who become frustrated by racism in large corporations, those leaving the military, and those retiring from various professions, especially from teaching, comprise a very large proportion of new business owners. A 1987 study by Bennie Nunnally and Robert G. Hornaday reveals that the rate of success of these entrepreneurs is quite high relative to the "norm." (Normally, approximately one in four new businesses, white or black, survive the first three years.) Nunnally and Hornaday also found that there was "a relationship between the educational level of the owners and the size of both black-owned and white-owned small business" and that "black owners recognize that their firms need to grow and choose growth as a main goal," because, in contrast to white owners, they see "lack of growth/expansion capital and internal managerial problems as the most serious problems they face, both related to their desire to grow."

It is clear, therefore, that, in order for African Americans to succeed in business ownership, as noted again by Nunnally and Hornaday, "the emphasis placed by policy makers on providing new sources of capital to black-owned firms must be

Table I
Wealth Ownership 1984
(1989$)

	Black Mean	White Mean	Black %	White %	B/W	Black Aggregate*	White Aggregate*	Aggregate Gap*
Net Worth	$24,168	$103,081	100.00	100.00	23.45	$229,813	$7,766,444	$695,808
Interest Earning at Financial Institutions	3,743	20,137	43.80	75.40	10.80	15,590	1,143,952	128,787
Regular Checking	715	1,131	32.00	56.90	35.56	2,176	48,474	3,942
Stock & Mutual Funds	3,359	33,067	5.40	22.00	2.49	1,725	548,099	67,451
Equity in Business	40,593	77,008	4.00	14.00	16.06	15,440	812,278	87,077
Equity in Motor Vehicle	4,115	6,814	65.00	85.50	44.34	25,431	454,362	31,913
Equity in Home	35,718	62,016	43.80	67.30	37.47	148,762	3,144,555	248,111
Equity in Rental Property	45,542	88,155	6.60	10.10	33.75	28,582	670,827	56,083
Other Real Estate	17,221	41,901	3.30	10.90	12.43	5,404	344,198	38,037
U.S. Savings Bond	657	3,133	7.40	16.10	9.63	462	38,005	4,344
IRA or Keogh	4,109	10,802	5.10	21.40	9.06	1,992	174,168	19,989

* in millions

Source: U.S. Department of Commerce, Bureau of the Census, *Household Wealth and Asset Ownership: 1984*, Tables 1 and 3, quoted by David Swinton in *The State of Black America*, 1991, p.71.

Table II
Total Receipts (in Billions of 1989$) and
Number of Firms (1,000's) in 1987 by Industry

	Black Receipts	Total Receipts	B/T**	Receipt Gap	Black Firms	Total Firms	B/T**	Firm Gap*
Total	21.6	$10,828	0.016	$1,299	424	17,526	0.198	1,713
Construction	2.5	561	0.037	66	37	560	0.539	32
Manufacturing	1.1	2,899	0.003	353	8	642	0.102	70
Transportation and Public Utilities	1.7	827	0.017	99	37	735	0.412	53
Wholesale Trade	1.4	1,335	0.009	161	6	641	0.070	73
Retail Trade	6.4	1,641	0.032	194	66	2,658	0.204	258
Finance, Insurance, and Real Estate	0.9	1,652	0.004	201	27	1,426	0.155	147
Selected Services	6.7	907	0.060	104	210	7,095	0.242	656
Other Industries*	0.9	1,006	0.007	122	34	3,769	0.075	425

Note: 1987 dollars were converted to 1989 dollars using CPI-U.
* Includes Agriculture, Mining, and industries not elsewhere classified.
** This is black receipts or firms per capita divided by the complement for total per capita. Black population in 1987 29,417,000 total population in 1987: 241,187,000.
Source: U.S. Department of Commerce, Bureau of the Census, *Survey of Minority-Owned Businesses: Black, 1987,* and *The Statistical Abstract of the United States,* 1990, quoted by David Swinton, in *The State of Black America, 1991,* p. 73.

combined with a recognition of sociological conditions in the black community," and that capital made available to non-college graduates to open businesses will be unlikely to succeed in raising "the socio-economic conditions of blacks in the ghettos" of America.

African Americans in the Film Industry

The problems facing African Americans in the traditional business world are also discernible in the entertaining business world. The presence of African Americans in the film or motion picture industry is now taken for granted. Many black movie stars appear daily on the silver screen not only playing black roles in society or depicting African American life themes but, increasingly, assuming and portraying "crossover" roles and themes which were once reserved for whites. Their participation in the industry has been enhanced by the fact that blacks have finally become producers and directors, as is the case with such current household names as Sidney Poitier, Eddie Murphy, Spike Lee, and many others—some of whom have, in the process, become millionaires.

To get where they are in the movie industry, however, African Americans have had to wage an uphill battle for decades and have struggled constantly to gain recognition. The efforts of many groups have resulted in better and increased diversified roles for black actors and a less stereotypical portrayal of black life in America and elsewhere in the world. Changes in the film industry have been brought about by the National Association for the Advancement of Colored People, the Civil Rights movement (which often urged a boycott of the industry), the few black stars and producers themselves, the black press, and the International Film and Radio guild.

Until the end of World War II, the roles of blacks in the silent and sound movies were played at first by whites with black-painted faces, and then by a few blacks. African Americans, often dubbed "lackies," were usually depicted as loyal and obedient slaves, maids, servants, doorkeepers, singers of Gospel music on the plantations (of the *Yes, Master!* type) or they acted as clowns, imbeciles, and "Samboes" (as illustrated in the *Birth of a Nation*, 1915)—all reinforced by Tarzan pictures denigrating the African continent and its people.

This trend continued during the 1930s, although singing and dancing provided new roles for black actors, in tune with the stereotypical image of blacks as people of innate "beat and rhythm." Frustrated by Hollywood, hesitation, and racism, many African American actors and aspiring producers looked to Europe (Britain, France, and even Russia) as alternative outlets for their creativity, as was the case of Paul Robeson in England and expatriate Josephine Baker in France (with her *Siren of the Tropics*, for example). African Americans' active involvement in World War II, however, the continuing decline of overt racism in the South, and the effort of African American organizations contributed to the eventual acceptance of black Americans within the industry. Melvin Van Peebles's production of *The Night the Sun Came Out* in 1960 (which netted $10 million) has been heralded as signaling a new era for blacks, one crowned with brilliant performances by stars like Sidney Poitier (in *Lilies of the Field*, which won him an Oscar award in 1965) and by a score of others. The independence of African nations beginning in the 1960s also had its own positive impact, as Africans, in spite of the fact that they have never controlled or managed the movie industry on the continent, began to combat stereotypical Western portrayals of their lives and culture.

Unfortunately, this promising phase was followed, during the early 1970s, by a proliferation of the so-called "action" films with scenes of black life replete with violence, sex (pimps and prostitutes), and drug use and abuse, which later were dubbed as "blaxploitation." This trend elicited so much criticism from moviegoers and reviewers that it was replaced by comedy, musicals, and biographies played by black actors. These were followed, during the 1980s and 1990s, by a number of black stars, producers, and directors, including Spike Lee, Sidney Poitier, Richard Pryor, Billy Dee Williams, Cicely Tyson, Lou Gossett, Ossie Davis, James Earl Jones, Ben Vereen, Diahann Carroll, Arsenio Hall, Gordon Parks, Raymond St. Jacques, Pam Grier, and others. Hundreds of films depicting black life or dealing with non-stereotypical African Americans were also produced.

Barring unforeseen circumstances apart from recurrent economic downturns, the place of African Americans in the motion picture industry seems to be secure, and black actors and stars are poised to reach new heights, although parity with their white counterparts, given the prevailing social climate, seems to be out of the question. In fact, although figures are hard to come by, the financial share of the most successful black producers and actors is like a drop of water in the bucket, compared to the trillions of dollars the white-dominated film industry generates each month in Hollywood and elsewhere in the country.

African Americans in the Sports Arena

Although few can overlook the economic dimensions of sport, many refuse to see it as a political, cultural, and social institution, endowed with enormous power to influence people's lives. Perhaps the first African American to record such an understanding is Frederick Douglass, who viewed sport from the perspective of a slave employed by slaveholders. In their hands, sport was an oppressive instrument and a diversionary device to occupy the minds and energies of slaves, thus preventing them from pursuing more useful activities and of fully appreciating their horrible plight. Even more, Douglass believed that the "sports and merriments" sanctioned by the slavemasters were among the most effective ways of "keeping down the spirit of insurrection." Although one might disagree with Douglass's conclusions that the power of sport flowed in one direction, he deserves praise for recognizing that sports were far more than games people play.

Douglass's message of sobriety and industry seemed to resonate in the black community, and Booker T. Washington's teachings echoed those of his predecessor. Prayer, education, and work left little time for sport or leisure in Washington's puritanical worldview. Yet, his chief rival for the attention and allegiance of African Americans, W. E. B. DuBois, saw the need to address the problems of amusements among blacks. If not ahead of his time, DuBois once again proved himself ahead of Washington as a modern man. Writing on the subject in 1897, DuBois did not pretend that amusement was "one of the more pressing of the Negro problems, but it is destined as time goes on to become more and more so." What DuBois saw in blacks was a tendency to "depreciate and belittle and sneer at means of recreation, to consider amusement [including sport] as the peculiar property of the devil, and to look upon even its legitimate pursuit as time wasted and energy misspent." While DuBois understood that too much of anything could be intoxicating, he not only urged moderate participation but also analysis, for "proper amusement must always be a matter of careful reasoning and ceaseless investigation, of nice adjustment between repression and excess." DuBois's prediction proved prophetic, as sport has become a serious issue in the black community and, unfortunately, given little of the "careful reasoning" and "ceaseless investigation" he urged.

Historians of the African American athletic experience once asserted that there had been a slow but steady progress in the elimination of racial discrimination in sport and that, since the late nineteenth century, athletic competition has been essentially democratic. More recent and careful studies reveal that the history of race relations in American sport often imitated and influenced the cultural patterns of the larger society. Moreover, sports sometimes serve to affirm the cultural patterns residing in that society's institutions, but they might also provide a forum for the expression of different values and behaviors. In other words, sport can be an instrument of oppression and conformity and one of liberation and resistance.

The African American experience in sport cannot be fully appreciated without defining the meaning of sport in the larger, white male-dominated society. Once seen as repulsive and counterproductive, if not a threat to survival, sport found little support among the so-called respectable elements of American society until the mid-nineteenth century. Concern with morality and health did much to change opinion. With popular amusements rising rapidly in America's burgeoning cities, many saw the need to control and regulate the activities of the masses. Moreover, with an eye to foreign developments, many observers believed that Americans were becoming dissipated. Their reliance on curative medicines and quack remedies (often one-and-the-same) alarmed the new proponents of physical fitness. In some ways, these concerns converged in a movement known as "Muscular Christianity." To it, the body was the temple of the soul. Before long, a rage for competitive athletics swept across the land finding sanction among high public officials such as Theodore Roosevelt. In his "Strenuous Life" speech of 1899, Roosevelt, as the Governor of New York and with a national reputation, commanded his audience to "boldly face the life of strife," for strife was necessary to winning the goal of true national greatness. Implicit in the new emphasis on athletics and physical development was the alleged building of manhood, character, and leadership. It was a doctrine that applied only to white males.

The nineteenth century was an age of endless measurement. Human beings were ranked on the basis of anatomical, mental, and moral criteria; on all scales blacks were founding lacking. These pseudo-scientific findings of difference and inferiority justified segregation and discrimination and hindered blacks in their attempts to disprove these tragic conclusions. These "findings" found popular currency in social Darwinism, in which theories of survival of the fittest came to apply to humans.

Despite the fact that blacks had demonstrated competence in boxing during the early part of the nineteenth century (in the persons of Tom Molineaux and Bill Richmond, among a host of others), whites, on the one hand, maintained that they were exceptions to the rule and, on the other, that success in sport did not transfer outside of that context—at least not for blacks. In the face of white defeats and black champions, the dominant discourse still maintained that white physical and intellectual superiority would triumph always, while dismissing or ignoring setbacks.

Race relations in sport around the turn of the century revealed the shallowness of the myths that abounded in athletics and the larger society. Contrary to the often-held view, evidence indicates that there has not been slow and steady progress in the elimination of racial discrimination in sport, nor has athletic competition since the late nineteenth century been egalitarian. From 1880 to 1900, blacks were at the nadir of their post-slavery experience. Changing attitudes, laws, and treatment in the North and South, brought about disfranchisement, segregation, and economic hardship while reversing black gains in the athletic arena. Prior to this time, blacks participated freely in, and excelled at, horse racing. The most outstanding jockey of his day was Isaac Murphy, who rode three winners in the Kentucky Derby. African American jockeys won twelve of the first fifteen "Derbies," but were a rarity by the turn of the century.

At the same time, whites tolerated some black participation in baseball. Brothers Moses and Welday Walker both played for the Toledo Mudhens of the American Association, a major league in the 1880s, but an incident occurred which served as the pivotal event in determining black-white relations in American sports for more than a century. When the Chicago White Stockings visited Toledo in 1887, Adrian "Cap" Anson refused to take the field until the Walkers were removed. They did not play that game and, within a week, they were banished from the sport. Anson's actions were accepted, even preferred, in the harsh racial climate of the times. Worse, the Supreme Court of the United States confirmed this hateful sentiment in a series of decisions upholding segregation and discrimination from 1875 to 1898, culminating in *Plessy vs. Ferguson* in 1896, which nationally codified the doctrine of "separate but equal" and ensured second-class citizenship for blacks.

No matter the sport, the "color line" became increasingly difficult to cross as the African American athlete was called "a growing menace" and symbol of "a black rise against white supremacy." Thus, whites no longer wanted to watch blacks dominate athletic encounters or even have them participate. Individuals such as the pioneering speed cyclist Major Taylor, at the beginning of the twentieth century, and Jack Johnson, heavyweight boxing champion of the world from 1908 to 1915, were exceptions. They were allowed to participate and excel because their economic value to sports and related enterprises outweighed racial considerations. Yet, both men still suffered extreme persecution and hardship for their success in areas reserved for whites. All that was left for most black athletes was the acceptable realm of comedy. Many black athletes resorted to entertaining whites who gladly paid to watch the "darkies" perform in the stereotypical role of clown. Others avoided such humiliating displays by forming barnstorming teams for the benefit of appreciative black audiences, yet another example of parallel institution building.

The plan for one of the greatest of these enterprises was laid by Beauregard F. Moseley who had promoted a successful all black baseball team in Chicago. In 1910, Moseley called together a group of black baseball officials from throughout the Midwest and South to organize a National Negro Baseball League. Moseley's plans and goals reflected a more widespread concern among blacks for self-help and racial pride to counter the exclusionary practices of white America in and out of sport. Unfortunately, financial problems prevented materialization of the plan until 1920, when Rube Foster, one of baseball's great pitchers and a resourceful promoter, revived Moseley's blueprint for a black baseball league. The new league, which lasted into the 1950s, produced such legendary figures as Josh Gibson, James "Cool Papa" Bell, Leroy "Satchel" Paige, and many other great stars.

Less known is the fact that blacks created successful golf and tennis circuits, proving that they could both organize and master the more genteel forms of sport and recreation. Virtually absent from the game's history and popular lore, blacks long have been associated with golf as more than servants. One of the game's first and best professionals was John Shippen, who played in the 1896 U.S. Open and enjoyed a lifetime association with the game as a player and teacher based at the black controlled and operated Shady Rest Country Club in Scotch Plains, New Jersey. The inventor of the first golf tee was a black dentist, Dr. George F. Grant of Boston, whose creation has received little credit. Excluded from the Professional Golfers Association (PGA) and the United States Golf Association (USGA), blacks formed the United Golf Association in 1928. The UGA had amateur and professional divisions and hosted local, regional, and national tournaments for men and women. Ted Rhodes, William Spiller, Pat Ball, and Howard Wheeler stand out among the men. Although Ethel Funches and Anne Gregory were two great female champions, women were not altogether pleased with their standing or treatment within the organization. In 1937, black women golfers in Washington, D.C., and Chicago established their own clubs affiliated to the UGA. Through these groups, they negotiated (with black men) gender roles in and out of sport. Many of these women went on to become leading opponents of racial discrimination in the sport and leaders of the UGA. Thus, black men and women carried out legal assaults on segregated public golf facilities in the 1950s, aware that second-class status anywhere extended it everywhere. Despite the breakthroughs of professionals such as Pete Brown, Charlie Sifford, Lee Elder, and Calvin Peete, among males, and Renee Powell and Althea Gibson among women, golf at its highest levels remains a white preserve, and black participation has been (and continues to be) largely separate, unequal, and invisible even though estimates of black golfers range from 400,000 to 2,000,000. The fact that so much attention is being paid to Eldrick "Tiger" Woods and basketball superstar, Michael Jordan, underscores the sad state of affairs.

A similar story emerges in tennis. Denied membership in the United States Lawn Tennis Association, blacks formed the American Tennis Association (ATA) in 1916. Its membership was composed mostly of professional blacks and collegians. Early stars were Talley Holmes, Reginald Weir, Gerald Norman, Jr., and James McDaniels, but none was allowed to reach his full potential. The same held for Lucy Diggs Slowe, Ora Washington, and Isadore Channels who dominated the ATA. Only after persistent pressure did the USLTA open its tournaments, played at prestigious private clubs, to blacks. Largely responsible for the breakthrough was Althea Gibson who would emerge from the ATA to become a two-time Wimbledon and U.S. Open champion. Arthur Ashe remains the only other African American to win a "Grand Slam" event—the U.S. Open and Wimbledon. No other men have come close to reaching this level, although MaliVai Washington is a rising star on the men's circuit. Zina Garrison and Lori McNeil have fallen just short on several occasions.

Until fundamental socioeconomic changes occur in this country, blacks will not and cannot represent the sports of golf and tennis in large numbers. Both are capital intensive, requiring expensive equipment, expert instruction, quality facilities, high level competition, and parents with the time and resources to travel with players to tournament sites. Adequate income is not the only obstacle. Racism remains a serious impediment to participation in and mastery of these games. Residential segregation hinders access to golf courses and tennis clubs, which still might deny entry strictly on racial grounds. Inherent in the exclusion is a desire to maintain social distance and to reinforce notions of difference. For blacks to excel at sports supposedly requiring certain traits found among the dominant group would help undermine racial myths. On the flip side, without prominent and numerous role-models, exposure, and encouragement, neither familiarity nor cultural acceptance is likely among members of the excluded group.

Baseball, which had sought bright, educated, disciplined athletes, had similar reasons for denying opportunities to blacks. Billed as the "national pastime," baseball had no room for blacks as tried to project a cerebral and wholesome image to the American people. Despite Jackie Robinson's historic breakthrough in 1947 with the Brooklyn Dodgers, baseball has been slow to integrate the front office and managerial ranks. Studies have also pointed to salary inequities and segregation by position or stacking. The baseball establishment's true feelings were revealed by Al Campanis of the Los Angeles Dodgers, in his unguarded statement that blacks "lacked the necessities" to be managers. Blacks are, however, breaking into the managerial ranks as evidenced by Cito Gaston, the manager of the 1992 World Series winner, the Toronto Blue Jays.

Perhaps no sport is more identified with black Americans than boxing. The domination of boxing by blacks in the twentieth century is at once a measure of black achievement and an index of the black plight. While African Americans have taken pride and found encouragement in the triumphs of champions such as Jack Johnson, Joe Louis, Sugar Ray Robinson, and Muhammad Ali, boxing is a sport of the desperate. Sometimes glamorous, empowering, artful, and lucrative, boxing is more often ugly, debasing, brutal, and costly. No modern sport more closely approximates the gladiatorial spectacle, in which slaves fought to the death at the pleasure and profit of others. Few white young men see more than pain and suffering in such a sport, but African Americans, who remain near or at the bottom of the socio-economic ladder, will be attracted to the illusory quick fame and wealth the game offers.

Today, basketball has also become a sport closely identified with blacks. The college and professional games are dominated by blacks to the extent that white players are often viewed as "tokens" and their presence often gives rise to cries of reverse discrimination among black athletes and fans. In this societal mirror image, white athletes are stereotyped for lack of jumping ability called "the white man's disease." Yet, what white athletes are purported to lack in natural talent is more than compensated for by media commentary about their intelligence, grit, and discipline, positive traits rarely ascribed to blacks. Thus, even in a sport with so many black stars and a relatively high number of black coaches and executives, traditional images are perpetuated. It is probably no accident that the Harlem Globetrotters, a comedic team, still draw fans and that the Harlem Renaissance squads of the 1930s and 1940s, famed for their discipline and teamwork, are hardly known.

Not to be overlooked in this discussion is the minority within a minority—black women. Not only has sport been racist, it is even more sexist. Women who engage in athletic activities often do so at risk of reputations and, in the minds of some, femininity. For black women, femininity has always been at issue, having been forced to labor under degrading and harsh conditions outside "the cult of true womanhood" promoted by white males and subscribed to by many white females in the nineteenth century. Thus, whether they would be condemned for participation in sport has been less a concern for them. Since so few professional sport's opportunities exist, African American women have been most prominent in track and field, even reaching celebrity status in the persons of Wilma Rudolph, Florence Griffith Joyner, and Jackie Joyner-Kersee.

Today, blacks who have believed that sport, like military service, is a way of proving worth, ability, and even loyalty (as indicated by their stellar record in the nationalistic, quasi-military Olympic Games), are caught in a serious dilemma over the place of sport. Although African American athletes dominate the collegiate basketball ranks and represent other sports in large numbers, the overall black college population is declining, especially among males. Many of those athletes attending college are not being graduated, some hardly educated. As African American sporting prominence grows, so does homelessness, crime, drug abuse, and early death. Although not the cause of these social ills, sport is not the solution to them. African Americans must remember the warnings of Douglass and DuBois to place sport in perspective.

Summary

The role of African Americans in science has usually been neglected in the European-American science literature, although African Americans have been prominent in physics, chemistry, biology, medicine, and mathematics. In spite of institutional obstacles, for example, African Americans have been able to patent numerous inventions which have greatly improved the quality of life in America. The contributions of African Americans will continue to be significant, as long as they are given equal opportunities in the realm of education.

A cursory analysis of black ownership and entrepreneurship in America confirms the sad fact that African Americans, although 12 percent of the population in the United States, own less than 1 percent of the business in the country. A combination of historical factors and changing economic conditions (which always affect the black community negatively) warrants several conclusions on African American ownership and control of the means of production, namely: 1) that there is a disproportionate and lopsided advantage given to European-American ownership and management of business ownership in the country; 2) that most black-owned businesses are of sole proprietorship, employing, on the average, three to four persons; 3) that blacks are unable to compete in wholesale trade, finance, manufacturing, and heavy industry (which requires considerable capital), and therefore concentrate their business in the service sector and retail trade; and 4) that 90 percent of the time black-owned businesses serve black communities which are, in general, poor in resources; the businesses are rarely patronized by the black middle-class. The implication of this situation is that African Americans remain consumers rather than owners, which gives them very little power in attempting to change the economic and political direction of the country.

Given that the world is becoming much more interdependent, particularly now with the collapse of the communist bloc, the skills of African Americans can be put to good use in Africa and other parts of the developing world. While their contribution should be primarily to their communities here in the United States, African American business men and women should also venture abroad to enhance the restricted opportunities they have at home.

The athletic experience of African Americans has been one filled with both tragedy and triumph, not unlike the historical plight of this long scorned and persecuted minority group. Like modern day gladiators they have often performed for the profit and pleasure of others and to the detriment of their own selves and family. Some, such as Joe Louis, have risen to the very pinnacle of success in their sport, becoming national heroes and symbols in the process, only to be cast aside by the dominant majority when no longer needed. Yet, blacks remain intensely loyal, finding in these individuals proof of black capability and achievement.

Individually and collectively, blacks have proven that given the opportunity to excel in the athletic arena their potential is unlimited. More than in most other activities, sports have proven highly rewarding in terms of fame and fortune. Yet, both can be fleeting and, for the majority, illusory. The publicity afforded athletes far exceeds that given to blacks in any other field with the possible exception of a few in entertainment. Unfortunately, educators, scientists, lawyers, civil rights leaders, and other very successful professionals are largely unknown and often unrecognized for their contributions. Moreover, the chances for success in these fields greatly outnumber those in sport. While some might be persuaded that the massive inclusion of blacks in some sports is positive, one must also understand that the terms of this arrangement have their costs. Only through a close examination of the historical record can sport and the African American experience be understood for what it is and has been.

Study Questions and Activities

1. Explain why it has been so difficult for black people to own and run businesses in the United States. What solutions do you propose to remove the obstacles?
2. Compare and contrast the factors that led to Reverend Leon Sullivan's Opportunities Industrialization Centers, Oprah Winfrey's television program, and George E. Johnson's "Johnson's Products."
3. Why have African Americans been so successful as boxers and basketball players? What have been the benefits and costs of that success?
4. Why have so few blacks reached the highest levels of success in golf and tennis? What must happen before change occurs?
5. How has the plight of African Americans in sport reflected conditions in the larger society for blacks, particularly females? How has it differed?
6. What would Frederick Douglass and W. E. B. DuBois think of African Americans and sport today? Why?
7. What has been the role of African Americans in the film industry?

References

Arthur R. Ashe, Jr. *Hard Road to Glory*. New York: Warner Books, 1988.

William J. Baker. *Jesse Owens: An American Life*. New York: Free Press, 1986.

H. G. Bissinger. *Friday Night Lights*. New York: Harper, 1991.

Krin Gabbard. *Black Magic: White Hollywood and African American Culture*. New Brunswick, NJ: Rutgers University Press, 2004.

Darnell M. Hunt (ed.). *Channeling Blackness: Studies on Television and Race in America*. New York: Oxford University Press, Inc., 2005.

Onnie Kirk et al. *Contemporary Black America*. Nashville, TN: The Southwestern Company, 1980.

W. Augustus Low and Virgil A. Clift (eds.). *Encyclopedia of Black America*. New York: McGraw-Hill Book Co., 1981.

National Urban League. *The State of Black America, 1989, 1991*. New York: National Urban League, Inc. 1989, 1991.

Bennie Nunnally and Robert Hornaday. "Problems Facing Black-Owned Businesses." *Business Forum*, vol. 12, 4(Fall 1987): 34-37.

Harry A. Ploski and James Williams (eds.). *The Negro Almanac*. New York: Gale Research, 1989.

Donn Rogosin. *Invisible Men: Life in Baseball's Negro Leagues*. New York: Atheneum, 1983.

Edna and Art Rust, Jr. *Art Rust's Illustrated History of the Black Athlete*. Garden City, NY: Doubleday, 1985.

Jeffrey T. Sammons. *Beyond The Ring*. Urbana, IL: University of Illinois Press, 1988.

David Swinton. "Economic Status of Black Americans." *The State of Black America, 1991*. New York: National Urban League, 1991.

U.S. Department of Commerce, Bureau of the Census. *Money Income and Poverty Status, 1982, 1985, 1987, 1990*. Washington, DC: Government Printing Office.

Walter B. Weare. *Black Business in the New South: A Social History of the North Carolina Mutual Life Insurance Company*. Urbana, IL: University of Illinois Press, 1973.

PART V

SOCIETY AND VALUES IN THE BLACK WORLD

20

The African Family

Mario Azevedo

Introduction

Just as elsewhere in the world, the traditional African family setting is under assault from many factors, some unique to the continent, others brought about by external forces. These include children leaving home at an early age and moving to the cities; a lessening of the gap between men and women regarding roles and responsibilities in the household; the practice of polygyny being challenged by educated women and enlightened men; both men and women working away from home, from 9 a.m. to 5 p.m., in order to feed the family members and afford the necessities of modern life; the diminishing influence of the elders and traditional authorities in the village setting; the impact of Westernization arriving through Western education, radio, television, magazines, and books, which, in the eyes of the elders, encourage lax morals; and increased poverty, particularly in the inner city slums and the remote areas, all of which present immense obstacles to the proper functioning of the family.

As a result, the question is often asked whether the family, as we know it today in Africa, will survive and function normally, keeping the values it cherishes at present. This essay attempts to portray the present structure of the African family, its function in society, and the challenges it faces.[1]

Major terms and concepts: family, marriage, matrilineage, patrilineage, clan, lineage, bridewealth, initiation or rites of passage, polygyny, bigamy, inheritance.

Family Structure

It is universally acknowledged that, in every society, the family is of major importance, though its forms and functions may vary. There are two functions of the family that are widespread among African families. First, much as in American

---

1. Portions of this essay have been adapted, expanded, and reprinted with permission of Kendall-Hunt from Mario Azevedo's and Gwendolyn S. Prater's (eds.) *Africa and Its People* (Dubuque, IA: Kendall-Hunt, 1982), pp. 9–19 (authored by Robert Daniels et al.)

society, the family is the social unit primarily responsible for the early development and socialization of the child. Second, unlike most families in American society, African families are the primary economic units of production in their societies, and thus are organized according to the rules surrounding corporate property and the behavioral requirements of producing a livelihood.

In almost all cases, African families are in a very real sense also family businesses, as the issue of marriage illustrates. There are several characteristics of African marriage which differ significantly from what is commonly thought to be typical of marriages in Western societies. In almost every African society, marriage is universal; older bachelors and spinsters are practically non-existent on the continent. One of the reasons for this situation is that African marriage is not a private matter or a relationship between two people alone. Marriage focuses upon the individual, but each individual represents a larger group. African marriages are alliances between families through the conjugal union of a female from one family and a male from another. It follows that marriage and divorce decisions involve many people and are usually not left to the young people to make on their own.

Marriages are arrived at after a series of formal arrangements have been made between the bride's and groom's parents and other relatives. In some cases, the young people may have little personal knowledge of each other before the marriage is arranged (if, however, parents will not accept their children's choice, the young people may elope, just as happens, on occasion, in American society).

Another common characteristic of African marriage systems is polygyny, the practice which permits a man to have more than one wife. Polygyny is an accepted practice in practically all African societies. For polygyny to be possible, there must be more married women than married men, and this can only happen if women marry at an earlier age than their brothers. Consequently, first wives tend to be younger than their husbands, and second wives still younger. Although, even at present, there are chiefdoms in which the ruler may have as many as fifty wives, this is obviously exceptional. Even in societies with a great deal of polygyny, it is not possible for more than a quarter or a third of the men to take a second wife, and very few ever take a third.

Although polygyny is allowed, it does not mean that, whenever a man wants another wife, he can simply go to the village and get himself one. Just as in monogamy, courtship precedes consent of marriage, and a marriage ceremony must be arranged in order for the union to be socially accepted. For centuries, experts have tried to understand the reasons for polygyny (a practice which was upheld by the Old Testament). Since the need for manpower is great in farming societies, the desire to have many children in one household is understandably strong: one more child is two more hands in the field. Polygyny allows this to happen in a household or homestead in Africa. Likewise, because infant mortality rates have been generally high on the continent, having many children born in one household does offset the losses, which is indirectly guaranteed by the marriage of a man to more than one wife.

Finally, the practice of ceasing sexual activity as long as the baby is being breast-fed, as is customary in many African societies (up to three years among the Sara of Chad, for example), makes it extremely difficult for the male to remain within the socially accepted mores, unless he can legitimately satisfy his human needs through relations sanctioned by tradition. Polygyny is not, therefore, the same as concubinage, which is morally frowned upon in African societies, although, in the past, it was tolerated for chiefs and kings, particularly in Muslim societies.

It must also be said that being polygynous requires not only wealth but also interpersonal relations skills. The husband must be able to balance the needs of all his co-wives and keep them in harmony. One thing he must constantly keep in mind is never to show preference for the children of one of the wives at the expense of those of the others. Such behavior would necessarily disrupt household relations. Usually, the first wife maintains some authority over the wives, which often spares the husband the headaches brought about by sometimes insignificant domestic quarrels. Anthropologists also observe that polygyny guarantees steady companionship among the wives and is a source of assistance when one of them falls sick, has a child, or is unable to perform expected tasks.

A universal feature of traditional African marriage is the provision of bridewealth by the groom's parents to the bride's family. In some societies, bridewealth amounts to a little more than a token gift, while, in others, it involves a very significant amount of property. (The implications of this variation will be discussed on the following pages.) Whatever the amount, however, bridewealth has a number of functions beyond those we might consider economic. Most generally, it constitutes a legal guarantee of good faith, a warranty for good behavior, and insurance of the stability of the marriage.

In all African societies, whatever the bridewealth arrangements, husbands are directly responsible to their in-laws for the proper treatment of their wives, and a woman's father or brother will not hesitate to reprimand her husband, if he feels that she is being mistreated. In this sense and others, African marriages are very much public, and not private, arrangements involving many people.

Patrilineal and Matrilineal Societies

In Africa, as elsewhere on the planet, the family is the basis for social relationships, but one's roots and kinship are of paramount importance. African societies trace family membership through males (patrilineal descent), through females (matrilineal descent), or through both equally (bilateral or cognatic descent). The latter is common to Western tradition but extremely rare in Africa, one example being the BaMbuti of the Ituri forest in Zaire. In a patrilineal society, children (both sons and daughters) belong to their father's kin group. Thus, among a man's various cousins, his father's brother's son and daughter (technically his "patrilineal parallel cousins") will be in his own kin group, and are called brother and sister. This idea is easy for us to understand since it corresponds to our system of passing on family names patrilineally. American society differs from patrilineal African societies, however, in that it reckons kinship equally through the father and mother. Consequently, although only a few of our cousins share our last name, all are treated equally and addressed by the same name in our system.

Examples of patrilineal societies in Africa include the Tiv and Yoruba of Nigeria, the Tallensi of Ghana, the Kikuyu of Kenya, the Swazi of Swaziland, the Mossi of Burkina Faso, the Malinke of Senegal, Mali, Guinea-Bisssau, and Côte d'Ivoire, the Nuer of Sudan, the Zulu of South Africa, and the Gala of Ethiopia.

Authority can be systematized in a patrilineal system among highly segmentary or stateless societies with no central power just as satisfactorily as it can in a patrilineal kingdom. In the latter, authority is centralized in the person of the king who is recognized as a representative of divine power and is elevated above the subjects by rituals and sacred regalia. African kings rarely held dictatorial power, however. The day-to-day operation of the kingdoms relied on the delegation of power, in a system of checks and balances, between members of the royal family, representatives of other leading families, and commoners who were appointed to high office because of personal talents.

In societies in which family property belongs to patrilineal kin groups, and marriage involves the exchange of bridewealth, it often happens that there is a preference for arranging marriages between certain pairs of cousins, specifically the children of a brother and sister. Anthropologists call this pair crosscousins because they belong to different kin groups. Such marriages lead to strong bonds between different segments of the society. Since the children of such a marriage will have only six great-grandparents rather than the usual eight, the effect of crosscousin marriage is to increase their inheritance and keep the family property from being dispersed too widely among the younger generations.

In a patrilineal society, there are generally three levels of relationships. First comes the immediate family which is made up of the man and his wife (or wives) and their children. If a man has two wives, each has her own household even if they live on the same homestead. Next in size, and often of great importance, is the lineage, made up of all those of a local area who can trace themselves through men to a common forefather. In many societies, men live near their fathers and grandfathers, and the lineage becomes a local focused around a shrine to their common ancestor, and held together by joint property and shared rituals.

Finally, on a more general level, there is the clan. This consists of all the people in the society who recognize that they belong to a common kin group no matter where they live and even if they cannot trace their exact relationships to one another. Kinsmen share moral responsibility. A man may be held accountable for the crimes committed by his kinsmen. Similarly, if one man sins, divine punishment may strike anyone in his kin group. It follows that kinsmen are not only expected to help each other but also to govern each other's behavior.

In patrilineal societies, women's duties are much the same as they are elsewhere in Africa. Women are responsible for taking care of the household, collecting firewood for cooking, growing and preparing food. Other children share much of the work of minding younger children as well as helping with household chores. Pastoral people eat milk products along with staple grains, supplemented with vegetables from women's gardens, and, when an animal is slaughtered for an occasion, meat. A lightly fermented beer, which is rich in vitamins and protein, is drunk by many Africans. In West Africa, palm wine and kola nuts also play an important role in hospitality patterns and family rituals.

Married and unmarried men eat together, separately from the wives and children. The head of the household often eats alone or may share his meal with a male visitor of equal rank. Children of both sexes eat in their mother's or grandmother's house. The immediate patrilineal family lives in a compound or joint homestead. In many patrilineal societies, an elder's married sons may live with him as well. Large compounds are subdivided into several enclosed courtyards, and each married woman lives in her own house. Another house is set aside for the unmarried sons of the compound's head and his younger brothers who choose to remain with him. Sometimes, older girls will sleep together in a house where they are chaperoned by a grandmother. Associated with each married woman's house are a few buildings used for storage, and a granary. There is also an ancestral shrine or sacred family symbol.

As noted earlier, Africans see marriage as a union between two families as well as between two individuals. Before a family can give consent to a marriage, long discussions must be held in which each family considers the other's history and background. In some societies, the ancestors are also consulted through oracles. In fact, when the issue of bridewealth is settled, the groom's parents assure the other family that their daughter not only has good morals and manners but is also in good health and will be able to have children. Proven future sterility and adultery are serious grounds for divorce and partial or complete return of bridewealth. The rituals have to be arranged, and economic obligations of the groom to the parents of his future wife must be settled in detail according to the local traditions of their group. In societies with a great deal of moveable wealth, especially the pastoralists who herd large numbers of cattle, bridewealth can amount to a significant block of property, in some cases up to twenty or thirty head of cattle.

The obvious economic importance of such large bridewealth provisions led some Europeans in the colonial era to think that the groom's family had somehow purchased the wife. In fact, the bride is not his property in any case, but his dependent and partner to whom he is responsible for providing the material and social support to raise and feed a family. The critical problem for pastoral families is to determine the link between father and son, which is so necessary for the continuity of family herd, in a way that will never become ambiguous. Yet, marriages can go astray, and people's personal lives can get as complicated in Africa as they do in America. Among pastoralists, the marriage contract designates the woman's husband as the legal father of all her children come what may in their personal lives. Put another way, one can say that what is purchased in a marriage contract involving a large amount of bridewealth is the right to paternity over all the children born of the woman.

Since a bride's family gives the cattle received from her marriage to still other families when her brother marries, divorce (which requires total or partial return of bridewealth) is nearly impossible in such societies. In fact, a woman remains married if her husband dies. His brother or kinsman assumes responsibility for her and, if she is still young, she continues to bear children in her dead husband's name. (Some call this a *ghost* marriage.) While this may strike us as odd, the same pattern is found among the Old Testament Israelites who were also pastoralists (Deuteronomy 25:5).

Although a husband is said to own all the cattle, a wife is permanently assigned a share of his herd which she controls until they are inherited by her sons. A man with more cattle than are needed by one household naturally uses the "extras" to support more dependents by taking a second wife. Although there will always be some men with more cattle than others, polygyny ensures that the key resources of milk and meat are distributed among the women and children of the society as evenly as possible.

What about matrilineal societies? When social anthropologists began intensive study of African social organization in the 1930s, a great deal of interest in different descent systems developed. These systems include: 1) patrilineal, already discussed (tracing descent through only the father and his kinsmen), 2) cognatic (tracing descent through both parents, as in America), and 3) matrilineal (tracing descent through the mother and her female kin who are descended from a common ancestress.)

Among the matrilineal societies stand the Yao of Malawi, Mozambique, and Tanzania, and the Bemba of Zambia. Among the Wolof of Senegal, kinship is also reckoned matrilineally, and the Baule of Côte d'Ivoire are predominantly matrilineal. In some matrilineal societies, the bride continues to live with her parents, and her husband takes up residence with them. It is rare, however, that this is typical of most marriages throughout their duration. More often, men seek to live near their sisters and their own kinsmen. As a result of the various, at times contradictory, attractions which people feel in matrilineal societies, it is not unusual for a person to live in three or more different places in a lifetime. Yet, although descent is reckoned through women, it is men and not women who dominate the public forums of power. In family affairs, it is not the woman, but her brother who exercises ultimate authority in her house (instead of the husband) and looks after his sister's affairs. It is a woman's brother who belongs to the same kin group as her children, and not her husband.

Hence, in matrilineal societies, it is the uncle who disciplines the children and arranges their marriages as the representative of the family. Within this context, men find their attention divided between their wives and children on one hand and their sisters and their children on the other. While patrilineal societies, particularly those that stress the local lineage, are marked by highly stable local groups, matrilineal descent results in more flexibility, and the membership of a matrilineage in any local area is likely to change from year to year.

Matrilineal descent is relatively rare in Africa, being found in only 14 percent of the societies. In all cases, these societies are associated with hoe agriculture, and almost all of them are in the "matrilineal belt" of the southern savanna. Throughout Africa, most people live on small family farms, and most of the daily agricultural work is done by women. In the southern savanna, however, a number of special circumstances combine to make matrilineal descent adaptive. Goods cannot be stored for long, and the tse-tse fly makes it impossible to accumulate wealth in cattle. Soil conditions are poor and the population is relatively sparse. Thus, there is no shortage of land, but there is a shortage of the one asset families do have, which is labor.

The most important function of a matrilineal grouping is to serve as a means by which economic resources, especially men's and women's labor, can be pooled and redistributed. Few people are willing to give up precious time during cultivating season to work for others, even for pay, since they can easily find land to work on their own. As a result, an ambitious cultivator can only increase his agricultural income by marrying more wives or by controlling the labor of his unmarried children, especially his daughters.

The forces at work make it difficult to keep extended families together. Young men wish to exert their independence of their fathers, and end their economic dependence on their mothers by marrying, for, in Africa, a man is not fully adult until he has his own household and children. Young women realize that children are their major source of prestige, influence, and long-term security. So, marriages are often arranged for a number of social and economic purposes, as they are in patrilineal societies, but the interests of the young people do not always match those of their elders.

Since there is a shortage of labor in matrilineal societies, heads of families try to attract as many people as possible to their villages. While this presents people with options about where to live, it also creates certain contradictions. A big man will try to keep his sisters and the other females of his lineage with him (whether or not their husbands are willing to join him instead of living with their own people), while at the same time trying to keep his brothers and other male kinsmen with him (although their wives are being pressured to return to their own brothers). Obviously, everyone cannot have it both ways at once. The bond between brother and sister is considered stronger than that between husband and wife, and since there is little property to use as bridewealth, divorce is easy and occurs quite frequently. In such societies, it is not uncommon for a woman whose children are approaching maturity to leave her husband and return to the security of her brother's community.

Husbands also try to bargain for the best economic arrangements when they marry. Sometimes they work for a number of years in the wife's matrilineage (in what has been called brideservice), and are then allowed to take their family back to their own communities. Such arrangements, however, are highly varied. On the one hand, elders of a young man's matrilineage may control his labor by contributing heavily to his bridewealth on the promise that he bring his wife to live with them. On the other hand, elders of the bride's matrilineage may keep control of her by accepting very little bridewealth on the premise that her husband move in with them.

Given that women's contributions to the economy are so important, there is competition for marriages, and, in some cases, this reaches the point at which options to marry elders' daughters are agreed ahead of time while the girls are still very young, or even before their birth. This is not as odd as it sounds when we reflect that, in that part of our society which is also based on highly competitive recruitment such as professional sports, the "big men" also deal in future options over potential team members.

Matrilineal societies arrange social life to facilitate production in a difficult and uncertain environment. While the conflicting pulls of different groups may sound chaotic when described one by one, people in these societies make choices, and those choices are made according to their assessment of where they can find the most socially satisfying and economically secure life. Since the fortunes of any community are likely to fluctuate from year to year with the uncertainties of farming in a marginal area, the various choices open in matrilineal societies allow people to adjust by changing communities.

In patrilineal societies, men gain power and prestige by amassing wealth and using it to support large numbers of dependents and heirs for whom they are permanently responsible. In contrast, in matrilineal societies, a man gains power and prestige through his leadership in keeping a number of people with different interests working together as a team. To be successful, one must have a great deal of interpersonal skill, wisdom, and political savvy. When it works, people cooperate. Unfortunately, as in every society, people sometimes choose not to follow the rules.

In both patrilineal and matrilineal societies, the primacy of the child is incontrovertible. No family is a family until it has its first child. In fact, no one is completely a man or a woman until a child is born, particularly a male child. Thus, pregnancy is welcomed because it publicly declares that the union has been consummated, confirms the fertility of the wife as claimed by her parents, and affirms the husband's "virility" and procreativity. Names of children are carefully chosen, and in many African societies, a special ceremony is held, often eight days after birth, to name the child and present it to relatives and friends. It is also at this time that the seclusion of the new mother, imposed immediately after childbirth (which Eric Ayisi calls the period of separation) ends. It is worth dispelling, at this juncture, the myth that all African names have a meaning. Only a few ethnic groups have such a practice, as is the case among the Yoruba of Nigeria, who may name a child after the day of the week it was born or create a name that conveys a special message. In East Africa and Southern Africa, children are usually named after important individuals, deceased or living family members, or persons whose lives the parents would like the child to emulate in his or her adult life.

Modes of Transmission of Tradition

Before closing this section, an important traditional educational process, responsible for the transmission of culture and kinship bonds from one generation to another should be mentioned. Anthropologists have called it initiation, initiation ceremonies, or rites of passage, common in some African societies in the past as well as in the present, particularly in the countryside.

Initiation is a ritual and a period of formal training for young boys and girls between the ages of nine and sixteen and, depending on the society, occurs every three to five years and lasts from two weeks to two months. Among the Sara of Chad, for example, the yondo, from which no young person could escape, was the most important event in the community. It was the rite of transition (passage) from childhood to manhood or womanhood. The ritual was designed to teach youngsters how to survive in the real world, it exposed them to the secrets of life and to the traditions of their society, and told them what the community expected of them. Among the Sara, the initiates were also trained in a secret male language that bound them forever. (During the ceremonies, it was not rare for entire villages to be completely empty of youngsters for 45 days or more.) While boys were trained in seclusion by male elders, young girls were entrusted to female elders. Among the Maasai of East Africa, circumcision is still part of this formal educational process. In Sara society, clitoridectomy was required of girls on that particular occasion, while circumcision was required of boys.

Interestingly, among the Maasai warriors, a boy must undergo circumcision and other rituals without complaint, before he is declared a Maasai warrior, a man. In most societies, however, one should emphasize, initiation was a very limited and temporary aspect of a youngster's life. In fact, many societies did not or do not have one. Invariably, youngsters learned more from observing, from listening to the elders in their daily counseling and pronouncements, and by following the example of the adults—parents and older brothers and sisters. This partly explains the absence of formal teachers and missionaries or preachers in traditional African societies. The child grew naturally and, without realizing it, he or she became the preserver and the transmitter of his or her people's traditions. Societies without initiation might have other types of organizations based on age set and gender. The secret societies of the Dan of Côte d'Ivoire, for example, commonly known as *poro*, reinforce the bonds between individuals and perform important social functions.

The Impact of Modernization on the Family

Any discussion of changes in Africa must encompass the recognition that "traditional" African cultures were associated with a vast array of different social organizations and ways of life, including many bands of hunter-gatherers, hundreds of different societies based on self-sufficient farming villages, and several multi-ethnic empires using special currencies and trading over vast areas. Africans living below the Sahara, particularly in the Western Sudan, have been in contact with the Mediterranean world since time immemorial. While societies along the West African coast have been involved with direct European contacts for five hundred years, those on the east coast similarly had a long history of contact with Arab, Indian, and even Chinese trade. Much of the interior of Africa, however, was not directly contacted by colonial powers until the start of this century.

The most important force in the modernization of last century has been the involvement of almost all of rural Africa in the worldwide economy. This has come about in two main ways: 1) wage labor, almost always outside people's home areas, and 2) the expansion of traditional agricultural production or, more often, the adoption of new cultivated plants, to be grown for outside markets. While some areas are heavily involved in migratory wage labor and others have specialized in cash crops, most African families find themselves trying to strike a balance between both methods of raising cash for the many expenses that have become necessities: taxation (which was often introduced with the intention of forcing people to seek employment with outsiders), imported goods (the earliest ones, such as cloth, salt, sugar, and metal, are now augmented by thousands of others including bicycles, trucks, radios, and televisions), educational costs, and many more.

At first, wage labor took place on colonial plantations growing such crops as coffee, tea, rubber, sisal, and cotton, in the mining industries of Central and Southern Africa, and on the European-owned farms in East and Southern Africa. Now, of course, millions of Africans work in cities in jobs ranging from bus boys to corporate executives and presidents, from skilled traders to professionals.

Perhaps the most striking aspect of African migrant labor is that people involved did not cut themselves off from their rural homes, but sought, through wages, to supplement their families' economic position in the countryside. Once cash became a necessity, the number of men seeking work has always exceeded the available jobs. This has led to a number of negative results: since wages were sought as a supplement to what the family produced outside the cash economy, wages for most Africans have fallen far less than the amount needed to support families adequately, especially in the cities where life is expensive. As a result, most men leave their families at home, causing much separation, and resulting in large numbers of single men living in substandard conditions at the workplace.

Meanwhile, the development of the rural areas has meant that women, who did much of the traditional agricultural work and provided much of the day-today support for their children, now find their work expanded to include responsibility for growing even more crops for sale. In areas where population pressure is greatest because of improvements in public health, land is scarce, a large population of the younger men are away at work, and many children are in school. In order to cope with these problems, Africans have adopted traditional ideas of communal support to form migrant associations (sometimes voluntary associations) in the new cities or networks of friends and relatives who help each other find housing and employment and assist one another in maintaining contact with their families back home. While these responses have been very effective, it is still true that involvement in wage labor has caused many strains for the cohesiveness of the African family and community patterns. Rapid change also alienated younger people from elders, particularly when the young adopted a Western, individualist economic philosophy of life, which is in sharp contrast to the spirit of communal responsibility that characterizes traditional African thought.

Cash cropping, or commercial agriculture, has also become a mixed blessing. In many areas, agricultural land has been converted from growing local foods to growing export crops—a particularly serious problem given the rapid increase in population throughout most of the continent. People who farm to supply foreign markets also find that they are at the mercy of price changes caused by forces beyond their control. While many Africans have risen to the top of their national governments and business corporations, and some independent African nations are major producers of oil and minerals such as copper, the vast majority of families in Africa find themselves caught up in an economic squeeze which threatens to overwhelm the resources of the traditional family life.

However, what seems to give hope to the continuity of the African family is the fact that the sense of communalism is still strong as is the primacy of the child, and respect for human life and age. Other positive factors include the relative absence (at least for the present) of substance abuse by the young, homelessness, serious violent crime, and teenage pregnancy. Yet, the issues of population explosion and the spread of AIDS and poverty (the latter sometimes induced by nature and other times by unwise government policies), present a challenge which the continent cannot ignore, if generations to come are to maintain a viable family and national life.

Summary

As is true in every society, the African family is the most basic human institution. In Africa, in spite of changes brought about by colonialism and the pressures of contemporary life, the family has remained relatively strong and still tends to be extended (rather than nuclear), encompassing all kin members who live in proximity, such as brothers, cousins, grandparents and great-grandparents, uncles, nephews, and other known relatives. African societies are still polygynous in theory (a man has the right to marry as many wives as he wishes), although most men do not choose or cannot afford more than one wife. In fact, the ratio between polygynous and monogamous married males is estimated at 33 percent to 60 percent, respectively, the remainder being non-married individuals, due to various reasons.

Since marriage is an obligation in Africa, one does not find many bachelors within the marriage age, although modern changes, especially in the cities, have forced many men and women to delay marriage or a few not to marry at all. It is still true that, in most African societies, marriages are seen as alliances strengthening the bonds between families, friends, or even clans, which explains why young men and women are not at liberty to plan their wedding without considerable family input. Families also discuss the type and amount of bridewealth to be given by the groom's family to the bride's parents. (Some governments are attempting to pass laws to forbid the practice.) This physical token represents compensation to the parents for the "loss" of their daughter, while serving, at the same time, as a guarantee that he has the right to paternity over every child born of his wife-to-be. As a result of the deep involvement of several families and the practice of bridewealth, which, in most cases must be returned when things go wrong, divorces are not as common in Africa, particularly in patrilineal societies, as they are in the Western world. But divorces do occur, especially in cases of proven adultery, impotence, and sterility. Sometimes, serious disagreements with the husband or among wives in a polygynous household may also lead to divorce.

Major differences in family members' relationships occur between patrilineal and matrilineal societies. In patrilineal societies, for example, descent is reckoned on the father's (male) side, and usually the bride must join the husband's kinsfolk, whereas, in matrilineal societies, the tendency is to compel the man to join his wife's people, although there are many intervening variables that may prevent this from occurring. In matrilineal societies, however, the man is more at the mercy of the wife's brothers or uncles than in patrilineal societies, as the latter not only make sure that they continue to have control over their kin, but even assume responsibility in disciplining the children and in arranging for their marriages.

The primacy of the child in the African family milieu is acknowledged by anthropologists and by careful observers alike. In fact, there is no family if there is no child, and men and women are not considered adults, even if they have undergone the rites of passage, until they have had a child. Parents, on the other hand, are not content until they become grandparents. In some African societies, children go through a formal period of training for life, called initiation, while in others, simple observation, direct experience, and daily admonitions from parents, elders, and others through various means (conversation, stories, legends, songs, and assignment of certain responsibilities) prepare the youngsters to become productive individuals and to transmit social traditions. The child is, in most cases, a type of social "insurance" for old age, a guarantee of manpower in farming communities (as is the case in most of Africa), and the assurance, particularly in nonliterate societies, that the name of the family will be perpetuated indefinitely.

There is no doubt that, as elsewhere, the African family faces tremendous problems. However, most experts hold the view that, in general, African families are stronger and more stable than families in the West—poverty being the number one enemy. The relative absence of serious and violent crime, of substance abuse, of teenage pregnancy, or of out-of-wedlock motherhood (although these are increasing in the urban areas), assures that African families will survive.

It is comforting to know that, even in the midst of extreme poverty, an elderly person, a widow, a divorcee, a child out-of-wedlock, and a handicapped person, are all taken care of by family members. In the words of Paul Bohannan and Philip Curtin, "loneliness is not an indigenous African problem."

Study Questions and Activities

1. How is the family in Africa different from that in the Western world?
2. Discuss the role of marriage, bridewealth, and divorce in Africa.
3. Compare and contrast polygyny with monogamy. Can you see the reasons why societies in Africa have preferred polygyny in the past?
4. What roles do patrilineage and matrilineage play in African societies?
5. Compare and contrast the problems of the African family and those of the African diaspora in America.

References

J. F. Ade Ajayi and Toyin Falola (ed.). *Tradition and Change in Africa: The Essays of J. F. Ade Ajayi.* Trenton, NJ: Africa World Press, 2000.

Eric O. Ayisi. *An Introduction to the Study of African Culture.* London: Heinemann, 1988.

Mario Azevedo and Gwendolyn Prater (eds.). *Africa and Its People.* Dubuque, Iowa: Kendall/Hunt, 1982.

William Bascom and Melville Herskovits. *Continuity and Change in African Cultures.* Chicago: University of Chicago Press, 1959.

Edna Bay and Nancy Hafkin (eds.). *Women in Africa: Studies in Social and Economic Change.* Stanford, CA: Stanford University Press, 1976.

Paul Bohannan and Philip Curtin. *Africa and Africans.* Prospect Heights, IL: Waveland Press, 1988.

Vigdis Broch-Due (ed.). *Violence and Belonging: The Quest for Identity in Post-Colonial Africa.* New York: Routledge, 2005.

P. H. Gulliever. *Tradition and Transition in East Africa.* Berkeley, CA: University of California Press, 1969.

Philip Kilbride. *Life in East Africa: Women and Children.* London: Longman, 1990.

Ron Lesthaeghe. *Reproduction and Social Organization in Sub-Saharan Africa.* Berkeley, CA: University of California Press, 1989.

Joseph Lijembe (ed.). *East African Childhood.* New York: Oxford University Press, 1967.

Michael Meeker. *The Pastoral Son and the Spirit of Patriarchy: Religion, Society, and Person Among East African Stock Keepers.* Madison, WI: University of Wisconsin Press, 1989.

Christian Oppong (ed.). *Female and Male in West Africa.* Boston: Allen and Unwin, 1983.

David Parkin and David Nyamwaya (eds.). *Transformations of African Marriage.* Manchester, UK: Manchester University Press, 1989.

Torild Skard. *Continent of Mothers, Continent of Hope: Understanding and Promoting Development in Africa Today.* New York: Zed Books, 2003.

Thomas S. Weisner, Candice Bradley, and Philip L. Kilbride. (eds.). *African Families and the Crisis of Social Change.* Westport, CT: Bergin & Garvey, 1997.

Elizabeth Wheeler. *Women of Modern Africa.* New York: Women's African Committee, 1956.

21

The African American Family

Gwendolyn Spencer Prater

Introduction

Since the mid-1960s, the African American family has attracted considerable attention from scholars as well as from politicians. Tragically, during this same period, black community members have continued to be victims of increased crime, of substance abuse, of unemployment, and ultimately, of untold poverty. The size of the black community's male population continues to dwindle. The impact of the provocative works by E. Franklin Frazier and Melville Herskovits during the 1940s seems to have opened the debate on the black family. Franklin, after a careful study of the impact of the slavery era and the conditions of the black family in the periods thereafter, concluded that slavery contributed to a loss of traditional African family values within the black community, forcing African Americans to assimilate the values of the white family structure, a trend that was accelerated by continued racism and the deplorable conditions of the inner city (the destination of most urban migration). Alternatively, Herskovits stressed the strength of the black family even in slavery and pointed to the survival factor that Frazier had overlooked.

Unfortunately, Frazier's conclusions were subsequently misinterpreted and misused by Daniel Moynihan who, as a member of the Nixon Administration, argued that the detrimental matriarchal nature of the black family was responsible for the disintegration of the black community. The debate has resulted in a serious questioning and criticism of the methodology used by the students of the African American family and therefore of the validity of their conclusions. Many black sociologists argue against sweeping generalizations based either on the black middle-class family or the premise that the white middle class model—monogamous, nuclear, and self-sufficient—is the model family against which black families should be measured to determine success or failure.

The continuing debate has generated two major schools of thought: one which sees the black family as sick (the pathological theory, advanced by Moynihan and others) and therefore negatively affecting the soundness of the whole black community; and the other stressing the strengths of the black family as an adaptive institution (the adaptability theory, advanced by scholars such as Robert Hill and John Blassingame). Most other scholars can be placed between the two extremes, as they are able to find both positives and threatening negatives in the institution of the black family.

An important often-asked question is: Will the black family be able to survive the onslaught on its stability coming from so many directions? Because the issue has become so prominent and troubling among African American researchers and professionals, particularly social scientists, social workers, public policy makers, and community leaders, the following chapter will be devoted entirely to the black family — its history, its nature, its strength and weaknesses, and its ability to survive and thrive, as America continues its path throughout the twenty-first century. The author hopes that this introductory treatment of the black family will lead students to more advanced studies on the topic.

Major terms and concepts: slavery, emancipation, family, nuclear vs. extended family, monogamy, African survivals, pathology, adaptability, teenage pregnancy, single-headed household, racism, unemployment, child welfare system, adoption, foster care, guardianship, empowerment, family-preservation services, family-centered services.

The Black Family from Slavery to Freedom

Much of the study that followed Frazier's and Moynihan's rejoinder has attempted to rehabilitate the black family by exposing the fallacies upon which the pathology and instability claims of the African American families were based. In his several studies, Billingsley, for example, has denied the premise that the black family, even during slavery, was unstable and matriarchical, pushing the argument to the point of almost denying the cultural and psychological destructive nature of slavery in the United States. He has argued that black families, in spite of slavery, kept kinship ties, maintained solidarity, respected their traditional mores, and never abandoned the mutual assistance tradition, much of which, he added, were African survivals. Atwood and Genovese advanced a similar argument when they concluded that commitment to marriage was always present in the majority of black families and that, rather than a matriarchy, there was partnership, flexibility, and equalitarianism in marriage, as a complementarity in household roles, out of which came families that were as stable as white families as America entered the post-World War II era.

Other scholars, including Herbert Gutman, took pains to demonstrate that, contrary to what we have been led to believe, black families, from the civil war to civil rights, even though the large majority were of lower class, remained overwhelmingly, both in the urban North and the rural South, two-parent headed households kept together by extended, "multigenerational" kinship networks, just as continental African families have been over the centuries. Allen (1978) and Harriet Pipes McAdoo have also derided the generalizations of the first studies because these were based on the lower class black family and used the white family or the upper middle class black family as a median model. While Allen stressed variance or the adoption of a "variant perspective," which underscores the diversity but also the normalcy of all types of families, including the African American family, McAdoo has noted that "there are several distinct groups within the

African American community, yet when we are able to relate only to mean or median statistics, the wide diversity of family experiences becomes buried." Yet, she finds a major common thread in the fabric of black communities, reflected in the crucial role of such African survivals as the importance of "oral traditions, reliance on extended families (consanguinal relationships), spirituality, rhythmic-movements expression, and communalism."

McAdoo further stresses the fact that earlier studies contributed to unproven stereotypes about black families when they failed to differentiate between family stability and marriage stability. She and many other scholars have emphasized the important point that, in the black community, kinship relationships have often kept family relationships stable in the face of rising divorce and separation rates. The most important requisites for stability and proper functioning of the family, scholars add, are love and adequate resources to raise the children.

Historians John Hope Franklin and John Blassingame and the late sociologist E. Franklin Frazier have provided a comprehensive view of the black family in antebellum America. Their studies demonstrate and underscore both the obstacles to the continuation of the family traditions brought from Africa and the slaves' resilience in their attempt to maintain a modicum of kinship ties despite the brutal system under which they lived. The picture that comes out of the slavery experience, studied by so many others, has shaped many of the treatises advanced by contemporary social scientists.

When slaves arrived on the shores of America, they were, in most cases, not kept as a family but were split up and sold or auctioned to eager slaver masters. Although keeping families together should have been simply a matter of common sense if the plantation productivity through stability of manpower were to be facilitated, masters feared that a stable and close family could become a nucleus for conspiracy based on kinship, culture, and common language. Separating individuals who might have come from the same African region, who spoke the same language, or who were members of the same family was thought to be the safest way to ensure the survival of the peculiar institution. It was believed that a slave, placed in a totally new social and physical environment without the solidarity brought about by family bonds, would not be as likely to muster the inspiration and strength to escape or rebel.

John Hope Franklin writes that, among most slave owners who specialized in slave-breeding in such states as Virginia and South Carolina, the tendency was to sell slaves as individuals rather than families, some of which had emerged on the plantations, because retailing individual slaves was more profitable. Although some states had laws prohibiting the sale of children under the age of ten, in most, the laws were "almost wholly disregarded." In most cases, except among some extremely religious master's households, slave families were never taken seriously. In those cases where slave unions were somewhat respected, economic rather than moral considerations were the basis. Marriage, the most important aspect of family formation, was not taken seriously by slave masters, even when they allowed a special ceremony to mark the event. Marriage was simply viewed as a search for companionship to make plantation life more bearable. In fact, slave accounts confirm that most of the marriage ceremonies that were allowed turned out to be an entertainment for the master's household.

Slaves wishing to marry always had to have permission from their masters. Because most masters preferred marriages of slaves living on the same plantations, it became extremely difficult for most male slaves to find suitable mates, since the master himself quite often maintained his most attractive female slaves as concubines. This high incidence of concubinage is confirmed by the numbers of mulatto children in the antebellum period: out of 3.2 million slaves in 1850, 246,000 were registered mulattoes, according to John Hope Franklin. By 1860 the figure had risen to 411,000 (or 588,352 according to DuBois) out of a slave population estimated at 3.9 million. Adding to the difficulties surrounding marriages between enslaved African Americans was the fact that, when marriages were allowed by the slave masters, necessary courtships were often missing. Furthermore, children were not properly cared for because of the work the mother had to perform for her master in the household or in the fields. Slave children, except perhaps among certain mulatto households, were given tasks (errands, fetching water, taking care of the master's other children, traveling with his wife) as soon as they reached the age of seven or eight, spending very little time with their own parents. Lack of prenatal and postnatal care for the mother and neonatal care for the newborns resulted in high infant mortality rates which further destabilized many slave families.

One other factor contributing to the erosion of family ties prior to emancipation was the separation of slaves during the settlement of an estate even if the slaves were from the same household. In addition to this, because many slave masters maintained a special relationship with their female slaves, particularly those assigned to domestic chores, the women became heads of families. They assumed authority over the children while the father, feared and relegated to the fields, was reduced to the role of a breeder. The presumed predominance of a matriarchal system in the slave family prompted Frazier to declare the weakness of the institution within the black community and to posit that mulatto families, favored by slave-owners, were stronger because they were predominantly patriarchal.

Franklin, Frazier, Blassingame, and Gutman are quick to add, however, that even during slavery—in the midst of oppression and repression—the black family remained relatively strong in the North and where it was allowed in the South. Mothers loved their children (the primacy of children has remained one of the major characteristics of the black family); under adverse circumstances, fathers did what they could to protect their households; brothers and sisters took care of each other; and when they were separated, siblings quite often attempted to find one another. Using the Underground Railroad, siblings looked for each other in such large northern cities as Philadelphia and New York. Thus, the family, as an institution, continued to be cherished within the slave community, notwithstanding the legal system that did not recognize it as valid and legal. This reality prompted Blassingame to write:

> Although it was weak, although it was frequently broken, the slave family provided an important buffer, a refuge from the rigors of slavery. While the slave father could rarely protect the members of his family from abuse, he could often gain their love and respect in many ways. In his family, the slave not only learned how to avoid the blows of the master, but also drew on the love and sympathy of its members to raise his spirits. The family was, in short, an important survival mechanism.

With emancipation, the situation of the African American family was radically altered, and the union of the emancipated could now evolve from an "invisible" and oppressed family to a full-blown, self-sustaining free family. Several factors assisted the newly freed slaves in starting a new family or reinforcing the one maintained during the slave years. It must be noted that, although a period of theoretical freedom for the slaves, emancipation proved very trying for many former slaves. Many remained on the plantation against their will; others decided to stay with their masters because they had nowhere else to go or owned nothing; and many others, some of whom had families, remained literally hopeless. The federal government and some states stepped in to protect the freed families and instill in others the sense of building a monogamous household, because many polygynous and polyandrous practices had existed among both the white and black plantation dwellers. Thus, deserting a wife or the children became a criminal offense in ✓ many states, and bigamy and polygyny were punishable by law.

In order to allow a smooth transition, beginning in 1866, several states compelled the male ex-slaves to select only one mate in cases where they may have had several wives. In South Carolina, for example, polygamous slaves had until April 1, 1866 to select a mate, otherwise their children would be declared illegitimate. Marriage registration was made easier at state, county, and municipal offices. In this effort, the churches (independent African American Churches) and the missionary schools (especially those run by missionaries from New England) contributed greatly to the stabilization of old and new marriages. As Jessie Bernard (in *Marriage and Family Among Negroes*) notes on the role of the Church, "in many cases the idea of marriage dignified by a minister appealed to the newly freed Negroes, for it implied equality with whites. Official marriage became a status symbol, and weddings became occasions of great gaiety." The Church was empowered by states to dissolve polygamous or abusive marriages whenever it made sense to church officials.

The military establishment also had a positive role in this endeavor, as it insisted on marriage registration and family responsibility toward wife and children, and often returned any fees charged to the soldiers who attempted to obtain marriage certificates. This was reinforced by the establishment in 1866 of the Freedmen's Bureau. The Bureau was an early significant government-sponsored child welfare service that had a positive impact on African American families. Not only did it clarify and facilitate rules governing marriage for the newly freed slaves, it secured land, work, and direct relief to poor children within their families. Within the context of the time, the creation of the Bureau was a revolutionary development in child welfare services since it was financed by the federal government and provided in-home service to African American children and their families. Its demise in 1871 came too soon, and was a result of inadequate financial support and the belief that, Andrew Billingsley and Jeanne Giovannoni state, the Bureau's work encouraged "the natural slothfulness of the Black race."

Other early community efforts in the late 1800s were led by African American organizations such as lodges (the Masons, the Odd Fellows, and the Knights of Pythias); women's clubs (the National Association of Colored Women); and educational institutions which were instrumental in meeting the needs of freed or newly established African American families. These measures certainly strengthened the post-emancipation African American family. Thus, although Billingsley calls emancipation "a catastrophic social crisis for the ex-slave," and the Reconstruction period "a colossal failure," he is compelled to add that "at the same time, there were some 'screens of opportunity' which did enable large numbers of families to survive, some to achieve amazingly stable and viable forms of family life, and a few to achieve a high degree of social distinction."

A discussion of the African American community following Reconstruction, particularly in the South, must take into account the devastating psychological and social impact of racism and violence on the family unit. In its worst form, violence against blacks and the black family manifested itself in lynching, which became an all too common occurrence. Present records suggest that between 1882 and 1968 some 4,000 cases of lynching of African American men, women, and children took place in the United States, including 581 cases in Mississippi, 531 in Georgia, 493 in Texas, and 347 in Alabama, as the following table illustrates.

Incidence of Lynchings in the United States (1882–1968)

States	Total	States	Total	States	Total
Ala.	347	Md.	29	Ore.	21
Ariz.	31	Mich.	8	Pa.	8
Ark.	284	Minn.	9	S.C.	160
Calif.	43	Miss.	581	S.D.	27
Colo.	68	Mo.	122	Tenn.	251
Del.	1	Mont.	84	Texas	493
Fla.	282	Neb.	57	Utah	8
Ga.	531	Nev.	6	Vt.	1
Idaho	20	N.J.	2	Va.	100
Ind.	47	N.M.	36	Wash.	26
Iowa	19	N.Y.	2	W. Va.	48
Kan.	54	N.C.	101	Wis.	6
Ky.	205	N.D.	16	Wyo.	35
La.	391	Ohio	26		
Maine	1	Okla.	122	TOTAL	4,709

Source: *U.S.A. Today*, September 25–27, 1992, pp. 1, 2, 4A–5A (from 1990 U.S. Census figures).

Added to the terror of lynching, was the fact that little was done by the government to protect by law and through enhancing programs the African American community and its family units.

During the early and mid-1900s, authorities continued to exclude African American families from the formalized child welfare service systems. As a result, national black community organizations, such as the National Urban League, founded in 1911, and the National Association for the Advancement of Colored People, created in 1909, struggled for the provision of economic opportunity and civil rights for African American families. Since that time, African American families have become more visible in the child welfare system. However, adequately meeting African American families' and children's service needs in the current system of service delivery remains inadequate.

The Black Family from Freedom to Civil Rights

The past four to five decades have also witnessed broad societal changes that influenced the status of the African American family—the Civil Rights movement, urban unrest, political discontent, the War on Poverty programs of the 1960s, school busing to achieve integration, the Voting Rights Act of 1965, affirmative action and the affront to its existence and an employment-focused child and family welfare system. The United States has also experienced the numerical predominance of African Americans in major cities, the expansion of the black middle class and a stable working class, the achievement of a nearly one million-plus enrollment of African American youth in higher education, in addition to the exponential increase in the number of African Americans holding elected office. The Joint Center for Political and Economic Studies released its 2000 figures, showing a six-fold increase since 1970 to 9,040 of black elected officials. Perhaps, surprisingly, the top five states with the largest number of black elected officials are Mississippi, Alabama, Louisiana, Illinois, and Georgia. Furthermore, Black Issues in Higher Education has reported the striking progress of African Americans in degree attainments. Specifically, the number of blacks earning bachelor's degrees has doubled over the past two decades and includes more than 100,000, while the number of blacks earning master's degrees is up 141 percent since 1985. The most frequent degrees awarded to blacks were business management, social sciences, such as psychology, education, and health sciences. In 2002, according to census information, 17 percent of young blacks received bachelor's degrees. Although black women are earning almost double the baccalaureate degrees as black men, black men earning degrees are also increasing in number. Other striking news is that, during the same period, black doctoral degrees were up 110 percent. Yet, the African American community itself continues to face significant problems. For example, although African American teen birth rate is reportedly the lowest in the 40 years for which data has been available for African American women, the percentage of births to unmarried teens remains high. In 2000, the birth rate for African American adolescents 15–17 was 50.4 per 1000 compared to 23.6 per 1000 for white teens, according to the Sexuality Information and Education Council of the United States. This phenomenon accounts, in part, for the rate of out-of-wedlock pregnancies and subsequently for an increase in single parents.

Further, the number of children in need of child protective services has soared. Maltreatment categories typically include neglect, medical neglect, physical abuse, sexual abuse, and psychological maltreatment. The National Clearinghouse on Child Abuse and Neglect Information revealed that, in 2001, 3 million referrals concerning the welfare of approximately 5 million children were made to child protective services agencies throughout the United States, with two-thirds being screened on and one-third screened out for service. Additionally, more than 2 million children and families were provided services to prevent abuse and neglect. According to the National Child Abuse and Neglect Data System (NCANDS), investigations confirmed over 903,000 children were found to be victims of child maltreatment in 2001. The highest percentage of victims was white (half), African American (one-quarter), and Hispanic (15 percent). Child fatalities are the most tragic consequences of maltreatment. Approximately 1,300 children died of abuse or neglect during 2001, a rate of 1.81 children per 100,000 children in the population. Neglect, difficult to clearly define, usually referred to as deleterious acts of omission (inadequate care) rather than commission, was the largest single discrete category of children noted to be in need of protective services, comprising 57 percent of the total number of abused and neglected children.

As Robert L. Hampton has noted, it is risky to draw conclusions solely from official reports about the rates of child maltreatment among African American families because the poor and racial minorities are typically over represented in official reports of deviant behavior. Reflecting the high rates of poverty in the black community, African American children do, unfortunately, enter the child protection system in disproportionately large numbers. As the National Center of Child Abuse and Neglect has previously indicated, parental abuse of alcohol and use of other drugs during pregnancy and after has been identified as a major factor contributing to child abuse, neglect, and death. Child maltreatment has negative short- and long-term effects on children's mental health and development, including drops in intelligence quotient (IQ) and increases in learning disabilities, depression, suicides, delinquency, and drug and alcohol abuse.

During the 1980s, African Americans experienced a growing "underclass," high rates of unemployment and underemployment, and a high rate of school drop-outs. Clearly, the African American community is in transition. Yet, African American families are retaining their strength to "make it against all odds." In 2002, there were 8.8 million black families and 53.6 million white families in the United States. According to the U.S. Census Bureau, also in 2002, the Hispanic population became the largest population of color in the U.S., with about 13.5 percent of the population. This was up from about 4.5 percent in 1970. Simultaneously, the black population comprised about 13 percent of the total population, comparable to the 1990 percentage, although the black population increased faster than the population as a whole, at 21.5 percent for African Americans versus 13 percent for the entire population. Yet, black families faced odds that have been difficult to overcome, as the following statistics underscore.

The income for African American households increased 4.3 percent between 1996 and 1997 and has not drastically changed since. The real median income rose from $24,021 to $25,050 making the income surpass 1989 levels. Receipt for all African American firms increased by 63 percent, from 19.8 billion in 1987 to 32.2 billion in 1992, and in 1998 nearly 23 percent of African American women and 17 percent of men, in 1998, worked in managerial and professional jobs. Between 1996 and 1997, the number of poor African Americans dropped to 9.1 million and poverty rates dropped for African Americans from 28.4 percent to 26.5 percent. In 2001, census statistics indicate that an estimated 32.9 million people lived below the poverty level, including 8.1 million blacks, and 15.3 million non-Hispanic whites. The poverty rate, which was 12 percent for the total population, was 23 percent for blacks and 8 percent for non-Hispanic whites. Thus, the attainment of economic parity with white American families continues to elude African American families. As the Census Bureau indicates, over one-half (52 percent) of all black married-couple families had incomes of $50,000 or more and 27 percent of them had incomes of $75,000 or more; conversely, 64 percent of non-Hispanic white families had incomes of $50,000 or more, while 40 percent of white families had incomes greater than $75,000. Clearly, black married couples fare better economically than all variations of black family structures combined, as indicated by the lower percentages of all black families with incomes reaching $50,000 (only 33 percent) annually and those attaining a $75,000 (only 27 percent) yearly income.

Indeed, not withstanding the above, still a larger proportion of black married-couples (8 percent) than their white counterparts (3 percent) were poor in 2001.

There were 6.8 million families in the United States with incomes below the poverty level, and 1.8 million of these families were black. Twenty-one percent of families in poverty were black. In 1997, the nation's African American population consisted of 12,109 million households of whom 3.85 million were married couples, 3.94 million were headed by women, and 757,000 were led by men. Furthermore, also in 1997, African American families with children under 18 were comprised of 1.97 million married couple families, 2.59 million female-headed families, and 1.70 million were headed by males. Among African American families, which consisted of families with children less than 18 years of age, 58 percent were headed by females who had no spouse present and had never been married, as compared with 41 percent of mother-child family groups in the total population. The number of families headed by African American women and women in the general population has increased dramatically over the past several decades. For example, Family Services America reported that the number of families headed by African American women significantly increased, from 30 percent in 1970 to 42 percent in 1987. In 1997, all married couples with children less than 18 years of age had declined to 25 percent, down from 40 percent in 1970. With the growing unemployment, single female heads of families in the black community is likely to increase. Robert Hill notes that the poverty rates among female-headed African American families edged upward by 1 percent, from 51 percent to 52 percent, between 1978 and 1987, while recent census reports (2001) indicate that 35 percent of black families maintained by women were in poverty and 19 percent of black families maintained by men with no spouse present lived in poverty. The comparable rates for white families were 19 percent and 10 percent, respectively.

Statistics also prove that both African American males and females are likely to be employed in lower paying occupations and to receive lower wages within many occupations. According to Jesse McKinnon, in 2002, the unemployment rate for blacks was twice that for non-Hispanic whites, 11 percent and 5 percent, respectively. Recent history shows that the African American community lost about $15.2 billion in income due to high rates of unemployment (from 6 percent in 1969 to 12 percent in 1988). This increase from 570,000 unemployed to a record high of 1.7 million resulted in zero earnings for a significant number of black American individuals and families. African American males and teenagers were the hardest hit by unemployment. Overall, the most recent census figures reveal that the number of black families under the poverty level was 20 percent in 1969 and 21 percent in 2001, thus emphasizing that the economic racial divide for a significant minority of the black population continues. These adverse circumstances have also been detrimental to the life expectancy of the black population, particularly for males, whom death prematurely takes from the family. Life expectancy for black males has declined over the years, from 69.7 years in 1984 to 69.5 in 1985 and to 69.4 in 1986 and, according to the Centers for Disease Control and Prevention (CDC) in 2000, to 68.2 versus 74.8 for white males.

As though these misfortunes were not enough, the African American male has been hardest hit by drugs, crime, unemployment, lack of educational opportunities, prison sentences, and diseases, conditions that have created a severe shortage of prospective spouses within the black community. In 1983, it was estimated that, although the black male population accounts for only 6 percent of the U.S. population, about 50 percent of the U.S. prison population was black—about

80,671 black male prison inmates (contrasted to 6,836 black females). Delgado, in 2001, reported that, although blacks were 13 percent of the U.S. population, they represented 45 percent of those arrested for violent felonies and roughly half of those held in state and federal prisons. Ergo, no decrease in the percentage of blacks in the prison population over the past two or more decades is discernible. African American overrepresentation in prisons and jails is none less than startling. Even worse, historically, men of color have been overrepresented on death row, comprising 50 percent of the total of 5,416 persons sentenced to death from 1877 to 1997. This period also witnessed an overwhelming number of those who were executed—181 of the 432 men and women, or 44.2 percent.

The impact of these conditions on the number of males has been well documented. Thus, for example, in 1989, there were 95 white men to every 100 white females but only 90 black men to 100 black females. This shortage was most acute within the 24–45-year-old range, where the ratio was 85 for every 100 females. Interracial marriages have also had their impact on the black family and the availability of male partners. According to Lee, in 1990, black males were 2.5 times more likely to be married to a white female than black females married to a white male. The author reports, in accordance with the official 2000 census count, that black men are 2.82 times more likely to marry outside of their race, predominantly to white women, than black women are to marry outside of their race. According to the Bureau of the Census, in 1985, the black-white interracial married couples in the United States, the number of black male-white female unions was more than double the number of black female-white male unions." From 1970 to 1985, the number of black husband-white wife rose from 41,000 to 122,000 respectively, while that of black wife-white husband grew from 24,000 to 47,000 respectively during the same period. The interracial marriage trend continues, while drug use erodes the community and the black family. At the height of the war on drugs, from 1986 to 1991, the number of white drug offenders in state prisons increased by 110 percent. The number of black drug offenders grew by 465 percent. African Americans account for 14 percent of the nation's drug users, yet they make up 35 percent of those arrested for drug possession, 55 percent of those convicted for drug possession, and 74 percent of those sentenced to serve time according to Charles Shaw. According to the Federal Bureau of Prisons (2003), males represent 71.8 percent of those sentenced to serve time. In his study of the ratio between black males and females, Michael Williams warns of ominous consequences for the future of the black family and concludes by noting:

> When the numbers of black men who are homosexual, already married, uninterested in marriage, and for other reasons, unacceptable as mates, are excluded from the official Census Bureau statistics, the male to female ratio in the African-American community, in real terms, declines even more. In fact, Robert Staples has suggested that, in practical terms, there may be no more than one black man for every five single women in the United States.

The impact of disease on the black community is becoming clearer as more studies are completed. According to the CDC, in 2001 African Americans accounted for more than 833,000 estimated AIDS cases diagnosed since the beginning of the epidemic. By the end of December 2001, more than 168,000 African Americans had died from AIDS. In 2001, African Americans accounted for about

21,000 or 50 percent, of the more than 41,000 estimated new AIDS cases diagnosed among adults. The CDC also reported that African American men accounted for 43 percent of HIV cases among men in 2001, and African American women accounted for nearly 64 percent of HIV cases among women in the same year. The Black AIDS Institute has further documented that African American children represented almost two-thirds (62 percent) of all reported pediatric AIDS cases in 1998. Serious attention and collaborative intervention efforts on the part of stakeholders in the African American community including spiritual and religious leaders and organizations, educational systems, family systems of diverse structures, professional practitioners, and those directly impacted by the HIV virus or AIDS itself must become involved in preventive efforts to reverse this destructive occurrence in the black community.

The Survival of the African American Family

Many of the problems within the black community have an economic and racial bases. Thus, to understand and appreciate the economic difficulty of African American families, four social and economic disadvantages that have plagued African Americans must be understood.

First, African Americans own or control few businesses or other economic enhancing or job-creating institutions. Second, African Americans have had little accumulated wealth. Third, they have historically experienced racial discrimination in their attempts to gain equal access to education and employment opportunities controlled by whites. Finally, African Americans have traditionally had lower levels of formal training and education than their white counterparts. The impact of these economic circumstances on family functioning is negative. The primary functions of the family are: 1) to provide for the basic physical needs of its members and 2) to nurture them. Adequate income is required to fulfill the provider role which, if accomplished, raises the self-esteem of parents and consequently increases their ability to nurture their children. As job opportunities decline and unemployment gains momentum, a simultaneous decrease in two-parent families, increases in out-of-wedlock births, and the growth of an underclass of families in poverty can be seen.

The federal government has, over the years, provided some assistance to poor white and poor black families. As noted by Prater, the three primary forms of services historically offered by child and family welfare agencies are supportive services, supplemental services, and substitute services. These services are generally mandated at the micro level (individual and family) while using an ameliorative or restorative approach to service delivery for the purpose of improving family functioning. Supportive services, such as child care and counseling, provide help to families that are carrying out the basic caretaking role and providing for the principle needs of their members. Supplemental services are made available to families by the child welfare system to aid them in meeting the basic family functions of feeding, clothing, housing, and ensuring that adequate healthcare services are provided for their members. These services are offered through programs such as Medicaid, Food Stamps, and the Temporary Assistance for Needy Families (TANF) created by the Personal Responsibility and Work Opportunity Reconciliation Act of 1996. The latter replaces the former Aid to Families with Dependent Children, the Job Opportunities and Basic Skills Training (JOBS), and the Emergency Assistance Programs. Both supportive and supplemental services are usually provided to families in their own homes. Moreover, there is increased overlap of supportive and supplemental services as the federal guidelines for states link supportive and supplemental services such as child care with economic assistance such as TANF.

The final primary service category is substitute services. These are generally out-of-home services provided to children and families, when, for a myriad of reasons, families are unable to provide for the basic needs of their members. Examples of these services are foster care, group homes, and other institutional care, adoption, and other permanency planning options such as guardianship. A significant number of African American families interface with the child and family welfare system in the supportive, supplemental, and substitute service areas. Of importance is the fact that African American children are disproportionately represented in the foster and group home and other institutional care arenas. It should be further noted that extensive culturally competent service delivery and policy formulation and implementation are required to reverse this occurrence.

Child care provisions are especially important to support the goal of promoting self-sufficiency through work. The law (PRWORA: P.L. 14–193) is designed to streamline the federal government's role in child care services and increase flexibility to states. Historically, "states' rights" over federal government leadership have often not served the best interests of African Americans. Implementation issues that disproportionately affect black families include the extent to which child-care resources will be adequate to meet the needs of eligible low-income families including those who receive welfare and those who do not. Important factors for analysis and assessment are the specific work requirements developed by the states for welfare recipients, whether states comply with the federal work requirements, the amount of non-federal resources committed to child care, and whether states will use all child-care funds available from the federal government. Child care, including Head Start and Early Start, is especially important for African American low-income and poverty-stricken families, since the key to an economically self-sufficient and stable family in the African American community is usually comprised of both parents working in two-parent families. Further, it is necessary for a low-income female-headed family to maintain a job or participate in education and training for meaningful employment in order to approach sustainable economic self-sufficiency. Therefore, available, affordable, quality child care is necessary if this quest for self-sufficiency and family stability is to be achieved.

There is no doubt that, although the black family will survive, it will continue to face tremendous obstacles, both from within and from without, and solutions must be found to make its path more certain. In his article, "Critical Issues for Black Families by the Year 2000," Robert Hill outlines the problems the institution will face: 1) recessions and inflation which, in the past, have been extremely detrimental to the black community; 2) industrial shifts, particularly of industrial jobs from the inner city to the suburb, a shift that has always benefited the white middle class; 3) job mismatches, due to lack of adequate training; 4) new immigration patterns, which will see an increase in other minorities such as Hispanics and Asians fiercely competing with African Americans in education, employment, and housing; 5) federal budget cuts and tax reforms which could have an adverse impact on blacks; and 6) uncertain welfare reforms and non-cash benefits, for which the black community must be prepared.

Hill lists several important issues to be addressed by both the public and private sectors in order to strengthen and stabilize the African American family for the twenty-first century. These include: single parenthood, adolescent pregnancy, sensitive child support policies, available quality child-care services, formal foster care and adoption policies that build upon the informal adoption practices of the black community (permanency planning for African American children), family violence, drug and alcohol abuse, and the shortage of marriageable men.

Minimizing the impact of the serious problems that plague the African American family requires resources that build on the strengths of African American cultural experiences. These include strengthening the delivery of services to children and their families (which enhances family integrity and decreases the risk of inappropriate placement) and promoting prevention and early intervention services. Viewing the family as a system that deserves and should receive services based on need is an important philosophical stance to embrace if the goal is to improve the functioning of the African American family. Family preservation services or family-centered services embrace this philosophy and are designed with the intent of keeping families together and preventing out-of-home placement in child welfare protective services, juvenile justice, and mental health systems. The service providers (usually professionally trained social workers) offer intensive, time-limited, family-focused, and home-based services, including concrete and psycho-educational services, and often achieve positive outcomes for troubled African American families.

Empowering families is a common theme used in the family preservation or family-centered therapeutic model. As Carol Williams indicates, the lack of supports for families necessitates reshaping an impoverished policy environment by creating a policy context that is supportive of families and that minimally guarantees access to adequate income through training and employment, prenatal and postnatal health care, adequate housing, early intervention services of improved family functioning, and mental health, and drug-treatment services based on need. This form of public policy agenda requires restructuring the delivery of services to abusive and neglectful families so that families are preserved and reunified whenever feasible, while ensuring protection of the children. It calls for the expansion of the permanency options for children, which would include the following: 1) preservation of the family of origin; 2) adoption, if the former is not feasible; and 3) legal guardianship (a legal guardian is a person who has control over a minor's person or estate or both by decree of the court for purposes of protecting the minor).

Hill sees the "attainment of economic self-sufficiency, strengthening and stabilizing families, and developing viable and healthy communities" as the most important broad tasks of the black community for it to survive during the twenty-first century. Most scholars tend to agree that education, elimination of racism (the problem of twentieth-century America, in DuBois's view), and the provision of job and wealth creation opportunities (including economic development within the African American community) will go a long way in solving the problems facing the black family today.

Summary

The nature and the viability of the black family has been a focus of a heated debate among scholars and community leaders. While a few see it as pathological and decaying, the majority of the experts view the institution of the black family as vibrant, but facing strong challenges resulting from racism, inner city neglect, low income, and unemployment. Years of indifference on the part of the federal government and state agencies as far as correcting the shortcomings that have resulted from centuries of oppression have also contributed to the difficult plight of the black community.

Among the weaknesses often pointed out are the high rates of unemployment and illiteracy among blacks, drug use and prison occupancy, the shortage of black men, high teenage pregnancy rates, and the increasing number of female-headed households. However, those who believe that the black family is viable emphasize that most black families are resilient and demonstrate considerable strengths; that caring is certainly visible — particularly the love for children (perhaps an African carry- over which puts primacy on children); and that the sharing of responsibilities among the family members ensures its survival.

Some even point to major differences between the nature of the black family and that of the white family: that the black family tends to be an egalitarian unit in the decision-making process and, in the tradition of African families, it is extended and cherishes kinship bonds (no matter how distant they might be), and a sense of community. They further remind us that the successful struggles the black family has endured to survive and provide shelter, food, clothing, and emotional nurturing for each member of the family prove that it is here to stay. The debate is not over yet, and more research is currently being conducted on this critical issue. The methodology used and the assumptions of the researchers have added to the debate, some arguing that there is no typical African American family, and others rejecting the tendency to view the white middle class or, for that matter, the black middle class, as the ideal family — monogamous, small, and able to provide all the necessities of life, including leisure opportunities for the members of the household.

Study Questions and Activities

1. Compare and contrast the conditions of the black family during slavery and emancipation.
2. What are the factors that account for the high rate of poverty within the black community, and what are some of the solutions proposed by the experts and community leaders?
3. Read the writings of E. Franklin Frazier and those of Melville Herskovits and assess their positions on African survivals in the black community in America.
4. Why do you think the welfare of children is crucial to the survival of the black community?
5. Would you agree with the view that the African American family is sick and in danger of extinction or do you believe that it is alive and will continue to survive and thrive as it adapts itself to new circumstances? Why?

References

W.R. Allen. "The Search for Applicable Theories of Black Family Life." *Journal of Marriage and the Family* 40 (February): 117–29, 1978.

Black Issues in Higher Education. "The Top 100: Interpreting the Data." 19 (June 20, 2002)

American Humane Association. *Child Neglect Fact Sheet.* Washington, DC: U.S. Department of Health and Human Services, 2003.

Joan D. Atwood and Frank Genovese. *Counseling Single Parents.* Alexandria, VA: American Counseling Association, 1993.

Jessie Bernard. *Marriage and Family Among Negroes.* Englewood Cliffs, NJ: Prentice-Hall, 1966.

Andrew Billingsley. *Black Families in White America.* Englewood Cliffs, NJ: Prentice Hall, 1968.

Andrew Billingsley and Jeanne Giovannoni. *Children of the Storm: Black Children and American Child Welfare.* New York: Harcourt Brace Jovanovich, 1972.

Black AIDS Institute. *Helpful Factoids on the AIDS Crisis Among Africans and African Americans.* Author. http://www.aaapti.com/durban/fast_facts.htm, 2003.

John Blassingame. *The Slave Community.* London: Oxford University Press, 1972.

Centers for Disease Control and Prevention. Life expectancy Statistics: CDC, *National Vital Statistics Report (NVSR) vol. 50. Deaths: Final Data for 2000.* (April 24, 2003) Retrieved on December 2, 2003 AT http://www.healthgap.omhrc.gov/talfact03.htm.

Centers for Disease Control and Prevention. *HIV/AIDS Among African Americans.* National Center for HIV, STD and TB Prevention. http://www.cdc.gov/hiv/pubs/facts/afam.htm, 2003.

Neil A. Cohen (ed.). *Child Welfare: A Multicultural Focus.* Boston: Allyn and Bacon, 1992.

Melvin Delgado. *Where Are All the Young Men and Women of Color?* New York: Columbia University Press, 2001.

W. E. B. DuBois. *Black Reconstruction in American 1860–1880.* New York: Atheneum, 1962.

Federal Bureau of Prisons. *Federal Bureau of Prisons Quick Facts.* Washington, D.C.: U.S. Government Printing Office, 2003.

John Hope Franklin. *From Slavery to Freedom.* New York: Alfred Knopf, 1974.

Joint Center for Political and Economic Studies. "Number of Black Male Elected Officials Declining Says Joint Center Report." http://www.jointcenter.org (December 3, 2003).

E. Franklin Frazier. *The Negro Family in America.* Chicago: University of Chicago Press, 1939.

Herbert Gutman. The Black Family in Slavery and Freedom, 1750–1925. NewYork:Pantheon, 1976.

Robert L. Hampton. "Child Abuse in the African American Community," in Joyce E. Everett, Sandra S. Chipungu, and Bogart R. Leashore (eds.). *Child Welfare: And Africentric Perspective.* New Brunswick, NJ: Rutgers University Press, 1997.

Melville Herskovits. *The Myth of the Negro Past.* New York: Harper and Row, 1941.

Robert Hill. *Critical Issues for Black Families by the Year 2000,* in National Urban League. *The State of Black America, 1989.* New York: National Urban League, 1989.

———. *The Strengths of Black Families.* New York: Emerson Hall, 1972.

Dana Hughes and Elizabeth Butler. *The Health of America's Black Children.* Washington, DC: Children's Defense Fund, 1988.

B. Lee. (June/July 2003). "The Reality of Interracial Marriages." *The Multiracial Activist.*

Harriet P. McAdoo. *Black Families.* Beverly Hills, CA: Sage, 1981.

Jesse McKinnon. *The Black Population in the United States: March 2002.* (Current Population Reports, SeriesP20–541). Washington, DC :U.S. Census Bureau, 2003.

U.S. Department of Health and Human Services. National Child Abuse and Neglect Data System (NCANDS). *Child Abuse and Neglect Fact Sheet.* Washington, DC 2003.

———. *The State of Black America, 1989.* New York: National Urban League, 1989.

National Urban League. *The State of Black America*, 1991 New York: National Urban League, 1991.

Gwendolyn S. Prater. "Child Welfare and African American Families," pp. 377–389 in Neil A. Cohen (ed.). *Child Welfare: A Multicultural Focus.* Boston: Allyn and Bacon, 2000.

Lee Rainwater. "Crucible of Identity: The Negro Lower-Class Family." *Daedelus 95* (Winter 1966): 172–215.

Sexuality Information and Education Council of the United States. "Teen Pregnancy, Birth and Abortion," SIECUS Report, 30 (3), (February/March 2002).

C. Shaw. War on Drugs Unfairly Targets African-Americans. *St. Louis Dispatch*, 2000.

David Swinton. "Economic Status of Black Americans." In National Urban League. *The State of Black America, 1989.* New York: National Urban League, 1989.

The State of Families 2: Work and Family. Milwaukee, WI: Family Service America, 1987.

U.S. Bureau of Census. American FactFinder. *People: Race and Ethnicity.* Washington, D.C: U.S. Government Printing Office. http://factfinder.census.gov/jsp/saff/SAFFInfo.jsp?geo_id+01000US&_geoContect+&_stree..., 2002.

U.S. Bureau of Census. *Current Population Report Series: Household and Family Characteristics.* March 2002. Washington, DC: U.S. Government Printing Office.

U.S. Bureau of Census. *New Facts about African Americans: 1999.* Washington, DC: U.S. Government Printing Office, 2000.

U.S. Department of Health and Human Services. Administration for Children and Families. *Preventing Child Abuse and Neglect Reporting 2004.* National Clearing House on Child Abuse and Neglect Information (NCCANCI) webmaster_nccanch@caliber.com, 2005.

U.S. Department of Health and Human Services. *2001 National Statistics on Child Abuse and Neglect.* National Clearinghouse on Child Abuse and Neglect. http://www.calib.com/NCCANCH/Statutes, 2003.

Carol C. Williams. "Expanding the Options in the Quest for Permanence," in Joyce E. Everett, Sandra S. Chipungu, and Bogart R. Leashore (eds.). *Child Welfare: An Africentric Perspective.* New Brunswick, NJ: Rutgers University Press, 1997.

Michael Williams. "Some Empirical Dimensions of the Declining Male to Female Ratio in the African American Community." University of North Carolina at Charlotte, Department of African American and African Studies *Newsletter I* (1), (Spring 1989): 1–3.

Charles Vert Willie. *A New Look at Black Families.* Dix Hills, NJ: General Hall, 1988.

22

Religion in Africa

Mario Azevedo

Introduction

Throughout the centuries, religion has played a crucial role in the destiny of man. It has shaped his outlook of the universe, provided an explanation of his existence, and impacted his political, social, and economic behavior. While, on the one hand, religion has brought harmony, strengthened the bonds of brotherhood among peoples of the world, and fought racism and oppression, it has, on the other hand, fostered injustices (as was the case with slavery, colonialism, and apartheid), and reinforced global polarizations. On occasions, it has likewise caused untold suffering, as illustrated by the impact of the inquisition in medieval Europe, the crusades and the *jihads* (Islamic holy wars), the wars and the unending conflicts between Catholics and Protestants, and the vicious splits between moderates, fundamentalists, and the orthodox within the Christian denominations themselves as well as within Islam. More recently, religion has exacerbated the violent political cleavages among continental Africans, Nigeria, Chad, and Sudan being the prime examples. The following chapter takes a broad look at the state and role of three major religions in Africa, Islam, Christianity, and Traditionalism.

Major terms and concepts: Islam, Christianity, Traditionalism, ancestor, *sasa, zamani, jihad,* Muslim brotherhood, *Qur'an,* colonialism, monotheism, polytheism, slavery, civil rights, the five pillars of Islam, pantheism, ontology, cosmology, eschatology.

Traditional Religion

In contrast to both Islam and Christianity, it is much more difficult to discuss Africa's traditional religion. First of all, what has been called Traditionalism does not have a sacred book as does Islam or Christianity, no known religious founders, no proselytizers or missionaries coming from foreign lands roving in the countryside to secure coverts, and no *marabouts* (hermits, saints), or priests on the Western model. Furthermore, to the outsider, it looks as if African religion has no temples of worship, no representations of God, no reformers or prophets, and

to others

no complex dogmas. African religion prescribes no specific days of worship consistently held during the week, month, or year, as in the West. To add to the confusion of looking for uniform, organized religious practices, the first missionaries realized that virtually no traditional African society subjects children to formal and consistent "catechetical" training and drilling about religious beliefs and dogmas as is the standard practice in Christianity, Judaism, or Islam. To the outside world, especially Euro-Christians, Africans either had no religion or theirs was an "invisible" one.

This seeming void frustrated Christian missionaries as they began their work on the African continent, especially in Sub-Saharan Africa, and searched for authentic African religious beliefs they could contrast to their own. The problem was and still is compounded by the fact that little is written about Traditionalism (formerly labeled as paganism, heathenism, or even animism) because most literate Africans tend to be either Christians or Muslims, or, occasionally, atheists, and therefore are rarely interested in preserving or clarifying the African supernatural belief system.

Experts such as John Mbiti, Placide Temples, Geoffrey Parrinder, Benjamin Ray, and others, however, tell us that African religion is as complex as other religions of the world, in its attempt to explain humankind's existence on the planet and the issues of life and death. Unfortunately, a discussion of the African religious system must always carry the following caveat: one is entitled to talk of African religion only if one stresses the common elements of religious beliefs in Africa. If the emphasis, however, is on the differences (specific beliefs, rituals, responsibilities, for example) from region to region and from ethnic group to ethnic group, then the expression "African religions" is more appropriate, although it renders matters more complicated. Thus, while Mbiti writes of *African Religion*, Benjamin Ray titles his book *African Religions*. Therefore, only the common elements of traditional religion are discussed in this essay. Interestingly, as David Westerbund has uncovered in his study, continental African scholars tend to see similarities rather than differences in African religious practices. He attributes that to the fact that African scholars are more interested in creating or preserving the sense of nationhood and in fostering social solidarity in Africa than in pointing to differences, which can only perpetuate the strength of the ethnic group's affiliation.

The term Traditionalism in the present context refers to those supernatural beliefs and rituals that have existed on the continent since time immemorial without being intrinsically tampered with by foreign influences. Consequently, the word "indigenous" describes the concept better. An analysis of Traditionalism in Africa, particularly in Sub-Saharan Africa, reveals the following common features. First, African religion postulates the existence of one Supreme Being, God in Western terminology, for which every African language has its own term. This God is creator of the universe, omniscient, omnipotent, omnipresent, and caring. Perceived in anthropomorphic (human-like) form, He lives way up in the skies, and therefore stands remote from his creatures. Accordingly, only on special occasions man appeals or prays to Him directly (e.g., when a community is threatened by such calamities as epidemics, continued drought, and unexplained deaths that befall members of a family), as is the case among the Kikuyu and Maasai of Kenya. Otherwise, man must avail himself of His intermediaries: the spirits (sometimes inappropriately labeled by Western experts as deities, gods or lesser gods, making African societies polytheistic). In this context, therefore, the over-

whelming majority of African societies are essentially monotheistic in the sense
that they worship only one Supreme God.

In the traditional setting, true worship is only reserved to the Great God, because everything else is subordinate to Him. The spirits are designed to protect
humankind or to punish evil-doers, and serve as intermediaries or mediators between God and man, playing a role similar to that of Christ or the saints in Christianity. Ancestors, who are venerated rather than worshiped, are important
people who lived in the community, left their offspring, led an exemplary life, and
have joined the everlasting world of spirits. They are the protectors of the community and guarantors of morals. As such, they are the living-dead, who can also
reward and punish. Evil-doers are quickly forgotten by the community, since the
eschatological (related to the end of time) concepts of final judgement, purgatory,
eternity, hell, and heaven are not part of African religious traditions. Thus, while
going to hell in Africa can be equated to being forgotten by one's community because of the evil deeds one committed on earth, being in heaven is remaining in
the memory of the living as the "living-dead." In this context, God is not a capri-
cious and an imperfect being that constantly changes his mood by getting mad or
happy, and spending His time determining how to punish or reward humans. This
function is essentially reserved for the ancestors.

Mbiti makes an interesting point about the African concept of time. He claims
that Africans are mainly concerned with the recent past, the present, and the immediate future (two years at maximum), which he calls the micro-time or *sasa* (a
Swahili word). The remote past, the macro-time, or *zamani* (another Swahili concept), equivalent, at maximum, to five generations, is meaningless or incompre-
hensible to them. Thus, the relevant immortality of the soul applies only to *sasa*,
which Mbiti calls personal immortality. Once the last living member who might
remember the deceased dies, the living-dead (ancestor) falls into *zamani*, achieving collective immortality as a spirit, and becomes irrelevant to his or her community. If Mbiti is correct, therefore, the limited number of eschatological concepts
(those that refer to the future) in African Traditional religion may be well explained. In fact, Mbiti attempts to prove his point by noting that the future tense
in most African languages applies only to up to two years. It is within the context
of *sasa* and *zamani* that deceased individuals, no matter how virtuous they might
have been during their life time on earth, never share of the divinity of the creator
or the place (heaven) where God is thought to live. We might say, therefore, that,
if there are irreconcilable differences between Christianity or Islam and Traditionalism, they lie mainly in the nature of the after-life (if Mbiti's study is accepted).

On the other hand, however, African Traditionalists, just as the Christians do,
make sacrifice, involving 1) the shedding of the blood and the viscera of an animal
or bird, usually a lamb, a goat, or a chicken and 2) consumption of meat by those
officiating the ritual, who may be priests, elders, or selected others. Offerings to
the spirits consist of foodstuffs, during harvest, e.g., water, milk, honey, drinks (as
a libation) or even money. Prayers for good health, rain, success, and protection
against the elements are usually accompanied by offerings and sacrifice and by
singing and dancing. Africans may worship at specific places (such as a forest, a
tree, a shrine, a cemetery, a simple altar, or the back of the household dwelling),
as is the case among the Yoruba of Nigeria. In the past, many societies built elaborate temples, as was the case in Ghana, Nigeria, Tanzania, Zimbabwe, and Zambia. As a result of Western intrusion, says Mbiti, very few of these are left or built

Temples 〟

these days. Shrines, both private and communal, are the most common religious places, and are found all over Africa. Africans also perform rituals that are specifically related to birth or death, adulthood or marriage, and the seasons, and thus may be related to agriculture (planting and first fruits), stock-keeping, milking, bloodletting, health, and other occasions that follow the rhythm of life. African Traditionalists may use images as well to represent the spirit or the spiritual world (e.g., sculpture, masks, and statuettes) and symbols that carry spiritual content and message. On such occasions, "priests" (rarer now with the fading of the temples, especially in East and Central Africa), elders, chiefs, or heads of the family may be officiating. These may be called "specialists," to use Mbiti's terminology.

Contrary to Western or Middle Eastern tradition, in traditional Africa, children are exposed to religion in their daily lives and not necessarily through special sermons, daily chanting or memorization (as with Islam), or through years of schooling. The constant indirect or direct, brief admonitions from the parents and the clan, the songs, the proverbs, the riddles, and the rituals, all reinforce the religious message about God, the spirits, or the ancestors. In this sense, therefore, children grow up in a religion which permeates their entire life cycle. As some experts put it, "African religion is life and African life is religion." Among societies that practice initiation ceremonies or rites of passage that mark the transition from childhood to adulthood, religious instruction simply becomes not a lesson apart from but a part of the process of learning about one's responsibilities and rights as a member of society.

Africanist theologians tell us that African cosmology (view of the universe or cosmos) evolves around the idea of a God who is (or transmits) a vital force, which in turn informs everything living or non-living. This is not, however, conceived in a pantheistic sense (or that everything is God and can therefore be worshiped). It is this ontological (relative to being) view that has led Western theologians and philosophers to use the word *animism* for African religion(s). Actually, animism is an inaccurate concept that does not express the true meaning of African belief systems. Indeed, African traditionalists do not believe that a man, a lamb, a bird, a stone, the wind and water, the sun and the moon all have souls or that they are gods (which must be worshiped), as the word animism, derived from the Latin word *anima*, implies.

It must also be acknowledged here that, because African traditional religion is not compartmentalized, scholars find it hard to classify certain traditions (sorcery, for example) as religious or simply as aspects of culture which would have endured even if Africans were atheists. For example, the Western beliefs that a black cat crossing the street or the number 13 are omens of bad luck are characterized as superstition in Western tradition because they have no provable basis. However, to the extent that sorcery, witchcraft, divination, and magic contain elements of the supernatural (as naturally inexplicable) and are sometimes a part of the religious ritual in Africa, they may be discussed in the context of traditional religion.

To be sure, sorcery is a willfully acquired power to cause evil in others. A sorcerer, usually thought to be a female, is believed to travel even long distances at night, causing death, illness, injuries or bad luck to enemies, animals, and even crops through secret spells and poisoning. Witchcraft, on the other hand, is an inborn (innate), uncontrollable power to cause evil in other people through words, rituals, incantations, and magical objects such as nails, hair, cloth, and other people's possessions, according to Mbiti. Both powers are, of course, socially unacceptable and are viewed as evil states of mind and immoral behavior which must be eradicated or whose potential harm must be prevented by securing (in most cases) the help of medicine-men (often pejoratively labeled as witchdoctors), oracles, mediums (those who can establish contact with the spirit world), diviners or fortune-tellers and seers (those able to see things others cannot see), both of whom can also be medicine-men. The triad of sorcerer, witch and medicine-man or traditional healer (TRH) exists in every Sub-Saharan African society. While sorcery and witchcraft are symptoms of a sick society, medicine men or medicine-women exist to mend society both physically and spiritually. Some studies have shown, for example, that the frequency of sorcery and witchcraft cases increased with the advent of colonialism due to the unique suffering it caused and that, in time of crises, the cases tend to intensify. This seems to have been the case during the German occupation of Tanganyika, which led to the 1905–1907 Maji Maji Rebellion against the Germans, and during World War I, with the so-called War Effort. Thus, sorcerers and witches, once discovered, are brought to public trial, ostracized, and sometimes killed through poisoning or deadly rituals. They may also be forced to pay compensation proportional to the evil or misfortune "inflicted" on the victim, the family, or the clan.

Magic, on the other hand, is the ability to manipulate the powers of nature or the vital force, to use Father Temples's expression. As such, magic can be good, as is the case when a chief is believed to bring rain after a period of severe drought, or bad, as when a medicine-man might "inflict" pain in a patient who refuses to pay promised consultation or treatment fees. Beliefs in the supernatural powers of the witch, the sorcerer, the medicine-man, or the healer, the diviner, and the fortune teller are widespread and strong in Sub-Saharan Africa, and are therefore hardly abandoned totally even by devout Christians or Muslims. This reality has caused great frustration and discouragement among Western missionaries some of whom have concluded that an African, even after generations, can never be a true Christian. In fact, one may find Catholics who receive Communion at Mass at 10:00 a.m. on Sunday or speak in tongues during an Apostolic Church service and then go home and pour libations to the spirits or the ancestors. Interestingly, TRH's, who incurred the wrath of the missionaries, are now being officially rehabilitated all over Africa because of their knowledge of human nature and familiarity with the curative power of certain trees, roots, and leaves. It is acknowledged now that they can successfully diagnose and treat several blood diseases. As a result, they remain very popular even among the educated Africans, who go to them when Western medicine is unavailable or ineffective. This explains why so many African religious beliefs remained among transplanted Africans in the Americas — in the Voodoo rituals of Haiti, for example, in the *Santeria* of Brazil, and in the highly emotional Baptist and Pentecostal Churches of black Americans in the United States, in which the state of "possession" by the spirit among the worshippers, as in Africa, is common.

Finally, it should be said that, because religious beliefs are absorbed naturally and become an intrinsic part of the self of the African child as he or she grows to become a man or a woman, traditional religion, contrary to what we are told by partisan Muslim and Christian statistics alike, presently marshals more followers on the continent than the two faiths. However, the future of Traditionalism in Africa is at risk stemming from several forces, including: 1) absence of a proselytizing zeal; 2) lack of an effort to religiously organize across clans; 3) eternal tolerance for other religions on the part of Traditionalists (who, for example, have never gone to war to stop foreign crusaders or to impose their beliefs on others); 4) and the fact that education has meant Westernization, which has meant the abandonment of essential traditional teachings. Indeed, while Africa faces growing atheism on the part of its young men and women who live in the large urban centers, the roots of Traditionalism are constantly weakened by aggressive attempts by both Christianity and Islam, in particular, to find new followers. To its credit, however, it must be said that Traditionalism has never been a religion of divisiveness on the continent. By contrast, even though Christians are supposed to be united by their belief in Christ's incarnation, death, resurrection, and second coming, they are nevertheless desperately disunited, making the recent ecumenical movement inconsequential. The controversial ordination of a gay bishop in the US Episcopal Church in October 2003 proves the point beyond a doubt. Likewise, the rivalry between Christianity and Islam in Africa has contributed to wars in Nigeria, Sudan, and Chad, and to riots and military coups in other parts of the continent. What did Christ say about loving one's neighbor?

Impact of Christianity

Christianity has become one of the oldest major religions in Africa. This has prompted renowned Kenyan theologian and philosopher John Mbiti to note in his *African Philosophies and Religion* (1969) that "Christianity in Africa is so old that it can rightly be described as indigenous, traditional and African religion." Three major phases characterized the spread of this religion on the African continent. First, was the arrival of Christianity in North and Northeast Africa, as early as the first century A.D. The Coptic Church in Egypt and the Orthodox Church in Ethiopia claim that St. Mark, the Gospel writer, evangelized the area and converted many Africans. It is also known that, during the fourth century, Ezanas, Emperor of Ethiopia (or Abyssinia), made Christianity the religion of the state, as depicted in the Ethiopian flag and the symbols of the era. Likewise, Nubia and parts of present Chad had become Christian enclaves up until the coming of Islam during the seventh century. Northern Sudan did not succumb to Islam until the sixteenth century, while, in Ethiopia, Islam made limited inroads (except in parts of Eritrea, where both Islam and Christianity have maintained a strong foothold).

Interestingly enough, the earlier African Church was much more creative and vibrant than the present, taking part in the most important activities of the Church of Rome. Thus, the contributions to theology, asceticism, and monasticism by famous African clerics such as Saint Augustine (a Berber who became Bishop of Hippo and turned out to be a renowned theologian who wrestled with the mystery of the Trinity), Tertullian (150–258), Cyprian (200–258), Origen (182–251), Clement of Alexandria (d. 215), and others have not gone unnoticed among informed and interested scholars. Their writings, their influence in Church synods and councils, their defense of the Christian doctrine as they interpreted it, and their sometimes independent thinking, notwithstanding the position of Rome, attest to the extraordinary role the early African Christian Church played in Christendom. While Augustine attempted to explain the Trinity, for example, Clement and Origen synthesized Platonism and Christianity. As a result of the theological and philosophical activity of the early Church Fathers in North Africa, for a long time it was not clear whether Rome would continue to be the seat of Christianity. However, the invasion of North Africa by the Vandals in 429 and the subsequent fall of the city of Hippo in 431 (St. Augustine died during the siege of the city), the seventh-century Islamic onslaught, and theological differences with Rome, contributed to the decline of the primordial Christian Church and to the ultimate independence of the Coptic Church (centered in Alexandria, Egypt). Leaders of the new Church eventually refused to recognize the authority of the Bishop of Rome, the Pope, as the successor to Peter.

The second phase was spurred by the arrival of the Portuguese on the coast of Africa after 1415. Officially, the Portuguese voyages were intended primarily to reach India by sea and to fight the so-called Moors or African Muslims who threatened Western Europe and the Holy Land. Increasingly, however, the voyages became religious crusades, designed also to spread Christendom and allow the forging of an alliance between the Portuguese and the legendary Christian king Prester John, identified as the emperor of Ethiopia only in 1505. As a result, not only was the Church of Ethiopia revitalized with the coming of the Portuguese, but the newcomers established missions in Angola, Congo, Mozambique, Benin, Mwenemutapa, Mombasa, and other parts of Africa. In the Congo, for example, they converted the royal family and one of the kings, Afonso (baptized a Catholic with this Portuguese name), had one of his sons ordained a priest. In Mwenemutapa, Father Gonçalo da Silveira converted the king, his family, and his court in 1560. (In 1561, however, the Jesuit priest was murdered, and the Portuguese implicated the king in the plot, even though some accounts blame the murder on the jealousies and intrigues of Arab merchants.) During this phase, the Portuguese did most of the missionary activity. The Spanish, the French, the Dutch, and the British focused mainly on legitimate trade. The decline of the Portuguese in Europe, the intensity of the Atlantic slave trade, which replaced earlier trading activities, the anti-clericalism of the Marquis of Pombal, once Prime Minister of Portugal (1750–1777), and subsequent anti-religious actions undertaken by the Portuguese government contributed to the rapid deterioration of the Church in Africa. Dominicans, Jesuits, Franciscans, and other religious orders, for example, were expelled from the Portuguese colonies during the eighteenth and nineteenth centuries, leaving hundreds of churches totally abandoned.

One of the root problems encountered by these Euro-Christian Churches in Africa was the failure to train and ordain an indigenous clergy. Unfortunately, the same problem was to plague the next phase, particularly within the Catholic Church. There was a minor revival of Christianity at the end of the eighteenth and early nineteenth centuries, when Sierra Leone and Liberia were created, ushering in a good number of African Americans and West Indians, such as Bishop Edward Wylmott Blyden (1832–1912), whose mission, as they stated it, was to "civilize and Christianize Africa." However, the era of real revival of Christianity in Africa coincided with the advent of colonialism, following the Berlin Conference (1884–1885). The Berlin Act forbade discrimination of religious activity on account of denomination both on the coast and in the interior of Africa.

In this effort, Protestant missionaries outdid the Catholic Church in most of Africa. The Anglicans (in West and Central Africa) and the Baptists, the Seventh-Day Adventists, the Methodists, and the Presbyterians (in South-Central Africa) outpaced the work of the Catholic missionaries who became active mostly in the Portuguese, Belgian, and some French colonies, and in Uganda. (In South Africa, the Dutch Reformed Church had been taking root since 1652, but Anglicans and Catholics also established missions and parishes there during the nineteenth century.) As a result of colonial occupation, missionaries found it easier to gain access to Africa's remote areas to the extent that, prior to independence, Africans were being converted to Christianity in unprecedented numbers. Yet, it was feared that, after independence, Africans would abandon the old Euro-Christian tradition along with its various denominations and sects. However, the prophets of doom saw the numbers of conversions soar after 1960 as the Church continued to Africanize itself in ritual and personnel, while simultaneously attempting to meet the social needs of the faithful. Consequently, during the early 1990s, the number of Christians on the continent was estimated at more than 200 million out of a total population of 750 million Africans and, accoring to the *Encyclopædia Britannica Almanac*, as of 2003 there were 394 million out of a total population of 851 million.

Notwithstanding the controversy over the methods, the role played by the Church in Africa's development, particularly in health and education, has been heralded even by critics as pivotal. Indeed, it is acknowledged that Christian missions educated more Africans than the colonial governments. Missionaries established the first schools in most areas, including the remote hinterland; built the first health care centers; and promoted several indigenous languages through the collection of folklore and translation of the Bible. Many religious orders, such as Cardinal Lavigerie's Missionaries of Africa (also known as White Fathers), urged their clergy to learn and speak African languages so they could better communicate with the faithful. In spite of the emphasis missionaries laid on religion to the neglect of the political and social well being of the Africans, it is a known fact that, in most of Africa, the first African nationalists and leaders were products of mission schools. Skillfully using the arguments of equality preached but rarely observed by the missionaries themselves or the colonial government, the new nationalists successfully challenged the imposed European presence on the continent. Even the late Walter Rodney who, in general, argued against the colonial Christian Church in almost every respect, admitted that the Church contributed to the end of the killing of twins and trials by ordeal among certain African societies.

Unfortunately, however, missionary work was also plagued with many shortcomings. As noted earlier, most mission schools and parishes made little attempt to train a local clergy and adapt the Church to African cultures and realities. The continued use of the Latin in Catholic liturgy, even when Vatican II had lifted a ban on the use of vernacular languages, the wholesale adoption of European hymns in Church celebrations and services, the use of white images and symbols in churches and in teaching, and proscription of African musical instruments in worship proved that the Church was insensitive to Africa's valued traditions. There were other problems: The proliferation of denominations, which desperately confused the uninformed faithful; the emphasis on elementary education to the neglect of secondary or university education for Africans; the constant chastisement of African values and customs, particularly the practice of polygamy; and the deliberate restraint imposed on the expression of spontaneous emotions in church services, particularly among the Catholics, Lutherans, Anglicans, and Methodists—all constituted insurmountable contradictions for the institution.

More importantly, the racist attitude of many of the missionaries, ministers, pastors, and priests became a major issue for Christians Africans.

The most severe problem facing the Church on the continent, however, was the (often correct) African perception that the Church was in collusion and in alliance with the colonial authorities—hence the experts' fear that the end of colonialism in Africa also meant the eventual demise of Christianity on the continent. As Professor Nyang in his *Islam, Christianity, and African Identity* (1984) puts it, "When Africa finally came under colonial rule, the European missionary found himself in a very difficult position. Though protected by the colonial regime from the attacks and harassments of an unruly population somewhere within the newly established colony, his national and racial association with those manning the colonial apparatus soon exposed him to African suspicion and hostility." These contradictions and shortcomings account for the rise of African independent (Ethiopian or Zionist) churches on the continent, especially during the 1920s and 1930s. For example, the racist attitudes of the American Zulu Mission founded in Natal, South Africa, in 1844, which refused to ordain black ministers, lost many of its members who joined other churches or founded their own. In 1888, the Lagos Baptist Church led by Rev. D.B. David, a segregationist American missionary, saw 200 of its 204 members leave and follow Moses Stone and D.B. Vincent, who established their own Native Baptist Church. The Methodist Episcopal Church founded in Inhambane, Mozambique, in 1895 and supervised by an American racist missionary by the name of Erwin H. Richard, lost in 1917 many of its members, who went on to found the Mozambique Independent Methodist Episcopal Church under the leadership of Muti M. Sikbele. Richard is said to have been such a racist that he once wrote that the African "...is stark naked for the most part and full of lecherous sores and his spiritual nature is so very low that his breath would pollute the waters of the Stygian Lake—of which it is said that it stunk so bad the birds were unable to fly over it" (Gershoni, 1997: 19).

One recalls also the outcome of the 1920s and 1930s fight between Christian missionaries and African converts over the issue of circumcision and clitoridectomy in Kenya, which led to the creation of several independent African churches and schools. The African Inland Mission, the Gospel Mission, and the Church of Scotland Mission (CSM) in Kikuyu country, the latter led by zealot crusader Rev. John Arthur of the CSM in 1929, lost 90 percent of their members and almost 80 percent of their African school children, whose parents and teachers refused to sign a pledge to abandon the rites of passage to adulthood. Some independent churches, as was the case of Simon Kimbangu's in the former Belgian Congo during the 1920s, became veiled nationalist stages, prompting the colonial administration to incarcerate the leaders. (Kimbangu died in jail after being incarcerated for 30 years.) Other independent Churches and sects that sprang up in Central and East Africa were genuine attempts at creating indigenous African Christian institutions, just as the Europeans had created theirs, which they subsequently propagated with racial overtones in Africa. Independent churches were established as an attempt to explain African suffering under colonialism and its organized religious institutions. In the process, the leaders of Kimbanguism, Khakism, Tonsism, Mpandism, and several others weaved together selected Christian teachings and African traditional beliefs.

Interestingly, many of the churches were also millenarian and messianic in character extracted from the cheaply available American Watch Tower writings (in African languages) and the preaching of the Seventh-Day Adventists, predicting that the impending thousand years were at hand and that the Messiah would come to end the rule of the white church and liberate Africans from the shackles of colonialism. Watch Tower followers, some of whom had familiarized themselves with the Marcus Garvey's radical racial philosophy embedded in his Universal Negro Improvement Association (UNIA), rejected the church hierarchical structure and embraced the "more fundamentalist, egalitarian interpretations of the Scriptures," considering all governments as Satanic and the organized churches as "Satan's emissaries." Basing their teachings on the Old Testament, they predicted an Apocalyptic (God-revealed) Armageddon (i.e., the last battle between evil and good) that would pit Goliath (the white world) against David (the suffering African people) and end in David's victory! In fact, in the process, some leaders proclaimed themselves the anointed Messiahs and incited their congregations to take up arms against colonial rule only to be incarcerated and at times killed by the colonial administration. For example, Tomo Nyiremba of Nyasaland, educated at the Scottish Livingstonia Mission, formed a very popular millenarian sect in the then Northern Rhodesia during the mid-1920s, where people considered him to be "the resurrection of their traditional god [sic]" (Gershoni, 44). His Nyasaland Tonga friend, Elliot Kamwana, also educated at the same mission, had founded his own messianic church as a local branch of the Watch Tower in October 1908. Nyiremba changed his name to Mwana Lesa, meaning the Sun of God in the Lala language. Some of the leaders were so zealous that they went after those who were accused of witchcraft, which they considered to be anti-social and anti-Christian. Thus, while Tomo Nyiremba, mentioned above, led a crusade against it and executed 174 "witches" in Northern Rhodesia and former Belgian Congo before the authorities stopped him, William Wade Harris, calling himself a "prophet in Cote d'Ivoire (1913–1915), "destroyed fetishes and offered baptism as protection from evil spirits." For obvious reasons, the independent church movement has continued to spread in Africa even today, and it is reported that, during the 1990s, a total of some 4,000 independent churches and sects flourished on the continent.

In an effort to learn from its past mistakes, Christianity in Africa today is becoming an action-orientated institution. In order to be relevant, it is making strides to preserve those cultural elements that are not specifically condemned by the Gospels; allows the laity to take an active part in matters and decisions that affect their various dioceses, parishes, and congregations; and stresses the importance of achieving happiness in this life, if at all possible. In fact, as David Thebehali asks (in *A New Look at Christianity*, 1972):

> Why should not a black man be called to church by a big drum, as he was generally called to any public meeting? Why in the name of reason and common sense should not a black man bear his name, and wear his own garments? Why, indeed, other than that the simple missionaries had from the beginning ruled that all these things were against the spirit of the Gospel which they saw as inalienably wedded to their Western culture?

As a result, today's Church in Africa is increasingly being staffed totally by Africans, whose leaders are finally becoming bishops, cardinals, deacons, and pastors in their own countries, positions which had been reserved for the white clergy in years past. The Anglicans, for example, demonstrated their commitment and pragmatism even in apartheid South Africa with the consecration of now retired Desmond Tutu as their first African Archbishop. To the extent that Christianity attempts to adapt itself to the African reality, as is now the trend, and continues to provide educational opportunities and health care for the needy, as it did prior to independence, it has a bright future on the continent. In this context, is it not amazing that in 2005, within the Catholic Church, before the election of Benedict XVI, there was talk that the next Pope could have been an African cardinal.

The Expansion of Islam

In an article on Islam published in *The Cambridge History of Africa* (1986), C.C. Stewart echoes what many experts on Islam have observed, namely, that "the most remarkable feature of Islam in twentieth century Africa has been the rapidity with which diverse communities embraced the faith." Unfortunately, most estimates of the Muslim population in Africa are results of guess-work and are often contradictory. While Ali Mazrui, himself a Muslim, quotes the figure of 80 million in 1951 (from 40 million in 1931), and notes that, at that time, out of 130 million Africans in Sub-Saharan Africa, 28 million were Muslim, 17 million Christian, and 85 million Traditionalist, Geoffrey Parrinder estimates that there were more than 83 million Muslims in Africa in 1966, 68 million Christians, and 130 million Traditionalists, out of a total population of 280 million Africans. John Mbiti, on the one hand, believes that, in 1969, the number of Muslims and Christians in Africa approached the 100 million and the 70 million mark respectively, while M. Ali Kettany, on the other hand, provides the following figures: 202 million Muslims in 1971, rising to 276,190,000 in 1982, out of a total African population of 508,700,000 that year. Kettany adds in his *Muslim Minorities in the World Today* (1986) that "Africa is the Muslim continent of the world." It would seem, however, that the true Muslim population of Africa stood at less than 250 million during the late 1980s.[1] The *World Almanac* cites the figure of 264,132,000 Muslims for the year 1992, but this number is still unreliable because it is based on an estimated total population of 647,518,000 for Africa, when the UN figure was around 750 million for the continent in early 1991. As of mid-2003, the *Encyclopædia Britannica Almanac*, counts 344 million Muslims out of a total population of 851 million.

In spite of its foreign origins and the uncertainty over the numbers of its adherents, there is no doubt that Islam has become one of the most widespread religions on the African continent. The North, comprising Egypt, Tunisia, Algeria, Libya, and Morocco, is practically all Muslim, while Nigeria, Senegal, Sudan, Guinea, Sierra Leone, Niger, Somalia, Tanzania, Djibouti, Mali, and Chad have large Muslim populations. At present, some studies predict that Islam will continue to gain grounds over Christianity and Traditionalism. How did Islam spread over Africa and why has it been so successful on the continent?

Islam, meaning "submission" (to Allah), originated in what is now Saudi Arabia, in the city of Mecca. Islam is based on the teachings of Muhammad

1. References to Islam in East Africa, co-authored by Mario Azevedo and Gwendolyn S. Prater in the *Journal of Islamic Minority Affairs*, vol. 12, 2 (1992): 482–97, are printed here with permission of the *Journal*.

(570–632), who proclaimed himself the last of the prophets in the line of Moses and Jesus, entrusted with a message from God by Archangel Gabriel. The message purportedly entrusted to him is contained in the Islamic holy book known as the *Qur'an*. Following his marriage at the age of twenty-five to a wealthy forty-year old widow, Muhammad began preaching his new religion in Mecca. Persecuted there, he was forced to seek refuge in Medina in 622. Here, his new religion was well received, which allowed him to return to Mecca and succeed in his previously failed religious crusade.

As a result of its successful religious and political sweep over most of the Arab Middle East, Islam, after sanctioning the use of the "holy war" (*jihad*) to convert "pagans," penetrated North Africa around 640 and reached the shores of the Atlantic Ocean within the next 50 years. Through force and persuasion, traveling often on camels, the adherents of the new religion prevailed over the indigenous inhabitants of North Africa, who were mostly Berbers rather than Arabs, converting the whole Maghrib (Libya, Tunisia, Algeria, and Morocco) to Islam. Thus, by the end of the sixteenth century, Islamic Arabs had taken over the Maghrib religiously and politically, and from there succeeded in converting the Berbers. Islam then pushed southward to Sub-Saharan Africa through the Sahara desert—not only to find new converts but also to subjugate new peoples and lands in the name of Allah.

Two major sects developed among the Berbers: the Almoravids, who, following the teachings of Abu Bakr (d. 1087) and Imam Al Hadrami (d. 1096), preached a strict interpretation and practice of Islam; and the Almohads, who instead espoused a more liberal theology, stressing the importance of a personal and individual relationship with Allah as opposed to the external observance of rituals and ancient teachings. It was the Almoravids who took the initiative to penetrate West Africa. After successes in Mauritania, Mali, and Niger, they invaded Ghana, which fell to their armies in 1076. Although evicted from Ghana in 1087, the Almoravids had laid the foundations for Islam to subsequently spread to Mali and Songhay. There, such Muslim rulers as Mansa Mussa of Mali (1312–1337) and Askia Muhammad of Songhay (1493–1538)—both of whom made celebrated pilgrimages to Mecca—attempted to impose the new religion on Traditionalist Africans. From there, Islam penetrated—through the work of Muslim merchants, *marabouts* (saints or hermits), learned men, and proselytizers—to other areas of West Africa, including Senegal, Sierra Leone, Liberia, and parts of Côte d'Ivoire.

The *jihad*, as an arm of Islam, was extensively used in the Senegambia area, where the converted pastoral Fulani of Futa Jallon (1725) and of Futa Toro (1775) defeated their Traditionalist rulers and imposed on them their new religion. In parts of Nigeria, where such Hausa states as Kano, Katsina, Gobir, and Zaria had nuclei of Islamic communities, in Northern Cameroon, and in Northern Chad, the nineteenth century *jihads* (initiated or authorized by the now famous Usuman dan Fodio) assured the total victory of Islam over the Traditionalist rulers and institutions. Dan Fodio, a Fulani learned man, a teacher, and a protege of the king of Gobir, did not hesitate to revolt against his master to restore pristine Islam as he saw it. Toward that end, he called on his fellow Fulani to join him in a crusade against the Hausa rulers in 1804, an appeal that attracted even non-Muslims who were overburdened by taxes and tired of tyrannical rule. Having won the war, dan Fodio established himself as the *Caliph* (head of a Muslim state) of Sokoto, in what is now Northern Nigeria, making his son Mohammad Bello his *emir* (viceroy, governor, prince) at Sokoto and his brother Abdallah *emir* at Gwandu. His followers continued the "crusade" into Northern Cameroon (particularly in Adamawa) and in Northern Chad where they established strong centralized systems based on the law of Islam (*shari'a*).

Along with the *jihads*, several Muslim orders or brotherhoods (known as *tariqa*, meaning path)—including the Qadiriyya (founded in Baghdad during the twelfth century), the *Tijaniyya*, and the *Ahmadiyya*—became powerful and fervent weapons in the spread of Islam in West Africa, particularly in Senegal and Nigeria. Ira Lapidus (in his *History of Islamic Societies,* 1988) notes that Islam experienced three major phases before it became a part of African life, namely: 1) the acceptance of its "material culture" (food, ornaments, and concepts); 2) formal conversion, including the worship of Allah and the acceptance of the *ulama* (Muslim scholars); and 3) adoption of Islamic law and the five "pillars" of Islam, "as well as the introduction of Islamic customs in "rituals of circumcision, marriage, and death." The five pillars of Islam are: 1) belief in Allah as God and Muhammad as his Prophet; 2) prayer held five times a day; 3) observance of Ramadan, a month-long fasting; 4) pilgrimage to Mecca at least once in one's lifetime; 5) and giving alms to the poor.

In Sudan, Islam encountered serious difficulties in its attempt to dislodge the Christians in Nubia, where Christianity had taken roots as early at the fourth century. Constant intercourse between Egypt and Northern Sudan, however, assured by the sixteenth century the ultimate victory of Islam in what is now Northern Sudan. When the Turks, in 1820, followed by the Egyptians and the British in 1898, imposed their rule over Sudan, Islam had already prevailed in the north, while the south continued to be mostly Traditionalist and Christian. This religious and cultural dichotomy later exacerbated the country's political problems, as the Muslim rulers insisted on imposing the *shari'a* on all regions. In Ethiopia, Islamic crusaders also met the resistance of the Amharic emperors and kinglets who had converted to Christianity and had formed the Orthodox Church (until 1959 hierarchically subordinate to the Coptic Church of Alexandria).

The east coast and, to a certain degree, the hinterland, had established and maintained trade relations with India, China, and the Arabian Peninsula well before the beginning of the Christian era. The now famous *Chronicle of Kilwa* indicates that, during the eighth century, Arabs had already settled on the Somali coast, joined a century later by Shirazi traders and immigrants. The *Periplus of the Erythrean Sea*, a Greek merchant's maritime guide, and the writings of Arab trader Ibn Battuta, confirm these early movements and settlements of Arabians and Persians on the east coast of Africa. Given the success of the trading activities on the coast, more immigrants, particularly Muslim Arabs from Hadramaut in Southern Arabia, Aden, and Yemen arrived on dhows propelled by the monsoons on the East African coast as traders and seamen, some of whom settled on the islands, married African women, and helped establish permanent trading posts (Lamu, Pate, Shango, Zanzibar, Manda, Mafia, Mombasa) and create a unique language and culture known now as Swahili. A surge in trading activity resumed after 1698 when Omani Arab soldiers and mercenaries chased the Portuguese out of Mombasa and settled there permanently. In 1840, Sultan Sayyd Said moved his Omani capital from Muscat to promising and secure Zanzibar.

A unique feature of the newcomers, however, was the fact that, contrary to what happened in North and West Africa, they came as individuals, without their families. East Africa's universally precious and exotic trade items attracted the attention of a large number of seafaring Muslim entrepreneurs, searching for incense, ambergris (ninth century), and leopard skins and gold, particularly from Zimbabwe down to Sofala in Mozambique (tenth century), iron (twelfth century), gum and myrrh (thirteenth century), cotton cloth, grain, corn, rice, millet, sorghum, sugar cane, coconut palm, orange, sesame, timber, dyes, perfumes (fourteenth century), tortoise shell, slaves, ivory, and cloves (fifteenth century). Imports included swords, food stuffs, cloth, wine, guns, and gunpowder, from Europe and the Middle East, lances, glass, porcelain from China and Arabia, copper, hatchets, and cannons. However, the Bantu-speaking, non-Muslim populations remained the major link and middlemen between the hinterland and the coast and (at times) coastal *sheikhs* (Muslim officials, heads of family or clan) made specific agreements with the chiefs of the interior to preserve this status quo. Thus, only during the nineteenth century (1870s) did caravans of Islamic Arabs such as Tippu Tib go inland as far as Tabora, Nyangwe, Buganda, Lake Nyasa, and even Katanga, in pursuit of slaves and ivory.

Among the factors that slowed the spread of Islam stood out the absence of strong state societies in the hinterland. This fact, in contrast to the situation in West Africa, made it almost impossible for any chiefs who might have converted to Islam to force their new religion upon their scattered and few subjects. In East Africa, conversions seemed to have been individual. Generally, as in West Africa, analysts have emphasized that the adaptability and tolerance of African traditional religion to either Christianity or Islam (though Islam seemed the greater beneficiary) was one factor in the spread of Islam. Mazrui calls this tolerance the "ecumenic element" of African religion. Edward Alpers, in his study of the phenomenal conversion of the Yao of Mozambique to Islam during the nineteenth century, cites cultural affinity, reinforced by commercial links with the Muslim east coast, as the most important factors predisposing Africa's positive response to the new faith. Other experts point to the attractive character of Islam as a modernizing force, a vehicle allowing Africans to belong to a more international community — the learned pan-Islamic world — with its pilgrimages to Mecca, while Sulayman Nyang speaks of African exposure to "a brotherhood of Islam whose borders were beyond what he [the African] could be and see."

A major debate arises when the colonial factor is brought into play to explain the rapid expansion of Islam in Africa, particularly East Africa. One theory claims that colonial penetration assisted the expansion of Islam through its pacification process. The other posits that the social and economic dislocation brought about by the oppressive colonial system forced many Africans to join the religion of their Muslim neighbors, some of whom had successfully halted the tide of colonial penetration in their areas. Upholding the first view, Trimingham argues that the *pax colonica* (colonial peace), which enabled the rapid improvements in communication and transportation and the founding of new towns and commercial centers, created an atmosphere that assisted Islam in its sweep over the coastal areas and the interior of East Africa during the 1880–1930 period. In the same vein, Humphrey Fisher gives credit to the quasi-political autonomy given to Muslim areas by the colonial policy of indirect rule, and the direct employment of Muslims in government positions as clerks, policemen, soldiers, teachers, prison wards, and interpreters, as the Germans and the British did in Tanganyika and the latter in Kenya and Zanzibar, by-passing the Africans. In general, where Europeans found a well-organized Muslim society, they feared changing the status quo. In Northern Cameroon, for example, the Germans (1884–1916) declared the Muslim areas off limits to Christian missions, while in Northern Chad, the French were powerless when the Muslim hierarchy refused to send their children to Western schools (seen as culturally poisonous) and began sending, instead, the sons of their slaves.

At the other end of the spectrum, however, G.E. Grunebaum credits indirectly the European system for the spread of Islam—not for its *pax colonica* but for the *odium colonicum* (colonial hatred, author's expression) it provoked in the colonial subjects. He argues that African social and political systems, unable to cope with the threats posed by colonialism, opened the door to "transformation or even displacement" by Islam. More recently, Ira Lapidus, embracing the same thesis, noted that "it seems likely that the spread of Islam was facilitated by political instability, by the need for a common identity for heterogeneous peoples, and by the need for new bases of social and political organization." August Nimtz takes issue with the *pax colonica* advocates, and posits instead that "the evidence... [particularly, for the 1916–1924 period] indicates that Islam's vigorous expansion occurred not during tranquil times but, on the contrary, during periods of upheavals and crisis." Edward Alpers, although unwilling to generalize on the crisis theory, concludes that the massive conversion of the Yao occurred after the conversion of their chiefs who faced a challenge from their village headmen over the issue of "ancestors' veneration." The most likely hypothesis to explain Islamic expansion, however, seems to lie elsewhere, for colonialism impeded as well as facilitated the popularity of Islam in Africa. For example, the employment of Muslim agents was counterbalanced by the admission of Traditionalist Africans into Western colonial and European schools. On the other hand, as Mbiti observes, the fragile colonial peace, which supposedly created a favorable atmosphere for Islamic expansion, found a fierce competitor in Christianity, which was often protected by the colonial state, as was the case in the Portuguese colonies, and in former Belgian Zaire, Rwanda, and Burundi.

In view of the inadequacy of the hypotheses presented above, one must look elsewhere for the most important factor (beyond Islam's natural appeal to Africans) to explain its unprecedented rise during the nineteenth and twentieth centuries. It would appear that, unlike in West and Central Africa, where Muslim traders, *sheikhs*, and the *jihad* played a major role, on the east coast the answer lies in the activity of the Muslim brotherhoods (*turuq*; singular, *tariqa*). The *Qadiryyia*, for example, the most popular brotherhood in East Africa, did not reach Zanzibar until the nineteenth century, but by 1950 it had become extremely popular in the Tanzanian hinterland, with major strongholds in Dar-es-Salaam, Bagamoyo, Kilwa, Lindi, Northern Mozambique, and Nyasaland. The *Shadhilyyia*, which also admitted women, presumably spread from Comoros during the First World War and became the second most popular *tariqa* in East Africa, with major chapters in Kilwa, Zanzibar, and northern Mozambique. The brotherhood leaders, although often only half-educated, were egalitarian, mystically oriented, and self-made missionaries, who were well versed in the *Qur'an*. They were also healers, charmers, and eloquent talismans, attributes that intrigued the Traditionalist African. As a result, *tariqa* leaders in the hinterland eventually became local Africans. Had it not been for these newly arrived missionaries of the faith, notwithstanding the so-called *pax colonica* or the social crisis (*odium colonicum*) it caused, Islam might have been still confined to the islands of the Indian Ocean.

Elsewhere, it is generally acknowledged by scholars that in several areas of Southern Africa the Portuguese succeeded in slowing down the spread of Islam.

In South Africa, where there were some 300,000 vocal Muslims in 2003, the repressive apartheid regime also prevented Muslims from worshiping freely and gaining converts easily, while in Central Africa the strong alliance between the colonial state and Christianity (as was the case in the Belgian Congo) made it extremely difficult for Islam to expand. Mazrui says that Islamic expansion in North and West Africa was facilitated by the camel, which was able to crisscross the Sahara desert but not the forest: Where the camel stopped, Islam stopped!

The impact of Islam in Africa cannot be underestimated, as being a devout Muslim is not just believing in and practicing the "five pillars" of the faith, but embracing a whole new way of life. In fact, Islam has increased the international dimension of the continent through links with the pan-Islamic world, has contributed to literacy, and dictated new codes on health (emphasis on cleanliness, for example), dressing, and eating habits (prohibition of the consumption of pork, for example). It has, at the same time, strengthened the patrilineal societies through emphasis on man's undisputed authority in the family and reinforced inheritance traditions, which favor the male, while weakening the traditional role of women in matrilineal societies. It has also given stronger sanction to certain long-standing African traditions such as polygamy, circumcision (where practiced), and the use of charms, amulets, and certain types of symbols and signs which "guarantee" success and good luck. While, politically, Islam provided a strong basis for resistance against colonialism and, therefore, became inspiration to all African state as well as stateless societies, it also ushered in severe obstacles to the nationalist movement during the 1950s and 1960s and to the nation-building effort following the achievement of independence. In Nigeria, Ghana, and Tanzania, for example, Islam militated against the nationalist movement and, quite often, as was the case in Northern Nigeria, Northern Mozambique, and Chad Muslim leaders either opposed independence or attempted to postpone its arrival. This created much internal discord and recrimination.

The reasons for such behavior on the part of Islamic leaders are easy to find. First, Muslims feared that their privileged positions, protected in most cases by the colonial government, would disappear as the new leaders took over the reins of power. Furthermore, the emerging nationalists, most of whom were Christian, insisted that all future citizens would have to come under one government with no political or cultural privileges reserved for any community, religion, or region. Second, many of the new nationalist leaders embraced the concept of a secular state, in which all religions would be treated equally. This emphasis threatened the position of many Islamic elites who, in the tradition of Islam, maintained both political and religious power, making the distinction between church (religion) and state almost meaningless. Third, the long-standing tension between Arabs and Sub-Saharan Africans was aggravated by Islam's close association with the Arab Middle East, culturally and religiously, thus heightening African nationalists' suspicion, both prior to and after independence, of the loyalty of Muslim citizens, particularly if they were of Arab descent, as was the case in Northern Chad and parts of East Africa. Finally, the philosophical dispute over the role of race and color in nationalist pronouncements heightened the political differences between African Muslim and non-Muslim believers. Islam sees the world as primarily divided on the basis of religion and not color, whereas some radical nationalists have used race and color to advance their objectives, making Muslim nationalists uncomfortable to join the mass parties which led the colonies to independence.

At present, in Sub-Saharan Africa, where Islam has remained the religion of a minority (as is the case in Mozambique, Kenya, Cameroon, Chad, South Africa, and even Nigeria), the political and social tensions of old have surfaced from time to time, and have either contributed to war (Sudan, if one locates in Sub-Saharan Africa, being a classical case) or heightened tensions which have led to violence (exemplified by incidents in Nigeria in 1992 and Kenya in 2002). Overall, however, orthodox Islam has not been a disruptive but a positive force in Africa, and, usually, Christians, Muslims, and Traditionalists have been able to live in a semblance of harmony. Senegal (predominantly Muslim but for long led by a devout Catholic president and then by a Muslim head of state) and Côte d'Ivoire, until the death of Christian President Felix Houphouet-Boigny in 1993), have been perfect examples of harmonious religious coexistence. The deadly bombings of the American embassies in Kenya and Tanzania in 1994 and the World Trade Center and the Pentagon on September 11, 2001 by Islamic fundamentalists and the retaliatory measures undertaken by the United States against Afghanistan in 2002 and Iraq in 2003, in the name of the war against terrorism, represented a new challenge to African Muslims, to Christian and Muslim leaders in Africa, and to the ecumenical movement on the continent. For the foreseeable future, and as long as the fight against terrorism is linked to religious fundamentalism, the dilemma will be quite obvious for Africa. For a leader with a large Muslim population, the fear may stem from the actions of a small radical Islamic group that espouses the religious fundamentalism associated with Osama bin Laden's and his follower's ideology. This fear will be heightened if the population is entirely Arab, since, understandably, Arabs tend to associate some of the latest global terrorist acts with the explosive unresolved Palestinian issue. Palestine has worried the Africans since the beginning of the Arab-Israeli wars in 1948 to the point of breaking relations with Israel after the June 1967 Israeli War. The stakes of anxiety and non-action rise if the leader is a non-Muslim governing a Christian and a large Muslim population. As a result, the Christian West cannot expect much cooperation from Africa, even if a fundamentalist group threatens the established internal order. Religion and Palestine have always been a double sword in many African countries.

By contrast, in a state where the Muslim population is a minority, the leader straddles a fine line between peace and cooperation with the Christian West and the fight against terrorism, if linked with Islamic militants, a potentially vocal minority that may be ready to resort to violence. Indeed, the African Arabs and Muslims see the current avowed assault on terrorism as an indiscriminate, deliberate affront, designed to cleanse all the continents, including Africa, from the Muslim presence. Either way, for the presidents of Kenya, Nigeria, Egypt, Senegal, Uganda, and even South Africa, the issue is how to pursue a strong anti-terrorist policy without offending their Muslim populations or giving their Christian and religiously traditionalist citizens the impression that they are not placating their Muslim constituency. How does one react to Ugandans and Kenyans who are making Osama bin Laden a hero by naming their children little Osama's? Because the recent terrorist events have strained intra-Islamic relations, mainstream Islam has made a concerted effort to distance itself from the extremist positions taken by its marginal or "outlawed" elements that are intent on making their point heard at all cost. Within the *ulamma* (community of scholars) and the *umma* (Islamic community) rages the debate as to the true meaning of the *jihad*: is it, asks Walter Laqueur (1999), a "*jihad bi al saif*" (holy war by means of the sword) or "*jihad al nafs*" (struggle of one's soul against one's own base instincts)? In sum, for the African masses, the two imported religions, Christianity and Islam, are at a crossroads, and the future of peaceful co-existence seems to be bleak, as demonstrated by the continued failure of the ecumenical movement trying to bring Christians and Muslims in Kenya, Uganda, and Nigeria closer together.

Summary

This chapter outlined the major tenets and current (and historical) state of three major religions in Africa: Traditionalism, Christianity, and Islam. Traditionalism is indigenous to the continent of Africa and, contrary to myths and stereotypes perpetuated by European traders, explorers, missionaries, and early ethnographers, it enshrines the essential elements of any religion in the world, namely, the belief in a creator and in a world of spirits (often wrongly labeled by Western scholars and their early African disciples as gods or deities), and the use of sacrifice, prayer, and ritual. Africa's ancestral veneration and invocation could be compared to the prayers addressed to saints among some Christian denominations. The strength of Traditionalism on the continent is illustrated by the fact that, notwithstanding the cultural and political onslaught of colonial Christianism and Arab Islam over the centuries, most Sub-Saharan Africa remains Traditionalist. Furthermore, the resilience and strength of African religion can still be detected among Diaspora Africans in the United States, the Caribbean, and Latin America, especially Brazil. Yet, the lure of Western culture and technology and the continued appeal of both Islam and Christianity threaten the future of Traditionalism.

The issues of witchcraft, sorcery, divination, magic, and fortune telling, often labeled by the West as superstition, must be understood in their proper context to make sense. The concept of the vital force in the universe, emanating from the almighty Creator, seems to be crucial to the understanding of African traditional religion into which children are born and in which they live, grow, and die. Because religion is not compartmentalized but still permeates the individual inner self and is, in a sense, the soul of the traditional community in Africa, outsiders find it difficult to differentiate religious from secular cultural practices. This was, in fact, the major reason why missionaries and colonial administrators showed such contempt for what has come to be known as Traditionalism. On Islamic and Christian expansion in Africa, the chapter pointed out that, even though North Africa and Ethiopia experienced Christianity perhaps as early as the first century, Islam enjoyed a more rapid and sustained expansion after its founding in Mecca during the seventh century. It spread first throughout North Africa, then to West and Central Africa, and finally to coastal East Africa. Whereas in North, West, and Central Africa, Islam was assisted primarily by the *jihad* (holy war), particularly during the late eighteenth and early nineteenth centuries, and the trans-Saharan trade, in East Africa the holy war was less important than the work of Muslim brotherhoods and the impact of the caravan trade, which, by the twelfth century, had created an African-Arab Islamic culture and language called Swahili. Here, proximity to the Middle East, the birthplace of the faith, was another important factor.

Colonialism, on the one hand, indirectly assisted the spread of Islam through improved communication networks, the creation of new urban centers, and the special role it entrusted to Muslims, most of whom were literate in the Western sense. Islam also skillfully exploited the misery caused by the colonial situation and often convinced mainly its destitute urban listeners that Christianity was nothing more than the other face of colonialism. European occupation, on the other hand, brought an influx of mission churches, schools, and health care centers which, protected by the colonial state, became a fierce rival to Islam, clearly demonstrated by the sparsity of Muslim communities in Southern Africa.

It would appear more plausible, therefore, to hold the view that, apart from the Muslim orders or brotherhoods, the most important factor in the spread of Islam where it succeeded was its very nature which seems to elicit a positive response from the Africans—the simplicity of its dogma, its success in portraying itself as a non-racialist, a non-colonial, and an egalitarian religion, and its affinity with long-standing African cultural practices and symbols such as circumcision, polygamy, and amulets as was, according to Alpers, the case among the Yao of northern Mozambique, and the lure of its learning and cosmopolitanism. In both colonial and post-colonial Africa, the political, social, and cultural impact of Islam has been greatest in all of North Africa and in such countries as Senegal, where the population is predominantly Muslim, and in Nigeria, Chad, Cameroon, and Tanzania, to cite a few examples, where there are large Muslim communities.

Christianity in Africa is almost 2,000 years old, having made its inroads, as noted above, in North Africa and Ethiopia perhaps as early as the first century of the Christian era. However, the destructive nature of the Vandals during the fourth century and the pressure from Islam after the seventh century, dealt a severe blow to its presence. It was only after the fifteenth century, with the arrival and the activities of the Portuguese, that Christianity flourished, but only temporarily and only along the coastal areas. By the end of the seventeenth century, a combination of factors, including the rivalry between the Christian religious orders, anticlerical metropolitan tendencies, lax morals among the European clerics in Africa (some of whom were even involved in the slave trade), and the absence of trained indigenous personnel, contributed to a total decline of Christendom on the continent. However, the implantation of colonialism in Africa during the nineteenth century contributed to an unprecedented revival of the Christian Church with all its antagonistic major denominations.

Notwithstanding their shortcomings in Africa, missionaries not only concerned themselves with converting the Africans, but they also built schools and contributed to the education of Africans, created dispensaries for the treatment of the sick, and initiated the use of African languages in texts such as the Bible, while often collecting the rich folklore of the people they encountered. Unfortunately, missionaries often allied themselves with the colonial state, did not forcefully combat racism among themselves and the colonialists, and never took seriously the indigenization of the African Church. Instead, they constantly fought against African cultural manifestations and rarely listened to the warnings of their faithful, even after the proliferation of independent Christian Churches on the continent. (Their fate is well dramatized and depicted, for example, in such African novels as Mongo Beti's *The Poor Christ of Bomba* and Chinua Achebe's *Things Fall Apart*.) Thus, when independence came, it was feared that the Church might one day disappear altogether. However, this fear did not materialize, even though in the Portuguese colonies, where the alliance between Catholicism and the colonial regime was tighter than anywhere else in Africa, the

Church suffered severely following independence. The new revolutionary Marxist regimes declared war against organized religion, while attempting to deprive the few African priests of any power, freedom of worship, or role in the new society they were forging.

In spite of obvious problems, however, Christianity continues to be popular in many parts of the continent, and therefore still poses a "threat" to both Islam and Traditionalism. A major challenge to the ecumenical effort put forth during the past four decades by leaders of Christianity and Islam both in the Western world and in Africa has been made tenuous by the resurgence of fundamentalist Islam. Islamic fundamentalists have declared war on the West, using terrorist acts and demand, among other things, the establishment of religious rather than secular states in the Muslim world, the imposition of the law of Islam or *shari'a,* elimination of Christianity, and the abandonment of some modern technological innovations that corrupt the youth, oppose the education of women, and would like to see a strict enforcement of the medieval dress code, especially for women. In Nigeria, Kenya, Uganda, and South Africa, and many other countries in Africa where there is a vocal Muslim population, the recent terrorist acts and American retaliation have strained the relations among Muslims, Christians, and Traditionalists, even if feelings are not always expressed in public. It is clear that the period following the 1994 embassy bombings in Africa and the 2001 attacks on the World Trade Center and the Pentagon in the United States have created more divisiveness than harmony in Africa. The future of religious relations on the continent is therefore gloomy.

Study Questions and Activities

1. Do further research on African traditional religion and compare it with Christianity in the following aspects: the concept of God and the role of the spirits, the dead, sacrifice, and prayer.
2. Compare and contrast the spread of Christianity and Islam in Africa. What were the elements that made both religions attractive to the Africans?
3. What were the major shortcomings of Christianity in Africa during the colonial period? Have these disappeared on the continent?
4. Do research on the following African theologians: St. Augustine, Origen, and Tertullian.

References

Chinua Achebe. *Things Fall Apart.* New York: Fawcett, 1959.
Abdullah Ahsan. *Ummah or a Nation: Identity Crisis in the Modern Muslim Society.* Leicester: Islamic Foundation, 1992.
Edward Alpers. "Toward a History of Expansion of Islam in East Africa," in T.O. Ranger and I. Kimambo (eds.). *The Historical Study of African Religion.* Berkeley, CA: University of California Press, 1974.
C.G. Baeta. *Christianity in Tropical Africa.* Oxford: Oxford University Press, 1968.

Mongo Beti. *The Poor Christ of Bomba*. Paris: Presence Africaine, 1976.

Basil Davidson. *The African Genius*. Boston: Little, Brown, 1969.

Stephen Ellis and Gerrie ter Haar. *Worlds of Power: Religious Thought and Po-litical Practice in Africa*. New York: Oxford University Press, 2004.

Encyclopædia Britannica Almanac 2004. Chicago: Encyclopædia Britannica, Inc., 2004.

Allan Fisher and Humphrey Fisher. *Slavery and Muslim Society in Africa*. New York: Doubleday, 1972.

Kwesi A. Dickson and Paul Ellingworth (eds.). *Biblical Revelation and African Beliefs*. Maryknoll, NY: Orbis Books, 1969.

Humphrey Fisher. "The Western and Central Sudan," in P.M. Holt et al. (eds.). *The Cambridge History of Islam*, vol. 2. Cambridge: Cambridge University Press, 1970.

Yekutiel Gershoni. *Africans on African-Americans: The Creation and Use of an African-American Myth*. New York: New York University Press, 1997.

Martha Greenshaw (ed.). *Terrorism in Africa*. New York: Macmillan Publishing Company, 1994.

G.E. Grunebaum. *Islam and its Cultural Divergence*. Urbana, IL: University of Illinois Press, 1971.

Isichei Elizabeth. *A History of Christianity in Africa from Antiquity to the Pre-sent*. Lawrenceville, NJ: Africa World Press, 1995.

Neil Kasfelt (ed.). *The Role of Religion in African Civil Wars*. London: Hurst & Co., 2003.

M. Ali Kettany. *Muslim Minorities in the World Today*. London: Mansel, 1986.

Giles Keppel. *Jihad: The Trail of Political Islam*. Cambridge, MA: Belknap Press, 2002.

Ira Lapidus. *A History of Islamic Societies*. Cambridge: Cambridge University Press, 1988.

Walter Laqueur. *The New Terrorism: Fanaticism and Arms of Mass Destruction*. London: Oxford University Press, 1999.

W.H. Lewis. "Islam and Nationalism in Africa," in Tibor Kerekes (ed.). *The Arab Middle East and Muslim Africa*. New York: Praeger, 1961.

Ali Mazrui. *The African Condition: A Political Diagnosis*. London: Cambridge University Press, 1980.

————. *The Africans: A Triple Heritage*. Boston: Little, Brown, 1986.

John Mbiti. *African Philosophies and Religion*. New York: Praeger, 1969.

August Nimtz. *Islam and Politics in East Africa: The Sufi Order in Tanzania*. Minneapolis, MN: University of Minnesota Press, 1980.

Sulayman Nyang. "Sub-Saharan Africa: Islamic Penetration," in Philip H. Stod-dard (ed.). *Change in the Muslim World*. Syracuse, NY: Syracuse University Press, 1981.

————. *Islam, Christianity, and African Identity*. Brattleboro, VT: Amana, 1984.

Arye Oded. *Islam and Politics in Kenya*. London: Lynne Rienner Publishers, 2000.

Geoffrey Parrinder. *Religions in Africa*. Baltimore, MD: Penguin, 1969.

Kimberley C. Patton and Benjamin C. Ray (eds.). *A Magic Still Dwells: Compar-ative Religion in the Postmodern Age*. Berkeley, CA: University of California Press, 2000.

Randall Powells. *Horn and Crescent: Cultural Change and Traditional Islam on the East Coast 800–1900*. Cambridge: Cambridge University Press, 1987.

Cora Pressly. *Kikuyu Women, the Mau Mau Rebellion, and Social Change in Kenya*. Boulder, CO: Westview Press, 1992.

Benjamin C. Ray. *African Religions: Symbol, Ritual, and Continuity* (2nd edi-tion). Upper Saddle River, NJ: Prentice-Hall, 2000.

Walter Rodney. *How Europe Underdeveloped Africa*. Dar-es-Salaam: Tanzania Publishing House, 1972.

Aylward Shorter. *African Christian Theology*. Maryknoll, NY: Orbis Books, 1975.

C.C. Stewart. "Islam," in J.D. Fage and Roland Oliver (eds.). *The Cambridge History of Africa, 1905–1940*. Cambridge: Cambridge University Press, 1986.

David Thebahali. "Has Christianity Any Relevance and Any Future?" in World Student Christian Federation. *A New Look at Christianity in Africa*. Vol. II, 2(1972): 40–45.

John Trimingham. *Islam in East Africa*. Oxford: Oxford University Press, 1964.

John Voll. *Islam and Continuity and Change in the Modern World*. Boulder, CO: Westview Press, 1982.

David Westerbund. *African Religion in African Scholarship: A Preliminary Study of the Religious and Political Background*. Stockholm: Almquist & Wiksell International, 1985.

David Westerland and Eva Evers Rosander (eds.). *African Islam and Islam in Africa: Encounters Between Sufis and Islamists*. Athen, OH: Ohio University Press, 1997.

World Almanac. New York: Pharos Books, 1992.

World Student Christian Federation. *A New Look at Christianity*, vol. II, 2(1972). Geneva, Switzerland: WSCF, 1972.

23

Religion in the Diaspora

Mario Azevedo
Gregory Davis

Introduction

Since, historically, the African American Church is believed to have played a significant role in the shaping of the black community, it deserves closer attention from both religious and secular scholars. Islam, on the other hand, is a recent phenomenon among black Americans but, relatively speaking, its impact has also been considerable in certain areas of the country. This chapter traces the origins and the role of the black Church in the United States and the Caribbean, from its beginnings to the present. It also assesses the Church's impact on black people and briefly outlines the origins, the nature, and the relevance of Islam to the black community.[1]

Major terms and concepts: the "invisible" Church, Baptist, Methodist, Episcopalian, Congregationalist, Catholic, NAACP, Civil Rights movement, front store Church, "separate but equal," black Muslims, Nation of Islam, Bilallian, slavery, nationalism, Caribbean, Liberation Theology.

One may define the black Church as that gathering of like-minded African American faithful who accept and profess the principles of Christianity, by and large, organized around a particular structure. The Church structures relevant to the present discussion fall into one of three general types: Congregationalist, Episcopalian, and Presbyterian, with each structure denoting a particular form of government based on a constitution.

The first is known as the Congregationalist, where Church officials are accountable to the entire membership, which has complete authority over every aspect of Church life: calling a minister, hiring staff, and approving or rejecting budgets. In the Congregationalist system, exemplified by the Baptist and Pentecostal Churches, there is no structured hierarchy, and affiliation with a higher body is strictly voluntary. The Episcopalian system, which encompasses the Roman

---

1. The section on the black Church in the United States was written by Gregory Davis. Mario Azevedo authored the section on black Catholics in the United States and religion in the Caribbean.

Catholic Church, is characterized by a hierarchy that falls under the control of what is known as a bishop who is the head of the church. For Roman Catholicism, the Pope (known as the Bishop of Rome) is the ultimate human authority. The concept of a bishopric comes from the belief that the bishop has a line of authority that extends far back to the time of Saint Peter to whom Christ entrusted his Church. The clergy, therefore, is legitimized only by the authority of the bishop.

Among the Presbyterians, in contrast, the congregation elects the elders who, along with the minister, make up what is known as the session, which is the lowest governmental body but controls all local church activities. The Presbyterian Church is sometimes called a connectional church because, within its structure, several layers interrelate, making sure that decisions made by a lower body are fair, sound, and just. Overall, the Presbyterian Church has a four-tier structure: the session, which is the lowest body, followed by the presbytery, the synod, and the general assembly (the highest governing body).

Today, the largest number of African Americans is affiliated with the Congregationalist and the Episcopal models, partly as a result of their less complicated form of worship, and partly due to their insistence that members participate fully in the life and mission of the Church. This point cannot be emphasized enough, given that, in the early days of the Baptist and Methodist Churches, the largest percentage of African Americans who identified with the Church were untrained, unskilled, and felt less threatened by the Methodist and the Baptist internal structure. (Today, there are 8.7 million black Baptists in the United States, the largest number of black adherents of any denomination in the country.)

The Church in the United States

The Church and Slavery

It is often said that the African American Church was formed in protest against the inhumane treatment African Americans received from their white Christian brothers during slavery, especially prior to the mid-eighteenth century. The issue of Christianizing the slaves sparked a heated debate among slave owners because some Christians argued that, once baptized, a slave could no longer be held in bondage. As a result, some masters even refused to allow their slaves to hear the gospel preached by traveling preachers.

The Church often responded to the problem by issuing printed sermons and pamphlets which argued that the enslavement of African Americans was compatible with Christianity; that African Americans were bound to the system of servility by some God-given decree that resulted from sin; and that baptism in no way affected their servile status. According to this line of reasoning, the only freedom that one received from baptism was spiritual freedom, the masters serving as mediators between their slaves and God.

As the slave masters slowly became comfortable with the idea of their slaves converting to Christianity, however, they began to develop means by which African Americans could hear the gospel under controlled circumstances. Some allowed their slaves to listen to itinerant (traveling) evangelists who preached to the slaves submission and the virtues of hard work, while others took their slaves to church with them. In church, as expected, slaves sat separately from their masters. While some churches assigned slaves seats around the wall, some gave them seats in the front of the church, and others preferred to seat them in the balcony.

Yet, of what they heard preached to them, slaves were able to redefine the gospel to meet their own particular situation and turned the call to submission into a word of liberation, which they preached and sang in their own secret services, sometimes called the "invisible Church," held in the swamp, the brush arbor, and other locations away from their masters.

This secret worship played a significant role in the slaves' attempt to overthrow the institution of slavery. There are indications, for example, that the Gabriel Prosser insurrection of 1800, in Richmond, Virginia; the Denmark Vesey conspiracy of 1822, in Charleston, South Carolina; and the Nat Turner rebellion of 1832, in Southampton, Virginia, were inspired by the Bible. Prosser was fascinated by the Book of Judges and the story of Samson, while Vesey quoted the writings of Joshua and the story of the Battle of Jerico. Turner, on the other hand, was knowledgeable, and read the Old and New Testaments. In addition, particularly in the North, the "invisible" black Church not only spoke against slavery but also served as a facilitating vehicle for the Underground Railroad, providing food and shelter along the way to freedom for southern slaves. On some occasions, masters allowed their slaves to preach the gospel, as happened to Richard Allen, the organizer of the African Methodist Episcopal Church, in Philadelphia, who eventually converted his own master, and, as a result, was allowed, along with his brother, to purchase his freedom.

The Roots of the Independent Black Church Movement

During the celebration of the American revolutionary spirit, in the eighteenth century, the prevailing attitude of most Americans was that the Declaration of Independence and the United States Constitution guaranteed equal rights to all, as it proclaimed that "all men are created equal" and endowed by their creator "with the right to life, liberty, and the pursuit of happiness." However, such thinking did not last long, for the United States Constitution considered an African American to be only three-fifths of a human. Yet, in the area of worship there was some measure of equality between blacks and whites, based not on the conviction that the two were equal, but on the need to maintain some sense of control over them.

Having "feasted" at the table of equality during the revolutionary era, African Americans were unwilling to give up their seat at the "table" of human rights. It was against this backdrop that the independent African American Church was born, with Richard Allen as the pioneer in the North. Allen grew up a slave in Delaware and, upon reaching his manhood, converted and began to preach the gospel as announced by the Methodist Church. (The Methodist Church—founded by John Wesley in England in the early 1770s and brought to the United States in the 1780s—attracted more blacks than other Christian denominations before emancipation because it was the only one that stood firm against slavery.)

A man of unusual talents, Allen drew the attention of Bishop Ashbury of the (white) Methodist Church. Ashbury allowed Allen to travel throughout the Northeast, and occasionally let him deliver a sermon. His preaching was so successful that he soon developed his own following in Philadelphia.

During this period, it was customary for African American preachers who had sponsors to preach in some of the white churches. Allen became so popular as a preacher that he began to draw large crowds of African Americans in the white local church he attended. Threatened, the white leadership of Saint George's Methodist Church decided to segregate the two races. The policy was carried out with such zeal that Richard Allen and others were interrupted even while on their knees in the midst of prayer, because they were sitting on pews reserved for whites. This sparked the origins of the separate African Methodist Episcopal (AME) Church.

Allen and his followers first formed what was called the Free African Societies, which were similar in function and style to communal societies, with membership greatly determined by acceptance of Christianity. The designation highlighted the desire for freedom and underscored the African roots of the members. In fact, the Free African Societies could best be described as welfare agencies which provided aid only when members needed it, such as when one was widowed.

These societies were actually meant to make a statement regarding the social, economic, and political status of African Americans in nineteenth century Philadelphia, as Allen and his followers held the view that a community of believers had both a religious and a social responsibility toward the members. In short, he preached that the Church must be relevant to the community.

In Allen's case, the Free African Society also served as a bridge between the departure from St. George's Methodist Church and the establishment of the African Methodist Episcopal Church. While, on the one hand, Allen was uncomfortable with the involvement of non-Methodist groups in the Free African Society, on the other hand, he felt uneasy leaving the Methodist Church, primarily because he liked the structure and the functioning of Methodism. He was therefore interested in creating a church that would be concerned with both the spiritual and the secular needs of the members and of society at-large. To achieve his goal, he first organized a Sunday School and a night school for African Americans. His efforts culminated with his ordination as a deacon by Bishop Ashbury in 1799. From this period to the early 1800s, Allen continued to preach and develop contacts which resulted in the creation of his Bethel African Methodist Episcopal Church in Philadelphia in April 1816. Richard Allen was elected bishop and adopted the same principles and discipline used by the (white) Methodist Church.

The growth of the African American AME Church was not restricted to the North. In spite of the institution of slavery, the AME churches enjoyed a level of success in the South. In the city of Charleston, for example, Morris Brown, a black Methodist minister, was the pastor at a church said to have 1,000 members before the Vesey insurrection. It is estimated that, by 1820, there were 4,000 black Methodists in the city of Philadelphia alone. Today, AME membership in the United States is 3 million blacks, with several thousand in the Caribbean and in Africa.

At the same time that the AME Church was being organized, a group of African Americans living in New York walked out of St. John Methodist Church in 1794. This group left, not because of any pressure from their white Christian brothers, but simply because they wished to have a place where they could worship on their own, away from whites. Led by Francis Jacobs, William Brown, Peter Williams, James Varick, and others, the group was eventually able to secure a building in 1800, and adopted the articles of discipline and governance and the principles of faith of its white Methodist counterpart. It adopted the name of AME Zion, and elected its first bishop in 1822. (Today, the AMEZ Church has some 400,000 members in the United States and about 100,000 in Africa and the West Indies.)

The religious independent movement continued, however. In 1870, black members withdrew, with the blessing of their white fellow members, from the Southern Christian Methodist Church and formed the Christian Methodist Episcopal Church (CME) in Jackson, Tennessee, which changed its designation to the Christian Methodist Church in 1954. Its first bishops, elected in 1870, were William H. Miles and Richard Vanderhorst. As Eric Lincoln notes, the CME, headquartered in Memphis, Tennessee, has remained the smallest of the three major branches of the Methodist Church, with some 850,000 members in the United States and 75,000 abroad.

The successful birth of Baptist Churches was primarily due to the freedom of Church discipline and the uncomplicated nature of the denomination. The Silver Bluff Church, established by George Liele and Andrew Bryan, in 1773–1774, but relocated to the Savannah area in 1794, was the first organized Baptist Church in the South. George Liele, a deacon of a local Baptist Church in Virginia, was ordained a Baptist minister soon thereafter. Aware of his slave's unusual talents, Liele's master gave him permission to preach at the plantations located along the Savannah River, and later freed him so that he might be able to pursue his religious career freely. Liele's master was killed during the Revolutionary War, however, and a question arose about the deceased's estate, and whether Liele was actually a free man. As a result, the black minister was jailed. Fortunately, however, a British Army General released him from jail and subsequently freed him.

While in Savannah, Liele came in contact with Andrew Bryan who was born a slave in Goose Creek, South Carolina, in 1730. Through the influence of George Liele, Bryan became a Christian and was ordained a minister in January 1788, and began preaching to both black and white listeners. With the help of some white admirers, Bryan was able to build his church. Subsequently, his master allowed him to buy his freedom. As his church grew, Bryan split its membership and formed another church which he named the Savannah African Baptist Church. His pioneering effort led to the establishment of a number of black churches in the state of Georgia, and other southern states. Eventually, therefore, black Baptist churches sprang up everywhere in the South as well as in the North.

As one would expect, black Baptists in the North also encountered difficulties with their white brothers. For example, in Philadelphia, in May 1800, a number of blacks left the (white) First Baptist Church and formed the First African Baptist Church of Philadelphia. Likewise, in Boston, Massachusetts, black Baptists, in an effort to form their own community of worship, called upon the services of the Reverend Thomas Paul. Paul was ordained in 1804 and immediately organized the African Baptist Church on George Street in Boston. Subsequently, in 1808, he assisted in organizing the Abyssinian Baptist Church in New York, where he served as a pastor.

The Church of God in Christ originated in 1897 through the work of Baptist minister Charles Harrison Mason, who had been banished from his church in Arkansas in 1893. The number of his followers grew rapidly, compelling representatives of twelve churches to meet in Memphis in their first General Assembly in 1907 to proclaim the official founding of the denomination, which at present, rivaling only the Baptists, counts more than 3 million members, 9,000 churches, and 10,000 members of the clergy. (The Church of God in Christ has strong affinities with Pentecostalism, from which it borrowed many of its teachings and practices.)

Pentecostals are the only significant denomination that did not originally derive from a white church. Pentecostalism started in Los Angeles during the 1906–1908 Holiness revivals preached by black minister William Seymour, who added to the Holiness dogma of salvation and sanctification the phenomenon of speaking in tongues. The new brand of Christianity known as Pentecostalism spread like fire throughout the world, and is estimated to have a membership of 35 million, most of whom are in the developing world.

The nineteenth century was perhaps the most important period in the history of the African American Church, as it was during this time that the Church carved out themes that would characterize its existence through the struggle for equal rights for black Americans, and fulfilled four major functions: it served as a place for social development; it provided educational opportunities for blacks; it enhanced their economic development; and it promoted and fought for their political emancipation. Thus, from its origins, the black Church has played a significant role in maintaining the family structure in the black community, and provided assistance long before the government had enacted its welfare and social programs. As a social institution, it set the standards by which families and people were to behave, sanctioned an evolution of patterns of behavior which at times were unpopular, and served as a social clearinghouse for better relations among Americans.

The economic role of the black Church, on the other hand, grew out of necessity, as a result of the system of Jim Crow. Through mutual associations, burial societies, and band and insurance companies, the Church helped foster an incipient black middle class, and, with time, it became the most important economic institution in the black community.

Of course, no institution can expect to play a significant role in the community if it does not have an educational component and thrust. At the conclusion of the Civil War, the black Church immediately stepped in to shape the development of independent educational institutions for the black community, spending millions of dollars to provide educational opportunities for the newly emancipated slaves. Thus, in most cases, educational institutions were Church-based, and trained black men for the ministry and others for the teaching profession. It was through these Church-based institutions that a great number of Afro-American leaders of the third-quarter of the twentieth century received their training, thus laying the foundation for the black Church's involvement in the political arena. To be sure, the educational efforts of the black Church materialized in the establishment of several Church or Church-related institutions over the centuries among which stand Johnson C. Smith University, Livingstone College, Shaw University, and Hood Theological Seminary in North Carolina; Miles College in Alabama; Morris Brown, the Interdenominational Theological Seminary, in Atlanta, Georgia; Wilberforce University in Ohio; Allen University in Columbia, South Carolina; and dozens of other colleges throughout the United States.

The black Church has also served as the training ground for political action and participation. Through their Church affiliation during Reconstruction, for example, many African Americans became delegates to the various state conventions and held seats in the United States Senate. Since, at the conclusion of Reconstruction, African Americans lost their right to participate in the political process, they had to come up with alternate strategies to be involved in state and national politics. Again, the Church came to the rescue, becoming the major political vehicle. Church preachers struggled for political roles and forcefully addressed those political issues that directly affected their constituency. Indeed, direct participation in Church affairs taught the masses of African Americans how to effect political change. Here they learned how to negotiate, while putting together a church budget, and learned how to lobby and build a consensus, as they served on a particular church committee. The wide array of political leaders from the Church throughout the decades attests to the Church's impact: from Rev. Hiram R. Ravels and Rev. J.W. Hood to Rev. Clayton Powell and Rev. William Gray, and from Rev. Walter Fauntroy to Rev. Benjamin Hooks and Rev. Jesse Jackson, to name just a few political giants of the black community. It was the strength of the black Church which forced several southern legislatures to pass restricting laws on black religious worship during the 1820–1860 period. This happened in Charleston, South Carolina, where it was feared that churches had become sources of rebellion. The restrictions temporarily weakened the effectiveness of the institution on the eve of the Civil War.

Unfortunately, beyond the social, economic, educational, and political role it played in the development of the black community, the black Church was equally responsible for causing African Americans to retreat from the realities of the present and to look instead toward a life in the hereafter. This was particularly true in the case of the rural Church, as it became primarily concerned with issues of suffering in this world and told the faithful to look forward to a better time to come, an emphasis that may have hindered its effectiveness in changing the condition of blacks in the nation. Simple-minded ministers often preached that affirming faith in God would solve all problems. In spite of this apparent "otherworldly" view, the rural Church strengthened all African American institutions and contributed to the struggle for equality for and by African Americans. The lessons of hard work and determination that emerged in the antebellum rural South and the comforting nature of the Church enabled preachers, teachers, and laborers to work together and survive the hostilities of nineteenth and twentieth century America.

When the African American Church moved northward, it was responding to the masses of immigrants searching for a new life in the promised land. In large numbers, blacks moved to the urban areas of the North and the West, and to the centers of the southern cities. A number of factors contributed to this sudden shift in population: 1) a need for cheap labor in the war industry of the North which lured many unemployed blacks; 2) the massive floods in the South which diminished agricultural opportunities; 3) the loss of cotton crops due to the boll weevil; and 4) the persistent view of the North as the promised land. In fact, it was not uncommon for whole communities to pick up their belongings and move North, often taking their ministers with them. Unfortunately, what they found in the North was not the expected promised land but high unemployment, lack of health care, crowded living conditions, and police brutality.

Responding to these conditions, the urban Church developed social programs designed to deal with the new situation African Americans faced in the northern cities. Unlike the rural minister, the urban minister became involved in the struggle for black liberation by lobbying for open house, health care, police review boards, and political participation. Yet, as the Church became more socially oriented and membership increased, it began to lose the personal relationships that were part of the rural experience. This caused many of those who had migrated from the South to disassociate themselves from the traditional denominations — Baptists, Methodists, and Presbyterians — which they viewed as too large and unresponsive to their spiritual needs. The dissidents often chose to associate themselves with indigenous urban churches, commonly referred to as Store Front Churches (so designated because they were organized in renovated houses or stores). Members of these new churches were often conservative in their behavior and dress, and shunned such practices as smoking, drinking, and dancing.

As a result, the traditional role of the Church in the black community continued to evolve downward. Its influence began to wane at the turn of the century, and such secular organizations as the Urban League, Greek sororities and fraternities, the National Association for the Advancement of Colored People (NAACP), and the Garvey Movement became more popular resources for the advancement of the black cause. In this new environment, the Church was seen as a do-nothing, unresponsive institution, and it was not until the 1950s and the outbreak of the Civil Rights movement that it resumed its role as the dominant, long-lasting black institution.

Indeed, by the 1950s, the African American community had become more action oriented or activist in its approach to social conditions. Its activism was sparked by the 1954 *Brown vs. Board of Education* decision that struck down the concept of "separate but equal" (upheld by the Supreme Court in *Plessey vs. Ferguson* in 1896) and propelled by the success of the Montgomery Bus Boycott in 1956. These two factors, along with others that followed, gave rise to the modern Civil Rights movement. The Civil Rights movement had a salutary impact on the African American Church itself because it forced the institution to move from the back to the forefront of the struggle, as it had done in previous centuries in America.

Prior to the 1950s, the major organization at the vanguard of social change was the NAACP, which had made its name in the African American community by winning landmark cases that struck down all-white primaries, poll taxes, and the cornerstone concept of "separate but equal." Yet, despite its success, the NAACP never took root among the African American masses because its primary strategy for change was legal action, which usually took a long time and did not involve the direct participation of ordinary African Americans.

In fact, the Civil Rights movement differed from the NAACP in a number of other ways: 1) it became a Church-based movement in origin and organization; 2) it was controlled primarily by the African American community; 3) it depended on financial support from the black masses, generated through the Church; 4) it advocated direct, rather than legal, action; and 5) it adopted non-violent direct action, rooted in love, as its tactic.

The major personality in the movement was a young Baptist minister, Martin Luther King, Jr., who was educated in southern religious traditions, but was also trained as a philosopher and theologian in the finest white schools of the North. This background helped him forge a new approach to southern white domination. He argued that, if the laws made by the southern power structure were unjust and resulted in the oppression of God's people, then every child of God had a moral obligation to disobey them. He also held that it was wrong for people to participate in their own oppression, and that Christians who gave into violence were as wrong as those who perpetrated violence upon them. Finally, King preached that religion had a social as well as a spiritual mission and that it should be concerned with the whole person and not just the soul.

The Civil Rights movement led by King transformed the African American Church, moving it from the passive institution that it had become to an instrument for social change. Its mark on the Civil Rights movement was underscored by the fact that the major leaders (Joseph Lowery, Ralph Abernathy, and others) who formed the Southern Christian Leadership Conference, were all southern ministers. One might say therefore that, during this period, the Church served as an institutional center. It was through the Church that mass rallies were organized; economic boycotts planned; registration drives coordinated; and resources secured.

A logical consequence of the Civil Rights movement of the mid-1960s was the emergence of the Black Power movement, that had a profound impact on several aspects of black social life and institutions including the black Church, which saw the rise of the black liberation theology movement. The concept of black liberation theology, advocated by such black theologians as James Cone and Albert Cleage, is best expressed in the philosophy that black Christians, rather than being subservient and docile, are called upon by a black God to take total control of their destiny and to struggle against social, political, and economic oppression and cultural subjugation, which are perpetuated by an insensitive and racist power structure.

The teachings of the theology of black liberation went counter to Martin Luther King's core theology and philosophy of "love thy neighbor" and peace, and the Civil Rights leader rejected the concept of black power advocated by such aspiring young leaders as Stokeley Carmichael. Yet, the new theological thinking strengthened rather than weakened the black Church. It helped mobilize those African Americans who were turned off by traditional Christianity which they viewed as European-based, manipulated by the white power structure, and unresponsive to the needs of the black community. In fact, the popularity of the black Church is confirmed by the fact that, of the approximately 15 million black Christians, some 13 million attend African American churches.

Although the focus of this essay has been the fate of blacks in the Protestant Church, black Roman Catholics, who constitute 2 million of the 53.4 million Catholics (the largest Christian denomination) in the United States, were not meant to be ignored. What was the position of the American Roman Catholic Church toward slavery and the fate of black Catholics who, by 1836, numbered about 100,000? Unfortunately, its position and practice were no different from those of the other Christian denominations in the Union. Historically, Catholics have been a persecuted and scared religious minority in the United States, rendering the overall impact of the Catholic Church on American life minimal. Thus, when government officials attacked a statement by Pope Gregory XVI against slavery during the 1840s and labeled the Pontiff an abolitionist, Bishop England attempted to exonerate the Pope by declaring that the Head of the Catholic Church condemned not slavery in the South but the further illegal importation of slaves. There were other revealing statements from the hierarchy. During the Civil War, for example, Archbishop Hughes noted that, if the war was being fought to end slavery, then "our Catholic soldiers would not fight with enthusiasm." *The Baltimore Catholic Mirror* clarified the position of the Church on slavery thus:

> Never has the Catholic Church condemned domestic slavery, and equally never has she condoned it. There are many things in the world that have to be taken as they are...and among them the Church has reckoned slavery. The Catholic Church looked up to the lot of slaves as accidental. Our priests in the north... have not desecrated their pulpits with slavery harangues. Our clergy in the south, who have a true appreciation of the facts, preach to the slaves obedience, and to the masters clemency.

Yet, what hurt the Catholic Church in the black community was not just its position on slavery and racism, but its neglect to accept and train a black clergy. The first seminary for this purpose was established only in 1920, in Greenville, Mississippi, by the Divine Word Missionaries. It moved to Bay St. Louis, Mississippi, in 1923, due to harassment by the local white population and the Ku Klux Klan. The results of the effort in Mississippi and the rest of the country were meager: between 1930 and 1950, fewer than 35 black priests had been ordained.

The insignificant number of ordained black priests was due not just to racism on the part of the institutional Church but also to its inflexible and perhaps unreasonable discipline and the vows of poverty and obedience (and celibacy, for that matter). Such strictures were all too familiar to the black community during slavery, nor did the long years of training required to prepare for the priesthood appeal to many. Although a black separatist movement for a Church, independent from the institutional hierarchy, has been almost non-existent within the African American community, segregated parishes abound in Catholic dioceses. For example, in 1974, there were 900 segregated black parishes, but only 40 of them were pastored by black priests.

Notwithstanding the obstacles, however, black Roman Catholics have not been a passive flock. For example, their frustration from continued discrimination in Church-related institutions led them to join the Knights and Ladies of Peter Claver founded in Mobile, Alabama, in 1909, shunning the white dominated Knights of Columbus. In 1925, black Catholics founded the Federated Colored Catholic Council in Washington, D.C., later becoming the Catholic Interracial Council. Furthermore, taking note of the Civil Rights movement, the few black priests organized themselves into the National Black Clergy Caucus in Detroit in 1968, harshly indicting the Catholic Church in the United States as "primarily a white racist institution, [which] has addressed itself primarily to white society and is definitely a part of that society." Likewise, in 1968 black nuns organized the Catholic Sisters Conference in Pittsburgh, while, in Washington, D.C., in the following year, the National Catholic Black Caucus came to fruition, followed, in 1970, by the establishment of the National Office of Black Catholics. (During the late 1980s, a group led by a black priest in Washington, D.C., detached itself from the official Catholic Church assuming the designation of the Imani Catholic Temple. Although it favors the ordination of women, the Africanization of the Church and its liturgy, and repudiates celibacy, the Imani Temple has attracted only an insignificant number of black Catholics.)

The action of the black Catholic clergy and laymen, however, has bought about some minor changes within the U.S. Catholic Church. Thus, in the early 1980s, of the 350 bishops in the country, 5 were black (1.4 percent); out of 58,485 priests,

300 were black; of 3,200 deacons, 161 were black, with 110 as candidates for the deaconate; among the 8,460 religious brothers, 100 were black; and of the 129,391 sisters, 700 were black. Finally, out of 14,909 seminarians, 200 were African American.

In its annual meeting, in New Orleans, in July 1992, the National Black Catholic Congress, with support from prominent members of the white clergy, decided to propose to the Church the establishment of an African American rite "which might include a new form of worship or a separate jurisdiction of black American bishops, dioceses, and parishes," which would become, if approved by the Vatican, the eighteenth rite within the Catholic Church.

The statistics presented above and the impact of the activity of black Catholic lay men and women in the United States represent progress, when compared to prior years. Yet, for the Catholic Church to be totally accepted in the black community, it must become much more socially and politically active (it has shunned political action in the past), revolutionize its dead and monotonous liturgy in worship, fight racism in its own midst and in society more vigorously, and somehow increase the number of black priests (priests are in general an endangered species within the Roman Catholic Church itself) and empower them by making them an integral part of the hierarchy.

Overall, the 1970s through the 1990s, the religious and secular role of the black Church continued to be equally vital, especially on the political level. It became the vehicle for black massive voter registration and political education and mobilization, quite apparent during presidential elections. The nationally perceived strength of the Church is demonstrated by the fact that, during the last twenty years, practically every presidential hopeful has had to address a black Church and actively solicit the support of its members. It can be successfully argued, therefore, that whenever previous social and political gains have moved into retreat, the black Church has attempted to fill the vacuum and retain, sometimes with great success, center stage and realize its full potential. This has been particularly true in the South, in such states as Mississippi, Alabama, Tennessee, and South Carolina.

Thus, since the beginning of the African American experience to the present, the black Church has remained, by and large, the most enduring black institution, which has put forth an agenda for black action, and suggested and implemented strategies designed to uplift the condition of black people in America. Of course, not every scholar would agree with this positive assessment of the Church in the United States. For instance, Eric Lincoln, noted black scholar, writes in his *The Black Muslims in America* that:

> The Negro church has never been a significant instrument of effective protest. Furthermore, the Negro clergy has yielded a considerable amount of its influence in recent years to business and to other professions. Only lately are there some indications of a renaissance in clerical leadership; and even now, the most significant social leadership is offered by those denominations that lack institutionalized hierarchy.

Lincoln's analysis may have applied to periods earlier than 1961 (the time he wrote his brilliant piece) but one could dispute its validity for the 1956–1965 period, the height of the Civil Rights movement. In fact, in his most recent analysis of the black Church which appears in *The State of Black America, 1989*, published by the National Urban League, Lincoln writes that "...the Black Church is alive, alert, and addressed to the realities of our times," and that:

> Perhaps most significant of all is the fact that the black churches are not only cooperating with each other, they are increasingly willing to work closely with secular institutions in the struggle against the mundane changes to the physical well-being of the black community.

The Church in the Caribbean

The conduct of the Church in the Caribbean or the West Indies was not much different from that of its counterpart in the United States. As in North America, in the Caribbean most Church leaders sided with the planters in what counted most for black people: freedom from bondage. Just as in America, prior to the eighteenth century, there was very little effort on the part of the Church to Christianize the slaves. As experts point out, the reasons were many: planters' objections, who feared that eventually Christianity would give slaves a special status in the eyes of Christendom and therefore undermine the plantation system; planters' concern that, with Christianity, would come literacy and widespread knowledge of the English language, both of which would foster cohesiveness among the slaves and cause them to organize against the established order; and slave masters' realizations that Christianity would have an immediate impact on the pace of work and production in the plantations, as slaves, if baptized, could not be forced to work during the many Christian holidays and on Sundays.

Missionary Work on the Islands Prior to Emancipation

As a result of the prevailing conditions, both the Roman Catholic and the Protestant Churches often became the allies of the plantocracy. What compromised the position of the Catholic Church was the fact that, as Eric Williams writes in *Capitalism and Slavery* (1964), its religious orders (Jesuits, Franciscans, and Dominicans), backed by the Society for the Propagation of the Gospel, owned slaves on their plantations and were told not to Christianize the slaves, as was clear in the case of Barbados. As we are reminded by Professor Noel Leo Erskine, the Catholic Church's attitude had been compromised even much earlier when Bartholomeu de las Casas, Bishop of Chiapa, had convinced Charles V of Spain that it was alright to enslave the Africans (the king subsequently allowed four thousand Africans to be exported from the continent of Africa to Hispaniola, Jamaica, and Puerto Rico in 1517), while, at the same time, forbidding the enslavement of Amerindians.

On the Protestant side, it is known that the Moravian missionaries, who arrived on the island of Jamaica in 1754, "held slaves without hesitation," says Williams, while the Baptists, who started their missionary work in 1814 (although black Americans such as George Lisle and Moses Baker had attempted to establish Churches as early as 1783), "would not allow their first missionaries to deprecate ownership of slaves." The same attitude prevailed within the Scottish Missionary Society after it began its work on the islands in 1800. Even the Quakers are said to have owned slaves and engaged in the North Atlantic slave trade between 1756 and 1784, opposition to the institution having come mainly from American and not English Quakers. The Church of England, for its part, had made its position clear when Bishop Sherlock of London had told his flock and missionaries on the islands during the 1820s that "Christianity and the embracing of the Gospel does not make the least difference in civil property."

Up until the early nineteenth century, therefore, the missionaries had done little worth mentioning to alleviate the condition of the slaves in the Caribbean. Their sectarianism, "indolence and absenteeism," as J.H. Parry and P.M. Sherlock note in *A Short History of the West Indies*, their attachment to material things (symbolized by ownership of slaves), and fear of the plantocracy, which accused the few missionaries opposed to slavery as contributing to slave unrest, prevented the Church from playing a useful role on the islands. However, certain factors beyond the control of the Church were to revolutionize, in a sense, at least temporarily, the position and status of the Church in the eyes of the planters and their slaves in the whole of the West Indies.

Many factors forced the established Caribbean churches to take a stand against slavery and begin to educate the slaves as part of their mission: 1) the Evangelical movement in England, during the latter part of the eighteenth century; 2) continuous revolts on the plantations such as that of Toussaint L'Ouverture in 1801 and the so-called Baptist War in Jamaica in 1831 which had far-reaching consequences; 3) the impact of the French Revolution; and 4) and the work of the abolitionists at the beginning of the nineteenth century. When Britain and France outlawed slavery in the West Indies in 1833 and 1848 respectively, the clergy, particularly the Baptist, because of the pressure it exerted upon the established Church in England and the British government on the issue of emancipation, gained new importance among the newly emancipated blacks. Although all along the Church had generally sided with the planters and had preached submission and obedience to the master and the virtues of hard work, the slaves now saw it as an ally in their struggle for liberation and freedom.

Emancipation and the Church

Following emancipation, the Church's major effort, apart from imparting religious values, focused on teaching blacks how to read and write and on securing land and housing for their families. (In fairness, it must be noted that some denominations had insisted on providing education to slaves, as the Moravians had done, beginning in 1760, but the results were negligible.) Thus, as Professor of Theology Noel Leo Erskine puts it in his work *Decolonizing Theology: A Caribbean Perspective* (1981), the Church was instrumental in securing not the important "social space" (equality with whites) for blacks but the necessary "physical space" for displaced former slaves whose masters let them go either without a plot of land or attempted to sell them several acres for which the slaves could not afford to pay.

Consequently, on many occasions, missionaries became the trusted mediators between the master and his soon-to-be-free slaves. In this capacity, by 1839, Baptists had, for example, created some 200 villages (about 100,000 acres of land), entirely occupied by former slaves and their families. Around the same time, as a result of the concerted effort by the Church and the government, particularly in the British-controlled islands, 70,000 students were enrolled in the newly established school system, and, in 1843, when they severed their ties with the London Baptist Missionary Society, the Baptists founded Calabar College in Jamaica for the training of black ministers.

Statistics show that the popularity of the established Church caused its black membership to soar, doubling at times, as was the case with the Baptists whose black membership rose from 10,000 between 1831 and 1841. Thus, by the mid-nineteenth century most Caribbeans professed to be either Catholic (in the French Antilles, Santa Lucia, Grenada, Dominica, and Trinidad) or Protestant (in Barbados, Guyana, and Jamaica). In fact, the Church gained so much in stature after emancipation that Erskine states that "with the confidence placed in [the ministers] by the planters and black people alike, there is a sense in which they and not the black people were the greatest beneficiaries of emancipation."

The popularity of the established Church did not last long, however, as, by 1845, membership had plummeted by half. It would appear that, by then, with education, black members had understood more clearly the role the Church had played in the sanctioning of slavery in the Americas, its discriminatory practices even after emancipation, the provision of an education which was inferior to that of whites, and the continuous preaching of religious equality between black and white while upholding the cultural and social inequality between the former masters and the freed slaves. Furthermore, as we are reminded by Franklin Knight and Colin Palmer, the new Christians had never abandoned the African religious beliefs and practices (such as the use of charms, spiritual possession, sacrifice of animals or birds to ancestors and spirits, and dancing in rituals) which they had brought to their confined new island habitat.

This, as expected, elicited a condemning response from the established churches. For example, the Baptists, generally more tolerant of such practices than their Christian counterparts, were accused of allowing un-Christian practices in their churches. Paradoxically, the Baptists as well as the Methodists, had unwittingly created a favorable atmosphere for black religious adventurers to rebel and establish churches of their own. According to Erskine, because of their absenteeism, missionaries in these two denominations had traditionally divided their Afro-Caribbean members into classes on the basis of regions, and appointed leaders who would replace the clergy when absent, carrying on the responsibility of convening meetings, visiting the sick, and even preaching on certain occasions.

As a result of these factors, the independent or separate black Church movement spread so rapidly that, by 1860, in Jamaica, for example, one half of the Baptist churches were run by black "ministers." Within the Catholic Church, on the other hand, several indigenous church organizations emerged on the islands and skillfully syncretized Catholicism with African religious survivals. The result was what is now known as *Vodun* with its priests (or *hongans*) and its divinities (or *loas*) in Haiti; Shango in Trinidad; comania in Jamaica; Macumba in Brazil; and Santeria in Cuba. In Jamaica, Revivalism with an infusion of African religious residues became the most popular brand of Christianity between 1841 and 1860.

The free spirit of American black independent Baptists, Pentecostals, Methodists, Seventh-Day Adventists, and followers of the Church of God and the

Church of Nazarene, also had an impact on the number and fervor of Caribbean black churches. Pentecostals, in particular, who favor the speaking in tongues phenomenon and prophesying, spiritual possession and trance, healing miracles, and open emotional responses during worship, gained considerable following. The centuries-old religious syncretism, we are told by Knight and Palmer, is still visible in the Jamaican Christmas festival called the Jonkonnu and the Carnival (Catholic) lent celebrations of many of the islands.

The independent movement away from the established, transplanted European Church, and the obvious religious syncretism have remained as the two most important features of the type of Christianity prevailing in the islands at present. Thus, although practically everyone in the islands professes to be Christian, Afro-Caribbeans have created a Church with its own unique identity, one which became, over the centuries, a vehicle for the ventilation of frustration under slavery, colonialism, and racism, and the reaffirmation of the African roots of the former slaves.

The Rastafarian movement started forming in the 1930s. The movement interpreted the scriptures in its own way, proclaimed the late Emperor Haile Selassie the black Messiah, and believed that Ethiopia was the land of the chosen people. It should be considered the most radical offshoot of Caribbean Christianity, started by people who were stirred by the Garvey movement and frustrated by the depression of the 1930s. As Erskine once again informs us, the Rastafarians reacted to economic hardships and longed for true freedom, identity, and unity, as well as economic emancipation and prosperity. Notwithstanding the fact that Rastafarianism never spread to the islands beyond its Jamaican birthplace, it is still a powerful reminder of the tragic consequences of the encounter between Africans and Europeans.

The Nation of Islam

Islam has existed in the United States for centuries, but it did not attract a significant number of African Americans until the 1930s. Although it is known that the first (Moorish Science) Temple espousing Islam was founded by Drew Ali in Newark, New Jersey, in 1913, the precise origins of the Nation of Islam as an organized institution within the black community are still clouded in mystery. Renowned black scholar Eric Lincoln, the best living authority on black Muslims in the United States, tells us that the founder of the Lost-Found Nation of Islam was Wali D. Fard, who, though without much proof, was believed to have come from Mecca to save what he called the "Negroes," whom he held as descendants of the ancient "tribe" of Shabazz. Following his mysterious disappearance in 1934 in Detroit and a split in the movement, Fard's lieutenant, Elijah Muhammad (formerly, Elijah Poole) of Sandersville, Georgia, took over the leadership, and established his residence in Chicago, with Temple Number Two as the movement's headquarters.

Under the able leadership of Elijah Muhammad, the Nation of Islam grew to some 10,000 members during the post-World War II period, to 100,000 by the 1960s, to close to 200,000 during the late 1980s, and to one million in 2005, with temples spread throughout the major cities in the United States and even abroad, in Africa, Europe, and Asia. Experts claim that the relatively accelerated growth of the Nation had its roots in the continuing discrimination and racism in the country, black unemployment during the 1930s (particularly with the Depression), and the apparent weakening of the Civil Rights movement during the late 1960s and 1970s.

Lincoln's study shows that most members of the organization have tended to be young black males, southern migrants, and from the low-income class within the black community, many of whom are also ex-Christians. Those who have studied Islam have generally viewed the Nation of Islam as a brand of nationalism within the black community using religion (Islam) as the vehicle for the achievement of its goal—the liberation and independence of the black race in the United States. Harold Cruise maintains, for example, that, in the case of the Nation of Islam, "religion took the place of a cohesive political creed which neither Marxism, socialism, communism, nor black nationalism alone could do." With its founder and his immediate successor, the Nation of Islam stood for economic independence of the members and, by extension, the whole black community. Since its inception, Islam has exacted fixed financial contributions from its members. These assets have turned the organization into a multi-million dollar religious-economic enterprise, owning businesses, lands, estates, tax-exempt schools, temples, and a university.

Its philosophy stands for total racial separation, as it considers whites "devils" whose rule of the world will disappear, and blacks as the chosen people, the inheritors of the earth, whose God—Allah—is also black, with the leader of Islam as the Prophet who received his message from Him directly. The Nation of Islam rejects and ridicules Christianity as the religion of the devil but respects the Bible and takes inspiration in the *Qur'an* and its teachings.

Consequently, the Nation of Islam uncompromisingly rejects integration, which it considers to be the goal of "Negroes" and not of blacks, and, until recently, it aspired for a separate state for black people in the country. Although many people tend to fear the members of the Nation of Islam (mainly because most do not know what they stand for), the leaders have always forbidden their followers from carrying weapons or engaging in violent acts, although, as Lincoln observes, "they do believe in keeping the scores even," namely, in the concept of a tooth for a tooth. Yet, Muhammad had taught members that, because America was a country controlled by the "devil," black people had no allegiance to the flag, and discouraged the use of the ballot, except on those occasions the Prophet deemed it necessary to vote. Black Muslims were also compelled to keep a strict discipline: they could not drink alcohol, smoke, gamble, eat pork, or engage in premarital sex, and they had to observe a dress code and a separation of sexes in schools.

As the Nation grew and became a multi-million dollar business, problems, common to most organizations, began to crop up, from disagreements on the role of material things to charges of corruption and immorality on the part of the leadership, including the Prophet himself, and from non-adherence to the doctrine of strict racial separation and demand for statehood to the control of the organization itself. Thus, the official spokesman for the Nation of Islam, Malcolm X (converted while in prison in 1947), raised his concerns and encountered the wrath of the conservative leadership and, in 1964, he was censored and eventually ousted from his position, allegedly for making disparaging remarks following the assassination of President Kennedy (namely, that "the chickens have come home to roost"). Malcolm X, who had become the most eloquent defender of the Nation, left the organization and founded his own Temple in New York City, where, unfortunately, he was assassinated in 1965. However, his departure underscored the deep philosophical and organizational divisions within the Nation of Islam, which came to the open immediately after the death of Elijah Muhammad in 1975. The conservatives or the moderates had secured victory with the accession to leadership by Muhammad's fifth son (he had six), Wallace Muhammad.

In an attempt to align the Nation with Orthodox Islam, Supreme Minister (later Imam) Wallace Muhammad changed the name of the organization to The World Community of Islam in the West, becoming The American Muslim Mission in 1980, a designation which was also dissolved in 1985, when black Muslims were renamed Bilallians (after Bilall, allegedly, as Lincoln notes, the first Muslim African *muezzin* or crier). In a reversal of long-standing policies, whites, at least in principle, could be admitted into the organization, and the dress and eating codes and voting restrictions became voluntary. As expected, the new direction was opposed by many members including the spokesman who succeeded Malcolm X, Minister Louis Farrakhan. Farrakhan rejected the changes, continued to use the designation of The Nation of Islam for the organization, and has since then considered himself to be the true representative of Elijah Muhammad.

Islam is a fascinating phenomenon within the black community, but black scholars are divided in their assessment of its impact and appeal. While many applaud its emphasis on racial solidarity, discipline, and the call for economic self-determination, they question its extreme views on race and its advocacy of a philosophy of political and social separatism. In fact, Lincoln considers Islam in the United States a "religion of protest," a religion that is propelled by racism, as he writes that:

> We must confront the issue of racism and discrimination. When we have done so with the determination and moral conviction so brutally the problem deserves, there will be no black Muslims. There will be no need for them. And America will be a better place for us all.

Harold Cruise, on the other hand, comments that "under the ideology of Islam we find the same economic and educational philosophy of Booker T. Washington in more updated trappings." In short, he doubts its practical value for the masses of the black community.

The lack of total acceptance of the Nation of Islam by Orthodox Islam is also attributed to the stand on the racial issue, although Bilallians, who do not seem much concerned about their worldwide acceptance, hold that the world is divided into two camps: the whites and those of the Third World who must join in solidarity. Robert Allen also sees shortcomings in Islam as a provider of solutions to black people's problems in America, namely, the "religious mysticism" of black Muslims; the failure to come up with a realistic strategy to "change power relations" (black Muslims do not protest with sit-ins and marches); and the image that, by and large, the organization seems "simply to supply an alternative route to middle-class status for some blacks, rather than actively attacking the problem of general black oppression."

Despite their small number, however, and their slow inroads into the black community, particularly into the black middle-class, black Muslims are a group to contend with: very dedicated, disciplined, which cannot but instill pride among blacks all over the country. Whether they would, indeed, disappear when and if discrimination and racism would be done away with, as Lincoln predicts, is an imponderable. It is clear, however, that, for the establishment, black Muslims have become less of a threat than used to be perceived.

Summary

Insofar as African Americans are concerned, the position of Christianity, as preached and practiced by both the Roman Catholic Church and the Protestant denominations (except for the Methodists), has been one of simultaneous ambiguity and contradiction—of defending and condoning both human dignity and oppression; of preaching and living both equality and discrimination; and of cherishing and rejecting both brotherhood and racism. A study of antebellum Church documents in America demonstrates that the institution was divided on the issue of slavery: while a few enlightened clergy in all denominations condemned slavery since its beginning, until the latter part of the eighteenth century, however, the majority of the Church hierarchy and membership condoned and defended institutional slavery. In the South, in particular, many slave masters, afraid that Christianizing the slaves might entitle them special social status and perhaps give them a stronger claim to freedom, refused to have them baptized, and restricted their exposure to the teachings of Christ, constantly quoting the Apostle Paul who once admonished servants to obey their masters. Realizing, however, that those who advocated freedom for slaves once Christianized had no impact on the fate of the "peculiar institution," many slave masters began allowing their slaves to hear the message of the Church, but only that of submission and not of equality, brotherhood, and love among humankind.

Despite the constraints, an "invisible" Church emerged among the slaves even prior to emancipation, one which, in its own peculiar way, provided solace, racial and social solidarity, and the hope that things would get better, if not here, at least in the afterlife. On the eve of the Civil War and during Reconstruction, tired of continuing discrimination and racism not only in society at large but in the very bosom of the Christian Churches, which preached human equality before God, black men and women of courage and determination succeeded in founding independent black Churches both in the North and the South. Richard Allen (who established the Bethel African Methodist Episcopal Church in 1816) was one of the major inspirations for the expansion of the movement in the United States.

Although the role of the black Church has had an uneven evolution and impact, and has been challenged by other black organizations such as the NAACP, it is generally acknowledged that the Church has been crucial in the preservation and the strength of the black family and community. Indeed, throughout the centuries, the black Church has fostered and provided educational opportunities for African Americans; it has helped uplift their economic and social conditions through special programs such as those sustained by the Free African Societies, the mutual associations, and Church-sponsored welfare insurance agencies; and, most importantly, it has remained in the frontline in the struggle for equal rights and political participation not only for the masses of the black people but for all

Americans. Its involvement in the Civil Rights movement of the mid-1950s and 1960s, and the resulting civil rights legislation, and the role the black preacher has played on the political, state, and, national arena are ample proof of the black Church's enduring and cherished mission among diaspora Africans in the United States.

In the Caribbean or the West Indies, the ambiguities of the Roman Catholic and the Protestant Church toward slavery and in its social teachings and practices were similar to those in North America. Although its effort toward the education of black people and its assistance to the newly emancipated slaves must be recognized, the established Church's refusal to adapt to the indigenous cultures and the contradiction between its theory and practice forced Caribbean blacks to break away and form their own Churches which would cater to their true social and spiritual needs.

In the process, on one hand, the syncretized Church assisted the Afro-Caribbeans in the quest for their roots and identity. Although Rastafarianism, on the other hand, did not take much hold in the islands, it stands as a clear manifestation, albeit an extremist one, of the longing for Africa and the search for relevant religious and secular institutions able to provide more meaning to the lives of these forcefully transplanted Africans.

Islam in the black American community is a recent phenomenon which dates back to the 1930s. Until the 1970s, Islam was viewed as an extremist organization, preaching strict racial separation (and, in the eyes of some, racial hatred), economic independence, political separatism, and upholding one of the strictest eating, dressing, and pleasure-related codes. As a result of such an image, the Nation of Islam remained the "religion of protest," to use Eric Lincoln's expression, and was unable to compete with the Christian black Church for a wider membership, and faced a problem of recognition by Orthodox Islam both in the United States and abroad. Yet, Islam has managed to attract some of those young men and women who have lost faith and hope in the American system.

Despite the fact that there are still those who advocate the brand of Islam preached by Wali Fard and Elijah Muhammad, as is the case of Minister Louis Farrakhan, the new Bilallian Nation has become less of a threat for the system and the black middle class than it was prior to the mid-1970s. However, this does not mean that its controversial nature has disappeared completely, as one can detect from the reaction to Minister Farrakhan's indirect involvement in the 1988 presidential campaign, when Jesse Jackson was asked to disassociate himself from the minister and from the statements on the race issue and the Jews. Perhaps the most significant role of Islam in the black community has been the contribution to racial pride and solidarity and the struggle toward economic independence.

Study Questions and Activities

1. Compare and contrast the three governmental structures which characterize the Christian Church in America.
2. How did the "white Church" justify slavery?
3. What were the four major functions of the African American Church in the rural South?

4. How did the Civil Rights movement and the black Church impact each other?
5. Discuss the origins, the success, and problems of black Muslims in the United States.
6. Compare and contrast the features of the Church in North America and the Caribbean and its treatment of black people.

References

Robert Allen. *Black Awakening in Capitalist America*. New York: Doubleday, 1970.

Yvonne Chireau and Nathaniel Deutsch (eds.). *Black Zion: African American Religious Encounters with Judaism*. New York: Oxford University Press, 2000.

Harold Cruise. *Rebellion and Revolution. The Crisis of the Negro Intellectual*. New York: William Morrow and Co., 1968.

Noel Leo Erskine. *Decolonizing Theology: A Caribbean Perspective*. Maryknoll, NY: Orbis Books, 1981.

Toyin Falola and Matt D. Childs (eds.). *The Yoruba Diaspora in the Atlantic World*. Bloomington: Indiana University Press, 2004.

Yvonne Haddad (ed.). *The Muslims in America*. New York: Oxford University Press, 1991.

———. *Islamic Values in the United States: A Comparative Study*. New York: Oxford University Press, 1987.

Vincent Harding. *There is A River: The Black Struggle for Freedom in America*. New York: Harcourt Brace Jovanovich, 1983.

James Hennesey. *American Catholics: A History of the Roman Catholic Church in the United States*. New York: Oxford University Press, 1981.

Linda M. Heywood (ed.). *Central Africans and Cultural Transformations in the American Diaspora*. New York: Cambridge University Press, 2002.

Franklin W. Knight and Colin Palmer (eds.). *The Modern Caribbean*. Chapel Hill, NC: University of North Carolina Press, 1989.

Waltraud Kokot, Khachig Tölölyan and Carolin Alfonso (eds.). *Diaspora, Identity, and Religion: New Directions in Theory and Research*. New York: Routledge, 2004.

Eric Lincoln. *The Black Muslims in America*. Boston: Beacon, 1961.

Luis Martinez-Fernández. *Protestantism and Political Conflict in the Nineteenth-Century Hispanic Caribbean*. New Brunswick, NJ: Rutgers University Press, 2002.

Randall Miller and Jon Wakelyn. *Catholics in the Old South*. Macon, GA: Mercer University Press, 1983.

National Urban League. *The State of Black America, 1989*. New York: National Urban League, 1989.

Timothy Jon Nelson. *Every Time I Feel the Spirit: Religious Experience and Ritual in an African American Church*. New York: New York University Press, 2005.

Stephen Ochs. *Desegregating the Altar*. Baton Rouge, LA.: Louisiana University Press, 1990.

Margarite Fernández Olmos and Lizabeth Paravisini-Gebert. *Creole Religions of the Caribbean: An Introduction from Vodou and Santería to Obeah and Espritismo*. New York: New York University Press, 2003.

J.H. Parry and P.M. Sherlock. *A Short History of the West Indies*. London: Macmillan, 1957.

James Roohan. *American Catholics and the Social Question, 1865–1900*. New York: Arno Press, 1976.

Milton C. Sernett. *Black Religion in American Evangelicalism: White Protestantism, Plantation Missions and the Flowering of Negro Christianity, 1787–1865*. NJ: Scarecrow Press, Inc., 1975.

Thérèse Smith. *Let the Church Sing!: Music and Worship in a Black Mississippi Community*. Rochester, NY: University of Rochester Press, 2004.

Laura de Mello e Souza; translated from the Portuguese by Diane Grosklaus Whitty. *The Devil and the Land of the Holy Cross: Witchcraft, Slavery, and Popular Religion in Colonial Brazil*. Austin: University of Texas Press, 2003.

James H. Sweet. *Recreating Africa: Culture, Kinship, and Religion in the African-Portuguese World, 1441–1770*. Chapel Hill: University of North Carolina Press, 2003.

Patrick Taylor (ed.). *Nation Dance: Religion, Identity, and Cultural Difference in the Caribbean*. Bloomington: Indiana University Press, 2001.

———. *The Narratives of Liberation: Perspectives on Afro-Caribbean Literature, Popular Culture, and Politics*. Ithaca, NY: Cornell University Press, 1989.

Earl Waugh et al. (eds.). *The Muslim Community in North America*. Alberta, Canada: The University of Alberta Press, 1983.

Eric Williams. *Capitalism and Slavery*. London: Andre Deutsch, 1964.

Gayraud Wilmore. *Black Religion and Black Radicalism*, New York: Doubleday and Company, 1972.

Gayraud. S. Wilmore. *Pragmatic Spirituality: The Christian Faith Through an Africentric Lens*. New York: New York University, 2004.

Carter G. Woodson. *The History of the Negro Church*. Washington, DC: The Associated Publishers, 1972.

Henry Young. *Major Black Religious Thinkers*. Nashville, TN: Abingdon Press, 1977.

24

African Women

Hazel M. McFerson

This chapter examines the status and roles of women in traditional and contemporary African societies. At the outset, it is important to emphasize that in Africa, as elsewhere, the social status and economic position of women is determined by the interaction of a variety of factors, and not by any single factor. Among these, the most important are the criterion for tracing genealogical descent and group membership; the nature of economic organization; religion; history and culture; and geography. Other things being equal, women have higher status in pastoral systems than in agricultural societies; under Christian or animist religions than under Islam; and in matrilineal cultures than in patrilineal ones. As a general proposition, kinship-based ethnicity is basic to social and economic relations in Africa. Consequently, the rules determining lines of descent and kinship relations are particularly important determinants of African women's status.

The first section of the chapter introduces the concepts of kinship, lineage, ancestry, and matrilineal and patrilineal descent systems. These concepts are important for understanding women's roles and status in marriage and the family, as well as the importance of fertility and children, and their roles in economic activities, and authority systems in traditional society. The richness and complexity of the situation of women in Africa is illustrated in the second and third sections of this chapter, with discussions of Ashanti women in Ghana (a matrilineal, agricultural, largely Christian society in West Africa), and of women in Somalia (a patrilineal, pastoral, Islamic society in East Africa). The final section discusses women in contemporary Africa, with particular attention to their roles as peace activists and advocates of nonviolent conflict resolution. We will also examine are the consequences of war, particularly the plethora of unexploded antipersonnel land mines, for women and children.

Major terms and concepts: kinship, ascribed and achieved roles, matrilineage, patrilineage, matriarchy, lineage, chiefdom, queen mother, mobility, polygamy, pastoralism, ancestor, golden stool, bridewealth, descent, *Asantehene*, female genital mutilation, nonviolent conflict resolution, peace advocates, antipersonnel land mines.

Gender, Lineage and Kinship

Kinship and lineage are important in traditional African societies. *Kinship* is the network of relatives—fathers, uncles, brothers, nephews, mothers, sisters, daughters, nieces, cousins, etc.—who share a common ancestor or ancestress. *Ancestry* is a method of tracing descent from a common ancestor or ancestress, who is considered the founder of the group. *Ancestor "worship,"* as it is called by some anthropologists, is the practice of venerating and honoring the dead ancestors, who continue to be important members of the family. Their spirit remains with the group, and their protection and involvement in the activities of the family is essential. A *descent group* consists of individuals who are related by blood, and who trace their lineage back to a single ancestor, who can either be male (patriliny) or female (matriliny). *Matriliny* traces lineage exclusively through the female line, based on a common female ancestress, usually for a period of ten to twelve generations. ("Matrilineal" is the adjective.) Although women generally do exercise comparatively greater influence in a matrilineal system, this should not be confused with *"matriarchy,"* a system in which women wield formal authority over the family, the state and the nation. *Patriliny* is a method of tracing ancestry through the male line, based on a common male ancestor.

The ancestor is the link between past, present and future generations in a descent group. In reciting their origins, people will speak of an ancestor. For example, in a biography of African American entertainer Lena Horne, mention is made of a founding female ancestress, a grandmother from Madagascar, from whom the Horne family in America descended. In contrast, Alex Haley's *Roots*, named a male African ancestor, Kunta Kinte, as the founder of his lineage. Lineage, ancestry and descent are important for establishing social rules, such as those governing inheritance, succession, residence, formal authority, and women's roles in matrilineal and patrilineal societies.

The rules and customs governing kinship in traditional society are complex. They regulate behavior in a variety of contexts, and determine status, rights, and obligations. A *role* is a pattern of behavior, and can either be *ascribed* or *achieved*. An ascribed role is one into which an individual is born, or succeeds to at a certain age (as in a royal lineage). An achieved role is one that an individual earns, or otherwise works for, as in becoming an engineer. *Status* is a position in the social hierarchy of a group or of a society. Status, too, can either be achieved, or ascribed. The obligations of kin toward one another are specified by traditional customs, but always kin are expected to help one another in times of trouble, to share their possessions with each other, and to share in happiness, sorrow, wealth and poverty.

The concept of the individual has little meaning in traditional Africa. The survival and property of the individual depend on the survival and property of the group. The family and the kinship group are primary. Kinship is the cement which binds individuals to family, clan, village, and ultimately the nation. (A *clan* is an extended kinship group based on either matrilineal or patrilineal descent.) Kinship groups, such as clans, function as a kind of social safety-net. For example, when an individual travels from the village to the city, he or she expects, and receives, assistance from city-based relatives who provide free lodging and food, and tips on employment opportunities and the ways of city life. It is this aspect of traditional society which points up the importance of gender and women.

In Africa, because family is one of the most important traditional institutions, motherhood is the most important role and source of personal identity for women. Women in Africa are responsible for perpetuating the group and the family, especially by producing sons. This applies to both patrilineal and matrilineal societies. The *reproductive* role of women, as bearers of children, is essential to insuring the continuity of the family. Fertility is important and barren women are stigmatized. The number of children a woman bears is important for her status; the emphasis is on the number of living children. Because of high infant death rates, it is expected that a woman will bear many children to increase the number of those who survive. Motherhood is revered, and the term "mother" or "mama" is one of respect throughout Africa. In addition to their reproductive role, women also have important productive roles in subsistence and market agriculture and in other income-generating activities. In both matrilineal and patrilineal societies custom and tradition insure that women have gender-specific roles in almost all aspects of social, cultural and political organization.

Case Studies: Women in Ghana and Somalia

The Ashanti are the largest group among the Akan-speaking peoples, who live in an area of southern Ghana around Kumasi, the historical capital of the Ashanti Kingdom. The Ashanti are predominantly agricultural people, who grow maize, manioc, plantain, bananas, yams and cocoa, which is their principal export crop. In traditional society gold was an important economic commodity, and the British referred to the country as the *Gold Coast*, until it became independent in 1957, and took the name Ghana after the ancient kingdom.

While many economic, cultural and religious aspects influence a woman's role and status, lineage and ancestry are especially important. Among the Ashanti, an individual is a member of his mother's lineage, which consists of all the descendants of both sexes who trace their genealogy *through women* to a common ancestress. Matrilineal descent is the key to Ashanti social and political organization, and it determines, in turn, clan affiliation. The mother-child bond (see below) incorporates a man into his mother's clan, as every lineage belongs to one of seven clans, which form the basis of Ashanti social and political life.

In fact, the mother-child bond is central to Ashanti social organization. An Ashanti proverb summarizes its importance: "*wo na awa a, wo abusua asa.*" ("If your mother dies you have no lineage kin left.") Every Ashanti is by birth, a member of the mother's lineage (*abusua*). As K.A. Busia points out, this bond illustrates the importance of women in Ashanti society. The Ashanti believe that a human being is formed from the blood of the mother and the spirit of the father. In addition to inheriting his mother's blood, every man is believed to receive a *kra,* a life principle bestowed by the Creator. It is through the matrilineal line, or the mother's blood, that an individual inherits status and membership within the lineage, the clan, the ethnic group, and ultimately the nation. The Ashanti believe that because a person's status, rank and fundamental rights stem from the mother, she is the most important person in an individual's life.

The mother-child bond establishes a wide network of relationships, rights, obligations and status. In particular, matriliny determines the rules of inheritance and succession (the transmission of property and accession to public office). For example, a man would succeed his mother's brother in holding office. The line of succession and of obligation are described by an eminent Ghanaian sociologist, the late K.A. Busia:

> In this group the closest bond is that which exists between siblings: children of the same parents or of the same mother. A man's potential successors are his brothers in order of age, his mother's sister's son, his sister's son, his mother's sister's daughter's son, his sister's daughter's son, his mother's sister's daughter's daughter's son, his sister's daughter's son, his mother's sister's daughter's daughter's son, his sister's daughter's daughter's son, or his mother's sister's daughter's daughter's daughter's son, in that order of preference.

By Ashanti law, the right of inheritance is matrilineal, and brothers take precedence over sisters in inheriting property. However, sisters can inherit property in the absence of a male descendant from the mother. The lineage is also the basis of a political unity. The clan system is common to all Akan people, and is an important source of cultural unity.[1] The central bond underlying the genealogical aspect of Ashanti society is the institution that some have called *ancestor worship*. This is reflected in the following poem, taken from Birago Diop:

> Those who are dead are never gone,
> They are in the breast of the woman,
> They are in the child who is wailing,
> And in the firebrand that flames.
> The dead are not under the earth;
> They are in the fire that is dying,
> They are in the grasses that weep,
> They are in the whimpering rocks,
> They are in the forest, they are in the house,
> The dead are not dead.

Ancestors serve as links between the living and the past. The spirits of the dead are the source of the continuity of the group. Ancestors are always with the group in spirit, and are involved in daily life, as the living appeal for the ancestors to intervene on their behalf and help in solving problems, and otherwise invite them to participate in family business. Periodically, libations (offering of food and drink) are offered to the ancestors, along with prayers that they protect members of the lineage, bless them with health and long life, that the women bear many children, and farms yield sufficient food.

Lineage, through the mother-child bond, is the basis of the political unit, the chiefdom. Despite the cultural importance of women, formal authority in Ashanti matrilineal society is held by men, rather than by women. The highest authority is the head of the Ashanti people (and of Kumasi State), the *asantehene*, who is closely linked in Ashanti tradition with the Golden Stool. The status of the *Asantehene* and other chiefs is ascribed, although achievement also plays a role. They are chosen from a particular lineage by the heads of other lineages on the basis of personal skills and abilities. A chiefdom consists of an aggregate of several social

---

1. This section is based in part on K.A. Busia, "The Ashanti of the Gold Coast," in Forde, Daryll, ed., *African Worlds: Studies in the Cosmological Ideas and Social Values of African Peoples*, published for the International African Institute by Oxford University Press, London: 1954, reprinted in 1970.

units: the lineage, the village and the sub-division. A chiefdom is a combination of localized lineages which live in a given territory, and which constitute a political community based on kinship. The Ashanti kingdom is composed of a number of different chieftaincies (*oman*), governed by a chief (*asantehene*), and a queen-mother (*asantehemma*), the senior woman of the royal lineage, who is generally the sister or the mother of the chief (Sarpong, 77:3). The *Asantehene* is the head of the national Council, composed of the heads of the various states. Every lineage has a male head (*abusa panin*), who is assisted by a senior woman (*obaa panin*).

As noted, even in matrilineal societies men generally wield formal authority exercised through the state, but women have a comparatively significant symbolic role. All chiefs are male, with queen mothers playing advisory and ceremonial roles among the Ashanti. In a broad sense, they personify motherhood. (A recent attempt by queen mothers to improve their representation in the National House of Chiefs failed.) The Queen Mother is the "stool mother" of the chief, and she can be the birth mother, an aunt, a sister or a cousin of the reigning chief (Amoah: 1988, 174). Traditionally, the queen-mother owned a stool—a symbol of authority among the Ashanti. Her authority depended on moral rather than legal sanctions and she symbolized the importance of matriliny in the social system. However, the office of the queen mother was not merely an elevated domestic position. In traditional society it was a vital public political office, and she was an important political figure, especially in verifying lineage. She also played an important role in nominating candidates, in consultation with the "stool family," to fill the vacant stool. The nominee not only had to be formally approved by the *asantehene's* advisors, but also by the Union's Chiefs of State. Thus, the Queen Mother shared important duties with the male lineage head. Her role in the hierarchy is described by G. Y. Amoah:

> Though she was not necessarily next in importance to the chief, she seemed to exercise more rights than most of the sub-chiefs. She played an active part in the business of government of the chiefdom. She sat with the chief in court and in council and always to the immediate left of the chief. She maintained linguists and councilors of her own who could be either males or females.

Similarly, each village has a queen mother, who performs ritual rites of worship and has a main role in settling divorce cases. Her duties include watching over the morals of the woman and girls, supervising girls' puberty rites, and representing women in political and domestic affairs. As a stool mother, she is the recognized head of the ruling family. She is also an authority on matters relating to genealogy and the chiefdom, and she educates the chief in the history and the custom of the chiefdom. She also exercises some control over the women in the chiefdom. When they are called upon to perform communal work, she supervises them. However, although she has a general supervisory authority over women, she does not represent women's interests *as such* in state government. Her position is based on ascribed, rather than representative, power.

Agnes Aidoo notes that the Queen Mother is independently wealthy, deriving her wealth, in part, from Ghana's vast gold mines. In addition, as in most societies, personality, skills and other attributes are important in determining the personal popularity of queen mothers. Within all Ashanti states (which comprise a number of villages), one clan provides the royal lineage, and a candidate for the chieftaincy is nominated by the queen mother. The queen mother does not control the women of the state. And, as Sarpong observes, every lineage has its own Senior Woman, who is responsible for the women of the lineage and concerned with their marriages and divorces, and general status. The queen mother is not a figurehead. She is expected to play a strong, active role in matters of state including hearing judicial cases involving the sacred oaths of the state. Rev. Peter Sarpong writes: "The Queen-Mother is consulted on matrimonial affairs within the royal lineage. She hears 'household' cases, usually matrimonial cases and disputes between members of the royal household" (77: 4). From the earliest times, the queen mother ruled when the king died or was deposed and no successor had yet been appointed.

Studies by Meyer Fortes, K.A. Busia, and others make it clear that the symbol of the Ashanti nation is the *Golden Stool*. A chieftainship, lineage or other public office held by a man or a woman is always referred to as a stool (*Kunnua*). According to legend, a wooden stool adorned with gold was brought forth from the sky by Anokye (the king's priest), before a great assembly of chiefs and people, and it descended, amidst thunder and dust, to land before King Osei Tutu. The stool is believed to contain the soul of the Ashanti people, as well as their health and welfare. It also contains *sunsum* of the people, which, according to Busia, is "a man's . . . ego, his personality, his distinctive character." The chief's authority as guardian and the continuity of chieftainship is symbolized by the stool, which must, however, never be sat upon. The golden stool was more revered than was the person of the ruler. Removing the stool from the chief ("destooling") means that he has lost the confidence of the Ashanti people.

During numerous attempts to bring the Ashanti under their domination, the British demanded the Golden Stool. In 1900, on a visit to Kumasi, the governor of the then-Gold Coast, Sir Frederic Hodgson, declared that it was an insult to the British queen that he was not permitted, as her representative, to sit on the stool. This was blasphemy and the Ashanti buried the stool to prevent its desecration. The failure of the British to understand the significance of the stool contributed to the series of wars between the British and the Ashanti, and to the colonizer's unsuccessful attempts to break the spirit of the Ashanti. As part of this effort, the British sought to remove or destool Prempeh I, the young *Asantehene*.

A woman, Yaa Asantewa, was deeply involved in attempts to preserve the integrity of the Golden Stool and the Ashanti nation. She is one of the most important female leaders in Ashanti history. As Sweetman notes: "When all seemed lost, their power broken and their king in exile, the Asante put themselves under the command of a woman, Queen Yaa Asantewa, who led them in their last desperate attempt to keep foreigners at bay." She was the mother of the young Asantehene Prempeh I, who was finally destooled in 1894, and exiled to the Seychelles Islands. The loss of her son did not endear the British to Yaa Asantewa. The bereaved and proud mother eventually declared war upon them (the "*Yaa Asantewa war*"). She did not live to see her son return from exile a few years after her death. As Sweetman further comments, the Ashanti still sing of her: "*Yaa Asantewa*, the warrior woman who carries a gun and a sword of state in battle."

An important watershed in the lives of Ashanti women is the nubility rite, which is performed in preparation for the transition from childhood to womanhood, and which illustrates the importance of fertility and motherhood. In Ashanti society, as in Africa generally, a barren woman is disgraced, as the bearing of children is essential for perpetuating the lineage. Thus, the entry into womanhood is marked by complex ceremonies and nubility rites, entailing much preparation and ritual, beginning after the onset of the first menstruation. The queen-mother plays an important role in determining the girl's readiness for the ceremony. She examines each of the girls who are about to go through the nubility rites, to insure that their menstruation has in fact begun, or to determine if they are pregnant. Abortions are frowned upon. The Ashanti revere life, and the rites are intended to involve the ancestors in the all-important issue of fertility and children. It is important to note that the Ashanti do not practice female genital mutilation or circumcision as a rite of passage from childhood to womanhood. They believe that a clitoridectomy would deplete the personality of the woman.

Nubility rites consist of a series of life-affirming spiritual and religious activities, which are carried out over a period of days. Preparations for the ceremony consist of the following: spiritual preparation, which involves properly consulting a spirit to insure that the celebration will not be harmful to the girl; material preparations and assembling a large number of items, such as *kente* cloth (a hand-woven multi-colored cloth for which the Ashanti are famous), as well as gold necklaces, expensive beads, blankets, mats and pillows for the attendants, cooking pots, and other items (some of the items are for immediate use, while others are used in later life); choice of day and invitations follow the material preparations, and depend upon the advice of a deity (the Ashanti favor Monday, which is considered to be a propitious day of the week); and ceremonial dancing led by the leader of a woman's dancing group, the *Bragorofua*.

The long-awaited ceremonies consist of: 1) an announcement of the event— the girl is awakened early in the morning by her mother, and asked to take a cold bath, following which people are given the signal to attend the events; 2) the enstoolment—after the bath, the girl is seated on a white stool, and assisted by an old woman who first lowers and raises the girl three times upon the stool, taking care that her buttocks make contact with its surface; and 3) dancing and libation—the head of the girl's matrilineage takes a bottle of liquor (usually palm-wine) and pours a libation (or offering) to thank God, the earth, the ancestors and others for having looked after the girl.

Other important ceremonial activities include the presentation of gifts from guests, ceremonial dressing of the girl, distribution of food on behalf of the girl, a ritual bath, in which she is immersed in purifying water, the ritual eating of a meal ("dedication"), and a closing dance. Following this, the girl retires to her home, where she is treated like a chief or queen mother for six days, because she is in a transitional state. Thus, the girl is purified and oriented into adult womanhood, with certain privileges, including the right to marry. As Sarpong writes:

> The [nubility rites]...serve as an instrument of instruction in the qualities of a wife, in motherhood, and in maternal attributes. Educators of children use the rites to maintain the accepted standards of morality and good behavior. The... rites engender social solidarity and reciprocal assistance among members of a community. They also act as sanctions against bad husbands, and provide a sense of security that all is now right with her (89).

In addition to guaranteeing the legitimacy of children, and perpetuating the family name, it is through marriage that a woman plays another important role, that of cementing alliances among groups. In recognition of her important productive and reproductive role, a ceremonial exchange of pre-nuptial gifts is made to the bride's family from the groom's family. Without these gifts the marriage is not complete. The gift is passed to the bride's family on behalf of the husband by the head of his lineage to the head of the bride's lineage. Fortes and others have noted that the bride's father, mother, lineage head, and brothers are also entitled to customary gifts from the bridegroom. In the event of divorce, these gifts must be returned to the groom.

Polygyny is a form of marriage in which a man is allowed to have two or more wives, provided that he can care for them equally. The basis of polygyny is usually economic, and practical. (Polygamy is the practice of having more than one husband *or* wife at the same time; polygyny refers only to the practice of multiple wives. Polyandry refers to the practice of several husbands to one wife.) A man with several wives commands more land, can produce more food for his household, and can achieve high status due to the resulting wealth. Most importantly, he can father many children, which is essential for his status, and the perpetuation of his name. Polygyny is permitted by the *Qur'an* in Islamic societies, and by custom elsewhere. Usually, each wife and her children live in separate compounds, which the husband and father visits on a regularly scheduled basis.

Finally, women in traditional Ashanti play an important economic role as cultivators of the land, processors of food, suppliers of water and firewood, maintaining the household and related activities. Of particular economic significance is their role in cultivating, harvesting and processing cocoa, the country's major cash crop. Ghanaian women are also important traders, market women, and laborers in cash crop agriculture.

Somalia is a Muslim country located on the Horn of Africa. It is a *pastoral* society in which the major economic activity is herding camels, cattle and sheep. Unlike most African countries, Somalia is culturally and linguistically homogeneous, although there are clans, and rural and urban differences. The southern section of the country, which includes Mogadishu, the capital city, is less pastoral than is the northern region of Hargeisa. The south is also agricultural, and almost 80% of the population are rural. Farmers (who are mostly women) grow maize, sesame, and fruit and vegetables. The principal export crops are bananas and grapefruit. Livestock (cattle in particular) are important export commodities, and camels have a high social value in Somali culture. Somalis share a common culture, institutions and language, although this is obscured by the ongoing civil war which began in 1991, and which resulted in an American Intervention, Operation Restore Hope, launched in December 1992. All Somalis trace their origins to two brothers, Samaal and Sab, who established six clan-families. These four largest are the Dir, Darod, Isaaq, and Hawiye. Sub-clans view themselves as related, but have distinct and different interests. Clan group loyalties are strong, and membership brings with it a range of responsibilities, rights, and obligations towards other members of the group.

Clans are the basis of socio-political organization in Somalia. Descent is traced through the *patrilineal* line from a male ancestor. Patriliny determines an individual's social position and relations with others. Within each clan there are more specific groups such as primary lineage, *dia*-paying groups, and the extended family. ("*Dia*" means "blood wealth" or compensation.) The *dia*-paying group consists of a few small lineages, that trace descent through from four to eight generations to a common ancestor. These units have memberships ranging from a few hundred to a few thousand people. A primary function of the group is to support its members in collective political and customary responsibilities, in particular, in paying and receiving compensation for transgressions against one's group by outsiders. The *dia*-paying group, which is larger than the extended family but smaller than a clan, is composed of members who are obliged to support each other in paying and receiving customary compensation for acts of war or other hostile acts.

In a nomadic society, in which groups compete for access to water and pasturage, conflict is an ever-present reality, and there are many mechanisms to regulate and moderate this (McFerson: 1996). One of the most important traditional practices in this respect is marriage, in which women play a crucial role in cementing alliances between potentially warring factions. Another mechanism is the custom of paying "*dia*," or compensation to a victim's family by his assailant's group. In the event that a member of one clan is killed by someone from another clan, the latter group has to compensate to the victim's *group* for the loss. This is an important tool for conflict resolution for, in its absence there would be a never-ending cycle of violent retribution. Traditionally, *dia* consists of livestock, particularly camels and cattle. Compensation for a murdered woman is about 50 camels; the survivors of a man receive 100 camels. The difference is based, in part, on perceptions of the value of the contributions of men versus women. In nomadic society, the loss of a man (a potential warrior) is considered a more serious blow to the group.

The membership of *dia*-paying groups is male, although all Somalis are affiliated with a group by birth. Women leave on marriage when they join the lineages of their husbands, consistent with the rules of *patrilocal* residence: men stay, women move. Married women do not become exclusive members of their husbands' groups; rather, they retain some degree of membership in the group of their birth, because a woman's ties to her lineage are not fully severed by marriage.

Reflecting the values of a patrilineal Muslim nomadic society, traditional Somalia has no centralized authority system. I.M. Lewis called traditional Somalia "a pastoral democracy." Thus, the centralized and repressive regime of General Mohamad Siad Barre (from 1969 until his overthrow in late 1991) was a historical aberration in Somalia. There is an administrative hierarchy of officials, and no single cultural symbol of unity. There is no equivalent of the Golden Stool, or the queen-mother. The "Sultan," or clan-head, has almost exclusively moral authority, and no formal legal or political power *per se*.

The primary social unit is the immediate family, *qoys*, which consists of one father, up to four wives and their children — if the marriage is polygynous, as is permitted under Islam — and his parents. Children live with their mothers in separate compounds. A *reer* is the extended family unit that includes distant male relatives. Socio-political organization is based on clan affiliation, an aggregate of interrelated families bound together by blood, which, in the past, lived, traveled, camped and went to war together.

Male superiority is inextricably woven into nomadic customs and Islamic tradition. A prominent Somali woman describes the status of women in her country:

> The father is head of the family, and the ultimate arbitrator and controller of family property. The woman has no legal identity in the strict sense of the word, although they can, and do, inherit property in the absence of male heirs. The property of families and their assets are handled by the male head of the family, whether father, brother or husband.

For Somali women, as studies by UNICEF confirm, their role as sister and aunt to their brother and his family is the basis of their authority and responsibility in family decisions. As a sister, or mother of grown children (preferably males), she is consulted in all decisions made by her brothers or sons. A common view is that the social status of the family is determined by the husband, but it is the wife who makes a family. Nevertheless, in many ways the status of Somali women still corresponds to that described 150 years ago by the British explorer Richard F. Burton (the first European to discover the sources of the Nile):

> In muscular strength and endurance the women of the Somal are far superior to their lords: at home they are engaged all day in domestic affairs, and tending the cattle; on journeys their manifold duties are to load and drive the camels, to look after the ropes, and, if necessary, to make them; to pitch the hut, to bring water and firewood, and to cook.

Nomadic women personify the virtues of Somali womanhood. For, unlike other societies, the Somalis look up to nomads, who are considered the embodiment of Somali ideals. Nomadic women are widely admired for their strength, dignity, intelligence and beauty, and the central role they play in the survival of their family in an arid and unfriendly terrain. Family cooperation is necessary because of the harsh environment and the conditions which this imposes upon the family, particularly women. The ideal Somali woman is described in classic Somali poetry as possessing six attributes, each consisting of a blend of white, black, long, short, slender, slim and rounded elements. These are described by Mohamed Hamud Sheekh, a Somali anthropologist. The four white parts are teeth, nails, eyeballs, and clear (i.e. reddish, unblemished) skin. The four dark parts are hair, gums, nipples, and pupils. Long parts are height (tall), limbs, hair, and neck. Short parts consist of low voice, pleasant smile, and furtive glance. Slim parts are the body, waist, fingers, and nose, and the rounded parts are buttocks, calves, cheeks and bosom.

Although the emphasis is on men, in their nomadic society women play an important role in traditional life in Somalia, particularly in the economy. As noted by Burton above, women are depended upon to perform a number of chores necessary for maintaining the pastoral family as they move in search of pasture land and water. The traditional duties of women include moving the family encampment, fetching water, collecting firewood, milking and maintaining responsibility for dairy products, such as milk, and *ghee*. One of a woman's most important roles is the assembling and dismantling of the portable family home, the *aqual*, as the family moves in search of better range land, similar to the traditional practices of the Sioux nation in North America. Nomadic families follow the seasons, and the decision of when and where to move is made by men. Consistent with nomadic society, patriliny and Islam, women play a subordinate role to men. Another important, yet heavy burden on women, is their job to find water for the family's use, which they transport in large (12–20 liter) wooden containers called *haan,* and to find firewood for cooking, which they carry on their backs. Watering of household stock, the responsibility of women and children, sometimes takes up to twelve hours, depending upon the season.

Marriage is expected of all individuals of good health and sound mind and character. As in most African societies, traditional marriage is not exclusively a relationship between two individuals, but an important link in expanding kinship, and cementing alliances between potentially warring clans. Marriage and the family are the foundations of society, and it is this institution which highlights the important role of women in expanding family and kinship ties, solidifying alliances, and bearing legitimate children. On the average, women marry for the first time at about age 20, which is late compared to most of Africa. In Somalia, traditional marriages occur within a context of mutual obligations and the exchange of reciprocal gifts. The husband is obligated to make a personal gift to his bride consisting of the *meher*, or bride wealth, without which marriage does not occur. The union is not considered legally binding until the wife receives the *meher* to which she or her family have previously agreed, and if there is divorce, this is returned. The value of the *meher* varies, and is determined by, among other things, the precedent established by older sisters, and virginity. It is important to stress that the *meher* is *not payment for the woman*. Rather it is compensation to the woman's family for the loss of her labor, and a recognition of her virginity.

As this writer found out, the complexity of marriage in traditional nomadic society creates a range of economic and contractual obligations between families of the bride and groom. The value of exchanged gifts in arranged marriages, which have declined in contemporary society, are important indicators of the personal status of the bride and her family. Bridewealth is presented by the groom to the bride's family; this can be given in installments, and in a variety of forms, including cash. The *yarad* is an important gift traditionally consisting of the nomadic house, household effects and camels. In *Sisters of Affliction* (1982), Dualeh Abdulla, as well as I.M. Lewis (1961), and Mohammed Sheekh (1980) observe that the *meher*, given at the time of betrothal, and returned upon divorce, must be paid according to the terms of a marriage contract. In traditional society, a respectable *meher* could consist of up to 100 camels. The amount is now regulated by the government not to exceed So. Sh. 1,000 (before the civil war in Somalia, at the mid-1989 exchange rate—the ratio at which money of one country can be exchanged for money of another country—1 Somali Shilling was equivalent to about US $2.00).

Female circumcision is a near-universal practice in Somalia, with a wide-ranging negative impact on the role and well-being of women. The procedure amounts to radical mutilation performed on 99% of young girls between the ages of 7–14, and is considered an important rite of passage to womanhood. Circumcision in Somalia is of the "pharaonic" type (also called infibulation). It consists of the total excision of the clitoris, the labia minora and the inner walls of the labia majora. The two sides of the vulva are then stitched together, leaving only a small opening, which serves as an outlet for urine and menstrual blood. As Raqiya Haji Dualeh Abdalla, a Somali critic of the practice, has written, circumcision leaves scars which are a seal that attests to the intangible, but vital property of the social groups' patrimony, the honor of the family and patrilineage. This seal and a woman's sexual purity must be transferred intact upon marriage into another lineage. Should either not be intact, the girl will be unacceptable to the husband's lineage. Thus, Abdulla adds: "Preservation of purity and honor is essential if her patrilineage is to maintain its social status, broaden its kinship ties and enhance its patrimony."

Islam also plays a role in the lives of Somali women, particularly in matters relating to their modesty and social behavior. Abdalla further comments that the code of modesty includes concern with chastity before and after marriage, fidelity, purity, genital mutilation, virginity, marriage, polygamy, divorce and the legitimacy of children. Polygyny is in accordance with Islamic principles, which permit a man to have up to four wives—provided that he provide equal financial support for each. Polygyny is also associated with patrilineal society. Older and wealthy men commonly marry younger women especially for reproductive reasons. The desire for sons is strong, and it is hoped that young wives will bear many sons during their reproductive years. Likewise, a man with more than one wife commands more labor to help in herding and agriculture. Mohamed Hamud Seekh summarizes the economic aspect of polygyny:

> In the southern agricultural communities, a man marries several wives with the aim among others, of [availing] himself of their additional farm services. In the nomadic society the need for more womanpower who take care of the livestock, especially sheep and goats, which are usually under the woman's domain, encouraged polygyny.

African Women in Contemporary Society

Throughout Africa, women today are involved in a variety of economic and social activities. The continent has been severely affected by civil war, political oppression and corruption, an adverse economic environment, drought and famine. In the face of these adversities, African women have emerged as the backbone of contemporary society. Their contributions to family and society are essential. Women in rural areas, in particular, maintain an arduous schedule working in the home and in the field. At home they cook, fetch water and firewood, maintain the household and care for children. In the field they perform tasks ranging from planting to food cultivation, food preservation and storage, in addition to caring for livestock. Most African farmers are women. Women in urban areas are often more educated than their rural counterparts, and may work outside the home as professionals, government workers, businesswomen, university professors, and health care providers. The primary identification of women in both sectors of society, as in traditional society, however, is still that of wife and mother. This section examines some of the areas in which African women in contemporary society are involved, as the following poem vividly portrays:

WHERE are those songs

> my mother and yours
> always sang
> fitting rhythms
> to the whole
> vast span of life?

> What was it again
> they sang
> harvesting maize, threshing millet,
> storing the grain....

> And the rows of bending women
> hoeing our fields
> to what beat did they
> break the stubborn ground

as they weeded
our shambas?

Rural agriculture is the most important economic activity in Africa and involves more than 80 percent of rural women as farmers (compared to about 65% of men who farm). Women play a pivotal role, both in cash and subsistence farming, and in raising and caring for livestock. Women raise crops to feed their own families (*subsistence agriculture*) and for sale in the market (*cash crops*) which they either market themselves, or sell to middle-marketers in the urban areas. Women farmers perform a variety of activities, and it is widely recognized that without their significant contributions agricultural production in most African countries would suffer. Women in Ghana, Somalia, Madagascar, Nigeria, Zimbabwe, Kenya and a number of other countries, plant, weed, harvest, process, and store agricultural produce ranging from cocoa to tea and rice.

In traditional societies of an earlier era, many of these activities, such as hoeing, weeding, and preparing the land for planting, were distributed on the basis of custom, which often called for gender-specific roles. Men performed certain tasks — usually heavier jobs — such as preparing the land for cultivation, hunting, night-watching for marauding animals, and irrigating land. More recently, gender-based roles have become less common, as social change, war, male migration, divorce, death, female-headed households, and other events have made women assume additional tasks in the rural household. This is often the case, even when a woman lives with her husband. If he is a wage-laborer, she often works on his plot of land as well as on hers, and the allocation of her time is a problem, for a woman who must labor in the fields from dawn to dusk, and then maintain a household and care for children. Easily accessible clean water, reliable sources of fuel, and labor-saving devices are typically non-existent in villages with erratic supplies of electricity and a lack of basic amenities. As a result, women must grind and pound grain, and walk miles to find and bring back water and firewood, often while carrying babies on their back.

Women farmers in Africa face many constraints, some of which are rooted in culture, and others the result of government and donor agency policies. For example, even though women constitute the majority of farmers, official recognition is seldom given to their role, because they are perceived primarily as wives and mothers. This has serious implications for their economic well-being, and that of their children. International development agencies often assume that because men control land, they are also the primary farmers. As a result, assistance is targeted to men, who often have different interests from those of women, and who, in fact, are not the actual farmers. This distorted view of who actually farms has been documented in a number of countries including Somalia, Kenya, and Ghana.

Land-tenure laws and customs affect women in a number of ways. Because of customary restrictions, African land is almost entirely controlled by men. The well-being of female-headed households is also particularly compromised by deficient land-tenure laws, which permit land to continue to be registered in the name of absentee husbands, thereby limiting a woman's legal claim. Because they lack legal claim to land, women cannot apply for credit using land as collateral. This is a serious matter, because credit is often necessary for women who are short of cash. They need to purchase equipment for farming, such as seeds, hoes, axes, fertilizer, grinding mills, churns for making butter and ghee, transport vehicles, for household chores, and for seasonal family support while the crops are still in the ground.

Ownership of land also means control of the crops which are grown. This affects the nutritional health of farming families, particularly young children, for whom good nutrition is critical. Six out of every ten Africans are children, and providing adequate resources for women has a trickle-down effect to children, who are Africa's future. Agricultural extension programs are needed to assist women farmers in a number of ways, ranging from nutrition education to helping women organize into cooperatives, pooling limited resources, and learning new skills.

Of particular note are the rotating credit unions (*esusu* or tontines), which provide capital for women members. Although there are variations, rotating credit associations consist of a core group of women who agree to make regular contributions into a fund which is then allocated, on a rotating basis, to each contributing member. The important aspects of the association are rotation and regularity. Members agree in advance on the amount of contributions, on the time intervals between collections, the position of individual members in the sequence of rotation, and on the cycle of the group. Ten members, for example, might agree to contribute $10 each week during a ten-week cycle; in any given week's rotation, one member will collect the pool of $100. The order in which rotation is determined depends as much on the members' needs for immediate cash, as it does on personal reliability. In West Africa, associations are often organized on the basis of kinship, reflecting the significance of strong personal bonds to other members.

Paradoxically, even though the majority of farmers in Africa are women, men constitute the majority of agricultural extension agents and the "contact" farmers, who work directly with extension agents. In Somalia, for example, in 1987, as the researcher learned, there were only four women extension agents, even though about 65% of Somali women are farmers. Because of custom, African women are often reluctant to discuss certain issues with male agents, and this is compounded by religion in Somalia. For obvious reasons, many women relate better to female agents, who, recognizing the varied needs of women, often advocate an "integrated" approach to extension activities, which range from planting to nutrition education, to improving homemaking skills, and improving child care. Female agents are also important for female-headed households, which are increasingly frequent in many countries owing to male migration and the toll of wars. In Kenya, for example, 31 percent of an estimated 1.7 million households are female-headed; in Botswana one in ten households is headed by a woman; in Mali, one in six; and, in Southeast Ghana, almost one half fall within this category. Male migration in Somalia has produced similar results. Recognition of these changes in family structure is not only an issue of fairness, but important for the economic development of rural women as well.

African women are becoming increasingly active on their own behalf, and are seeking solutions. Educated urban-dwelling women often articulate concern for other women not able to speak on their own behalf. For example, the issues of hunger and malnutrition are of special concern to women of high-status and high visibility, such as Maryam Babangida, Nigeria's former First Lady, and Wangari Muta Maathai, a Kenyan environmentalist. Both are the 1991 recipients of the

$100,000 Africa Prize from the Hunger Project, annually awarded by the New York-based international non-profit organization.[2]

Other activist women include Esther Ocloo of Ghana, who with 14 other women, founded an international financial institution to service women entrepreneurs through the establishment of a branch of the American-based Women's World Banking (WWB). Ocloo was joined in this endeavor by former Ghanaian Supreme Court Justice Annie Jiagge.[3] Important recent achievements of Ghanaian women include 1) securing an amendment to the rape law in the Criminal Code, to ensure a minimum of three years in jail for individuals found guilty of the crime; 2) securing legislation in Parliament proscribing female circumcision; 3) the passage of Article 22 of the Fourth Republican Constitution making provisions entitling a spouse (of either gender) to a reasonable proportion of an estate whether or not the deceased person made a will; 4) permitting both spouses, upon dissolution of the marriage, to have equal access to and a share of property acquired during marriage. As Aya Okwabi notes, however, much remains to be done to further improve women's rights. The causes of the continuing inequality between the sexes are rooted in cultural and religious factors, including strong religious beliefs which discourage a questioning attitude on the part of women.

The position of women in the southern African mountain Kingdom of Lesotho is also worth noting. Dr. Khauhelo D. Raditapole, the country's only female cabinet minister (Minister of Natural Resources), and a former Minister of Health, reports that, until recently, married women in the Kingdom were still legally regarded as minors (*The Courier*: 1995). Lesotho recently signed the United Nations Convention on Discrimination against Women, however. This means that the country will be obliged to repeal discriminatory laws against women. While the monarch must be a man and men are dominant in political decision-making, women occupy a large number of key civil service posts in a country where female heads of household predominate, as many men have migrated to South Africa to work in the mines. But Basotho women, Dr. Raditapole notes, tend to be better

---

2. Mrs. Babangida founded the Better Life for Rural Women's Program, which promotes women's social, economic and political advancement in Nigeria. The group has established over 7,600 cooperatives, 1,700 new farms and nearly 1,000 cottage industries, as well as shops, markets and women's centers. Mrs. Babangida has also raised funds to construct an international women's center in Abuja, Nigeria's new federal capital.

Wangari Muta Maathai is a noted environmentalist, who founded Kenya's Green Belt Movement, which has mobilized 50,000 women to plant 10 million trees throughout the country and has set up 1,500 nurseries. Maathai recently led a successful campaign against the construction of a multi-million dollar skyscraper complex and super shopping mall in downtown Nairobi, Kenya's capital, which incurred the wrath of Kenyan men, especially President Daniel arap Moi, who were forced to succumb to international pressure generated by the activist.

A 1995 co-winner of the prize for leadership is Joyce Mungherera, the Executive Director of the YWCA in Uganda. She is cited for her dynamic leadership of the local YWCA, and its work on behalf of literacy, family planning, and improved incomes of rural women.

3. WWB has created a network of over 90 local groups, extended 56,000 loans, and established 25 loan programs for women around the world. The program's priority is to assist poor rural women in obtaining access to credit. The Africa branch of WWB originated in Ghana in 1974, when a group of women decided that access to credit was women's most important need. The group consisted of small-scale entrepreneurs, such as local market women, and leaders of women's organizations. The group decided that before education or health care or family planning, women needed money in their pockets, which would then allow them to make their own decisions and take care of their other needs.

educated, with more girls than boys attending primary and secondary school. Females are beginning to outnumber males in tertiary education, because the latter are more likely to drop out of school early to take up the traditional practice of cow-herding.

The role of women traders and entrepreneurs in Africa is significant. West African market women are known throughout the world for their effective participation in retail trade. In Nigeria, for example, women traders are chiefly engaged in the sale of textiles purchased from large urban firms, which they then sell at retail in rural markets and small towns.[4] Throughout the continent women also play important economic roles in fisheries, in palm oil production, as owners of trucking and other businesses. Many of these women are illiterate, but their ability to conduct business is remarkable and widely-recognized.

Although West African women have been particularly active in retail trade, they are also similarly engaged in Zimbabwe, Malawi, Kenya, Cameroon, South Africa, Somalia, Ethiopia, and Madagascar, to mention just a handful of countries. Important assistance for these women comes from cooperatives which will help aspirants start a business, or enlarge existing enterprises. Cooperatives have been organized in a number of countries, and they are recognized as vital in helping women establish contacts, network with other women, identify prospective clients and markets, and even assist in maternal and child health care. These associations also provide credit and other market supports, and their role in economic development is invaluable.

Of the many problems affecting African women, none has been more devastating than the conflicts that have erupted in a number of countries. Although too numerous to mention, these include countries in Southern Africa, Ethiopia, Angola, Burundi, Chad, Liberia, Mozambique, and Somalia. Wars have disastrous consequences for all of a country's citizens, but women and children bear a particularly harsh burden, and they constitute the majority of refugees seeking asylum in neighboring countries. Women are also the victims of rape at the hands of roaming bands of soldiers, and many endure the resulting unwanted pregnancies. Refugees, an increasing number of whom are widows with their young children, are often the poorest of the poor, and suffer from inadequate nutrition, disease, and a host of other ills. In addition to refugees, African women have also been involved in rural to urban migration in search of economic opportunities. This removes them from the support of their extended families. If their children accompany them, they are often without adequate child care. Inadequate maternal and child health care, even in peacetime, and the lack of access to clean and safe water, shelter, education and jobs have disastrous consequences.

A particularly cruel consequence of war is the number of unexploded antipersonnel landmines in Africa, which injure, maim, and kill men, women, and children — the noncombatants of war — indiscriminately. Because of the gendered division of labor, rural African women are particularly vulnerable, as it is they who must search for wood and water, often in unmarked mine fields (McFerson: 1995). Living in societies which value health and the able-bodied, the plight of female landmine victims is grim. Marriage becomes an unlikely proposition for

---

4. The experiences of one woman who aspires to become an entrepreneur in this tradition are depicted in Nigerian novelist Cyprian Ekwensi's classic novel *Jagua Nana* (London: Hutchinson, 1961).

many, and this problem is compounded not only by physical disfigurement, but by the void left by the high numbers of male casualties in combat. The women who have not been victims of antipersonnel landmines are the more desired marriage partners in societies which esteem women as wives, mothers, and providers. Female landmine victims are marginalized, with severe consequences for them and their children. Women are also affected by the significant numbers of children who are also maimed and injured by landmines. For these children, the primary caretaker is an impoverished woman in a female-headed household, thereby spreading even thinner scarce financial resources.

According to the United Nations, there are between 85–100 million landmines planted in at least 30 countries on five continents (DHA/UN/ICRC.) The problem is particularly acute in Africa, because of the legacy of the Cold War, and the many ongoing civil conflicts. The United Nations and the International Committee of the Red Cross have ranked the severity of the landmine problem in African countries in three categories, based on the estimated number of mines in each country:

Extremely Severe		Severe		Moderate	
Angola	9–10,000,000	Chad	(unknown)	Djibouti	(no data)
Mozambique	2,000,000	Rwanda	60,000	Libya	(no data)
Sudan	1,250,000	Egypt	22,000	Mauritania	(no data)
Somalia	1,000,000	Liberia	18,250	Senegal	(no data)
Eritrea	500,000	Morocco	10,000	Uganda	(no data)
Ethiopia	500,000	*including*		Malawi	(no data)
		Western		Zambia	(no data)
		Sahara		Namibia	2,000
				Tunisia	300

Equal access to education for women and girls is the key to improving the overall status of African women, especially as the numbers of female-headed households increase. The position of girls and women in education is an important indicator of both development and the status of women in society. Statistics on the rate and pace of socioeconomic development indicate that in developing countries the percentage of women over age 15 who have completed secondary school varies from 2 to 15 percent. At the level of higher education, women are generally under-represented compared to men, reflecting discrepancies which often start in the lower grades. Although there is variation among and between countries, the education of African women in general has not kept pace with that of men. The highest discrepancies favoring boys' education have been identified in Guinea-Bissau and Togo—each accounting for gender-based differential access to education at around 46% (Robertson, 85:91). The next highest rates of gender-based differentials have been identified in Algeria, Benin, Central African Republic, Congo, Ethiopia, Ivory Coast, Liberia, Morocco, Tunisia and Congo-Zaire, where a 20 to 30% differential in the education of girls in comparison to boys was noted. Discrepancy rates were also marked in Angola, Cameroon, Chad, Ghana, Guinea, Malawi, Mali, Mozambique, Senegal, Sierra Leone, Somalia, Sudan, Uganda, and Zambia.

The reasons for these gender differentials vary, and include cultural and religious customs of different ethnic groups, the greater demands placed on young girls to help in household chores, the legacies of colonial policies, the rate and pace of urbanization, levels of economic development, and the presence or absence of Christian missionaries, who educated both male and female converts at about an equal rate. The absence of female role models also impedes girls from getting an education, as does the widespread belief that an educated woman will, through marriage, benefit another family, while a son will carry out his obligation to the welfare of aging parents; thus educating him is an investment for the future. Another factor preventing many women from obtaining an education is pregnancy and motherhood, which forces them to leave school and lower their expectations. This results in lower retention rates for women, and wastage.

In Islamic countries, colonial governments tended not to encourage the presence of missionaries. Koranic schools were relied upon to educate Muslim children and these often favored boys. A notable exception was pre-war Somalia, where the data indicates that there was parity between boys and girls up to certain levels. For example, at the pre-primary level, girls accounted for 52.0% of the total enrollment (McFerson, 89:25). In primary school enrollments girls accounted for 34% of the students in 1981–82, and women constituted 34.1% of the primary-level school teachers. At the intermediate level, 26.7% of the students, and 38.7 teachers were female. Females constituted 32% of the secondary level students, 52% of the vocational education students, and 13% of the technical school enrollments. Finally, the status of women in higher education in Somalia is illuminating. Male-female enrollments at the National University of Somalia dating from 1971, when the first degrees were awarded, indicate that the largest number of women graduates have been in the School of Education, followed by Economics, Law and Veterinary Science. The lowest number of female graduates have been in the Schools of Engineering and Geology. The school of Education has the lowest on-time graduation rates, and the lowest entrance scores. Women accounted for 9.8% of the assistant lecturers, 6.3% of the lecturers, 10.1% of the full-time instructional staff and 4.2% of the part-time faculty. Female students represented approximately 30% of the senior high school class from which the July 1983 admissions pool was drawn, but only 18.1 percent of those admitted to the university (McFerson, 27). Equality of opportunity benefits not only women, but the family, and ultimately the nation. As the saying goes, the education of a woman benefits everyone, and educated women are better able to safeguard their family's welfare and health.

Female Genital Mutiliation (FGM) and International Law

The issue of female genital mutilation has been mentioned frequently in this chapter. A young woman refugee from Togo scored an impressive victory for international women's health and legal rights in 1996. Fauziya Kasinga fled her country to avoid the ritual practice and sought asylum in the United States. Ms. Kasinga, who was jailed after arriving in the United States on a false passport, argued that the certainty of being subjected to genital mutilation if she were to return home met the U.S. standard of a "well-founded fear of persecution." Her initial request was rejected by a Philadelphia judge, who expressed disbelief that such practices could possibly exist. The judge was ignorant of the reality that an estimated 80 million women worldwide have experienced genital mutilation. The issue is compounded by the reality that female genital mutilation, the cutting or removal of genitals, is practiced "legally" throughout Africa. In the case of Fauzia Kasinga, she was undoubtedly influenced by her father, a man opposed to the practice. But after his death, she was forcibly married to a man who insisted on it. She fled the country, and in seeking asylum in the United States posed a dilemma: what should a global superpower which is dedicated to human rights do about the practice which condemned many girls and women to death, or to a lifetime of physical and mental pain?

In its decision[7] the Board of Immigration Appeals ruled that a well-founded fear of female genital mutilation (FGM) can be a basis for a grant of asylum under Section 208 of the Immigration and Nationality Act. The Board concluded that FGM as practiced by an ethnic group in Togo, of which Kasinga was a member, constituted a level of harm sufficient to constitute "persecution" under the Act. The Board granted her asylum, holding that she was a member of a particular social group, consisting of young women of her ethnic group who have not been subjected to FGM, but oppose the practice. She, therefore, had a well-founded fear of persecution (WILIG Newsletter, Vol. 8. No. 2, September 1996, p. 1.) Finally, Meserak "Mimi" Ramsey, an Ethiopian living in California, has emerged as a prime mover in urging the California legislature to outlaw female genital mutilation in immigrant communities in the United States. The founder of an organization, Forward USA, she notes that the "evil custom" has made its way to California through immigrant communities and has become prevalent. Governor Pete Wilson signed legislation outlawing the practice in September 1996.

Women, War, and Peace

As the year 2006 approaches, African women are moving to the forefront of efforts to end the many wars plaguing the continent, and to peacefully end conflicts. Surprisingly, though, scant attention has been given to the efforts of these women. Academic studies on conflict, its management, resolution and peace in Africa are mostly silent on the role of women. Yet the evidence vividly illustrates the far-reaching involvement of women, both as peace activists and as advocates of violent conflict resolution. Consider, for example, the views of two women activists for peace. Nana Konadu Agyeman Rawlings, the First Lady of Ghana: "In every conflict situation, be it Angola, Bosnia or Somalia, Rwanda or Liberia, it is always the women who bear the brunt of the suffering. The legacies of cruel socio-cultural practices and prejudices which humiliate women and deny them their most basic rights, worsen the situation. It is in the small towns and villages of the rural areas, within developing countries, that the plight of women can be seen most vividly. The ravages of malnutrition, disease, illiteracy, unemployment and absolute poverty take a heavy toll" (quoted in *West Africa*, 1995). Gertrude Mongella, the African Secretary General of the Women's Conference in Beijing (1995), offers a complementary view. A trained teacher and a former parliamentarian in her home country of Tanzania, she is a strong advocate of women in the peace process and in conflict resolution. She attributes a special role to women: "We ... bring the spirit of serving people which men don't have. Men are used to being served by women, so even when you're in power, you only want to be masters. We are used to serving people, so that when we are in power, we use that position to serve everybody" (*The Courier*, November–December 1995, p. 3).

---

7. *In re Fauziya Kasinga*, Bd. of Immig. Appeals, File A373 476 695 (June 13, 1996).

African women attending the Beijing conference passed resolutions demanding commitments from their governments to allow a greater role for women in conflict prevention and resolution (Tafadzwa Mumba, September 1995). They argued that, while they and their children suffer most in times of war, the continent's male-dominated governments were slow in acting to resolve conflicts. They noted that Africa is home to more than 75 percent of the world's 24 million refugees and displaced people. Women caught up in armed conflicts are often raped and tortured, noted Stella Mukasa, a consultant with the Women in Law and Development in Africa Fund in Uganda. She cited the consequences of civil wars in Uganda between 1962 and 1986: "Women were given to men for whom they had to perform sexual services, cooking, cleaning and other conjugal duties. Women had to collect food, water and firewood from forests and were exposed to dangers such as attacks from wild animals, rape by civilian men, government soldiers or insurgents and worst of all, death from landmines or getting caught in crossfire" (*ibid.*). Another participant, Mary Yakobo, a Sudanese, questioned: "Why should a country like Sudan be having war for 40 years? There must be something wrong and we women have fallen victim to that."

Consider the life story of one Sudanese woman who has known little peace during her 38 years of life. She notes: "All my life I have been a refugee. When I was five years old my family fled to Uganda. I had to walk all the way because there were younger children to carry, and there was no one to carry me. Fear is always in our hearts. We never know what tomorrow will bring, although we always live in hope" (*West Africa*, 1995). Women and children in southern Sudan, which has one of Africa's longest ongoing wars, have borne the greatest brunt of the fighting, drought, famine and displacement. The majority of refugees are unaccompanied minors or women, either widows or women whose husbands have been away fighting for years. Consider the views of Mary Nyankuer, aged 39: "I have lost two children…they have been killed. Most of my relatives have been killed. If there are people left alive, they will have been displaced into the bush. I don't know where they are now. This war doesn't differentiate between a child, a woman or a man. These militias kill everybody. A war that kills women is not a good war. We don't want this war that kills women and children, that kills people who have no arms."

The war in Sudan, as elsewhere in Africa, is a man's war. Few women are actively involved in the military action. Few hold senior political or civilian posts within either of the warring factions, the Sudanese People's Liberation Army or the Sudanese People's Liberation Movement (Mary Evans, *ibid.*). Monika Yom, a Dinka whose ethnic group has borne the brunt of the war, laments that "this war has affected women greatly in southern Sudan because women are mothers of the children who are now fighting. Before the factions split the war was mainly a war of struggle against the oppressor in Khartoum….But now women are asking themselves whether their children have died in vain, fighting each other." In response to the devastation experienced by women and children, a small but vocal group of women has emerged, the Sudan Women's Voices for Peace. Their aim is to stop the factional fighting and to "make our men listen. They are fighting about who is to be leader and building castles in the air, when the battle with Khartoum is still to be won." Another organization, the New Sudan Women's Association, is a network of women's groups in the south. They hope to reintegrate women who have been marginalized by the war back into the decision-making process. The process is being repeated throughout the continent, as women in Angola, Namibia, Eritrea, Ethiopia, Somalia and a host of other countries become advocates for peace.

Finally, women throughout Africa are organizing to facilitate nonviolent conflict resolution. During the Beijing Conference, the wives of the leaders of Benin, Botswana, Burundi, Ghana, and Nigeria held a meeting to develop a plan for peace on the continent. Mrs. Rosine Soglo, then first lady of Benin, complained that "Women are never included in peace negotiation teams." The women decided it was time for them to become advocates of peace, and they agreed to organize a Peace Mission to several warring countries. The meeting, which was chaired by Mrs. Nana Konadu Agyeman Rawlings of Ghana, also appointed Mrs. Maryam Abacha of Nigeria to head the newly formed Conflict Resolution Committee. Thus, African women are increasingly viewing peace and conflict resolution issues as women's issues.

Study Questions and Activities

1. "Somalia is a predominantly patrilineal society where the life-style is primarily suited to men's conveniences, and the traditional role of women buttresses and supports this orientation. Women are depended upon to perform [certain labor tasks] for the pastoral family, including moving the family encampment, fetching water, collecting firewood, cooking family food and milking the sheep, goats and cows entrusted to their care." (UNICEF, 84:7)

   a. How would you describe the role of women in Somalia? Is it peripheral, or central to social organization? Is this type of responsibility necessary for survival in nomadic society? Why?

   b. Can you make comparisons between the exchange of pre-nuptial gifts and similar practices in western societies?

2. *Discuss* the poem on page 446 in terms of the role of ancestors, ancestor-worship, and matriliny in traditional Ashanti society.

3. What is the link between ancestry and gender in traditional Ashanti society?

4. Discuss the features of a matrilineal society in terms of: (a) the mother-child relationship; (b) titles to traditional office; (c) social organization and politics, (d) the role of queen mother and (f) the significance of nubility rites.

References

Ghana and Somalia

Abdulla, Dualeh Haji Raqiya, *Sisters in Affliction*. London: Zed Press, 1982.

Burton, Richard F., *First Footsteps in East Africa: Or, An Exploration of Harar*. London: Tylston and Edwards, 1894, reprinted 1987.

Lewis, I.M., *A Pastoral Democracy*. London: Africana Publishing Company for the International African Institute, 1961, reprinted 1982.

Little, P. D. *Somalia: Economy Without State*. London: James Currey Publishers, 2003.

McFerson, Hazel M., "Women in the Economy of Somalia." Washington: U.S. Agency for International Development, 1989.

Menkhaus, Kenneth John . *Somalia: State Collapse and the Threat of Terrorism.* New York: Oxford United Press, 2004.

UNICEF, *Women and Children in Somalia: A Situational Analysis.* Mogadishu: Ministry of National Planning and UNICEF, 1982.

United Nations. *The United Nations of Somalia 1992–1996.* New York: UN, 1996.

Sheekh, Mohamed Hamud, "The Somali Traditional Marriage." Mogadishu: Unpublished B.A. thesis, December 1980.

Dirie, Mahdi Ali, Dr. *Female Circumcision in Somalia: Medical and Social Implications.* Mogadishu: SOMAC, December 1985.

Contemporary Society

Aidoo, Agnes Akosua, "Asante Queen Mothers in Government and Politics in the Nineteenth Century", in Steady, Filomina Chioma, (ed.), *The Black Woman Cross-Culturally.* Rochester: Schenkman Books, Inc., 1981.

Brown-Radcliffe, A.E., and Forde, Darryll, eds., *African Systems of Kinship and Marriage.* Published for the International African Institute, by London: Oxford University Press: 1950.

Busia, K.A., "The Ashanti of the Gold Coast", in Forde, Daryll, ed., *African Worlds: Studies in the Cosmological Ideas and Social Values of African Peoples.* Published for the International African Institute, by London: Oxford University Press, 1954, reprint 1970.

Fortes, Meyer, "Kinship and Marriage Among the Ashanti" in Brown-Radliffe, op. cit.

Parrinder, Geoffrey, *African Mythology.* London: Paul Hamlyn, 1967.

Sarpong, Peter, *Girls' Nubility Rites in Ashanti.* Tema: Ghana Publishing Company, 1977.

Sweetman, David, *Women Leaders in African History.* Portsmouth: Heinemann Educational Books, 1984.

25

Women of the Caribbean

A. Lynn Bolles
Barbara Shaw Perry

Introduction

Until recently, Caribbean women did not receive the kind of attention they deserve in the historical or socio-cultural scholarship on the region. The reason women were left out has much to do with who was documenting the events of any particular era, and what they deemed to be valuable knowledge. Since the 1970s, however, researchers (primarily women) have brought women's histories and experiences to the forefront of the academic forum in efforts to construct a more accurate picture of the Caribbean. From a Western perspective, the experiences, the lives and the world views of women were not seen as equal to those of men. And, in a colonial context (the historical memory of the region) subjugated women, especially those of dark skin color, were even more debased than their Caucasian counterparts. In combination, all of these factors limited the range and scope of the scholarship concerning women of the Caribbean. This essay discusses some of the historical, social scientific, and literary cultural work designed to redress this imbalance.

When writing and reading about women's lives, as Johnnetta Cole notes, no one model or theory is adequate because of the intersection of class, race, color, ethnicity, religion, geographical location, and sexual preference. This means that we must analyze women from the standpoint of the multiple positions that they occupy in society. Moreover, when Caribbean women are the subjects of comparative analysis, social factors, nationality, and geopolitical influences must be examined. For example, one must consider whether the area is on the mainland or is a big or small island and whether it is a Department of France, a Commonwealth of the United States, a member of the British Commonwealth, a colony of the Netherlands, or an independent country. And if it is one of the oldest black independent republics, like Haiti, it is critical to understand why it is one of the poorest countries in the Western hemisphere. For our purposes here, we will give a cross-cultural overview of Caribbean women's lives and experiences through the following subject areas: 1) the legacies of Caribbean history, 2) the European "ideal" versus the Caribbean "reality" in the social structure, family and kinship, 4) tourism and work, 5) health, sexuality, and HIV/AIDS, and 6) a brief overview of Caribbean women's literature. In the remainder of this essay, these topics will be discussed through examples taken primarily from the English-speaking areas, and to a lesser extent from the Spanish, French and Dutch Caribbean. Before going further, however, let us take time to locate Caribbean women in the broadest sense of that sociocultural term.

Legacies of Caribbean History

The Caribbean region, named after one of its indigenous groups, the Caribs, includes 27 island and mainland territories, 4 major European language groups, countless vernaculars, and a myriad of races and cultures. Despite these differences, the people of the region have a shared identity—a West Indian or Antillean, or a Caribbean one—that results from a shared history. There is no denying that the Caribbean region experienced two of the most extreme forms of exploitation known in human societies—slavery and colonialism. Contact between Europeans and the indigenous populations almost eradicated the latter through warfare, forced labor, diseases, and genocide. Slavery and colonial oppression introduced two additional cultural systems—West African and European—which, through the process of creolization, gave rise to particular geographically and historically complex social formations. Consequently, because of the legacy of slavery, that marked free and non-free on the basis of phenotype (skin color), Caribbean societies are highly stratified by race, color, class, ethnicity, and gender inequality.

In the Caribbean, women descend from various ethnic backgrounds including Africa, Europe, the Indian subcontinent, China, and the Middle East. In fact, the majority of contemporary Caribbean women can trace their cultural heritage to the largest forced migration in modem history (arising from the enslavement of the African peoples) and of the coerced relocation of nineteenth-century indentured East Indians. They are the victims and survivors of European expansionism and its annihilation of Amerindians.

For most Caribbean societies, the Amerindian (namely the Arawak, the Taino, and the Carib) contribution to culture is reduced to a faint memory inscribed in archeological sites, and evident in some cultural traits such as language, geographical names, home furnishings, and some food customs. However, the recognition and pride of Taino heritage is resurfacing in certain quarters in the Dominican Republic and Puerto Rico. For contemporary Carib women from St. Vincent, and their relatives, the Garifuna from coastal Guatemala and Belize, Amerindian culture is alive and well. There is no doubt that these indigenous groups paid and continue to pay a high price for their survival. Caribs who survived battles against the French and the English were forcibly removed and relocated. Britain moved Carib peoples beyond the tropics and even resettled a group to their northern colony of Nova Scotia (Canada). However, the Caribs did not go quietly. In 1650, the Caribs of Grenada allowed a French expedition from Martinique to buy extensive land holdings. A year later, however, hostilities resumed between the indigenous people and the French. Seeing their efforts had become futile, the last 40 Caribs jumped to their deaths from a precipice on the extreme north of Grenada. They suffered this extreme sacrifice rather than submit to French rule.

In Guyana and Trinidad, the East Indian population is the numerical majority in the former, and is the largest ethnic group in the latter. Clearly, those societies exhibit critical cultural contributions from the subcontinent, including both Hindu and Muslim. The vicissitudes of British colonial rule, the political economy, and immigration flows impact the indentured populations. Many more men than women were conscripted, thereby skewing the demographics and altering cultural expectations for both men and women. Only when the male-female ratio evened out did the Hindu and Muslim prescribed role of women and men become possible in the Caribbean. Gender constructs of the sending society weigh heavily on how Indo-Guyanese and Indo-Trinidadian women are viewed historically and how they are understood at present.

Caribbean women of European descent are predominant in the Spanish-speaking countries of the Dominican Republic, Puerto Rico, and Cuba, although these societies are primarily mestizo. Mestizo means that the majority of these societies reflect the sociocultural and racial context of creolization—in this case the blending of African, European, or Amerindian. Here, as in the rest of the region, class and color are fundamental indicators of a woman's social position. There are also Caribbean women of Chinese and Middle Eastern descent, among others, who have different ethnic and religious affiliations. Ironically, notwithstanding the creole nature of these societies, in the official census there are categories of people designated as "mixed."

When all is said and done, however, the majority of the women who live in the Caribbean are of African descent. The sociocultural contributions of different African (e.g., Akan, Yoruba, Ibo, and Twi) ethnic groups in the early days were quite significant. Subsequently, language, music, religion, and other aspects of social organization contributed to the creolization process in all island and mainland territories. In addition, the intensity of particular African ethnic cultural contributions is often most pronounced. For example, there are Trinidadian Yoruba songs, and religious practices of Kumina in Jamaica, Vodun in Haiti, and santeria in Puerto Rico and Cuba.

Regardless of racial or ethnic background, the brutal force of slavery and the aftermath of uneven social, and economic development propagated by colonial administrations and the landed elite influenced the shape of livelihoods and options available to peoples in Caribbean societies. However, the social divisions of society (race and color, class and gender) assign black women to the low end of the socioeconomic ladder.

The pioneer work of Jamaican feminist historian, Lucille Mathurin Mair (1974), brought the "invisible" black women into Caribbean history. The images about women found in conventional historical texts convey the idea that either the experiences of slavery and post-emancipation life were homogeneous (essentially those of men) or that black women and men had different aspirations, needs, and functions in West Indian societies. It becomes evident that, by reducing women's experiences to a generic one, the texts denied the role of female participation in resistance, in the development of culture and society, and advanced male-centered interpretations of history.

The focus of our attention here, however, is the positive nature of the cultural patterns of Afro-Caribbean people, specifically, how West African heritage influenced women's position in culture and society during Caribbean culture building. How did these new cultural forms provide the basis for future generations of black Caribbean women? Men and women labored side by side in the sugar cane fields. Some occupations were gender-specific to women, such as midwifery. And in some cases, other production-related jobs on sugar estates were exclusively performed by men, especially those of artisans (such as coopers, blacksmiths, and carpenters). In the French Antilles, men were also given tasks as drivers of the first gang, coach drivers and messengers. However, for the majority who labored in gangs, only age and health differentiated one slave from another. And as the time period of slavery extended into the 19th century, often this unidentified, undifferentiated slave was female.

In most areas of the Caribbean, especially in the early days, as Mair notes, men outnumbered women. In 1789 in Jamaica, for example, the ratio was 2:1. Slave mortality was high throughout the region, and some slave holders took extreme measures to increase their slave populations. Historian Bernard Moitt tells us that in 1775 in Guadeloupe, the slave master paid 15 livres to the midwife for a live birth and gave the mother cloth. If the baby died, both women were whipped and "the one who lost the child placed in iron collars until she became pregnant again."

After the abolition of the British-controlled slave trade in 1807, women became important as breeders to maintain the number of slaves needed for labor. Thus, the enslaved woman who bore six children became "privileged" by law. Such a clear recognition of the black woman's vital role as mother indirectly helped to keep alive her awareness of herself as a woman. As Mair comments, "it is essentially such awareness of oneself as a human being which makes the individual refuse to be reduced to the level of a non-human being, in the way that slavery attempted." West African traditions of production, kinship, and family also supported the positive valuation of motherhood and the "equality" fostered by the estate labor force.

The following two examples taken from Caribbean history illustrate how an alternative view can bring people, especially women, and events into their proper light, and, at the same time, provide a more inclusive vision of society. While the first illustration comes from the slavery period and focuses on women and resistance, the second example is an account of the experiences of women leaders in the trade union movement in the post-World War II era.

Conventional histories of slavery assert that women in slave society were "more readily and firmly" attached to white society; in other words, that black women accommodated more readily to slavery than their male counterparts. Presumably, a domestic slave woman's physical proximity to white men placed her in a contradictory position of devotion and betrayal. However, as the records of slave revolts in the British and French West Indies swell with accounts, there is no doubt that there was an outright rejection of slavery by peoples of African descent in the region. Furthermore, both men and women found many ways in their everyday lives to frustrate their masters. Planters needed the psychological and physical security of believing behavioral stereotypes of blacks to retain their own honor and power in slave society. Daily resistance on the part of women slaves was the response to this denigration. In fact, resistance to enslavement began from the moment of their capture, through the middle passage, and onto emancipation which began with the Haitian revolution in 1801 to 1886 when Cuba finally freed its slaves.

Female insubordination took on various forms, including shamming illness, refusing to go to work, using abusive language ("tongue lashings"), leaving the estate without permission, losing articles of clothing from the master's laundry, withholding or using their sexuality for their own benefit, and using the slave codes in their own favor, especially concerning maternity rights. One of the most powerful weapons in the hands of women cooks was their skillful use of poisons.

Around 1769, in Saint Domingue (Haiti) a group of women who pounded grain and did other domestic chores, was persuaded by another group of women to become maroons. Maroons were groups of people who escaped slavery and set up their own communities, usually in inaccessible areas such as swamps, forests and mountains. Although women refrained from running away in large numbers, because of their kinship ties and children, it is now clear that they engaged in daily resistance and were often severely punished for these offenses against the planter class.

As the documents show, including the work by Barbara Bush, women on a daily basis caused more trouble than the men. According to contemporary histories written by men, few women seem to have taken part in the uprisings that plagued the Caribbean during the days of slavery. Yet, as Bush adds, the absence of the names of female slaves from official records and contemporary accounts of slave uprisings and conspiracies does not constitute proof that they played no active part. Nanny, the legendary Jamaican Windward Maroon, provides an example of the role women played in their baffle for freedom from slavery in the region.

Nanny was known by her own people and the British as an outstanding political and military leader. As cited by Bush, a junior British officer described her in the following way: "(She) had a girdle round her waist, with nine or ten different knives hanging in sheaths to it, many of which I doubt not had been plunged into human flesh and blood." Legend also has it that Nanny slew captured English soldiers with impunity and that she had supernatural powers. Yet, in 1739, when the British were finally defeated, they refused to recognize Nanny as the Maroon leader during the signing of the treaty. Nonetheless, stresses Caribbean scholar Rhoda Reddock, Nanny figures prominently in Caribbean women's history because she led her people with courage and religious conviction, and inspired them to maintain that spirit of independence which was their rightful inheritance.

It was only after the tremendous social, economic and cultural change that took place in the 19th century (e.g., the Haitian revolution, the independence of the Dominican Republic, the emancipation in the English, Danish, Dutch and French colonies, the rise of the peasantry, indenture, the wars of independence with Spain at the end of the century), that the region would be in a position to look for a female figure who could reclaim the spirit invoked by Nanny. One such figure is Doña Mariana Grajales de Maceo of Santiago de Cuba. Born a free woman of color in the early 19th century, Doña Mariana was the mother of 13 children, 9 of whom lost their lives in Cuba's independence wars (1868–78), including the most famous, Antonio and Jose Maceo. Antonio Maceo (the Bronze Titan) has military standing that is likened to that of Toussaint L'Ouverture of Haiti's revolution. Caribbean historian Jean Stubbs remarks that Mariana, "the mother of Cuba" has acquired legendary proportions akin to Nanny, "but the focus is on her status as a self-sacrificing mother, and not as a political or military leader."

Both Nanny and Mariana Grajales de Maceo each represent an aspect of womanhood that is fostered in the region. Each worked exceptionally hard to reach her own goals. Mariana nursed her sons, as well as other wounded soldiers, in the fight for independence. She lived in exile and her own life was in jeopardy for decades. Nanny's status as a warrior mother rekindles the heritage of the Akan peoples, who were prominent in the early enslaved populations. Nanny fought the battles, but was denied recognition because of her gender by the British. Both women are now valued by their respective countries. One of the highest accolades bestowed to a Cuban mother is in the name of Mariana Grajales de Maceo. Nanny is Jamaica's only National Heroine, and her visage is on the Jamaican $500 bill.

During the worldwide Depression of the 1930s, Anglophone Caribbean women were really ready to reclaim the political spirit invoked by Nanny of the Maroons. It is in the labor unions that the public role of women is quite evident. The general strikes and worker insurrections, which blazed across the English-speaking Caribbean in the late 1930s, gave rise to two things: a more self-confident working class demanding its rights, and trade union workers calling for the right to strike for labor representation, adequate pay, and decent working conditions. Work situations had not improved since the days of slavery, which had ended 100 years earlier in the British territories. The trade unions, following British organizational structures, considered men as the primary workers, although they did recognize the fact that women constituted a major segment in the British West Indian labor force. During the strikes, there were women on the picket lines engaged in their own anti-colonial struggle and exerting their right to self-determination.

Feminist anthropologist Lynn Bolles's study underscores the view that early women trade union leaders were fiscally responsible for those fledgling labor organizations. Yet, these women are absent from Caribbean history. Like the men in the labor movement, trade union women leaders continue to have a sense of collective consciousness; they recognize the benefits of collective action on behalf of the common good of working people. Once they were members of a trade union and their talents apparent to those in leadership positions and their peers, these women took on responsibilities beyond mere membership. To this day, however, only a handful of women trade union leaders are included in the highest levels of decision-making in their organizations. Again, it is not a question of women's capabilities but the nature of the deterrents that impede their progress.

Family Structure and Kinship

Much of the social literature from the 1930s to the early 1970s stresses the differences that appear between aspects of culture which are perceived as ascriptive, "European" features (white or light-skinned, upper- or middle-class), and as the social "norm," on the one hand, and the African-based creole cultural systems of the majority on the other. Over four centuries of European colonization resulted in the socio-political hegemony of the upper classes and accompanying derision of the cultures of the masses. Light skin color and middle-class status approximated the socially approved "norm," while the African cultural patterns and dark skins of the black majority were causes of disparagement. In the case of Trinidad and Guyana, the Indo-West Indians were allotted a rank below that of Afro-Caribbeans, while Chinese, Lebanese, Jews and Portuguese were below that of "whites."

Family forms were couched in "ideal" topologies. For example, decades of social science research categorized West Indian family forms and household organizations in three patterns, listed here in descending order: nuclear family (wife, husband, children); common-law (nuclear without legal sanctions); and visiting unions (woman and children with a non-resident boyfriend, or nonresident children's father). Research in the French and Dutch Antilles followed the British model, while studies in Cuba, the Dominican Republic and Puerto Rico utilized the Spanish class/color specificities of mestizo culture.

Often, marriage is neither economically feasible (cost of a wedding, setting up a household) nor a given in the Caribbean reality of gender relations. Indeed, having child does not connote or necessitate the forming of a nuclear family and therefore counter the normalization of what "family" means. Within domestic organizations, there is the prevalence of female-headed households and other variations in household structures, the double standard in mating relations, the normative experience of extra-marital mating, and the commonplace acceptance of birth outside of wedlock.

The West Indian Family, the topic and title of a book set in Martinique, reminds us that the very notion of West Indian-ness refers primarily to peoples of African descent, or of mulatto or mestizo origins. To a large extent, the terms exclude the Indian experience. This is particularly true in the discussion of family organization. The East Indian family structure was able to draw on its south-Asian foundations when the ratio of men and women was less skewed. When there were twice as many men as women, there were a variety of relationships, none of which even came close to approximating traditional ones. Hindu and Muslim marriages were not legally sanctioned in Trinidad and Guyana until the mid 20th century. For those living primarily on sugar plantations, marital disputes and other domestic conflicts were settled according to Eurocentric family norms and values, usually by the estate manager. In contrast to sub-continent practices, couples resided with their paternal parents for only a few years, the father was no longer the sole "trustee" of family resources, and wives were given more say in family events. The caste system, caste endogamy (marrying within your own group by Hindus) was undermined and arranged marriages became impossible to attain.

When the balance between males and females was finally established, it became a catalyst for the revival of Indian culture in the West Indies. Pride over India's independence in 1947, and the arrival of Muslim religious preachers and artists made family and religious ceremonies once again the center of Indian life. However, Indo-West Indian culture had evolved its own creolization due to influences of the wider society. Marriage was one of the first traditions to be compromised. While parents' criteria for selection of marriage partners emphasized security, wealth and family status, the younger generation looked for new and modern ways, similar to creole styles. The legally-sanctioned nuclear family is still the most popular marital union, although common-law and visiting unions are becoming more prevalent than before. Young Indo-West Indians are also experiencing greater equality between spouses. A 1992 study notes that "the wife's selfless devotion" to her husband is attributed only to those 40 years and older.

The domination of European constructs of gender-appropriate role, status and proper place in society can be seen in the laws and policies enacted throughout the region at the turn of the century. For example, mass-marriage campaigns of the postwar period attempted to convince Jamaicans to transform common law relationships into patriarchal legal marriages, and enlisted churches, schools, the press, the radio, and welfare agencies in the effort. This effort also legitimized off-spring who were deemed bastards under the law. Despite the media "blitz," the mass-marriage campaign was a failure, because of the popular economic require-ments necessary for legal marriage, and the social acceptance of all children, re-gardless of the circumstances of their birth. As a matter of fact, since the late 1970s, starting with Jamaica, most Commonwealth Caribbean governments have enacted a "status of the Child" law which states that a person cannot be held re-sponsible for the consequences of his/her birth. In effect, "illegitimacy" is now a moot point and all children are legitimate under the eyes of the law. Mindie Lazarus-Black studied how poor women, legally married or not, are taking their "baby father" to court and demanding child-care payments because they are legal heirs to the man's property.

However, it was not the question of children that was viewed as a "problem," but the prevalence of female-headed households that concerned first colonial and now duly-elected governments. Furthermore, this situation, most prominent for poor and working class women, dovetailed with the increasing levels of social in-equality.

Detailed investigations by anthropologists and sociologists eventually chal-lenged the notion that Afro-Caribbean families represented disorganized or pathological adaptations to the conditions of slavery. Such a view resulted from looking at female-headed households in the Caribbean through Euro-American eyes. For example, the model household of a family as two adults of the same generation, but different sexes, who are the biological parents of children with whom they live, rests in part on a gendered division of labor requiring a male breadwinner and a female homemaker, as well as on the belief that conjugal rela-tions are more important than consanguineous ones. The creole West Indian fam-ily differs from this not only in reality, but in beliefs about what a family is and what is appropriate for its members to do. Anthropologists learned that, in at-tempting to understand both the economic support of households and children, and the performance of domestic responsibilities such as laundry, meal prepara-tion, and childcare, they could not assume that the boundaries of a dwelling de-fine a family and what it does. Often, eating, sleeping, financial support, and child rearing were shared among a network of male and female relatives and neighbors.

The complexities of West Indian plantation life distorted the African heritage division of labor, while ironically reinforcing it. For example, many mothers felt the deep cruelty of bringing children into slavery and resisted the master's encour-agement to do so. The use of women as laborers in the fields beside men also re-vealed biases of color and gender; the majority of field slaves were black women. Although men and women labored equally in the field gangs, the chances of fe-males doing any other task were slim. Further, there is a sharp division in the or-ganization of household labor. Dorian Powell's study stresses the point that women perform a disproportionate amount of work and usually carry the enor-mous responsibility of ensuring the survival of family members, a set of activities which Victoria Durant-Gonzalez calls "the realm of female responsibility." She states that a large proportion of women in the English-speaking Caribbean are "in charge of economics of producing, providing, controlling, or managing the re-source essential to meeting daily needs."

Helen Safa did a comparative study of contemporary women, family and factory work in Cuba, the Dominican Republic and Puerto Rico. She notes that women assume more authority in the household than was culturally prescribed in the past when they were employed in jobs outside of the home. The additional authority does not necessarily come from their economic contribution, but more from the fact that now there was more than one source of family income. It is not only the erosion of the man's role as the economic provider that is at issue, but his ability and willingness to share this role with his wife. It makes for more equitable marital relationships. In Puerto Rico and the Dominican Republic, where male marginalization was most severe due to unemployment, the percentage of female-headed households was on the rise. As a matter of fact, women headed 25% of all households in these three countries. In contrast to the prevailing cultural patterns of male dominance within families, the question is: will these trends start to approximate martial patterns found in other areas of the Caribbean, or will new forms appear?

With the predominance of women heading households, we see the reality of the "price" of the inclusive concept of motherhood that pertains in the West Indies. Since most Caribbean women are either employed in low-paying, low-skilled, and menial jobs or unemployed, how can they fulfill all that is expected of them? The ideological support mechanisms found in the African-based traditional role of women in Caribbean societies prove to be invaluable cultural assets. Work, regardless of what tasks it is tied to, has meaning in terms of how a woman attempts to meet her familial responsibilities and is an essential part of her self-image and conception of womanhood. As a result, "independent" is a word often used to describe West Indian women and how they carry out their responsibilities. As used by Christine Barrow, it is a quality based on having one's own source of economic support—from employment, other income-generating activities, and, where possible, savings—while at the same time organizing and utilizing support from others. Autonomy, on the other hand, implies exercising options while making decisions for oneself and having control over one's own destiny with no strings attached.

Independence, then, is not coterminous with female autonomy. Economic self-sufficiency is far beyond the grasp of most to whom the term independent has been applied in the Caribbean context. Rather than acting on behalf of a single person, autonomy implies interdependence among a number of individuals. Autonomy is highly valued, and lifetimes are spent fulfilling obligations to others so as to reinforce that reciprocal support in time of need. Barrow says: "one is considered foolish to refuse support from those who give, especially if they have a culturally prescribed obligation to do so."

One mechanism used to preserve autonomy in the Caribbean is the maintenance of reciprocal relationships with the networks. Again, to borrow from Barrow, there is an etiquette to network exchanges such that "independence," or at least the public image of it, is maintained. The most critical characteristic of successful network management is avoiding total dependence on one source of support, particularly a male partner. If a relationship endures over the years, the mate support tends to become secure. However, it can never be fully relied upon, since at any stage of marital union-visiting (where the man visits his girlfriend and perhaps their children), common-law (where a couple lives together), or points in between—the relationship can be temporarily or completely terminated. Therefore,

Caribbean women's control over their lives is a function of their degree of economic autonomy, which includes the nature of their earning, spending, saving, property ownership, and the sexual division of "money matters." According to Barrow, female autonomy in the English-speaking Caribbean is encouraged from an early age, and education is emphasized as the means to get a good job. Although the notions of independence and autonomy are essential aspects of women's survival in the region, they should not be romanticized.

Women of the region, whether poor or from the working or the upper classes, are subject to iniquities based on their gender. They are denied access to resources (relative to their class position), and their potential minimized because they are not full participants in the development of their countries. Economic opportunities for women also do not mean the reduction of their domestic duties at home. As we learn more about the past, and the contributions women made to Caribbean life and culture, we will be better equipped to answer the questions for contemporary problems and those that may rise in the future.

Tourism and Women's Work

Tourism, that broadly-defined, service-producing sector, has for the past 10 years been the largest earner of foreign exchange (US 1.3 billion in 2001 for Jamaica). Further, the country as one of the "mature" Caribbean destinations, leads the way with the tourist sector being the Caribbean's biggest employer (Ferguson 1999). For the most part, the majority of workers in Jamaica's tourist sector are women, yet rarely are the dynamics of gender, class, and race analyzed in most of the tourist academic literature, or that of the promotional literature coming from the industry itself. Certain questions need to be asked: what do these women think about their relationship between themselves and tourists? How do they equate their hard work with someone else's pleasure and adventure?

Tourism, like the other sectors of the economy, features sex-segregated occupations (housekeeping, bar maids, craft vendors) as well as those that are considered non-traditional ones (hotel managers, dive shop owners, and head cooks). All of these jobs are subject to the variances of hurricanes, seasonal business cycles, and overall international economic conditions that allow or discourage individuals from taking a vacation far away from home. In addition, tourism is embedded in the society in which it is located. Places like Jamaica are highly stratified on the basis of race, class, ethnicity, gender and other marked and unmarked differences. The culture, with its legacy of slavery, indenture, 350 years of colonialism, and neo-colonialism frames a society that is also secured by a social system that allows upward mobility to be a real possibility. As a service sector, tourist work fits neatly into Jamaica's gender segmented labor market. Low skill jobs are the backbone of the business, and according to GOJ data, 1 out of 4 in the country is now related in some fashion with the tourist industry. Women have numerous roles to play in tourism. Not only do they represent "natural" service worker (based on being women), but also because they are non- white, they represent "the exotic islander" to tourists—another set of criterion for "consuming the Caribbean." Tourism requires not only being an expert in one's own job, but also being an accomplished actress so that the tourist, no matter where they are from in the world, will return to the Caribbean again and again to seek the "pleasures" of the islands.

Tangentially related to women and tourism is sex tourism. It is a thriving business in the Caribbean, and as a result, contributes substantially to the annual income of the islands. Whilst prostitution is illegal in Jamaica, it is decriminalized in the Dominican Republic, Belize, Aruba and Curacao, and widely practiced in Cuba and Puerto Rico (Mackay 66). Such industries make a profit from women's labor and their exploitation, and as detailed in the following section, compromise women's physical and mental health. Sex tourism and prostitution depends on the ready-supply of women's bodies, and it comes as no surprise that countries that see high sex trafficking (that is the sending of women to Western Europe, Israel, Puerto Rico, Panama and Venezuela) also support the growing sex tourism industry.

Health, Sexuality and HIV/AIDs

The primary indicators of women's health according to world organizations—maternal mortality and HIV/AIDS—is connected directly to issues of sexuality, world economics, and the global structures of poverty. According to geographer and women's studies scholar Joni Seager, "[o]f all the health measures monitored by the World Health Organization, the largest discrepancy between rich and poor countries occurs in maternal mortality" (38). Since Haiti is one of the poorest countries in the Caribbean, it should come as no surprise that it has one of the highest maternal mortality rates in the Caribbean. According to mid-1990s data, Haitians experience 1100 deaths of mothers per 100,000 live births whereas Guyana is 150/100,000, Jamaica is 120/100,000, and the Dominican Republic is 110/100,000. According to researchers, most of these deaths could be prevented if basic prenatal health care, nutrition, and education and support were provided. However, for the government, non-government organizations (NGO's), and/or private industry to implement such programming, it must have financial backing and the countries themselves are not in an economic position to support such endeavors.

Due to the very same social structures that contribute to maternal mortality (women's social status, economic disempowerment, and sexual status), women are also at high risk for contracting HIV/AIDS. As Seager suggests, "sexual relations between men and women are often framed by violence, coercion, and the presumption of men's 'right' of sexual access to women. Many women are not able to negotiate safe sexual behavior with male partners. Higher illiteracy rates for women and certain social arrangements (such as multiple partnering) add to their burden of risk" (48). In the Caribbean, there are at least 50,000 women living with HIV and again, a disproportionate number of cases exist in Haiti. According to UNAIDS, 6.1% of the Haitian population is infected with HIV/AIDS, and in 2001, 30,000 people in Haiti died of AIDS. In the Dominican Republic, 130,000 are living with HIV/AIDS, 2.5% of the population is infected, and 7,800 people died in 2001. The numbers in Jamaica drop off fairly dramatically whereby 1.2% of the population is infected with HIV/AIDS and 980 people died in 2001, and is most likely connected to the increasing number of health programs designed to educate the public as well as variations in the construction of gender and sexuality across the islands.

Given the processes of globalization described above, combined with complex social factors and personal choices, women have been and continue to make difficult decisions to leave their homes in the Caribbean in order to better support their families and take care of themselves. For example, according to the United States Immigration and Naturalization Service, 400,879 migrants from the Americas and Caribbean were admitted to the US alone in 2000. However, in looking to statistics, it is important to keep in mind, as women's creative expression shows us, migration does not mean that the Caribbean is left behind. Rather, their connections, memories, and travel back and forth become a part of women's diasporic experiences and constitute an increasingly important part of the scholarship on the Caribbean.

Overview of Caribbean Women's Literature in the Diaspora

As Joan Anim-Addo writes in her introduction to her edited text, *Framing the Word*, women's literature *as a body of work* is becoming more representative of women's diverse experiences in the Caribbean. Moreover, she asserts that the "range and vitality" of women's creativity is attracting new readers and scholarly interest globally (Anim-Addo, ix). Central themes of this body of literature include domination and resistance to colonial power; back and forth migration in the Diaspora; female sexuality and relationships; the significance of land and space in understanding social interaction and power; the centrality of storytelling and spirituality in understanding the Caribbean; nationalism and transnational connections; neocolonial relationships; and Caribbean peoples' subjectivities in the construction of home and identity. Some of the notable authors and their creative work that have received quite a bit of scholarly attention include but are not limited to Michelle Cliff's *Abeng* and *No Telephone to Heaven* (Jamaica); Merle Collins' poetry *Rotten Pomerack* and novel *Angel* (Grenada); Maryse Condé's *I, Tituba, Black Witch of Salem*, *Segu*, and *Windward Heights*; Edwidge Danticat's *Breath Eyes Memory* and *Krik Krak* (Haiti); Beryl Gilroy's *Frangipani House* and *Boy Sandwich* (Guyana); Cristina Garcia's *Dreaming in Cuban* (Cuba); Lorna Goodson's *I Am Becoming My Mother* (Jamaica); Merle Hodge's *Crick Crack, Monkey* (Trinidad); Jamaica Kincaid's body of work, particularly *Annie John*, *Lucy* and *A Small Place* (Antigua); Andrea Levy's *Fruit of the Lemon* (Jamaica); Audre Lorde's *Zami: A New Spelling of My Name* (Carriacou); Paule Marshall's *Brown Girl, Brownstone*, *The Chosen Place, The Timeless People*, and *Daughters* (Barbados); Pauline Melville's *The Ventriloquist's Tale* (Guyana); Grace Nichols' *Whole of a Morning Sky* (Guyana); Elizabeth Nunez's *Bruised Hibiscus* (Trinidad); Joan Riley's *The Unbelonging* (Jamaica); Jean Rhys' *Voyage in the Dark* and *Wide Sargasso Sea* (Dominica); Esmeralda Santiago's *When I Was Puerto Rican* and *America's Dream* (Puerto Rico); and Jan Shinebourne's *Timepiece* and *The Last English Plantation* (Guyana). It is worth noting that many of the above titles were written in Spanish or French before being published in English.

Writer and literary scholar Merle Collins states in "Framing the Word: Caribbean Women's Writing" that Caribbean women writers today, much like in the past, are engaged in framing that "which is distinctively Caribbean, shaped by the

Caribbean experience" (Anim-Addo, 4). As Collins details, Caribbean women's writing emerges from its patriarchal and white-centered history and creates a vibrant and differently told history of the region. Connected to expanding notions of education for girls and women, as well as international women's movements and the expansion of publishing houses titles, women today have some outlets (though still not enough) to weave their stories of family and kinship, connection to the land and Caribbean space, colonization and racial power, and subjectivity and independence.

Study Questions and Activities

1.   Given the history of slavery and colonialism in the Caribbean, discuss two examples of how Caribbean women actively resist(ed) Western domination?
2.   Discuss the variations in family type across the Caribbean and how this differs from patriarchal, Western marital arrangements?
3.   What is the relationship between women and tourism? What does Esmeralda Santiago's novel, *America's Dream*, add to the scholarly literature on tourism?

Glossary

Caribbean: complex term that can refer to (1) the Caribbean Sea, its islands, or its Central or South American coasts or to the peoples or cultures of this region; (2) indigenous Carib peoples, their language and culture.

Caste: (1) a social class separated from others by distinctions of hereditary rank, profession, or wealth; (2) a social system or the principle of grading society based on castes; (3) the social position or status conferred by a system based on castes.

Common-law family: a family in which a man and woman are not legally married by state and/or religious codes but bound together by choice and years of living in the same household

Commonwealth: The people of a nation or state; the body politic. In the case of the English-speaking Caribbean, the commonwealth refers to those lands that were and are, in principle, self-governing but under the rule of the English Monarchy. Commonwealth can also describe the relationship between the Spanish-speaking island of Puerto Rico and the United States.

Creolization: the blending together of two or more cultures to create a new one.

Female-headed households: Sociological term that describes the economic and social arrangements of families where the woman/mother is the primary economic provider and care-taker.

Male breadwinner: Sociological term that describes the economic and social arrangements of families where the man/father provides the sole or majority income for the household.

Maroon: (1) a fugitive Black slave in the West Indies in the 17th and 18th centuries and (2) a descendant of such a slave.

Mestizo: a person of mixed racial ancestry, especially of mixed European and Native American ancestry.

Nuclear family: a family in which a man and woman (1) are legally married and thus bound together by state and/or religious codes and (2) have children.

Resistance: the act or instance of resisting or opposing a given force. In this case, resistance refers to collective and individual acts. For example, Caribbean peoples fought back or resisted oppressive institutions such as slavery (e.g. through slave revolts) and an individual might resist slavery by poisoning the master's food.

Sexuality: Complex term that has social, political, and biological connotations. On the surface, it might appear that sexuality refers to how one is characterized by sex (female or male) and engages in sexual activity. However, sexuality is broader than this and must consider relationships and identification beyond heterosexuality to include lesbian, gay, bisexual, trans-sexual, and transgendered persons. Sexuality and its perceptions are deeply connected to power within any given society.

Social divisions of society: The social system in which societies are built upon hierarchies connected to race, class, gender, sexuality, religion, ability, and education.

Visiting unions: family structure whereby mother/female guardian and children live together in a domestic dwelling whilst the woman's mate/children's father is a non-resident in the home.

References

Joan Anim-Addo, ed. *Framing the Word: Gender and Genre in Caribbean Women's Writing*. London: Whiting and Birch, 1996.

Paula L. Aymer. *Uprooted Women: Migrant Domestics in the Caribbean*. Westport, CT: Praeger, 1997.

Edna Acosta-Belen. "Puerto Rican Women in Culture, History, and Society." in A. Acosta-Belen (ed.), *The Puerto Rican Woman*. New York: Praeger, 1986 (pp.1–29).

Violet Eudine Barrieteau. "Confronting Power and Politics: A Feminist Theorizing of Gender in Commonwealth Caribbean Societies." *Meridians: feminism, race, transnationalism* 3:2 (2003): 57–92.

Christine Barrow, ed. *Caribbean Portraits: Essays on Gender Ideologies and Identities*. Kingston, Jamaica: Ian Randle Publishers, 1997.

Christine Barrow. *Family in the Caribbean*. Kingston: Ian Randle Publishers, 1996.

Lynn Bolles. "Flying the Love Bird and Other Tourist Jobs in Jamaica: Women Tourist Workers in Jamaica." In *Sister Circle: Black Women and Work* edited by S. Harley and the Black Women and Work Collective. New Brunswick, NJ: Rutgers University Press, 2001.

———. "Women Workers and Global Tourism in Jamaica." In *Black Women, Globalization and Economic Justice* edited by F. Steady, Rochester, VT: Schenkman Books, 2002.

———. We *Paid Our Dues: Women Trade Union Leaders in the Caribbean*. Washington, DC: Howard University Press, 1996.

———— and Deborah D'Amico-Samuels. "Anthropological Scholarship on Gender in the English-speaking Caribbean." in S. Morgen (ed.). *Gender and Anthropology*. Washington, DC: American Anthropological Association, 1990 (pp. 171–288).

Barbara Bush. *Slave Women in the Caribbean Society*. Bloomington, IN: Indiana University Press, 1990.

Barbara Christian. *Black Feminist Criticism: Perspectives on Black Women Writers*. New York: Pergamon Press, 1985.

Johnnetta B. Cole. *All American Women*. New York: The Free Press, 1986.

Maryse Condé and Thorunn Lonsdale, eds. *Caribbean Women Writers: Fiction in English*.

London: Macmillan Press Ltd, 1999.

Selwyn Cudjoe, ed. *Caribbean Women Writers*. Wellesley: Calaloux, 1990.

Arlene Davila. *Sponsored Identities*. Philadelphia: Temple University Press, 1997.

Carole Boyce Davies and Evelyn Fido, eds. *Out of Kumbla: Caribbean Women and Literature*. Trenton, NJ: Africa World Press, 1990.

Nancy Foner. *Islands in the City: West Indian Migration to New York*. Berkeley, CA: Universityof California Press, 2001.

Vera M. Green. *Migrants in Aruba*. Assen, Netherlands: Van Gorcum, 1974.

Michael Horowitz. *Morne-Paysan: Peasant Village in Martinique*. New York: Holt, Rinehart & Winston, 1967.

Mindie Lazarus-Black. *Legitimate Acts and Illegal Encounters*. Washington, DC: Smithsonian Institution Press, 1994.

Oscar Lewis. *La Vida: A Puerto Rican Family in the Culture of Poverty*. New York: Random House, 1966.

Lucille Mathurin Mair. *The Rebel Woman*. Kingston, Jamaica: Institute of Jamaica, 1974.

Irma McLaurin. *Women of Belize: Gender and Change in Central America*. New Brunswick, NJ: Rutgers University Press, 1996.

Patricia Mohammed, ed. *Gendered Realities: Essays in Caribbean Feminist Thought*. University Press of the West Indies, 2002.

Bernard Moitt. "Women, Work and Resistance in the French Caribbean during Slavery." in V Shepard, B. Brereton, B. Bailey (ed.), *Engendering History*. Kingston, Jamaica: Ian Randle Publishers (pp. 1S5–175).

Susheila Nasta, ed. *Motherlands: Black Women's Writing from Africa, the Caribbean and South*

Asia. London: The Women's Press, 1991.

Marysa Navarro and Virginia Sánchez Korrol, eds. *Women in Latin America & the Caribbean: Restoring Women to History*. Bloomington, IN: Indiana University Press, 1999.

Dorian Powell. "The Role of Women in the Caribbean," *Social and Economic Studies*. 33: 2 June, 1984.

Rhonda Reddock. *Women, Labour, and Politics in Trinidad: A History*. London: Zed Books, 1994.

Helen I. Safa. *The Myth of the Male Breadwinner*. Boulder, CO: Westview Press, 1995.

Seager, Joni. *The Penguin Atlas of Women in the World*. NY: Penguin Books, 2003.

Verene Shepherd, ed. *Women in Caribbean History*. Kingston, Jamaica: Ian Randle Publishers, 1999.

————. Bridget Brereton, and Barbara Bailey, eds. *Engendering History: Caribbean Women in Historical Perspective*. Kingston, Jamaica: Ian Randle Publishers, 1995.

Jean Stubbs. "Social and Political Motherhood of Cuba: Mariana Grajales
    Cuello" in V. Shepard, B. Brereton, B. Bailey (ed.), *Engendering History*.
    Kingston, Jamaica: Ian Randle Publishers, (pp. 296–319) 1995.
Kevin Yelvington. *Producing Power: Ethnicity, Gender, and Class in a Caribbean
    Workplace*. Philadelphia: Temple University Press, 1995.

26

Lifting As We Rise: Black Women in America

Marsha Jean Darling

Introduction

There is little question that African American females share a common heritage with African American males. Together, as people still striving to attain equality and freedom from persecution and white domination, human and civil rights, and personal and collective advancement, black women and men have endured and resisted centuries of enslavement, exploitation, disfranchisement, and *de facto* and *de jure* segregation. Collectively, black women and men have also sought to develop their own institutions, defined with values arising from the empowerment they have evoked in changing and evolving participatory democracy in the United States. Indeed, for a very long time, it was the practice to speak of an African American nation as a people with one voice, one set of goals, and one identity. In this regard, efforts to promote race upliftment, nation building, and an emphasis on the similarities and differences in male leadership in African American communities preoccupied most "progressive" historical accounts of black peoples' "history." Consequently, until fairly recently, African American women have been rendered invisible in African American and American historiography.

This chapter is not an attempt to write African American males out of African American history, but rather it seeks (as do quite a few other scholars) to write African American women into the historical narrative as subjects of "herstory."[1] Having taken on the challenge to present African American women as more than appendages of men in history, it must be said that the experiences of African American females have differed from those of African American males. In other words, as unaccustomed as some people are to asking how the experience of female gender has created a different historical reality for African American women, sex and the construction and definition of gender have not been inconsequential matters.

---

1. The term "herstory" is purposely used here to underscore the differences between the traditional deficient historical accounts of women and the contemporary historical writings on women, particularly African American women.

Thus, the following chapter begins by seeking to address important conceptual and theoretical questions regarding African American women, chiefly: How has the experience of being female, coupled with the experience of being a women of color, shaped the historical experiences of African American women? What unique and different issues arise when we consider African American females as subjects in the historical narrative? Stated differently, how have the experiences of females (and the cultural realities of their world) shaped the "herstory" of Africa, and the experiences of African American female diaspora? What unique experiences have shaped African American female consciousness and action? Why? In what ways has the conquest of people of color affected females of color, in particular, in this chapter, African American women? What values, beliefs, and commitments have influenced both responses and initiatives in the actions of African American females during the past several centuries?

So, with the central task of exploring the "herstory" of African American females, the following is an inquiry into the positive and negative experiences, the challenges, and the struggles that are embodied in the sexual exploitation and oppression experienced by African American females. This chapter looks at the initiatives, the commitments, and the achievements embodied in the organizations, institutions, and actions undertaken by African American women both on their own behalf and with an unerring commitment to advance African American people. It also looks at the collective, and where known, individual efforts of millions of African American females during the past several centuries.

Major terms and concepts: Invisibility of African American females in black history; African American females as historical subjects with a "herstory" of their own; cultural roots for gender identity; double jeopardy — sexual and racial exploitation in the Americas; resistance of African American women against enslavement; stabilization of African American familial groups on plantations, matrilineal descent, incest taboo, black naming patterns; African American women as abolitionists and women's rights advocates; African American female mutual aid, benevolent, and educational societies; black women in the black Church; black Women's Club Movement; black women in the Civil Rights movement.

Key Conceptual and Methodological Issues

Before one can undertake to chronicle the historical legacy of African American women in the United States, one must address a few critically important conceptual and methodological issues. Until recently, many scholars of American "history" began their discussions of African peoples in the year 1620. For a time, white scholars wrote textbooks that celebrated European military conquests over the indigenous peoples of North and South America. In the same way that American Indian "history" was distorted to conform to the white image of Amerindians as the "noble savages," African peoples were presented as unorganized "savages" living in primitive barbarity. White supremacists argued that the conquest and domination of Amerindians was a cultural imperative, and that the enslavement of African peoples was not only benign, but, quite possibly, a service to humanity and an aid to black progress. Against such a distorted backdrop, many white scholars and leaders have portrayed Africa as a "dark continent" and Africa's sons and daughters (whether remaining in Africa or abroad in the African diaspora) as having come from nothing worthy of note, much less a cultural respect. In essence, any black "history" worthy of note was purported to have begun with the European trade in African flesh—the slave trade.

An important question emerges for the student interested in "herstory:" What does it mean to "start" the "herstory" of the people who have become African American in the year 1620? To do that is to start a "herstory" of women and men that has no initial point of reference than enslavement, and the *objectification* of African people into a European white settler's concept of property. For example, one notices the frequency with which publishers, editors, and scholars refer to black people who lived during America's antebellum slavery period, as either "free blacks" or "slaves." In this context, the use of the word "slave(s)" does not describe a person with a national origin, but one whose legal and social status is enslavement in the country or in the culture under description. It imparts no immediate identity, reflects no national origin, and infers no active presence amongst the living as a sentient human being or a person. Indeed, the word "slave" masks the overt and explicit act committed against African females and males (persons who had a national origin), namely, the explicit political, social, cultural, economic, and ideological process of "enslavement." The word "slave" is impersonal and non-sentient, reflecting the writer's sense that what is being described is a unit of production in the context of plantation capitalism. It is important to sit with these conceptual issues for a while, for they are essential to the task of reassessing what we have been told is the process of "naming" and, hence, describing and assessing African American historiography.

On the other hand, to insist that African people have been subjects and not objects in "herstory" is to insist that our language convey the precision to which scholars are held accountable. Consequently, the language that directly conveys the historical reality of the betrayal that African females and males endured begins with words that assess what happened to *people*, real live men and women, not units of production. In a changed and far more accurate context, "enslavement" describes something that happened against the will and the well being of African peoples for nearly 300 years in this county, and much longer elsewhere in this hemisphere. "Enslavement" is what happened to females and males who had, in fact, come from Africa, where they possessed, as Americans say, an Old World cultural identity. Hence, it is important to use broader, more meaningful and reconsidered concepts and approaches to identify the people abducted into slavery; to highlight the system of values, beliefs, and concepts regarded as First Principles in African societies; to bring forth the social, legal, economic and cultural experiences of subordination and exploitation that African females experienced in slavery; and to note the resistance they displayed against the institution.

The larger problem is that enslaved Africans are often reduced to passive objects or units, while white settlers are described and analyzed as active subjects who grapple with difficult choices on the stage of "history." Certainly, the effect of an historiography that has presented images of white settlers as paternalistic should be noted, if only because it has influenced scholars to see what might be called "becoming benevolence" where they should see a bizarre, yet conscious attempt by many white settlers to relegate humans to the level of animals or chattel.

Also, dwelling on white settler paternalism, does more to ameliorate contemporary guilt amongst whites than it does to explain the emergence of an institution predicated on white denial of the African personhood.

As bizarre as it may seem to our rational minds, European settlers—many themselves in search of freedom from persecution and access to the opportunity for economic advancement—undertook to define their own status in such a manner as to negate the likelihood that the very concepts of freedom, equality, and opportunity they valued would ever be societal in scope. The enslavement of Africans occurred against a background of racial and gender-defined entitlements. Persons and subjects under American law were first white and Christian, then male, and then white *and* female. Chattel and objects under the law were brown and black, male and female. In essence, white settlers undertook to establish freedom in an unfree society, equality in the slave society of their creation (with denial of African humanity at its center), and participatory democracy (based on white-skin-privilege in a multi-racial social setting).

Contrary to the representation of Africans as "savages," African females and males who were transported to the Americas against their will had a frame of reference that was distinctly African. A few first-person accounts by Africans have survived, and we are prompted by wisdom to ask different questions from those previously asked by the majority of scholars who engage in what might be called "victim studies." Since 1620 marks the beginning of a point in black "herstory" then, where racial betrayal and the persecution and humiliation of ever increasing numbers of Africans commenced, beginning black "herstory" then, as noted earlier, deprives black people of a past unpillaged by European greed for profit at someone else's expense, and lust for power in the name of white nationalism. Seeing Africans in the diaspora as lacking a home, a "herstory," and a culture is tantamount to engaging in "victim studies."

While elsewhere this volume provides readers with a fully developed essay on the black woman in Africa, this chapter presents a methodological case which prefaces African American women's "herstory" with a reference to an African Old World connection. As such, it presents a model for "how" to begin African American "herstory," and, in this specific instance, a chronicle of African American females. Therefore, no matter how brief an overview of the most significant values and belief systems that formed the cultural basis for an African Old World connection might be here, our discussion begins neither with European domination and exploitation nor with the betrayal of African against African (that accounts for some of the captive Europeans transported to the Americas and the Caribbean). It begins, instead, with an exploration of the major themes and issues in the "herstory" of African women living in African social systems, prior to being involuntarily and forcibly conveyed to the West. Some enslaved African females in the diaspora would subsequently give birth to a generation of children in the Americas. Others would die a wretched death during the Middle Passage or at the hands of white settlers intent upon stripping African women of their human dignity.

Assessing African Roots

African American women did not come from a nameless void—from cultures without values, belief system, institutions, obligations and commitments—doomed to live out the pitiful and degrading experience of enslavement and servitude derived from European settlers' beliefs about a master race that reproduced itself in near total segregation, and a servant race, whose only right to life rested on its enslavement in perpetuity. Such pretensions tell us more about white settler desire to erect a privilege system without responsibility, accountability, or guilt. Nor did African American females, once in America, simply evolve as an extension of African American males, invisible and spoken for at all times by the voices, interests, beliefs, and aspirations of African American men.

As a result of a shared exploitation and subordination based on race, enslaved African females and males share a common experience of racial oppression. Yet, African American females are not males in a world where race *and* sex are at the center of nearly all levels of personal and group definition and interaction. Indeed, throughout the last 500 years, many African American females have been victimized and traumatized by rape and sexual violence. No man, of whatever race or class, can speak definitively for the experience of black women's pain and struggle, and only African American women have borne the children of their beloved and the children of their oppressors.

The following brief discussion of African thought and social systems that preceded the horrifying experience of enslavement and involuntary transmigration to the Americas references values and beliefs that formed the social boundaries held in place by African females and males, for their benefit and the benefit of their children, their elders, and their ancestors. In the African cultural milieu, the needs, the values and the respectful place accorded to each member of society—incarnate and discarnate—defined the philosophical context which shaped the values and the expectations. They also sanctioned peoples's decisions and actions—a factor of crucial importance—because there is a fundamental difference between "dominator societies" and "partnership societies."

In contemporary times, we are often confronted with the consequence of the historical evolution of the white Euro-American cultural value placed on "unrestrained individualism." Students of "herstory" know that the enslavement of Africans was defended in part by white male claims that they were "individuals" above and beyond question, moral persuasion, or individual accountability. For instance, throughout the 245 years of the American institution of slavery, if a white man killed an enslaved African, no law in the land held him to any measure of justice. It was even the case that in some colonies, and, later states, the public treasury reimbursed the white man whatever monies he had originally expended on"purchasing" the enslaved African man or woman. Another example can be gleaned from more recent years. Anyone familiar with the Joanne Little court case, dating back to the mid-1970s, remembers that what was really on trail was Joanne Little's *right* to have killed a white man who, holding her imprisoned in a local jail in North Carolina, attempted to rape her. Had it not been for a short ice pick (with which Ms. Little defended herself from rape) she would have been one of the many nameless black women and girls raped at the whim of white men. It almost goes without saying that, in many places in the country, though in the South in particular, white men continued the "presumed individual right" of raping African American females beyond the 245 years in which they did so with little, if any, impunity. Such examples bespeak how far ranging and often out-of-ethical-control is the cultural value of "unrestrained individualism." Historically, "unrestrained individualism" has not been a part of black people's "herstory" of evolving a tradition of protest and resistance to unrestrained greed and white nationalism.

The concept of thinking for oneself and acting for the benefit of a "common good" more aptly describes traditional African societies. An emphasis on acting for "individual advantage" renders the social environment highly competitive and undermines all but a very narrowly construed sense of other people's worthiness. An unquestioned defense of individualism leads, invariably, to the refusal to ask what impact, not intention, one's actions really had on another person or group. In essence, moral boundaries that respect and protect the vulnerable—children, women, the aged, and those with different abilities—and our links with our ancestor crumble when eroded by unrestrained negative and destructive emotions. At issue here is the fact that many African social systems provided an institutional structure which allowed actualization of the concept of a "common good": mechanisms for sharing resources, provisions for shared family maintenance responsibilities, and many other more equitable, and (in the context of non-Muslim African societies), egalitarian traditions and norms, which most of the Africans where were forcibly transported from West African villages and towns brought with them to the New World.

A second important aspect on non-Muslim African social systems is the far greater equality between women and men. West African females lived for centuries without the yolk of oppression later imposed by the construction of European oppositional thinking regarding sexuality, wherein gender relations were perceived in dualistic terms, creating an image of women and unworthy and undeserving—the opposite of the image of men as good and deserving. At issue is also the emergence of male-controlled religions that have denied women their "worthiness." And yet, among many ancient religions (some of which so strongly influenced the development of Christianity and Islam), goddesses and women were revered. Nut, Isis, Ashtar, Diana, Hathor, and Maat—all reigned fully endowed with the powers, gifts, and blessings of the sacred. Historical fact simply does not support the evolution of those religions (to which Judaism, Christianity, and Islam owe much of their structure and codes of conduct) as belief systems where women are fallen, lesser, and persecuted rather than valued for being born female—an irony, when one considers that all men and women come through and by the presence of a woman.

That is not to say, however, that African societies were without ascribed male privileges, but there is no question that the pernicious persecution of women, and the denial of their equality before the sacred speak to the differences in status and in conditions of worthiness and value accorded to females in European and African societies during the 1500s. West African women outside of Islamic influence lived in social systems where their sex and sexuality, their bodies, the unity of body and mind, and the expression of emotions and feelings were believed to be positive and, hence, accepted, not repressed or denied manifestations of the natural world.

In patriarchal societies, which are prevalent in West African regions where most enslaved Africans originated, variations and distinctions in the evolution of male entitlements were and are still important. Essentially, West African societies were significantly more egalitarian in the range of rights and levels of respect accorded to women. In many places, patriarchy existed alongside matrilineal descent. It must be remembered that, while most of the world values women for their reproductive capacity, women's productive capacities, at the material level, have made significant contributions to the development of traditional subsistence societies. Studies have shown, for example, that 80 percent of Africa's subsistence-scale agricultural productivity has, for centuries, come from the work done by women. In addition to crop cultivation, West African women have been instrumental in processing, storing, bartering, and marketing food, and in selling grains, cloth, and other items at stalls in open air markets. Because their work in the cultivation of grains and cereals and their knowledge of food, herb, and root nutrients sustained the daily needs of most villages, women earned the respect of all in their communities. It was in their capacity as workers, not just as mothers, that they derived their status, for, while men's work of hunting (in hunting societies) was indeed important to the nutritional needs of members of the village, it was a task that took them away from the village for days or even weeks. Were it not for the daily gathering and subsistence agriculture that women undertook, starvation would have been widespread. Furthermore, in traditional Africa, women were the midwives, and, in many villages, trusted mediums and diviners.

The phenomenon of African market women, particularly in West African, undertaking increasingly sophisticated roles in providing some of the material level needs of families, is time-honored. Essentially, West African women have been instrumental and significant in the entire food chain, and, along with men, have served their families as "providers." Needless to say, with such essential roles as workers, particularly in West African societies, women have earned levels of respect and deference that established their mentoring of younger females and males as an important and far greater balance in the distribution of power and authority.

Hence, because scholars sometimes hold patriarchy constant (and assume that the distribution of power between the sexes has been the same in African, European, Asian, and Amerindian societies), important distinctions that bespeak structural differences in the social status and personal recognizance of women in different parts of the world prior to the 1500s have not really been explored. The penchant for some scholars toward immersion in European culture is in part the issue, alongside the presumption that African societies were about at the same (or much lesser) degree of state formation as the European nation-states when they sought out Africans in the fifteenth century. The tendency to "universalize" the austere treatment of women under European male patriarchy is also embodied in European assumptions, and it is the idea that women's status under a male defined nation-state apparatus must also have been, or should have been, the same in Africa as in Europe.

Yet, many West African ethnic groups had partnership structures prior to the arrival of the Europeans and the Arabs, in which the legal status of children was derived from matrilineal descent. In a world now preoccupied with images and validation for patriarchy, matrilineal descent is inaccurately compared and assessed in the context of patriarchal control and subordination of women. As a matter of historical record, it would also be inaccurate to assume that non-Islamic traditional rural West Africans practiced any sex-specific subordination of women common to Western Europe and Islamic societies. The fact of matrilineal descent evolved not only from women's real and symbolic relationship with the survival of the lineage, but also from women's direct link with fertility. Matrilineal descent insures that the social group will always be more certain of the identity of a child's mother than of the child's father. In addition, since children were the primary responsibility of their mothers, guaranteeing them linkage to the mother's family insured their access to people and resources not arranged for by marriage vows, but by direct blood lineage.

Hence, many West African women functioned in a far more egalitarian social and political environment than women in Europe or in Asia. In Africa, women served as co-regents, queens, and heads of state, from the earliest times through the recent centuries. At issue, quite simply, is the fact that women's status in the Middle Ages deteriorated everywhere that a belief system evolved which valued the idea of "owning" things. Property relations were applied to people—for example slavery, female concubinage, and prostitution. Patrilineal descent through the oldest son became the dominate form of passing authority from one generation to the next. This development was contrary to the traditional worship of a Supreme Creator with a female *and* male sacred aspect (like the Orisha and the Obasum in areas of West Africa). Judaism, Christianity, and Islam created and sustained female subordination and undermined the significance accorded women's work and their religious identification with the sacred.

The Enslavement of African Females

Slavers did not carry off old, sick or disabled people. Neither did the slave trade begin and then taper off after twenty years. Much to the detriment of Africa's development, the enslavement and forced transportation of Africans in the Atlantic slave trade lasted anywhere between 245 and 300 years continuous years. In essence, millions of Africa's youths were carried away for three centuries. Africa's development was partially arrested, as the continent lost the productive capacity of many young minds and hands. In conquering the Amerindians and forcibly transporting millions of Africans into the New World, European settlers expropriated the reproductive, earning, and inventive capacity of the enslaved African women who survived the horrible Middle Passage. Enslaved African women were victimized culturally and sexually. Slavery meant the loss of personal and familial control over African female reproduction, and the significantly diminished capacity to influence key events in a child's passage into young adulthood. For instance, an incest taboo was meant to protect children from sexual abuse and to teach them the inappropriateness of sexual involvement with a close blood relative. However, enslaved African women were forced to engage in sexual relations with men not of their own choosing, and hence to conceive and bear children at the whim of white settlers who themselves often arranged their own first-cousin marriages and often insisted on having affairs with their mulatto female children.

African women transported to the New World were treated and defined as beasts of burden, even when they resisted such degradation. African American females were targets of the full force of a virulent white male patriarchy that has been institutionalized into much of the American culture and gradually absorbed by many black men in their quest o be acceptable as "males" on terms set down and defined both explicitly and implicitly by white male misogyny towards women.

The idea that all women are property lies at the root of white male misogyny, which, since 1620, has defined and represented black women as "common property"—as promiscuous, ugly, and undesirable. The idea that white women, on the one hand, are the mothers of white children is the basis for white female "worthiness" and redeems some of the "lost" value white male patriarchy has imposed on women. The idea that white women, on the other hand, are beautiful must begin by the acquisition of skin color privilege, then by possession of sexuality that white males value for their sexual enjoyment. These value-laden criteria lift white women, particularly those with blonde hair and blue eyes, to "cult" level.

It is the European creation of "fallen" womanhood that is responsible for the transmission of misogynist beliefs brought over to the Americas and instilled in the social ordering of colonial American society. Enslaved African women's vulnerability as females, as legally enslaved foreigners, and their subjugation as objects of white male lust who could be violated without moral censure that would follow such violation of even poor white women, affixed a racial *and* sexual oppression. Thereafter, successive generations of enslaved African American women were persecuted by racists and misogynist actions. Deliberate violations of black female personhood conveyed the idea that black women were unacceptable to look at and fit only (to put it in frank language) to serve a white man in his fields or in his bed.

The rape and physical violations of enslaved African women were intended to insure that their sexuality and reproductive capacity belonged to white males. One tires, therefore, of hearing some white scholars strain both the historical realities of what black women endured under slavery and of white male domination of their sexual and reproductive experiences, in order to assert a comparable female oppression among white women settlers who lived as wives. Alongside a cadre of white women who committed themselves to abolitionism as they saw and reported on the degradation of enslaved African women were many white men and women who purported their own greater moral and physical "worthiness" and value precisely because of black women's degradation. Such an attitude is consistent with the evolution of some white settlers' attitudes that someone must be degraded and made into scapegoats for them to feel worthier. Indeed, a pivotal question in examining America's past is how persistent were white men and women in both attempting to instill in African American women racist and misogynist projections (to fear their sexual organs and hate their hair, noses, skin, buttocks, and hips) and in encouraging white women to belittle the value of other females, especially black women. Thus, regardless of the skill, intelligence, and moral fiber a number of enslaved African American women might have possessed, most white settlers displayed their most negative emotions towards the slave trade's most vulnerable people.

The decision to exploit the sex and color of enslaved African women marked the beginning of an African nation in the diaspora—Africa was picked up and forcibly transported across the Atlantic Ocean, forcing its daughters to experience dramatic changes in their personal, legal, social, economic, political, and spiritual status, as well as in the treatment accorded to their persons. Liberal historians have often made a distinction between the status of Africans in 1620 and the decades that followed. While such a distinction has some merit, particularly when one considers the unchecked movement toward enslaving Africans *in perpetuity*, it is important to ask what and whose perspective is being used to consider the issue of the declining status of enslaved Africans. Humanists must attempt to contemplate the experience of enslaved African females as though they were in touch with their values, and beliefs, and not from a detached Eurocentric perspective. Simply put, from an African woman's point of view, forcible removal from Africa under the barbaric and cruel conditions of capture, separation from significant others, white male sexual violence, branding, and other forms of personal degradation and humiliation, remained traumatic and debilitating throughout the period of slavery.

There is little question that African women were outraged, terrified, and brutalized, even with the first boat's arrival in Jamestown in 1619. Already without a country, without a village, without elders (both female and male served as mentors), and without warriors to protect their persons and children, captive African women were vulnerable misunderstood, despised, and mistreated. What was yet to follow was the gross exploitation of forcing black women into legal and social postures for the economic profit and lust of white men. Consistently raped and labeled as "wenches," African women were regarded as sub-human and became the property of white men. White men, ever accustomed to holding white women to a monogamous standard of sexuality, availed themselves of a captive and powerless group of women. As a result, black women gave birth to mulatto children, clear evidence that white males, though professing cultural supremacy and hence disdain for "African wenches," nonetheless maintained sexual relations with them. These actions prompted colonial courts and legislatures to write into law statutes that defined the status of mulatto children, as well as those whose color resembled that of their mothers.

Some historians have argued that the status of black children born in the Americas would await colonial law anyway. One should bear in mind, however, that because significant numbers of the newborn children of African women consistently looked like the white men who had sired them (by force of social practice in sexual relations with enslaved African women) white men, who controlled the Virginia House of Burgesses (where much of colonial law regarding race an sex was first written), provided any white male settler with a legal and economic cover for illicit sexual relations with African women. In 1662, as notes A. Leon Higginbotham, Jr. (in *The Matter of Color*, 1978) the Virginia House of Burgesses ruled that all children born to African women would follow the legal status of their mother: "1662. Act. XII. Children got by an Englishman upon a Negro woman shall be bond or free according to the condition of the mother..." Master-class white males (in opposition to the doctrine embodied in English Law whereby the status of children followed that of their father) wrote colonial law to specify the subjugation of African women. Hence, all children born to enslaved African women followed the status of their mothers, while the color, religion, or legal status of the children's fathers were inconsequential in the sight of the law.

With such a law, Virginia and all of the colonies that followed its lead, tacitly sanctioned the sexual exploitation of African women. At the same time, the states insured that white settler males who sexually used enslaved African women could reproduce the slave population without bearing the expense of "purchasing" abducted Africans at slave markets.

On an interpersonal level, white males vulgarized reproductive sex by insisting on establishing a system of concubinage without any moral imperative to take responsibility for the consequence of their control over African females. As a matter of fact, countless of their control children grew to adulthood looking at their fathers, only to have their fathers deny that English fatherhood meant anything but the ability to exploit women and children of color. Unlike some other places in the Americas where mulattoes were enumerated as a separate segment of the population—thereby, acknowledging the incidence of interracial sexual liaisons—white males in colonial America insisted on defining even their own children by African women as black. Hence, instead of the status, race, and religion of males imparting a definitive interpretation to justify the status of children and, thus, their ownership (under the European system of thought, people were owned), children born of enslaved African women on colonial soil had no father as far as the law was concerned.

Essentially, since law follows social custom, the act of sexually exploiting african women well preceded the perceived need to legislate the matter on behalf of the sexual and material interests and passions of white settler males. The denial of white male paternity was one of the early influences that molded the boundaries of American slavery. Sexually exploiting African women while holding constant the value of the white, male head of household, the monogamous, Christian family exposed the contradiction laid down as a part of the founding of the Republic. The reality was that, at any given moment, enslaved and free children—brothers and sisters who looked alike, except for skin pigmentation—existed in a colonial world where the promiscuous sexual conduct of white men went largely unnamed as the rape of captive African women.

Enslaved African women were already desperately exploited and sexually oppressed long before most American historians mark the point of legislation that set down in writing what was already crystallizing in social practice—that Africans would be debased, subject to cruelty, and enslaved *in perpetuity* Indeed, as we are once again reminded by Higginbotham, the sexuality and reproductive behavior of African women was dominated by white males long before the Virginia status of 1691 that stated, "A great inconvenience may happen to this country by the setting of Negroes and mulattoes free."

Assessment of the codification of racism and sexism into American social practice and law must acknowledge the incipient racism *and* sexism of the colonial era. In her groundbreaking book on enslaved black women, *Arn'n't I a Woman?: Female Slaves in the Plantation South* (1985), Professor Deborah Gray White argues that "...color was the absolute determinant of class in antebellum America. To be of Color was mark of degradation, so much so that in most Southern states one's dark complexion was *prima facie* evidence that one was a slave. Black in white society, slave in a free society, woman in a society ruled by men, female slaves had the least formal power and were perhaps the most vulnerable groups of antebellum Americans."

At the same time that enslaved African women's reproductive rights were controlled by white men, the work that black women performed was parallel to that of enslaved African males. Commenting on Black women's work under American slavery in her book, *We Are Your Sisters* (1984), Professor Dorothy Sterling asserts that "By the time she was ten years old, a slave girl was classified as a half-hand. At puberty she was doing the work of a woman, and a woman's work was scarcely distinguishable from man's." Indeed, enslaved African females were worked as hard and steadily as men. Narratives are replete with explicit accounts of enslaved African women performing labor-intensive agricultural work in the fields, while being responsible (simultaneously) for sewing, cooking, cleaning, and caring for children.

The "double duty day" meant that black women toiled under the grueling demands of the white settlers all day, and usually in the evenings, set about doing what was needed to help keep themselves, men, children, and elders. In Sterling's book, black women speak for themselves on this matter:

> This race coming up don't know nothing 'bout hard work. Over there, see a road all turned up and you would see men and women both throwing dirt and rocks; the men would haul it off and the women would take picks and things and get it up. You could, any day see a woman, a whole lot of 'em making on a road. Could look up and see ten women up over dar on the hill plowing and look over the other way and see ten more. I have done ever thing on a farm what a man done 'cept cut wheat. I split rails like a man. I used a iron wedge and drove into the wood with a maul. I drive the gin, what was run by two mules...I fired de furnace for three years. Standin' front wid hot fire on my face. Hard work, but God was with me.

The toll exacted from enslaved African women must have been enormous because labor-intensive work is exhausting. We will probably never really know the extent of miscarriages and health problems borne by black women being worked as mules. Indeed, it is a testament to the black women's resolve and resistance to enslavement—and not to white settler paternalism—that the institution of the black family was sustained at all.

Enslaved African women were instrumental in fashioning an experience of family that resembled the value structure not of white settler communities, but of traditions long cherished, learned and internalized from African First Principles. As captives, black women, like black men and black children lived in two worlds: the highly restrictive and exploitative world that white settlers made, and the close-by world of black people who lived together in the plantation "slave quarters." Herbert Gutman's pioneering book on black families in slavery and freedom underscores the fact that much of the previous scholarship on enslaved African understated the significance of cultural values, structures, and forms that black women had some direct hand in helping to shape. Indeed, because black women and men labored similarly and worked collectively to survive enslavement, egalitarianism between the sexes often prevailed.

Documentary evidence cited in Professor Gutman's copious book, *The Black Family in Slavery and Freedom, 1750–1925*, notes that several important characteristics of African social systems were valued by enslaved Africans, and, when possible, replicated by the sampling of black families that his research uncovered. In researching several plantations located in different areas of the South, Professor Gutman found evidence of enslaved African women and men tracing their descent by organizing their naming patterns in a manner similar to West African matrilineal descent. They used the naming patterns to keep a knowledge of kinship boundaries, sufficient to enforce an incest taboo amongst kinfolk. Not only does Professor Gutman's research provide clear evidence of "organized" attempts to create and sustain meaningful beliefs, values, and "responsible" behaviors, but, very significantly, the enslaved Africans he reported on *were not* emulating, white settler values and beliefs. Hence, black people in some communities in the "slave quarters" created and sustained African-derived beliefs and values, sufficient to create and sustain the basis for a black culture.

Clearly, maternal bonds established during pregnancy and a child's infancy were often disrupted by slave owners. Knowing that white settlers greedily took possession of the fruits of enslaved African women's labor in the fields and the children born from their wombs, most black women set about to define the nature of their emotional relationship with their children from as early in childhood as a child's understanding would permit. Essentially, black children had to learn early on in their youth that they lived in two worlds. Living in a white world of oppression, often brutal and physically controlling at a personal level, and a black world of personal survival and collective group empowerment through self-determination and resistance to exploitation, required dual consciousness. While the responsibility to convey a folklore of resistance to their young rested with all members of enslaved black communities, the mother-child dyad let itself particularly well to black women introducing and affirming important lessons about identity to their young children.

The received historical traditions has most often presented enslaved and free Africans of both genders as victims. Much of this "history" rests on an over simplified assessment and aggrandizement of white settler authority *and on* a gross misunderstanding and underestimation of African women's and men's capability and willingness to resist and challenge the imposition of domination. This legacy of racism has produced a scholarship that presents African women as black "blackboards" without a sense of separateness, significance, and importance in the presence of white settlers. It is the folly of seeing omnipotence as a cultural characteristic of whites that has prompted the legacy of depicting African women and men without any redeeming cultural endowments of their own. Much of the scholarship written within this view of African inferiority assumes: 1) that white culture erased whatever little of Africa remained in the minds of enslaved Africans, and 2) that white authority, institutions, and values became as important to enslaved Africans as they were to white settlers. Therefore, it is against such a values backdrop that we pose the question: What was the nature of African American female resistance to enslavement?

White settlers often represented enslaved African women as chattel. While pigs and chickens might reasonably be thought of as animals who without rational thought allow themselves to be pinned up, enslaved Africans acted in ways that subverted slavery. Africans organized overt and covert resistance to being held in bondage against their wills. So, contrary to the mythology of slavery, the reality was that from the start of the institution, white settlers maintained their system of forced servitude with violence, cunning, and, where possible, cooptation of black self-help. While many scholars have accurately described the many contrived boundaries—some very inhumane—the white men, often with the complicity of white women, imposed on enslaved African women, some scholars have presented white valued constraints and physical domination as though blacks obediently obliged because whites willed it so. Again, one might argue that the tendency to see whites as omnipotent often blurred the separate and often uncontrolled black identity and will that characterized the anger and distance between the races almost everywhere that there was plantation slavery. Simply put,

Africans understood that slavery was wrong, and captive Africans knew why white people practiced physical and sexual violence against them.

Enslaved African women knew, therefore, that white settlers (through the institution of slavery) sought to betray and rob them of their productive lives; it was clear that many settlers constantly compromised their humanity for greed, lust, and domination over a captive people. African women and men created oral narratives and a folklore tradition that conveyed the moral and ethical issues involved in their struggles against captivity and exploitation. The most fundamental act of struggle is survival, and enslaved Africans in America constantly sought to protect their own humanity from exploitation and cruelty, while also insisting on creating structures for shared communities defined by self-help and philanthropy towards others. Indeed, enslaved African women occupied and utilized a unique place in the enslaved black community. Professor Angela Davis observes in her article "Reflections on the Black Woman's Role in the Community of Slaves" that:

> Even as she was suffering under her unique oppression as female, she was thrust into the center of the slave community. She was, therefore, essential to the *survival* of the community. Not all people have survived enslavement; hence her survival-oriented activities were themselves a form of resistance. Survival, moreover, was the prerequisite for all higher levels of struggle.

As such, even when enslaved African women were legally prohibited from learning to read or write, owning or conveying property, testifying against a white person, serving on juries, defending themselves from white violence, or obtaining patents for their numerous inventions, unknown numbers of enslaved African women somehow taught themselves to read. They usually read *The Bible*, and then they and others taught still others adults and children.

On a spiritual level, enslaved African women struggled to see themselves as "worthy" human beings because violence hurt, injured, and belittled their lives. Most enslaved Africans knew that white people lied to themselves when they denied what orally transmitted African traditions—the oldest on the planet—had for centuries taught African peoples about the soul and one's eternal relationship with one's ancestors and the deities. Even as white settlers initially insisted that enslaved Africans were ineligible for baptism, and decades later insisted that, even with baptism, their status would remain unchanged, black people had to sustain a spiritual awareness, inextricably connected to the spirit and the discarnate world to which we all return.

Since it was clear that many white settlers made religious principles follow their greed and penchant for violence, black people perceived an awareness of the difference and distance between being white and being black. Accordingly, spiritual, moral, and ethical world views became crystallized as racial groups identified values and actions, and over many decades the enslaved became the champions and guardians of the concepts of justice, freedom, equality, equity, human civil rights, disobedience and nonviolent direct action protest, and violent struggle against any form of oppression.

Black people readily understood that dual nature of providing for themselves so as to empower their own self-determination whenever possible (given the very real limitations and constraints that pushed in on their consciousness and persons everyday) and insisting on resisting white control and enslavement by acting to weaken and destroy slavery. Out of the many decades of enslavement, there emerged a deeply ingrained and passionately pursued commitment to resistance, protest, and individual and collective empowerment. This active tradition of protesting subjugation and exploitation and resisting injustice and inequality has factored significantly in the participation of African American women in the evolution of the black Church, and in the many spiritual rituals and practices that draw on the traditional religions of West African peoples, particularly the Yoruba and the Akan. Essentially, worshiping the sacred realm and pursuing freedom and equality on the earthly realm have always been inextricably linked and an unmistakably black aspiration.

Clearly, enslaved African women had to conspire against oppression in order to do something good for themselves and others. Ultimately, one conspired to escape enslavement and to somehow bring (or await) loved ones to a place of safety. Many did. However, sometimes enslaved African women, exhausted and desperate from being forced to use their bodies as "baby breeders" on plantations, aborted fetuses or killed infants and themselves rather than continue in a seemingly unending nightmare. On plantations where enslaved African women were forced to undergo one pregnancy after another, it was not uncommon for them to birth twenty or more babies. It was the kind of experience that devoured a woman's body, mind, and soul.

Alongside many forgotten women whose struggles for dignity and self-direction in their own lives prompted their covert and even overt resistance to enslavement, appear strong black women whose escape from slavery informed their insistence to aid in the liberation of others. Harriet Tubman (1820?–1913) was one of many enslaved African American women whose insistence on being free of slavery's cruel domination prompted her attempted escape to freedom. In a daring, willful, and persistent manner, Harriet Tubman succeeded in escaping captivity, and returned repeatedly to liberate both her family members and others, despite serious and dangerous obstacles. She was one of the driving forces in the effectiveness of the Underground Railroad.

Black women who displayed courage and risk-taking in challenging slavery and escaping enslavement and captivity were most certainly mentors for others, as were previously enslaved African American women who spoke publicly or wrote articles and books in the struggle against slavery. Sojourner Truth (1797–1883), born Isabella Baumfree, a committed and effective abolitionist and women's suffrage advocate, was freed by a 1827 New York Emancipation Act. Once the shackles of slavery were removed, Sojourner Truth began to renounce slavery and the absence of women's rights. Truth lectured publicly, often appearing before white audiences who were silenced by her moral conviction, candor, accuracy, and intense commitment to see all forms of slavery, including the subjugation and sexual domination of women, abolished. She is here quoted (in Marilyn Richardson's book, *Maria W. Stewart: America's First Black Woman Political Writer*, 1987) from two public addresses, the first recorded by Francis D. Gage, at the Akron Women's Rights Convention on May 29, 1851, and the second recorded in Battle Creek, Michigan in 1856, by Thomas Chandler, recording secretary for the Michigan Friends of Human Progress:

> Dat little man dar, he say women can't have as much rights as men cause Christ wasn't a woman! Whar did Christ come from? From God and a woman! If de

fust woman God ever made was strong enough to turn the world upside down all alone, dese women togedder ought to be able to turn it back, and get it right sid up again...I have had children and yet never owned one...I did have love for them, but what was become of it?...I have had five children and never could take one of them up and say, "My child' or 'My children," unless it was when no one could see me....

In a book edited by Maria Child, *Incidents in the Life of a Slave Girl*, Linda Brent (1818–1896), an enslaved African American woman who escaped enslavement in South Carolina, presented a scathing indictment of the brutality and misogyny directed against black females. Her autobiography is a call to anti-slavery activism in its poignant and sincere personal account and description of the physical and sexual exploitation directed against enslaved African American females by white males. Brent's contribution to the Abolitionist Movement was important, for her words countered the denial of southern whites and the mythology of black female promiscuity deliberately fostered by white supremacy misogynists.

It is important to bear in mind that the struggles of many other enslaved women were much more difficult than the challenges of either free African American women, or the numbers of progressive white women who also worked to abolish slavery. The obstacles that confronted enslaved African American women who *took* their freedom, or were granted liberty, were often numerous; overcoming or working despite illiteracy, delivering speeches or lecturing often to literate audiences that valued book learning, working as activists with little if any material or financial support, and traveling around to meet and talk with other anti-slavery advocates, often alone and at risk of physical violence.

Free African American Women

From a demographic standpoint, free African Americans were always a minority of the black population in the United States. In the decades following the Revolution, African American advocacy on behalf of emancipation in many northern states prompted the abolition of slavery, thereby freeing the black populations in those states. By 1800, there were approximately 47,000 free blacks in the North, living mostly in cities. Contrary to popular belief, the free African American population of the South was substantial. Professor Ira Berlin, author of *Slaves Without Masters*, cites the figure of 250,000 free African American in the South by the middle of the nineteenth century.

Life was hard, perhaps nowhere as difficult as under slavery, but free African Americans lived in a tenuous existence in the United States throughout the years of slavery. Many places forbade free African Americans to settle, and, after 1830, cities like Richmond, Virginia, required that free blacks post a monetary bond in order to remain in the cities. Many whites made their animosity toward free African Americans very clear. Free black women were discriminated against at all levels of society except in their own communities. Even in some free black communities, status distinctions based on skin color, literacy, and class differences emerged. African American women lived in a society committed to "racially defined" slavery, which meant that, at any given moment, the freedom so preciously appreciated by free blacks could be compromised or even withdrawn. And so, free African American women took working to promote the development of services and community facilities very seriously. It bears remembering that, since there was an absence of any system of state or local financial intervention, black women and men understood the imperative of working to sustain their own self-help.

In fact, much of the work to support, nurture, and sustain black families was done by African American women, as many free black families in the antebellum period included female and male working adults in the household. Most black families would not have survived without both adult members working and without African American women engaging in a double-duty day, once at home.

With their numbers increasing naturally, free black communities engaged in self-help development and created their own organizations and institutions. Free African American women worked; participated in mutual aid societies; paid dues to benevolent associations; initiated their own women's educational and benefit organizations; wrote and published articles, speeches, and books; supported philanthropic efforts to assist those in need; and helped to institutionalize free black churches. In some instances, free black women started and operated their own businesses, schools, health facilities, and burial associations.

Most free African American women worked in the only jobs available to them: washing, sewing, cooking, cleaning, nursing, and caring for other people's children. Even into the twentieth century, black women were relegated to service jobs such as those described above. More prosperous free African American women were able to acquire an education, often at colleges like Oberlin that opened their doors to blacks in the nineteenth century. For the most part, they worked as teachers, or started businesses or organizations, or both. The businesses operated by free African American women included catering, bakeries, hair salons, boarding houses, milliners, and dressmaking. The women used their earnings to start institutions such as schools, burial insurance companies, societies for the educational improvement of girls and women, churches, and board and lodging houses (modern precursors to inns and motels). A partial list of organizations that African American women supported in the antebellum era include:

> 1790 — Brown Fellowship Society, Charleston, S.C.
> 1815 — Burial Ground Society of the Free People of Color, Richmond, Va.
> 1828 — African Educational and Benevolent Society, Providence, R.I.
> 1832 — Afric-Female Intelligence Society, Salem, Mass.
> 1837 — Madame Bernard Couvent Institute for Colored Youth
> 1838 — Female Benevolent Society of Troy, N.Y.
> 1843 — New York Benevolent Branch of Bethel
> 1843 — Ladies Union Benevolent Society, Charleston, S.C.
> 1843 — Union Band Society of New Orleans (secret society)

Professor George F. Jackson (in his *Black Women Makers of History*, 1975) has cited the research of Benjamin Quarles to identify the significant efforts of numerous self-help and philanthropic organizations, many involving African American women's efforts and support:

> Philadelphia...outstripped all other cities, nearly one-half of it's adult Negro population holding membership in mutual aid societies in the 1840s. In 1838 the city could count 80 such organizations, with an average membership of 93.

Ten years later the roster of mutual benefit societies had risen to 106, comparing favorably with the total of 119 such groups in the entire state of New York in 1844. Most of the groups were related Dorcas groups comprised of women.

After attending the everyday survival needs of their community, many African American women were preoccupied with destroying slavery, not only because free blacks would not ultimately be safe until slavery was gone, but also because all black people comprehended the horror that enslavement imposed on the majority of African Americans living in the United States. While many more free African American women than can be profiled here worked assiduously to abolish slavery *and* improve the status of black women, the published speeches of Maria Stewart provide a poignant and forceful narrative reflecting the views they held. According to Marilyn Richardson's published volume of Maria Stewart's (1803–1879) speeches,

> Stewart, the first American woman to lecture in public on political themes and leave extant copies of her texts, was a woman of profound religious faith, a pioneer black abolitionist, and a defiant champion of women's rights...Likely the first black American to lecture in defense of women's rights, Stewart constructed a series of arguments citing feminist precedents from biblical, classical, and historical sources.

Maria Stewart and other African American women committed themselves to actions that positively influenced the black community and challenged the continued existence of slavery. Stewart delivered public speeches, some of which were later published in the *Liberator*, the anti-slavery publication edited by William Lloyd Garrison.

Historians have been slow to report that, so far as we can ascertain at this time, the Afric-American Female Intelligence Society, founded in Salem, Massachusetts in 1832, was the first female anti-slavery organization in the United States. When the organization met in the Spring of 1832, Maria Stewart addressed the black women present and implored "...O woman, woman! Upon you I call; for upon your exertions almost entirely depends whether the rising generation shall be any thing more than we have been or not. O woman, woman! Your example is powerful, your intelligence great..."

African American females actively resisted the institution of slavery and the propaganda of pro-slavery men and women in the country that argued that enslavement was good for black people. Many women of color invested large amounts of their time and resources toward the destruction of slavery. It must be remembered that overt and covert resistance *together* undermined slavery. It can never be said, therefore, that enslaved and free African American females did little to weaken the institution of slavery. It can also never be asserted that African American women were not almost everywhere actively involved in self-help work, mutual aid assistance, and philanthropic giving and charity to the needy. Most important is the fact that black women ignored the illusion of invincibility that the white settler imposed slavery presented. Many may attribute the actual collapse of the institution of slavery to the Confederacy's defeat, but, in significant ways, slavery died as each day of subversive thinking, speaking, and acting empowered black people and their progressive white allies to persistently and continuously weaken the basis of its mental hold on the nation.

Freedwomen

Freedom from enslavement was legislated by Congress following the Civil War. African American women were among the 4.5 million freed persons who needed help and encouragement, and constituted a significant number of those who offered and were called upon to "administer" much needed assistance. Educated African American women immediately turned their attention to assisting in the massive effort to provide for millions of black people, emancipated, and yet poor, largely illiterate, and in need of communities that could nurture and support them. Sizeable numbers of these women worked as schoolteachers, nurses, and missionaries.

Efforts to promote the civil and human rights of African Americans, preoccupied African American women in the decades following Emancipation. The most dramatic and significant work undertaken by them in the years between emancipation from enslavement and the turn of the century arose from focused efforts on behalf of promoting self-determination within black rural and urban communities. For the first time on American soil, African American women joined with African American men in celebrating a new found freedom. The challenges before them were numerous, but none so ominous as the challenges they had already faced in helping bring down slavery. Nonetheless, hard times followed slavery's demise, primarily because a nation of white people set about either to promote, or watch and tacitly condone, racial segregation and second-class citizenship for black Americans.

Organized white terrorism emerged as the agenda of white supremacy in such groups as the Ku Klux Klan. Violence against African American peoples intensified in the form of lynching, rape, burning, mutilation, and sexual assault against African American girls and women. An African American female leadership remained committed to realizing the rights and privileges of citizenship for African Americans. Black women like Ida B. Wells-Barnett (1862–1930)—journalist, lecturer, social activist, clubwoman, feminist, and anti-lynching crusader—worked assiduously to publicize and expose the atrocities being committed against black people in the South. When personal friends of Ms. Wells-Barnett were murdered by and angry white mob in Memphis for no reason other than that the black men operated a successful business that the whites envied, Wells-Barnett understood for the first time that the allegations of black men raping white women were actually clandestine maneuvers by violent whites to shroud their violence against successful blacks in ambiguity and denial.

It was in her capacity as a journalist that she worked most effectively documenting white terrorism against black people in the South. Her accounts of the barbaric treatment directed at hundreds of African Americans contributed significantly to an increasing anti-lynching movement in the U.S. and abroad amongst progressive-minded white newspaper editors and their constituencies in countries like England. Thus, Ida B. Wells-Barnett, just as the African American activist women who preceded her in their struggles against injustice, often risked injury or death to challenge the lynching and physical violence directed against African American initiative.

Mary Church Terrell (1863–1954) was yet another vibrant, active, and committed African American women who, in the years following emancipation, worked as an educator, clubwoman, writer, and activist. For the most part, black women's historians have been the scholars and writers who have brought many of the African American clubwomen out of obscurity. Intensifying their efforts between 1890 and 1895, African American women sought to use the club movement to build a national self-help movement. Ms. Terrell is credited with working with many other women to help empower black women, who had fewer rights than black men. By the 1890s, Ms. Terrell was a founder and the first president of the National Association of Colored Women (NACW). Terrell, Wells-Barnett, Josephine St. Pierre Ruffin, and Anna Julia Cooper were among the African American women instrumental in establishing a black women's club movement around the myriad and varied activities in which black women involved themselves following the demise of slavery.

For many of them, their involvement as "clubwomen," signaled the continuation of the race and gender activism that had evolved earlier in the century. Indeed, the dual agenda of racial uplift *and* progress for the race's girls and women rang clear as necessary goals of the African American women's club movement. The clubs and the movement stood for anti-racism work, while at the same time the movement promoted the uplift, education, and protection of African American girls and women from virulent white male sexual violence. Indeed, clubwomen pressed for reform as an active part of good civil leadership. Thus, Josephine St. Pierre Ruffin (1842–1924), emerged as a powerful and enigmatic activist on behalf of black women's rights. She is also recognized, as Jessie Carney Smith points out in *Notable Black American Women* (1992), as "a charter member of the Women's Era Club, the National Federation of Afro-American Women, the National Association of Colored Women, and the Northeastern Federation of Women's Clubs."

The African American women's club movement, embodied in the formation of the National Federation of Afro-American Women and the Colored Women's League, existed alongside other women's self-help efforts. African American women started schools and colleges, and engaged in financial ventures. Francis Jackson Coppin (1836–1913), who was born enslaved, attended Oberlin College to fulfill a desire to become a teacher after her aunt purchased her freedom. In fulfilling her life's goal, Coppin eventually founded the Institute for Colored Youth, which would later become Cheyney State College in Pennsylvania. Also born enslaved, Anna Julia Cooper (1858–1964), activist, feminist, writer, and Pan-Africanist, graduated from Oberlin College and earned a doctorate in 1925 from the Sorbonne, in Paris. She was an eloquent speaker and prolific writer, authoring significant works such as *A Voice from the South: By a Black Woman from the South* (1892), *Slavery and the French Revolutionist* (doctoral thesis), *Life and Writings of the Grimke Family*, *The Third Step*, and *Le Pelerinage de Charlemagne*. Most important is the fact that Cooper, like so many other African American women, never faltered in her dual commitment to the racial uplift of all black Americans *and* to women's self-help empowerment.

It bears remembering that, through much of the twentieth century, the issue of racism and Jim Crow segregation has severely limited opportunities and options for the majority of African Americans. Throughout the decades of racial exclusion from all but the most marginal levels of economic development in America, African American women and men struggled to survive and pave a way for their children. Many working-class African American women living in the deep South had taken their children and moved north to escape the debilitating effects of the crop-lien system. While historians have emphasized the "lure" of jobs and education opportunities in the cities, one should be mindful that tenancy, share-cropping, white greed, and violence all conspired to "push" thousands of African Americans out of the South. The vast majority of African American women worked just to make ends meet, doing the most menial work in the society. In fact, through the nineteenth, and into most of this century, working-class African American women have been virtually excluded from union membership, as have been large numbers of African American men. Most important, white racism worked to obstruct black talent from taking its rightful place in American society. Even as lynching and sexual violence against African American men and women continued, and economic marginality in a society that professed opportunity for all was held constant by the ideology of white supremacy, African American women were among those persons who stood up for civil rights and racial uplift.

The survival of the black family has been a major issue in this century. In many ways, African American communities resemble colonized communities of people of color in what is often called the Third World. Why? Because, until very recently African Americans and other people of color in the United States were specifically excluded from economic development and participatory democracy, in a situation reminiscent of Third World past colonial conditions where skin color *and* gender became defining and qualifying personal attributes. In the U.S., one sees a historical pattern of internal colonialism, whereby black labor and productive capacity have been held captive to white nation-building goals and strategies. While an enforceable body of human and civil rights law has made the essential difference in the capacity of African Americans to change the operation of the law, and to some extent the operation of social custom (that is, some discernible barriers to inclusion have come down, like signs marking segregated public facilities), large numbers of black Americans have been held in poverty by policies and practices that maintain systemic disadvantage and exclusion. We have to begin to name this process of exclusion from development in urban ghettos and impoverished rural areas, so as to see through the illusion of "lazy, shiftless, bad people" to a more astute understanding of how the system excludes and marginalizes people it targets as "unworthy" because of skin color and sex.

In this century, there have been civil rights activists who have worked assiduously to strengthen and protect the very fabric of the black family, for, at some point, unmitigated poverty destroys peoples' capacity even to stay together as a family. While many Americans have suffered, during hard times, racism and sexism have acted to accentuate suffering for people of color, and in the context of this anthology of essays, for African American peoples in particular. For example, historians of African American "history" have often focused their attention on black male leadership in this century—Washington, DuBois, Garvey, Powell, Randolph, King, Malcolm X, Jackson—often to the exclusion of identifying and assessing the work of African American women who either attained positions of authority or marked the decades in which they lived with personal commitments that helped "race uplift" move forward.

As a civil rights activist, government official, educator, and women's rights advocate, Mary McLeod Bethune (1875–1955) became one of the most important African American women in the country. Born as the fifteenth of seventeen children in Sumner County, South Carolina, Ms. Bethune grew up on a small family farm. Her parents had been emancipated by the Union victory over the Confederacy in the Civil War. Fortunate to attend a small rural mission school, the young

Bethune, like so many of her age, was tremendously influenced by the ideas and the knowledge she gained while in school. Although she initially prepared herself to serve as a missionary in Africa, Bethune was gravely disappointed when her application was turned down on the grounds that the Presbyterian Mission Board did not appoint African Americans to such positions. It would not be the first nor the last time the exclusion based on race would disappoint the young activist.

Having been turned away from service in foreign missions, Ms. Bethune turned her attention to becoming a teacher in Georgia and South Carolina. Her experiences as a teacher convinced her to start an educational institution. Thus, in a rented house with barely the essentials, Bethune started the Daytona Educational and Industrial Institute in Daytona, Florida, in 1904. The school proved a success, and by 1922 it had registered three hundred girls. Among other subjects, the Institute taught nursing and teacher preparatory training. In 1923, Bethune's Institute merged with the coeducational Cookman Institute in Jacksonville, Florida, becoming the Bethune-Cookman College in 1929.

B. Joyce Ross, in an article in *Black Leaders of the Twentieth Century*, describes the hard-working and enigmatic Mary McLeod Bethune as having been someone who, rising from poverty to distinguished leadership, had several careers: "as an educator, she was the architect of Florida's Bethune-Cookman College; as founder and president of the National Council of Negro Women, she was a central figure in the development of the black women's club movement; and, as a worker in politics, she was one of the few blacks who held influential posts in the federal bureaucracy during the administration of Franklin D. Roosevelt." Bethune is credited with working to insure that African Americans received the relief and recovery provisions (food allowances, clothing, commodity surpluses, and low-cost housing) allocated by the federal government during the New Deal era. Very real constraints operated to thwart the work of Bethune and that of others. On paper,, benefits and provisions were to be dispensed according to the white racial dogma of "separate but equal," which ordered *all* social relations in America. In reality, the grossly unequal distribution of subsidies, rations, and allocations of spending for basic services predominated everywhere. Bethune used her appointment and involvement in the Roosevelt cabinet to press national state, and local governments to do as much for the nation's suffering black communities as was being done to assist white communities.

While the 1950s are acknowledged as the decade of change, it should be remembered that significant events in the 1940s intensified the relationships of people of color to power. By the 1940s, significant events absorbed many African American women in work, war, and activism on behalf of change. Between 1942 and 1944, the Department of War organized the Women's Reserve of the Navy (WAVES) and the Women's Reserve of the Coast Guard (SPARS) and admitted African American women, though into segregated units. With large numbers of American men at war in Europe, including nearly 980,000 African American men, as many as 1 million more African American women entered civilian jobs in 1944 than in 1940, although it should be noted that they were seldom ever paid the same wages as the men who performed similar tasks.

As the decade of the 1940s unfolded , an increasing African American females militancy began to explode into action that prompted and reinforced the existing dissatisfaction felt by African American women. In addition to their increased involvement in the club movement, sororities, mutual aid societies, and numerous other African American self-help activities, African American women emerged as forceful agents of change in the lives of rural and urban black Americans. Many African American women and men knew and understood that they were never going to break even, let alone get ahead in the rural South. Many of these were working women who for the most part raised large numbers of children on barely subsistence wages. While their lives were not filled with social festivities and the honors earned by working to build educational institutions, many were instrumental in the survival and uplift of large numbers of black children who grew up understanding that their task was to insist on inclusion in American society. For those dreams to become a reality, many of them had to impress their mark on American society by pulling down the contrived boundaries of racial exclusion and sexual subjugation.

Generally, students of "herstory" think of Rosa Parks as the first black woman to refuse obedience to the white South's adherence to strict observance of segregation in public facilities. Yet, eight years prior to Rosa Parks's daring act of disobedience, a courageous and determined African American women named Irene Morgan sued a bus company and the Commonwealth of Virginia over her right to challenge segregation laws when traveling via interstate carriers. Like several other landmark Supreme Court cases in the 1940s, *Morgan vs. Virgina* (1946) opened the way for still greater activism by African Americans on behalf of realizing long-denied civil rights. Progressive precedents often enable people to keep the momentum of positive change ever moving forward. Many African American women understood that a system of second-class citizenship had to be challenged for the good of black people then, as well as for the future of as yet unborn black children who would inherit the same nightmare in the American society that black adults struggled to reform. Hence, all civil rights activism in this century has been undertaken with a sense of purpose and purposefulness.

African American women have also distinguished themselves as civil rights activists and human rights advocates. Few realize that the Great Awakening of the twentieth century—the Civil Rights movement—stands as one of the important precursors to the contemporary human rights movement. Forceful and often intensely purposeful African American women, like their predecessors, rightly answered the marginality that white America imposed on the majority of black people with political protest, community organizing, and advocacy for women's rights. It was an everyday woman—Rosa Parks (1913–)—who got tired of segregation and who, by refusing to move to the back of the bus in Montgomery in December 1955, became a Civil Rights activist. Ella Baker (1903–1986), educated at Shaw University, distinguished herself as a movement theoretician and grassroots level organizer.

As important as Ella Baker was to the Civil Rights movement, however, it was not until PBS produced the documentary *Fundi* that people understood Baker's central importance to many of the movement's key activities and achievements. For instance, having graduated from Shaw University in the 1920s, Baker busied herself in helping to organize the Young Negro Cooperative League in 1932. By the 1940s, she was very much involved in the National Association for the Advancement of Colored People (NAACP) and, following *Brown vs. Board of Education, Topeka, K.S.* in the 1950s, committed herself to assisting in the formation of the Southern Christian Leadership Conference (SCLC). It was from her vantage point as associate director of the newly formed Civil Rights organization that Baker traveled to her alma mater in the winter of 1960 to meet with black student

activists who would eventually, with her support, form an new organization—the
Student Nonviolent Coordinating Committee (SNCC).

It is interesting that, against the wishes of many of her own peers and colleagues in SCLC, Baker chose to support African American students who met in
Raleigh, N.C. in their quest to fashion an organization where their voices would
shape policy. Many of Baker's contemporaries, including Dr. Martin Luther King,
Jr., wanted to see the students who met at Shaw University in February 1960 form
themselves into a youth chapter of the SCLC. Essentially, her leadership style
helped pave the way for a bridge between the older adult leadership of civil rights
organizations like the NAACP, SCLC, and CORE, and the student-led SNCC.
Still later, in 1964, the enigmatic Baker was pivotal in the establishment of the organization which, presided over by Fannie Lou Hamer, represented the political
aspirations in Mississippi, namely, the Mississippi Freedom Democratic Party. As
an organizer, Civil Rights activist, and educator, Ella Baker was, indeed, one of
black America's most precious and prized leaders.

Other African American women activists in the Civil Rights movement include Daisy Bates (1920–), a journalist; Fannie Lou Hamer (1917–1977), a
grassroots organizer; and Diane Nash (1938–), a student organizer who inherited the legacy of struggle and resistance. Unfortunately, many of these women
are unknown to the average student, and yet the very progress that many now
celebrate following the tumultuous years of the Civil Rights movement. Simply
stated, the movement could not have gone forward without the vision, foresight,
commitment, courage, and organizing skills of these and many other African
American women.

Alongside the women who were visible in local, organizational, or student leadership in the movement, have been African American women like Dorothy Height
(1912–), civil and women's rights activist, and president of the National Council
of Negro Women since 1957; Shirley Chisholm (1924–), author and elected official to the New York State Assembly and the United States House of Representatives, and founder of the National Political Congress of Black Women (NPCBW);
Barbara Charline Jordan (1936–), lawyer, educator, appointee to the Lyndon B.
Johnson Centennial Chair in National Policy, and elected official to the Texas State
Senate and, in 1973, to the United States House of Representatives ; Eleanor
Holmes Norton (1938–), attorney, head of the New York City Human Rights
Commission in 1970, and most recently, delegate to Congress on behalf of the District of Columbia; and Marian Wright Edelman (1913–), lawyer, children's rights
activist, and president of the Children's Defense Fund. While these few names
highlight very visible African American females leadership, it is important to note
that many others in civil rights, education, business, entrepreneurship, science, law,
medicine and technology, government service, the arts, sports, and entertainment
have contributed accomplishments and service to their families and communities.

Despite the obstacles to racial uplift and women's rights presented by very real
impediment to participatory democracy in this century, many African American
women have worked to provide a way for their children and the children of those
who will come in the future to have a meaningful first class citizenship in American society. It is imperative that black people's tradition of struggle and resistance
be documented, so that they will be mindful of where they have come from. It is
also vital that opposition and risk do not deter them, and that individual achievements on behalf of a "common good"—racial uplift and women's and children's

rights—and a collective whole continue in the minds, hearts, and actions of African American females. It has been and is quite literally the case that African American females hold up one-half of black people's destiny.

Summary

It is clear by now that this essay is much more than a chronological examination of the major themes in African American women's "herstory." Elsewhere in this volume, this writer has analyzed the chronology of African Americans, dating from the Reconstruction era to the recent decades in this century. There is a discernible difference between the two chapters presented in this anthology, not just because one chapter is on black women's "herstory," while the other chapter presents an encompassing assessment of the African American nation, but also because this chapter is part of the scholarship that charts new ground in its presentation as a separate chapter on black women's "herstory." This chapter is important precisely because it seeks to set out the major theoretical *and* conceptual issues, even as it also presents a brief chronology of the major events in the scholarship that relates to African American women, major issues, themes, and personalities in African American women's "herstory." Hence, the chapter requires the student to examine: 1) one's assumptions about the consequence of the intersection of race and sex; 2) the impact of the societal construction of the meaning of gender; 3) the myriad experiences deriving from female gender that have been shaped and influenced by misogynist beliefs and practices; 4) perceptions about white cultural values and beliefs; 5) assumptions that undergird imprecise language and biased naming; 6) the consequence of starting a people's history in their experience of domination and exploitation; and 7) the uses of "history" and "herstory" for those living now, as the past lives among us in the present in the form of beliefs and attitudes about what is and what is not so.

It is because African American women have been marginalized in African American history that this chapter is so necessary. (The editor is to be commended for his insight in perceiving the importance of this chapter to the volume.) In recent years, scholars of history and a variety of other academic disciplines have been challenged to reconsider the consequence of the invisibility, or objectification of females, and, in this instance, African American females in the historical narrative. Too often, African American females have gone unidentified as persons and as active subjects in history. For instance, throughout most of the scholarship on American or African American history, the habit of referring to *enslaved African females* as "slaves" thoroughly obscures the personhood, nationality, and consequences of the experience of female sexuality for enslaved African, and then subsequently, African American females. A "slave" is the *object* of beliefs about owning people as property. Scholars who uniformly reference an enslaved people as "slaves," tacitly or explicitly objectify the persons they are discussing. The habit of doing this to black people's "history" is so widespread that picking up almost any American history book will illustrate the point.

Because our thinking has been so influenced by the tendency to see women as passive "objects" that men act upon, we need to be mindful that the illusion of passivity creates "victims" in our own understanding of history. In much the same way that white scholarship has encouraged us to see all people of color as "objects," always acted upon by the will and actions of white males, so, too, sexism encourages us to see all women as "objects" who are acted upon by white men, and all other males of color. Such thinking about black people and especially about black women, who have so intensely resisted oppression belongs in the realm of mythology.

At issue is the inherited tradition in American history of seeing white males as active subjects on the stage of evolution, doing, controlling, conquering, always dominating others. At the other end of the "mythological" spectrum are people of color (women and men), and all women, who are represented as idle, lazy, passive, compliant, acquiescing, waiting to be led, and eager to be dominated and told what to do. Such a mythology ends with white males ordering the world and white females being the objects of white male desire and the receptacles of white male children, while everyone else is on a lower level. Men of color either never achieve manhood, and are perpetually called and treated like "boys," or are perceived to be "bestial," thereby justifying the very worst animalistic impulses of white males to castrate, lynch, and burn alive black men.

Women of color, especially African women in America's history, have been treated as breeding machines, white men's prostitutes, work mules, and as ugly "caldrons" against which the virtues of white womanhood, (beginning with the white female's skin being the ticket to acceptability or privilege) could be compared and exalted. In other words, the oppression of African women in North America has been intensely physical, psychological, and spiritual. Racial slavery, *evolved*, that is, a captive labor force grew naturally because of the existence of captive African women, on whose backs rested the full burden of reproducing an African American labor force in the New World.

Treated as objects of sexual license from the moment of capture, we will never know or feel the misery suffered (perhaps to the point of death) by countless, now nameless and faceless African women. Ironically, the writer can barely remember a scholarly examination of slavery that stated that African women were most certainly used as sexual objects in the baracoons (fortress-like encampments along the West African coast where captive Africans were forcibly detained) and on the slave ships that crossed the Atlantic Ocean. Nor has there been a penetrating analysis of how white males used coerced authority—such as withholding food from black women who resisted or refused the sexual overtures of white males.

We know that, wherever African women were held in slavery, white men talked and wrote innocuously about white male propriety to the point where whites, and apparently some blacks, came to believe that it was promiscuous black women who presented such a problem for civilized white Christian males. This kind of "blaming the victim" mythology has taken hold in American culture because of the relatively unquestioned sexism that has existed alongside a virulent racism—licensing and re-enforcing the institution of slavery *and* concubinage in America. It has even been the case that some black male scholars and writers in this century have directed their anger at black women for being vulnerable to white men. Hence, black women have been violated and exploited by white men, and, in the twentieth century, sometimes scorned by black males and blamed for their *own* victimization. There is much work to be done to clarify the basis for this new direction in black male anger. As far as the historical record is concerned, however, there appears to be no evidence, either in published sources, letters, or the slave narratives that African American males blamed African American females for the power the white settler males exerted over black females in earlier centuries.

Misogyny, like racism, transfers the blame for oppression not onto those who exploit and victimize, but onto those who do not control the production of information, and, hence, image and myth making. For as long as racist, misogynist, and sexist views obstruct the historical record, then females and males of color will be victimized by the historical record, after having been victimized by the oppression that the historical record obscures.

If African peoples in African American history have been reduced to non-humans — productive unites because of the imprecise use of language — and if the tendency is to attribute more power to white settler culture than it is due and to make assumptions about the absence of a black culture, then scholars have also been remiss in their assessment of issues that involve an analysis of the intersection of race and sex. In other words, misogyny is as powerful as racism in obscuring or denying that there are significant issues that are particular to women of color, that should concern us all. "Herstory" means that the facts about the experiences of female sex, and, in the context of African American females, what the intersection of race and sex has come to mean, are examined in a serious way.

For too long and in too many varying contextual situations, the issues that are significant in the lives of African American females have been ignored or presumed to be addressed by a concern to articulate a voice for racial uplift of the "nation." At issue is the fact that the practice of speaking in a monosexual voice about an entire people obscures the diverse range of real life issues that the construction of gender has generated. The student explores issues that are significant to African American females not just to illuminate how the experience of being a person of color and a female in a society that is intensely anti-female and anti-people of color complicates matters, but also to assess how the experience of being a female in black communities that have internalized misogyny brings it own set of issues and problems. We might wish that racism and sexism were only issues that affect black people across racial and sexual lines, but the truth of the matter is that misogyny undermines and destroys the viability of relationships between African American females and males.

Between 1620 and 1865, the majority of African women, whether involuntarily transported via the Middle Passage, or born to African women in white settler colonies, were enslaved. Two points stand out in stark contrast to many scholarly discussions about slavery that linguistically de-gender slaves, but actually hold male issues constant. For instance, in most history books on slavery, the discussion about slavery generally proceeds with an analysis of the intensification of racism in white settler attitudes towards blacks and native people of color. Many scholars either look for examples of overt resistance or protest to slavery's domination, or they attempt to document some amount of kindly white paternalism. The student must question what is missing from such analyses.

This chapter has suggested, to begin with, that discussing slavery *only* from a series of questions that assume gender uniformity is theoretically problematic and inaccurate. African women were treated with a degree of violence against their persons that not only differed from the violence transferred onto African males, but was far more corrosive of personal dignity. To be sure, the European white males who came face-to-face with African women were, socialized to see their women as their own property. Captured, vulnerable, and enslaved women could be and most often were seen and treated as common property and raped by white men. That is, European male patriarchal beliefs pre-dating the Middle Ages by centuries had long encouraged the treatment of captured women as objects of violence and sexual license. Humans who are, in fact, treated as non-humans are the most vulnerable since it is precisely their humanity that is categorically denied. Many scholars have for a very long time denied the manner in which captive African women, obliged to bear the sexual violence of white men who cared no more for them than if they were animals, were treated.

This chapter has placed African American females in an Old World cultural context. Not without a cultural past, African First Principles everywhere influenced the formation of values about personal identity, and the significance of kinship and one's family. African First Principles shaped the development of people's values and beliefs about the material world, resources, and institutions of governing. Many traditional West African societies were more like "partnership societies" than "dominator societies." Within these, the austere forms of patriarchy associated with European male domination of women did not exist. For instance, European men created a belief system in which they are purported to "own" European women and possess the legal power of life or death over women and children. In the centuries before European penetration of Africa's interior, most West African women did not live under a system of individual male domination over others through property relations in persons and things. In addition, many West African women earned and accrued respect as workers, traders, mothers, mediums, and healers.

The concept of a "common good" served as one of the foundations of African philosophy, and it has continued as a highly valued concept and guide for personal action towards one's familial and communal good. Many historians have long been more interested in perceiving black Americans to be without culture, than on identifying and articulating the mechanisms for the conveyance and transference of the African First Principles — principles that were apparent in the formation of black self-help, mutual aid, benevolent, and secret societies during the antebellum period. It is important to remember that culture is ideas, that ideas travel in people's heads, and that peoples's commitments to ideas travel in their hearts. Culture is destroyed when a people is destroyed. Enslavement, however, was not analogous to genocide, for, if it were, African Americans would not be here today.

Although the mythology created by white southerners invoked images of either a docile Mammy or a harlot Jezebel, the reality of black women's lives (where plantation slavery defined sexual and material exploitation) required black women to find and use whatever well springs of personal power they possessed. Simply stated, enslavement robbed each successive generation of black people of an unfettered freedom. Enslavement also meant underdevelopment for black people and self-development for whites, not because, as whites insisted, Africans were an inferior people destined to be dominated by whites, but because whites were an aggressive nationalistic breed determined to expropriate other people's lifetimes in order to erect their own entitlement privileges. As each decade passed, the deepening of white settler resolve to hold African women in slavery was met with the evolution of a pronounced and willful tradition of resistance.

Just because white settlers were inhumane towards enslaved African females, it should not be assumed the African American females became inhuman. Black women resisted enslavement and white settler attempts to destroy the souls of black people. While white males controlled black female reproductive capacity, black females chose who they would love and to whom their primary commitment belonged. Free and enslaved African American women were also instrumental in organizing a kinship system around their children and the children of other black women. By such actions, they often named and taught their children in ways that served the kinship needs of black people, not white settlers.

Whether born free, manumitted, or escaped, free African American women worked to build the black communities in which they lived, worked, raised children, and built institutions along with African American men. Many African American women involved themselves in the nineteenth century's liberation struggle by working to undermine and abolish the institution of slavery. Harriet Tubman, Sojourner Truth, Maria Stewart, Linda Brent, and many other African American women deserve recognition as abolitionist and women's rights advocates.

Emancipation brought African Americans immense joy and, at the same time, great concern to protect their human and civil rights and to uplift and improve themselves. The growth of the Black Women's Club Movement provided a national organizational forum through which to address the joint goals of "race uplift" and "women's rights." Many women worked hard to build the self-help movement that historically has always been so important to African American progress. Ida B. Wells-Barnett, Mary Church Terrell, Francis Jackson Coppin, Anna Julia Cooper, the enigmatic Mary McLeod Bethune, and many other African American women have been instrumental in forging organizational and self-help efforts on behalf of all African Americans.

Throughout the decades of this century, the vast majority of African American women have always worked a double-duty day. In addition to being partners who toiled to help make ends meet, African American women have been the cornerstones of black families, and black extended kinship networks, without which many black children and adults would have perished. Educated, working, middle-class African American women have been instrumental in prompting and promoting civil rights reform, and in starting organizations to channel reform efforts in black communities. Some acted as individuals like Irene Morgan and Rosa Parks; others, like Ella Baker, Diane Nash, Daisy Bates, Fannie Lou Hamer, Dorothy Height, Marian Edelman, Elizabeth Duncan Koontz, and Faye Wattleton, mobilized the creative energies of others and profoundly influenced the Movement and its aftermath. And, finally, there are an increasing number of African American women who have been elected to public office; Shirley Chisholm, Barbara Jordan, Eleanor Holmes Norton, and Maxine Waters, whose terms in service to black people and the nation exemplify the progress that has been made in civil and women's rights during the later decades of this century.

As African American females look to the future, longstanding issues such as civil rights and women's rights remain as important as ever, and access to education and entrepreneurship as significant aspects of economic development must be pursued. Finally, in addition, African Americans need to know that African American females have contributed to a tradition of protest, resistance to oppression, commitment to African American familial viability, and creative initiative in organization building.

Study Questions and Activities

1. What are the issues of contention in the present historiography on African-American Women?
2. Discuss how enslaved African women survived the institution of slavery: What were the obstacles and what were the values which kept their hopes throughout the period?
3. What has been the impact of African American women—both during the slavery period and thereafter—on the uplift of the black communities?
4. Compare and contrast the philosophy and impact of Harriet Tubman and Fannie Lou Hamer on their times.

References

Ira Berlin. *Slaves Without Masters.* New York: Pantheon, 1974.

L. Maria Child (ed.). *Linda Brent: Incidents in the Life of a Slave Girl.* New York: Harcourt Brace Jovanovich, 1973.

Anna Julia Cooper. *A Voice From the South: By a Black Woman from the South.* The Schomburg Library of Nineteenth-Century Women Writers. New York: Oxford University Press, 1988.

Angela Y. Davis. "Reflections on the Black Woman's Role in the Community of Slaves." *The Black Scholar.* December, 1971.

———. *Women, Race, & Class.* New York: Random House, 1981.

Marianna W. Davis (ed.). *Contributions of Black Women to America: The Arts, Media, Business, Law, Sports,* Vol. 1. Columbia, SC: Kenday Press, 1982.

———. (ed.). *Contributions of Black Women to America: Civil Rights, Politics and Government, Education, Medicine, Sciences.* Vol. 2. Columbia, SC: Kenday Press, 1982.

Paul Finkelman (ed.). *Women and the Family in a Slave Society,* Vol. 9. New York: Garland Publishing, Inc., 1989.

Paula Giddings. *When and Where I Enter: The Impact of Black Women on Race and Sex in America.* New York: Wm. Morrow & Co., 1984.

Herbert G. Gutman. *The Black Family in Slavery and Freedom, 1750–1925.* New York: Pantheon, 1976.

A. Leon Higgenbotham, Jr. *In The Matter Of Color, Race & The American Legal Process: The Colonial Period.* New York: Oxford University Press, 1978.

Gloria T. Hull, Patricia Bell Scott, and Barbara Smith (eds.). *All the Women Are White, All the Blacks Are Men, But Some of Us Are Brave: Black Women's Studies.* Old Westbury, NY: Feminist Press, 1982.

George F. Jackson, *Black Women Makers of History: A Portrait.* Oakland, CA: GRT Book Printing, 1975.

Gerda Lerner (ed.). *Black Women in White America: A Documentary History.* New York: Pantheon, 1972.

Bert James Loewenberg and Ruth Bogin (eds.). *Black Women in Nineteenth-Century American Life: Their Words, Their Thoughts, Their Feelings.* University Park, PA: Pennsylvania State University Press, 1976.

(Mrs.) N. F. Mossell. *The Work of the Afro-American Woman.* The Schomburg Library of Nineteenth-Century Women Writers. New York: Oxford University Press, 1987.

Jeanne Noble. *Beautiful Also Are The Souls of My Black Sisters: A History of the Black Woman in America.* Engelwood Cliffs, NJ: Prentice-Hall, Inc. 1978.

Marilyn Richardson (ed.). *Maria W. Stewart: America's First Black Woman Political Writer—Essays and Speeches.* Bloomington, IN: Indiana University Press, 1987.

LaFrances Rogers-Rose (ed.). *The Black Woman.* Beverly Hill, CA: Sage Publications, 1980.

B. Joyce Ross. "Mary McLeod Bethune and the National Youth Administration: A Case Study of Power Relationships in the Black Cabinet of Franklin D. Roosevelt," in John Hope Franklin and August Meier (eds.). *Black Leaders of the Twentieth Century.* Urbana, IL: University of Illinois Press, 1982, pp. 191–220.

Sandi Russell. *Render Me My Song: African American Women Writers from Slavery to the Present.* New York: St. Martin's Press, 1990.

Six Women's Slave Narratives. The Schomburg Library of Nineteenth-Century Women Writers, New York: Oxford University Press, 1988.

Jessie Carney Smith (ed.). *Notable Black American Women.* Detroit, MI: Gale Research Inc., 1992.

Dorothy Sterling (ed.). *We Ar Your Sisters: Black Women ink the Nineteenth-Century.* New York: W. W. Norton & Co., 1984.

Deborah Gray White. *Ar'n't I a Woman? Female Slaves in the Plantation South.* New York: W. W. Norton & Co., 1985.

27

The Health of Africa and its Diaspora: Confronting Crisis and Charting New Directions

Almaz Zewde

Introduction

Health is the foundation of human well-being and progress. Nowhere is this realization more ingrained in the very fabric and consciousness of society than in Africa. There is a great deal of preoccupation with health and remaining healthy in African communities. Certain metaphysical practices, often misunderstood as negative superstition by outsiders, are mechanisms to attain holistic healing and attempts to ward off potential afflictions.

Africa's health and healing practices benefit from both biomedical (western) and traditional medical systems. The application of western medicine and medical technology has been most successful in the control or eradication of menacing epidemic diseases like measles, small pox, malaria, schistosomiasis (bilharzia), polio, river blindness and other communicable diseases. In most African countries, people seek traditional and biomedical or western style medical services in closely comparable proportions (Warren, 1982, table 1, Kramer and Thomas, 1982, 166, Reid, 1982, 121). But a number of researchers find that both supply constraints of western medicine (Reid, 1982, 129, Warren, 1982, World Bank, 2004 table 3) and the trust people have in the holistic approach of traditional medicine (Reid, 1982, 130–137, Kramer and Thomas, 1982, 166–169) steer people toward traditional medicine in ever greater numbers. The problem of scarcity and lack of expansion of western-type medical services has worsened since the start of implementation of World Bank Structural Adjustment Programs (SAP) starting in the early 1980s (Koblinsky, Timyan and Gay, 1993, 6–8). Part of the SAP requirement is trimming down all government expenditures on social services such as health and education. Without people's heavy reliance on traditional medicine, hospitals and clinics organized in the western medical tradition would simply be overwhelmed by demand and unable to provide even the meager services they render to the few.

In many Sub-Saharan African countries, as much as 85% of the health budget is used to organize hospital and out-patient facilities that effectively serve no more than 10% of the population (Warren, 1982, 94). Warren gives some glimpses at rural-urban disparities in the availability of western style medical services. He provides a picture for Ghana during the early 1980s, putting the urban physician/population ratio at 1/ 10,000, but that for rural areas at 1/100,000. Even in the new millennium, this great rural/urban divide persists. Rural people generally, and a significant portion of Africa's urban poor rely on traditional medicine to meet their health needs.

Western type health service in Sub-Saharan Africa has somewhat expanded during the 1990s. During 1990–1999, the average physician/population ratio for countries that provided data stood at around 6/100,000 (UNDP, 2002, Table 6). More recent averages put the ratio at 1/15,000.[1] The important role played by traditional medicine notwithstanding, medical education, research, and institution building in all African countries neglected, even actively marginalized, traditional medical systems (Reid, 1982, 128) until very recently. Medical education, research, and institution building, whether governmental or private, were all oriented toward western medicine at the expense of traditional medicine and healing systems. This picture, however, has started to change, in a number of African countries quite dramatically. Given the multiple epidemic challenges (HIV/AIDS, Malaria, Tuberculosis and other epidemic diseases), the continent has been obliged to look at its own traditional resources, in addition to western ones, to help confront the enormous health threats it faces. The Organization of African Unity (now the African Union) underscored this need to take a serious look at traditional medicine as a component of Africa's strategy to meet its health challenges. It deliberated on the centering of African Traditional Medicine at its Summit in Lusaka, Zambia, held during July 9–11, 2001.[2] The Summit launched the 2001–2010 decade of African Traditional Medicine. One of the most enthusiastic countries to embrace the new drive for research and application of traditional medicine systems is South Africa[3]-a country hard hit by the HIV/AIDS pandemic and other diseases.

Africa's health problems, which seriously affect its society, family structure, and economy, have reached crisis proportions. Africa has finally realized that without resorting to its own medical wisdom, knowledge, and resources, it cannot hope to effectively fight and defeat the serious threats of diseases including HIV/AIDS. This awareness is critical as the long subdued communicable diseases like malaria and tuberculosis are on the rise and provide mutually reinforcing effects with HIV/AIDS. Reliance solely on Western medicine is too expensive and beyond Africa's reach to make a significant dent in the problem in the long run, no matter how generous Western responses have been in the short run.

This chapter will look at the major health campaign successes of the past and the new health challenges facing Africa. Attention will then be focused on the cur-

---

1. Twentieth African Health Congress, 19–23 April, 1999, Accra, Ghana, http://www. idb.org/v1/geo/Africa/#af_gen

2. "Canada to participate in the Decade for African Traditional Medicine", http://www.web.idrc.ca/en/ev-41556-201-1.DO_TOPIC.html retrieved, 12/19/ 004. Posted 7,11,2001

3. Traditional Medicines: South Africa Health Info. http://www.sahealthinfo.org/traditionalmeds/traditionalmeds.htm

rent HIV/AIDS crisis in Africa. By all accounts, Sub-Saharan Africa is the world's hardest hit by the HIV/AIDS pandemic. It is curious that the rate of HIV/AIDS infection in Africa compared to global distribution of the problem mirrors the rate of infection among African Americans in the United States context. Though race and ethnic disaggregated data for the Caribbean area and Brazil are not yet available, some inference on disease impact on black people in the region will also be included. Where the race and disease data is explicit, comparisons will be made between this and disease incidents in Africa. Of course, any comparative parallels will stop at proportionality of rates of infection, and trends, since the magnitude of the problems and other circumstances in Africa and communities outside are different. The chapter will conclude by highlighting new trends in responses to epidemics by the international community, African governments, NGOs and grassroots or civil society, especially as this relates to the HIV/AIDS crisis. A number of positive trends appear to emerge from the current health crisis which involve spontaneous mobilization of indigenous people's own resources in ways not seen before. The implication of this indigenous mobilization at different levels for different African issues will be briefly reflected on.

Major terms and concepts biomedical (Western) medicine, traditional medicine, traditional healers, epidemic, UNAIDS, World Bank, UNDP, USAID, NGOs, international cooperation, Bill and Melinda Gates Foundation, Global Fund to fight HIV/AIDS, malaria and tuberculosis, research into traditional medicine, regional cooperation, Independent Group for Health in Africa (IGHA), Mobile Task Team (MTT), DOTS strategy, indigenous knowledge, heuristic and symbolic value, African paradigm, paradigm shift, community mobilization, river blindness, polio, measles, small pox, disease eradication, capacity building, Multi-Sector Approach to AIDS (MACA), schistosomiasis (bilharzia)

Africa's Major Health Challenges: Past and Present

Africa has been challenged by a number of diseases prior to the emergence of the HIV/AIDS crisis (Azedevo, M.J, 1978). Much of the African region being hot and humid most of the year, the climate is conducive for many disease-causing microbes and parasites to breed and infect people. Thus, such diseases as malaria, tuberculosis, bilhazia and river-blindness were rampant in addition to global diseases like small pox, measles, and polio which attacked large numbers of people, especially children. Africa has a record of success in fighting these diseases.

Small pox, polio and measles have largely fallen under control, though malaria and tuberculosis which were nearly eradicated during the 1970s have re-emerged as major health threats in recent times. There is one area where western medicine has been fully instrumental in helping vast numbers of people. Western (biomedical) medicine produced some miraculous successes in Africa in the area of mass disease eradication. Nowhere is this better illustrated than by the eradication or near eradication of measles, small pox, and polio.[4] Small pox was actu-

---

4. Polio was scheduled to be eradicated by the early years of the new millennium. But hampered vaccination drives, especially in Northern Nigeria and neighboring countries, have forced postponement of the target date.

ally eradicated in 1977 through vaccination campaigns in Africa and globally. This was followed by a goal to eradicate measles by 2000. Except for a few occurrences in Nigeria in 2004, measles has more or less been eradicated.[5] Polio, a crippling disease that attacks and weakens human limbs, was also successfully subdued. Through persistent vaccination campaigns spearheaded by the World Health Organization at a cost of $4.6 billion, the disease was to be eradicated by 2000. This target was extended to 2005 as some anti-polio vaccine attitudes were spread in major population centers of Northern Nigeria which happens to be predominantly Muslim. Suspicion on the negative health effects of the polio vaccine developed resulting in mistrust fed by negative rumors.[6] This resulted in the obstruction of necessary vaccination and follow-up leading to new infections in the region. Of the 667 global cases of polio recorded in 2003, Nigeria accounted for 300, triggering stern blame from the World Health Organization[7]. As of late 2004, Nigeria has launched a vigorous information campaign to get the entire child population of northern Nigeria vaccinated against polio. The World Health Organization Report on global health conditions affirms the success of the Nigerian vaccination drive[8]. On the whole, Africa, with international cooperation and assistance, has largely rid itself of the menace of small pox, polio and measles.

It is estimated that malaria alone kills 3,000 children under the age of 5 years every day and that 900,000 adults die each year from the disease.[9] According to another source, malaria kills one child every thirty seconds and accounts for one fifth of all child deaths in Sub-Saharan Africa. The updated figure estimates that 1 million adult deaths are caused by malaria.[10]

Tuberculosis (TB) is also a re-emerging threat. The World Health Organization estimates that one third of the world's population is presently infected with the tuberculosis bacillus.[11] Africa accounts for 26% of all the infections and tuberculosis-caused deaths averaged 83/100,000 in 2002. Globally, it is estimated that 2 million deaths resulted from TB with the highest number of deaths in South-East Asia. Still, the highest mortality rate is in Sub-Saharan Africa. Experts believe that TB vulnerability in Africa is exacerbated by the prevalence of HIV/AIDS.[12] There is, however optimism that TB can be contained and even reversed. Efforts have been under way since 1991 to control TB through an inexpensive strategy that could prevent "millions of TB cases and deaths over the coming decades". This strategy is called DOTS and consists of a number of key elements:[13]

---

5. Assistant Secretary for Legislation, Department of Health and Human Services, Sept. 23, 1998 http://www.hhs.gov/asi/testify/1980923a.html (retrieved, Dec. 15, 2004).

6. Dr. Mrs.Dere Awosika, Minister of Health, Nigeria posted on web November 29, 2004 thhp://allafrica.com/stories11290744.html.

7. UN Wire (United Nations Foundation) http://www.unwire.org/unwire/20040112/449/11955.asp (retrieved Dec. 19, 2004).

8. UN Wire, http://www.unwire.org/unwire/20040112/449/11955.asp World Health Report, Geneva.

9. Africa News, September 21, 2003..

10. United Nations Chronicle Online Edition, http://www.un.org/pubs/chronicle/2004/issue1/0104p72.asp (retrieved, 5/6/05).

11. WHO Fact Sheet no. 104, revised March 2004; http://www.who.int/mediacenter/factsheet/fs104/en/index.html.

12. Ibid.

13. Ibid.

- government commitment to sustained TB control
- detection of TB cases through sputum smear
- uninterrupted supply of cheap but highly effective drugs for 6–8 months treatment (6 months sully costs $6/ per person)
- Monitoring and reporting system installation

Already, the DOTS strategy has reportedly produced 95% cure rate even in the poorest countries. The picture is so optimistic that the United Nations Millennium Development Goal includes the halving of TB prevalence by 2015.

In the same vein, the African Summit on Roll Back Malaria, held in Abuja in 2002 has endorsed inexpensive but effective strategies for malaria control.[14] These include insecticide-treated nets (ITNS) most of it scheduled for production in Africa. In addition potent drugs to treat drug-resistant strains is in use. An African group of scientists and doctors petitioned WHO to allow indoor spraying of DDT (IRS) to increase malaria control effectiveness.[15] Still, malaria and tuberculosis are big concerns in Sub-Saharan Africa, next to HIV/AIDS.

Recognizing the triple threat of HIV/AIDS, malaria and tuberculosis, the Global Fund to Fight HIV/AIDS, Malaria and Tuberculosis has been established.[16] The goal of the Global Fund is to expand international resources for the treatment and research of HIV/AIDS, malaria and tuberculosis. The target was to raise $10 billion a year towards this goal. The Fund so far has been able to raise only a little over $4 billion annually. The Bill and Melinda Gates Foundation is a major contributor to the Fund. Of the $1 billion the Gates Foundation donated in 2003, $120 million was allocated to fight malaria in Africa alone. [17]

Whether African countries' budgets' reflect the same level of concern is a matter of judgment. Below is the health budget allocation rate for selected African countries

As experience demonstrates, generous international cooperation and assistance in Africa's health challenges has been forthcoming to enhance Africa's health expenditure. Sachs (2001, 56–57) advocates even greater international contribution to strengthen African health service delivery and research.

Economic Empowerment and Development Through Health: Moving Africa Beyond the Scourge of River-Blindness

Despite the many diseases that confront Africa, Sub-Saharan Africa has a huge and growing population. Africa's population in 1980 was 379 million which grew to 614 million by 1997 (World Bank, 1998/1999, table 3, p 194–195). This repre-

14. UN Chronicle Online edition Malaria in Africa Today, http://www.un.org/pubs/chronicle/2004/issue1/0104p72.asp.

15. Africa fighting malaria, April 20, 2004 http://www.fightingmalaria.org/petition.php (retrieved 5/6/05).

16. Africa News, Sept. 21, 2003.

17. Ibid. Also The Global Fund to Fight AIDS, Tuberculosis and Malaria, http://www.theglobalfund.org/en/publication/....

National Health Expenditure of selected African countries

Country	Health expenditure As % of GDP					Health expenditure as % of Govern. Expenditure				
	1997	1998	1999	2000	2001	1997	1998	1999	2000	2001
Angola	3.9	3.5	3.3	3.5	4.4	4.6	2.5	2.4	3.3	5.5
Botswana	5.7	5.5	6	6	6.6	7.8	7.2	7.4	8.8	7.6
Cote d' Ivore	6.2	6.4	6.3	6.2	6.2	5.4	5.9	6.4	5.3	6
DRC*	3.3	3	3.1	3.2	3.5	10.3	8.3	8.7	9.7	10.3
Ethiopia	3.4	3.6	3.5	3.2	3.6	5.8	5.9	4.3	3.2	4.9
Malawi	8.7	8.5	8.7	8.2	7.8	12.2	12.9	13.9	12.2	12.3
Nigeria	2.8	3.1	3	3	3. 4	2.1	2.3	1.7	1.7	1.9
South Africa	9	8.7	8.8	8.7	8.6	12.4	11.3	11.1	11.2	10.9
Zimbabwe	9.3	11.4	7.9	7.4	6.2	15.4	12.2	10.	7.1	8.

* Democratic Republic of the Congo.

Source: WHO World Health Report 2003. WHO, Geneva, table 5

sents an average growth rate of 2.9 for 1980–1990. For 1990–1997, this rate of growth was 2.7% an observable decline in growth rate. Despite this apparent growth decline, Sub-Sahara's population had grown to 688 million by 2002 (World Bank, 2004, table 1, p. 253).

Disease control and prevention work in relatively dense population settlements requires a number of things. First, the people's economic prosperity and level of education needs to be such that they are able to actively seek and acquire information about critical diseases. Secondly, they need to be economically able to afford the preventive health measures and essential treatments to keep them and their surroundings healthy. Thirdly, they need to have developed institutions of medicinal production on the scale necessary and the essential network of health institutions to distribute medicines safely.

In the pre-colonial spacious villages, Africans could meet all of these conditions through their traditional medical and economic institutions.[18] But then, traditional methods, skills, and institutions were not what Africa invested in and developed since its contact with the west as colonial and post-colonial states. Medical services and institutional forms have been developing along western methods. But the scope of western style medical services remains very limited, leaving an estimated 85% of the African population to rely primarily on traditional medicine and traditional medical healers.[19]

One of the major achievements of Africa's concerted health campaigns using western style prevention and treatment has been the control of river-blindness. The fight against the scourge of river-blindness which had devastating social and

---

18. Many researchers on African traditional medicine discuss this. Among the major ones are Gills Bibeau, "A Systems Approach to Ngbandi Medicine", John Jazen "Lubanzi : The History of a Kongo Disease" and a number of others. The three works mentioned here appear in *African Health and Healing Systems: Proceedings of a Symposium"* edited by P. Stanley Yoder, Crossroads Press, University of California, Los Angeles, 1982.

19. Bob Stanley, http://web.idrc.ca/en/ev-55582-201-1-Do_topic.html. 2004-02-13 (retrieved on Dec. 10, 2004)

economic impacts on a huge region spanning west, central, and north-eastern Africa is nearing successful conclusion. An initiative to eradicate this disease and free hundreds of millions of people from this permanently disabling disease and allow the reclamation of millions of hectares of fertile land, abandoned because of the disease, was urgently needed. African states, local communities and international donors cooperated to tackle the problem of river-blindness. The success of the international and local cooperation against river-blindness, which achieved freedom from the disease for millions and the reclamation of millions of hectares of fertile land for production, is well documented in a documentary video produced by the External Affairs Office of the World Bank entitled *Optimism for Africa*. Much of the account below is derived directly from this documentary.

In 1968, the United States Agency for International Development (USAID), the World Health Organization (WHO) and some African countries, concerned with a variety of growing health threats in Sub-Saharan Africa, initiated discussions in Tunisia on the assessment of priorities. By 1972, Robert MacNamara, then president of the World Bank, joined the conversation and together, the African and international groups determined that river-blindness, which was disrupting the lives of millions of people across the continent, needed to be addressed as a priority.

River- blindness is caused by a parasitic worm which latches itself to nodules on and in the human body. The eggs of the worm hatch and breed in the human body eventually causing irreversible blindness. The disease is transmitted by the female black fly which sucks blood from infected patients and spreads the disease to healthy people. The parasite favors shallow banks of rivers to breed and thrive. The river banks of Africa's networks of large rivers are fertile agricultural life lines for large population groups. The river banks and their contiguous river-fed lands, therefore, become the favored habitat of the disease-causing parasite and farming communities attracted by the fertility of the land and the availability of water. Disease and man compete for the same natural environment and resource. In this struggle the disease had won and chased people out . In rural Ivory Coast, Ghana, Burkina Faso, Niger, Togo, Mali, and many other countries, this disease chased people out of fertile river banks and adjacent agricultural areas. The people escaped to arid, infertile lands that proved safer from river-blindness.[20] Poverty was severe and endemic for tens of millions of people, a large group of whom continued to suffer from river-blindness already contracted before their escape to dry lands.

Multilateral aid to start intervention to eradicate river blindness started in 1974 with concerned African countries and communities as full partners in the effort. This was an exemplar model of successful cooperation between African governments, local communities, international donors and even a private pharmaceutical corporation. USAID, the World Bank, and the European countries made necessary finances available, The Pharmaceutical giant MERCK provided free medicine to eradicate the parasite causing river blindness from the waters of the rivers and to treat people already infected. African governments and civil societies played key roles by providing critical and accumulated local knowledge about the etiology of the disease. The people willingly participated in trials and experiments and volunteered for activities asked of them. Governments trained national staff,

---

20. This story is colorfully documented in a World Bank documentary video, issued by the External affairs Office of the Bank under the title *Optimism for Africa*. The date of the video is 1995.

and built national capacity to run and maintain the program. They made whatever resources they had available for the effort.

By 1993–1995, the disease was virtually eradicated from the initially participating countries which included Ghana, Burkina Faso, Mali, Benin, Guinea Bisau, Siera Leone and a few others. Thirty million people afflicted by the disease were cured, 24 million hectares of fertile land abandoned owing to fear of river-blindness, were put back to agricultural production, and some 10 million children were seen healthy and prosperous. By the end of 1995, 220 million people living in 11 participating African countries were looking at the early stages of their fast advancing agricultural development and economic activities inter-linked with agricultural prosperity. The people had already started to produce wondrous varieties of vegetables, fruits, nuts, and grains in such surplus that they were beginning to look for inter-regional and extra-regional markets for their surplus produce.

Chad, Cameroon, Nigeria, Sudan and Zaire (the Democratic Republic of Congo) were later added to the project. Already, their affected people have become direct beneficiaries. Yet, all this successful work was estimated to cost only $550million by the end of 2002. This is why many development experts hope that this tripartite model (involving the partnership of local people, government, and the international donor community) becomes a standard for designing development and international cooperation in Africa in the future.

The Present and Future Health Challenge: HIV/AIDS

It is dispiriting to observe, that all of the above disease control and eradication successes notwithstanding, Africa has faced multifaceted health crises again. The current crises arise from the HIV/AIDS pandemic, exacerbated by the re-emergence of epidemics of malaria and tuberculosis. While all of these afflictions menace other regions of the world, none is as hard hit as Africa. It does not seem to be a mere coincidence that Africa, which is the most disadvantaged and marginalized in the global economic arrangement,[21] is also the region most savagely ravaged by HIV/AIDS, malaria and tuberculosis. [22] Poverty increases people's vulnerabilities in so many ways and the direct association of poverty and disease prevalence in Africa seems to affirm this. Among the reasons of this association of disease and poverty is poor peoples' lack of timely access to information on diseases and the ways diseases could be prevented or minimized. Disease vulnerability is also aggravated by lack of adequate and well balanced nutrition among the poor. Table 1 below provides a summary of the HIV/AIDS infection situation in selected Sub-Saharan African countries.

The staggering nature of the HIV/AIDS crisis is clear from the figures in table 1. Figures for different years vary. No matter what year we look at, the rates re-

---

21. Mkandawire, Thandika and Soludo, Charles C. (1999), *Our Continent Our Future: African Perspectives on Structural Adjustment* Africa World Press Inc.,Trenton NJ, Foreword.

22. Global Fund to Fight AIDS, Tuberculosis and Malaria: http://www.theglobalfund.org/en/in_action/stories/ retrieved 12/13/004.

Table 1. HIV/AIDS Infection Among Selected ub-Saharan African Countries (2003)

Country	Adult	%	AIDS death	AIDS orphans
Botswana	3,330,000	37.3	33,000	120,000
Ethiopia	1,400,000	4.4	120,000	720,000
Lesotho	300,000	28.9	22,000	100,000
Malawi	810,000	14.2	84,000	50,000
Mozambique	1,200,000	12.2	110,000	470,000
Namibia	200,000	21.3	16,000	57,000
Nigeria	3,300,000	5.4	310,000	1,800,000
South Africa	5,100,000	21.5	370,000	1,100,000
Uganda	480,000	4.1	78,000	940,000
Zimbabwe	1,600,000	24.6	170,000	980,000

Source: http://www.avert.org/subaadults.htm, posted January 28, 2005.

main frightfully high, especially given two facts on the ground: a) the underdeveloped nature of African economies; b) the fact that the HIV/AIDS crisis is attacking the economically most productive class (see table 3 below). This will be discussed later in this article under the subheading "HIV/AIDS and The African Paradox." We should here consider one more telling fact about the scale of damage the epidemic has done to the hard-won life expectancy improvements. Life expectancy is an important social measure for, beyond its intrinsic value in extending human life, it also means that people have the opportunity to make their learning and experience to bear fruit for society over a longer period. Table 2 shows the reduction in life expectancy resulting from HIV/AIDS.

In Africa, poverty and ignorance are not the only engines for HIV/AIDS expansion. The population sector most seriously affected since the beginning of the epidemic has been the educationally and economically better off class. As far back as 1988, it was broadly evident that Africa's professional and scientific core had become the victim of HIV/AIDS. In a book edited by Norman Miller and Richard C.

Table 2. Life Expectancy Decline in Selected Southern African Countries hard hit by the HIV/AIDS epidemic

Country	1996	2001
Botswana	65.2	41.9
Lesotho	60.8	47.9
Malawi	45.5	40.3
Mozambique	46.4	39.8
Namibia	59.1	44.9
South Africa	63.2	53.9
Swaziland	57.8	47.0
Zimbabwe	53.4	42.9

Source: One Step Further Responses to HIV/AIDS Sidastudies no.7, Anne Sisaka editor, 2nd.

Cromwell (1988)[23], it was documented that the highest risk of infection was found among 20–40 year olds, predominantly urban, generally better educated, and relatively well paid. In some countries, the whole professional core of some institutions had already succumbed to the disease. For instance, during 1986 in Zaire, a bank president, two vice presidents and a prominent executive secretary died of AIDS within one month. The bank lost virtually its entire experienced professional leadership.[24] The same trends emerged within the military, police, teachers, medical personnel in other countries of Sub-Saharan Africa. Botswana, Africa's most admired development success story became the most HIV/AIDS ravaged country with estimated infection rates of 38.8%, by the early years of the new millennium, according to UNAIDS figures. Botswana's prosperity led to disproportionate burden of the disease instead of reducing it.

The explanations for this perverse condition are varied. But one sociological factor can be considered to have played a key role in the accelerated spread of the disease in African communities of relative affluence and social and physical mobility. First, this class of people has the financial and material means to want to seek leisure and pleasure more readily than people struggling for survival. Second, segments of this population travel far and wide within and between countries in pursuit of economic opportunities or as truckers, businessmen and government officials. Traveling away from family and community leads to liaisons with strangers including prostitutes. Combined with lack of information on HIV/AIDS transmission, such population mobility becomes a powerful engine for accelerated disease expansion. Fear of stigma of infidelity and HIV/AIDS infection leads to secrecy of the infected, thereby helping the further spread of the infection.

The Sociology of Stigma: Delaying Prevention Responses

Until very recently, most African governments were stoutly reluctant to take the necessary steps to contain the HIV/AIDS crises in their midst (World Bank, 2004, 21).[25] Among local communities too, there existed superstition about the causes of the disease. All sorts of belief systems were constructed to attach the disease to anything but the real cause-uninformed and unprotected sex with multiple partners. Instead of curiosity about its nature and modes of transmission, a great

---

23. In their introduction to their edited work, AIDS in Africa: The Social and Policy Impact, Norman Miller and Richard C. Rockwell illustrate how Africa loses its scientific, technical, managerial, military capacities to HIV/AIDS, xxiv–xxviii.

24. Ibid, pp. xxiv.

25. Bertil Egero writes on this in his article " To fight AIDS successfully requires unconventional approaches", chap. 10 in Sidastudies no.7. The author even documents that in Ethiopia, the public education programs finally started by Mengistu's regime was undermined and reversed by the Tigre People's Liberation Front government that, with the help of all the people, fought to power in the country in 1991. Instead of caring for the health of the people that trusted it and assisted it to power, the regime dismantled the few AIDS programs instituted by the defunct regime and pushed the population into unprecedented harm of HIV/AIDS. (p. 209).

deal of social and medical stigma developed. Those infected, therefore, hid and denied their status until they succumbed to the disease.

HIV/AIDS was reported in parts of Africa between 1982–1984.[26] In most African societies, the formal and informal responses to the threat was not alarm, or mass education on its prevention. Writing as late as 2002, Virginia Bond observes the problems of stigma and ostracism that prevent people from seeking help and adopting necessary behavior modification and safe sex practices in the most HIV/AIDS devastated Southern Africa region.[27] Uganda was an exception.[28] The first case of HIV/AIDS in the country was identified in 1982. Explanatory superstitions and attribution to witchcraft developed in affected Ugandan communities as responses to the disease. The government did not respond even as these unproductive popular responses flourished. By 1986, the prevalence rate was nearing 30% and whole villages were being decimated.

It was at this point that realistic, spontaneous community responses emerged reversing the myth, denial, superstition, and witch-hunt. The practical community response and change of attitude soon resulted in group formations to care for AIDS victims. The government of the National Resistance Movement, which had assumed power right about that time, joined the popular response. The new Government and its health institutions were reinforced to join community initiatives to build a strong information dissemination campaign, and HIV/AIDS control programs. The news from Uganda has been encouraging since. In some places the rate of infection has been reported as reversed (see table 1). Uganda's response and results will be revisited later when we examine broadly emerging continent-wide responses to the HIV/AIDS threat.

The fear of stigma and government neglect have raised the death to unprecedented levels (table3) with enormous social and economic consequences.

Clearly, HIV/AIDS is targeting the most productive age group (15–49), leaving behind the old and very young who depend on this productive age group.

The World Health Organization Commission on Macroeconomics and Health completed a study in 2001. It estimated that in Sub-Saharan Africa, AIDS caused the loss of 72 million workdays adjusted for days lost due to other disabilities. This is the equivalent of 11% of GNP loss.[29] If the disease is not controlled, South

---

26. Weddy Silomba, 2002, HIV/AIDS and Development-the Chikankata Experience, chapter 4 in One Step Further-Responses to HIV/AIDS, Sida Studies no.7 edited by Ann Sisask, printed by Elanders Novum AB, Gothenburg, Sweden. Gloria White discusses the first years of HIV detection in Rwanda, Uganda, and Zaire, around 1982–84. In her piece "The Politics of Disease: The AIDS virus and Africa" in AIDS IN AFRICA: The Social and Policy Impact (1988), edited by Norman Miller and Richard C. Rockwell, Gloria White discusses that Uganda and Rwanda, unlike other countries, took relatively early steps to good effect; government sponsored education programs started around 1985–1986.

27. Bond, Virginia, The Dimensions and Wider Context of HIV/AIDS Stigma and Resulting Discrimination in Southern Africa, Chapter 2 in Sidastudies no.7, edited by Anne Sisask. Because the author of the present article picked this undated material in the Fall of 2002, and because a number of the authors cite materials from 2001, and 2002, it is assumed that the date of publication may be early 2002. In the same work, Minou Fuglesang also discusses related and wider problems of communicating with youth about the problems in effective manner, using some successful media formats addressing youth.

28. Uganda AIDS Commission http://www.aidsuganda.org/ retrieved on 12/10/2004.

29. World Health Organization Commission on Macroeconomics and Health: "Macroeconomics and Health: Investing in Health for Economic Development, Geneva, 2001,

Table 3 Age and Sex Distribution of People
Living with HIV/AIDS in Sub-Saharan Africa at the end of 2001

	Age		Adult Sex	
Total no. living with HIV/AIDS	**0–14**	**15–49**	**M**	**F**
28.5 million	2.5mil.	26 mil.	11 mil.	15 mil.

Source: UNAIDS Report on Global HIV/AIDS epidemic 2002, GENEVA Page 190

Africa, Africa's economic powerhouse, representing 40% of Sub-Saharan African economic activity, will have its GDP reduced by 17% by 2011, something that would not happen without the effect of HIV/AIDS. [30] This reflects the effect of so many productive people dying as we saw earlier in table1. Another effect is life expectancy decline we saw in table 2.

The US Census Bureau calculation projects that in Southern Africa, hardest hit by the HIV/AIDS epidemic, life expectancy by 2010 will be worse than the scenario presented in table 2 above.[31] Any data one picks up at this time shows the grim social and economic reality of the continent.

Sub-Saharan Africa has about 10% of the world's population but hosts about 70% of all people living with HIV/AIDS[32]. If we put a numerical face to the problem, we can appreciate its gravity. UNAIDS estimates that at the end of 2002, about 40 million people were HIV positive globally. Of these, Sub-Saharan Africa owned about 28.5 million[33]. Of this overwhelming HIV/AIDS infected population, only 30,000 were estimated to benefit from anti-retroviral drugs by the end of 2001.[34] Eleven million African children have been orphaned by the epidemic and this is out of a global population of 14 million HIV/AIDS orphans.[35] Eighty per cent of all AIDS orphans are African. Botswana, Africa's development success story, is the hardest hit among African countries devastated across the board. Here, the median HIV prevalence rate among urban pregnant women was estimated to have reached the astounding 38.5% already in 1997. By 2001, it had reached 44.9%. The country has started to see some decline in HIV/AIDS occurrence, its rate at the end of 2003 being around 35% as shown in table 1 above. Zimbabwe's pregnant women were infected to the tune of 29% in 1997, which rate climbed to 35% in 2000. South Africa, Namibia, all countries with promising transformational prospects, have been hard hit.[36]

---

quoted in Allan Whiteside and Mary O'grady in One Step Further- Responses to HIV/AIDS, Sidastudies no.7

30. UNAIDS 2002 Report on Global HIV/AIDS Epidemic, Geneva. Page 57.

31. the US Census Bureau World Population Profile, 1998 cited in Allan Whiteside and Mary Ograly, Sidastudies no. 7 puts 2010 life expectancy in Botswana at 37.8; South Africa at 42.4; Zimbabwe at 38.8 and so on.

32. UNAIDS Fact Sheet "AIDS epidemic in Sub-Saharan Africa" http://www.unaids.org/html/pub/publications/fact-sheets04/FS_SSAfrica_en_pdf/FS_SS...(retrieved 10/26/2004)

33. UNAIDS, Report on the Global HIV/AIDS epidemic, UNAIDS/02.26E (English original), July 2002, Geneva, Switzerland p. 22.

34. Ibid, p.23.

35. Ibid.

36. Ibid, 23–24.

Some Transatlantic Comparisons

Africa's globally disproportionate share of the HIV problem seems to parallel somewhat the trend in the African American community at the national level. According to the 2000 US Census, African Americans constitute about 12.3% of the US population. But when it comes to HIV/AIDS, this population accounts for more than 39% of all cases diagnosed since the beginning of the epidemic[37] The Centers for Disease Control and Prevention statistics[38] show that of all the population groups diagnosed with HIV/AIDS since 1994, African Americans had the poorest survival rates. Only 55% of African Americans testing positive for HIV survived for 9 years, compared to 61% for Hispanics, 64% for whites and 69% for Asian Pacific Islanders. In 2002, African Americans accounted for 50% of all adult cases diagnosed with full fledged AIDS in the United States.[39] Quoting Centers for Disease Control and Prevention statistical projections, the Kaiser Family Foundation warns that 54% of the 40,000 new HIV infection estimated to occur in the US each year in the future will be African American.[40]

Though the numerical magnitude of HIV/AIDS among African Americans pales when seen against the African situation, it should be great cause for concern since, in the US, the disease seems to focus on the African American community just as it focuses on Africa in the global context. The correspondence is curious only for that reason. Current CDC statistics portray the accelerating rate of "African Americanization" of the disease in the US. By 2002, for instance, AIDS prevalence rates among African Americans became eleven times the rate for whites, with African American women having HIV/AIDS infection rate of 23 times greater than white women[41]. Not only do African Americans bear the heavy brunt of HIV infection and AIDS, they also get diagnosed late according to CDC and the Kaiser Family Foundation.

A compelling case can be made from these data that economic and social factors which disfavor Africans globally and African Americans nationally must figure prominently in the health status of these communities, the peculiar case of the African paradox notwithstanding. Health and well-being are part of economic and social well-being and we see this relationship emerging clearly in the African American and African situations. In both cases, the affected populations in the aggregate, find themselves on the low end of the income and wealth ladder. Andrew Hacker (1995) shows that 33.3% of African Americans live under poverty compared to 9% of whites, with the median income for black families being $21,161 compared with $38,900 for their white counterparts. While black income may not seem bad looked at in the international context, the national context of affluence with its implied cost of living gives it a different picture . Growing African

---

37. Fact Sheet-HIV/AIDS Among African Americans-CDC-NCHSTP-Divisions of HIV/AIDS. http://www.cdc.gov/hiv/pubs/facts/afam.htm retrieved 12/13/2004.
38. Ibid.
39. The Kaiser Family Foundation, September 2003 HIV/AIDS Policy Fact Sheet, *African Americans and HIV/AIDS.*
40. Ibid.
41. Fact Sheet-HIV/AIDS Among African Americans-CDC-NCHSTP-Division of HIV/AIDS. http://www.cdc.gov/hiv/pubs/facts/afam.htm.

Table 4 HIV/AIDS Infection in Brazil and the Caribbean (2001)

Country/ Region	Infected	%	AIDS Death	Orphans	Population
Brazil	610,000	.7	8,400	130,000	172,559,000
Caribbean	420,000	2.3	40,000	250,000	32,480,000

Source: UNAIDS Report on the Global HIV/AIDS Epidemic, Geneva 2002, p. 198

American children who form the next generation appear especially vulnerable; 46.3% as compared 12.3% of their white counterparts live in poverty (106).

Africa's integration into the global economy is very weak,[42] in fact marginal, in that its role is only to provide unprocessed raw materials that do not produce jobs and wealth for the people on the continent. It is common place knowledge that the average African lives on less than $2 a day with some countries having per capita income of around $100 even in 2003 (World Bank, 2004).[43] Poor people not only lack the economic means to protect themselves from disease and sickness, their poverty becomes the reason for being exposed to easily transmittable diseases such as HIV/AIDS. Poor women can be apt examples here. They become sex workers who help spread diseases from ill to well people who patronize them which in turn triggers the multiplier effect in the spread of the disease to the general population. Poverty, powerlessness and lack of self-worth push poor women to behaviors that others with better choices would disdain.

Brazil and the Caribbean are two other areas in the western hemisphere with a preponderance of people of African decent. Though there is some re-emergence of malaria and tuberculosis in the Caribbean region especially, the major health threat recognized in the region and internationally is HIV/AIDS (UNAIDS, 2002, Caribbean Health, 2005). Compared to Sub-Saharan Africa, the magnitude of HIV/AIDS infection in the Caribbean, and even more in Brazil, appear modest as shown in table 4. The Caribbean authorities, however declare that the region's infection rate is second only to Sub-Saharan Africa (Caribbean Health, 2005)

While the magnitude of infection is not as overwhelming as Sub-Saharan Africa, there is concern that the disease burden may be concentrated within communities of African decent. It is difficult to make a firm ethnic case as there are no ethnic-specific data on health, or for that matter other social and economic variables. But certain inferences are emerging to suggest that gross inequalities persists between Whites and Blacks in the region (Barros et al, 2001, World Bank, 2003, Giovanella et al, 2002). The same sources are urging the dis-aggregation of health, education, and other data by race and ethnicity.

A seminar entitled "Health and Inequality: Institutions and Public Policy", sponsored by the Brazilian National School of Public Health and the Pan American Health Organization, was held in Rio de Janeiro from November 29 to December 1, 2001. The seminar examined the relationship between health, inequal-

---

42. Economic Commission for Africa, *Economic Report on Africa 2002: Tracking Performance and Progress, p. ix* Economic Commission for Africa, Addis Ababa, Ethiopia, 2002.

43. World Bank, *World Development Report 2004: Making Services Work for Poor People*, The World Bank, Washington DC. Table 1 Size of the Economy (pp. 252–253)

ity and poverty and found that the important variables of gender, race and ethnicity, generally lacking in current statistics need to be developed in the region.

Brazil's population of nearly 173 million is 54% white and 45.3% black. It is disconcerting that 30% of the population live below poverty (Global Snapshot). A Brazilian scholar once told me that depending on the definition of blackness, the country's population can be as much as 70% black or African descended which would imply that the vast majority of this population is poor and vulnerable to diseases.

Brazil and the Caribbean do much better than Sub-Saharan Africa in the level of health budget allocation. In 2002, for instance, Brazil allocated 8.8% of total government expenditure to health while the Caribbean figure was 14.1% for the same period (WHO, 2003, 170 & 172). Despite this generous allocation, the Caribbean needs significant external assistance to cope with HIV/AIDS and other communicable diseases and is included in the $15 billion that the United States government under the administration of President Bush has allocated for African HIV/AIDS assistance.

The Caribbean, in particular, is determined to confront the challenge of HIV/AIDS. Plans have been completed to create a Pan-Caribbean Partnership against the disease. This partnership is to be launched in July of 2005. Health Ministers of the region reiterated that the Caribbean region was second only to Sub-Saharan Africa in HIV/AIDS prevalence and that a combined effort was needed to confront the threat.

Challenges and Promising Multi-level Responses

In this section, we will take a brief look at innovative responses to the HIV/AIDS challenge by local communities, formally and informally organized groups and government agencies, and where applicable, regional and international organizations. Indigenous or local initiatives are becoming so prominent in facing up to the health challenge that the new international buzz phrase is "the community-based approach" (WHO, 2005, 392–394) or "local pathways" (World Bank, 2004).

The African American responses to the HIV/AIDS challenge are multi-layered. At the national level, The CDC and the Kaiser Family Foundation are active in researching and disseminating information on the accelerating rate of HIV infection among African Americans and urging awareness by all concerned. They make efforts to point to policy directions to control the problem. At the community level, groups from within the African American community are vigorously organizing and mobilizing themselves to challenge the threat. For instance, the Black AIDS Institute which is very active in this area, was organized by volunteers in Los Angeles to raise funds for HIV/AIDS work and to disseminate information to the African American community. Their Web site "BLACKAIDS.ORG is an effective and efficient medium for their work. The motto of the Institute and the web site is "Our People Our Problem Our Solution". Gilbert and Wright (2003) also write of many community initiatives to face up to the challenge from within the African American community. The growing consensus seems to be that much can be accomplished to control and reverse the HIV/AIDS threat by grassroots advocacy initiatives. Government measures alone cannot do the job of slowing down and eventually eliminating the problem. Given the resource and technological abundance to deal with the problem and the potential responsiveness of policy makers to their voting constituencies, grassroots and advocacy innovations from within the African American community are likely to produce positive results.

Information on grassroots activities in the two areas is not readily available to researchers, perhaps owing to language problems. But the activism of intellectuals and medical professionals is evident from the many workshops and advocacy activities some of which were cited earlier. Specifically, the demand for ethnic-specific data compilation on health comes from such groups. This too is a trend towards grassroots involvement in policy and delivery of services.

Africa: International, Government, Civil Society, and Health Professionals' Response

Internationally, the Global Fund to fight HIV/AIDS, malaria and tuberculosis was created to increase resources to fight these three epidemic diseases with particular emphasis on the AIDS crisis. The fund had hoped to raise $10 billion a year but has so far managed to raise $4.7 billion. It plans to allocate 61% of the $4.7 billion in its support programs through 2008 to Africa.[44] The proportion of fund allocation is indicative of the disproportionate prevalence of the epidemic diseases in Africa. Within this resource allocation, two thirds is committed for HIV/AIDS; Malaria and Tuberculosis being allocated 17% and 14% respectively. It is clear that HIV/AIDS is considered a serious and immediate threat to Africa.

Under the administration of President George Bush, the United States government has allocated an emergency fund of $15 billion to combat HIV/AIDS in Africa,[45] with some of this money to be allocated for the Caribbean region. The Bill and Melinda Gates Foundation generously endows different initiatives to combat HIV/AIDS, malaria, and tuberculosis in Africa. UNAIDS coordinates the efforts of its constituent UN agencies (listed below) and the World Bank. It is difficult to enumerate the number of international non-governmental organizations that have been working on the African AIDS crisis. Some estimates put the number of international non-governmental organizations from North America alone, working in this field at 2000, with Kenya estimating the number of such NGOs it hosts at 600 (Gowan and Reining 1988, 312). Their contributions in the on-going battle against HIV/AIDS are said to be very significant.

UNAIDS, which comprises the United Nations Children's Fund (UNICEF), United Nations Development Program (UNDP), United Nations Fund for Population Activities (UNFPA), The International Labor Organization (ILO), the World Health Organization (WHO) and the World Bank, has been targeting Africa's HIV/AIDS crisis for a number of years.

---

44. The Global Fund to Fight HIV/AIDS, malaria and Tuberculosis (see note no. 16 for address).

45. http://www.usaid.gov/locations/sub-saharan_Africa/.

As far back as 1996, the UNDP had foreseen the urgent need to effect local mobilization against the HIV/AIDS epidemic. UNDP wrote "...the role of the outsider in identifying social change agents is, to a large extent, indirect. The aim is not to go into other peoples' contexts (countries and communities) and identify individuals as social change agents, but rather to establish partnerships which facilitate communities identifying and working with their own...agents" (UNDP, 1996 p. 37) In 2004, a UNAIDS fact sheet affirms "...the past two-to-three years have seen an upsurge of political support, stronger policy formulation, boosted funding, and moves towards cushioning societies against the epidemic-a momentum that has to be maintained to reverse the epidemic."[46] Initiatives from small local groups organized to assist the sick and orphans and to disseminate information on how to avoid HIV transmission and infection are proliferating with the help of international donor resources. There is evidence of growing awareness of the need for essential behavior modification with regard to sexual activities in Africa as a result of combined efforts of local communities, international NGOs, and international organizations. International voices urging recalcitrant African governments [47] to be engaged are now joined by local groups gaining increasing influence because of their organized and coordinated presence among the people and the international support they receive. Such pushes for collaborative processes are ubiquitous on the continent. [48] This popular involvement is reportedly making international and NOG assistance more effective.[49]

A number of African countries have finally woken up to the real dangers of the AIDS crisis, not just for their development but even for their survival as viable, self-sustaining states. For instance, the South African government, till recently noted for its ambivalence towards HIV/AIDS prevalence and needed treatment, is now in the forefront of African countries in the fight against the crisis. It leads in the most innovative responses to combat HIV/AIDS. The University of Natal Mobile Task Team on HIV/AIDS (MTT) and Education was formed in August of 2000. Its main objective was, and remains, to reinforce the expertise of professionals of the University of Natal's Health Economics and AIDS Research Division so that it could help South Africa and other African countries in HIV education and training of personnel. Personnel training is linked to education systems and is de-

---

46. UNAIDS   Fact   Sheet   http://www.unaids.org/html/pub/publications/fact-sheetso4/FS_SSAfrica_en_pdf/FS_SS...The fact sheet adds other positive observations regarding African responses. Of course this is long overdue, as the disease has already caused irreversible damages to African society, economy, education and other institutions.

47. The 2002 Economic Commission For Africa titled "Economic Report on Africa: Tracking Performance and Progress" mentions the non-timely responsiveness and reluctance of all African countries included in the report, vis-à-vis action on the HIV/AIDS crisis Many authors in the compiled work of Sidastudies no.7, extensively cited in this piece also record similar complaints. Note especially Minou Fuglesong, chap.7, p. 139; Bertil Egero, chap.10, p. 209. UNAIDS report 2002, p. 174 also affirms African governments' reluctance to face up to the HIV/AIDS challenge early enough.

48. Minou Fuglesong, Voices of FEMINA HIP Magazine; chap.7 in Sidastudies no.7 n.d, USAID Office of Sustainable Development for Africa 2002, Africa Bureau writing on Tanzania also mentions this phenomenon.

49. USAID Bureau for Africa (2002) Africa Bureau Brief no.2, 2002 "USAID Responses to the Impact of HIV/AIDS on Basic Education in Africa"; Weddy Silomba in Sidastudies no.7, chap. 4 makes the same observation.

signed to achieve multi-tasking capabilities that help education establishments to both deliver education programs and HIV/AIDS prevention methods throughout the education community[50]. The population group most vulnerable to the HIV/AIDS epidemic in Africa being the 15–49 age category, one can readily appreciate the enormous impact an education-based program can have. The USAID has become vital partner in the spread of the MTT innovations throughout Africa.

Typically, a USAID mission approaches the ministry of education in an African country with proposals on how to benefit from MTT resources. African countries thus approached have been prompt in their receptivity to ideas of working with MTT. Upon government acceptance, an MTT team of four experts from the University of Natal is attached to the ministry of education to work with teams composed of ministry of education employees, and USAID mission on preparing a 3–5 day workshop. The workshop is designed to "develop a vision statement and strategic plan" for each country involved. Workshop participants are selected from among ministry of education planners, educators, NGOs, UNAIDS workers, personnel of other agencies involved in HIV/AIDS work and other stakeholders in the country such as local groups formally and informally organized to fight HIV/AIDS and to assist AIDS victims and orphans. USAID funds the MTT workshop organizers and facilitators while the ministries of education fund expenses of other local participants and provide logistical support.

In addition, to technical training of personnel, the workshops also help participants to assess the particular country's current HIV/AIDS status and unique problems, evaluate existing programs in each country and then develop a comprehensive nationally prioritized and achievable plans.[51] Plans include measures for monitoring and evaluating program outcomes.

Through such broad-based, continentally linked and internationally supported programs, many African governments are finally participating fully in the urgent effort that the HIV/AIDS crisis demands. The USAID observes that there already are signs that the MTT approach is proving effective in countries reached, including South Africa itself.[52] By 2002, Zambia, Malawi, Namibia, Ghana, and South Africa had implemented this integrated and locally rooted approach to fighting the HIV/AIDS epidemic. Requests from Ethiopia, Guinea, and Uganda were already in the pipe-line by 2002 and other countries were expected to follow suit. This innovation of researchers at the University of Natal is, thus, traversing Sub-Saharan Africa with its unique model for fighting the HIV/AIDS threat.

Even before its involvement in the MTT methodology and strategy, Uganda had relied on the spontaneous self-mobilization of grassroots to fight the HIV/AIDS crisis. During the mid and late 1980s, the Ugandan government had overcome its reluctance to act because of the pressure of grassroots mobilization. The disease was first diagnosed in 1982. Because of government reluctance, denial, and neglect, whole villages were decimated. The national infection rate reached 18.3% within a few years, with some regions of the country registering infection rates as high as 30% by 1992.[53] By 1987, the new government of president Uri Museveni vigorously joined the grassroots movement and reinforced it

---

50. USAID Bureau for Africa, Office of Sustainable Development; Africa Brief no.2, 2002.
51. Ibid.
52. Ibid p. 6.
53. http://www.aidsuganda.org/ retrieved on 12/10/2004.

with a Multi-sector Approach to Control AIDS (MACA). This involved the inte-grated effort of different government departments and NGOs to build on the ef-forts and experience of the grassroots movement and to add a vigorous education campaign to the mix of services being given. By 1992, the MACA- grassroots col-laborative matured into an effective instrument to fight HIV/AIDS. During the same year, the Ugandan AIDS Commission was established by parliament under the office of the President.[54] The Commission promoted open discussion on the disease and widely disseminated information on its nature, avenues of transmis-sion and methods of prevention. The results were demonstrably impressive.

By the beginning of the new millennium, Uganda became the only African country to have generally reversed the spread of HIV/AIDS. The infection rate, al-ready under control by the early 1990s at 12% was reduced to 4.1% by 2003. The rate even for the capital city Kampala was reduced from 29% in 1992 to about 8% in 2002.[55] With the added expertise of the MTT, Uganda is likely to de-feat the disease at some point in the future. Many African countries are trying to follow the footsteps of Uganda.

A few other HIV/AIDS- inspired local initiatives and local professional organi-zations need to be mentioned briefly to underscore the positive trend in Africa. The heretofore neglected indigenous medicine and healing systems are receiving new vitality in many African countries as part of the strategy to defeat first the HIV/AIDS epidemic and then expanding to cover the malaria and tuberculosis threats. At the Eighth International Congress of the World Federation of Public Health Associations held in Arusha, Tanzania, from October 14–16, 1997, a group of Africans raised questions about the role of African health professionals in Africa's unique health challenges in an ad hoc committee meeting.[56] They asked self-challenging questions like "How can African health institutions and experts best contribute to building a healthy Africa?" The ad hoc committee meeting ac-knowledged the salience of these questions to the African continent and sup-ported a Rockefeller Foundation gesture to finance a series of workshops to fur-ther examine the questions the Africans raised.

Among the highlights of deliberations made by the African group at the Arusha Congress were: a) encourage African experts to work diligently on topical health problems like HIV/AIDS, tuberculosis and malaria and come up with African so-lutions; b) foster strong working partnership between government, the private sector and non-governmental health sector agencies operating in the region; c) es-tablish an expert group, independent from government and UN agencies, to ad-vise African governments on health issues

Out of this exercise has emerged the Independent Group for Health in Africa (IGHA) to be initially registered as a non-governmental organization in Zim-babwe, and later in each African member country. The founding leadership of the IGHA consists of medical specialists and researchers in different African coun-tries and members of the medical profession of the African Diaspora. Among the

---

54. Ibid.

55. UNAIDS Fact Sheet, AIDS epidemic in Sub-Saharan Africa http://www. Unaids.org/html/pub/publications/fact-sheets04/FS_SSAfrica_en_pd/FS_SS . . . retrieved 12/10/004.

56. Afro-Nets:African Networks for Health Research and Development-Independent Group for Health in Africa http://www.afronets.org/egha.php retrieved 12/10/004.

latter are notable personalities with admirable records working in health fields in
renown American institutions like Harvard University and Tulane University.[57]
    The updated Web information on the group states its aims as:

> *monitor health problems, policies, strategies and programs (including re-
> search) in Africa and
> *advocate for improved health policy, strategy, programs, and research in
> Africa:

Its more specific objectives are stated as follows

- audit international organizations involved in the health sector in Africa
- assess regional and national health policies and programs including research
- monitor the role of the private sector in health
- advocacy for action on audited issues
- promote networking among health institutions, agencies and experts in Africa
- advocate for capacity-building of relevant local health institutions.

It remains to be seen how much of these ambitious objectives with huge time
and resource implications the group will be able to achieve. Perhaps more than its
immediate impact and outcomes, the most important significance of this initiative
may lie in its heuristic and symbolic value. The story of post-independence Africa
has been one of dependence on donors and short on local initiatives that intervene
in critical issues of the continent and its development. Governments, with violently imposed political hegemony have neither welcomed nor tolerated organized
public participation in societal affairs. It seems that Africa's threatening health
challenges topped by HIV/AIDS has inspired concerned people of all stripes and
level of expertise to force open the threshold of official tolerance for people's initiative and participation.
    It is interesting to note that the international community is generally encourag-
ing of this trend towards popular initiative and participation. Because of the new
found energy of civic activism, traditional/indigenous medical systems and practices on which the majority of the rural people rely (note earlier discussion in this
chapter), are receiving new levels of attention and respect in many African countries. A number of African countries are now embarked on new paths of research
and application of traditional medicine and training traditional/indigenous medical practitioners. Traditional/indigenous medical systems are being mainstreamed
as complements to the national health system generally organized along western
lines.[58] Canada is one of the countries supportive of African efforts to incorporate
traditional medicine into the health care system and to advance scientific knowledge in this area through joint African and Canadian research enterprises.[59]
    The major impetus for this new trend of incorporating traditional medicine
into the health care system comes from the peoples' insistent reliance on it and the

---

57. Ibid.
58. Robert, Stanley writing of Dr. Hills Sekagya-African dentist and traditional healer
who made a presentation at the International Symposium on Biodiversity and Health in Ottawa in October 2003 discusses this new trend and documents that Dr. Sekagya is invited
around the world to present his ideas and model for streamlining traditional/indigenous medicine and medical practices to play important roles in Africa. http://www.web.idrc.ca/en/ev-
55582-201-1-DO_TPOIC_html. 2004–02–13 Retrieved December 10, 2004.
59. Ibid.

advocacy of professionals like Dr. Hills Sekagaya-African dentist and traditional healer who has become a noted authority on research and application of traditional medicine.[60] Referring to an AIDS conference in Nairobi, Kenya in September 2003, Bob Stanley of Canada posts information on the Web affirming the positive engagement of traditional medicine in the fight against HIV/AIDS. African initiatives in research on traditional medicine have not only received bilateral support, but also the support of the World Health Organization.[61]

At the Summit of the Organization of African Unity in Lusaka, Zambia, held during July 9–11, 2001, the Decade of 2001–2010 was proclaimed as African Traditional Medicine decade.[62] The Canadian government expressed interest in cooperating with African countries towards to the goal of the decade. South Africa also places emphasis on research and application of traditional medicine to fight HIV/AIDS and other diseases. Speaking confidently about the useful role traditional medicine will play in the future, the South African Minister of Health said that the use of traditional medicine may eventually replace anti-retroviral drugs in the treatment of HIV/AIDS.[63] The research unit at the University of Cape Town, School of Pharmacy, the University of Western Cape, School of Pharmacy are conducting extensive research in anti-malaria plant derivatives.[64] Early results of these efforts are reported to be promising. This encouraging outcome has led to the publication of the first journal ever on the subject of traditional African medicine. The publication of this journal entitled *African Journal of Traditional, Complementary and Alternative Medicines* volume 1, no. 1 came out in October 2004. The table of contents of this journal shows an impressive array of research articles.[65]

The World Bank (2004) has embarked on the study of the emerging phenomenon of indigenous knowledge building and utilization processes in Africa. Two striking things are evident from the observation on the trends recorded in this work by the World Bank entitled *"Indigenous Knowledge: Local Pathways to Global Development"*. The first striking thing is that for the first time in the post-independence history of the continent, indigenous knowledge and approaches to human, social, and economic problems are considered primary in the search for solution for these African problems. In the foreword to the study, James J. Wolfenson, President of the World Bank declares the necessity of learning from "...the practices of communities so as to leverage the best in global and local knowledge systems" (VII). This is revolutionary. For too long, African people and communities with their age-old knowledge and skills were marginalized as irrelevant to the continent's development and transformation. At its hour of HIV/AIDS trial, the indigenous knowledge resources emerged as essential components of the solution to the challenge. For instance, the Africa-Wide, Senegal-based NGO, PROMETRA, is coordinating AIDS programs that "involve indigenous African

---

60. Ibid.
61. Ibid.
62. http://www.web.idrc.Ca/en/ev-41556-201-1.DO_TOPIC.html/ posted on 7–11–2001
63. South Africa: Traditional Medicine to Fight AIDS, Poverty http://www.newmediaexplorer.org/Sepp/2004/02/16/south_africa_traditional medicine_to-fight-aids_poverty.htm.
64. Traditional Medicines South Africa Health Information: http://www.sahealthinfo.org/traditionalmeds/traditionalmeds.htm retrieved 12/12/004.
65. Ibid.

healers throughout the continent" (21). The World Bank encourages this and finds that in general, "African paradigms work best" (20).

It is difficult to do justice to the burgeoning grassroots and indigenous groups movements to face up to Africa' current health crisis in a limited work like this one. It is hoped that the glimpses provided here will stimulate and spur interest in some readers to do further investigation.

Summary

People of African decent everywhere seem to be more vulnerable than others to health challenges, especially the epidemic of HIV/AIDS. It is heartening to note that this situation may change due to many factors, not the least of which is the peoples' own initiatives and ownership of their issues.

Because of the magnitude of the HIV/AIDS crisis and other diseases like malaria and tuberculosis, Africa is made the main focus of this study. We saw that Africa had overcome a number of epidemics like small pox, measles, river-blindness and brought under control malaria when the HIV/AIDS crisis hit to reverse many gains.

The HIV/AIDS crises that started in the early 1980s has assumed an unprecedented challenge to Africa's human, social and economic prospects. Early neglect and ambivalence of African governments and civil society presented unique opportunities for the disease to proliferate unchecked. The result has been that hard earned life-expectancy improvements have taken a beating and economies have started to decline. Africa is feeling the strain of the crisis. This inescapable strain has finally driven first, grassroots and civil society groups to organize and act spontaneously, forcing governments to move on the disease. In cases like South Africa, Uganda and a few other countries, robust efforts and creative initiatives are helping to contain the rate of spread of HIV/AIDS.

While mobilization in the African American community is poised to tap into the enormous national resources to reverse the spread of HIV/AIDS, and Brazil has many resources and capabilities to deal with the problem, Africa and the Caribbean face a different situation. The international community is actively assisting and the African social landscape is changing very fast in the direction of involving and empowering people to make international assistance effective. Remarkably, indigenous medicine and medical healing are becoming important components of the new indigenous paradigm. Some civil society initiatives against the HIV/AIDS epidemic appear to be looking beyond the immediate concerns and aiming to be part of future policy and program processes for building a healthy Africa. The African way of approaching and solving health problems is being acknowledge as the most effective for the continent. This will enhance the credibility of indigenous claims for partnership with international and governmental programs. This could well mark a turning point in how the African people deal with their governments and other problems of development and underdevelopment in the years to come.

References

Aggleton, Peter, Davis, Peter and Grahm Heart eds. (1997) *AIDS: Activism and Alliances.* Taylor and Francis, Bristol, PA.

Almeida-Filho, Naomar, Ichiro Kawachi, Alberto Pellegrini Filho and J. Norberto W. Dach (2003) Latin American Social Medicine "Research on Health Inequalities in Latin America: Bibliometric Analysis (1971–2000) and Descriptive Content Analysis (1971–1995)" December 2003, *Vol 93, No 12 American Journal of Public Health 2037–2043*

Azevedo, Mario, J. (1978) *Disease in African History: An Introductory Survey and Case Studies;* edited by Gerald W. Hartwig and K. David Patterson, Duke University Press, Duke University Center for Commonwealth and Comparative Studies #44.

Biggar, Robert J (1988) "Overview: Africa, AIDS, and Epidemiology" in Miller, Norman and Rockwell, Richard C. eds. *AIDS in Africa: The Social and Policy Impact*, The Edwin Mellen Press, Lewiston, New York

Brokensha, David (1988) "Overview: Social Factors in the Transmission and Control of AIDS" in Miller, Norman and Rockwell, Richard C, *AIDS in Africa: The Social and Policy Impact*, The Edwin Mellen Press

Caribbean/Health: Pan-caribbean Partnership against HIV/AIDS, file://c:\windows\TEMP\8MJRVAPK.htm (retrieved 6/3/05)

Sachs, Jeffery, D. (chair and presenter) *Macroeconomics and Health: Investing in Health for Economic Development* Report of the Commission on macroeconomics and Health, World Health Organization, Geneva 2001

CDC (Centers for Disease Control) (2002) *HIV/AIDS Special Surveillance Report, N0. 5 HIV Testing Survey,* 2002, Department of Health and Human Services, Public Health Services.

CDC, National Center for HIV, STD and TB Prevention, Division of HIV/AIDS PREVENTION (2003?) hip/aids Among African Americans http:www.cdc.gov/hiv/pubs/facts/afam.htm

Dancy, Barbara L (2003) " Focus on Solutions: A Community Based Mother/daughter HIV Risk Reduction Intervention" in Gilbert, Dorie J. and Wright Ednita M. eds. *African American Women and HIV/AIDS: Critical Responses,* Prager Publishers, 2003

Dawson, Mare H (1988) "AIDS in Africa: Historical Roots" in Miller and Rockwell eds. *AIDS in Africa: The Social and Policy Impact*

Foster, Geoff (2002) "Understanding Community Responses to the Situation of Children Affected by AIDS: Lessons for External Agencies" in Sisask Anne ed. *One Step Further-Responses to HIV/AIDS.* Sidastudies no.7

Gilbert, Dorie J. and Wright, Ednita M eds. (2003) *African American Women and HIV/AIDS: Critical Responses* Prager Publishers

Giovanella, Ligia, Vaitsman, Jeni, Escobar, Sarah, magalhaese, Rosana and Nilson do Rosario Costa (2002) *Health and Inequality: Institutions and Public policies in the 21st Century* http://www.scielosp.org/scielo.php?pid=S1020-49892002000500026&scripy=sci_arttex&tlng=en (retrieved 5/7/2005)

Global Snapshot: Brazil, a rich country full of poor people http://www.studentbmj.com/back_issue10503/life/160a.html (retrieved 5/6/05)

Good, Charles (1988) "Traditional Healers and AIDS Management" in Miller, Norman and Rockwell, Richard C. eds. *AIDS in Africa: The Social and Policy Impact*...

Gowan, Ann and Reining, Priscilla (1988) "Resource Guide to Non-Governmental Organizations Concerned with AIDS in Africa Based in North America" in Miller, Norman and Rockwell, Richard C. *AIDS in Africa: The Social and Policy Impact*...

Hacker, Andrew ((1995) *Two Nations: Black and White, Separate, Hostile, Unequal*. Andrew Hacker, Balantine Books, N.Y.

Kaiser Family Foundation (2003) HIV/AIDS : *HIV/AIDS Policy Fact Sheet: African American and HIV/AIDS* September 2003, Henry J. Kaiser Family Foundation

Koblinsky, Marge, Tinyan, Judith and Jill Gay eds. (1993) *The Health of Women*, Westview Press

Kramer, Joyce and Thomas, Anthony (1982) "The Modes of Maintaining Health in Ukambani, Kenya" in Yoder, Stanley ed. *African Health and Healing System: Proceedings of a Symposium*

Crossroads Press, University of California, Los Angeles

McElmury, Beverley J. Norr Kathleen F and Parker, Randy Spreen (1993) *Women's Health and Development: A Global Challenge*, Jones & Bartlet Publishers, London, Boston

Miller, Norman and Rockwell, Richard C eds. (1988) *AIDS in Africa: The Social and Policy Impact*, The Edwin Mellen Press, Lewiston, New York

Merritt, Gary, Lyerly, Williams and Jack Thomas (1988) "The HIV/AIDS Pandemic in Africa: Issues of Donor Strategy" in Miller, Norman and Rockwell, Richard C. eds. *AIDS In Africa: The Social and Policy Impact.*...

Reid, Marlenne B (1982) "Patient/Healer Interactions in Sukama Medicine" in Yoder, Stanley ed. *African Health and Healing Systems*

Sisask, Ann, ed. n.d., *One Step Further-Responses to HIV/AIDS*. Sidastudies no.7, Swedish International Development Cooperation Agency, Stockholm

UNAIDS (2002) Report on the Global HIV/AIDS Epidemic, Geneva

UNDP-United Nations Development Program (1996) *Development and the HIV Epidemic: A Forward Looking Evaluation of the Approach of the UNDP HIV and Development Programme*, UNDP. N. Y.

——— (2002) *Human Development Report 2002, Deepening Democracy in a Fragmented World*, UNDP N.Y.

UN Chronicle Online Edition: Infectious Diseases-Malaria in Africa Today.

United Nations Economic Commission for Africa (2002) *Economic Report on Africa 2002: Tracking Performance and Progress*, UNECA, Addis Ababa Ethiopia

USAID Bureau for Africa, Office of Sustainable Development (2002) Africa Bureau Brief no. 2, 2002,

USAID Responses to the Impact of HIV/AIDS On Basic Education in Africa, USAID, Washington DC

Yoder, Stanley, P. ed. (1982) *African Health and Healing Systems: Proceedings of a Symposium* , Crossroads Press, University of California, Los Angeles

Wallman, Sandra (1996) *Kampala Women Getting By: Wellbeing in the Time of AIDS*, Ohio University Press

Warren, Dennis M (1982) "The Techiman-Bono Ethnomedical System" in Yoder, Stanley ed. *African Health and Healing Systems: Proceedings of a Symposium*, Crossroads Press, University of Clifornis Los Angeles

WHO (2003) *The World Health Report 2003: Shaping the Future*

WHO (May 2005) *Bulletin of the World Health Organization, The International Journal of Public Health*, Volume 83, Number 5, May 2005

Williams, Dana (2003) "Focus on Solutions: Blacks Assistig Blacks Against AIDS-Taking Care of Our Own" in Gilbert, Dorie J. and Wright, Ednita eds. *African American Women and HIV/AIDS: Critical Responses*...

World Bank (1999) World Development Report 1998/1999, *Knowledge for Development*, World Bank, washington DC/Oxford University Press
——— (2000) World Development Report 1999/2000 *Entering the 21st Century*, World Bank, Washington D.C/Oxford University Press
——— (2002) *World Development Report: Sustainable Development in a Dynamic World-Transforming Institutions, Growth, and Quality of Life*, World Bank, Washington D.C/ Oxford University Press
——— (2003) *World Development Report 2004: Making Services Work for Poor People*, World Bank, Washington D.C./ Oxford University Press
——— (2003) Inequality in Lation America and the Caribbean: A Break with History?
——— (2004) *Indigenous Knowledge Local Pathways to Global Development*, The World Bank, Washington D.C.

PART VI

APPENDIXES

Appendix A

Selected Maps

Physical Map of Africa

Pre-Colonial Africa

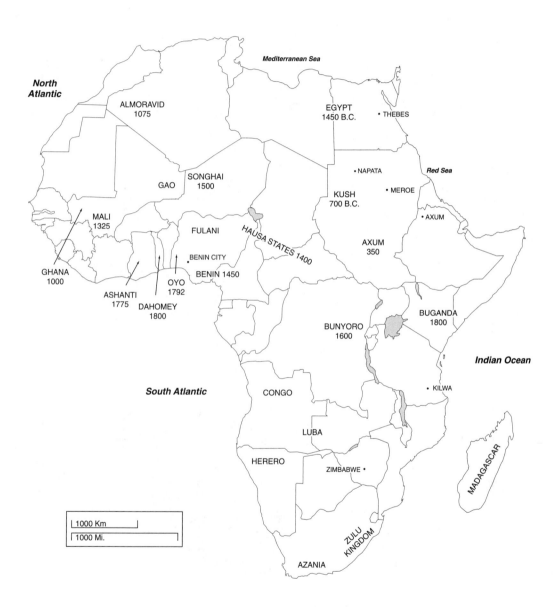

Mediterranean Sea

North
Atlantic

ALMORAVID
1075

EGYPT
1450 B.C.

• THEBES

SONGHAI
1500

GAO

• NAPATA

Red Sea

KUSH
700 B.C.

• MEROE

MALI
1325

FULANI

HAUSA STATES 1400

AXUM
350

• AXUM

GHANA
1000

BENIN CITY

BENIN 1450

OYO
1792

ASHANTI
1775

DAHOMEY
1800

BUNYORO
1600

BUGANDA
1800

Indian Ocean

South Atlantic

CONGO

• KILWA

LUBA

HERERO

ZIMBABWE •

MADAGASCAR

| 1000 Km |
| 1000 Mi. |

ZULU
KINGDOM

AZANIA

Colonial Africa

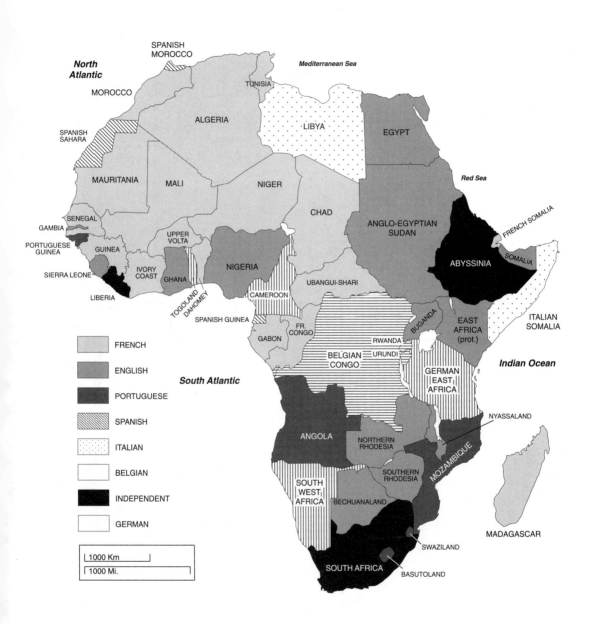

SPANISH MOROCCO

North Atlantic

MOROCCO

TUNISIA

Mediterranean Sea

ALGERIA

LIBYA

EGYPT

SPANISH SAHARA

Red Sea

MAURITANIA

MALI

NIGER

CHAD

ANGLO-EGYPTIAN SUDAN

FRENCH SOMALIA

SENEGAL

GAMBIA

PORTUGUESE GUINEA

GUINEA

UPPER VOLTA

ABYSSINIA

SOMALIA

SIERRA LEONE

IVORY COAST

GHANA

NIGERIA

UBANGUI-SHARI

LIBERIA

TOGOLAND

DAHOMEY

CAMEROON

EAST AFRICA (prot.)

ITALIAN SOMALIA

SPANISH GUINEA

GABON

FR. CONGO

RWANDA

BUGANDA

FRENCH

ENGLISH

BELGIAN CONGO

URUNDI

GERMAN EAST AFRICA

Indian Ocean

PORTUGUESE

South Atlantic

SPANISH

ITALIAN

BELGIAN

INDEPENDENT

GERMAN

ANGOLA

NORTHERN RHODESIA

NYASSALAND

MOZAMBIQUE

SOUTHERN RHODESIA

1000 Km

1000 Mi.

SOUTH WEST AFRICA

BECHUANALAND

SWAZILAND

MADAGASCAR

SOUTH AFRICA

BASUTOLAND

544

Present-Day Africa

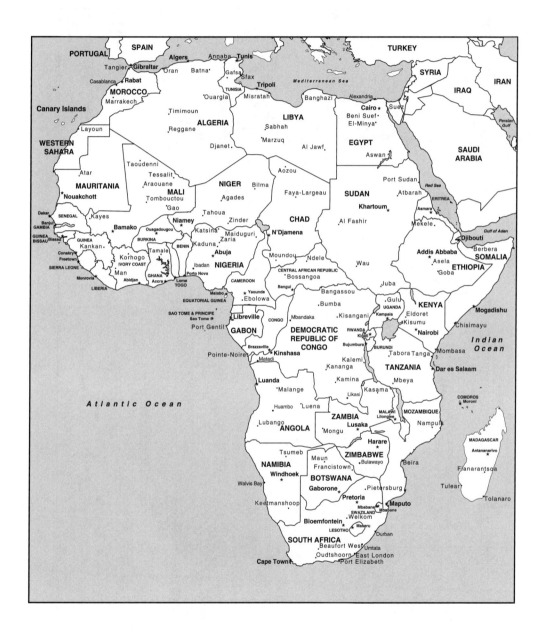

The Caribbean

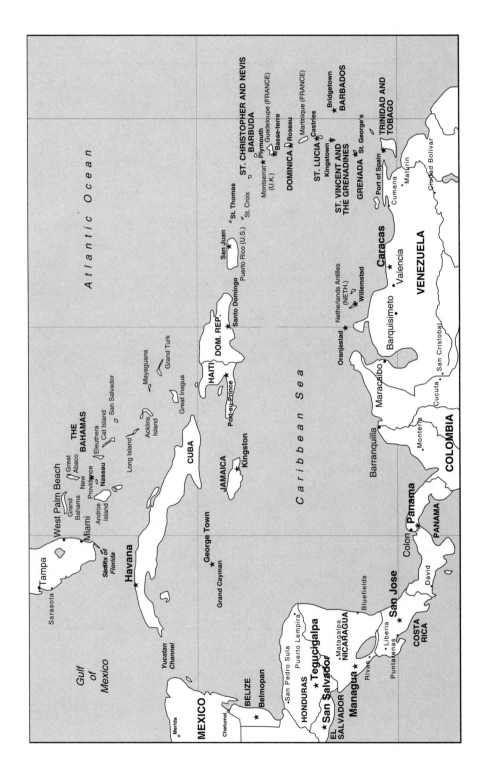

Appendix B

Landmarks in the History of Peoples of African Descent

B.C.
5000   Agriculture in Egypt
3100   Unification of Egypt under Menes
1000   Founding of Axum (later Ethiopia)
814   Founding of Carthage
750   Kashta of Kush begins conquest of Egypt
600   Egyptians circumnavigate Africa
538   Napata abandoned in favor of Meroe in Kush
332   Alexander the Great conquers Egypt
218   Second Punic War: Hannibal threatens Rome,
        but is not defeated until 202
200   Nok culture: knowledge and use of iron in West Africa
90   Introduction of the camel into the Sahara
31   Rome conquers Egypt

A.D.
100   Beginning of Bantu migrations
230   Origen exiled from Alexandria for heresy
330   Donatist Council held at Carthage with 270 African
        bishops attending
350   Axum destroys Meroe after battle of Fort Kemalke
396   Augustine consecrated bishop of Hippo
429   Vandals arrive in North Africa with 20,000 soldiers and
        60,000 "Barbarians" under Genseric
622   Founding of Islam in Mecca
690   Founding of Gao
706   Arabic made official language of Egypt
800   Founding of Ghana
975   Founding of Kilwa in East Africa
900   Founding of Benin
1077   Ghana temporarily conquered by Almoravids
1235   Founding of Mali by Sundiata
        Probable Founding of University of Senkore in Mali
1350   Beginning of the Congo dynasty
1415   Portuguese conquest of Ceuta in Morocco
1441   First capture of Africans by the Portuguese
1445   Fort Arguin built by the Portuguese

1450s	Probable date for the building of the Great Zimbabwe
1492	First blacks reportedly arrive with Columbus in the New World
1497	Vasco da Gama begins his expedition to India by sea; disembarks in 1498
1526	First blacks arrive in the future United States
1593	Fort Jesus in Mombasa under construction until 1639
1595	Moroccans overrun Songhay
1597	Augustinian friars arrive in Mombasa
1619	First twenty indentured Africans land in Jamestown, Virginia
1625	The French take Haiti from Spain
1641	Massachusetts becomes first colony to legalize slavery
1642	The French introduce African slaves in Martinique
1652	The Dutch begin settlement in the Cape
1669	Beginning of nine slave uprisings in Jamaica, ending in 1734
1679	Slave revolt in Haiti
1688	Mennonite Quakers sign anti-slavery resolution in Germantown, Pennsylvania
1697	Osei Tutu founds Kumasi
1711	Pennsylvania Assembly outlaws slavery; nullified by the British government
1712	Slave revolt in New York
1721	The French occupy Mauritius
1725	Founding of First Church of Colored Baptists
1738	Signing of a treaty between the Maroons and the British, giving autonomy to the former in Jamaica
1770	Crispus Attucks killed in the Boston Massacre
1780	Founding of African Union Society
1787	Prince Hall founds Grand Masonic Lodge 3459, Boston, Massachusetts
1788	Andrew Bryan founds Bryan Baptist Church, Savannah, Georgia
1790	Founding of Brown's Fellowship Society, Charleston, South Carolina
1791	Absalom Jones founds St. Thomas Episcopal Church, Philadelphia, Pennsylvania
	L'Ouverture's unsuccessful uprising in Haiti
1793	Fugitive Slave Act enacted by Congress in Philadelphia
1795	Toussaint L'Ouverture wins the first battle against the French in Haiti
	Mungo Park explores Senegambia
1796	First Zion Methodist Church founded
1800	Gabriel Prosser's conspiracy suppressed
1803	L'Ouverture dies in prison
1804	Usuman Dan Fodio declares a holy war against Gobir
	Haiti's independence
1807	Parliament abolishes the slave trade in the British dominions
1808	Gambia and Sierra Leone become Crown colonies
	Rev. Thomas Paul founds what is now known as the Abyssinian Baptist Church, New York City
1810	Founding of African Insurance Company

1815	Founding of Burial Ground Society of the Free People of Color, Richmond, Virginia
1816	Founding of first African Methodist Episcopal Church in Philadelphia
1818	Founding of Zulu kingdom by Chaka
1820	Missouri Compromise
	Slave revolts in Martinique, Puerto Rico, Antigua, Cuba, Jamaica, Tortola, and Demerara
1821	Founding of first African Methodist Episcopal Zion Church
1822	Denmark Vesey conspiracy
1822	Founding of Liberia by ex-slaves
	Dom Pedro proclaims Brazil's independence from Portugal
1827	Freedom Journal published
1830	David Walker's Appeal published
1831	Nat Turner revolt
1832	Founding of Afric-American Female Intelligence Society, Salem, Massachusetts
1833	Founding of Anti-Slavery Society
	Slavery abolished in Jamaica
1837	Madame Bernard Couvent founds Free School for Black Orphans
1838	Founding of Female Benevolent Society of Troy, New York
1840	Pope Gregory XVI declares slavery incompatible with Christianity
1841	Slave revolt on the ship Creole
1843	Founding of Ladies Union Benevolent Society, Charleston, South Carolina
	Founding of New York Benevolent Branch of Bethel for Women
	Founding of Union Band Society of New Orleans
	Founding of Colored Missionary Society, Mobile, Alabama
1844	The Dominican Republic proclaims independence
1847	Liberian independence
1849	Harriet Tubman escapes from slavery in Maryland and initiates the Underground Railroad, eventually freeing three hundred slaves
1850	The Clay Compromise, reinforcing the 1793 Fugitive Act
1851	Edward Wilmott Blyden settles in Liberia
1854	Kansas-Nebraska Act passed
1856	Under Kabaka Suna, Buganda reaches its zenith
1857	Dred Scott decision
1859	John Brown with thirteen whites and five blacks assaults Harpers Ferry arsenal: two blacks killed, two blacks captured, and one black escapes. Brown hanged in Charlestown (in present-day West Virginia)
1861	Civil War begins
1863	Emancipation Proclamation in effect
1865	End of Civil War
	Founding of the Ku Klux Klan in Tennessee
1865	Thirteenth Amendment approved
1866	Fourteenth Amendment ratified
1867	First Reconstruction Act

1868	Fourteenth Amendment ratified
	Fifteenth Amendment ratified
1869	Completion of the Suez Canal
1875	Civil Rights Bill against discrimination in public facilities
1876	King Leopold II takes the Congo Free State as a personal possession after Henry M. Stanley secures fraudulent treaties with African authorities
1881	The Mahdi Rebellion in Sudan ends on January 28, 1885 with the slaying of British Governor-General Gordon
1883	Supreme Court declares the 1875 Civil Rights Bill unconstitutional
1884	Berlin Conference; ends February 1885
1886	Slavery abolished in Spanish dominions
1888	Slavery abolished in Brazil (750,000 slaves freed)
1892	Defeat of Italians at Adowa by Menelik II of Ethiopia
	Helen Cook elected first President, Colored Women's League, Washington, D.C.
	Founding of Loyal Union of Brooklyn and New York Black Women
1893	Founding of Harper's Woman's Club, Jefferson City, Missouri
1894	Founding of Belle Phoebe League, Pittsburgh, Pennsylvania
	Founding of Woman's Mutual Movement Club, Knoxville, Kentucky
	Founding of Phyllis Wheatley Club, New Orleans, Louisiana
1895	Josephine St. Pierre Ruffin founds National Federation of Afro-American Women in Boston
	Founding of Women's Club of Omaha, Nebraska
1896	Mary Church Terrell founds the National Association of Colored Women
	Plessy vs. Ferguson ("separate but equal" doctrine decided)
	Founding of Sojourner Truth Club, Providence, Rhode Island 1898
	Fashoda Incident
	Cuban independence
1899	Beginning of Boer War; ends in 1902
1900	First Pan-African Congress in London (gathering of African and New World intellectuals)
1902	End of Cuban Occupation by the United States
1904	Mary McCleod Bethune founds Daytona Educational and Industrial Institute; later merged with Cookman Institute to become Bethune-Cookman College in 1929
1905	The Niagara Movement established in Fort Erie, N.Y.
1905	Beginning of Maji Maji Rebellion against the Germans in Tanganyika, ending only in 1907
1908	Due to scandalous treatment of Africans, the Belgian government takes the Belgian Congo from King Leopold II
1909	Founding of the NAACP
1911	Founding of National Urban League
	Founding of UNIA by Garvey in Jamaica
1912	Founding of the South African Native National Congress, later known as the African National Congress (ANC)

1915   Carter G. Woodson founds the Association for the Study of
       Negro Life and History and the Journal of Negro History
1919   Paris Pan-African Congress
       Lynching of eighty-three African-Americans in the South
       Founding of the National Congress of British West Africa
       (NCBWA) in Accra, Gold Coast
1921   The Harlem Renaissance begins
1923   Garvey sentenced to five years in jail for mail fraud in New York
       Founding of Nigerian National Democratic Party in Lagos
1926   Founding of Negro History Week by Carter G. Woodson
1927   Garvey deported to Jamaica
1930   Founding of Temple of Islam by Fard Mohammed in Detroit
1933   Elijah Muhammed founds the Nation of Islam
1935   Mussolini overruns Ethiopia (until 1941)
1941   Announcement of the Atlantic Charter
1942   Founding of CORE
1944   Nnamdi Azikiwe founds National Council for Nigeria and
       the Cameroons
1945   Black troops distinguish themselves in Germany and Northern
       Italy Manchester Pan-African Congress
       Founding of the United Nations in San Francisco
       International Bank for Reconstruction and Development—IBRD
       (World Bank) created
1946   Felix Houphouet-Boigny of Côte d'Ivoire and leaders from
       French-speaking Africa launch the Rassemblement Democratique
       Africain at Bamako, Mali
       End of forced labor (corvée) in the French territories
1948   Founding of the Union des Populations Camerounaises
       Victory of the Nationalist party in South Africa: formal
       apartheid begins
1949   Kwame Nkrumah founds the Convention People's Party (CPP)
1951   Independence of Libya
1952   Beginning of Mau Mau uprising in Kenya; ends in 1956
1953   Central African Federation (Nyasaland, Northern Rhodesia,
       and Southern Rhodesia) formed
1954   Brown vs. Board of Education
       Establishment of Tanganyika National Union (TANU)
       Gamal Abdel Nasser wrests power after 1953 coup against
       King Faruk of Egypt
1955   Rosa Parks refuses to sit in the back of the bus in Montgomery,
       Alabama
       Martin Luther King, Jr., initiates boycotts and marches for
       civil rights
       First Non-Aligned Movement Conference in Bandung, Indonesia
1956   Independence of Morocco, Sudan, and Tunisia
       Establishment of Loi Cadre, giving autonomy to French colonies
       and abolishing the dual college (which was based on race)
1957   Federal paratroopers force Central High School in Little Rock,
       Arkansas to integrate eighteen black students

1957   Ghana's (Gold Coast's) independence
        Martin Luther King, Jr., founds the SLCC
1958   General de Gaule's referendum on French-speaking Africa
        (only Guinea, under Sekou Toure, opts for independence)
        Economic Commission for Africa created
1959   The Leakeys find the remains of Zinjanthropus (1.7 million
        years old)
        Conseil de L'Entente created
1960   Four black students "sit-in" at a Woolworth counter in
        Greensboro, North Carolina
        First wave of African independence in Sub-Saharan Africa:
        Cameroon, Chad, Central African Republic, Congo (Brazzaville),
        Benin, Gabon, Cote d'Ivoire, Malagasy Republic, Mali, Mauritania,
        Niger, Nigeria, Senegal, Somalia, Togo, Burkina Faso, and Zaire
        achieve independence
        Sharpville Massacre in South Africa
1961   Central African Federation dissolved
        Formation of Zimbabwe African Peoples Union (ZAPU)
        Founding of Kenya African National Union (KANU)
        Beginning of war of liberation in Angola by the MPLA
1962   Federal marshals force integration at University of Mississippi
        (James Meredith attends classes)
        Independence of Algeria, at war with France since 1954
        Uganda's independence
        Emperor Haile Selassie annexes Eritrea to Ethiopia
        Beginning of Eritrean liberation war (by the Eritrean
        Liberation Front)
        Jamaica's independence
        Trinidad and Tobago achieve independence
1963   Medgar Evars assassinated in Jackson, Mississippi
        First military coup in Sub-Saharan Africa: President Sylvanus
        Olympio assassinated
        Kenya's independence
        Establishment of the Organization of African Unity
        Formation of Zimbabwe African National Union (ZANU)
        PAIGC, under Amilcar Cabral, wages guerrilla war against
        Portugal in Guinea-Bissau
        African Development Bank (ADB) created
1964   Civil Rights Bill approved by Congress
        Tanganyika and Zanzibar united as Tanzania
        FRELIMO under Eduardo Mondlane declares liberation war
        against Portugal
1965   Selma-Montgomery March
        Voting Rights Bill
        Assassination of Malcolm X in Harlem
        White settlers in Southern Rhodesia announce their independence
        (Unilateral Declaration of Independence, simply known as UDI)
        United Nations Development Programme created
        Organisation Commune Africaine et Malgache created

1966   Kwame Nkrumah overthrown by the army
        Military coup in Nigeria
        Stokely Carmichael heads SNCC
        Founding of FROLINAT in Sudan and beginning of civil war
        in Chad
1967   Biafran War in Nigeria begins and continues until 1970
        Arusha Declaration
1968   Assassination of Martin Luther King, Jr., in Memphis, Tennessee,
        April 4
1969   Eduardo Mondlane, FRELIMO's President, is assassinated in
        Dares-Salaam
        Civilian government restored in Ghana under Dr. Busia as
        Prime Minister
1971   Anguilla's independence
        The Commonwealth of Nations created at Singapore's meeting
        of Heads of State
1972   Coalition against Blaxploitation in L.A.
        Shirley Chisholm runs for U.S. president
        Amilcar Cabral of the PAIGC is assassinated
        Lt. Col. Ignatius Acheampong overthrows Busia's civilian
        government
1973   Independence of the Bahamas
        Arab Bank for Economic Development in Africa (BADEA) created
        at Algiers Arab Summit Conference
1974   Independence of Grenada
        Communeauté Economique de l'Afrique de l'Ouest (West African
        Economic Community) created
        Overthrow of Emperor Haile Selassie of Ethiopia
1975   Independence of Portuguese-speaking Africa (Guinea's was
        recognized in 1974)
        Establishment of the Economic Community of West African
        States (ECOWAS) at a Lagos meeting
        Comoros independence
1976   Spain withdraws from Spanish (Western) Sahara and conflict
        begins among Morocco, Mali, Algeria, and the POLISARIO
        Angolan civil war
1977   Ogaden War between Somalia and Ethiopia begins but does
        not end until 1978
        RENAMO is created
1978   Allan Bakke Supreme Court decision
1979   Amin overthrown by Tanzania's and Milton Obote's armies
        Lt. Jerry Rawlings assassinates Acheampong in Ghana and
        takes over the government
        Nigerian civilian government restored, with Shehu Shagari
        as president
        Southern African Development Coordinating Conference
        created (SADCC)
1980   Independence of Zimbabwe

1980   Sam Doe overthrows Tolbert in Liberia and becomes the
        first non-Americo-Liberian leader in the country
        President Leopold Senghor of Senegal resigns from power
        voluntarily, the first to do so in Africa, and is replaced by
        Abdou Diouf
1981   Reagan initiates review of civil rights regulations
1982   Hisseine Habre's victory in Chad over Gukuni Weddey and Libya
        President Ahmadou Ahidjo resigns and hands over power to
        Paul Biya in Cameroon
1983   Saint Kitts-Nevis's independence
1984   Jesse Jackson runs for president of the United States
1985   President Julius Nyerere retires, replaced by Ali Hassan Mwinyi
1986   The Reagan administration bombs Libya in April
        President Samora Machel of Mozambique dies in airplane crash
        in South African territory and is succeeded by Joaquim Chissano
1988   Jesse Jackson again runs for president, winning primaries in
        five states
        Beginnings of pluralistic democratic movements in Africa
1989   Douglas Wilder elected first black Governor of Virginia
        Ronald Brown appointed National Chairman of the Democratic
        Party
        First African-American Summit in New Orleans
        Nelson Mandela released from jail
1990   Independence of Namibia
        Liberian civil war
        Hisseine Habre is overthrown by Idris Deby in Chad
1991   First African and African-American Summit in Abidjan
        Africa's international debt estimated at $272 billion
        Conservative Clarence Thomas takes seat on the Supreme Court
        Siad Barre of Somalia is overthrown: violence, chaos, and
        famine follow. UN relief effort begins in August
        President Kenneth Kaunda of Zambia is defeated in the
        country's first fair presidential elections
1992   First presidential and parliamentary elections in Angola
        Peace negotiations concluded between FRELIMO and RENAMO
        UN massive food assistance to Somalia
1993   Second African and African-American Summit, Libreville, Gabon
1994   US troops leave Somalia
1995   Ethnic warfare erupts in Rwanda, with thousands massacred
        The University of California ends all Affirmative Action policies
1996   University of Texas Law School Affirmative Action policy struck
        down by Federal Appeals Court
1997   Laurent Kabila ousts through war Joseph Mobutu, President of Zaire
1998   President Clinton's 12-day visit to Africa
1999   Thebo Mbeki elected President of South Africa, succeeding Nelson
        Mandela
2001   World Conference Against Racism, Racial Discrimination, Xenophobia
        Related Intolerance convened by the UN in Durban, South Africa

Kabila assassinated and son, Joseph Kabila, succeeds in Democratic Republic of Congo (DRC), former Zaire. Civil war ensues, with neighboring countries involved

2002 Launching of the African Union in Durban, South Africa
Jonas Savimbi assassinated by Angolan government troops
Luiz Inacio Lula da Silva: Brazil's first president to declare himself black

2003 Supreme Court's decision on the University of Michigan Affirmative Action
Joseph Kabila inaugurates power-sharing government, but violence continues in DRC

2004 Haiti's President Jean-Bertrand Aristide ousted; US troops and UN intervene to restore law and order; yet, instability continuing even by mid-2005
Sporadic war continues in DRC; 3.8 million estimated people to have died since 2001

2005 Ratification of the agreement between the Sudanese government and the Sudanese People's Liberation Movement; Darfur refugee situation worsens
Edgar Ray Killen, former pastor and KKK leader, found guilty in Philadelphia, MS, for the 1964 murder of civil rights workers James Chaney, Michael Schwerner, and Andrew Goodman, with an imposed sentence of 60 years in jail
Tony Blair's Commission for Africa pleads for forgiveness of all Africa's external debt; the G8 decide to follow-through for several developing countries.

Appendix C

Selected Periodicals and References in Africana Studies Available in the United States

Africa (News)

Africa: South of the Sahara (Reference)

Africa Confidential (News)

Africa Contemporary Record (Reference)

Africa Currents (News)

Africa News (News)

Africa Press Clips (News)

Africa Report (News and Articles)

Africa Research Bulletin (News)

Africa Today

African Affairs

African Arts/Arts d'Afrique

African Economic Digest (News)

African Economic History

African Historical Dictionaries (References)

African Language Studies

African Literature Today

African Studies Review

African Writers Series

Afrique Contemporaine

Art Journal

Black Enterprise

Black Music Research

Black Scholar

Black Studies Journal

Cahiers d'Etudes Africaines

Caribbean Economic Almanac (Reference)

Caribbean Insight

Caribbean Journal of Education

Caribbean Journal of Religious Studies

Caribbean Quarterly

Caribbean Review

Caribbean Review of Books

Caribbean Studies

Caribbean Update (Reference)

Canadian Journal of African Studies

A Current Bibliography on African Affairs

International Journal of Modern Historical African Studies

Jamaican Journal of African Music

Jamaican Journal of Modern Historical African Studies

Jeune Afrique

Journal of African History

Journal of African Languages and Linguistics

Journal of African Music

Journal of African Studies

Journal of Asian and African Studies

Journal of Behavioral and Social Sciences

Journal of Black Music

Journal of Black Music Research

Journal of Commonwealth Literature

Journal of Modern African Studies

Journal of Negro History

Journal of Religion in Africa

Journal of Southern African Studies

Liberian Studies Journal

Marchés Tropicaux et Méditerranéens

New African (News)

Phylon

Quarterly Conflict

Research in African Literature

SAGE: A Scholarly Journal of Black Women

Sierra Leone Language Review

Social Science and Medicine

Third World Quarterly

TransAfrican Journal of History

Western Journal of Black Studies

West Africa (News)

Contributors

RUSSELL L. ADAMS, Chairman, Department of Afro-American Studies at Howard University, earned a B.A. degree at Morehouse College and M.A. and Ph.D. degrees from the University of Chicago, all in Political Science. A political sociologist, Adams has written extensively on the influence of social status and ethnic background in shaping analytical perspectives in the social sciences, especially in the field of African American Studies. Adams's research interests include minority institution building, epistemology, and cultural diversity in the African diaspora. He is also known for his widely used reference work, *Great Negroes Past and Present*, a standard in its genre. Adams is a consultant to and advisor of African American Studies departments as well as public school systems in the area of multicultural education.

MARIO AZEVEDO, originally from Mozambique, is Professor and Chair in the Department of Afro-American and African Studies at The University of North Carolina at Charlotte. He holds a B.A. degree in History from The Catholic University of America, an M.A. in History from American University, and a Ph.D. in African History from Duke University. His recent publications include: *The Returning Hunter* (Interculture Associates, 1978), contributor; *Disease in African History* (Duke University Press, 1978), contributor; *Independence Without Freedom* (ABC-Clio Press, 1980), contributor; *Africa and Its People* (Kendall-Hunt, 1982), editor; *Historical Dictionary of Mozambique, Cameroon and Chad in Historical and Contemporary Perspectives* (Mellen Press, 1989), editor; *Roots of Violence: A History of War in Chad* (Gordon and Breach, 2003); Tragedy and Triumph: Mozambique Refugees in Southern Africa (1977–2001) (Heine Mann, 2003) and articles in *African Studies Review, Journal of African History, African Affairs, Journal of Southern African Affairs, The Researcher, Current History, Western Journal of Black Studies, Journal of Muslim Minority Affairs, Africa Today, Africa In the World, Journal of Social Science and Medicine, Conflict Quarterly* and *Journal of Negro History*. Azevedo has been a recipient of major grants on Africa from the Department of Education (four Fulbright-Hays to Africa), the Lilly Endowment, the National Endowment for the Humanities, and U.S.A.I.D.

M. ALPHA BAH, Associate Professor of African History at the College of Charleston, was born and reared in the Mano River area (Guinea, Sierra Leone, and Liberia). He studied in Sierra Leone, Egypt, and the United States. Bah graduated from Howard University (B.A. in French, M.A. in French, M.A. in History, and Ph.D. in African History). He also taught History and French at the University of Liberia (1978-1985), where he served as department Chair (1984-1985), and was a Fulbright Scholar at Villanova University (1985-1986). Bah's articles have appeared in the *Liberian Studies Journal* and the *Journal of Muslim Minority Affairs*. His interest in traditional ethnic and modern colonial boundaries in Africa has led to his first book, *Fulbe Migration and Settlement Among the Kissi of Eastern Sierra Leone* (Peter Lang Publishers, Inc., forthcoming).

NIKONGO BA'NIKONGO has a Ph.D. in International Relations, Political Economy, and Comparative Politics from Howard University and is a Professor in the Afro-American Studies Department at Howard University, where he teaches courses on the African American and Caribbean experience and the Third World. He has also taught in the University of Maryland system and at the University of Hartford, Connecticut. His most recent publications include: *The Ultimate Dilemma* (University Press of America, 1986) and *Debt and Development in The Third World: Trends and Strategies* (IAAS Press, 1991). Professor Ba'Nikongo also served as a consultant for the Institute for Urban Affairs and Research in Washington, D.C.

KENNETH BILBY received his Ph.D. in Anthropology from Johns Hopkins University and works at the Smithsonian Institution, Office of Folk Life Programs, Washington, D.C. He has conducted field research in New Mexico, Sierra Leone, and Jamaica, published articles in academic journals, made a number of ethnomusicological phonograph recordings, and produced (with Jefferson Miller) a documentary film about the Jamaican Maroons, *Capital of Earth*. He is currently carrying out research among the Aluku (Boni) Maroons of French Guiana.

A. LYNN BOLLES is Professor of Women's Studies and Affiliate Faculty member in Anthropology, and Comparative Literature Departments and Afro-American Studies Program at the University of Maryland, College Park. She received her A.B. from Syracuse, and her M.A. and Ph.D. Rutgers. From 1980–89, she directed Africana Studies at Bowdoin College. Bolles is the author of *Sister Jamaica: A Study of Women, Work and Households in Kingston* (1996), *We Paid Our Dues: Women Trade Union Leaders in the Caribbean* (1996), and co-author of *In the Shadows of the Sun* (1990). Her work has also appeared in *Caribbean Studies*, *Review of Radical Economics*, *Transforming Anthropology*, *American Anthropologist*, *American Ethnologist* and *New West Indian Guide*. Her professional activities include the Scholars Council of TransAfrica Forum, 1996 Program Chair for the American Ethnological Society, elected member of the Executive Council of the Caribbean Studies Association, and member of the editorial board of *Feminist Studies* and *Urban Anthropology*. Bolles was the President of the Caribbean Studies Association, 1997–98.

MARSHA JEAN DARLING is Director of the Center for African American and Ethnic Studies, at Adelphi University, New York. She earned an A.B. degree in History from Vassar College and an M.A. and a Ph.D. in History from Duke University. She taught previously at Wellesley College, Hunter College, and the University of Maryland at College Park. She is the recipient of a Fulbright Award, a Rockefeller post-doctoral fellowship, and an NEH summer award.

She has also held research appointments at the W. E. B. Du Bois Institute for Afro-American Research at Harvard University and the Smithsonian Institution. Darling has worked as a consultant on the *Eyes on the Prize* documentary series, and most recently served as co-principal investigator on a post-Croson study on the history of minority and women-owned business enterprises. She is the author of numerous papers, and has published articles in the *Michigan Quarterly Review, The Encyclopedia of Southern Culture*, and the *Women's Review of Books*.

GREGORY DAVIS is Adjunct Assistant Professor and Minority Student Advisor for the Academic Advising and Learning Assistance Services at the University of North Carolina at Charlotte and teaches "Introduction to African American and African Studies" and other courses on the black experience. He also serves as Pastor of Bellefonte Presbyterian Church in Harrisburg, N.C. He received his B.A. degree in Religious Studies at the University of North Carolina at Charlotte, a Master's of Divinity at Duke University Divinity School, and a Ph.D. in American Religious History at The Union Institute, Cincinnati, Ohio. He has contributed encyclopedia articles for Salem Press.

R. HUNT DAVIS, JR., is Professor Emeritus of History and African Studies, former Interim Director of International Studies and Programs, and former Director of the Center for African Studies at the University of Florida, Gainesville. He is also the former Editor of the *African Studies Review* and served as the Coordinator of the University of Florida-Cornell University project that published *Global Research on the Environmental and Agricultural Nexus for the 21st Century* (1995). He holds a B.A. in history from Grinnell College and an M.A. and Ph.D. in History from the University of Wisconsin, Madison. His publications include *Bantu Education and the Education of Africans in South Africa* (1972), *Apartheid Unravels* (1991), *Mandela, Tambo, and the African National Congress* (1991), which he co-edited with Sheridan Johns, and numerous chapters in edited books, journal articles, and reviews. He is also the senior author of the last two volumes of the forthcoming five-volume *Encyclopedia of African History and Culture*.

RAYMOND GAVINS is Professor of History at Duke University. His research focuses on the African American experience in the Jim Crow South. Gavins has a B.A. in History from Virginia Union University and an M.A. and Ph.D., also in History, from the University of Virginia. He is author of *The Perils and Prospects of Southern Black Leadership: Gordon Blaine Hancock, 1884-1970* (Duke University Press, 1977) and *Black North Carolina: A History* (University of North Carolina Press, forthcoming), and has several articles in renowned journals.

TRUDIER HARRIS is J. Carlyle Sitterson Professor of English and former Chair of the African and Afro-American Studies Curriculum at the University of North Carolina at Chapel Hill, where she has taught courses in African American literature and folklore since she joined the faculty in 1979. She earned her B.A. from Stillman College, Tuscaloosa, Alabama, and her M.A. and Ph.D. from The Ohio State University, Columbus. Author, co-editor, and editor of eleven volumes, her most recent critical work is *Fiction and Folklore: The Novels of Toni Morrison*, published by the University of Tennessee Press, 1991. Harris has also done research in Kenya.

ALPHINE W. JEFFERSON is Associate Professor of History, Black Studies, and Urban Affairs, at the College of Wooster, Ohio, where he teaches interdisciplinary courses on Race, Class, and Gender as well as Afro-American and Urban History. He received his bachelor's degree in American Colonial History from the University of Chicago and M.S. and Ph.D. degrees in Social History from Duke University, where he was a Fellow in the Oral History Program and the Center for the Study of Civil Rights and Race Relations. Jefferson has also taught at Northern Illinois University and served as Director of African American Studies at Southern Methodist University in Dallas, Texas. Recipient of numerous fellowships and awards, including an NEH Fellowship for Independent Study and a Mellon Fellowship at Harvard, Jefferson has published widely. He has articles in *Oral History Review, The Black Scholar*, and the *Journal of American Ethnic History*, and is contributor of chapters in *Illinois: Its History and Legacy* and several Encyclopedias and Abstracts.

RODERIC KNIGHT is Professor of Ethnomusicology at the Oberlin College Conservatory of Music. He worked first in Africa as a Peace Corps music teacher and band director in Sierra Leone, turning later to field research with Mandinka musicians in the Gambia and Senegal for M.A. and Ph.D. degrees from UCLA. More recently, he has conducted research on music in India. He has written numerous articles and produced three LP recordings.

HAZEL M. McFERSON is a Commonwealth Associate Professor of Government and Politics and Conflict Analysis and Resolution at George Mason University, Fairfax, Virginia. She has over twenty years of professional experience in teaching, consulting, and university administration. She has taught at Southeastern Massachusetts University, North Dartmouth, Massachusetts, at the University of the South Pacific, Suva, Fiji Islands, and, at the University of Maryland, College Park. Her administrative experience includes the position of Associate Director of Academic Affairs at the Massachusetts Board of Regents of Higher Education, Boston, and as Program Social Science Analyst for the U.S. Agency for International Development, Mogadishu, Somalia during 1985-1987. Her duties included evaluating refugee programs and assistance projects in Somalia and women in development issues. Ms. McFerson, born in Boston, was educated in Boston, Massachusetts. She holds a Ph.D. in politics from Brandeis University, a Masters in international politics from the Fletcher School of Law and Diplomacy, Tufts University and a B.A. in Sociology from the University of Massachusetts at Boston. She has written on ethnic and race relations in the United States, Africa and the South Pacific, on African American and African politics, on women in development, and conflict analysis and resolution in the United States, the Caribbean, Africa, and the South Pacific. She has traveled extensively and lived in Africa, the Caribbean, the South Pacific, Central and South America, Europe, and India.

EDDIE S. MEADOWS is Professor of Ethnomusicology at San Diego State University. He completed his B.A. at Tennessee State University, an M.A. at the University of Illinois, and a Ph.D., in Music, at Michigan State University, and has done postdoctoral studies in Ethnomusicology at UCLA with J.H. Kwabena Nketia and Kobla Ladzepko. Meadows has held several visiting professorships including such institutions as The University of California, Berkeley, University of Ghana, and

Michigan State University. He has published some one hundred articles in reputable journals and encyclopedias, including the *Western Journal of Black Studies*, the *National Association of Jazz Educators Journal*, and *Jazzforschung*. He is author of *Jazz References and Research Materials* and *Theses and Dissertations of Black American Music*, and contributed an article in Talmadge Anderson (ed.), *Black Studies: Theory, Methods, and Cultural Perspectives* (1990), and is completing a manuscript which will be published by Garland Publishers.

JULIUS E. NYANG'ORO is Chair and Professor of African Studies at the University of North Carolina at Chapel Hill. He holds a B.A. in Political Science from the University of Dar-es-Salaam, Tanzania, and an M.A. and Ph.D. in Political Science from Miami University, in Ohio. He also holds a J.D. from Duke University. Among his publications are *The State and Capitalist Development in Africa; Corporatism in Africa*, co-editor (1989); and *Beyond Structural Adjustment in Africa*, co-editor (1992).

F. UGBOAJA OHAEGBULAM is emeritus Professor of Government and International Affairs and former Chair of the African/African American Studies at the University of South Florida. He received his B.A. in Arts and Sciences from Evangel College, an M.A. in History from Fordham University, and a Ph.D. degree in International Studies from the University of Denver. He is an active researcher and is author of *The Nigeria UN Mission to the Congo* (1982), *Nationalism in Colonial and Post-Colonial Africa* (1977), *The Post-Colonial Era in Africa; Traumas and Opportunities: A Foreign Affairs Special Anthology* (1990), and *Towards an Understanding of the African Experience: From Historical and Contemporary Perspectives* (1990). His articles have appeared in *TransAfrica, Journal of Modern African Studies, Africa Today, Western Journal of Black Studies*, and *African Studies Journal*. He has also been a recipient of several NEH and NSF grants.

TANURE OJAIDE is Professor in the Afro-American and African Studies Department at the University of North Carolina at Charlotte. Ojaide was educated in Nigeria and the United States, where he received an M.A. in Creative Writing and a Ph.D. in English from Syracuse University. He has been a Fellow in Writing of the University of Iowa; has been inducted into the Ahmadu Bello University Creative Writers' Club's Roll of Honor; and he was winner of the Africa Regional Commonwealth Poetry Prize in 1987 and of the All-Africa Okigbo Prize for Poetry in 1988, as well as the 1988 Overall Winner of the BBC Arts and Africa Poetry Award. His publications include: *Children of Iroko, Labyrinths of the Delta, The Eagle's Vision, The Endless Song, The Fate of Vultures*, and *The Blood of Peace*. Ojaide's poetry has been described by the veteran American poet Hayden Carruth as "strong, supple, various, colorful, moving, invariably interesting," while Joseph Bruchac of The Greenfield Literary Center has commented: "I personally regard [Ojaide] as perhaps the most important voice in the generation of African writers following Chinua Achebe and Wole Soyinka."

BARBARA SHAW PERRY, a Ph.D. candidate in the Department of American Studies at the University of Maryland, College Park, collaborated with Dr. Lynne Bolles on the chapter on Women of the Caribbean.

GWENDOLYN S. PRATER is Professor and Dean of the College of Public Service at Jackson State University. She has a B.A. degree in Sociology from Tougaloo College, an M.S.W. from Ohio State University, and a D.S.W. from the University of Southern California. Her publications include *Africa and Its People* (1982), co-editor; *Child Welfare: A Multi-Cultural Focus*, contributor; and articles in *Journal of Social Work, Western Journal of Black Studies, African Studies Journal, The Researcher, Journal of Social Science and Medicine, Comprehensive Psychiatry*, and *Journal of Islamic Minorities*. She has been a recipient of numerous grants from the Department of Education (including two Fulbright-Hays to Africa), the Department of Transportation, and U.S.A.I.D., and has done research in Cameroon and Kenya.

SHARON PRUITT is Associate Professor of Art History at East Carolina University. She received a B.S. in Art Education from Case Western Reserve University, an M.A. in African Studies from Howard University, and a Ph.D. in Art History, following field study in Nigeria, from The Ohio State University. Pruitt has done research in Kenya and teaches and researches both the traditional and contemporary arts of Africa. Presently at East Carolina University, she teaches West and Central African Art, Art Appreciation, and Art History Survey. Prior to coming to East Carolina University, Pruitt taught African and African American Art at Spelman College.

JEFFREY SAMMONS is Professor of History at New York University. He received his Ph.D. in History from the University of North Carolina at Chapel Hill and has authored and edited works on the history of African Americans in sports. He is author of *Beyond The Ring: The History of Boxing in American Society*, and has been commissioned by Macmillan to edit an encyclopedia on African American life and culture. Sammons also serves on the editorial board of the *Journal of Sport History*. He is currently preparing a socio-cultural history of blacks and golf.

LUIS B. SERAPIAO, Professor in the Department of African Studies at Howard University, has an M.A. degree in International Relations from The Catholic University of America and a Ph.D. in International Relations from American University. He is co-author of *Mozambique in the Twentieth Century: From Colonialism to Independence*, (1979), and has also published articles in several journals including *Africa Quarterly, Conflict, A Current Bibliography on African Affairs, Issue, Journal of Church and State, Lusophone Area Studies Journal*, and *Munger Africana Library Notes*.

MICHAEL W. WILLIAMS is Director of the American Exchange Program and Professor at the University of Ghana at Legon, Ghana, Massachusetts. He received his M.A. and Ph.D. degrees in Sociology from the University of Notre Dame. Williams's research is in the areas of African American families, race, and ethnic relations, the sociology of knowledge, and Pan-Africanism. He has published in numerous scholarly journals, and his most recent book-length manuscripts include *Pan-Africanism and Zionism: Political Movements in Polarity* and *Pan-Africanism: An Annotated Bibliography*. He is currently working on an edited volume on Malcolm X.

ALMAZ ZEWDE is Assistant Professor at Howard University, Washington D.C. She earned her B.A. in Sociology at the University of Washington, Seattle, WA, one M.S. from Columbia University, N.Y., in social research and community organization, and another M.S. in Agricultural Economics from Michigan State University, East Lansing, and her Ph.D. from Michigan State University. She has taught at Michigan State University, in the Department of Sociology, at Georgetown University, in the African Studies Program, at George Washington University, in the Department of Sociology and the Graduate Program in Women Studies. Dr. Zewde has also worked in international development in the U.S. and Africa and has published works on North East African Studies and the Third World Spectrum.

Index

Levinson, Stanley, 140
Lewis, Edmonia, 317-318
Lewis, John, 292
Lewis, W. Arthur, 158, 162
Liberation, 22, 51, 65, 94, 98, 101, 104, 135,
      141, 143, 181, 183, 209, 213, 215, 222,
      231-232, 235-236, 238, 362, 421, 423,
      428-429, 433, 436, 441, 462, 495, 509,
      522, 552, 555
   of blacks, 23, 39, 41-45, 47, 83-85, 92, 94,
      96, 98-99, 103-104, 125, 127, 129-130,
      134-137, 139, 142-143, 146-148, 175,
      201, 207-214, 216-223, 229-234, 243,
      262, 317-319, 333, 344, 347, 351-352,
      356-357, 360-367, 389-390, 392, 396,
      423, 425, 427, 429, 433, 436-437, 468,
      483, 502, 507, 510, 536, 548, 564
   theology of, 32, 404, 410, 421, 429, 433
Liberia, 71, 85, 88-89, 113, 164, 168, 171, 174-
      175, 177, 182-184, 190-191, 196, 230-
      232, 234, 236, 259, 405, 410, 458-459,
      461, 549, 554, 559-560
Libertaçao de Mocambique (FRELIMO), 169,
      552-554
Liele, George, 425
Lincoln, Eric, 425, 431, 435, 439-440
Lincoln, President Abraham, 102
Literacy, rates of, 129
Literature, 5, 7, 11, 18, 23, 26, 28, 37-38, 42,
      102, 261, 266, 309-310, 315, 321, 325-
      350, 366, 441, 465, 470, 474, 476-477,
      479, 557-558, 560-561
   African and Caribbean, 332, 337
   African, 7, 11, 18, 23, 26, 309-310, 315, 325-
      332, 335-341, 343, 345, 347-350, 366,
      557-558, 561
   African American, 11, 315, 339-341, 343,
      345, 347-350, 561
   Afro-Caribbean, 325, 332-337, 441
   Caribbean, 261, 321, 325, 327, 329, 331-
      333, 335-337, 465, 476-477, 479
   creole and, 325, 334
   improvisation in, 325, 328
   Mandingo Epic, 325
   oral and written, 325-327, 330, 332, 335-336
   patois in, 325
   protest, 339
   slave narratives, 339
   Sundiata Epic, 325
   traditional African, 325, 327-328, 330-331
   women in, 11, 26, 331, 337, 465, 476, 479,
      558
Little, Malcolm. See X, Malcolm
Livingstone, David, 110, 120
Lloyd Gaines vs. University of Missouri, 139
London Baptist Missionary Society, 434
Lost-Found Nation of Islam, 435
Lott, Cary, 230
Lovejoy, David, 116

Lugard, Lord Frederick, 116
Lumumba, Patrice, 207
Lusaka Conference, 196
Lynch, John R., 128
Lynchings, 131, 388

Madubuike, Ihechukwu, 326, 337
Mair, Lucy, 13
Maji Maji Rebellion, 113, 403, 550
Makeba, Miriam, 253
Malaria 513
Mali, 8-9, 42, 67, 75, 114, 167, 182, 193, 255,
      257, 259, 320, 373, 409-410, 456, 459,
      519-520, 547, 551-553
Mali Ensemble, 259
Mandela, Nelson, 201, 203, 207, 247, 554
Manley, Michael, 215
Mansfield, Lord, 83
Manumission, 91, 94, 96, 99-100, 102, 105
Marcus, Robert, 248
Marriages, African, 73, 372-373, 381, 386
   bridewealth in, 373, 375, 377, 381-382
Marsalis, Wynton, 287, 294
Marshall, Thurgood, 139, 145, 351
Marxism, 6, 21, 163, 171, 436
Mason, Charles Harrison, 425
Matrilineal societies, 373, 375-377, 381, 414,
      444-445, 447, 488
Mau Mau War of Independence, 169
Mazrui, Ali, 172, 409, 419
Mbari Mbaya (Mbari Mbayo), 314
Mbari, writers in, 315
Mbira, 253-255, 258, 268, 282-283
Mbiti, John, 19, 31, 400, 404, 409, 419
Mboya, Tom, 167, 170, 235
McFerson, Hazel, 443, 464, 562
McGowan, Patrick, 16
McKay, Claude, 133, 333, 343, 345
Meadows, Eddie S., 285-286, 304-305, 562
Measles 513
Mento, 268, 273, 275
MERK 519
Methodism and Methodists, 83, 98, 405-406,
      424, 428, 434, 438
Methodism, abolition and, 83
Methodist Churches, 422
Metuge, Wang, 20
Middle Passage, 71, 77, 81-82, 90, 97, 341, 344,
      468, 484, 488, 507
Miley, Bubber, 289-290
Military, African Americans and, 135
Military, the, 6, 15, 22, 64-67, 78, 100, 102, 118,
      124, 134-136, 147-149, 158, 164, 169,
      177, 180, 193-194, 196, 202-204, 212,
      214, 270, 311, 343, 347, 357, 387, 404,
      462, 469, 482, 522, 553
Miller, Joseph, 77, 85, 90
Miscegenation, 208, 216-217